Praise for *Promissio*

Dr. Silcock has provided this carefully crafted translation of Oswald Bayer's magisterial study of the decisive turn in Luther's theology that was triggered by his insight into the performative function of God's word as his promise that conveys what it pledges to give in its oral proclamation and liturgical enactment. The translation is distinguished by Silcock's close reading of the text and clear presentation of its somewhat difficult academic syntax in lucid English.

—**John W. Kleinig**, emeritus lecturer in the Old Testament and biblical studies, Australian Lutheran College, Adelaide

In this book, Oswald Bayer, a foremost German Luther scholar, pinpoints how Luther, early in his career, became distinctively gospel-centered. This turn happened when Luther realized that the gospel is a promise, a word that neither merely describes reality nor directs behavior but instead actually delivers forgiveness, life, and salvation. Bayer's lucid survey of Luther's early works not only engages scholars but also supports pastors eager to preach good news. Given that many crave to see the church rekindle its sense of mission, this book is poised to help energize its witness.

—**Mark Mattes**, Lutheran Bible Institute Chair in Theology, Grand View University

Finally! English-speakers can how read Oswald Bayer's groundbreaking work *Promissio* in their own language! Here Bayer follows the appearance in Luther's theology of the core reformational teaching that God's word does what it says. This work should be read and studied not just by Reformation scholars and theologians, but by all who value and trust the promise of the gospel, which actually bestows what it proclaims: the forgiveness of God won by Christ crucified!

—**Joshua C. Miller**, pastor, Jehovah Lutheran Church, St. Paul, and adjunct professor of theology, Concordia University, St. Paul

Oswald Bayer has put the motif of promise at the center of Luther's doctrine of justification by faith. Here is an instance of an interface of theology and piety. Theologically, promise supplies proper substances to Luther's doctrine of God as active agent and God's actions in Christ for us, and to the meaning of the human person as passive agent before God. Experientially, the stress on the word of promise does two things: It places us under that word, allowing it to do its task on us; it accentuates hearing ("ear") as essential to formation of faith, even contrary to what we see ("eye"). Promise and faith form a seamless unity: Without promise, there is nothing to believe, while without faith, promise is useless. By grace, God's promise seizes us, and we in turn seize him back by faith. The Christian life receives its nourishment from the bountiful blessings that inhere in the various forms that God's promise assumes: preaching, confession and absolution, baptism, the Lord's supper. Bayer calls us to heed Luther's fundamental assertion that the subject of theology is God's promise, which delivers what it says. Because God does not lie, faith can be certain of what God promises, despite our fickle emotions and despite all appearances to the contrary.

—**Dennis Ngien**, Distinguished Professor at the Institute of Lutheran Theology, South Dakota; former Alister E. McGrath Chair of Christian Thought and Spirituality, Tyndale University, Toronto; and author of *Grace and Law in Galatians: Justification in Luther and Calvin*

Bayer is a meticulous and insightful Luther scholar, documenting the Reformer's path in coming to an understanding of the gospel as God's performative promise. Not only is *Promissio* a foundational contribution to Luther research, but it is also a book that demonstrates the vitality of Luther's understanding of the divine promise for preaching, liturgy, and pastoral care in the twenty-first century.

—**John T. Pless**, assistant professor of pastoral ministry and missions, Concordia Theological Seminary, and author of *Martin Luther, Preacher of the Cross: A Study of Luther's Pastoral Theology*

The Western shift to postmodernity has made contemporary theologians afraid to make any claims about reality as a whole. Bayer is different. Through Silcock's groundbreaking translation of a new and expanded English edition of his classic *Promissio*, Bayer dares to show a whole new generation of readers and scholars how Luther's reformational understanding of the unity of God's word of promise and the certainty of faith not only unlocks the Reformer's whole theology but touches on every aspect of our lives. A tour de force!

—**Leopoldo A. Sánchez M.**, professor of systematic theology and Werner R. H. Krause and Elizabeth Ringger Krause Professor of Hispanic Ministries, Concordia Seminary, and author of *T&T Clark Introduction to Spirit Christology* and *Sculptor Spirit: Models of Sanctification from Spirit Christology*

Oswald Bayer's *Promissio* is a masterful, groundbreaking study that offers a new perspective on Luther's theological development compared to previous research. It stands out by extraordinary exegetical precision in the interpretation of Luther's texts, by in-depth systematic reflection of its observations as well as by pointed summaries of its results. Even more than fifty years after its first publication, it has not been outdated. The excellent English translation allows for and encourages a broad reception in the English-speaking world. Whether one agrees with Bayer's view or not, serious research into Luther must take into account his perspective on the "reformational turn" in Luther's theology.

—**Theodor Dieter**, director emeritus, Institute for Ecumenical Research, Strasbourg

It is a rare thing when a book on Luther grows rather than recedes in importance fifty years on from its publication. Bayer's *Promissio*, now rendered in clear and precise English in Silcock's masterful translation, still inspires fresh research. For the attentive reader, its significance may far exceed a study of Luther's early development—this is a book about the heart of the gospel and the great struggle to speak it clearly.

—**Adam T. Morton**, lecturer in Christian theology, University of Nottingham

LUTHERAN QUARTERLY BOOKS

Lutheran Quarterly Books will advance the same aims as *Lutheran Quarterly* itself, aims repeated by Theodore G. Tappert when he was editor fifty years ago and renewed by Oliver K. Olson when he revived the publication in 1987. The original four aims continue to grace the front matter and to guide the contents of every issue, and can now also indicate the goals of *Lutheran Quarterly Books*: "to provide a forum (1) for the discussion of Christian faith and life on the basis of the Lutheran confession; (2) for the application of the principles of the Lutheran church to the changing problems of religion and society; (3) for the fostering of world Lutheranism; and (4) for the promotion of understanding between Lutherans and other Christians."

For further information, see www.lutheranquarterly.org.

The symbol and motto of *Lutheran Quarterly*, VDMA for *Verbum Domini Manet in Aeternum* (1 Pet. 1:25), was adopted as a motto by Luther's sovereign, Frederick the Wise, and his successors. The original "Protestant" princes walking out of the imperial Diet of Speyer in 1529, unruly peasants following Thomas Müntzer, and from 1531 to 1547 the coins, medals, flags, and guns of the Smalcaldic League all bore the most famous Reformation slogan, the first Evangelical confession: The Word of the Lord remains forever.

For the complete list of *Lutheran Quarterly Books*, please see the final pages of this work.

Promissio

Oswald Bayer

Promissio

The Reformational Turn in Luther's Theology

OSWALD BAYER

TRANSLATED BY JEFFREY G. SILCOCK

FORTRESS PRESS
MINNEAPOLIS

PROMISSIO
The Reformational Turn in Luther's Theology

First published 1971 in German as *Promissio: Geschichte der reformatorischen Wende in Luthers Theologie*.

This translation is based on the second revised edition with an expanded preface

31 30 29 28 27 26 25 2 3 4 5 6 7 8 9

All translations are by Jeffrey G. Silcock.

Library of Congress Cataloging-in-Publication Data

Names: Bayer, Oswald author | Silcock, Jeffrey G. translator
Title: Promissio : the reformational turn in luther's theology / Oswald Bayer ; translated by Jeffrey G. Silcock.
Other titles: Promissio. English
Description: Minneapolis : Fortress Press, [2025] | "First published 1971 in German as Promissio: Geschichte der reformatorischen Wende in Luthers Theologie. © 1971 Vandenhoeck & Ruprecht, Göttingen"--Title page verso | Includes bibliographical references and index.
Identifiers: LCCN 2024060982 (print) | LCCN 2024060983 (ebook) | ISBN 9798889833987 paperback | ISBN 9798889833994 ebook
Subjects: LCSH: Luther, Martin, 1483-1546
Classification: LCC BR333.2 .B3813 2025 (print) | LCC BR333.2 (ebook) | DDC 230/.41--dc23/eng/20250407
LC record available at https://lccn.loc.gov/2024060982
LC ebook record available at https://lccn.loc.gov/2024060983

Cover design: Josh Eller

Print ISBN: 979-8-8898-3398-7
eBook ISBN: 979-8-8898-3399-4

In Memory of Ernst Bizer

CONTENTS

ABBREVIATIONS

(See Bibliography for Publication Data)

AKG	*Archiv für Kirchengeschichte*
AL	The Annotated Luther
ARG	*Archiv für Reformationsgeschichte*
AWA	Archiv zur Weimarer Ausgabe, Luthers Werke
BC	*The Book of Concord*, ed. Robert Kolb and Timothy J. Wengert (2000)
BoA	*Bonner Ausgabe* (Luthers Werke in Auswahl)
BSLK	*Die Bekenntnisschriften der evangelisch-lutherischen Kirche* (1992)
CCL	*Corpus Christianorum, Series Latina*
cf	compare
chap.	chapter
Denz.	*Enchiridion Symbolorum*
Dt Wb	*Deutsches Wörterbuch von Jacob und Wilhelm Grimm.* I–XVI, Leipzig 1854–1960
EKG	*Evangelisches Kirchengesangbuch, Ausgabe für die ev. Landeskirche in Württemberg*
EvTh	*Evangelische Theologie*
FC	*Fathers of the Church*, ed. Ludwig Schopp
LR	*Lutherische Rundschau*
LW	Luther's Works, American Edition
Melanchthon, 1	*Der junge Melanchthon zwischen Humanismus und Reformation* (vol. 1, 1967)
Melanchthon, 2	*Der junge Melanchthon zwischen Humanismus und Reformation* (vol. 2, 1969)
MPL	Minge, *Patrologia Latina*
para.	paragraph
RE	*Real-Enzyklopädie der classischen Alterthumswissenschaft*
RDK	*Reallexikon zur deutschen Kunstgeschichte*
RGG	*Religion in Geschichte und Gegenwart*
sec.	section
ST	*Summa Theologiae*
s.v.	see under
ThEx	*Theologische Existenz heute*

ThR	*Theologische Rundshau*
trans. alt.	translation altered
VD	*Verzeichnis der im deutschen Sprachbereich erschienenen Drucke des XVI. Jahrhunderts* [*VD* 16]
WA	Weimar Ausgabe
WA Br	Weimar Ausgabe, Briefe
WA Db	Weimar Ausgabe, Deutsche Bibel
WA TR	Weimar Ausgabe, Tischreden
ZAW	*Zeitschrift für die alttestamentliche Wissenschaft*
ZKG	*Zeitschrift für Kirchengeschichte*
ZNW	*Zeitschrift für die neutestamentliche Wissenschaft*
ZThK	*Zeitschrift für Theologie und Kirche*

TRANSLATOR'S PREFACE

The notion of promise (*promissio*), as it is explicated in this book, has been foundational for all of Oswald Bayer's subsequent theological work, as his afterword bears witness. More specifically, as the author amply demonstrates and as Luther himself shows in his 1520 *The Babylonian Captivity of the Church* (also referred to as *The Babylonian Captivity*), promise and faith together constitute the new approach, the new starting point or organizing principle (*Ansatz*) of Luther's reformational theology.

The reader needs to be alert to certain key terms, apart from *promissio*, such as the *external word* (also called the *oral, spoken*, and *public word*), *faith, certainty, comfort, trust, gifting word(s), confidence*, and *binding* (as in God binds himself to his promise). All these words, which are characteristic of Luther's reformational theology, run like a *cantus firmus* through the whole book. They are all linked with the promise and explicate its significance. Looking out for these terms is a good way to understand the significance of the promise in all its dimensions and connections. Studying them in their context will also show how, for the reformational Luther, the promise is always specified in a concrete way and often occurs in connection with the oral word of the sermon and the enacted word of the sacraments. These key terms not only explicate the promise but also help the reader to distinguish between how Luther understands *promissio* in his early works (notably his first Psalms lectures and the Romans lectures) and how he understands it later in his reformational writings (as in his normative 1520 treatise *The Babylonian Captivity of the Church*, especially its section on baptism, which has criteriological significance for his understanding of the promise as well as the relation between word and faith). For a concise guide to the way that the *promissio* concept is developed in the book, the reader should consult the summary, especially the second part, where each chapter of part 2 is summarized.

The other thing the reader should keep in mind is that central to Luther's reformational insight is the sacramentality of the word. This stresses that the word should never be separated from the sacraments of baptism and the Lord's Supper, as well as confession and absolution (for Luther, the sacrament of penance), and conversely, that the latter should never be seen apart from the word. To speak of word and sacrament (as Lutherans often do) is open to misunderstanding as it suggests that the sacraments are an (optional) extra to the word. This would not only be thoroughly un-Lutheran, but it would also completely contradict the notion of the sacramentality of the word that Luther clearly teaches in 1520. To avoid this misunderstanding, it would be better not to use the cliché "word and sacrament" altogether in public discourse and to speak instead of the word that is enacted in different ways in the divine service (*Gottesdienst*): through baptism, absolution, the Bible readings, the sermon, and the Lord's Supper.

Another key aspect of the book is that the author convincingly demonstrates that, contrary to common opinion, justification by faith does not constitute Luther's breakthrough; rather, the turning point in his Reformation theology coincides with his discovery of a special understanding of the biblical term *promise* (*promissio*), which as the author shows, can be precisely located in connection with Luther's radical reconfiguration of the sacrament of penance in the early summer of 1518. The reader will enjoy discovering how Luther gradually applies this crucial insight to the key areas of his theology.

Translating Bayer is never easy, and *Promissio* presents the translator with some special challenges because of the complexity of its sentence structure and the density of its footnotes. My aim, as always, has been to make the German (and in this case the Latin also) clear and accessible to the English reader. It is encouraging to be told that even many German students struggle with Bayer's German (as well as Luther's German) and that some of them are looking forward to reading the English edition of *Promissio*! Bayer's language is precise and elegant and his style elevated and succinct. But these highly commendable literary qualities can make the book difficult to translate. However, that notwithstanding, I gladly took on the task because I was convinced, and still am, that even more than half a century after its initial publication, this book still makes an indispensable contribution to Luther research and needs to be read, especially by scholars and students of Luther in the English-speaking world. To revel in the plethora of Luther quotations, many of which have never before been translated, is a good enough reason alone for reading the book.

Although translators are servants of the text, they should not be its slaves, because translating with slavish literalism makes for a bad translation. In the case of this book, the use of dynamic equivalence has often been the best way to convey accurately the intended meaning of some of the author's long and dense passages. In the interests of comprehension and fluency, some sentences have been paraphrased (with the approval of the author) and in some cases, the author himself has revised and simplified the text during the translation process.

While many words present their own peculiar difficulties for the translator, one word in particular stands out that is worthy of comment because it is central to the book, and that is the German word *Buße* and its Latin equivalent *poenitentia*. These terms can be translated in one of three ways: the sacrament of penance, penitence, or repentance. The first presents no difficulty. Where the term refers to the sacrament, it will be translated as "the sacrament of penance." However, deciding between the other two is more difficult. I could have just translated them consistently with "repentance," but I wanted to provide more historical nuance in order to reflect Luther's change in understanding after his decisive reformational turn. Hence, I decided as a general rule to reserve the term *repentance* for texts that are clearly reformational in content and to use *penitence* to translate the equivalent German or Latin word in Luther's early pre-reformational writings. We need to remember that before his reformational turn, Luther understood "penitence," like "penance," in the sense of contrition, whereas after his decisive turn he understands penitence as inclusive of faith, which is how the English word "repentance" is understood in the Lutheran tradition. Thus, for example, the first of his ninety-five theses uses the term *Buße tun* (*poenitentiam agere*), which strictly speaking, should be translated as "do penance" even though it is usually translated as "repent." Historically, "do penance" is more accurate here because, as the author argues, this text is still pre-reformational. However, when we quote this thesis today, we usually say in English: "When our Lord and Master Jesus Christ said repent, he willed the entire life of believers to be one of repentance." But that translation, in light of Luther's reformational turn, is thoroughly justifiable because we understand the first thesis evangelically, which also reflects its biblical sense.

In most cases, where the American edition of *Luther's Works* (LW) is quoted, the translation has been altered (indicated by trans. alt.) to a greater or lesser degree because it is not precise enough to bring out the specific linguistic point the author is trying to make. Where a text is altered, I have taken the opportunity to update the language and bring the punctuation and capitalization into line with the publisher's preferred style (such as the use of an uppercase *W* for *word* only where it refers to Christ). At the time of publication, the second series of *Luther's Works* (LW) published by Concordia is still coming out. Since the early texts will be among the last to be translated, these future volumes cannot be referenced in this work.

Not only has the original German been translated but also all the Latin source material in the footnotes (such as the medieval commentators that Luther studied in preparation for his lectures). However, many Luther texts that Bayer works with are not translated in the LW, and so in these cases only the WA reference appears in the footnotes.

I normally only include the WA and LW abbreviations in the first Luther reference in a given footnote and then drop the WA and LW sigla for subsequent references in the same footnote, giving instead just the volume and page (and the line numbers in the case of the WA) unless I deem it necessary to repeat them for the sake of clarity.

Readers are advised that the full bibliographic reference of a given publication is not provided in the footnotes (which just cite the author and title of a book or article) but only in the bibliography. The same holds true for the list of abbreviations in the front matter.

The Bible verses that Luther cites do not follow any modern English translation but are my own. I have often been helped by two older versions: The Douay-Rheims Bible and the King James Version (minus the thous and thys), which usually come closer to the English equivalent of Luther's linguistic usage. All Psalm references in the German original are to the Latin Vulgate. In the translation, the versification has been changed to align with the English Bible.

References to the Lutheran Confessions conform to the latest Kolb-Wengert edition of the *Book of Concord* (2000). However, I have retained the references to the earlier 1992 edition of the *Bekenntnisschriften der evangelisch-lutherischen Kirche* (*BSLK*) rather than updating them to the new edition of 2014 (*BSELK*) as I see no compelling reason to do so.

I thank Paul Rorem, general editor of Lutheran Quarterly Books (LQB), for accepting this volume into the series. This is the third Bayer book to be published in LQB (the other two are *Living by Faith*, 2003, and *Theology the Lutheran Way*, 2007).

Thanks are due also to Philip Bartelt (Paul Rorem's assistant) for helping with the compilation of the indices and for reconciling the German and English page numbers at proof page stage.

Special thanks of course must go to the author, Oswald Bayer, who is not only a colleague but also a dear friend. I thank him for his help along the way in deciding the best way to translate certain key words and phrases and for leading me into a deeper understanding of his world of thought. We have had many lively discussions over the years, which have all proved very helpful. I thank him especially for contributing his retrospective afterword under difficult circumstances due to failing health. Even though this has meant delaying the publication date, in my opinion it was worth it. The pause has also enabled him first to bring out his final book, *Vernunft und Vertrauen: Zur Grundorientierung lutherischer Theologie* (De Gruyter, 2022). This magisterial compendium of Lutheran theology is the crowning achievement of the author's long and distinguished career and compellingly demonstrates the indisputable centrality of the concept of *promissio* for his entire theological work. The retrospective afterword, which forms a new chapter in this English edition, is in its own way also a splendid testament to the fundamental importance of the *promissio* concept in the life and work of the author since the beginning of his academic career. This afterword is unique to the English edition of the book and its greatest distinguishing feature. It not only reflects on the centrality of *promissio* in this book but is also a retrospection of Bayer's literary scholarship and demonstrates the way that each of his publications takes up and develops this crucial concept in specific ways.

Because the author chose not to engage with his critics, especially in the crucial but highly contentious matter of the dating of Luther's breakthrough or reformational turn (which is very important for him in order to be able to determine which texts are reformational and which are still pre-reformational), Theodor Dieter of the Ecumenical Research Institute, Strasbourg, has kindly taken up this challenge and will write an article for *Lutheran Quarterly* that will appear shortly after the release date of the book. He will not only discuss the impact and reception of *Promissio* but also offer his own critique of Bayer's work.

I thank Fortress Press for publishing the book, especially its editor-in-chief, Laura Gifford, and her team for their professionalism at all stages of production.

Last but not least, thanks are due to my loving wife, the newly minted Dr. Pam Zweck, who has been a constant support and companion throughout the book's long period of gestation and now rejoices that it has finally been "delivered" and that she can have her husband back—at least until the next project beckons!

Jeffrey G. Silcock
Rostrevor, South Australia
All Saints Day, 2024

AUTHOR'S PREFACE TO ENGLISH EDITION

It is a great joy for me to look at the finished book and do what is most important at this moment, and that is to give thanks where thanks are due—and that in the first instance is to the One who has given this book, himself a writer, and then to those through whom he has given it: friends and colleagues Jeff Silcock and Paul Rorem. Jeff has transformed the old German book into a new English one, and Paul, as editor of Lutheran Quarterly Books, has ensured that it can now serve many people who have no access to the original languages but are interested in the question of the reformational nature of Luther's theology.

My first encounter with Jeff goes back to the Tenth International Congress for Luther Research, held in Copenhagen in 2002. It was on the steps of the university's auditorium where he suddenly came up to me, as if in a hurry to catch a train, without even introducing himself, and said, "May I translate your *Theologie*[1] book?" I was almost left speechless for the moment because no one had ever asked me that before, but at the same time I was delighted and answered, "I can't see any reason why not." This was not only the beginning of a long and fruitful scholarly collaboration but also of a long and close friendship. It only came out later that he resonates deeply with my own theological perspective and has been using my insights in his own teaching at Australian Lutheran College, University of Divinity, where before his retirement, he was responsible for teaching systematic theology and Lutheran ethics as well as coordinating and supervising doctoral students in his role as associate dean for research.

Jeff started translating the first part of *Theologie* on Luther's theology, which contains a detailed interpretation of Luther's triad *oratio*, *meditatio*, and *tentatio* (prayer, meditation, and attack), which forms the basic elements of his concept of theology. However, at the same time and unbeknownst to both of us, Mark Mattes had nearly completed translating the final part of the book that represents my own constructive approach to theology, admittedly based on the exposition of Luther's theology in the first part of the book. These two parts were brought together to form an abridged version of the book for the American readership, which appeared under the title *Theology the Lutheran Way*.[2]

---

1. This volume is the first in the series *Handbuch Systematischer Theologie*, edited by Carl Heinz Ratschow (Gütersloher Verlagshaus, 1994).

2. Eerdmans, 2007.

At this point, it would be remiss of me not to acknowledge and thank others who have also contributed to translating my work over the years. Here I mention the former Tübingen theology students Christine Helmer and John Betz, who together with Mark Mattes, are now professors in the United States. To them and to any others who have contributed in some way to my writings becoming better known through the task of translation, I say a sincere thank you.

After working on the *Theologie* book and numerous other translations along the way, Silcock has now completed an incomparably larger project with this English-language edition of my first work, the *Promissio* book, in which my inaugural dissertation and habilitation thesis are combined—the habilitation (second doctorate) being a requirement for teaching in a German university. This has been an enormously time-consuming and demanding project and it is difficult for anyone who is not themselves familiar with the original work to properly appreciate this. Just the sheer volume and complexity of the footnotes is enough to put most translators off and is indeed one of the reasons that publishers could not find anyone to translate it fifty years ago, even though they made every effort to do so. While engaged in the *Promissio* project, Jeff has also translated several of my articles into English and more are planned.

Over the course of more than seven years, he has devoted himself tirelessly to this project, constantly checking with me about all manner of questions right down to the last detail so that he could make it as accurate and readable as possible. In addition to our regular emails, we both valued the face-to-face conversations that we could have whenever he was in Germany. All this is testament to his great scrupulosity and relentless effort to find the best translation for a particular word or phrase. Especially praiseworthy is his achievement in translating all the Latin quotations into English, which will be a great service to the reader. At the end of the day, his aim has always been to make the translation as fluent and accessible as possible. He used to say that the greatest compliment a translator can be given is to be told by readers that they didn't even realize that the book was a translation.

For me, Jeff's questions and our conversations over many years made me return time and again to the *Promissio* book and thus to the beginnings of my theological work. Last year, when my health was no longer as good as before and work came to a halt, he waited with patience and used the time constructively to check over and polish the translation. The fact that this book can finally appear is thanks to his tireless perseverance. The fact that he sacrificed the first part of his retirement for this project—time that he could have otherwise spent with Pam, his wife—and the fact that he did it freely for the sheer love of it because he was convinced that the book needed to be made available to the English reader, is an eloquent testimony that this translation is as important to him as it is to me. As I often told him, the concept of *promissio* is the foundation of all my subsequent work, and yet ironically, the very book that explicates and explains it has never been translated until now. I owe Jeff a debt of gratitude for the gift of this translation. I am also deeply appreciative that his dear wife, Pam, also a close friend, did not begrudge him the time spent on the project, even though with tongue in cheek she could refer to me as "the third person in our marriage"! I honor Pam for the singular support she has given Jeff throughout this project and highly value their friendship.

With these heartfelt words of thanks to my dear friend, Jeffrey Silcock, I cannot forget Paul Rorem, editor of Lutheran Quarterly Books, to whom I am also deeply indebted. While Jeff took care of the content and was solely responsible for it, Paul, who has always been solicitous of my work and keen to publish my articles in *Lutheran Quarterly* so that my theological work can become better known to the American readership, has taken care of all the logistics for its publication. I am understandably very excited about this book and look forward to seeing it in English dress. The success of Jeff's work is due not least to Paul's managerial skill and his dogged determination to get the book published.

Last but not least, I would also like to thank Fortress for agreeing to publish this English translation of my book.

The publication of this old book in English gives it a new lease of life. It brings together different interests that need to be briefly accounted for, because the question naturally arises as to whether its method and content have not become outdated by more recent scholarship. If I thought that this were the case, I would never have agreed to an unchanged translation. But as far as I can see, a revision is not necessary. New research has certainly expanded and deepened, for example, our understanding of the history of motifs with regard to the reception of Bernard of Clairvaux, Tauler, and the Franciscan concept of God's self-binding. But it has not resulted in a fundamentally new picture.

Apart from the many instructive Luther quotes, I think the book will be of interest because it approaches the topic of *promissio* both historically and systematically. From the former perspective, corresponding to my first doctoral thesis, I show, on the basis of a careful examination of the pertinent Luther texts, how Luther understood the promise in his early pre-reformational theology, while from the latter perspective, corresponding to my second doctoral thesis, I show how his early understanding of the promise is not yet reformational but changes once he started dealing with the sacrament of penance in response to the indulgence controversy, culminating in his new understanding in 1518.

I will not attempt to critically engage with my fellow Luther scholars in their critique and reception of my understanding of Luther's *promissio* concept but will leave that in the capable hands of my friend and colleague, Theo Dieter, former director of the Institute of Ecumenical Research, Strasbourg, who, as Silcock has already mentioned in his translator's preface, has kindly agreed to take on this task and to publish his essay in *Lutheran Quarterly* about the same time as *Promissio* comes out. He will critically reflect on my methodology and make some suggestions of his own as to how my approach could be made more fruitful for ecumenical engagement with the Roman Catholic Church. He will also include an assessment of my view of Luther's understanding of the promise in relation to the view of other scholars (especially Berndt Hamm) as well as of my stance on the question of whether, and if so when, we can speak of something like Luther's reformational turn. The critical question of course is this: Can Luther's theology really be organically situated in the context of late medieval piety or derived from it, or is there a point at which he breaks out of it with something absolutely new? I answer that question decisively in the second part of the book.

The question of the extent to which my own systematic way of thinking has been shaped by the research gathered together in this book cannot be answered any better than by pointing to the major impact that the findings of my inaugural dissertation and habilitation thesis have had on my own subsequent theological work. This has already been done by two of my closest interlocutors, Johannes von Lüpke and Edgar Thaidigsmann, who have pointed out that from the time of my initial doctoral studies, the word of God, understood as a promise, has formed the center of my theology. By focusing on this center and listening to the word of promise, a wide space opens up for theological reflection, in which it becomes clear who God is for humans and how humans can understand themselves in the midst of God's creation within the horizon of this promise. It shows that the whole of my theology can be seen from the angle of God's self-communication in his promise.

I hope that readers can see that my entire work is a thoroughly consistent—albeit contingent! (that is, not planned but, to a certain extent, given to me by God's providence)—development of what I once researched and identified under the concept of *promissio* as the core of Luther's reformational theology. How exactly my understanding of the promise has shaped my thinking and how I have built on this foundation, I have tried to outline in the retrospective afterword.

This approach to defining Luther's Reformation theology in light of its center located in the promise was still an almost completely new way of looking at things when my book was first published in 1971. My teacher Ernst Bizer was the first one bold enough to attempt it, and although it came under heavy criticism because many well-known Protestant theologians at the time did not share his opinion, it has now received a lot of attention beyond my own work and is widely accepted as the standard view of the "late daters" (1518). It thus takes its place alongside the old view that saw the reformational turn already present in Luther's Psalms or Romans lectures (1513–1516), as well as alongside the view of those who want to resolve the event character of Luther's one reformational discovery into a long process of development. That Bizer's view and my view, although not self-evident, should have found their firm place in Luther research fills me with great joy. Nevertheless, this definition of the Reformation and Luther's reformational turn is still the subject of controversy. And, as Silcock reminds me, this is especially the case in the English-speaking world, where the whole matter has not yet been thoroughly examined and discussed.

The present translation now offers readers the opportunity to examine independently the appropriateness and justification of my fundamental redefinition of Reformation theology in terms of the concept of promise. First, it presents the evidence of the sources (in English!), on the basis of which I developed all my future thinking in systematic theology, and second, it shows from a church history perspective that a new dating of Luther's reformational turn was necessary. The English-speaking readership can now form their own judgment as to whether my interpretation of Luther really has substance and is scientifically defensible and compelling or whether it is just another fanciful attempt to deal with Luther without strict reference to the sources. I have striven with might and main to avoid the latter judgment, since I have always understood all my work as detailed philological work, as I have explained elsewhere:

> The Luther references are . . . not just ornamental trappings nor are they merely preparatory to the real work of systematic theology. Rather, this textual work is properly the task of systematic theology: to listen to and examine the text and to let it call our conclusions into question. In short, the task of systematic theology is to shape ourselves and our own judgments based on the resistant text and not to bend the text to accommodate our own thinking. Anyone who always thinks they know everything or can see through the intuition of the moment without its historical context is in Luther's judgment "like fruit that falls out of season before it is even half ripe."[3]

Finally, I would like to leave my readers with a word from my teacher Ernst Bizer, which has stayed with me all my life. Speaking of his own careful and precise study of the sources, he says that he has tried to follow Luther's texts with his finger, so to speak, line by line.[4]

Oswald Bayer
Tübingen, Germany
October 2023

---

3. WA 48:141.

4. Bizer, *Fides ex auditu*, 14. The German sentence reads as follows: "Ich habe versucht, sozusagen mit dem Finger den Zeilen entlangzugehen."

AUTHOR'S PREFACE TO SECOND GERMAN EDITION

"On Seeking Out Truth and Comforting Terrified Consciences" (*Pro veritate inquirenda et timoratis conscientiis consolandis* [or *Pro Veritate*]). This is the title of the first reformational text in the story of Luther's theology. It describes in a nutshell the intention of this book also. The first part is my doctoral dissertation in church history while the second part is my postdoctoral thesis in systematic theology. The book documents my transition from the discipline of church history to that of systematic theology without ever leaving church history behind. In fact, the way I understand and do "systematic theology" is as "as a science of history," as I explain in an essay of the same name in the Festschrift for Gerhard Ebeling.[1]

Promissio (Latin for promise) has become the matrix of my entire work in systematic theology. It takes its bearings from God's promise, the comfort of salvation, which is determinative for Luther's reformational theology. In keeping with this, the central focus of my book *Was is das: Theologie?* (1973) is the concept of promise. The same applies to my dogmatics in outline: *Living by Faith: Justification and Sanctification* (2003; German 1984) as well as the monograph *Schöpfung als Anrede. Zu einer Hermeneutik der Schöpfung* (1986). It is my conviction that all dogmatic statements have their criterion in the story of the promise. Their reference to this setting in life (*Sitz im Leben*) makes them what they are. If Schleiermacher said that dogmatic statements are determined by their reference to the religious self-consciousness of an individual, I argue that this reference must be replaced by that of the gospel, understood as promise and comfort, in contradistinction to the law.

2.

If *Promissio* has now been reissued (in a revised edition, 1989), it has been born into a very different world, a world where the discussion has changed considerably from where it was almost twenty years ago, when the book first appeared (1971).

---

1. Bayer, "Systematische Theologie als Wissenschaft der Geschichte," in *Verifikationen*, ed. Eberhard Jüngel et al. (Mohr, 1982), 341–61.

At that time, the discussion centered on the content and date of the reformational turn in Luther's theology. This had been sparked by Ernst Bizer's book *Fides ex auditu* [*Faith Comes by Hearing*], in which he argued for a "late dating" of Luther's reformational insight, dating it to 1518. However, at that time, there was hardly any support for this view. Now the tide has changed, and the late dating has enjoyed a veritable "boom."[2] In the judgment of Otto Hermann Pesch, who wrote an instructive report on Luther research,[3] "the 'trend' is now in favor of the late dating."

The findings of the present book continue to be taken up, not least by Martin Brecht in *Martin Luther: His Road to the Reformation 1483–1521* (1985; Ger. 1981). Part of its significance lies in the fact that it explains the late dating in a way that is methodologically different from that of my teacher Ernst Bizer (see the "Retrospective Summary" p. 399 note 11). In what follows, I highlight the crucial points and arguments of the book.

3.

Protestant theology, insofar as it is committed to the theology of Martin Luther, is always faced with the task of presenting and explaining what it sees as distinctively reformational in the teaching of the reformer. This is all the more important since there is by no means a consensus on this question, and yet it is a question that goes to the very heart of the identity of Protestant theology itself. As Luther himself reports, he came to his crucial insight that defined him as a reformer through a surprising discovery, but only after long years of intensive work studying Holy Scriptures and engaging with the received tradition of the church. The knowledge he gained in the process pushed him to ask further questions and to sharpen them, but by themselves they never led to a solution. Rather, this came more like a sudden enlightenment that illuminated his question. But the source of this illumination cannot be traced and is as underivable as the divine answer to the human question. The closed gates have opened again.

Scholars have tried to find and identify the evidence for this event in the texts of the young Luther. Often, they took their bearings from Luther's self-testimony in the preface to the first volume of his Latin writings:

> So, I raged with a fierce and troubled conscience. Nevertheless, I persistently knocked on this very verse in Paul [Rom. 1:17], most ardently desiring to know what St. Paul could have meant.

2. Heiko Augustinus Oberman, in *Lutheriana* AWA 5 (1985): 21.

3. Pesch, "Neuere Beiträge zur Frage nach Luthers 'Reformatorischer Wende,'" *Catholica* 38 (1984): 121.

> At last, by the mercy of God, after meditating day and night on that text, I began to pay attention to the context of the words, namely, "In it the righteousness of God is revealed, as it is written, 'The righteous live by faith.'" There I began to understand that the righteousness of God is that by which the righteous live by God's gift, namely by faith. In other words, the righteousness of God as revealed through the gospel is the passive righteousness by which our merciful God justifies us by faith, as it is written, "The righteous live by faith." There I felt that I was altogether born again and had entered paradise itself through open gates. There I saw the whole of Scripture in a new light . . .
>
> The word "righteousness of God," became for me the sweetest word and I extolled it with a love as great as the hatred with which I had previously hated it. So that text in Paul was for me truly the gate to paradise. Later I read Augustine's *The Spirit and the Letter*, where contrary to all expectation, I found that he too interpreted God's righteousness in a similar way, as the righteousness with which God clothes us when he justifies us. Although this was said imperfectly and he did not explain all things concerning imputation clearly, I was nevertheless pleased that he taught there the righteousness of God by which we are justified.[4]

If we try to use the new understanding of Romans 1:17 outlined here as a measure of Luther's early interpretations of this verse, we see—as documented by many studies on the topic—that it leaves room for different interpretations that do not complement one another but are instead mutually exclusive. It thus proves to be so general that it is not suitable as a criterion within the Augustinian tradition. The retrospects, especially of the various table talks, in which Luther described his theological breakthrough as the discovery of a fundamentally new insight into the distinction between law and gospel, are more suitable for this. But even they are not sufficiently precise on their own. In addition, however, there is a yet third series of retrospective self-testimonies that until now have not been given their proper due; they are characterized by the keyword *promise*. The most important of these texts is a section of the Genesis lectures from the year 1545,[5] which from the angle of the text to be interpreted (Gen. 48:20–21), presents itself as a theological legacy and at the same time as a confession that manifests certainty, as an assertion of faith:

---

4. WA 54:185,28–186,20 = LW 34:337 (trans. alt.).

5. WA 44:711,7–720,36 = LW 8:180–94.

> I have been baptized. I have been absolved. In this faith I will die. No matter what trials and tribulations confront me, I will certainly not be shaken; for he who said: "Whoever believes and is baptized will be saved" (Mark 16:16) and "Whatever you loose on earth will be loosed in heaven" (Matt. 16:19) and "This is my body; this is my blood, which is shed for you for the remission of sins" (cf. Matt. 26:26,28)—he cannot lie or deceive. This is certainly true.[6]

The reformational discovery appears in the context of this confession, which is very close in time to the "preface," as a reillumination of God's forgotten promise:

> Formerly, under the papacy, when I was a monk, the word or promise was never spoken and never heard. I give thanks to God that I can live at a time like this when it resounds in my ears and in the ears of all Christian people. For whoever hears the word, easily understands the divine promise, which was obscure and unknown to all theologians throughout the papacy.[7]

The definition of the promise is here directly identical to the understanding of *promissio* that Luther had advocated in *The Babylonian Captivity of the Church* in 1520. Consequently, this is what is "distinctively reformational," which we also find in Luther's retrospective self-testimony and theological legacy.

We have here, then, a criterion that allows us to ask about *the* turn in the story of Luther's theology that has many turns, *the* turn that can be described precisely as his *reformational* turn. What we are looking for is a clear and coherent context, in which what is distinctively reformational is presented factually and linguistically in such a way that we can avoid generalizations as well as the introduction of decisive interpretations from later texts. The earliest text we come across that satisfies this requirement is the fifty theses of the circular disputation *Pro veritate* from the early summer of 1518.[8] They anticipate the understanding of the promise found in *The Babylonian Captivity*, in relation to the sacrament of penance, and at the same time serve to explicate Romans 1:17 in that this passage is used to sum up both of them at the end: "In summary, the righteous

---

6. WA 44:720,30–36 = LW 8:193–94 (trans. alt.).

7. WA 44:719,18–21 = LW 8:101 (trans. alt).

8. WA 1:630,1–633,12 = LW 72 (forthcoming).

will live, not by works or by the law, but by faith. Rom. 1."[9] The fact that the key term, the *righteousness of faith*, is presented as an abbreviation of the theses on the promise and faith but, on the other hand, wants to be interpreted by them, means that we can recognize the point of convergence between the retrospects of the preface and those of the Genesis lectures.

The late witness of the Genesis lectures is joined by that of the *Acta Augustana* (*Proceedings at Augsburg*), which appear almost at the same time as the theses *Pro veritate*. The significance of Luther's Augsburg meeting with Cardinal Cajetan in October 1518 for our question lies in the fact that the cardinal challenged Luther to confess what made him a Christian and what he therefore could not surrender:

> I will not become a heretic by contradicting the opinion that made me a Christian. I would rather die, be burned, banished, and cursed.[10]

This "conviction" is the particularity of word and faith in the saying about the keys in Matthew 16:19, which only dawned on him after a long tormenting search. In his written response before Cajetan, Luther defended the thesis this way:

> No one can be justified except by faith. Thus, it is necessary for us to believe with firm faith that we are justified and in no way doubt that we will obtain grace. For if we doubt and are uncertain, we are therefore not justified but reject grace. My opponents wish to consider this theology new and erroneous.[11]

Luther's justification for this thesis is based on Romans 1:17 ("The righteous live by faith"), which he calls an "infallible truth."[12] Among the numerous biblical authorities that he adduces, he gives special prominence to Matthew 16:19. Not to believe these words of Christ is to face the peril of eternal damnation:

> We must believe these words of Christ or otherwise risk eternal damnation and the sin of unbelief: "Whatever you loose on earth will also be

9. WA 1:633,11–12.

10. WA BR 1:217,60–63.

11. WA 2:13,7–10 = LW 31:270 (trans. alt.).

12. WA 2:13,12–13 = LW 31:270 (trans. alt.).

> loosed in heaven" [Matt. 16:19]. Therefore, if you go to the sacrament of penance and do not firmly believe that you are absolved in heaven, you go there to your judgment and damnation because you do not believe that when Christ said, "Whatever you shall loose," etc. [Matt. 16:19] he spoke the truth, and so through your doubt you make Christ a liar, which is a terrible sin. If however you say, "What if I am unworthy and do not have the right disposition for the sacrament?" I answer as I did above. No disposition will make you worthy and no works will make you fit for the sacrament, but only faith makes you fit and worthy, for only faith in the words of Christ justifies, makes us alive and worthy, and only faith is the right preparation. Without faith everything else is an act of presumption or desperation. The righteous live not by their disposition but by faith [Rom. 1:17].[13]

Here Luther connects Matthew 16:19 with Romans 1:17. In doing so, he retrospectively interprets this Pauline passage, which programmatically precedes his argument, in light of Jesus's words about the keys. He follows a similar strategy in his *Pro veritate* theses, which conclude with Romans 1:17 as a "final summary." In both cases, what the "righteousness of God" is, Luther specifically determines only through his new understanding of promise and faith.

4.

Luther's reformational discovery came about during a penetrating study of the sacrament of penance, which he was forced into because of the system of indulgences. He understood the priestly words of absolution—"I absolve you of your sins!"—initially as a speech act that establishes something that exists already. In other words, he understood these words as a declarative act: The priest sees the contrition, takes it as a sign of divine justification, the divine absolution that has already occurred in those to be absolved without them knowing it, and lets it appear as such. He declares it in order to give them the certainty that they have indeed been absolved. The words of absolution are understood as a judgment in the sense of a statement.

At first, Luther remained completely within the framework of the ancient understanding of language, especially that of Stoicism, which Augustine inherited, and that still largely prevails today. According to it, language is a system of signs that point to objects or facts, or signs that express an emotion. In both cases, the sign is a statement or expression, not the thing itself.

---

13. WA 2:13,31–14,9 = LW 31:271 (trans. alt.).

That the linguistic sign itself is already the thing, that it is not an absent but a present thing—that was Luther's great hermeneutical discovery, his reformational discovery in the strict sense. He made it (1518) initially as he reflected on the sacrament of penance. That the sign itself is already the thing has important implications for absolution. It means that the statement "I absolve you of your sins!" is not a judgment that merely declares what already is, thus presupposing an inner, divine, actual absolution. The absolution is not constative but constitutive. It is a speech act that creates a sphere of relations, indeed a relationship—between the person in whose name it is spoken and the one to whom it is spoken and who believes the promise.

The new understanding of the sacrament of penance also led to a change in the understanding of baptism and the Lord's Supper. The gospel has its specific *Sitz im Leben*. It is an oral, bodily word that we cannot speak to ourselves but must have spoken to us by another in the name of God. Only when we approach our topic from the perspective of form analysis (form criticism) that takes account of its *Sitz im Leben* is Luther's reformational discovery understood properly. Thus it also becomes clear that the reformational doctrine of justification is the general expansion of the specific reformational doctrine of the sacraments. But even in its generality, it remains special because it does not abstract from the specific form of faith, which is shaped and determined by the word.

This makes the concrete distinction between law and gospel possible. Only when Luther had discovered that God's promise is the unambiguous, oral word of salvation could he give a satisfactory answer to the question about the certainty of salvation, which was still not possible for him at the time of his early theology of the cross (before the spring of 1518). Luther's discovery of the *promissio* is therefore anything but a peripheral question and is certainly not a "technique of grace," as Leif Grane thinks (*Modus loquendi theologicus*, 1975, 148). Luther did not become a Christian through the discovery of a "technique." Even Cajetan did not criticize Luther in Augsburg for being a "technician of grace" but for being a theologian who demanded that "for a fruitful absolution in the sacrament of penance," faith is necessary "by which penitents can believe that they are most certainly absolved by God"—to which the cardinal could only say that "this is tantamount to founding a new church."[14]

Pesch[15] is correct: "We can finally only defend the early dating if we concede that the matter of certainty has no major importance. However, it is the strength

14. Cajetan, *Opuscula Omnia*, Lyon, 1575:111,3.

15. Otto Hermann Pesch, "Neuere Beiträge zur Frage nach Luthers 'Reformatorischer Wende,'" *Catholica* 38, no. 1 (1984): 66–134, here 128.

of the late dating [of Luther's reformational turn] to insist on what friends and opponents alike can agree on: that the matter of certainty is obviously central for Luther, irrespective of whether you link it to his understanding of the word, or to his understanding of righteousness, or to both at the same time."

Oswald Bayer
Tübingen, Germany
November 1988

AUTHOR'S PREFACE TO FIRST GERMAN EDITION

The topic and research question of this investigation as well as some of the text arose from the work done in the spring of 1962 following a seminar on Luther's doctrine of the Lord's Supper led by Ernst Bizer.

The two parts of the investigation were presented to the Protestant Theological Faculty of the University of Bonn. The first was the doctoral dissertation (completed in August 1967) and the second was the *Habilitationsschrift*, or postdoctoral thesis (completed in August 1969). The indices as well as the summary were added for the publication.

Promissio could not have been written without the Luther research of my teacher, to whom this book is dedicated. I must first thank him and his wife. I am also indebted to Dr. Friedrich Lang. He generously granted me, as his assistant, the leeway I needed to fully develop the method of the present work, determined as it is by the standards of New Testament exegesis, and at the same time to plan the dissertation. In addition to the work of Ernst Bizer, that of Gerhard Ebeling, with whom I was in constant dialogue, was a decisive influence on my book. So here I must also thank especially Professor Dr. Gerhard Ebeling.

My thanks also go to the members of the Bonn faculty, who took upon themselves the burden of the seminar papers: besides Professor Bizer, Professor Dr. Luise Abramowski (for the doctorate), Professor Dr. Dr. Hans-George Geyer and Professor Dr. Gerhard Krause (for the postdoctoral degree).

The *Studienstiftung des deutschen Volkes* [German National Academic Foundation], which I belonged to from 1961 to 1965, supported me and this work financially. In addition to that, a six-month research grant awarded by the *Deutsche Forschungsgemeinschaft* [German Research Foundation] was of great benefit to me while I worked on my postdoctoral thesis. I also thank the *Forschungsgemeinschaft* and the Protestant *Oberkirchenrat* [senior administrative body of the church] in Stuttgart for assistance in helping to defray the cost of publishing the book. Finally, I would like to thank the publisher Vandenhoeck & Ruprecht for including this work in the series *Forschungen zur Kirchen- und Dogmengeschichte*.

Oswald Bayer
Evangelisches Stift
Tübingen, Germany
November 1970

RESEARCH QUESTION AND METHOD[1]

Luther's treatise *The Babylonian Captivity of the Church* (1520) claims that *promissio*, (promise) and its counterpart *fides* (faith), is the canon of the sacraments and the epitome of the gospel. Ironically, however, what Luther himself declares to be the decisive driving force of his theology and its reformational heart[2] has never been deemed worthy of special study. If it was considered at all, Luther's special understanding of the promise was almost entirely incorporated into a general concept of the word and thus lost its sharpness. However, its great importance,[3] which only comes out in the above-mentioned treatise, requires us to study its history in Luther's early theology thematically to gain a proper understanding of its distinctive character.[3a]

---

1. The following considerations are taken up in a specific direction and in some cases put more precisely in my article "Die reformatorische Wende in Luthers Theologie" *ZThK* 66 (1969): 115–50, here 115–22. Above all, the notion of what is "reformational" is more clearly developed there and is assumed in the following wherever the term is used.

2. For the late period, we must remember here the moving outline of *promissio* theology in his Genesis lectures (WA 44:711,7–720,36 = LW 8:180–94; 1545), which throughout have the form and rank of a theological legacy. The *promissio*—"which was obscure and unknown to all the theologians throughout the papacy" (44:719,22–23 = 8:192)—appears here as almost the one great reformational discovery (see esp. 44:711,7–712,11 = 8:181–82; 44:714,27–715,10 = 8:185–86; 44:716,4–27 = 8:187–88, from which a few lines are taken up in Otto Scheel, *Dokumente* [under No. 516]; 44;719,18–23 = 8:192). Nowhere has Luther research shown the interest in this text that its subject matter deserves.

3. It was only Ernst Bizer, to whom this work owes the decisive insight in regard to the research question and method, who emphasized this. See his review of W. Jetter (*Die Taufe beim jungen Luther*), *ZKG* 67 (1956): 341–44, his essay "Die Entdeckung des Sakraments durch Luther," *EvTh* 17 (1957): 64–90, and his book *Fides ex auditu* (1958 1st ed.), especially the afterword to the 3rd ed. (1966), in which (180–84) the *promissio* concept is expressly introduced as an interpretative lens for the reformational understanding of righteousness (*iustitia*) in order to reformulate the result of his investigation to avoid misunderstandings. See further p. 121, n. 23, of my essay mentioned in n. 1, and the summary in chap. 11, p. 399.

3a. Understanding the term *promissio* in Luther's first Psalms lectures has been the focus of two recent works: Heiko Oberman, "Wir sein pettler. Hoc est verum. Bund und Gnade in der Theologie des Mittelalters und der Reformation," *ZKG* 78 (1967): 232–52, esp. 242–51, and James Samuel Preus, *From Shadow to Promise. Old Testament Interpretation from Augustine to the Young Luther* (1969). However, both convey a different picture to that presented in this study. Cf. my review of the work by Preus in *ZKG* 82 (1971): 380–82.

Our investigation of the history of the *promissio*-concept not only serves to understand a text from 1520 by moving toward it but also assesses the history of the understanding of the word that preceded it and is subsumed in it, albeit through many radical changes, by moving backward from it. In other words, we have found it useful to understand Luther's early texts developmentally as stages on the way toward the 1520 treatise as well as to see them retrospectively in the light of the treatise.

That means that a necessary aspect to the story of the *promissio*-concept that we find in 1520 is precisely also the understanding of the word that it corrected. For the most part, however, this does not depend on the texts in which the word *promissio* occurs. We therefore have to include the semantic field of *verbum* (word) in order to first determine starting points and differences to the later concept of *promissio* (part 1) so that this can then emerge in its specificity (part 2).

Since in every investigation of Luther's early theology some model of what is "actually reformational" comes into play, it has been rightly demanded that such a presupposition must be declared up front, so that everyone is aware of it from the start.[4] The question is, however, *Where* are we to find this model?

As we go through his early writings, we do not find it in a formula whose meaning is disputed,[5] but in a *textual context* that is clear in itself. The best example of this is *The Babylonian Captivity of the Church*.[6] That is, we find the crystallization point of Luther's reformational theology in the relationship between *promissio* and *fides* as understood by this treatise.

That this is not an arbitrary decision on our part (as is the case, for instance, with the popular canonization of the *Heidelberg Disputation*[7]) is evident from the historical position of our criterion. Despite his polemics, Luther shows in

4. A model of such reflection is offered by Wilhelm Link, *Das Ringen Luthers um die Freiheit der Theologie von der Philosophie* (1940) in the "introduction" to his book (1–77), esp. 66–77. We follow his "teleological" approach (74–76) but not in Link's sense. It seems more appropriate to see the aim as the criterion rather than as the "summary sentence" (75) and so instead of saying as Link does, "The aim becomes visible as the inner law of the whole movement" (74), it is better to say that, in accepting or rejecting this phrase, the aim becomes effective as the material criterion of the whole movement. This does not mean that the aim now is understood as an isolated result that has left its *Tendenz* behind. It cannot (not even in retrospect: so Link, 76) be seen as necessary, in the sense of the history of philosophy, but must be considered in its surprising contingency and thus seen as a discovery.

5. Link, for example, starts from the formula "*simul iustus et peccator*" (73–74,77).

6. In conjunction with the treatise *The Freedom of a Christian* (1520).

7. For example, in Walther von Loewenich's *Luther's Theology of the Cross* (Ger. 1929; Eng. 1976).

an almost detached manner that this is unmistakably his own position and so confers on it the power to distinguish between spirits. Thus it necessarily plays a significant role in the formation of our church confessions or statements of faith, as is evident from church history.[8] And it can also withstand the scrutiny of controversial theology, which highlights the differences between Protestant and Catholic, in that it cannot be slotted into Roman Catholic thought, which cannot be said of the theology of the cross.[9]

However, such a specific stance that has its roots in both church history and controversial theology cannot be abstracted from what is said in an endless regress to what is meant. The "actual reformational" aspect of Luther's theology cannot be chosen at will and found precisely in that which, for example, would make the break with Rome and the later doctrine of the sacraments completely incomprehensible.[10]

This also means we must reject the frequently used interpretative schema of "the seed and its development."[11] Certainly, there are numerous starting points or organizing centers (*Ansätze*) in the early texts that Luther later takes up. But this does not yet allow us to claim from his later understanding that these *Ansätze* form a corresponding *Tendenz*, if they are isolated in their context, if they lack decisive aspects, if they can only be compared with later statements when reduced to general concepts or basic structures, or if they are rendered ineffective by other, stronger aspects in the thought train of a section of text. If we want to determine the relationship between Luther's early theology and his reformational theology, we must not, therefore, compare individual motifs in themselves but only entire material contexts.

An exegetical approach that focuses on individual concepts, parts of sentences, and sentences only within entire textual contexts is therefore necessary. Of course, for the sake of clarity of presentation, these should not be too

---

8. We think of the impact that the appearance of this treatise had on Luther's contemporaries (see, e.g., Heinrich Boehmer, *Der junge Luther* (1962 5th ed.), 264–68.

9. It is significant that when Luther met with Cajetan in 1518 in Augsburg (on this, see Gerhard Hennig, *Cajetan und Luther. Ein historischer Beitrag zur Begegnung von Thomismus und Reformation*, 1966) the *theologia crucis* was not the stumbling block, but the new understanding of *promissio* that Luther had to publicly defend here for the first time.

10. As is evident from the careful work of Ulrich Mauser (*Der junge Luther und die Häresie*, 1968; see my review: *ZKG* 82 [1971]: 412–14) and Werner Jetter (*Die Taufe beim jungen Luther*, 1954).

11. This is how Ernst Bizer formulates it in the afterword to the 3rd ed. of *Fides ex auditu* (193) against Heinrich Bornkamm (see 191–92). Cf. Heinrich Bornkamm, "*Zur Frage der Iustitia Dei beim jungen Luther II*" (*ARG* 53, 1962):1–59, here 57.

numerous but must be exemplary, which can be shown, for example, by references to parallel texts in the footnotes.

In view of the structure of the investigation, this approach demands that we give up any attempt at systematization. Instead, we need to pay special attention to the texts, few though they be, in which Luther himself, so to speak, bundles different tendencies together, even combining several aspects of his word-concept into a single complex.

One such text is the *Sermon on the Prologue of John's Gospel* (1514), which forms the basis of the exposition for the first part of our investigation (chapter 1). Its development (chapter 2) shows that this is appropriate. However, with the analysis of a few texts, each one appears under as many different aspects as possible in order that its exemplary significance may been seen. The interpretation of the *Seven Penitential Psalms* of 1517 forms the conclusion of Luther's early theology before the Hebrews lectures; it concludes the first part of the book (chapter 3). Also in the second part, the structure of the investigation is determined by Luther himself. (Compare this with what is said below at the beginning of the second part, on the "Structure of the Presentation.")

In addition to making comparisons within Luther's writings to highlight their distinctiveness and focusing the presentation on representative texts, in what follows I will employ a further methodological principle to show as exactly as possible that the texts are deeply rooted in tradition history.[12] To this end, I had to work through the systematic, exegetical, and devotional literature (listed in the index of sources), paying particular attention to the sources that can be shown to have had a particular influence on Luther. In addition to Augustine's writings, these are Tauler's sermons and Gabriel Biel's Mass commentary. In contrast to the procedure often used of treating the representative of a tradition taken up by Luther and Luther himself separately (a method that can be eminently useful), this presentation focuses exclusively on the specific points of contact between them that can be established by the history of motifs or even understood directly by literary criticism, such as, for example, in the marginal notes on Tauler's sermons, and in his quotes of Augustine, Bernard, Gerson, etc.

The very broad framework of this investigation as regards its subject matter became necessary precisely because of a strict concentration on the understanding of the word, which however went beyond a conceptual monograph. However, there are still many individual interpretative tasks that need to be completed,

12. This includes the principles of historical methodology that Gerhard Ebeling sets out for research into Luther's theology; see his article "Luther II. Theologie," *RGG*, 3rd ed., IV, 496. See also Heinrich Bornkamm, *ARG* 53 (1962):53–55.

not only in relation to the tradition-historical background of the word. But to make a single text, such as the *Sermon on the Prologue of John's Gospel* discussed in the first chapter, the sole topic of a dissertation only makes sense once a methodologically and factually convincing overall perspective has been found for the interpretation of Luther's early writings. To map that perspective is the task of this work.[13]

13. Since the completion of the first part of this investigation (August 1967), several works on Luther have been published. Some are particularly important because they deal with problems that I also deal with in this study: Matthias Kroeger, *Rechtfertigung und Gesetz* (1968); Reinhard Schwarz, *Vorgeschichte der reformatorischen Bußtheologie* (1968); and James Samuel Preus, *From Shadow to Promise* (1969). On Preus, see the review mentioned in n. 3a. Schwarz goes into the tradition-historical background of penitential piety, which we will show to be pre-reformational (according to the definition given above); see chap. 4, n. 14. Kroeger, whose work deserves special mention here, comes to largely the same conclusions as the present study using similar methodological principles. This delightful agreement gives us reason to hope that research into the history of Luther's theology might now find a common path. This impression is confirmed by the recently published essay of Kurt Victor Selge, "Der Augsburger Begegnung von Luther und Kardinal Cajetan im Oktober 1518," in *Jahrbuch der hessischen kirchengeschichtlichen Vereinigung*, vol. 20 (1969): 37–54.

Part I

CHAPTER 1

Sermon on the Prologue of John (1514)

(In the Context of the First Lectures on the Psalms)

THE ONE TEXT that can best represent the understanding of the word in the first Psalms lectures appears in the *Christmas Sermon of 1514* on the Prologue of John.[1] Here the most important aspects, which are particularly prominent in individual scholia, are found in a comprehensive context, which makes it clear why the word must be spoken of in the singular and as a single concept, despite its different valencies of meaning.

Let us first briefly follow the course of the sermon (A), then look at its problems in more detail (B), and finally, inquire into the unity of its word-concept (C) and its significance for the understanding of the history of this concept in Luther's early theology (D).

(A) Luther begins with a long exposition of the first two verses of the text based on theological doctrines[2] of the Trinity and their discussion: the Word (*verbum*[3] = the Son of God, Christ) is eternal ("In the beginning was the Word"), distinct from the Father ("The Word was with God") and yet not separate ("God was the Word").[4]

But the main interest of the sermon lies in the question, Why does John call the Son of God the "Word"?[5]

---

1. More precisely, only John 1:1–14a. The sermon is given in WA 1:20–29 [= LW 70]. Its close integration with the first Psalms lectures, which the following section will demonstrate, especially in the footnotes, means that any dating other than that given by the WA (1:20:1514), such as 1516 or 1517 (as proposed by R. Schwarz, *Fides, spes und caritas*, 76, n. 1), seems impossible. If the sermon was written in either of these years, we know from the context of the texts of these years that it would be left in inexplicable isolation.

2. Latin: *propositiones*; see WA 1:22,28,11–12; 23,12–13.

3. The WA consistently uses an initial lowercase for *verbum* (word), even when it refers to Christ, the incarnate Word.

4. WA 1:20,13–22,28. [Luther translates the verse differently than the English Bible which renders it as "the Word was God"; trans. note.]

5. WA 1:22,30,37ff.

The first reason for this ("It seems to have been taken from Genesis, where we read: God said, 'Let there be,' and it was done"[6]) is only briefly examined.[7] The second reason, however, determines the sermon completely right up to the end: "Thus he prepared for us a better and more perfect way of understanding and ascending into the deity of the Son and the plurality of persons who share an identical nature."[8]

The fact that this way of speaking is possible lies in the capacity of the human word for analogy, which Luther says we find here in a double way: "First the word is internal, which most properly describes the word."[9] "Second the word is external."[10] This starting point (B1) is developed in two consecutive and parallel sections that allow Luther to assert that the understanding of the internal (or external) *human* word, which he explains in five (or six) points, is strictly analogous to the understanding of the internal (or external) *divine* word[11] (B2). A new series of arguments[12] leads back from the external word to the internal word and defines it basically as "motion" (B3). This prepares the way for the idea that dominates the final tropological part of the sermon: that humans become the word[13] (B4).

Thus Luther adheres, not formally and conceptually but thematically, to the traditional scheme according to which the Christmas sermon deals with the eternal, temporal, and spiritual birth of the Son of God, corresponding to the three different Christmas Masses.[14]

---

6. WA 1:22,38–39.

7. WA 1:22,38–23,18.

8. WA 1:23,18–20.

9. WA 1:23,21–22.

10. WA 1:25,14.

11. WA 1:23,35–40. "Think about God in this way" (1:23,40–24,1): 1:24,1–20 (in relation to the inner word). In relation to the external word: "However, let us see also here how the divine Word may be signified to us" (1:25,16): 1:25,17–24. "Since therefore the incarnate Son of God has all those attributes, he is best called the Word" (1:25, 24–25): 1:25, 25–36.

12. Their beginning (WA 1:25,36: Non . . .), which marks a decisive break in the flow of the sermon, is not indicated by Luther (and also not by the WA!). The execution of the theme announced in 1:25,11–13 begins with 1:25,36.

13. WA 1:28,25–29,30.

14. Thus, for example, Tauler (F. Vetter, 7–12; disposition of the sermon: 7–8), Gerson, *Sermon in Natali Domini* [Sermon on the Nativity of our Lord]: the Word was made flesh (*Oeuvres* 5:601) and Cusanus 1431 in Koblenz; *Predigten 1430–1441* (in German; the Latin text, to the best of my knowledge, has not yet been edited) by J. Sikora and E. Bohnenstädt. *Schriften des Nikolaus von Cues*, ed. F. Hoffmann on behalf of the Heidelberg Academy of Sciences (Heidelberg 1952):

(B1) The interweaving of the doctrine of the Trinity, Christology, the understanding of preaching, cosmology, and soteriology under the guidance of the "word" takes place according to a very specific understanding of human speech, which is developed briefly and concisely from two German expressions:

1. "My heart tells me so."[15]

   The inner word, the word of the heart that speaks to me, is the proper and complete word. Only later and in a broken way, does it find expression in the external word, the word of the mouth: "If your heart speaks to you, it is a word, indeed such a perfect word that you will perceive from your own experience that the word of the mouth is incomparably less and weaker."[16]
2. "It does not move the heart."[17]

   Since oral speech in the strict sense is not a "word" at all, but only its deficient mode, it, too, cannot establish genuine and full communication: "For you cannot move anyone's heart through a word spoken by the mouth, as much as your own heart is moved inwardly by your word . . . But it would be moved if we could send the internal word itself into their heart, but as it is we can only send the external word into their heart, and so their heart is moved incomparably less by it than our heart is by our own internal word."[18]

Thus the human word is not first and foremost binding oral and public speech but an inner, self-aware movement of the heart that can only be imperfectly transmitted. The understanding of the word is thus basically doomed to communication failure rather than communication success. Here, therefore, Luther operates entirely within the traditional Augustinian schema.[19]

85–90 (Disposition of the Sermon: 86). English: *Nicholas of Cusa's Early Sermons: 1430–1441*, trans. and intro. Jasper Hopkins (2003).

15. WA 1:23,25–26: "Mein Hertz sagt mir das."

16. WA 1:23,26–28.

17. WA 1:23,30–31: "Es geht ihm nit zu Hertzen."

18. WA 1:23,28–29, 31–34.

19. Cf. Nicholas of Lyra's approach in his Postil on John 1:1: The first thing to be noted is, "how the word is found in us," then, "how it is made in God." First, it must be understood "that a significative voice is called a word; but it is only this in a broad and denotative sense, inasmuch as it signifies the concept of the inner mind; just as urine is said to be healthy insofar as it is indicative of health. And therefore, just as what is indicated by the urine is properly called health, so too what is signified by the voice is properly called a word. But this is the concept of the inner mind, according to what Porphyry says in bk. 1 of *Peri Hermeneias* [*On Interpretation*]. Voices

This conception is seen in all its sharpness when compared with its antithesis, which in the later sermons on the same text[20] takes its place:[21] The spoken word—and here we see how the new understanding of the promise works itself out in a new concept of human speech generally—reveals the whole person; no one can hide themselves, but all are revealed unmistakably by the word they speak. Luther says in his paradigmatic *Christmas Sermon of 1522*:

> The human heart is known from the human word. As people commonly say,[22] "I know her heart" or "I know her mind," even though actually they only hear her word, since the mind of the heart follows the word, and is known through the word, as if it were in the word. Experience has taught the heathen, too, so that they can say, "A human being speaks what he or she is."[23] Likewise, "speech is the reflection of the heart."[24] If the heart is pure, it utters pure words. If it is impure, it utters impure words. The gospels agree with this, for

---

are known to be signs of those passions that exist in the soul. Therefore, the concept of the inner mind is indicated by the voice before it is properly called a word. And this is what Augustine says in bk. 15 *On the Trinity* (*De Trinitate*)" [then follows the beginning of sec. 19 (chap. 10), MPL 42:1071]: 5.185D. See also the article "verbum" in Johannes Altenstaig's *Vocabularius Theologiae* (Hagenau, 1517), which is an especially good indicator of the theological climate in which Luther grew up (Fol. 260v/261r). It is no accident that this work begins with the observation: "This vocabulary is frequently used by Augustine in his writings." As an indicator of the relationship between the internal and external word, the author quotes *De Trinitate* bk. 15, chap. 10: "The word that signifies outwardly is a sign of the word that is hidden within" (Fol. 261r; the correct reading of the passage is "The word that sounds without is a sign of the word that shines within" and comes at the beginning of chap. 11; the Latin [in the German original] is cited according to MPL42:1071).

20. See K. Aland, *Hilfsbuch zum Lutherstudium*, No. 316 (76). The sermons are likewise listed by W. von Loewenich in chronological order with their WA references; see p. 30, n. 3, of his publication *Die Eigenart von Luthers Auslegung des Johannes-Prologes* (Sitzungsberichte der Bayrischen Akademie der Wissenschaften. Philosophisch-historische Klasse, 1960, 8), 1960, which touches on the *Christmas Sermon of 1514*.

21. The following sermon extract is quoted from the archetype of Luther's later sermons, the 1522 Postil on John 1:1–14: WA 10 1/1:187,10–188,8 = LW 52:45–46 (trans. alt.).

22. Cf. Thiele, *Luthers Sprichwörtersammlung*, No. 412; Grimm, DWb 4:3,1211ff. With this and the following four proofs, I draw on the notes of the editor of WA 10 1/1, W. Köhler.

23. *Qualis quisque est, talia loquitur*: Seneca, *Epistle* 114 (ed. Hense, 1898, 533). See "This became a proverb among the Greeks: People's speech was just as their life [i.e., their character was revealed by their speech]," quoted in Erasmus, *Adagia* 1.i.98.

24. *Oratio est character animi*: Seneca, *Epistle* 115 (Hense, 542). Cf. "Language is the clothing of the mind" (*Oratio cultus animi est*).

> Christ says, "The mouth speaks from the overflow of the heart." And again, "How can you speak good when you are evil?" [Matt. 12:34]. Likewise, St. John the Baptist says in John 3[:31], "Whoever is of the earth speaks in an earthly way." Similarly, the German proverb says,[25] "What the heart is full of flows out of the mouth." So the whole world agrees that no image of the heart is so much like it or true to it as the word of the mouth. The bird is known by its song, for it sings according to the shape of its beak,[26] as if its heart were essentially in its words. The same is true of God. God's word is so much like God that the deity is wholly in it, and whoever has God's word has the whole deity.

(B2) The linguistic theoretical model of the *Christmas Sermon of 1514*, which has become even more clearly defined in its contrast, is now developed in five points with regard to the internal word and in six points with regard to the external word and then transferred step by step to the divine Word.[27]

The first thing to understand is that the *incarnation* is the extreme point of the internal word (a) and the *sermon* is the extreme point of the external word (b):[28]

---

25. German: *Weß das Herz voll ist, des geht der Mund über.* See Wander, *Sprichwörterlexikon* 2:611; Nos. 266, 267.

26. Cf. Thiele, *Luthers Sprichwörtersammlung*, Nos.167 and 121.

27. For the details, see n. 11.

28. Cf. on this Luther's interesting note on Ps. 29:3 in Faber's Psalter (*Psalterium Quincuplex*). [Biblical references in the psalms have been adjusted to match the versification of the English language Bible but do not follow any one version; the German follows the Hebrew and Latin versification; trans. note.] First, Luther refers the verse to the event of the incarnation and understands it from the language model presented above: "The Word of God takes on humanity as a word takes on a voice" (WA 4:485,21–22; see, on the same verse, 3:157,29–30: "As the word takes on a voice, so the Son of God takes on flesh." See 1:25,27: "He takes on a voice, that is, visible flesh"). Then it seems to him more correct to understand it with reference to the "published gospel" (4:485,22). In its characterization, the general understanding of language that gives the "inner word" priority over the "voice" is now intertwined with the notion of the incarnation in such a way that the deity takes on humanity, so that an understanding of the spoken word emerges, which seems superior to that of the (later!) Christmas Sermon: "The published gospel... was a word even before it was preached, but it assumed a voice when it was proclaimed publicly. And so it is the voice of power for the salvation of all who believe... Thus the voice was wordified, i.e. humanity was deified, and the word made vocal, i.e. incarnate" (4:485,22–27). How the phrase "the voice was wordified" is to be understood concretely, however, is not explained here, or even in the interpretation of Ps. 49:3 (WA 3:276–77; see esp. 276,37–41 = LW 10:228–29). So, the crucial point remains unclear.

(a) Just as the word of the human heart is only communicated to others in a broken form and is not "externalized,"[29] so God in the incarnation of Christ does not reveal his heart to us but basically keeps it to himself, only to open it up later. He does not bring himself to us but brings us to himself, "in the future": "We hope to look into this word in the future, when God has opened his heart, not simply to pour out his word, but to lead us into his heart."[30]

Thus the "word united with flesh or humanity" is only an outward "manifestation,"[31] only an improper word. It is therefore no coincidence that Christ's humanity is said to be "like a visible word."[32] This telling expression used by Augustine points to his idea of the sacraments.

(b) For the Augustinian understanding of the sacrament or word, the visible or audible word (= voice) is only a pointer to the inner, non-linguistic power of the word, the actual "word," which does not work as a voice but in parallel to it.[33] However, is Luther still operating with this schema when he says of the word: "It comes to be heard and makes itself heard, nothing more; that is, it only produces faith, not yet sight"[34]?

---

29. "It remains inside and cannot be poured out" (WA 1:23,36–37); correspondingly, the internal theological Word "remains in God and cannot be poured out, outside of God, but remains with God and is God. If God did not exist, it could be poured outside and separated and mixed with other words. But this is not possible, just as it is not possible with human words" (1:24,3–6). See Augustine, for example, *On Christian Doctrine* 1.13.12 (CCSL 32:13 [= MPL 34:24]): "It is like when we speak. In order for what we have in our mind to slip into the mind of the listener through the ears of their body, the word that we carry in our heart becomes a sound, which is called speech, and yet our thought is not converted into that sound but remains intact in itself and assumes the form of a voice by which it makes its way into the ears of another person without undergoing any change. In the same way, the Word of God was not changed, yet it was made flesh in order that it might dwell in us."

30. WA 1:24,13–15.

31. WA 1:24,9–11.

32. WA 1:24,9–11; on the following terms (1:24,11–13), "the work of God" and "the word, abbreviated and completed" (*verbum abbreviatum et consummatum*), see pp. 16–18.

33. We need here only refer to the classic passage in *Tractates on the Gospel of John*, tract. 80, chap. 3 (CCSL 36:529 [= MPL 35:1840]), where Augustine elaborates on John 15:3 ("Already you are clean because of the word that I have spoken to you").

34. WA 1:25,30–31.

This question becomes even more urgent when we also take into consideration the formulations of the scholia on Psalm 85:7–8, which are only slightly earlier than our text: "Faith comes from hearing";[35] "This mercy has been shown to us and this salvation of God given (!) to us for our hearing, but not yet for our seeing";[36] "The word of God is not perceived except by hearing. For it is the nature of the word to be heard . . . Therefore, to speak about the Lord himself is to declare his word and make it public (!), but only for hearing. Thus God the Father has spoken to us; that is, the Son has shown us his Word in the hearing of faith.[37] But faith does not stay with the spoken word but reaches "from the outside to the inside"[38]: "For this word cannot be spoken unless it is within you. Therefore, it cannot be heard by you unless you are within yourself and not outside of yourself."[39] What weight are we to give such a statement, and how are we to understand the sentence from our sermon, "In this inward hearing, the word effectually produces knowledge and salvation without merits"?[40] The answer to these questions is best seen from Luther's sharp statements on Psalm 45:1, which almost approach a definition—a verse, which from the point of view of its history of interpretation, is within the horizon of the theme of the Johannine

35. WA 4:8,34 = LW 11:159. Latin: *fides enim ex auditu est* (Rom. 10:17).

36. WA 4:9,14–15 = LW 11:160 (trans. alt.). "Given" is understandable from the text (v. 8): SHOW US YOUR MERCY, O LORD, AND GIVE US YOUR SALVATION (author's emphasis).

37. WA 4:9,18–23 = LW 11:160 (trans. alt.).

38. WA 4:11,3–4.

39. WA 4:10,38–11,1 = LW 11:162 (trans. alt.); see the context (4:10,26–33 and 4:11,1–15 = 11:162–63). The IN ME of Ps. 85:8: (I WILL HEAR WHAT GOD THE LORD WILL SPEAK IN ME) [The "in me" appears only in the Latin and is normally not translated in English Bibles; trans. note.] with reference to the inner word with which either the devil or God moves the human heart, also occurs in our sermon (at the end of Corollary 1: WA 1:25,8–9). According to the *Dictata*, the scholion touches on the *distinction between law and gospel*. "The law is the word of Moses to us, but the gospel is the word of God in us. The former remains outside and speaks of visible figures and the shadows of things to come, but the latter *comes inside* and speaks of inner, spiritual, and true things. For it is one thing to speak in us and another to speak to us. When God speaks *in* us, he is effectual and takes hold of us, but when he speaks *to* us, that is by no means the case" (4:9,28–33 = 11:160; author's emphasis; trans. alt.).

Luther cites this psalm verse, in agreement with the exegetical tradition (see the *Glossa interlinearis* and Lyra on Ps. 85:7–8; see his comments: 3:212), as evidence of the inner speaking of God in humans; it also occurs in Tauler ("I will hear what he is saying; I will hear what the Lord is speaking in me"; F. Vetter, 174,20–21) and in Staupitz ("I will hear, says David, what my Lord God will speak in me": J. K. F. Knaake, 165). See chap. 2, sec. C: "The Inner Word: Hidden Grace" and in chapter 3 B (2) "The Secret Whisper—The Forgiveness of Sins."

40. WA 1:25,32–36.

prologue,[41] but which lets Luther recognize and formulate a key question: "How is God's word to be heard or read?"

Psalm 45:1 (MY HEART HAS UTTERED A GOOD WORD): "In this verse he instructs us in a strange way how God's word is to be heard or read. He says that we should not attempt it by our own strength, nor should we be content with the letter and word heard from the outside, but should seek to hear the Spirit himself."[42] The "word heard from the outside" is therefore on the side of the "letter" in contrast to the "Spirit himself," to which all proper "hearing" is directed.[43] The vocal utterance is certainly necessary, but only as a secondary expression of the primary inner life: "To utter therefore is to bring out by means of the tongue the life that is hidden in the heart."[44] Under no circumstances should we be satisfied with the word heard as such, for it does not reveal the Spirit but hides him; the spoken word does not bring the Spirit with it but says, seek the Spirit. Therefore, the Spirit is not given through oral speech, for (as Luther says on Ps. 50:1) "God speaks without intermediary through the internal word, which is omnipotent and efficacious. But more often God also spoke many things that were not done and heard and received by humans. Therefore, there is a great difference between God's speech (*locutio*) and God's word (*verbum*)."[45] Thus

41. Saint Augustine, *Enarratio* on Ps. 44:2 (MPL 36:496–98), on which the *Glossa ordinaria* is heavily dependent (on Ps. 44:2, see 3.148F. 149A). In the Christmas sermon cited in n. 14, Cusanus also refers to this verse (*Predigten*, 86–87); likewise, in a Christmas sermon preached between 1441 and 1445 (*Predigten*, 442–63; here 450).

42. WA 3:255,41–256,2 = LW 10:211–12 (trans. alt.). [The significance of the point Luther is making here is lost in the English translations, which typically render Ps. 45:1 along the lines of: "My heart overflows with a goodly theme" NRSV; trans. note.]

43. Cf. (on Ps. 85:8): "The sense is that . . . we are to listen to the Spirit and not the letter, for the Spirit is the word of God" (WA 4:10:10–11 = LW 11:161; trans. alt.). See further the context of 4:9,28–10,12 = 11:160–61. The double schema discussed in 4:10,4–9 = 11:161, each part of which is again doubled in itself, shows that the sort of opposition that Luther sees existing within the gospel itself between outer orality and inner effect is analogous to the relationship between law and gospel! He speaks in an identical way in the marginal gloss on Ps. 71:15–16: WA 3:451,24–27, 32–39. When Luther here, speaking of the efficacy of Christ's Spirit baptism in contrast to John's water baptism, says that "Christ teaches inwardly with the living word," thereby referring to the IN ME of Ps. 85:8, and when he ranks the church's external rite of baptism with John's water baptism—"they all baptize with water only, like John"—that does not mean for a minute that "the word is given priority over the sacrament" (A. Brandenburg, *Gericht und Evangelium. Zur Worttheologie in Luthers erster Psalmenvorlesung*, 131) unless we understand "word" here in the sense of the Augustinian "power of the word." See also the scholion on Ps. 28:1, with its reference to Ps. 85:8: "God consoles inwardly, where he truly speaks with his invisible word, so that I hear what he is saying in me" (3:153,22–23 = 10:128; trans. alt.).

44. WA 3:256,23–24 = LW 10:212 (trans. alt.).

45. WA 3:281,3–6 = LW 10:230 (trans. alt.). This difference between the "word" (*verbum*) and "speech" (*locutio*) is typical of Luther's early understanding of the word. It is obvious that his later

the Spirit, in the sense of the Augustinian "power of the word," the power that produces immediate evidence, is the proper word, the "good word," the "word of grace" (again on Ps. 45:1): "For the Spirit is concealed in the letter, which is not the good word because it is the law of wrath. But the Spirit is the good word because it is the word of grace."[46]

(B3) That our interpretation is correct is clearly confirmed by the way the sermon continues. Suddenly,[47] the focus again shifts away from the external word back to the internal word in order to show in a far-reaching way why only the latter can be the word in the proper sense.[48]

At first, Luther had said that only the human word illustrated God's word, which corresponds to it in its double structure down to the last detail. But now, together with Augustine,[49] he sees God's word as basically represented by everything: "In everything and every creature, the procession of the word from the Father shines forth in many ways, though not equally in all."[50] When Luther says that "something similar to the word can represent God's word according to its degree of likeness, though less perfectly,"[51] he finds it—and now this is no

---

view cannot be derived from it. The "is" (*est*) of the Lord's Supper doctrine denotes a materially different theological position. The *coherence of the early understanding of the word* is remarkable. Luther has by no means unknowingly taken up the traditional motifs and formulations but strives intensely to clarify them both theologically and in terms of the philosophy of language. A most instructive testament to this is given by his interpretation of Ps. 71:15 (3:456,3–457,37 = 10:400–01), which leads to the following conclusion: "Here you must apply all your logic. A letter indicates a voice, and the voice an idea. Thus the law signifies the gospel, and the gospel, Christ. And just as an uneducated person sees and understands letters only as letters, not as signs of words, so the Jews see the law in the same way. And just as a barbarian hears a voice but does not understand it, so it is with the person who does not hear the gospel with understanding and growth" (3:457,33–37 = 10:401). This is a clear position that recurs in the sermon of Dec. 26, 1514, unchanged (1:30–37): "The letter is a dead word but the word a living letter, yet the thought is still dead. But the thought written by the finger of God is the life of the word and of the letter" (1:30,22–23; see ll.24–26). It is clear from this that the *Augustinian hermeneutic of signification* has not yet been overcome. We come across the schema again (57/2:94,20–26) in the Galatians lectures (1516/17) but no longer in the Galatians Commentary (1519) (see 2:548,30–549,9 = 27:308).

46. WA 3:256,28–29 = LW 10:212 (trans. alt.). Parallel to that (on Ps. 85:8: "The Spirit is the word of God" (WA 4:10,11 = LW 11:161). On the separation of "Spirit" and "word," see WA 4:57,34–58,21 = LW 11:201–02 (on Ps. 90:9).

47. See n. 12.

48. Cf. WA 1:23,22: "which is most properly called the word."

49. Augustine is only expressly named at WA 1:26,28 and 28,5.

50. WA 1:27,19–20. The general reference to Augustine's *De trinitate* should be enough to describe here the historical and theological background of this part of the sermon.

51. WA 1:26,2–3.

longer Augustinian—in the fact that everything that exists is realized, moves, without "losing itself";[52] in short, he finds it in motion. The Aristotelian concept of motion, however, connects the world with God in an ontological way; for according to Aristotle, "motion is the very essence of God."[53]

Let us briefly summarize Luther's remarks. All creation is one with God in the analogy of the word, where the "word" ontologically means "self-realization," "motion," and so is code for the fact that the being of God and of creation are in the process of becoming one.

It should be noted that Luther only arrived at such a general concept of the "word"[54] from the perspective of the internal word. If the binding oral and public character of the word were decisive factors in his understanding in 1514, as they are later, he could not have said that "the word is the intellect itself, insofar as it is such (i.e. insofar as it is realized)"[55] and that such a word is, "somehow,"[56] found in all beings.[57]

(B4) The concluding part of the sermon develops the formulaically tight but tropologically concise interpretation of John 1:14a: "The Word becomes flesh in order that the flesh may become the Word."[58]

The possibility of such an event can only be understood from its analogy with the word as presented above. The Word, God, does not change into flesh,[59] but persists in the incarnation so that the Word remains as movement. However, it can now be seen and viewed as united with the flesh[60] (that is, in its humiliation).[61] Thus its general concept is expressed in a concrete way: as a movement of weakness and humiliation.[62] In this concrete form, humans can and should take

52. On this expression: WA 1:27,17–18.

53. WA 1:27,23.

54. How enormously this general word (*verbum universale*) differs from the later special word (*verbum speciale*) (on that, see chap. 4)!

55. WA 1:27,35; cf. 1:26,33–34: "The word properly has the character of the intellect alone."

56. WA 1:26,9.

57. WA 1:26,3–25.

58. WA 1:28,27: *verbum fit caro, ut caro fiat verbum.*

59. WA 1:28,36–38.

60. WA 1:28,38.

61. "Its power becomes weak . . . it takes on our form and shape, our image and likeness" (WA 1:28,28–29). Thus for Luther, Phil 2:6–8 and John 1:14a clearly coalesce. See the scholion on Rom. 6:17 where it says: "'The Word was made flesh' and 'took on the form of a servant'" (WA 56:330,1–2 = LW 25:317); see pp. 21–22, 27, 65–67.

62. See n. 60.

on the Word, incorporate it by behaving in a way analogous to its humiliation, and so in fact become the weak Word that is presented to them: "But when we assume the Word, it is necessary to abandon and humiliate ourselves, retaining nothing of our frame of mind but renouncing everything. Thus without doubt we become what we assume; and so the Lord carries all of us in this life by the word of his power."[63]

The concept of word determined by its Aristotelian "motion" is so fused here in its concrete christological and soteriological form with the monastic idea of humiliation and the late medieval theology of suffering[64] that it is impossible to ask who is interpreting whom. Humans become the Word, not in an indefinite but in a definite movement: by "leaving and humiliating themselves, retaining nothing of their own but renouncing everything." *But this existential determination of the Word is not in addition to its motion; on the contrary, for Luther it is already part of its Aristotelian conception*, and so these two motives can hardly be unraveled:[65] Only as matter, understood as "pure potentiality," strives after its form does motion occur. "When the intellect and the affections desire their objects, insofar as they desire them, they, like matter, have a form that desires and according to it, that is, insofar as they desire, but not insofar as they subsist, they are pure potentiality, indeed, a kind of nothing and only become a kind of being when they attain their objects."[66]

The movement, the actuality (*actus*), in which the "pure potentiality" of the humble human being longs to look out from its nothingness, its *materia*, for its *forma*, its "object," is the human being becoming the word, is faith that presses on to the future.[67] This future means the unbroken validity—"without voice, sound, or letters"—of that internal word, which is now hidden in the flesh or "in sound, voice, letters" like a kernel in its shell.[68] But we already become one with it in that movement which, by virtue of its determining and thus desired

---

63. WA 1:29,6–10; the ending is based on Heb. 1:3. For an authentic comment on this by Luther, we can do no better than read the passage from his famous interpretation of Ps. 72 in WA 3:463,17–37 = LW 10:405, especially the addition "When the gospel is fulfilled in work, then the word of God is always incarnated spiritually. For work is like the flesh, and the word is like God's Son. Thus the fulfilled gospel is judgment and righteousness, and the work of God, the way of God, etc., just as Christ is literally all these things in his person" (ll.24–28) (trans. alt.).

64. On this, see in what follows, especially the intermediate chapter: "Sacramental Meditation on Scripture" and "The Understanding of the Mass."

65. *Among the most interesting passages in the first Psalms lectures are those in which Luther uses the concept of movement from Aristotle's Physics as a category of history* (see n. 89 and p. 142).

66. WA 1:29,22–26.

67. "The word is faith in future things" (WA 1:29,11).

68. WA 1:29,12–15.

"object,"[69] which is God, comes about from its potentiality, the humble human being, as an act, as faith.

We meet Aristotle most impressively where Luther draws on a train of thought from his epistemology in *De Anima* III[70] to determine what it means "to become the word"—that is, to believe, love, and hope.[71] He puts it this way:

> Do not be surprised when I say that we must become the word, since even the philosophers say that the intellect is the intelligible [or known] object through the actualization of the intellect [the act of understanding], and that the sense is the sensible [or sensed] object through the actualization of sensation [the act of sensation]. How much more then is it true of the Spirit and the Word! . . . So also, desire and the object of desire are one, as are love and the object of love.[72]

Thus, the unity-creating correlation of "word" and "humiliation" has found a clear expression.[73]

---

69. "Objects are their being and actuality, without which they would be nothing, just as matter without its form would be nothing" (WA 1:22,26–27).

70. *De Anima*, 425b: "The activity of the sensible object and that of the percipient sense is one and the same" (Aristotle, *Opera* [Bekker, 1831], vol. 3, 221,26–27); 426a: "The actuality of the sensible object and the sensitive faculty is one" (221,16); 431a: "For everything that comes into being from that which is in actuality is a whole. But the sensible object seems to draw the sensitive faculty itself toward its actuality from its potentiality and thus effect it in its actuality: yet the faculty itself is not affected or altered" (224,3–5).

The unity of movement that Luther spoke of in the passage referred to in B3 is, precisely as movement, the same unity as that characterized here in the final part; "every movement is easily understood from its identity with its movable object" (WA 1:27,35–36). *This is because the basic concepts of Aristotle's theory of motion and his epistemology are the same.* Thus Luther in his description of the "general word" (n. 54) can, in *one* train of thought, refer first to the *Physics* (27,23–24; E. Vogelsang mentions the place in Aristotle: *BoA* 5:415), and then shortly afterward to *De Anima* (see the passages mentioned above): "Sensation is nothing but the very essence of the sensitive thing, i.e., it is the actuality of the sensitive faculty inasmuch as it is such" (WA 1:27,33–34). *These are the philosophical lines Luther follows in his thinking about the "simul" (*at the same time*), "semper" (*always*), and "magis magisque" (*more and more*) in his early doctrine of justification.* "From this point of view, special attention must be given in the final part of the sermon to the sentence, 'the intellect and the affections . . . insofar as they desire, but not insofar as they subsist, are pure potentiality . . .'" (WA 1:29,22–25). See n. 89 and pp. 142, 146–153.

71. Cf. the texts mentioned in n. 73.

72. WA 1:29,15–18,20–21.

73. Otherwise, in this connection, apart from Aristotle, Luther also refers to Augustine: "We become what we love. 'If you love God, you are God; if you love the earth, you are earth,' says St. Augustine. For love is a unifying force, which makes the loved and the lover into one" (Scholion

(C) It has become clear that the sermon in its concept of the word is not dealing with a single problem but presents an entire theological outline that is extremely unified. It is noteworthy in itself that it speaks of *the* word throughout in the singular. For even this, which at first glance seems like a purely formal matter, shows that the sermon holds together a cosmos of theological topics and references[74] in nothing other than the *unity of the word*.[75] The word of course is that word that unites God and his creation. Precisely as the one and only word, it embraces and reaches eschatological fullness and completion. This as we see does not come out as clearly in our sermon[76] as it does in Luther's remarks on

on Rom. 3:12: WA 56:241,3–5 = LW 25:226–27); see J. Ficker's notes on Rom. 3:12 and G. Metzger, *Gelebter Glaube*, 25, n. 53). See further the scholion on Rom. 8:24 (56:374,8–21 = 25:364; for proof of the passages quoted by Luther, see also here again J. Ficker's prolific notes on Rom. 8:24 and R. Schwarz, *Fides, spes, und caritas*, 322, n. 202): "When the hope that arises from the desire for a beloved object is delayed, its love is made all the stronger. And so, what is hoped for, and the hoping person become one through intense hope, or as blessed Augustine puts it: 'The soul is more [at home] where it loves than where it lives.' Thus it is commonly said, 'My flame is here!' And the poet [Virgil] says: 'You are my flame, Amyntas.' And Aristotle in his *De anima*, bk. 3, says that the intellect and the intelligible [what it understands], sensory perception and the sensible [what it perceives] become one, as do potentiality and its object generally. Thus love changes the lover into the beloved. Accordingly, hope changes hopers into what they hoped for, but what they hope for is not apparent. Hope therefore transfers them into the unknown and hidden, into an inner darkness, so that they do not even know what they hope for, and yet they know what they do not hope for. Thus the soul that hopes has become hope and what it hopes for at the same time, because it remains in what it does not see, that is, in hope. If this hope were seen, that is, if hoping and what is hoped for mutually recognized each other, then hope would not be thus transferred into what is hoped for, that is, into hope and the unknown, but would be carried away to what it could see and would enjoy the knowledge of it." See the scholion on Rom. 5:5: WA 56:307,4–9, see LW 25:294 (chap. 2, n. 552).

74. In the same speculative and existential sense as our sermon, the interpretation of Ps. 64 sees the "work of God" from creation to the eschaton, unfolded according to the schema of the fourfold sense of Scripture, comprehended in "Christ" rather than in the "word": "All these things are Christ at the same time" (WA 3:369,1–10 = LW 10:312; trans. alt.). "Therefore, Christ is the end and center of them all. They all look and point to him, as if to say: 'Look, he is the one who is, but we are not; we are only signs" (3:368,22–24 = 10:311; trans. alt.). Corresponding to this is the statement (on Ps. 80:1) that "faith in Christ is . . . the fullness of all knowledge. And all other kinds of knowledge are like a figure of this knowledge and point to faith like a sign" (WA 3:606,31–32 = LW 11:95–96; trans. alt.). See p. 131.

75. Cf. on Ps. 62:11 (ONCE GOD HAS SPOKEN): "All the words of God are one, simple, the same, true, because they all tend to one word, however many they are. And all the words that tend to one word are one word" (WA 3:356,35–37). This one word of God has its unity in Christ: In Christ, all words are one word, and outside of Christ are many and empty, where even one word is many words, because it is turned to many. Thus in Christ, many words are turned to one, namely, Christ" (4:439:20–23).

76. WA 1:24,11–20; especially, however, 1:29,12: "the indivisible word."

Psalm 45[77]: "Then the Father will give us all things with his one word, for when his glory appears we shall be satisfied, and yet he will satisfy us with his single and most simple word,"[78] that he might be the same as always and the one who is "all in all."[79]

Luther will stress that the decisive hallmark of the later special word, the promise, is its *unambiguity*: God binds himself to it and with it,[80] and in this identification gives himself to us as the One, completely, so that we can seek after him and take hold of him with certainty. According to Luther's reformational view, the unity of God is thus given in the unambiguity of the oral word and so keeps us certain of our salvation. Our sermon, on the other hand, does not understand the unity of the word in such a narrow and specific sense, although for Luther later on, this is the crunch point on which everything depends.[81] It

77. The text that is materially closest to our sermon as a whole is the last of Luther's many attempts to understand Ps. 45:1: WA 3:261,18–262,29 = LW 10:220–21. The text that follows above is quoted from this "repetition" (WA 3:261,18 = LW 10:219).

78. WA 3:262,25–27 = LW 10:221 (trans. alt.).

79. WA 3:262:20–21 = LW 10:221 (trans. alt.).

80. We only have to think of those words "holding God to his word" and "taking hold of God with his promise of the forgiveness of sins" from the famous sermon on Matt. 15:21–28 (Lenten Postil, 1525, WA 17/2:200–04; here 204,2,9) or of the clear statements from *That These Words of Christ, "This is My Body" Still Stand Firm* (1527): There is a difference between saying "God is there, and God is there for you. For he is there for you when he adds his word and binds himself to it, saying, 'here you shall find me.' Now when you have his word, you can take hold of him and have him with certainty and say, 'here I have you'" (WA 23:150,13–17 = LW 37:68; trans. alt.). The understanding of the promise that God binds himself to his word of judgment certainly occurs already in the first Psalms lectures (and comes out especially clearly in the exposition of Ps. 51:4: 3:289,1–10 = 10:237; see chap. 2, sec. 1) but not the notion that God gives himself in a specific word of salvation and binds himself to it.

81. In view of what is being discussed here, it is highly instructive for determining the place of the first Psalms lectures in the history of theology to note how Luther, following the exegetical tradition, understands Ps. 62:11. (Some of the scholion has already been quoted in n. 75.) "ONCE, he does not repeat it or revoke it, GOD HAS SPOKEN, it is as if he said, hold on to what he says, for what God speaks, he speaks irrevocably; therefore, he does not change, but you can be changed (Job 33:14 follows, then:) THESE TWO THINGS HAVE I HEARD BECAUSE POWER BELONGS TO GOD (the following glosses take up Lyra [3:171G] almost word for word:) for punishing, as it does to the Lord [Christ]. AND MERCY BELONGS TO YOU, O LORD for the sake of rewarding, as it does to the Father: FOR YOU WILL RENDER TO EACH ONE ACCORDING TO THEIR DEEDS, good for good, evil for evil" (WA 3:354,2–8). In the marginal note, Luther refers to Augustine (see on this and on the scholion CCSL 39:786–91 [=MPL 36:741–46]): "These two things (according to Blessed Augustine) properly comprise the whole of Scripture: that we fear God's power and love his mercy, not that we so presume on his mercy that we despise his power, nor that we so fear his power that we despair of his mercy . . . these two things are in this article [of the creed] on God, the Father" (WA 3:354,32–37). The

rather sees the incarnation of Christ as the unique "work of God" in the midst of the times (Hab. 3:2),[82] that one and only "abbreviated and completed word" (Isa. 10:22–23 = Rom. 9:28),[83] the fullness in the One, which takes up and excludes confusing multiplicity, "so that the things that are done there (in the old

---

scholion first speaks about the *one* word of God with reference to the *ONCE* (see n. 74) in order then to explain THESE TWO THINGS. Here now Luther himself is unmistakably speaking: "Therefore, we must always stand between these two things, namely, the fear of God's power and the hope of his mercy so that we are ground in the Lord's mill between the upper and lower millstone, crushed between the upper and lower teeth, and passed through into the bowels of Christ. Indeed, the working of every created thing also teaches us this lesson, like gold in a furnace and every work in their factory" (WA 3:357,1–5 = LW 10:301; trans. alt.). The conventional picture of the two millstones [Deut. 24:6] is used in this connection also by Paul of Burgos in his addition to Lyra [3:171G]). The distance and proximity of this interpretation to Biel's understanding of "justice" and "mercy," as well as its difference to the later "to fear and love God" do not need to be discussed here in detail. In any case, the decisive step toward Luther's reformational theology only takes place when "the hope of mercy" is defined precisely as faith in the promise that delivers the forgiveness of sins. When Luther can say that, he will have also solved the problem of how we obtain certainty, which is still an open question in Biel (on that see H. A. Oberman, *Spätscholastik und Reformation* 1, 204–13) as in Luther's early theology. See pp. 73–75, p. 135, pp. 144–145, pp. 148–151.

82. "The incarnation of Christ is uniquely called God's work in Hab. 3: 'O Lord, your work in the midst of the years'" (WA 1:24,11–13). Compare this with the marginal gloss on Ps. 52:9: "[God] has done his work . . . At that time, you spoke in the law, then the word, now the work, then the promise, now the fulfillment, then the sign (*signum*), now the thing signified (*res*), then the figure, now the truth. Hence Hab. 3, 'O Lord, your work in the midst of the years'" (3:295,33–36; see further references to Hab. 3:2: 3:371,36–38). The clarity of this gloss is deceptive. Even if Christ is said to be the *res*, it remains to be seen whether as such it can also be promised and given, or whether the *res*, as Luther obviously means, is again just a *signum*. See especially the reference to Hab. 3:2 in the scholion on Ps. 82:1: "There are two years: one of the law, the other of grace, and in the midst of these, that is, at the end of the law and the beginning of grace, the mystery of the incarnation and redemption is completed: that is the work of the Lord" (3:621,1–4).

83. WA 1:24,13 (*verbum abbreviatum et consummatum*). Since Rom. 9:28 is only quoted briefly here for its understanding of the incarnation, the importance that this passage really has for Luther (see the section on the scholion to this text in the Romans lectures, pp. 130–135 is not clear. Therefore, we will draw on the context in which the quote is found in the interpretation of Ps. 45:1 (see n. 77) and use it as a commentary: "And just as God's first speech was wrapped in many figures and shadows, all of which are found and fulfilled in the one Christ—for whatever is done in the law, with so many words and deeds, the one Christ keeps in truth completely (for thus the Lord made a word that completes and abbreviates, so that whatever things are accomplished there [in the old covenant] in many ways, may be fulfilled here in the one faith and of course in love, thus bringing the burdensome host of laws to an end)—so in the future God will be one and the same, all in all" (WA 3:262,15–21 = LW 10:220–21; trans. alt.; the corrupted text in 3:314,6–8 seems to point in the same direction). That Rom. 9:28 and John 1:14 traditionally belong together is proved by Gerson's *Christmas Sermon* (*Oeuvres* 5:598): "The Word, it says, was made flesh. See what the apostle writes in Rom. 9: The Lord made an abbreviated word [the incarnate Word] upon the earth."

covenant) in many ways may be accomplished here in one faith and of course in love, thus bringing the burdensome host of laws to an end."[84] But this one word does not appear unambiguous but rather broken in the Augustinian sense of being "like a visible word" and so is only a pointer to its future unambiguity[85] or inner evidence.[86] Thus the Augustinian schema used by Luther does not preserve the unity of the word but breaks it precisely where it could, as the unambiguousness of the external word, embrace people in a salvific way. For the early Luther, however, the word, understood as an external word, is only an improper word, which compared to the internal word, is only equivocal but not univocal.[87]

But have we not been too hasty in our judgment? According to the concluding part of our sermon, does God's word not permeate us through its incarnation in such a way that it unites us with itself and so with God himself? Is the unity of the word not brought to bear here in a fascinating conception throughout so that 1) the monergism of the word overcomes the synergistic problem, 2) in its becoming, the future determines the present and the present lives from the future, so that 3) in the word, that is, in a single movement, God and faith belong together and are one? Is this not—formulated in the thought train of an Aristotelian epistemology—the same schema of a unity-creating correlation that becomes a decisive factor in Luther's later theology ("for the two belong together, faith and God")?[88]

The problem brought into focus with the last summary question encompasses almost all the points that are in contention in the research into the history of the reformational upheaval in Luther's theology.

It would be improper and methodologically wrong to pursue the schema of a unity-creating correlation alone as such, in its basic structure, as all that

84. See n. 83.

85. WA 1:24,13–20 (see p. 8); 1:29,10–13 (see p. 13).

86. WA 1:25,32 (see pp. 8–13).

87. Cf., on the other hand, again (see n. 21) the *Church Postil* of 1522: "His word is so much like God himself that the Godhead is wholly in it, and whoever has the word has the whole Godhead" (WA 10 1/1:188,7–8 = LW 52:46; trans. alt.; see 10 1/1:186,15–16 = 52:45). *Thus Luther here expressly refrains from making use of the concept of the "inner word"*: "They [the scholastics] have fiercely debated over the inner word of the human heart that stays inside . . . But the debate has been so deep and obscure so far, and no doubt will remain that way, that even they do not know what it is all about. Therefore, we will not bother about it either" (WA 10 1/1:188,18–23 = LW 52:46; trans. alt.).

In view of such a clear contrast to his earlier statements (see "the first is the inner word, which is most properly called the word": WA 1:23,21–22), we cannot agree with G. Ebeling that "later corrections . . . do not really contradict what he said earlier, but rather make his conclusions more precise" (Luther: *An Introduction to his Thought*, 107, trans. alt.; see 108–9).

88. Explanation of the first commandment in the *Large Catechism* (*BSLK* 560 = *BC* 386).

one could prove would be its continuity. Rather, an investigation of its history must not ignore the specific way in which it is expressed in each case. Thus in our sermon we must pay attention to *how* God and humans are related to each other in the unity of the Word.

God and humans are united in the word as a becoming, in a movement that embraces both. God is what he does when he is desired, humans are what they desire when they are affected by it. However, such an existential movement, which according to the Aristotelian conception of motion basically lasts "forever" (*semper*)[89]—as we would have to conclude from Luther's later theology—can only make us fundamentally uncertain because of its constant fluctuations,[90] since we never know how we "stand with God."[91] *The unity of the word does not come to a head in its unambiguity in an oral and binding promise, thus not at a fixed point, but spreads out in a movement of constant humiliation, where believers are not certain of their salvation and cannot not be certain of it, because they are always in*

89. The special significance of this adverb "forever" (*semper*), together with "at the same time" (*simul*), is known especially from the Romans lectures (on that see pp. 22–26). *According to its origin, it belongs to the ontological concept of the word understood as a movement.* We can observe this in many places in the first Psalms lectures (WA 3:223,16–28 = LW 10:185; 3:399,6–12 = 10:355; especially in the interpretation of Ps. 119: 4:362,32–363,5 = 11:494–95; 4:364,14–25 = 11:496; 4:365,5–29 = 11:497–98; 4:365,31–36 = 11:497–98; 4:366,3–4 = 11:498; 4:375,1–13 = 11:511 and elsewhere), but it comes out very clearly and precisely in a special way in our sermon: "For in all motion, it happens that the acquired part ceases to be acquired and there is a resting motion. And so the same thing, with respect to the end that it seeks, is moved, but with respect to what it has acquired, it rests. Therefore, it is both moved and at rest with respect to itself; it *always* begins and ends with respect to itself; it is *always* at the beginning and the end with respect to itself" (1:28,10–14; author's emphasis). Compare the striking passage from the interpretation of Ps. 119:125 (4:365,16–20 = 11:497; trans. alt.): "Just as in God, the Son is always born from eternity and to eternity, so we, too, must always be born, renewed, and brought to life. For every change in a creature signifies the Son's birth anagogically, our birth tropologically, and the church's birth allegorically. Therefore, it says of us in scripture that we are always like newborn babes."

90. We cannot deny this with the objection that Luther is here speaking of a "change and exchange" (*Wechsel und Tausch*) as he does in the freedom tractate (1520): "Since Christ's garment is righteousness and holiness and glory, and we are that garment itself, it follows then that we are righteousness and glory" (WA 1:29,5–6; see 28,32–33). However, the question that must now be asked is, *How* does that occur, and *what* causes it? The sentence immediately following our quote (mentioned above and referenced in n. 63) gives the answer: It happens through "humiliation" and "our self-denial"—which is still a long way from his reformational theology!

91. From Luther's *Sermon Preached in the Castle at Leipzig on the Day of St. Peter and St. Paul 1519* (WA 2:241–49 = LW 51:53–60; trans. alt.): "It is important to know whether we have received God's grace or not. For we must know how we stand with God, if our conscience is to be joyful and confident" (2:249,3–5 = 51:59). For how this sermon fits in, see chap. 4, p. 185.

humiliation.[92] Or to put it in expressly christological terms, the incarnated and preached word itself does not ultimately bind God to his promise;[93] it gives no guarantee of salvation but only a pointer to it (admittedly a unique pointer); and it offers no basis for unambiguity and certainty but only an occasion (admittedly unique) to wait for it, yearn for it, and thereby to persevere in the movement of humiliation that corresponds to Christ's own humiliation in the incarnation (Phil. 2:7; John 1:14).[94]

(D) The *Christmas Sermon of 1514* is an extremely important document for understanding the story of the concept of the word in Luther's early theology because it combines statements that occur only in greater or lesser isolation in the first Psalms lectures and then in the Romans lectures, to form a single clear *context.* Thus when we investigate the understanding of the word at the time of the Romans lectures, as we will in the next chapter, we do not have to construct presumed contexts but can adopt the outline of this sermon as a framework mapped out by Luther himself, as long as it is clearly not expanded or restricted and Luther's Romans interpretation does not introduce anything new and thus block an interpretation from his 1514 perspective. It remains to be seen, however, how well the statements from the time of the Romans lectures fit into this framework and really only become understandable in it.

However, as we will see, his statements at the time of the Romans lectures fit very well into this framework and can only really be understood within it.[95]

92. Cf. the "always seek," "always desire" of the first Psalms lectures (see n. 89) and esp. the Romans lectures (see pp. 146–153).

93. See B2 pp. 8–11 and pp. 15–18.

94. See n. 90.

95. This is not to say that, besides the differences due to the dissimilarity of the texts interpreted, the first Psalms lectures are not remarkably different from the Romans lectures in their conceptuality and motifs. However, to present these differences comprehensively would require a separate study. In our work, they should not be overplayed but can only be noted briefly at a few points. In terms of the overall context, this approach makes sense. It would only become problematic if the presentation of these differences between the first Psalms lectures and the Romans lectures were to correct the basic features of the picture of Luther's theology of the word prior to his *Explanations of the Theses on Indulgences* (also known as the Ninety-five Theses), as sketched out in the first part of this work, so that the reformational turn in Luther's theology would have to be defined differently than in the second part.

CHAPTER 2

The Time of the Romans Lectures[1]

1. Word—Humiliation

A) The Word as Movement: Penitence [Rom. 6:17; 12:2]

WE MEET THE train of thought and terminology of the final, tropological part of the *Christmas Sermon of 1514* again in the interpretation of Romans 6:17b, which is in large measure representative of his understanding of the word in the whole of his Romans lectures: YOU HAVE BECOME OBEDIENT FROM THE HEART TO THAT FORM OF TEACHING TO WHICH YOU WERE DELIVERED. The striking formulation of this text has theological importance for Luther: The "form of teaching" is not delivered to us, but we are delivered to it.[2] This means that "it is necessary for the wisdom of the flesh . . . to give up its own form and take on the form of the word. This happens when it

1. Luther began the Romans lectures after *Easter* 1515 and finished them in Sept. 1516 [with J. Ficker, WA 56: XII–XIII. E. Vogelsang, on the other hand (*BoA* 5:222), with H. Boehmer (*Luthers erste Vorlesung*, 6, n. 4) only has them beginning around Nov. 1515. H. Bornkamm ("Luther, 1. Leben und Schriften," *RGG*, 3rd ed., 4:482) supports J. Ficker's date, and Ficker in turn (56: XII) relies on Oldekop's account].

The main Luther sources used for this chapter, apart from the autograph and the dictation of the Romans lectures (WA 56 = LW 25 and WA 57/1), are the sermons of this time (WA 1; 4), the marginal notes on Tauler's sermons (WA 9), and the psalms revisions of autumn 1516 [WA 3:15,13–26,18; 39,21–60,7: cf. E. Vogelsang, *BoA* 5:40; the interpretation of Psalm 23 (WA 31/1:464–71) does *not* belong to this time: see n. 435b and chap. 5, pp. 235–236. *In a few places, we will have to reach back to the first Psalms lectures (WA 3; 4; 55) for the correct understanding of the texts from the time of the Romans lectures.*

2. Speech is more significant: "To which you were delivered rather than: what was delivered to you" (WA 56:330,5–6 = LW 25:317; cf. 56:329,25–27 = 25:317; trans. alt.); the gloss here reads: "For the word is not changed, but we are changed, and we yield to it" (56:62,14–15 = 25:54 n. 16). See the first Psalms lectures on Ps. 68:13: "The power of Scripture is this, that it is not changed into those who study it, but it transforms those who love it into itself and its virtues" (3:397,9–11 = 10:332) and on Ps. 119:24: "The testimonies should not enter us, but our meditation on them should enter the testimonies" (4:317,37–38 = 11:431; trans. alt.); see further 4:318,1–6 = 11:431–32; again from the interpretation of Ps. 1:2 (autumn 1516): "Theirs (i.e. the meditation of the perverse) is not a meditation on the law of the Lord but rather, on the contrary, the law of the Lord is in their meditation (which is a horrible thought). They . . . do not want to agree with their adversary on the way but want their adversary to agree with them"

takes itself captive and destroys itself through faith, conforms itself to the Word, believing it to be true but itself false. Thus 'the Word was made flesh' and 'took on the form of a servant'[3] in order that the flesh might become the Word and humanity take on the form of the Word."[4] The gloss puts it succinctly: "Give up your form and put on the form of the Word. For the 'Word was made flesh' in order that we might become the Word."[5] In that sermon, Luther had seen our becoming the Word, leaving our own "form" for the "form" of the Word, as a movement, according to the Aristotelian schema, in which the yearning matter and the form that realizes itself from it coincide. That this understanding also holds true for the Romans lectures can be seen from the scholion on the key phrase BE TRANSFORMED (Rom. 12:2):

> For just as there are five stages in the things of nature, according to Aristotle: nonbeing, becoming, being, action, and being acted upon, that is, privation, matter, form, operation, passivity, so also with the Spirit: nonbeing is something without a name and a human in sin; becoming is justification; being is righteousness; action is to act and live righteously; to be acted upon is to be made perfect and complete. These five stages are somehow always in motion in humans. And however we are to explain human nature—apart from the first nonbeing and the final being, for in between these two, nonbeing and being acted upon, the other three, namely, becoming, being, and acting are always in motion—through the new birth humans pass from sin to righteousness, and so from nonbeing through becoming to being. And having done that, they work justly. But from this new being, which is really a nonbeing, humans progress and pass to another new being by being acted upon, that is, through becoming new, they pass into being better and from there again into being new. Therefore, it is quite correct to say that humans are always in privation, always in becoming or in potency, matter, and always in action. This is the way Aristotle philosophizes about these things, and he does it well, but people do not understand him well.

(3:20,16–22 = 10:18; trans. alt.; important here is the reference to Matt. 5:25 at the end. It also occurs in the interpretation of Rom. 6:17b; see pp. 26–28).

3. It is not only the striking construction of Rom. 6:17b that prompts Luther to his interpretation but in conjunction with it the keyword *form*, which makes him think of John 1:14a via Phil. 2:7a (cf. chap. 1, n. 61). We could compare how *form*, for example, also leads the *Glossa ordinaria* at this point far beyond the text itself, certainly in a different way than in Luther: "Our teaching is a form that restores the deformed image of God" (4.15E).

4. WA 56:329,27–330,3 = LW 25:317 (trans. alt.).

5. WA 56:62,17–18 = LW 25:54 n. 16.

> Humans are always in nonbeing, in becoming, in being, always in privation, in potency, in action, always in sin, in justification, in righteousness, that is, they are always sinners, always penitent, always righteous. For by being penitent, the unrighteous person becomes righteous. Therefore, penitence is the medium between unrighteousness and righteousness. And so, people are in sin with respect to their starting point (*terminus a quo*), and in righteousness, with respect to their finishing point (*terminus ad quem*). Therefore, if we are always penitent, we are always sinners, and yet for that very reason, we are also righteous and justified, partly sinners and partly righteous, that is, we are nothing but penitents.[6]

Although the vocable "word" is not used, the same idea of the word as movement appears here as in the *Christmas Sermon of 1514* and, as there, its unity is emphasized, which is created by the correlation of matter and form. Even more clearly than there, we see here the movement described as a movement—that is, in its passage (*transitus*) from "nonbeing, through becoming, to being," which is constantly repeated. The importance of the statement lies in the repetition, not in the gradual progression; the "always" means "ever again" rather than "ever further." To put it pointedly, the "progress," which Luther will describe,[7] lies in the "repetition."[8] Admittedly, the starting point and the finishing point are marked

6. WA 56:441,23–442,22 = LW 25:434 (trans. alt.). For the period of the Psalms lectures, cf. besides the passages mentioned in chap. 1, n. 89, also the *Sermon on the Fear of God* of Dec. 27, 1514 (WA 4:659–66, esp. 665,2–5): "The righteous are called righteous not because they are but because they are becoming righteous, according to the text, 'Let the one who is righteous become more righteous still' (Rev. 22:11). For all motion is partly at the starting point and partly at the finishing point, just as sick people being healed are decreasing in sickness and increasing in health."

7. As he explains at the beginning and toward the end of the scholion. At the beginning, he says: "With this he is speaking in favor of progress, for it is speaking to those who have already begun to be Christians. Their life is not about being at rest but about being moved from good to better, just as a sick person proceeds from sickness to health" (WA 56:441,14–16 = LW 25:433; trans. alt.). Toward the end, he says: "Therefore, this life is a road to heaven or to hell. No one is so good that they cannot become better, and no one is so bad that they cannot become worse, until at last we reach our final form" (56:442,24–6 = 25:435; trans. alt.). In the main part quoted above, the notion of "progress" is only mentioned in one place: "humans progress and pass into a better being."

8. The same intention determines Luther's explanation of "first grace": "I call 'first grace' not the grace that is poured into us at the beginning of conversion, as in the case of Baptism, contrition, or remorse, but rather the altogether different grace that follows and is new, which we call a degree or increase of grace" (WA 56:379,10–12 = LW 25:368; trans. alt.: on Rom. 8:26). As also his following explanation (56:379,13–17 = 25:368–69) shows, Luther means in contrast to the concepts "degree" (*gradus*) and "increase" (*augmentum*) not a progression but the constant

by the "initial nonbeing" and the "final being," respectively;[9] but the movement that runs back and forth between them has in fact taken them into itself as its determinants. Thus it almost seems as if this movement, which is penitence, carries its meaning in itself.[10]

Here we must provide further clarity by distinguishing the scholion on Romans 12:2 from later comparable texts. But is this even possible? Has not Luther always understood penitence as "progress" in the sense of "repetition"? But also here,[11] finding what appears to be a constant basic structure will not help us gain a clear picture of the story of his theology. The decisive difference turns out to be a difference in the understanding of the word, according to which the "becoming" of penitence is understood once as a *repetition* but another time as a *return*. For the ever-repeated "passage from sin to righteousness" of this scholion is not the same as the return to baptism spoken of in *The Babylonian Captivity of the Church* (*De captivitate*). There Luther sees penitence (repentance) as an ever-new dependence on the baptismal promise once proclaimed,[12] as "a return to Baptism," which is granted again and again—by the promise of the Lord's Supper.[13] Baptism and the Lord's Supper work together to bring about

---

repetition of an initial "operative grace" and a diminishing "cooperative grace" (*gratia cooperans*). The "first grace" is therefore always understood as a new start. See further the well-known words on Rom. 13:11: "To make progress is nothing but always to begin anew" (*proficere, hoc est semper a novo incipere*) (56:486,7 = 25:478; trans. alt.).

9. In equivalent theological terms: "Thus (i.e. penitence) is in sin with respect to its starting point and in righteousness with respect to its finishing point" (WA 56:442,19–20 = LW 25:434; trans. alt.).

10. See the continuation of the sentence quoted in n. 9: "If therefore we are always penitent, we are always sinners, and yet *for that very reason*, we are righteous and justified, partly sinners and partly righteous, that is, nothing but penitents" (WA 56:442,20–22 = LW 25:434; trans. alt.; author's emphasis). These statements will appear in a broader horizon at the end of this chapter with the treatment of the scholion on Rom. 4:7.

11. Cf. pp. 18–19.

12. Cf. the whole section WA 6:528,8–19 = LW 36:59 and the beginning of the following section (6:528,20–24 = 36:59–60); for a brief definition, see 6:572,16–17 = 36:124: repentance is nothing but "a way and return to Baptism." Already the *Sermon on the Sacrament of Baptism* (1519) says that "the sacrament of penance renews and points again to the Sacrament of Baptism when the priest says in the absolution, 'Behold, God has now forgiven you your sin, as he promised you before in Baptism and has now commanded me to do the same, by the power of the keys. So you are now coming again into what Baptism is and does.' If you believe, you have it; if you doubt, you are lost" (2:733,31–36 = 35:38; trans. alt.). *On the whole matter, see chap. 7, from which alone it becomes clear that Luther was fully justified in asserting what he does here.*

13. WA 6:528,36–529,5 = LW 36:60.

what I call "wordtime."[14] In this unique time of the word, the "once" of the past promise, which is unsurpassable, is presupposed by the "always" of the new promises. But the always guarantees the once by continually reaffirming it, as happens in the public confession of the worship service. In this linguistic context, the saying from *The Babylonian Captivity* that "what Baptism signifies (*res baptismi*) should swallow up your whole life and give it back"[15] is referring to a different movement than the saying about "giving up its own form and taking on the form of the Word" from the Romans lectures. The latter is by no means based on a once-given comforting promise and in no way returns to it through ever-new comforting promises. Rather, this becoming the Word, this "being transformed," is a constant repetition. What is repeated is the possibility of the movement "from sin to righteousness, and so from nonbeing through becoming to being," but this possibility keeps fading with every new realization. What has happened becomes past with its repetition and therefore cannot itself be repeated. Repetition is only the response to what has happened, but since that was a unique event, repetition is the recalling of a past, unique reality.[16] Therefore, even if the scholion on Romans 6:10[17] retains the uniqueness of baptism and thus of the Christ event, this uniqueness in the schema of repetition only means an ideal possibility to be realized in each case but not a linguistic reality. Thus for the Romans lectures, the place of saving certainty accompanies the Lord's Supper, offering refuge again and again to sinners struck by the killing law, but it is not tied to baptism as an event that happened once in the past. At this time, Luther does not yet see the spoken word as the external place where God graciously gives

14. Cf. the immediate continuation of the text mentioned in n. 13: WA 6:529,5–6 = LW 36:60. [*Wordtime*, or *the time of the word*, is a term coined by the author to describe the eschatic time shaped and constituted by the word, specifically the word of baptism and the word of the Lord's Supper; trans. note.]

15. WA 6:535,12–13 = LW 36:69 (*The Babylonian Captivity*; trans. alt.); cf. the context, the two sections in 6:534,31–535,16 = 36:69.

16. The German formulation takes up Heidegger's thinking (*Sein und Zeit*, 9th ed., 385–86; cf. *Being and Time*, 7th ed., 437–38).

17. "The meaning is that we only have to undergo this spiritual death once" (WA 56:326,28–29 = LW 25:314; trans. alt.). "When a person sins again, their spiritual life does not die, but they themselves depart from it and die, while they remain in Christ forever" (56:327,13–14 = 25:315; trans. alt.). "Because they have Christ who cannot die again, they too cannot die again but live with Christ forever. Hence, we too are baptized only once, by which we obtain the life of Christ, even though we often fall and rise again. For the life of Christ can be repeated often but can only be begun once, just as someone who has never been rich can only begin to become rich once, although they can lose and regain their wealth again and again" (56:327,18–24 = 25:315; trans. alt.).

himself and where he can be found with certainty but still locates it, as in the Psalms lectures, in a hidden "illumination."[18] That is, law and gospel are still so deeply intertwined that we find them in the form of a single word, not the two words of the later Luther.

B) The Gospel as Enemy

The ever-repeated movement of penitence is therefore a becoming of the Word, because penitence agrees with the gospel, which encounters us as an enemy: "AGREE WITH YOUR ADVERSARY (= the form of the gospel), as if to say, give up your own form and take on the form of the Word," as it says in the gloss on Romans 6:17b.[19] As in the *Dictata*,[20] Luther, with the *Glossa ordinaria*[21] and Bernard,[22] amazingly sees here in the ADVERSARY of Matthew 5:25 the gospel, which (according to the interpretation of Ps. 78:25) embraces everything "that Scripture expressly contains and that the practice of the church clearly enacts."[23]

---

18. See section C: "The Inner Word: Hidden Grace."

19. WA 56:62,16–17 = LW 25:54 n. 16; parenthetical remark: l.13.

20. "The gospel has the name and word of God that says it is our adversary. Therefore, we must agree with every adversary on the way" (WA 3:574,10–12 = LW 11:57; trans. alt.; cf. 3:573,27–28 = 11:57). 3:32,2 = 10:35 (on Ps. 2:9): "The holy gospel is a 'rod of iron'" (l.2) "It does not permit soft things or feathers, but only everything hard, strong, and rough, and made of iron. Thus Matthew (5:25): 'Agree with your adversary on the way.' So too it is called a 'sword of salvation' and is doubtless made of iron" (3:32,9–12 = 10:35; trans. alt.). In 3:20–22 = 10:17–19 (1516), the "adversary" refers to the "law of the Lord" (as in the text being interpreted: Ps. 1:2), which means that there is no substantive difference here between law and gospel. On the importance of this passage for the "concept of heresy in the young Luther," see U. Mauser 61 (= *Der junge Luther und die Häresie*, 1968, 68).

21. 5.21 A: "The adversary is some person: or a divine word. Be kind and agree with the word of the gospel: because it commands many things contrary to the flesh . . . Otherwise, the adversary is God: or rather a divine word that opposes those who want to sin. It has been given for this purpose, that it may be with us on the way, and we must agree with it: lest we hate it that God does not spare us until we are healed." J. Ficker WA 56:447 on l.1 and U. Mauser (see n. 20) also draw attention to this passage. Lyra puts it much more cautiously than the *Glossa ordinaria*: "Morally, the adversary of the sinner may be said to be the divine command that accuses him." (5.21D).

22. On the Song of Songs, Sermon 85, 1:1 (*Opera* 2.307–8). For further passages, see R. Schwarz, *Fides, spes und caritas*, 309, n. 168.

23. WA 3:578,15–16 = LW 11:63 (trans. alt.). The "heretics" and the "proud" are not satisfied with this (ll.14–15). Instead of "taking their own thoughts captive to the obedience of Christ" (ll.19–20; trans. alt.), "they call into doubt and question everything that has been preserved through so many ages and for which so many martyrs have died (ll.20–21); "they should change

According to the scholion on Romans 6:17 now,[24] the gospel understood in this way is in conflict with human wisdom and demands its surrender. If the latter is captured and surrenders itself to destruction, the word of the gospel is vindicated. The way that wisdom believes is by acknowledging itself to be wrong and allowing the Word that is hostile to it to be true. In other words, faith agrees with the hostile Word and accepts it; that is, faith takes it on ("taking on the form of the Word") in lived self-surrender ("giving up its own form") and so becomes conformed to it. Then and in this way, the change takes place: "Then, as was said in chapter 3,[25] we become righteous, truthful . . . as is the Word itself, to which we conform ourselves through faith."[26] In its reversal, this change is exemplified ("*Sic* verbum caro") in the humiliation of the eternal Word and presented as a possibility to be realized ("*ut* caro verbum") by following the example of the Word. "Thus 'the Word became flesh' and 'took on the form of a servant,' in order that the flesh might become the Word and humans might take on the form of the Word."[27]

We must return to the topic of the christological aspect of the concept of the Word.[28] Here to begin with, we are only concerned with its expression at that point where judgment turns into grace, where the enemy becomes a friend: "We must agree with this adversary and thus (!) he will become a friend" (on 8:15).[29] The change in the statement indicated by the phrase "in this way" shows

their way of thinking and agree with their adversary, but they refuse to do so: therefore, they are offended by your word" (ll.30–32; trans. alt.). The intertwining of the word of judgment and ecclesiology is a topic that we will deal with later (see section D).

24. We have in mind the following related section from it: "The wisdom of the flesh is an enemy of God's Word, but the Word of God is immutable and insuperable. Therefore, it is necessary that the wisdom of the flesh be changed and give up its own form and take on the form of the Word. This happens when through faith it takes itself captive and destroys itself, conforming itself to the Word, believing the Word to be true and itself false. Thus 'the Word became flesh' and 'took on the form of a servant' in order that the flesh might become the Word and humans take on the form of the Word. Then, as is said in chap. 3, we will become righteous, truthful, wise, good, meek, and chaste, like the Word itself, to which we conform ourselves through faith" (WA 56:329,27–330,5 = LW 25:317; trans. alt.).

25. For a text directly parallel to the interpretation of Rom. 6:17, see the corollary in WA 56:226,23ff. = LW 25:211–12, from the interpretation of Rom. 3:4–5 (on this, see E. Bizer, *Fides*, 53–58). In spite of its terseness, the interpretation of 6:17 is more succinct than that of 3:4–5, because it also offers the christological dimension of the word, which is not made explicit at 3:4–5.

26. WA 56:330,3–5 = LW 25:317 (trans. alt.).

27. WA 56:330,1–3 = LW 25:317 (trans. alt.).

28. See the section "Word and Christ" and the whole intermediate chapter "Sacramental Meditation on Scripture" and "The Understanding of the Mass."

29. WA 56:368,28 = LW 25:358 (trans. alt.).

the difference to Luther's later understanding of law and gospel in an unsurpassably concise and sharp manner. We see this clearly looming, under Pauline and Augustinian influence,[30] at two points in the lectures, but there is no way that this means that the whole structure of Luther's theological thought is about to crumble here or has crumbled already. Rather, the understanding familiar to us from the *Dictata* and now presented here in the interpretation of Romans 6:17 still prevails: the gospel *meets* us from outside *in a single* form, as an adversary, but works through an inner change *in a double way*. In a nutshell, grace comes about through judgment. The gospel is proclaimed as a contradiction in complete openness[31] but as an acquittal in complete secrecy,[32] not loudly and audibly like "the other word."[33] However, this secrecy of the change that has no place for the oral promise is the reason for its fundamental uncertainty. Of course, the gospel must be believed. But since it is not heard as an unambiguous word, faith in the gospel remains uncertain and so lives in hope. But this hope has no more grounds for hoping than faith has for believing, because it has not been given any pledge, in the oral word. Like faith, hope is not directed purely to a promise but purely to the hiddenness of salvation—that is, to the future, which can only be anticipated "inwardly." The exclusive particle, the exclusion of everything, does not, as later, safeguard a single positive determination—namely, the unambiguity of the word of salvation—but is derived solely from its negation.[34]

Key for early Luther is the mystical idea of "un-becoming," which can also be expressed in the Aristotelian schema of form and matter.[35] How important a

30. In the scholion on Rom. 7:6 (WA 56:336,24–339,3 = LW 25:324–27 [esp. 56:338,13–339,3 = 25:326–27: strangely, not a word of this appears in the dictation (WA 57)!]; on that, E. Bizer, *Fides*, 44–45) and on Rom. 10:15 (56:424,1–426,9 = 25:415–18; esp. 56:424,7–17 = 25:416 [=57/1:211,2–12], but also 56:425,8–10 = 25:417). Cf. chap. 3 (B 5, on law and gospel).

31. See section D: "The External Word: Public Judgment."

32. See the next section: "The Inner Word: Hidden Grace."

33. *The Freedom of a Christian*, §9; WA 7:24,9–10; German); cf. LW 31:348 (Latin): "the second part of Scripture"; §25; WA 7:34,14–15 (in the context of ll.14–22; German); cf. LW 31:364 (Latin).

34. See the section "The Word and God" and the section on the scholion on Rom. 9:28: "The Word that Completes and Abbreviates."

35. Scholion on Rom. 8:26: "Think how an artisan looks over the material to see if it is suitable and ready to be turned into his work of art. The suitability of the material is a sort of irrational prayer for form, which the artisan understands and heeds when he decides to make what it asks for, because the material is well-suited for it. God considers our thoughts and feelings in the same way when he sees what we are asking for, what we are suited for, and what we desire. Then, heeding our request, he begins to impress on us the form of his artistic plan. Then the form and idea of our thinking necessarily vanish" (WA 56:378,2–9 = LW 25:367; trans. alt.). On the last sentence, cf. the marginal gloss on Ps. 75:3: "Those things [the earth and its inhabitants] that

role this idea plays here can be clearly seen from his marginal notes on Tauler's sermons; for example, "Opposites are from God, as it [Matt. 5:25] says, 'Agree with your adversary on the way.' Therefore, the whole of salvation is the resignation of the will in all things, as Tauler teaches, whether spiritual or temporal, and naked faith in God."[36] In fact, Luther does not distinguish between faith in the hostile word (= "resignation" = "giving up its form") and faith in the salvation hidden in it (= "naked faith"). Salvation is tied solely to the word of judgment and thus to self-surrender ("the whole of salvation is the resignation of the will"). Put in terms of the word, law and gospel are fundamentally the same.

C) The Inner Word: Hidden Grace

At this point we need to go back to the Psalms lectures because the Romans lectures presuppose what we must occupy ourselves with here, but nowhere do they explicitly reflect it. The matter then pops up again in the sermon on November 11, 1516, which we will therefore draw on in our conclusion.

There can be no doubt that the matter addressed with the terms *judgment* and *righteousness* must be regarded as the original motif of the early Luther 's theology. Already in his notes in Faber's *Psalter* and throughout the entire Psalms lectures, Luther was particularly interested in these terms—that is, according to Romans 8:10, the "mortification of the flesh" and the "vivification of the Spirit."[37]

The place of "vivification" is "not yet known," it is "secret,"[38] "before God," "in the sight of God,"[39] in one's "internal hearing" (on Ps. 51:8),[40] which then

---

have not first been melted cannot be made firm. For as the philosophers, indeed even nature itself, say: motion is not motion, but the birth of one is the corruption of the other" (WA 3:510,33–35). Besides the passage mentioned in n. 36 (9:102,17–36), see 9:97,12–16, which is also a passage from the marginal notes on Tauler's sermons; for the lectures on Hebrews, see the scholion on 3:7: 57/3:143,7–22 = 29:148–49.

36. WA 9:102,33–6, quoted in Steven E. Ozment, *Homo Spiritualis* (1969), 201. The train of thought in the terms *artisan*, *matter*, and *form* is somewhat different here (9:102,17–26) than in the similar passage in WA 56:378 = LW 25:367 (on Rom. 8:26) quoted in n. 35; cf. 56:378,13–17 = 25:367; 56:376,22ff. = 25:366 and J. Ficker's notes in 56:378 on l.13 = 25:367.

37. See only (on Ps. 1:5 in Faber's *Psalterium*) WA 4:468,1–5; 3:29,9–30,8 = LW 10:30–31 (on the same verse) and at the end of the lectures, the scholion on Ps. 122:5 in 4:403,27–407,17 = 11:544–49. See on this whole section now: R. Schwarz, *Vorgeschichte der reformatorischen Bußtheologie*, chap. 9.

38. WA 4:468,4–5.

39. On Ps. 9:1 in Faber's *Psalterium*: WA 4:477,3–7.

40. WA 3:285,15–16. Cf. the concept of *illustratio* (WA 3:290,33–5 = LW 10:239; on Ps. 51:4).

in 1517, in the German interpretation of the *Seven Penitential Psalms*, very significantly becomes the place of God's "secret whisper."[41] This is the nerve of the understanding of word and Spirit in the early Luther. He expressly and clearly reflects this point in three passages: with the interpretation of Psalm 77, Psalm 102:5, and Psalm 116:10–19. We also need to consider those passages in which Luther only briefly speaks of the "internal word,"[42] the "oracle of the heart,"[43] "illumination," and "enlightenment,"[44] or "internal inspiration,"[45] which takes us to the conceptual field of "conscience" and "synteresis."[46]

1. Luther interprets Psalm 77 in an unusually unified way compared with his other approach.[47] The whole psalm for him revolves around a single theme. The scholion begins programmatically: "I think the psalm describes a person meditating in remorse."[48] According to a marginal gloss, this "*remorse*" appears almost as a sacramental event ("Here remorse is described in terms of form and matter"[49]) but clearly does not mean the institutional sacrament, and yet it assumes its function—namely, "to heal and justify the soul"[50]—and causes the

---

41. WA 1:190,1 (on Ps. 51:8); on this, see pp. 163–164.

42. For example, WA 3:202,1–2 = LW 10:170. Where the verb *to teach* appears, Luther stereotypically adds *inwardly* (4:358,20–21 = 11:488; 4:445,6). On the schema "inwardly through the Spirit and outwardly through the ministry" (4:282,15–16; similarly, 4:90,2–3; 4:289,7–8), see the sermon for Nov. 11, 1516, which is treated on pp. 35–37.

43. WA 3:364,20–22.

44. WA 3:521,16–17 = LW 11:3 (*illuminatio*); 3:290,33–35 = 10:239; on Ps. 51:4 (*illustratio*).

45. WA 3:451,22–27; 4:444,17–445,2 (on this and the marginal gloss [4:444,39–445,26], cf. the passages listed in nn. 40 and 41).

46. On Ps. 112:7: "The *bad hearing* (*auditio mala*) is twofold, as is the good. First, there is the inward hearing of the conscience, which is the worm and murmuring of synteresis, or the joy and gentle whispering of the Holy Spirit. Ps. 51[:8]: 'You will give to my hearing joy and gladness'; and Ps. 85[:8]: 'I will hear what God the Lord will speak in me' (Ps. 51:8 and Ps. 85:8 obviously play an important role; see also n. 45 and chap. 1, n. 39). Then there is the outward hearing, as in the Last Judgment" (WA 4:253,23–27 = LW 11:389; trans. alt.). However, we cannot go into the terms *conscience* and *synteresis* in any more detail here. Cf. E. Hirsch's *Lutherstudien*, vol. 1, for our context, esp. pp. 109–16.

47. The question of the relationship of this interpretation to that discussed in WA 3:530–36 = LW 11:10–19 need not concern us here.

48. WA 3:537,3–4 = LW 11:19 (trans. alt.).

49. WA 3:526,34–35.

50. WA 3:543,15–16 = LW 11:28.

[righteous] person "to jump from wretchedness into the state of salvation"—that is, to jump "inwardly away from those things that are outside."[51]

The remorse that Luther finds described in this psalm has its *Sitz im Leben*, not in the institutional sacrament of penance but in a very specific *meditation*: "That beautiful Psalm teaches the modes and gestures of those who meditate as they are snatched up inwardly. And what should they be meditating on? What are the signs by which they will recognize that they are in meditation and remorse? If you want to know how a broken spirit and a contrite heart are sacrificed to God, consider this Psalm."[52] This meditation, understood as "a spiritual night," means that people are "to forget everything external and to be snatched up inwardly, and not to consider or look at anything visible."[53] It describes the place where people are alone with themselves in the ultimate depths and become aware of their time and history: "For they debate with themselves who they are, who they were, who they will be. It is a soliloquy of the soul where the soul exercises itself in hierarchical acts that happen most copiously and wonderfully. For whatever the office of preaching does for the people, this speaking with the heart does for the soul."[54] What humans thus experience in the sight of God in all their nakedness is the harshest judgment. "For those who are remorseful are thus snatched away to despair and hell."[55] What Luther actually means by this is that in the remorse that is lived out by means of inner and outer actions,[56] the final judgment is antic-

---

51. WA 3:549,2 = LW 11:36; WA 3:526,31–32. The verb *to leap across* (*transilire*), derived from the heading of the psalm, takes us into the semantic field of *transitus* (crossing) and *phase* (Passover). Luther explains his understanding of penitence in these terms in his letter of dedication to Staupitz accompanying the *Explanations of the Theses on Indulgences* (May 30, 1518) and refers expressly to this very psalm: "The heading of the Psalm also sings of this where the chief musician is introduced as Jeduthun, which means, 'one who leaps across.'" (WA 1:526,8–9 = LW 48:67; trans. alt.; see also LW 11:21).

52. WA 3:526,26–29.

53. WA 3:539,36–37 = LW 11:23 (trans. alt.); cf. 4:334,9–11 = 11:455; 4:519,20–30.

54. WA 3:540,4–8 = LW 11:24 (trans. alt.).

55. WA 3:540,18–19 = LW 11:24 (trans. alt.).

56. "This judgment however comes about like any virtue, namely, by an inner and outer act. The inner is always necessary, or at least not contrary, namely, that we hate ourselves and confess our sin with a true heart, and, in any event, punish ourselves inwardly . . . Conclusion: Therefore, the judgment is nothing else than the abasement or humbling of the self from the heart and the knowledge of the self, that we are indeed sinners and unworthy of everything. But the outer act is to live this way outwardly, that is, by choosing contempt, poverty, affliction, fasting, etc. For if we flee such things . . . we are not yet under God's judgment, and consequently, not yet under his righteousness" (on Ps. 36:11: WA 3:203,1–11 = LW 10:172; trans. alt.).

ipated, or (according to the note on Ps. 1:5 in Faber's Psalter) can be anticipated: "But the righteous rise up again and grow all the more by this judgment and so ask that their flesh be thus judged by the Lord. And if it does not please the Lord to do so, they judge and castigate themselves and subject their body to servitude to strengthen their spirit. As the apostle says: 'If we judged ourselves, we would not be judged by the Lord'"[57] (1 Cor. 11:31). In the interpretation of Psalm 77, Luther of course rejects any synergism: "This remorse does not come from me, for he (i.e. God) has changed me into a different person; for he has enlightened me so that I now know myself."[58]

With his understanding of remorse linked to Romans 8:10 and 1 Corinthians 11:31, Luther (in a gloss on Ps. 106:3) appeals to Bernard: "Bernard in a sermon on Advent . . . says, 'O happy the soul that always judges and accuses itself in the sight of God. For if we judged ourselves, we would not be judged by God.'"[59] Thus he locates himself in a tradition that reaches back to the monasticism of the ancient church.[60] Accordingly, Luther explained Psalm 102:10 this way: "I suffered all this remorse, all this I did, said, and endured so that I might not have to endure your coming wrath in its eternal severity, which I clearly recognize, but they have turned their back on it."[61]

---

57. WA 4:469,13–17. Cf. WA 4:343,22–25 = LW 11:468 and 3:291,14–21 = 10:240 (on that, see pp. 125–127.

58. WA 3:541,14–16 = LW 11:25 (trans. alt.); cf. 3:540,37 = 11:25.

59. WA 4:198,19–21. Bernard says literally, "He (i.e. God) loves a soul that examines itself in his presence without ceasing and judges itself without hypocrisy. He demands that judgment from us only for our sake, for if we judge ourselves, we will not be judged" (*De Adventu Domini Sermo* 3; MPL 183:47 A/B).

Cf. WA 4:198,19–21 with the scholion on Rom. 9:3: "The righteous . . . achieve this resignation [to hell] . . . And because of their readiness, they immediately escape this kind of penalty" (WA 56:392,1–4 = LW 25:382; trans. alt.). Again: "If therefore we sincerely want to persecute and destroy ourselves so that we offer ourselves to hell for the sake of God and his righteousness, we will have truly satisfied his righteousness, and he will have mercy on us and free us. 'For if we judged ourselves, we would not be judged by the Lord'" (56:393,29–32 = 25:384; trans. alt.).

60. Cf. *Vitae Patrum* [*Lives of the Fathers*] 5, *Verba Seniorum*, bk. 3 (*De Compunctione*), MPL 73:860–64, esp. the formulations "he was put into ecstasy" (*factus in excessu mentis*), "snatched away to judgment" (*raptus ad judicium*) (862–63). In the same context as WA 4:198,19–31, Luther himself in WA 3:433,24–434,1 = LW 10:374 expressly refers to the *Lives of the Fathers* (see n. 312); the Romans lectures (56:363,14–15 = 25:353), and the 1519 *Exposition of the Lord's Prayer* (2:124,26 = 42:73: *alt vatter buch* = "Book of the Hermits"; cf. 2:120,16–17 = 42:68) also betrays a knowledge of these lives. On the further use of the *Lives of the Fathers* in Luther, see E. Schäfer, *Luther als Kirchenhistoriker*, 159–69.

61. WA 4:158,30–32 = LW 11:311 (trans. alt.). Cf. the *Sermon on St. Andrew's Day* (Nov. 30) 1516: WA 1:102,20–26.

But we need to go into the interpretation of Psalm 102 in more detail since it gives an even clearer understanding of time than we get in Psalm 77. This is important because it is the understanding of time that gives us a window on Luther's experience[62] of this—what we will call "internal sacrament" of remorse.

2. Psalm 102:1,4–5 lets Luther see that "to stand before God" (*coram Deo*) means to have all time, which is equal in God's sight, behind us through true remorse. For "no one is in the presence of the Lord except those who have their backs not only to past and present days but to future ones too. For there we see them as God sees them. However, in his sight all the days are past and used up. But those who turn their face to the days themselves and their back to God think they are something."[63] Thus humans should expect nothing from the nothingness of history; they do not receive their destiny in the sight of the world (*coram mundo*). "But they are established in the sight of the Lord (*coram Domino*) through the understanding of faith and the intensity of their feelings,"[64] which in practice means through remorse: "In a mystical sense, the days vanish through the voluntary denial of them, by regarding them as smoke. This happens through genuine remorse, by which the days of the world are loathed, and the day of the Lord and his face are desired."[65] The lived negation, which as such stands under the sign of the cross,[66] brings salvation, but it is an anticipation of the end of

62. At the end of his interpretation of Ps. 77, Luther says: "If you want to have an example of this explanation, take the conversion of Saint Augustine in book 8 of his *Confessions*. There you will find an explicit and most felicitous practice of this psalm" (WA 3:549,26–28 = LW 11:37). Cf. 3:537,31–32 = 11:20 and 3:538,9–10 = 11:21, where Luther refers expressly to bk. 8 of the *Confessions*. The tradition history of this book is masterfully presented by P. Courcelle in *Les confessions de Saint Augustin dans la tradition littéraire*, 1963 (on Luther: pp. 353–70; esp. on his interpretation of Ps. 77: pp. 357–59). Further (3:549,30–37 = 11:37): "Hence one who has not experienced this remorse and meditation cannot be taught this psalm with any words. It is difficult for me, too, because I am outside of remorse and yet I speak about remorse. No one is fit to speak or hear any part of Scripture, unless their affections are in conformity with it, so that they feel inwardly what they hear and speak outwardly and can say, 'Yes, it really is so'! Therefore, since I cannot speak from the practice of my own remorse, I will demonstrate it by example and from the practice of blessed Augustine" (trans. alt.). However, Luther's confession that he has not experienced this remorse himself (or has not experienced it enough?) will not prevent us from considering it as authoritative for him and so representative of him.

63. WA 4:149,27–30 = LW 11:299 (trans. alt.).

64. WA 4:149,32–33 = LW 11:299 (trans. alt.) within ll.31–35.

65. WA 4:148,26–28 = LW 11:297 (trans. alt.).

66. Cf. (on v. 5): "I do not know anything in Scripture except Christ crucified. Therefore, I always taste the same thing everywhere, because the same thing appears everywhere" (WA 4:153,27–29 = LW 11:304). Cf. the section: "Word and Christ." It is especially clear in the Romans lectures on 9:28 that Luther defines faith as a "lived negation." Cf. the section: "The Word That Completes and Abbreviates."

history and so takes place in the eternal now. If humans are struck "intentionally, that is, while in ecstasy, they see a future striking as if it had already taken place, although in reality it has not yet happened: which is an effective and salutary striking. For thus the carnal will is struck down."[67]

3. The interpretation of Psalm 116:11 (I SAID IN MY ECSTASY: EVERYONE IS A LIAR) completes this picture and at the same time points ahead to the Romans lectures in which this psalm verse (Rom. 3:4a) is especially important."

> This is the ecstasy by which he [the psalmist] is elevated, through faith, above himself so that he may see the future blessings. Otherwise, he too was a liar, but when he was put in ecstasy, he transcended lying and was made truthful by faith . . . It is wonderful how he says that he is at the same time humbled and in ecstasy: but this is because he *recognizes* himself as humbled and wretched through his ecstasy. They, however, have not been humbled (that is, they do not recognize it), because they are not yet in ecstasy, but in the transitory state of lying.[68]

This review of the first Psalms lectures was meant to clarify what we called an "inner change" in the last section. Luther sees a sharp difference between "judgment" and "righteousness"[69] and carefully reflects on the point at which judgment becomes grace. But this turn does not occur constitutively[70] in an oral promise but in an "internal sacrament," the theological shape of which can be grasped especially in the interpretation of Psalm 77.

Until the spring of 1518, Luther gave the "internal sacrament" priority over the oral promise. Even in his "Explanation" of thesis 7 of the *Theses on Indulgences*

---

67. WA 4:151,31–33 = LW 11:302 (trans. alt.).

68. WA 4:273,14–17,19–22 = LW 11:408–9; cf. 4:265,32–33; 4:267,16–22 = 11:400–401.

69. For the most important text, see the famous interpretation of Ps. 72:1: WA 3:462,27–463,2 = LW 10:404 and further: 4:204,35–205,1 = 11:346 (on Ps. 106:3; the gloss on this verse is quoted above: see n. 59): "The truest gloss is to take 'judgment' as the condemnation of righteousness properly speaking and as self-accusation in a moral sense, and 'righteousness' as the grace of faith freely given" (trans. alt.). Cf. the reference to Ps. 106:3 in the *Exposition of the Lord's Prayer* (1519), which interprets the third petition by distinguishing between "two things, judgment and righteousness," which the word of God always does" (2:99,14–16, in the context of ll.13–23, = 42:42; trans. alt.). It is not the distinction between judgment and righteousness as such that is characteristic of Luther's early theology but the specific way of relating the phenomena in the "internal sacrament" that is distinguished by these two terms. Only when viewed in this way can we see the material contrast between Luther's early theology and his reformational theology.

70. Luther is speaking of course of the *indicative* function of the word: WA 4:272,16–31 = LW 11:407 (on Ps. 116:10).

(also called the ninety-five theses), *actual* justification is given priority over the *promissio*.[71] From this text alone and its clear antagonism between these two aspects, we have to assume a tense relationship between the "internal" word and the "external" word for Luther's early period. Not that he belittled the "ministry of the word"! Just the opposite in fact. But he had not yet recognized that God's speaking "inwardly through the Spirit" and "outwardly through the ministry of the word"[72] coincide not only in the word of judgment[73] but also in the word of salvation. The *Sermon of November 11, 1516, on Luke 11:34*,[74] which we discuss below, shows that this is true for the period after the Psalms lectures.

The text (YOUR EYE IS THE LAMP OF YOUR BODY) is to be understood "tropologically with reference to the eye of attention"[75]—that is, the place of illumination where we perceive ourselves by being perceived. This place is denoted by the phrase "outside of us" (*extra nos*), a formula that Luther never used in the first Psalms lectures but frequently uses from the beginning of the Romans lectures and which he probably found in connection with his study of Tauler's sermons.[76] It sums up what the first Psalms lectures present with terms such as *taken up (raptus)*, *departure (excessus)*, *ecstasy (ecstasis)*.

"Our eye is to be sought outside of us and not in us, and yet it is in us and is to be found in us."[77] The "illumination" ("eye") is not at our disposal, which is why when we look at ourselves, our light and our judgment, we have to despair completely and can only ask for God's direction and guidance.[78] "And yet the eye of the Lord is most present in us and is not found outside of us but within. This is clear from experience, because when people are illuminated, they never

---

71. See chap. 4.

72. WA 4:90,2–3; cf. n. 42.

73. On that, see the whole of the next section: "The External Word: Public Judgment."

74. WA 1:99–101.

75. WA 1:99,31–32. For a commentary, see WA 3:423,8–9 = LW 10:360: "Tropologically, the eyes of Christ are the senses and spiritual illuminations of faith" (trans. alt.) and 3:612,3–4 (on Ps. 81:11): "MY PEOPLE DID NOT LISTEN TO MY VOICE in the flesh of the speaker; AND ISRAEL DID NOT ATTEND TO ME with the eyes of her heart because that happens through faith which comes from hearing." The scholion on Heb. 9:2 (here on LAMPSTAND) gives information on the interpretative possibilities of the "eye" (57/3:198,1–16). Luther uses "eye" in a traditional way (see J. Ficker's reference to the *Glossa interlinearis* and Lyra: 57/3:198 on l.15 = 29:200) in connection with *intentio* = "attention" (on the different meanings of *intentio*, see the entry in J. Altenstaig's *Vocabularius Theologiae*, Fol. 119–20).

76. See the section: "The Word and God."

77. WA 1:100,14–15.

78. WA 1:100,15–21.

depart from their body or soul but remain as and where they are, and the eye of true direction is revealed to them inwardly."[79] It becomes clear here that the "*sola gratia*" (by grace alone) is not linked from the outset to the "*solo verbo*" (by the word alone). Luther can obviously use the *extra nos* without tying it to the oral word. The externality of the "illumination" lies in the fact that it does not arise from our own possibility and power[80] and that without Christ it is a deception.[81] Thus illumination happens "*sola gratia*" and "*solo Christo*": by grace alone and by Christ alone. But its unambiguity and certainty lie basically in itself and not in the external word, not in the promise—not *solo verbo*.

The second part of the sermon shows that we did not misunderstand Luther. As announced at the beginning,[82] the sermon text here is understood with reference to St. Martin, whom the day commemorates; it speaks "about the eye of the one who rules over others," which for Luther is its literal meaning.[83] The outer-inner schema undergoes an almost mechanical transposition. The second part of the sermon is thus made parallel to the first: "But literally, the eye is the bishop and prelate himself, who likewise is not to be sought outside of us but among us, not in heresy but in the church. And yet he is not within us but outside, because a bishop is not made by our power; for principalities and kingdoms are established by the Lord."[84] It is easy to see that the internality spoken of in the first sentence means something other than "illumination." It is different from the externality expressed in the second sentence. It addresses God's sole control and working. This is the point at which the two parts of the sermon meet and which makes their whole relationship with each other interesting. How does the

---

79. WA 1:100,21–24.

80. Cf. the text spoken of in n. 78.

81. WA 1:100,7–13.

82. WA 1:99,32–33.

83. The two interpretations can already be found in the *Dictata* (WA 3:170 = LW 10:142–43; trans. alt.; cf. esp. the following): "Mystically . . . the 'eye' of Christ . . . is his understanding" (ll.6–7). "Allegorically, the '*eye*' of Christ is the order of teachers and leaders, whose task it is to oversee and direct and be the eye of others" (ll.12–13). The different names given to the senses of Scripture need not detain us here. See further 3:117,4–5: "LIGHT . . . i.e. any preacher through whom I (Christ) appear to people." On Heb. 9:2 (57/3:198,11–12 = 29:200): "The eyes of the Lord are called the priests of the churches. For as the eye directs the body, so the priest the church." Luther shared the view with the tradition as if there was one system of fixed metaphors which allegorical interpretation could draw on and use to prove itself" (G. Ebeling, *Evangelienauslegung*, 164). This includes the interpretation that sees the eye as a reference to the preacher, which can also be found in the lexicon of Alain de Lille (G. Ebeling, 166).

84. WA 1:100:25–28. The concluding sentence refers to Rom. 13:1–7 (cf. the interpretation of the Lord's Prayer of the spring of 1517: WA 9:151,12–14)

externality of the illumination relate to the externality of the church's office? Seen as a whole, for Luther the two here still diverge.[85] But later, in his *promissio* theology, he succeeds in merging them in the oral and public promise. The illumination and the church's office will then both be critiqued on the basis of the *promissio*, because the promise is the criterion of both.

D) The External Word: Public Judgment [Rom. 3:20,22]

1. Tauler comments on 2 Corinthians 3:6 (THE LETTER KILLS, BUT THE SPIRIT GIVES LIFE): "Whoever wishes to come to the new must without any doubt be united with the old; they must suffer and bear the burden and bow under the mighty hand of God in order that they suffer both inwardly and outwardly when it comes—Children . . . submit to God and ask him to help you bear your suffering in all the ways in which it comes and through whom it comes. If you ever want to come to the new, you must first suffer the old and wait for it in humility."[86]

Luther adds: "Note this, because the whole of Scripture, every figure, and all of nature says the same thing."[87]

Not only the entire history of the old covenant, not only the whole of Scripture,[88] is impelled by God's word of judgment, but we also encounter it in the whole of nature[89] and in the whole world, symbolized by the cross of Christ: "The cross of Christ is distributed through the whole world."[90] Every insult, every injustice, every abuse, every illness, every calamity strikes us as God's word. "With all these things[91] (as with his words, for 'he speaks and it was done'), God

---

85. The statement "because he (i.e. the prelate) sees, the people also see" (WA 1:100,31) and the remainder of the sermon presuppose of course that the "illumination" (as in Augustine) is dependent on instruction and so on the word. But here the word is understood as a path that we must put behind us so that we can have the content without the word.

86. F. Vetter 395,19–27.

87. WA 9:103,20–21. Cf. n. 89.

88. Cf. WA 3:63,1–2: "For the cross of Christ crops up everywhere in the Scriptures."

89. Cf. WA 9:103,20–21 (see n. 87) with this sentence from the scholion on Ps. 84:3: "Why try to escape what every creature is teaching you? Why not accept the cross that is shown to you everywhere? (WA 3:647,3–4 = LW 11:142).

90. Thus Luther writes on Apr. 15, 1516, to Leiffer (WA Br 1:37,15). See WA 56:300,16 = LW 25:287 and on this J. Ficker in the apparatus. See further pp. 61–63.

91. WA 56:232,9–10 (*contumelia* = insult etc.) = LW 25:216 (trans. alt.).

can declare and confirm that you are a sinner."[92] In a lawsuit, "deeds" and "words" are one.[93] Luther had already emphasized this in the first Psalms lectures on Psalm 51:4: "But note: If God is to be justified in his words by which he declares us sinners, then he is certainly also to be justified in his works by which he asserts the same. But these works are scourges and crosses; when they come upon us, they are like God's word that declares and convicts our sin. Therefore, they must be received with all fear and humility."[94]

2. The omnipotence and ubiquity of God's word of judgment effecting our "humility" are not at all restricted when they are experienced in a special way in the church. Rather, we are opened up to this word of judgment in a specific place only so that it can be all the more certain and inescapable.

Luther's interpretation of *Romans 3:20,22*[95] states this most clearly. It is here that we come across important elements of his later doctrine of word and sacrament but oriented in a completely different way.

Only *complete* faith justifies. What this means Luther explains from James 2:10[96] (where admittedly the law and commandments are meant!): "'Whoever offends in one point has become guilty of all.' For faith is indivisible. Therefore, it is either whole and believes all that is to be believed, or it is nothing, if it fails to believe one part. The Lord therefore compares it to one pearl, one grain of mustard etc."[97] The apostle adds: "Since 'Christ is not divided,' therefore the whole Christ is denied or the whole Christ is affirmed in one point. He cannot

---

92. WA 56:232,12–13 = LW 25:216.

93. Luther will later bring this understanding of the word, obtained from Gen. 1 and Ps. 33, as an effective deed (already in the marginal notes on Lombard: WA 9:66,1–2; 67,25–31) into his determination of the oral word of salvation. In the early period, it refers only to the word of judgment and the "inner word" (on that, see pp. 9–11). From the first Psalms lectures, see 3:152,7–8 (on Ps. 28:1), where it says "God's works are his words ('for he spoke, and they were done') because God's doing and speaking are the same." See 3:152,26–30; 3:389,10,34–36; 4:458,27–29 and the notes in Faber's *Psalter*: 4:492,26–30 and 4:493,20–21.

94. WA 3:292,27–31 = LW 10:242 (trans. alt.). See from the notes in Faber's *Psalter* (on Ps. 111:7): "All the works and words of God are his judgments" (4:518,38).

95. WA 56:248,5–256,23 = LW 25:234–42. It is striking how little this text is considered (apart from E. Bizer, *Fides*, 38–39, and H. Bornkamm, who challenges Bizer, see *ARG* 53 [1962]: 1–60, here 11–13) in the literature (e.g., it is not in the otherwise extremely careful study *Fides, spes und caritas beim jungen Luther* by R. Schwarz). This is probably because this text, almost more than any other, resists being harmonized with Luther's later reformational theology. A harmonization has nevertheless been attempted, for example, by K. Holl (1:140) and R. Hermann (*Gerecht und Sünder zugleich*, 1930, 293–96; here 293: "The strong Catholic embellishment . . . need not bother us" or "But we do not need to adhere to this contemporary form today") and H. Bornkamm (see n. 122).

96. Cf. on Ps. 119:128 (WA 4:298,11–12).

97. WA 56:249,19–22 = LW 25:236 (trans. alt.).

be denied in one word and confessed in another at the same time."[98] This addition betrays the determining aspect of the whole argument, as we find it in the Augustinian idea of the whole and the one Christ. This means that Christ is necessarily represented by the church, which is expressed in the interpretation of Scripture by the principle "Whatever is said literally of the Lord Jesus Christ as to his person must also be understood allegorically of the help that is like him and of the church that must conform to him in all things."[99] The doctrine, with which Luther begins his interpretation of Romans 3:22, is to be understood from this program set out in the "Preface of Jesus Christ to the Psalter": "Since the faith in Christ by which we are justified is not a matter of believing only in Christ or in the person of Christ, but in all things that pertain to Christ."[100] In explaining this guiding principle, Luther then asks: "And what are these things? The church, of course, and every word that proceeds from the mouth of a prelate of the church, or of a good and holy person, for every such word is the word of Christ, who says, 'Whoever hears you hears me.'"[101] The mouth of the prelate and priest is the mouth of God,[102] and Christ is present in every word they speak, just as in a host.[103]

Luther seems particularly close to his later understanding of word and sacrament when he applies the figure of synecdoche,[104] which belongs to the rules

---

98. WA 56:249,22–24 = LW 25:236 (trans. alt.).

99. WA 55/1:8,8–10 (= WA 3:13,14–16 = LW 10:7; trans. alt.); (see the apparatus at WA 55/1:8 for ll.8ff.).

100. WA 56:251,12–14 = LW 25:237; emphasized by Luther (except for the "or in the person of Christ," which has been inserted).

101. WA 56:251,24–26 = LW 25:238 (trans. alt.). See 3:91,31–33 = 10:96, where Luther comments on "gates" in Ps. 9:13: "Every prelate or teacher who is over their people must be their door and entrance to life, just as Christ is our vicar to life" (trans. alt.).

102. Cf. WA 56:252,7–8 = LW 25:238 (trans. alt.).

103. Cf. WA 56:252,15–16 = LW 25:238 (trans. alt.). See on Ps. 122:5: "Christ sits among them (the church's leaders and priests) and is present, indeed the most present, since they are his seat" (4:403,34–35 = 11:544; trans. alt.; cf. 4:404,13–18,39–40 = 11:545–46).

104. Luther knows the fifth rule of Tyconius from *On Christian Doctrine* 3:35 (*CCL* 32:110–11 [= MPL 34:86]; but the figure of synecdoche is also included in the first and the seventh rule, which is a mirror of the first, as well as in the fourth). Synecdoche is, as Luther says, for example, in commenting on Ps. 52:2, a way of speaking peculiar to Scripture, "to express the whole by naming the parts" (WA 3:295,18–20 = LW 10:244; cf. 4:620,23: "through synecdoche, the figure used most frequently in the Scriptures"). "*First,* synecdoche is used because with the same words, the writer can include the literal, allegorical, tropological, and anagogical sense. For if you said, 'I have spoken,' you alone would understand 'spoken' literally. But when it is said that 'my tongue is the pen of a scribe,' there the tongue of the prophet is first understood literally.

of medieval scriptural exegesis, to the words "The whole Christ is in every word and wholly in every individual word."[105] When Luther later becomes interested in the content and form of the individual word—in the promise as a special word—it becomes for him the source of certainty that Christ promises and gives himself undividedly in it. That is, the one Christ as the placeholder for the one God gives himself completely precisely in a promise, a specific promise. And he does this unambiguously and in a way that gives us certainty.

If we think of this later function of the synecdoche, it is fascinating to see what it is used for here in the Romans lectures. Although Luther initially puts all the weight on the fact that Christ is completely present in a single word, he now turns this idea in a sense—and here he differs fundamentally from his later view—from a generic-specific understanding of the word to a numerical one. The uniqueness of the individual word is not given any further thought. In fact, it is actually neutralized again by the fact that suddenly the one Christ speaks not only in the uniqueness of the individual word but also and especially in the sum of all the individual words. The Neoplatonic-Augustinian "simple one" (*unum simplex*) used to integrate the "many"[106] is thus thwarted by the nominalist positivism of revelation, according to which everything "that Scripture expressly contains, and the practice of the church clearly enacts,"[107] is to be believed as willed by God's ordained power and to be believed in its entirety.

Second, allegorically, it means every teacher and preacher of the church; for in the body of the church, they are its tongue. Third, tropologically, it means the power of the soul, pondering and disputing in the heart, by which the words and thoughts of the heart are formed. Anagogically, however, it is the Son of God in divine things or the devil in evil things" (3:295,25–32 = 10:244; trans. alt.). "*Second*, synecdoche is used to express the unity of the soul in its many members, for the whole soul is in every part. And so, when the soul uses one member, the whole soul is in it; indeed, all powers work together to this end. And so all members in a certain way become one member, and, consequently, the whole person becomes like that one member, to which the soul transfers itself, and in doing so takes up everything with it" (3:296,1–6 = 10:244–45; trans. alt.). The hermeneutical model thus corresponds exactly to the anthropological one.

105. WA 56:252,11–12 = LW 25:238.

106. Cf. WA 56:253,7–14 = LW 25:239: "But you ask: If denial is so great, that a thing that has been denied in one point is denied in all, why is the affirmation not of equal force, so that a thing that has been affirmed in one point is affirmed in all? The answer is that the good is perfect and simple [= an absolute unity] and so is destroyed by one denial. But it is not established by one confession unless it is one complete confession without any denial. For two contraries cannot stand at the same time in relation to the same thing. And God wants to have all things pure and unstained. But denial is a stain and so it defiles a confession" (trans. alt.). On the "many," see 56:252,19–20 = 25:239. On 56:253,10 = 25:239 ("the good is perfect and simple"), see chap. 1 C, esp. n. 74.

107. This is how Luther had formulated his comments on Ps. 78:25 (WA 3:578,15–16 = LW 11:63; see p. 26 for the text and n. 108 for the reference to the context of this passage).

However, we need to carefully observe where Luther's train of thought leads. He is concerned neither with the content of the many words of God as such nor with their authority and that of their bearers per se but primarily with our obedience to them, with the impossibility of doing justice to them in their untold multiplicity and with the humility this causes.[108] Thus it is not certainty but uncertainty that has the last word:

Compare, for example, from Gerson's treatise on the *Declaration of Truths Which Must Be Believed by Necessity of Salvation* (*Oeuvres*, ed. Glorieux, 6:181–89): "The first degree of truths to be believed is the entire canon of sacred Scripture and every single thing that is literally asserted in it; thus, it is not consistent with faith for anyone to stubbornly disagree with anything contained in it" (181–82); "Scripture . . . in all its parts is the word of God" (182); "there are as many articles of faith as there are truths contained in sacred Scripture" (186; but the context is especially important here). "The second degree of truths are the truths determined by the church" (182). "The third degree of truths are the truths specially revealed to some people" (182). How Luther adhered to the "clearly" of the "practice of the church" can be seen specifically in his vigorous defense of the custom of silently praying the canon [from the Sanctus to the Pater Noster] in his sermon of Sept. 21, 1516, on keeping the Lord's Day holy (cf. the section: "Luther's Understanding of the Mass," p. 113 and in his reinforcement of the provisions of canon law in just this sermon (see esp. WA 1:444,14–17,26–27; note the reference to Matt. 5:25 [on this, see p. 26]).

108. In addition to the especially important passage in WA 3:578,14–579,28 = LW 11:63–64 (on Ps. 78:25: see n. 107), which is a parallel to our scholion, see the interpretation of Ps. 36:6: "The articles of faith or the virtues of faith are mountains, because all of them are arduous for faith. Likewise the very counsels of Holy Scripture" (3:202,19–21 = 10:171; trans. alt.), which become judgments: "The 'judgments' are the teachings and principles of the gospel, which are 'deeps, that is, spiritual things, such as the carnal-minded do not understand but regard as foolishness, according to 1 Corinthians 2[:14]" (3:202:26–28 = 10:171; trans. alt.). Regarding the words "your testimonies are strange" [Vulgate] in Ps. 119:129, Luther explains: "This is true not only of all the words of God in the Scriptures or wherever they are written, but also of the spoken words. When we hand on a teaching from the mouth of a prelate or counsel from the mouth of a neighbor, we always hand on something strange, that is, unless the hearers are humble and obedient, they fall and perish because the word we hand on is hidden from them and becomes a stumbling block and foolishness to them, since it sounds self-contradictory and seems to want to inflict great harm—although it claims to be doing nothing but what a word of judgment does—and requires our ejection that it may have a place. For it is an adversary, and so it appears as an adversary with whom we must agree quickly... Therefore, be humble and suspect that the word of the Lord is everywhere" (4:366,24–32,35 = 11:499; trans. alt.).

H. Bornkamm (*ARG* 53 [1962]: 14) misunderstands E. Bizer (*Fides*, 37). When Bizer speaks of "submission to authority," the emphasis is on "submission," not on "authority." That this is Luther's intention at the time of the Romans lectures is clear not just from the scholion on Rom. 3:20,22 but also from the revision of his interpretation of Ps. 1 (autumn 1516): "As with Adam in paradise, God does not always command through a prelate what is useful or necessary or great, but often a single sign is given to reveal the thoughts of the heart so that no other fruit is sought than that of obedience alone" (WA 55/2:11,2–5 [= 3:19,2–5] = LW 10:16; trans. alt.). "Therefore, it is the folly of fools (the following is especially emphasized by Luther) to measure the greatness of the obedience by the greatness of the work, or the smallness and worthlessness

> This being the case, we should humble ourselves immensely. For since we cannot know whether we live in every word of God or deny none (for many words are spoken by a prelate, many by brothers and sisters, many in the gospels and the writings of the apostles, and many are spoken to us inwardly by God[109]), we can never know whether we are justified or whether we believe. For that reason, we should consider our works as works of the law and be sinners, humbly desiring to be justified by his mercy alone. For although we may be certain that we believe in Christ, we may not be certain that we believe in all his words, and so for that reason, it is also uncertain if we actually do "believe in him."[110]

The idea that faith only justifies if it is complete faith leads to that famous[111] formulation of Lombard, which Luther had previously quoted: "It is one thing to believe that God exists (*credere Deum*), another to trust in God, that is, to believe what he says is true (*credere Deo*), and still another to entrust oneself to God (*credere in Deum*)."[112] Lombard, following Augustine[113] and followed by the whole of medieval theology, had interpreted full justifying faith, the *credere in Deum*, as "faith formed by love" (*fides charitate formata*): "To entrust oneself to God is to love him by believing, to enter into him by believing, and to cling to him and be incorporated into his members by believing."[114] Luther does not abandon the framework established by these statements when he understands

---

of the commandment by the worthlessness of the work" (55/2:11,12–14 [= 3:19,11–13] = 10:16); "God requires only obedience" (55/2:11:16 [= 3:19,15] = 10:16). For the whole context, see 55/2:9,12–11,25 [= 3:18,3–19,23] = 10:16–17. At the end of his interpretation of Ps. 122, Luther says similar things to what he said in relation to Ps. 119: "Therefore, in Ps. 119 (and this should be noted in a very special way), the psalmist very often puts his request above and before the commandments and the law, because he does not ask to do so many or such great things, but only for obedience to the law and for the knowledge of his obedience, so that his eyes may be directed not to the work that is to be done but to the obedience the law requires" (4:407,13–17 = 11:549; trans. alt.; the passage is emphasized by Luther).

109. Cf. on this Gerson's threefold division (see n. 107).

110. WA 56:252,17–25 = LW 25:238–39 (trans. alt.).

111. It determines, for instance, the disposition of the dictionary article on "*credere*" in Altenstaig's *Wörterbuch* (Fol. 57ᵛ).

112. WA 56:252,3–4 = LW 25:238. In Lombard (III/d.23/c.4), the phrases appear in reverse order (text in the Bonaventure edition [Quaracchi, 1882–1902], 3:467).

113. See the passages to which the Bonaventure edition (3:467 n. 4) refers. The path from Augustine to Lombard's formulation also led via the exegesis of Paul (see the *Glossa ordinaria* on Rom. 4:5; 6,10F).

114. III/d.23/c.4 (Bonaventure 3:467).

that the love that forms faith and makes righteous[115] is a humble desire for righteousness.[116] And he can find support for this in Augustine.[117]

Let us summarize: Although the worldwide judgment of God is meant to occur in a very specific place of the word, which is christologically and ecclesiologically determined, this place immediately disintegrates again into the points of many words and so scatters us in uncertainty instead of gathering us in certainty. Faith is then based not on a single word but on every word. "Therefore, we must accept every word that is spoken, no matter by whom, as if the Lord himself were speaking, and we must believe it, yield to it, and humbly subject our reason to it. For it is in this way that we will be justified and in no other. But 'who can understand' or everywhere pay attention to this? Therefore, cleanse me from my hidden [faults], Lord" [cf. Ps. 19:12].[118] We do not know "when, where, how, and through whom Christ is speaking to us . . . As he himself says, 'the wind blows where it wills . . .'"[119] (John 3:8). So here again we encounter[120] the primal motif of Luther's early theology: all his interest is directed to humility, which as God's work entirely, is for him the proper movement of faith. But faith determined by humility[121] must remain uncertain, and for the early Luther, the justifying faith of Romans 3:22 is just as uncertain.[122]

115. Like the exegetical tradition (cf. Lyra on Rom. 3:22: "The apostle speaks of faith formed by love, which is the faith that justifies": 6:9H), Luther also says (on Rom. 3:20; WA 57/1:157,10–11): "Faith or love in faith" (not, as later, by faith; cf. p. 44).

116. In addition to the text quoted above (WA 56:252,22–23 = LW 25:239) see WA 57/1:158,15–26. In relation to this, R. Hermann (*Gerecht und Sünder zugleich*, 1930) believes that our scholion is consistent with reformational theology (see n. 95). He expresses the result of his investigation as follows (p. 295): "Whoever does not ask is not righteous" (in the German original, Hermann spaces this out for emphasis) and (p. 296) "When we go to God for righteousness, our uncertainty is banished."

117. WA 57/1:158,18–19; cf. WA 56:280,14–281,4 = LW 25:267–68.

118. WA 56:253,16–20 = LW 25:239–40 (trans. alt.)—and this is the reason why the prophets only ever speak of the "word of the Lord" in the "absolute"!

119. WA 56:256,13–17; cf. the whole section ll.5–23.

120. Luther makes an annotation on Ps. 4:4 in Faber's *Psalter*, which is a particularly important verse to him: "Humility alone saves, so that you should submit yourselves and yield in all things, for you do not know how and where and when you may meet the truth. More often it will be in those cast down and humbled, as God is veiled in flesh, 'for you do not know when the Son of Man will come.' Therefore, those who understand this verse willingly consider themselves inferior to the whole world" (WA 4:473,17–21).

121. Cf. Augustine, *De trinitate* [*On the Trinity*] 4.1.2: "Let the virtue of love be perfected in the weakness of humility" (MPL 42:887), "so that through the same faith, those who have humbled themselves may be weakened, and the weakened may be perfected" (p. 888).

122. In the following quotation, Bornkamm's formulation accords with the substance of Luther's interpretation, even if he does not follow K. Holl (1:140) explicitly: "In the sense of a real fulfillment of what faith constantly requires of us, we can never really be certain of our faith and

E) The Word as Total Demand [Rom. 10:10; 10:6]

Luther's reference to John 3:8[123] made it clear once again that he was not exclusively interested in the word of a prelate as such. It interested him only because God humbles people through it. But God demands humble obedience not only in the church but everywhere and by everyone. It is not just an insignificant nuance but a profound difference when the Romans lectures claim for faith what the freedom tractate, for example, will ascribe to love. What the latter says of "love born of faith,"[124] the former sees in "faith" understood as "love in faith."[125] This becomes even clearer than in the interpretation of Romans 3:20,22 in its closest parallel, the interpretation of Romans 10:10 and of Romans 10:6, both of which are especially disputed in Luther research.[126]

1. But before we turn to these texts, we will look at the slightly later *Sermon on John 4:46–54* (of October 5, 1516).[127]

This story of the official describes "three levels of faith, namely, beginning faith, advancing faith, and perfected faith"[128]—that is, "believing in works,"[129] "believing in words,"[130] and "believing beyond words."[131]

> In the third faith, however, the ruler needs neither signs nor words to be given to him but shows that he believed Jesus beyond signs and words even down to the most minute movement of his will, and if he knew him, he would have most readily responded to him in every respect. Before, he was sought and called at a given time, but now he

our salvation" (*ARG* 53 [1962]: 12). He then (p. 13) refers to his own position when he asserts: "This is certainly not unreformational."

123. See p. 43.

124. "See here (cf. the preceding section WA 7:65,26–66,6 = LW 31:366–67), faith issues in love" (7:66,7 = 31:367; trans. alt.).

125. On Rom. 3:20; cf. WA 57/1:157,10–11 (see n. 115) and WA 56:249,10–11 = LW 25:235 ("living faith").

126. Cf. E. Bizer, *Fides*, 28–29, 36–37; on this, see H. Bornkamm, *ARG* 53 (1962): 1–60, here 10–11, 13–14; on this, again see Bizer in the afterword to the third edition of *Fides ex auditu* (195–98).

127. WA 1:87–88.

128. WA 1:87,15–16.

129. WA 1:87,16–28 (*credere operibus*).

130. WA 1:87:28–88,11 (*credere verbis*).

131. WA 1:88,11–31 (*credere ultra verba*).

> himself seeks and calls. This faith has nothing it believes more than him, because it is so absolute and complete that it believes more things than can be shown it to be believed, for it offers itself entirely without any exception. First Corinthians 13 speaks to this when it says that love believes all things, that is, accepts all things that are and that happen as coming from God alone and through its circularity refers all things to him, being ready to do whatever he wills in all things with all things.[132]

The fact that the second level of faith, faith in the word, can still be surpassed shows that words themselves are not the decisive thing but important only in their function as a means to the end of humble obedience. What they mean and do leads beyond them and is apart from them, so that we can speak of an "*absolute faith beyond words.*" This faith is no longer determined by the word but by love, understood as total surrender, as is clear from the reference to 1 Corinthians 13:7.

The notion of faith developed here obviously follows again the threefold formula "to believe God exists (*credere deum*), to believe what God says is true (*credere deo*), and to entrust oneself to God (*credere in deum*)." Traditionally, the second type is faith in the word.[133] The *fides perfecta* (perfect faith) surpasses it as *caritate formata* (faith formed by love). For Luther, however, love is not understood as broken down into individual summable acts, but as total surrender.

A comparison of our early sermon with later ones on the same text[134] that urge faith in the word in a most impressive and moving way can clearly illuminate the reversal that takes place in between at a specific point: the later sermons nowhere say that perfect faith can dispense with the word.

The same understanding of faith as that in the *Sermon on John 4* is expressed in the lecture on the interpretation of Romans 10:10 and 10:6. The two scholia revolve around the sharp contrast emphasized by Luther between work and word—that is, as will be shown, between self-assertion and self-surrender.

2. Concerning Romans 10:10, Luther claims, against the Aristotelian understanding of righteousness, that "true righteousness comes about by believing the words of God with all our heart, as has been said above in Romans 4[:3]: 'Abraham believed God, and it was reckoned to him as righteousness.'"[135] The

---

132. WA 1:88,19–29.

133. Cf. Altenstaig, s.v. "credere" (Fol. 57v): "*Credere deo*, according to Augustine, is to have faith in God's words or in the words of sacred Scripture and believe that all God's words are true."

134. Cf. the texts nicely compiled in D. Martin Luther's *Evangelien-Auslegung* (ed. E. Mülhaupt, part 4, 2nd ed., 1961), 183–205.

135. WA 56:418,30–419,2 = LW 25:410 (trans. alt.).

words of God permit no splitting up of righteousness, no partial obedience, no piecemeal action;[136] rather, they demand of us total abandonment of ourselves and complete surrender to God and his creatures:

> But in the case of God's righteousness, humans are indebted to all, because "they became guilty of all":[137] to their creator, whom they have offended, they owe glory and a blameless life; to their fellow creatures, they owe the proper use of things and cooperation in the service of God. Therefore, they are unable to pay the debt unless they subject themselves to all these and in humility take the lowest place, seeking nothing for themselves in anything. As the jurists say, "Those who surrender all their goods have made satisfaction." Thus those who surrender their earthly things, even themselves, to God, and gladly and willingly pass over into nothingness, freely confessing that they are worthy of both death and condemnation and judging themselves to be unworthy of sharing in any of these things, have plainly made satisfaction to God and are righteous. For they have kept nothing back for themselves but have surrendered everything to God and to their fellow creatures. This happens through faith, by which they take their reason captive to the word of the cross and deny themselves and refuse everything, having died to themselves and all things. And if you will, they live only to God.[138]

Not to be overlooked are the terminological and conceptual points of contact with the freedom tractate and the preface of the Epistle to the Romans in the

---

136. WA 56:419,2–6 = LW 25:410–11. Cf. on this and what follows the scholion on Rom. 12:2: "God does not care about partial righteousness or a righteousness in only one particular (WA 56:449,1–8 = LW 25:441; trans. alt.). "Therefore, the only complete righteousness is humility, which subjects everyone to everyone else and thus gives everything to everyone" (WA 56:449,8–10 = LW 25:441; trans. alt.).

137. We need to remember the context in which this passage from Jas. [2:10] occurs in the interpretation of Rom. 3:20 (WA 56:249,19–24 = LW 25:235–36; see p. 38).

138. WA 56:419,6–17 = LW 25:411 (trans. alt.). Cf. the scholion on Rom. 10:2: "Thus without understanding, without feeling, without reasoning, we must always be indifferent to everything, whatever may be required, whether by God or by humans or by any creature" (WA 56:413,22–4 = LW 25:404–5; trans. alt.). We find a less precise version of the same statement in the scholion on 1:9 in the Hebrews lectures (WA 57/3:110 = LW 29:120; cf. esp. ll. 15–16, 18–19). See from the first Psalms lectures: the saints "are humbled into nothingness, beneath every creature" (WA 3:126,32–33 = LW 10:122; cf. ll. 37–38).

September Testament of 1522:[139] We [are to] live free of self and of all things ("having died to self and all things")—"subject to all"—and free for God and our fellow creatures. Those who have been made free "keep nothing back for themselves but surrender everything to God and their fellow creatures." This happens through faith, which itself—and this is the difference to the freedom tractate[140]—consists in nothing other than what is supposed to happen through it (namely, "self-denial"). This is demanded by the "word of the cross," the word that exposes the total indebtedness of human beings ("We are indebted to everyone, because . . .") and thus enforces God's law in all its severity. *According to the Romans lectures, faith depends on the word of God encountered as law, not also and especially on the promise of grace.*[141]

3. But is this not implied by the scholion on Romans 10:6? Luther proceeds from the brief statement that concisely captures the train of thought in verses 5–8: "The apostle compares two kinds of righteousness with each other: works he attributes to the righteousness of the law but the word to the righteousness of faith."[142] He then draws the conclusion: "Therefore, the first kind of righteousness is based on the work that is done but the second on the word that is believed."[143] What, then, is this "word that is believed"? Luther finds

139. "Righteousness is such faith and is called God's righteousness, or that which avails before God; therefore, it is God's gift and makes us give to everyone their due. For through faith, we become free of sin and gain pleasure in God's commandments and so give God the honor due to him and pay him what we owe. But we willingly serve other people too wherever we can and so also pay our debt to everyone" (WA Db 7:10,28–33 = LW 35:371; trans. alt.).

140. See p. 44.

141. For the *Sermon on John 4* and on the scholion on Rom. 10:10, cf. the following passage from what would have to be the most significant sermon for the time of the Romans lectures (preached on St. Andrew's Day [Nov. 30,] 1516; the text, Matt. 4:20: THEY LEFT THEIR NETS . . .): "The most difficult thing is the cross, leaving everything, and faith. For it is the cross that mortifies this love of things so that he [Andrew] can leave everything, but faith sustains him in his mortification with other things that he does not see or experience . . . (To leave everything:) this is perfect faith. Therefore, the righteousness that comes from faith is strange, since it does not repay its debts to all, but leaves everything and surrenders all its goods. For even if we had to repay everyone everything we owed, we could never make satisfaction to God for even one hour of our life. Therefore, there is no better righteousness than this, that we surrender everything. Then we will be debtors to no one (WA I:102,10–19).

142. WA 56:414,21–22 = LW 25:405–6 (trans. alt.).

143. WA 56:414,25–26 = LW 25:406 (trans. alt.). Thus Luther has put Paul's antithetical terms in 10:5–8— namely, "writing" (= letter) and "speaking" (= spirit), work and faith, Moses and Christ—into a helpful formula. WA 56:415,4–5 = 25:406 ("the abridgment, the short way to salvation") also satisfies especially the intention of vv. 6b and 7—namely, to point out that not everything that is possible (indeed impossible and unnecessary, because salvation has been won

the answer in verses 6b and 7, which he links directly—although exegetically not really correctly[144]—to verse 9; that is, "Christ is dead and risen. That is why these negative and interrogative expressions include even stronger affirmative questions, such as, 'Who will ascend into heaven?' That is, you should most certainly say that Christ has ascended into heaven and that you will be saved. Do not doubt at all that he has ascended; for this is the word that will save you. This is what the righteousness of faith teaches."[145] Not only the last sentence (cf. verse 6a) but also the entire interpretation follows very closely the wording of the Pauline text. But if you also consider that it never goes beyond the traditional exegesis,[146] and especially that it never plays even the slightest role

---

already) should be undertaken to gain salvation. But of course, Luther has not yet made clear the mode in which salvation is present in the word (see the following note).

144. Verses 6b and 7 reject the opinion that salvation must first be obtained and brought here; it is already here, as vv. 8–13 make clear. Verses 6b and 7 are therefore virtually telling us what not to "believe." Luther, on the other hand, immediately understands them positively ("these negative and interrogative expressions include even stronger affirmatives"). Thus he deduces from these verses what words should be believed; namely, "He has ascended into heaven." But like the words "Christ died and rose again," so, too, the words "you will be saved" clearly show that he is looking ahead already to v. 9. Hence his exegesis, which is all about determining what words are to be believed, receives its relative due. But the decisive question, *how* Luther understood the words "Christ died and rose again" is by no means resolved (cf. n. 148).

145. WA 56:414,26–415,4 = LW 25:406 (trans. alt.).

146. a) Luther interprets Rom. 10:6b,7 like the *Glossa ordinaria*, which explains that "righteousness is based on faith, lest we waver in the hope that we have in God, which is grounded in Christ, lest we doubt that Christ has plundered hell and ascended into heaven. This is how we are made righteous." Lyra (on v. 7b) at first stays closer than Luther to the text by not turning it into an affirmation and having it speak only of the denial of Christ's resurrection from the dead. But then he, too, sees it in agreement with v. 9 (6.23D.F).

b) In view of Luther's formulation, "The righteousness (of faith) depends on . . . the word that we believe" (WA 56:414,25–26 = LW 25:406; trans. alt.), the interpretation of the *Glossa interlinearis* is remarkable: The word is near (v. 8), "because it justifies and saves"; it is "Christ: or the preaching of Christ." In Christ we have to do with "the Word that was in the beginning with the Father." The *Glossa ordinaria* (6.23E) says of the word that is near (on v. 8a): "It is spoken to us that we may believe." It is the word (on v. 8b) "about which the Lord says: 'You are clean because of the word that I have spoken to you.'" This word is the only thing that makes baptism into baptism, as the *Glossa* puts it with its literal, albeit abbreviated, quotation of Augustine's famous interpretation of John 15:3, to which Augustine himself had already referred in his treatment of Rom. 10:8b (+ 9–10) (in *Tractates on the Gospel of John*, tract. 80.3, *CCL* 36:529 [= MPL 35:1840]). What becomes clear here also applies to our assessment of Luther's exegesis: mere echoes of Scripture passages or their literal inclusion do not say anything clear about the theology of the exegete unless they are further explained, as here in the *Glossa ordinaria*, through the quote from Augustine (cf. n. 148).

in the body of the scholion,[147] then we cannot draw any reliable conclusions from it about Luther's understanding of the word in his Romans lectures.[148]

Luther then suddenly breaks off the discussion about the understanding of verses 6 and 7 and comes back to the statement he had started but this time with a new formulation: "But whatever the understanding, the intent of the apostle is that our entire righteousness for salvation is based on the word through faith and not on works through knowledge."[149] What Luther means here by "based on the word" is explained clearly: "God does not require a multitude of works but the mortification of the old self. But it is not mortified except by faith, which humbles its own mind and submits to the mind of another . . . which, as I said, faith in God's word does. Not that it only sounds forth from heaven, but to this day it proceeds from the mouth of every good person, especially that of a prelate."[150] This is the word that brings about humble obedience and *this* is the word that is contrasted with our works. It is a "most precious word"[151] and must be our focus. What matters first and foremost is not our *works* but our unconditional obedience, irrespective of whether our works are great or small.[152] That is, what matters is the demanding *word*, or more precisely, the word that *demands*. "Therefore, we

---

147. WA 56:415,22ff. = LW 25:406; cf. the following section.

148. *Mere scriptural quotations*, even passages like Rom. 4:25 (on 10:9: WA 56:100,24–25 = LW 25:90) and 1 Cor 1:30 (on 10:6a: WA 57/1:90,23–24), *do not convey an exact picture of Luther's Christology and his understanding of the word*, as H. Bornkamm (*ARG* 53 [1962]: 1–60, here 13) thinks. Even the extensive glosses of 56:99,26ff. = 25:89; 56:100,24ff. = 25:90; and 57/1:90,17ff., to which Bornkamm (p. 13, n. 64) points, offer nothing that would make them stand out from the traditional exegesis of Luther's day. The picture the *Glossa interlinearis* offers has the following features: the righteousness of God (on 10:3) that contrasts with the righteousness "BASED ON THE LAW (10:5), which arises from fear, not love," is the righteousness "by which God justifies those who believe." In other words, it is the righteousness "which is through faith in Christ." Christ is the "giver of righteousness, who fulfils what the law commands." It is now necessary to confess (on 10:9) "not the works of the law" but that "Christ has been raised, or that he is Lord." The *Glossa ordinaria* emphasizes (on 10:4; 6.23A) the phrase "without works": "*FINIS* not ending [the law] but perfecting it: therefore, he perfects righteousness through faith, without the works of the law." *Hence it is methodically necessary to formulate* (as E. Bizer does in his *Nachwort* to *Fides*, 198) *how Luther understood the biblical passages quoted at the beginning of his interpretation. This should be done in light of the thrust of the interpretation and its goal, which can be recognized clearly enough.*

149. WA 56:415,22–23. = LW 25:407 (trans. alt.). With the phrase "through knowledge," Luther takes up his scholion on Rom. 10:2 (WA 56:413–14 = LW 25:405; trans. alt.). Hence "word" can also mean the "humbling word."

150. WA 56:416,7–9; 12–14 = LW 25:407 (trans. alt.). See the scholia on Rom. 3:20,22, and on this, see section D 2.

151. WA 56:416,29 = LW 25:408 (trans. alt.).

152. WA 56:417,6–7 = LW 25:408.

must pay close attention to the word, with all zeal, with all our powers and all our wisdom, and with eyes completely closed. And whether the word commands us to do something foolish or base, great or small, let us do it, measuring our works by the word, and not the word by our works."[153] In other words, let us judge our works according to our obedience and not our obedience according to our works.[154]

In his interpretation, Luther does not yet give any prominence at all to the word that promises Christ (to use his later way of speaking), even though this is precisely what Paul, in verses 6 and 7, is leading to in verse 8. And the righteousness of faith, understood as "the shortest way to salvation" (cf. Rom. 9:28),[155] is revealed in all its power at one point, as a claim demanding unconditional obedience[156] but not[157] as a promise given in Christ, as the freedom tractate, for instance, will later make clear, with explicit reference to Romans 9:28 and Romans 10:[158]

---

153. WA 56:417,9–12 = LW 25:408–9 (trans. alt.).

154. This interpretation is corroborated by the slightly later (perhaps even contemporaneous) version of the interpretation of Ps. 1, to which reference has already been made in n. 108. The last quoted sentences of the scholion on Rom. 10:6 (WA 56:417,9–12 = LW 25:408) agree almost word for word with 3:19,11–15 = 10:16 (quoted in n. 108)!

155. "The righteousness of faith. This is the shortest way to salvation. But the righteousness of the law is a long and circuitous way, as figured by the wandering of the children of Israel in the wilderness" (WA 56:415,3–5 = LW 25:406; trans. alt.—this follows the text quoted in n. 143). With this, Luther briefly resumes his interpretation of Rom. 9:28 (on this, see section K), which in turn falls back on a motif that often occurs in the Psalms lectures (cf. esp. n. 518).

156. The line gloss on Rom. 10:3 should be read as an abbreviation of the scholia on 10:6,10: "The RIGHTEOUSNESS OF GOD which is through faith in Christ and the humility of obedience to God's word" (WA 56:98,10; 99,1 = LW 25:89; trans. alt.). Luther clearly says elsewhere that this understanding of the word means that the final sharpening of the law and its demand is the gospel: "Here we have the gospel (so begins the sermon on Jan. 25, 1517, on Matt. 19:29), and here also the purpose of all God's commandments: to strip us bare of all our desires; for we must be pure and holy and undefiled and cling to nothing at all of what we might desire. Therefore, the gospel is nothing else than the revelation and interpretation of the old law" (WA 1:126,4–8).

157. See, on the other hand, these words from the freedom tractate: "Christ . . . not only said, 'Repent,' but added a word about faith, saying, 'The kingdom of heaven is at hand,'" as well as the following section (WA 7:63,31–64,12 = LW 31:364; cf. WA 7:34,9–22). If the freedom tractate says "We are justified and saved, not by works or laws, but by the word of God (that is, by the promise of his grace) and by faith" (7:63,3–5 = 31:362–63), then this means something different from Luther's interpretation of chap. 10 in the Romans lectures, where he says, "that the entire righteousness of a person for salvation is based on the word through faith and not on works through knowledge" (56:415,22–23 = 25:407). See the interpretation of Rom. 10:4 given in §6 of the freedom tractate (7:22–23 [German]; cf. 31:346–48 [Latin]).

158. We should note the role played by these Romans passages in §§6–9 of the freedom tractate (WA 7:22–24 [German]; this is even clearer in the expanded Latin version: WA 7:51,12–53,14 = LW 31:346–49). The sections on the "two different words" of Scripture (§§8–9) are determined especially by Rom. 9:28 (cf. n. 159) and Rom. 10. Together with Mark 16:16, Rom. 9:28 (or Isa.

> Now when people have learned and felt their helplessness from the commandments and are worried about how to keep them . . . then they are truly humbled and reduced to nothing in their eyes and find nothing in themselves that would make them pious and godly. Then comes the other word, the divine pledge and promise that says: "If you want to fulfill all the commandments . . . look here, believe in Christ, in whom I promise you all grace, righteousness, peace, and freedom. If you believe, you have it; if you do not believe, you do not have it . . ." For I have compressed everything briefly[159] into faith, so that whoever has faith will have everything and be saved, but whoever does not have faith will not have anything! In this way, God's promises give what the commandments require and accomplish what they command, so that everything belongs to God, the commandment and the fulfilment. He alone commands and he alone is also the one who fulfils.[160]

God not only humbles and brings to naught; he also offers his fullness in an affirmative word—that is, a word that establishes a sure and certain foundation, a word that is orally proclaimed as a binding[161] promise. But the Romans lectures know nothing of such a word. This is also evident in the concept of God that we find here.

F) The Word and God (*nos extra nos in solo deo*) [Rom. 3:4; 9:3; 8:7]

What is meant by the formula "outside of us in God alone" (*nos extra nos in solo deo*) that Luther first used during the Romans lectures?[162]

10:22–23) and Rom. 10:10 completely determine the preparatory section §7b ("Therefore, true faith . . ."; cf. 7:52,12–19 = 31:347–48).

159. Cf. the "brief summary" and "briefly": WA 7:23,18–20 (in the interpretation of Isa. 10:22–23 = Rom. 9:28; on this verse, see section K).

160. §9 (WA 7:24) (German); cf. LW 31:348–49 (Latin).

161. Cf. the "if you believe, you have it; if you do not believe, you do not have it" (WA 7:24,13–14; cf. LW 31:349) with the verse Mark 16:16, cited just before (WA 7:23,16–17; cf. LW 31:347), which is the origin of this formula of blessing and curse. The precise proof for this is given in chap. 4 (pp. 224–225).

162. That this phrase has a formulaic character is shown by its frequent occurrence with almost the same wording in different texts. These are mostly sermons that underscore the importance of the formula. We will assemble several formulations in chronological order and in each case briefly draw attention to the context which is always materially the same:

a) "Tribulation . . . makes people despair of all creatures, turn away from them and from themselves, and seek help outside of themselves and of all things in God alone" (Scholion on Rom. 5:5; WA 56:305,24,27–306,1 = LW 25:292; trans. alt.;

As we saw from the interpretation of Romans 6:17b,[163] God in the word and humans in faith belong together in the event of justification, so that God judges and destroys in his word and humans submit to this judgment and destruction. "For now the word and the believer have a similar form, that is, truth and righteousness. Therefore, when God is justified, he justifies, and when he justifies, he is justified"[164] (on Rom. 3:4). In this double movement of the justification event, the formulation of which must be seen against the background of the tropological interpretation of the Scripture,[165] the difference between God and humans is said

---

see p. 54). For the importance of the formula for the interpretation of Rom. 4:7, see pp. 146–149. For further passages in the Romans lectures see: 56:264,20–21 = 25:252 (on 3:27); 56:386,25–27 = 25:376–77 (on 8:28): cf. on this, see pp. 72–73.

b) "Truthful people . . . acknowledge that they are all sinful and that all their good is not within them but outside of them in God, and that they want to be dependent on his mercy because the righteous will live by faith" (in the series of sermons on the Ten Commandments; here from a sermon probably preached on August 1, 1516 [WA 1:426, n. 2] on the first commandment): 1:427,31–33.

c) "Our eye is outside of us and is not to be sought in us, and yet it is in us and is to be found in us . . . Thus we are to despair utterly of ourselves and of our eye" (Sermon on St. Martin's Day [Nov 11,] 1516; WA 1:100,14–15, 19–20; cf. 1:100,27–28. On this, see pp. 35–37.

d) "This holiness is so excellent that it makes even righteous people sinners, because they live entirely outside of themselves in God, in his will, in his righteousness, and in his wisdom. And so they are not righteous because of their own righteousness, acquired or infused in them, but because of the divine righteousness in itself, before (*coram*) which and in which they lost their own righteousness and were made sin for it. Thus they no longer desire to live righteously but for God alone" (*Sermon on St. Andrew's Day* [Nov. 30,] 1516; WA 1:104,4–9).

e) "Where, then, is wisdom? Where is righteousness? Where is truth? Where is virtue? Not in us, but in Christ, outside of us in God" (Sermon on St. Matthew's Day [Feb. 24,] 1517; WA 1:139,34–35 = LW 51:28). Cf. 1:140,4,15 = 51:29–30.

f) "To put our trust in God: but this does not happen before we are outside of ourselves, abandon ourselves completely, comfort ourselves with our lack of virtue, and console ourselves only with the fact that we know someone who can help us, who for our sake bore all this oft mentioned pain and torment" (interpretation of the Lord's Prayer 1517: WA 9:147,27–148,3; the quotation: 9:147,30–34).

163. See pp. 21–22, 26–27.

164. WA 56:227,6–8 = LW 25:211 (trans. alt.).

165. Cf. the *Dictata* on Ps. 104:1: "God is *magnified* in us, that is, when we acknowledge him as magnified and confess him as magnified . . . This is tropology . . . But those who magnify him exceedingly are those who humble themselves exceedingly. For only the humble magnify him, and to them he is a great Lord and greatly to be praised, because they are exceedingly blameworthy in themselves. For the more you praise God, the more you disparage yourself; and the more he pleases you, the more you are displeased with yourself, and vice versa" (WA 4:172,5–12 = LW 11:316; trans. alt.). Likewise, v. 2 is interpreted thus: "*First*, with

to be the difference between the word that judges and faith that accepts it, between the revelation of God's judgment and the corresponding confession of sins.[166]

> So by going out of himself, God causes us to enter into ourselves, and through his knowledge he also gives us knowledge of ourselves. For if God had not first gone out of himself in this way and sought to be truthful in us, we could not have entered into ourselves and become liars and unrighteous persons. For none of us could have known by ourselves that we are such persons in God's sight if God himself had not revealed it to us . . . But now God has revealed what he thinks of us and has passed judgment, and that judgment is that we are all in sin. Therefore, we must submit to *this* revelation of his or to his words and believe them, and so justify and confirm them, and in this way confess that we are sinners according to them[167] (on Rom 3:5).

For in this way we are conformed to God, who does not consider or recognize anything good in us. And by this we are good, when we recognize nothing except God's good and our evil, for anyone who is thus wise with God is truly wise and good.[168] For they know that there is nothing good outside of God and that everything that is good is in God. As Christ says, "The kingdom of God is within you," as if to say, outside of you is only exile. But outside of you is everything that is only believed by faith[169] (on Rom 9:3).

This internality, in which humans in faith are one with the judging word—that is, "in God"—excludes all self-assertion and trust in everything that is not God and so includes leaving themselves and their world. However, internality in this sense is in fact externality, the very place where they are outside of themselves in God. This in turn means once again that they are "grounded" in the naked hope that is in God. "Therefore, tribulation . . . takes away everything they have and leaves them naked and alone, it does not permit help and salvation in either the physical or spiritual realm to those who seem deserving but makes

---

reference to Christ" (4:172,28 = 11:317). "*Second*, tropologically, when we offer him this kind of confession, praise, and honor, for then he is also in us what he is in his own person. And faith in him is then confession and the beauty with which he himself clothes us spiritually. For through faith we acknowledge, honor, and adorn him. But this does not happen unless we deny, confound, and defile ourselves" (4:172,35–173,4 = 11:317; trans. alt.).

166. Cf. pp. 116–117, pp. 120–130, 166–167.

167. WA 56:229,20–32 = LW 25:213–14 (trans. alt.; author's emphasis).

168. Luther here takes up 1 Cor. 3:18, as he does in a similar context in WA 56:229,32–33 = LW 25:214.

169. WA 56:393,13–20 = LW 25:383 (trans. alt.; the words from "kingdom of God" onward are especially emphasized by Luther).

them despair of all creatures, turn away from them and from themselves, and seek help outside of themselves and of all things in God alone"[170] (on Rom. 5:5).

Luther cannot say anything more specific about the place "in God alone" than that it is "outside of us and of all things." Thus, as in Tauler,[171] it is derived from pure negation or from the word of judgment. Nowhere in the Romans lectures is it linked to the word of salvation. This understanding of "externality," which Luther could never have used in his battle against the Enthusiasts (*Schwärmer*), should therefore not be automatically identified with the later "external word."[172] If the latter is an unconditional promise, which asserts and declares what it promises, then the former excludes all affirmations (even those of God's grace!) on the grounds that they offer false security:[173] "For our good is hidden, and so deeply, that it is hidden under its opposite . . . And in every way,

---

170. WA 56:305,24–306,1 = LW 25:292 (trans. alt.); (cf. 56:392,20–393,20 [esp. l. 26] = 25:382: "He loves himself not in himself but in God").

171. Cf. the marginal note on Tauler (WA 9:103,35–37): "The affections should be naked, stripped of all our wisdom and righteousness, and rely on God alone and be considered as nothing."

There can be no doubt that Luther, with his "outside" formula and the determinations it entails, is following Tauler. Cf. the following formulations of Tauler: "God leads people outside of themselves into him" (F. Vetter 162,5; cf. 162,4–22); "they go above everything, above themselves, and into God" (266,15–16.); cf. 306,1–4 (l.3: "they go out" [cf. l.10 and 307,28); 409,31–32: "they go into God, into his . . . good will, in a true departure from their own self-will" Basically, we would need to consider whether or not the concept "ground" (*grunt*) in Tauler corresponds exactly to the place "outside of ourselves in God alone" in Luther. The comparison is difficult because Tauler's statements cannot easily be brought to a common denominator. Particular attention should be paid to how Tauler interprets the "habit of the mind" (F. Vetter 350–52): it "is not in the reality, but in the essentiality, in the ground" (351,35–352,1). For the understanding of *grunt* in Tauler, see now Steven E. Ozment, *Homo Spiritualis* (1969), 15–21, and on "they go out" and "they go in," see 203–4.

172. G. Ebeling is of a different opinion. In considering the *extra* formula in the Romans lectures, he writes in *RGG*, 3rd ed., 4:501 (Art. "Luther 2. Theologie") that "the *extra nos* . . . influenced by mystical forms of thought, becomes the decisive catchword also in the battle against mysticism and the future Enthusiasm. It does not aim at an objectivity that disregards people, but at rightly understanding how human existence is affected by the word of salvation that creates faith." However, by speaking of the "word of salvation that creates faith," Ebeling imports Luther's reformational understanding of the word into the Romans lectures and then uses it as a decisive interpretative lens. But the texts will not permit it. The only context that Ebeling can have in mind here is the scholion on Rom. 4:7. Compare his formulation, "the justification of the person by faith alone (*sola fide*) . . . depends on the promise of God through faith" (*RGG*, 501) with WA 56:269,25–30 = LW 25:359; 56:271,27–272,2 = 25:260; 56:272,16–21 = 25:261. For these texts, see section I. 3.

173. We cannot say (with H. Bornkamm on Rom. 3:20,22 [*ARG* 53 (1962): 1–60, here 12–13]) that Luther only has a misunderstanding of true faith in mind (that is, its lapse into security): Luther's alternative to "security" (*securitas*) is definitely not "certainty" (*certitudo*), as it is later, but actual uncertainty. Cf. WA 56:281,16–21 = LW 25:268–69 (where *securitas* is rendered as "smugness"), see on this pp. 148–153.

all our affirmation of any good is hidden under the negation of the same, that faith may have its place in God, *who is a negative essence, and goodness, wisdom, and justice. But he cannot be possessed or touched except by the negation of all our affirmations*"[174] (on Rom. 9:3).

The fact that this concept of God, derived by way of negation,[175] is not of interest to Luther in and of itself but is always expressed immediately by an equivalent concept of existence[176] in no way deprives it of its philosophical, metaphysical character:[177] "And so 'our life is hidden with Christ[178] in God,' that is, in the negation of all that we can feel, possess, and understand. Thus, our wisdom and righteousness are not apparent to us at all,[179] but are hidden with

---

174. WA 56:392,28–393,3 = LW 25:382–83 (trans. alt.; author's emphasis).

175. The way of negation (*via negationis*) is praised most highly in the *Dictata*, for example, on Ps. 65:1 (WA 3:372,13–27 = LW 10:313). Cf. 56:299–300 = 25:287–88 together with the notes in the apparatus.

176. Luther of course always adhered to the principle that knowledge of God is not possible without knowledge of oneself and that knowledge of oneself is not possible without knowledge of God. Cf. the *Operationes in Psalmos*: "It is the same and both at the same time: the God who illuminates and the illuminated heart, the God who is seen by us and God who is present" (WA 5:118,20–22). The decisive thing, however, is the mode and medium of this simultaneity.

177. The Epiphany sermon of 1517 gives us an insight into the thoroughly philosophical structure of this thought: "As blessed Augustine is accustomed to saying in his meditations, if the good in the abstract is separated from its creaturely form, namely goodness, nothing but God would remain. The same is also true of wisdom and righteousness. For we are a shadow, but God is the true reality and substance (Col. 2:17 is no doubt in mind here) in us" (WA 1:125,6–9): A remarkable interweaving of the *via negationis*, the way of negation (of abstraction) and of the *via eminentiae*, the way of eminence (of limitlessness)! Expressed in existential terms, this means: "Those, therefore, who remove all good from themselves and ascribe it to God alone (as in truth he is), offer frankincense to Christ (the sermon theme!) and acknowledge God himself" (1:125:13–14). Cf. from the Hebrews lectures: "To cling to God is to be freed from the world and all its creatures" (on 9:23) (WA 57/3:214,20–21 = LW 29:216).

178. The christological form of the concept of God and of existence does not have to rob it of its philosophical character entirely; see n. 179.

179. Luther opposes the scholastic position, according to which infused grace inheres in the soul as a quality. Already for Tauler, the ground of faith, love, and hope lies beyond human possibilities, being neither visible nor certifiable—but also not audible as an oral word. What, then, is the mode of reality of this ground of ours that has been removed from us? Luther points to Christ. But how can that be, if "Christ," or the "cross," is nothing but the illustration of the negation, the "denial of the self"? Where exactly is the comfort? Where and how does certainty emerge concretely and unambiguously? Who has the power and authority to comfort me in the face of God's judgment (cf. on Rom. 9:3: those who hate themselves "truly love themselves, for they love themselves not in themselves but in God, that is, as they are in the will of God, who hates, damns, and wishes evil to all sinners, that is, to all of us" [WA 56:392,25–28 = LW 25:382; trans. alt.])?

Christ in God. But what does appear are their opposites, namely, our sin and foolishness"[180] (on Rom. 9:3).

What Luther is concerned about with his negative concept of God and its corresponding concept of existence, of humiliation (*exinanitio*)—the surrender of oneself—is clear: it is the one thing necessary, the Archimedean point. But nowhere can this be grasped as a promise. Even the Holy Spirit is not, as in Paul, the seal and pledge of salvation that guarantees that God will give it to us in full because of his promise. The wisdom given by the Spirit (on Rom 8:7) "has no other interest than God understood negatively (*Deum Negative*)"[181] and everything understood negatively with God, so that the person who has turned away "from everything, seeks only the one thing necessary with Mary. But Martha does not turn away from all these things but walks through them, even breaks through them, and is confused in many ways."[182]

Here as elsewhere,[183] Luther uses the Neoplatonic and Augustinian idea of the *unum simplex*, the notion that God is utterly simple, which can be very helpful for theological discourse. God is the one thing that is necessary, the one thing that excludes the many and ambiguous things, thereby taking us out of

180. WA 56:393,5–9 = LW 25:383 (trans. alt.). This is a continuation of the text quoted above and proved in n.174.

181. Cf. with this WA 56:393,1–3 = LW 25:383 (on Rom. 9:3). In contrast to the "*Deus negative*," God understood negatively, the scholion on Rom. 8:7 speaks of the "*Deus affirmative*, God as he is known from his divine properties" (56:362,11 = 25:351; trans. alt.), which is one of the "objects of extravagant enjoyment" (56:361,24 = 25:351)! (Cf. the scholion on Rom. 5:5: 56:305,10–18 = 25:292.)

182. WA 56:362,32–363,6 = LW 25:352 (trans. alt.). Cf. the *Sermon on the Assumption of the Blessed Virgin Mary* (see pp. 89–92): "If needs must have it that we are divided in many things outwardly and must be confused with Martha, it is far better to choose the best part with Mary and to be gathered into one from within" (WA 4:649,8–10).

183. From the first Psalms lectures, see the interpretation of Ps. 27:4 (ONE THING HAVE I ASKED OF THE LORD): "Here we are taught not to ask for many things, and that only 'one thing is necessary.' Martha is worried about many things, because she has asked for temporal things rather than spiritual things. For temporal things divide a person into many parts, but spiritual things gather the divided person into one, as the apostle says in 1 Cor. 7 [6:17]: 'Anyone united to the Lord becomes one spirit with him,' that is, they are one spiritually, but not temporally" (WA 3:151,36–41 = LW 10:127; trans. alt.). On Ps. 59:2: "Although turning toward the creature can happen many times, there is only one turning away, because God is one and the creatures are many" (3:331,13–14 = 10:274; trans. alt.). On Ps. 63:2: "The spiritual life is one, for it unites everything into one, that is, all saints into one, and all members into one etc. But the life of the world is manifold, for it scatters and makes many . . . However, the life of the saints is in the one Christ alone, for in him alone every soul also enjoys all its strength" (3:361,26–28,32–34 = 10:304; trans. alt.). See further chap. 1, n. 74. For the Romans lectures, we must remember especially the interpretation of Rom. 3:20,22; see section D 2, especially n. 106. Luther was confirmed in this way of thinking by the *Theologia Germanica* (see 9,3–4).

our "confusion" and making us certain. It is decisive that we experience the "one thing necessary" of God nowhere else, that the ground "in God alone" is offered nowhere else than in the existential exclusion of everything, in the "despising and renouncing of everything that is not God."[184] But who is able to mortify the old self in this way? Luther answers the question by referring to the Spirit of God.[185] But we can only be certain of this Spirit in mortification. Thus he says that the one thing necessary of God can only be experienced negatively as a *rejection* but not positively as a *promise*,[186] which according to Luther's later theology, is the only thing that can give certainty.

For the later Luther, rejection was a necessary flipside of the promise, because the unconditional validity of the promise called for the rejection of everything that is not God in his promise.[187] That is why he never stopped speaking about the necessity of mortification. But this discourse then takes place in a new frame of reference in which the Neoplatonic-Augustinian motif of the "one thing necessary" continues in a Taulerian form as the exclusion of everything. It becomes the exclusive particle, which is an important aspect of the reformational theology of the word, although the path to that is not without its twists and turns. The distinction between the word of judgment and the word of grace now finds its specific setting in life (*Sitz im Leben*) in an assertoric orality or oral proclamation.

On the other hand, it is typical of Luther's early theology that it does not distinguish between the word of judgment and the word of salvation, between rejection and promise, at least not in regard to their effect but only in the way we experience them. The rejection is, or more precisely becomes, in its innermost ground a "promise" and the law becomes "gospel."[188] But it is precisely this

184. WA 56:366,15–16 = LW 25:356 (trans. alt.), on Rom. 8:14.

185. WA 56:366,18–19 = LW 25:356: "freely to relinquish the good things and embrace evil things in their place. This is not natural, but the work of the Spirit of God in us."

186. It seems that only at Rom. 15:4 (THAT THROUGH PATIENCE AND THE COMFORT . . .) does Luther have a "positive" understanding of the word: "In place of material things he (i.e. Paul) gives words of comfort by which we are sustained so that we do not lack in patience. Thus to give up things for the words of Scripture is a great thing" (WA 56:520,8–10 = LW 25:515–16; trans. alt.; cf. the gloss: 56:137,5–7 = 25:119–20). But it is characteristic of Luther at this stage to immediately give this positive statement suggested by the text a negative twist: "And people do not do this unless they have died to all material things" (56:520,10 = 25:516).

187. Cf., for example, the impressive interpretation of Luke 2:49 in the Lenten Postil of 1525 (WA 17/2:24–6 = LW 76:199–201), especially, that "God will not tolerate us relying on anything else or clinging to something with our hearts that is not Christ in his word" (17/2:25,1–3 = 76:200). For you will only find help if *you go outside of yourself* and of all human comfort *and surrender yourself to the word alone*" (17/2:26,13–14 = 76:201; trans. alt.; author's emphasis).

188. See pp. 27–29.

mingling or confusion that causes the problem, because as the Romans lectures clearly show, it leads to uncertainty. This confusion has implications for Luther's concept of God. It means the equation of the "hidden God" and the "revealed God," which in turn means that only the judging God is revealed.

The difference between this understanding of the concept of God in the Romans lectures and *The Bondage of the Will* is clear. In the latter, the hidden and revealed (or preached) God are not intertwined but distinguished,[189] and it is precisely this distinction that gives us certainty. Revelation of course can also be hidden; otherwise, we could not speak theologically of unfaith.[190] But this hiddenness that the unbeliever experiences is by no means identical with, and must not be confused with, that fundamental hiddenness of God, which encompasses it and which is incomprehensible even to faith, which nevertheless still believes despite it.

This difference between the Romans lectures and *The Bondage of the Will* must be taken seriously and not glossed over.[191] It will be considered in the summary at the end of the book in a denser systematic context than here.[192]

G) The Word and Christ (nos extra nos in solo Christo) [Rom. 5:2–3; 6:17; 1:16; 8:26; 9:3; 2:15; 8:38]

The picture gained so far from the understanding of the word in the Romans lectures does not change when we consider their Christology—that is, that Luther interprets the "outside of us in *God* alone" as "outside of us in *Christ* alone."[193]

---

189. Cf. WA 18:682,26–686,13 = LW 33:135–40 (Luther's critique of the Diatribe's treatment of Ezek. 18:32).

190. Cf. WA 18:658,17–659,2 = LW 33:98; 18:689,26–31 = 33:146. See *An Exhortation to the Knights of the Teutonic Order* (1523): "But so it must be: God's word has to be the strangest thing in heaven and on earth. That is why it must at one and the same time do two opposite things: give perfect light and honor to those who believe it and bring utter blindness and shame to those who do not believe it. To the former it must be the most certain and best known of all things; to the latter it must be the most unknown and hidden of all things . . . As St. Paul says in 2 Corinthians 4[:3], if our gospel is hidden, it is hidden only to those who are lost" (12:235,35–236,8 = 45:146–47; trans. alt.; quoted in H. Bandt, *Luthers Lehre vom verborgenen Gott*, 1958, 85).

191. As G. Ebeling does in his *Luther: An Introduction to His Thought*, 210–11.

192. Pp. 393–394.

193. Cf. esp. from the *Sermon on St. Matthew's Day* (Feb. 24) 1517: "Where, then, is wisdom? Where is righteousness? Where is truth? Where is virtue? Not in us, but in Christ. It is outside of us, in God" (WA 1:139,34–35 = LW 51:28; see n. 162e). For the Romans lectures, according to the programmatic scholion on 1:1, it is a matter of destroying "everything that is within us"

The scholion on *Romans 5:2* turns emphatically against those "who follow mystical theology and rest in the inner darkness, neglecting the images of Christ's suffering and wishing to hear and contemplate only the uncreated Word itself, without first having been justified and having the eyes of their hearts purged by the incarnate Word."[194] This polemic is not specific to Luther's theology but is traditional and can already be found in Bernard,[195] Ludolf of Saxony[196] and Tauler,[197] to mention just a few important names.

What does the emphasis on the "incarnate Word" mean? It is not understood as the sign of a thing that is present but, as the *Christmas Sermon of 1514*

---

and of raising up "everything that is outside of us and in Christ" (56:158,7–9 = 25:136, trans. alt.; cf. 56:157,2ff. = 25:135–38).

194. WA 56:299,27–300,3 = LW 25:287; trans. alt. (cf. the *Sermon on the Assumption of the Blessed Virgin Mary*: 4:647,19–649,7). For the proof text from the *Opera Dionysii*, see J. Ficker WA 56:299 on l. 28. The "images of Christ's suffering" should be understood not least from their reification in the visual arts (on that: J. Ficker, on l. 28). But Luther, like Tauler, immediately turns this view mediated by the arts into a theological statement. See the intermediate chapter ("The Understanding of the Mass"), esp. n. 430 and Luther's interpretation of relics (on this, see pp. 62–63).

195. a) This is shown only by the text from the scholion on Rom. 9:16 (WA 56:400,1–12 = LW 25:389–90; here too, the copious notes of J. Ficker on l.3 should be esp. noted), which is parallel to the scholion on 5:2 (56:299,28–330,3 = 25:287). The "images of Christ's suffering" (on 5:2) find their counterpart (on 9:16) in the "wounds of Jesus Christ, 'the clefts of the rock'" (ll.9–10) or in our "meditation" on them (ll.3–4). Bernard is not expressly mentioned here but see the *Dictata* on Ps. 84:3: "According to Bernard, the soul does not have rest except in the wounds of Christ . . . and the Song of Solomon: 'my dove in the clefts of the rock'" (3:640,40–43; cf. 3:645,29–34 = 11:140; on that, see p. 107. Cf. the Hebrews lectures: 57/3:162,15–16 = 29:165; 57/3:164,16–17 = 29:166; 57/3:165,8–11 = 29:167. That Song of Songs 2:14 also plays a role in the piety of the Mass is clear from Biel's Mass commentary, Lect. 54 G (part 2:342).

b) Directly comparable with the scholion on Rom. 5:2 is Bernard's Sermon 62 on Canticles, especially (4:7): "What is more effective in healing the wounds of the conscience and purging the mind than constant meditation on the wounds of Christ? But until it (i.e. the mind) has been perfectly purged and healed, I do not see how it is able to say to him: 'SHOW ME YOUR FACE'" (*Opera* 2, 159).

196. With regards to the "highest majesty," Ludolf in the prologue to his *Life of Jesus Christ* says: "No one will be able to reach it rapidly except by advancing through this life of our redeemer" (Augsburg 1729, 2a).

197. Cf. in addition to F. Vetter 110,24–27; 112,4ff.; 141,12–13; 142,12–14; 166,7ff., esp. 111,29–30: "But all who will go there must enter through the door, which is Christ according to his humanity" (see as a commentary on it: 112,4–9). John 10:9, which Tauler refers to here, is the first scriptural passage quoted at the beginning of the preface to Luther's 1513 printing of the Psalter in which Jesus Christ himself speaks. Admittedly, there is no literary dependence here, but the parallels point to the commonality of a traditional motif.

has already shown, as the sign of a thing that is absent, to use a classic definition of the later Luther.[198] The "*uncreated* Word," the proper Word of God, is not given fully in the "*incarnate* Word."[199] Rather, the latter (and thus his sermon and meditation) points away to the uncreated Word and leads to it by "rapture," even if only in exceptional cases, so to speak, "by special revelation."[200] "For the incarnate Word is first necessary for the purity of the heart, and only when one's heart is pure can one then finally be taken up ("raptured") through this Word into the uncreated Word by anagogy."

Later, for Luther, faith is bonded to the incarnate Word and accordingly to the spoken word. For "his word is so much like him (i.e. God) that the Deity is completely within it, and whoever has the word has the whole Deity."[201] In contrast, for Luther's early theology, the incarnate Word is only the necessary path to the proper Word, the uncreated Word, which is difficult to reach. The latter is the province of mystical theology, "which is experiential wisdom not doctrinal."[202] "Dionysius calls it . . . *alogos*, that is, irrational or speechless, because

198. WA TR 4:666, no. 5106 (1540); hence: "A sign in philosophy is the mark of a thing that is absent, but a sign in theology is the mark of a thing that is present" (ll.8–9). Although Luther in the next sentence refers to Augustine for this definition, it in fact contradicts his hermeneutic of signification.

199. As it is, for example, according to the *Sermon on the Prologue of John* of 1522 (cf. n. 201 and chap. 1, n. 87).

200. Cf. the continuation of the above passage (WA 56:300,3–5 = LW 25:287–88): "But who is there who thinks that their heart is so pure that they could dare aspire to this level (i.e. the uncreated Word), unless they are called and carried away ('raptured') by God, as was the case with the apostle Paul [2 Cor. 12:2], or 'taken up with Peter, James, and John his brother' [Matt. 17:1]?" In short, that rapture is not called "access" (scholion on Rom. 5:2; trans. alt.). For our interpretive keyword *special revelation*, see in addition the marginal gloss on Rom. 8:38 (56:86,19–24 = 25:78), with its unsolved problem of certainty, from which also the scholion on 5:2 must be seen.

201. WA 10/1.1:188,7–8 = LW 52:46 (trans. alt.); (see n. 199).

202. With this and in what follows, we also include in the exegesis of the scholion on Rom. 5:2 a marginal note on Tauler's sermon written at about the same time. It is quoted here with its context to give the full picture: "It is true that God is to be born in us according to the state of the contemplative life and by spiritual anagogy [mystical rapture]. But morally he is born, not in rest but with the operation of the virtues, according to the state of the active life. The latter pertains to Martha, the former to Mary. The latter is easy, the former difficult; the latter is often, the former rare. The latter is easily understood by everyone, but the former is not understood except by those with experience. Hence this whole sermon starts out from mystical theology, which is experiential and not doctrinal wisdom. For no one knows except the person who receives this hidden matter. For it speaks of the spiritual birth of the uncreated Word. But proper theology, which speaks of the spiritual birth of the incarnate Word, has the one thing necessary and the best part. It is not anxious and troubled about many things but grows and fights in opposition to

it cannot be handed on or received by words or reason but only by experience."[203] "Proper theology" also has to serve this experience, but it makes use of "reason" and "words." It deals with the "spiritual birth of the *incarnate* Word,"[202] but as such already has, in terms of its subject matter, the "one thing necessary,[202] which traditionally is the prerogative of mystical theology with its focus on the *uncreated* Word.

At first it is difficult to see why Luther, on the one hand, very emphatically refers to the incarnate Word, particularly to the "images of the passion," but then, on the other hand, again gives preference to the uncreated Word,[204] without expressly balancing or even identifying these two interests (these being the *priority* given to the incarnate Word and the *prevalence* of the uncreated Word). But if we take into consideration the texts that speak of the knowledge of God on the path of negation, in which we only seek the "one thing necessary"[205] with Mary, then it becomes clear that there are not two different competing interests here but that "being taken up into the uncreated Word" is nothing but the way of negation, which Luther of course wants to see understood specifically as self-abnegation, which clearly is what we see in the image of the crucified one.

Since this self-abnegation lasts "forever" and never comes to an end, the uncreated Word is never reached. In this respect, it has an advantage over the incarnate Word and *cannot* be grasped in it.

But even if we could establish that, contrary to the thrust of this interpretation, the main part of the scholion[206] actually understands the intention of the

---

sin, and when it is anxious about its own virtue, it looks for where this victor triumphs over vices" (WA 9:98,14–27). We see here two dimensions of a threefold concept of theology (symbolic, proper, and mystical theology or alternatively, sensual, rational, and spiritual theology: see on Heb. 5:12: WA 57/3:179 = LW 29:179; trans. alt.), which Luther takes over from Gerson (*De triplici theologia*, Cons. 1, ed. Du Pin 1706, 3, 365: following J. Ficker WA 57/3:160 on l. 1).

203. WA 57/3:179,9–11 = LW 29:179 (trans. alt.; scholion on Heb. 5:12). Cf. n. 202.

204. The convergence, suggested above, of mystical theology (with its focus on the uncreated Word) and of proper theology (with its focus on the incarnate Word) in the "one thing necessary" is not expressly formulated by Luther himself but is already our interpretation.

On the prevalence of the uncreated Word, see, in addition to the scholion on Rom. 5:2, the scholion on Heb. 4:4, according to which the resting "inwardly" of the spiritual self happens "negatively" (privatively)—that is, "when it is lifted up by faith and the Word into the essential work of God, the work of God in his essence, which is the very birth of the uncreated Word . . . that is, the procession of the Son from the Father" (WA 57/3:159,19–23 = LW 29:162–63; trans. alt.).

205. See sec. F ("The Word and God"), esp. the proof text in n. 182.

206. WA 56:298,22–299,27 = LW 25:286–87.

Pauline text, that we *have* access to God through Christ and through faith,[207] we would still have to look again in more detail at the manner of this "access."

What does the incarnate Word specifically mean, and what do the images of Christ's passion mean, in which for Luther the Word is expressed? These questions are immediately answered in the following scholion on *Romans 5:3*. It says of our SUFFERING (*TRIBULATIO*)[208] that it "should be adored as the very cross of Christ."[209] Those who practice this adoration of the cross (according to the *Sermon on St. Andrew's Day* [November 30] 1516[210]) "say with St. Andrew, 'O noble cross, hail precious cross, you received grace and beauty from our Lord's limbs: now support me and restore me to my master who redeemed me through you.'"[211] Cross and suffering are the true most holy relics of the cross of Christ, whose splintered fragments, scattered throughout the whole world and throughout the whole of history, say to every person: "The cross of Christ has been distributed through the whole world; each person always receives their own portion. Therefore, do not throw it away but rather receive it as a most holy relic." Thus writes Luther on April 15, 1516, to Leiffer.[212] In a scholion he opines about "the hypocrites who venerate the relics of the wood of the holy cross only outwardly, and avoid and abhor the tribulations and adversities that it signifies."[213] And in a sermon he says that the true particles of the cross are "groanings," "vigils," "labors," "prayer," and "humiliation."[214] These are the things that we should regard as relics.[215] By means of the experience of our own suffering, the

207. That this is Paul's emphasis is clear from v. 2, with its use of the present perfect tense, and from the context, esp. v. 5.

208. We can ignore the distinction Luther makes here ("one kind of suffering comes from God's severity and another from his kindness": WA 56:300,11–12 = LW 25:288 [trans. alt.]) because it only highlights the problem without solving it. But the problem, how the cross can bring about salvation, is the question behind this whole section.

209. WA 56:300,16 = LW 25:288.

210. WA 1,101–4.

211. WA 1:102,27–30. Luther here quotes, as in the *Sermon on St. Andrew's Day* 1519 (WA 9:427,27–28), from the *Legenda Aurea* [*The Golden Legend*], chap. 2 (On St. Andrew, Apostle), Graesse, 17–18. See also chap. 137 (On the Exaltation of the Holy Cross): "Whence Andrew said: 'Hail, precious cross etc.'" (Graesse, 605). But the quotation is found neither in WA 1 nor in WA 9.

212. WA Br 1:37–38; ll.15–17.

213. Scholion on Rom. 5:3: WA 57/1:169,11–13 (cf. WA 56:301,20–21 = LW 25:288–89). For his interpretation, Luther wrongly refers to 1 Cor. 1:17 and Gal. 5:11 (ll.13–16).

214. WA 1:498,27–29 (Sermon on the Sixth Commandment, preached, according to Löscher, on St. Thomas Day [Dec. 21,] 1516: see 1:494, n. 1).

215. *Heiltumb*, or *Heilthum*, was the German word at the time for *relic* (see Grimm, *Dt Wb* 4:2,851). Grimm (851) gives the following saying from Johann Agricola's collection of proverbs:

cross of Christ, indeed Christ himself, is brought into the present.[216] Therefore, the cross that falls to our lot is, in the strictest sense, a means of salvation. It may but does not have to come to us as a word (a word of judgment), "because God's doing and speaking are the same."[217] The cross is salvific insofar as it is believed to be salvific, insofar as it is deemed salvific. However, we do not encounter the "relic" as such but only under the form of its opposite.[218]

Thus the Christ event contains the cross, every cross, archetypically, as Luther finds confirmed in Tauler's sermons: "Children, the cross stands for all the crosses that we may be called to suffer."[219] That the Christ event includes all

---

"The cross is evil, but if it is recognized as such and truly taken hold of and kissed, it is a pure relic that leads God-pleasing people to eternal life."

According to *On the Councils and the Church* (1539), the "relic of the holy cross" is the seventh sign by which the true church is recognized (WA 50:641,35–642,32 = LW 41:164–66 ["the possession of the sacred cross"]; cf. *Against Hanswurst* (1541), 51:484 = 41:197, and *The Babylonian Captivity of the Church* (1520), 6:571,35–572,9 = 36:123. The importance of this mark (*nota*) already indicates the *difference between the pre-reformational and the reformational understanding of the cross*. According to the latter, you do not *become* a Christian by means of your own cross, but you can, as a Christian (which you are through the word, see the first five marks in *On the Councils and the Church*: 50:628,29–633,11 = 41:148–54), bear the cross and its suffering. See the following examples.

The *Sermon on Suffering and the Cross* that Luther delivered at Coburg on April 16, 1530, is very instructive in the way in which it shows both its distance and proximity to his earlier theology of the cross (WA 32:28–39 = LW 51:197–208). In addition to the "promise" that makes your suffering and cross bearable, it especially emphasizes the need "to distinguish carefully between the suffering of Christ and the suffering of all others" (32:39,2 = 51:208). "The treasure and comfort that is promised and given to you is so great that you should suffer willingly and joyfully, because Christ and his suffering are given to you and will be made your own" (32:30,21–24 = 51:199; trans. alt.). On this premise, it can then be said, as earlier, that "through the suffering of Christ, the suffering of all his saints is also a pure relic (holy thing), for it is covered by Christ's suffering. Therefore, we should accept all suffering as nothing but a relic, for it is also truly a relic" (32:38,17–20 = 51:208; trans. alt.).

216. Luther can say one moment (in his Hebrews lectures; on 2:9), "To have Christ crucified in us is to live a life full of trials and sufferings" (WA 57/3:122,18–19 = LW 29:130; trans. alt.) and then simply reverse it and say, "Therefore we should welcome with open arms every trial, even death itself, with praise and joy, just as if we were welcoming Christ himself. For truly Christ always comes in the form he assumed when he 'emptied himself' of the form of God" (57/3:122,20–23 = 29:130; trans. alt.).

217. WA 3:152,7–8: see sec. D 1.

218. The term *sub contrario* (under its opposite) is typical of Luther's theology of the cross. On this whole topic, see the "Explanation" of thesis 58 of the *Theses on Indulgences* (WA 1:613,14–614,27 = LW 31:225–27). Luther here speaks about the matter in the greatest detail.

219. From the sermon *On the Exaltation of the Holy Cross* (F. Vetter 233,26). It continues immediately (26–32): "This bitter distress drives us closer to the source of living truth than any feeling. Our Lord God said: 'My God, why have you forsaken me'! and on Mount Olivet: 'Not my will but yours be done.' Children, fear not. Our Lord said: 'If anyone would come after me, let them

believers is a self-evident presupposition of all of Luther's theological thinking that he shares with the tradition. It comes out in the concept of the church with its idea of the "body," which in turn (especially since Augustine) decisively determines the interpretation of Scripture for the church and the individual.[220] No wonder that "the beginnings of Luther's Christology"[221] are shaped by the affective execution of his tropological interpretation of Scripture. Scholars agree on this point but not on what it means for the history of Luther's Christology. Do the christological-soteriological statements of his tropological exegesis lead directly to the conception of the freedom tractate, as is usually assumed? The problem that faces us here and is almost always glossed over[222] can be put even more pointedly: What does the "for me" (*pro me*) of his meditation piety[223] have to do with the "for you" (*pro te*) of his promise theology?[224] It is not simply a matter of assuming *that*, but of demonstrating *whether* both are basically identical. However, no one has yet provided this proof, and no one ever will. For the christological-soteriological statements of the *Dictata*, for example, only enter Luther's later theology in a very piecemeal way and then only after they have been refashioned. Crucially, this happens at the very point where our experience of Christ and his salvation shifts from the "internal sacrament"[225] to the "external word." We will now make this crucial correction clear from a comparison of texts.

According to the preface of the September Testament of 1522, we only hear the gospel in the strict sense "when the voice comes that says, 'Christ is your own, with his life, teaching, works, death, resurrection, and all that he is, has, does, and

---

take up their cross and follow me.' Children, that cross is the crucified Christ. He shall and must be borne" (i.e. his cross is to take shape in us, that is, in our life).

220. We need only think of the scholion on Rom. 3:20,22 (see sec. D 2, esp. n. 104).

221. See E. Vogelsang's book by the same name: *Die Anfänge von Luthers Christologie* (1929). Cf. further G. Ebeling, *Evangelienauslegung*, 281–82, and the literature mentioned there.

222. See, for example, W. Jetter, *Die Taufe beim jungen Luther*, 133.

223. See the intermediate chapter, sec. 1 ("The Sacramental Meditation on Scripture").

224. According to the sharp formulation of E. Bizer, who has repeatedly called attention to the problem. Cf. "Zur Methode der Melanchthonforschung," *EvTh* 24, no. 1 (1964): 1–24, here 8 (cf. 6–10): "Which way leads from the tropological method to the promise connected to the testament?" See, too, the report on the more recent Luther literature (*ThR* 31, 1966) with reference to L. Pinomaa, *Faith Victorious: An Introduction to Luther's Theology*: "The justification of the tropological method also seems to be taken for granted, as if it were self-understood that what is true of Christ is also true of the believer" (327–28; trans. alt.).

225. See sec. C: "The Inner Word: Hidden Grace."

can do," for it is nothing else than "a preaching of the benefits of Christ, gained for us and given to us as our own."[226] That Christ is present with all his gifts in the binding promise, orally and publicly proclaimed, is formulated even more succinctly in the freedom tractate: "The divine pledge and promise . . . says, 'Look here, believe in Christ, in whom I promise you all grace . . . If you believe, you have it; if you do not believe, you do not have it.'"[227] In the orally proclaimed word, faith becomes christomorphic; that is, it takes on the form of Christ. The connection between Christ and us is made by the word, so that we can believe. The certainty of faith depends exclusively on the orally proclaimed word and the Spirit working through it.

The validity of the tropological reference, on the other hand, is not made certain by the proclaimed word but by a disposition of our affects, our existence, which is presupposed when we hear and read the Scriptures. This disposition, which we do not create ourselves but is understood as the work of God, enables us to understand and verify what we have heard and read. "For no one is fit to speak or hear any part of Scripture unless their emotions are in conformity with it, so that they feel inwardly what they hear and speak outwardly, and can say, 'Yes, it is truly so!'" (on Ps. 77).[228] The tropological and ecclesiological reference already assumes what it is meant to establish and does not make clear who or what gives me the right to claim for myself what applies to Christ.[229] The efforts Luther expended in searching for an answer to the question of the certainty of salvation—and that amounts to nothing less than the story of his theology from 1513 to 1519—would make no sense if there were no fundamental distinction between the tropological reference (as in the *Dictata*) and the promise (as understood by the freedom tractate), between the "for me" (*pro me*) of his meditation piety and the "for you" (*pro te*) of his *promissio* theology.[230]

In his interpretation of Paul, Luther only rarely speaks of tropology and allegory,[231] because the literal sense of the text speaks clearly enough. However,

226. WA Db 6:8,18–19,23–24 = LW 35:361 (trans. alt.).

227. §9 (WA 7:24,10–13 [German] trans. alt.; cf. LW 31:348–49 [Latin]). [The words "divine pledge and promise" translate to "*vorheyschung* and *zusage*." The author says *Vorheyschung* (= *Verheißung*) stresses the future dimension of the promise, while *zusage* its present aspect. The latter is characteristic of Luther's reformational theology; trans. note.]

228. WA 3:549,33–35 = LW 11:37 (trans. alt.); cf. sec. C, esp. n. 62. See K. Holl, "Luthers Bedeutung für den Fortschritt der Auslegungskunst," *Aufsätze* 1, 547–49.

229. See n. 224.

230. The relationship and difference between these two types are discussed in chap. 8.

231. For example, WA 56:162,19ff = LW 25:141; 57/1:134,6ff.; 56:175,6ff = 25:155–56.

the theological thinking derived from his tropological interpretation of Scripture continues to play a role in determining the relationship between word and faith[232]—especially in justification[233]—but above all in determining the christological dimension of that relationship.

Keeping this tropological background in mind, let us now try, after having started with the scholia on Romans 5:2–3, to fully understand the Christology of the lectures in relation to our topic, using Luther's interpretation of the Christ hymn of Philippians 2 as a guide. We note that, as already in the *Christmas Sermon* of 1514, he deals with our topic in association with John 1:14. Here, too, we let the Christmas sermon of 1514, especially its tropological conclusion, outline the question that we need to answer.

1. When interpreting the scholion on *Romans 6:17*,[234] the text forced us to take a quick look at the christological side of the concept of the word, where we have the reverse picture of soteriology. There we saw that by taking on the form of a servant, humans share this servant form with the one who as God is righteous, etc. The fact that both take on the form of a servant—that is, that they are both united in cross and suffering—is the basis of their conformity. From this, Christians retrace the path of Christ. His divinity, his righteousness, is related to his humiliation just as our being humiliated is related to our justification. God and humans thus correspond to each other by means of the cross, his cross and our cross.

The pivotal point of this relationship interests us: Where and how does this reversal take place?[235] It is not announced and promised; it can only be "believed"—but not on the basis of a salvific word that brings and does exactly what it says but on the basis of the image of and the meditation on the crucified Christ and his wounds, on the basis of our own cross and suffering (and *thus* on the basis of the "word of the cross"), and thus on the basis of that which contradicts what we believe. There is a gaping difference between how we encounter the word and how salvation actually comes about, and this difference creates uncertainty. What is believed is a "meaning," which certainly does not come to us in audible words. For God gives "under opposites and the sign does not agree with what is signified" (on Ps. 92:5).[236] Salvation can only be revealed in a figurative

232. Especially in the scholion on Rom. 9:28; on that, see sec. K.

233. See pp. 52–53 and WA 56:224,20ff.= LW 25:209 and 57/1:147,15–18 (on Rom. 3:4): on this, see pp. 128–130.

234. See pp. 21–22, 26–28.

235. The reference to the tropological interpretation, which in this case would not mean a correlation running in the same direction but in the reverse direction (it would be too much of a short circuit to immediately see in it the "happy exchange" of the freedom tractate!), does not answer this question but only poses it in a different way.

236. WA 4:82,17–18 = LW 11:231; cf. the whole section 4:82,14–83,22 = 11:230–32. From that especially, we note that "truth is hidden under an alien form to the foolish, but to the wise,

way, in the cross. Thus at the heart of the theology of the cross (*theologia crucis*) there still lurks the Augustinian distinction between *signum* and *res*, between the sign and the thing signified, and it is only when Luther overcomes this split that he finally breaks free from Augustine.

2. In a different sense, Philippians 2 yields a more developed christological background in the scholion on *Romans 1:16.*

At first, however, the train of thought in which 1:16 is interpreted in a characteristic way on the basis of 1 Corinthians 1:27,25 runs in the same direction as in the interpretation of Romans 6:17: "Thus the final conclusion is that those who believe in the gospel must become weak and foolish in the sight of the world in order that they may be strong and wise in the power and wisdom of God,[237] as 1 Corinthians 1[:27,25] tells us."[238] An addition only explains the first part of this statement about "becoming weak":

> Thus all power, wisdom, and righteousness must be hidden, buried and not apparent, altogether in conformity with the image and likeness of Christ, who emptied himself that he might completely hide his power, wisdom, and goodness and instead put on weakness, foolishness, and hardship. In the same way, those who are powerful, wise, and sweet must have these things as if they did not have them.[239]

The christological illustration ("in conformity with the image and likeness of Christ") means that Christ's power is related to his powerlessness as our (supposed) power is to our (necessary) powerlessness. The image of Christ can and should teach us the need for humiliation: his self-abasement is an exemplary event, a great example for us to emulate. But there is no likeness beyond this crucial point of comparison ("*Thus* in the same way"). As Christ emptied himself

---

that is, to the humble and meek, it remains in its own form" (4:83,14–15 = 11:232; trans. alt.). Previously, Luther said: "What is done outwardly appears different from what is done inwardly" (4:81,27 = 11:230; trans. alt.). "For behold, God works glory and salvation in the spirits and the inner self... But still none of these things appears outwardly, but everything appears as its opposite" (4:81,28–30 = 11:230; trans. alt.). "For who would know that those who are visibly humbled are at the same time inwardly most exalted, unless they were taught by the Spirit through faith" (4:82,19–21 = 11:231; trans. alt.). Cf. 4:376,10–19 = 11:512 (on Ps. 119:148): The word is only a sign (*signum*), not the thing itself, not the reality (*res*)!

237. Cf. previously in the same scholion (WA 56,170,9–10 = LW 25:149): "But God completely emptied humans of their power through the cross of Christ that he might give them his power" (trans. alt.).

238. WA 56:171,8–10 = LW 25:149 (trans. alt.).

239. WA 56:171,14–19 = LW 25:151 (trans. alt.). The conceptuality of the last sentence is based on 1 Cor. 7:29–31.

of his legitimate glory, so we are to empty ourselves of our false glory ("Thus *in the same way*").

Luther had preached in the same vein on December 26, 1514: "This Word was made [flesh][240] and God's wisdom hidden and emptied in order to hide and empty this most inferior wisdom of ours as well, which is full of vanity, error, and sin."[241] This text with its "in order that," which goes beyond the "in conformity with (the image)" of the christological statements of the interpretation of Romans 1:16, shows that the correspondence to the exemplary Christ event was intended and brought about by Christ himself. Of course, it is still an open question whether this effect of the Christ event is not the effect of his summons to us to understand that the humiliation that we have not even sought but have experienced is based on the humiliation of Christ.

The fact that with this interpretation of Philippians 2, our humiliation appears as the purpose and fruit of Christ's humiliation cannot, in Luther's sense, be a contradiction to the scholion on Romans 6:17, where the train of thought does not stop with our humiliation but rather flows into our justification, retracing the path of Christ, as we said. For our salvation is actually hidden in our humiliation and is bound up with it in a communication of attributes (*communicatio idiomatum*), just as Christ in his humiliation is also the hidden God.[242]

3. Philippians 2 shows us the exemplary nature not only of Christ's action but also of his suffering in the sense of what God did through him. Through his humiliation God leads him to exaltation, and through contradiction to salvation. In this sense, the following passage from the scholion on *Romans 8:26* is also an interpretation of Philippians 2, although it contains no explicit reference to the wording of the text as in the passages we have discussed so far:

> It is necessary that God's work is hidden and not understood when it happens. But it is hidden in no other way than in a form that is the opposite of our conceptions and ideas . . . For that is how he acts in his proper work, which is the first, the exemplar, of all his works, that is,

---

240. Here *flesh* is probably meant to be inserted.

241. WA 1:34,4–7.

242. Cf. that well-known passage in Luther's interpretation of Rom. 7:18 (e.g., cited by E. Vogelsang, *Anfänge*, 178, n. 1): "This is how the communication of attributes takes place: the same person is spiritual and carnal, righteous and sinner, good and evil, just as the same person of Christ was at the same time dead and alive, at the same time suffered and was blessed, at the same time worked and rested etc, because of the communication of his attributes, although neither of his natures agrees with the property of the other but, on the contrary, they disagree with each other, as is well known" (WA 56:343,18–23 = LW 25:332; trans. alt.).

> in Christ. And when he wanted to glorify him and establish him in his kingdom . . . he made him die, be put to shame, and descend into hell, completely contrary to all our expectations. In the same way he also dealt with St. Augustine in a far deeper way than we can imagine and allowed him, against the prayers of his mother, to go astray so that he might give her more than she asked for. And this is how he deals with all the saints.[243]

Here Christ appears as the first among equals (cf. Rom. 8:29).[244] First of all, God's work is denoted as fundamental ("It is necessary"), then the destiny of Christ not only illustrates this but also reveals it precisely in its fundamentality ("*for* that is how"): In Christ, God did his proper work (*opus proprium*), the archetype of his actions; in him, he lays down, so to speak, the principle of his action. The archetype is explained with an arbitrary[245] example ("In the same way he also dealt with Augustine") and then appears in all sorts of other images ("and this is how he deals with all the saints").

Luther's Christology is not expressed here in words at all but only in images. But what guarantees the image? Who vouches for its correct understanding? How does it become the word?[246] And even if the image does come to us in the word, as of course it does in meditation and in listening to a sermon, the word is still not constitutive but only a vehicle to be left behind.[247]

---

243. WA 56:376,31–377,10 = LW 25:366–67 (trans. alt.). Cf. the scholion on Heb. 2:10 (57/3:124–25 = 29:132–33): "Here it is beautifully shown how we are saved, namely, through Christ as through an archetype and exemplar, to whose image all who are saved are conformed" (WA 57/3:124,10–11 = LW 29:131–32; trans. alt.).

244. Luther glosses FIRSTBORN (Rom. 8:29): "The beginning of the first fruits, the exemplar, the image of all, according to his humanity, because according to his deity he is the only begotten Son who has no brothers" (WA 56:84,1–2. = LW 25:75; trans. alt.).

245. For Luther, to see the life of Augustine as an archetype is purely arbitrary, but seen from the point of view of all saints, it is a model case of the "internal sacrament" of contrition. This is shown by Luther's interpretation of Ps. 77: see sec. C, esp. n. 62.

246. One way of solving this problem is found in the sermon on Ps. 19:12 for St. Thomas Day (Dec. 21) 1516 (WA 1:111–15 = LW 51:17–23). It succeeds in bringing the "twofold work of God" (his "alien work" in the cross and his "proper work" in the resurrection) together with the "twofold office of the gospel" and so soteriologically and anthropologically with "mortification" and "justification." See esp. 1:112,24–113,25 = 51:18–21. But here, too, "Christ" is the image of what happens with us soteriologically (see esp. 1:112,37–113,3 = 51:19–20). On "law and gospel," cf. chap. 3 B 5.

247. See pp. 76–119, esp. pp. 101–102 and chaps. 8 and 9.

4. The same question arises with regard to a passage in the interpretation of *Romans 9:3*, which closely follows Tauler,[248] in places word for word:[249]

> For Christ also suffered damnation and dereliction more than all the saints. And suffering was not easy for him, as some imagine, for he really and truly offered himself for eternal damnation to God the Father for us. And his human nature was no different than that of a human being eternally condemned to hell. However, because of his love for God, God immediately raised him from death and hell and thus devoured hell. All his saints should imitate him in this, some to a lesser degree, others to a greater degree.[250]

This text is of special interest because it more than adequately expresses christologically what is unique to the doctrine of justification in the Romans lectures. The Christ event is itself, archetypically, the justification event. Anyone who, like Christ, suffers the "harshest resignation to hell" and so experiences the "superabundant infusion of grace"[251]—that is, anyone who willingly and gladly takes damnation on themselves—no longer has to fear damnation[252] but is led back out

---

248. F. Vetter 371,13–26: "Listen to how Christ tricked the devil with his art or strategy when he overcame the devil's guile with his most bitter and shameful death, greater than any other person has ever suffered, and thus redeemed us all. And since he was the most forsaken of all, he was the most pleasing to the Father. When he cried 'God, my God, why have you have forsaken me!' he was forsaken more bitterly than any saint. He experienced this forsakenness when he sweated blood on the Mount [of Olives]. And yet at the same time he possessed, according to his highest powers, the very thing he needed: the divinity that he himself was. This is how Christ tricked the devil. This art, which surpassed all other arts, can also be used by his people so that although they are inwardly and outwardly inconsolable, forsaken and separated from all things, they can still experience the same serene composure as our Lord Jesus Christ did when he was forsaken. Thus whoever truly experiences this forsakenness and desolation is the most pleasing of all to the Father."

249. Cf. the phrase "Christ suffered . . . desertion more than all the saints" (WA 56:392,7 = LW 25:382) with "he was forsaken . . . more than any saint" (F. Vetter 371,17–18).

250. WA 56:392,7–13 = LW 56:382; trans. alt.

251. WA 56:391,22–23 = LW 56:381; trans. alt. The "or" in the Latin text in the sense of "or even" makes the "infusion of grace" and "resignation" equal. Luther here adheres to the scholastic principle that the "expulsion of sin" and the "infusion of grace" must take place at the same time. Cf. as Luther's own commentary, the scholion on Rom. 4:25 (56:296,23–24 = 56:284) from the context of the scholion on Rom. 9:3: 56:39/1:33–34 = 25:382 and further Tauler's maxim: "the greater the unbecoming (*entwerdendes*), the greater the becoming (*gewerdendes*)" (F. Vetter 314, 20–21).

252. "For they have no need to fear that they will be damned, for they willingly and lovingly submit to damnation for God's sake. Rather, those who flee from being damned are damned"

of death and hell by God.[253] What Christ suffered, he suffered "for us"—that is, as a model of our justification in which we "imitate" his sufferings. How Luther sees the relation of Christ to us and vice versa is explained even more clearly in the schema of sacrament and example, which we will look at more closely in the first part of the intermediate chapter after the section below.

However, the two following texts do not seem to fit the picture that has emerged so far.

The end of the scholion on *Romans 8:7* speaks about "blessed pride." It teaches about the trust that Jesus modeled for us in the face of his suffering and death:

> No one has conquered this fear (i.e. the last judgment, the final terror) except Christ alone who has overcome death and all temporal evils, as well as eternal death. Therefore, those who believe in him no longer have any reason to be afraid, but in their blessed pride they laugh with derision and rejoice in all these evils, for they will not be destroyed or swallowed up, but will experience, await, and see the victory of Christ wrought over these evils also in themselves. For that reason, they say: "Where, O death, is your victory? Where, O death, is your sting?" Therefore, death and evil are not overcome by power and might, nor are they evaded by flight and dread, but they must be endured in weakness (that is, powerlessness), and of course patiently and willingly, just as Christ teaches us by his own example, going confidently to his death and sufferings.[254]

Jesus's confidence should inspire our confidence. How this can happen and what function the word has in this will be clarified in a broader context in the intermediate chapter that follows.

The most strongly reformational text of the lectures, in which the ideas about externality, certainty, comfort, and the "happy exchange" seem to be clearly expressed,[255] is the second scholion on *Romans 2:15* (AND THEIR CONFLICTING THOUGHTS ACCUSE OR EVEN DEFEND THEM):

(WA 56:392,4–6 = LW 25:382; trans. alt.). The text quoted above follows immediately afterward ("For Christ also suffered").

253. Cf. WA 56:392,11–12. = LW 25:382: "Because of his love for God, God immediately raised him from death and hell."

254. WA 56:366,3–12 = LW 25:356 (trans. alt.).

255. In addition to the following text, see the marginal gloss on Rom. 5:14: "Indeed, Adam's sin is properly a transgression in his person, but in his children it is only the sin and guilt of that

> Where then do we get those thoughts that defend us (against the accusations of the conscience)? Only from Christ and in Christ. For if the heart of believers in Christ reprimands them and accuses them, testifying against them that they have done evil, they will immediately turn away from evil and turn to Christ and say: "But Christ has made satisfaction. He is righteous. He is my defense. He has died for me. He has made his righteousness my righteousness, and my sin his sin. If he has made my sin his sin, then I do not have it, and I am free. If he has made his righteousness my righteousness, then I am already righteous with the same righteousness that is his. My sin cannot devour him but is swallowed up in the depths of his infinite righteousness, for he himself is God who is blessed forever." Thus we can say, "God is greater than our heart." The defender is greater than the accuser, infinitely greater. God is our defender, our heart the accuser. Is this the balance of the relation? Yes, indeed it is! So "who will bring any charge against God's elect?" The answer surely is: No one. Why? "Because it is God who justifies. Who then is to condemn?" No one. Why? Because "it is Christ Jesus (who is also God) who died, yes, who was raised from the dead" etc. "Therefore, if God is for us, who can be against us?"[256]

It is striking that not a single sentence from all this preparatory material appears in the actual lecture that Luther dictated. Was what he wrote down there so unimportant to him? If we look at how he interprets Romans 8:31–39, which is the text he primarily uses to shape his conclusion to the scholion on 2:15, we find that there is only a brief reference to this scholion.[257] The fact is that the interpretation of *Romans 8:38* shows that the question of whether the scholion on Romans 2:15 teaches the certainty of salvation cannot and must *not* be assumed to be resolved.

---

same transgression, just as the righteousness of the saints is not the fulfillment of the law, for this belongs only to Christ, but the imputation and communication of that same fulfillment. Thus it says: "who is in the form of the one to come," etc. (WA 57/1:53,24–8) and the marginal gloss on Rom. 9:33 (whoever believes in him will not be put to shame): "For the righteousness of Christ belongs to those who believe in him and the sin of those who believe belongs to Christ in whom they believe. Therefore, sin cannot stay with the believer, just as it cannot continue in Christ' (WA 56:97,24–26 = LW 25:87; trans. alt.).

256. WA 56:204,8–29 = LW 25:188–89 (trans. alt.); the quotation: ll.14–29. Cf. H. Bornkamm (*ARG* 53 [1962]: 1–60, here 19), who uses especially this text to criticize E. Bizer's account of the Christology of the Romans lectures (*Fides*, 25–27).

257. WA 56:85,16 = LW 25:76.

Hence in his interpretation of Romans 8:38, Luther himself tests, so to speak, what he said in the scholion on Romans 2:15. He sees that Paul's I AM CERTAIN contradicts Ecclesiastes 9:1: HUMANS DO NOT KNOW WHETHER THEY ARE WORTHY OF LOVE OR HATRED[258]—a passage that forms one of the anchor points of the doctrine of conjectural certainty.[259] Luther resolves the contradiction in a quite traditional way[260] when he says: "The apostle is speaking of himself and of all the elect, because he was certain of himself by revelation, that he was a 'chosen instrument' (Acts 9), and we are all certain of the elect. Although it is certain that God's elect are saved, no one is certain that they are among the elect because of the general rule."[261] The scholion on the same text corresponds to this gloss. Surprisingly, for Luther the I AM CERTAIN does not speak, as at 2:15, of Christ's righteousness as the basis of Paul's certainty or of his "blessed pride," as at 8:7, but again only of our saving humility and the comfort of having been annihilated. By recognizing that "their salvation in no way rests on anything in themselves, but solely on what is outside of them, namely, the God who elects,[262] humans are completely throttled and reduced to nothing."[263]

Faith here does not cling to an assertoric or unambiguous word of salvation but identifies its trials and attacks (*tentatio*) paradoxically as the "sign of a loving God"[264] and takes comfort in God's love by virtue of its opposite:

---

258. WA 56:86.19–20 = LW 25:78; trans. alt. (Marginal gloss on Rom. 8:38).

259. Cf., for example, Lyra on Eccl. 9:1 (3:351D.E.): Only in the future "will you clearly see those whom God loves and those whom he hates. And although *humans cannot know about themselves with certainty*, much less about the way of another person, whether they are loved by God or not, *they may nevertheless have some conjecture* as to whether they themselves are conscious of their own mortal sin and whether they are willing to keep God's commandments. It is also possible for us to know with certainty from divine revelation, just as God revealed this same certainty to some of the saints by special grace for their consolation" (author's emphasis). Cf. further the relevant references of J. Ficker to Gerson, Biel, and Staupitz in WA 57/3:216.

260. Cf. Lyra (see n. 259) with the following Luther text.

261. WA 56:86,20–24 = LW 25:78 (trans. alt.). On the other hand, the *Glossa interlinearis* interprets the text in a way that is almost reformational: "I AM CERTAIN because of the promise of God who says: 'I will never leave you or forsake you'" (Heb. 13:5).

We should compare this with Luther's comments on Eccl. 9:1 in the Hebrews lectures (scholion on Heb. 9:24: WA 57/3:216,2–6 = LW 29:217): see chap. 5 C. The striking difference probably points to the decisive turning point in Luther's theology. In the second part of the book, we will have to deal with this in more detail.

262. WA 57/1:199,1–2. (= WA 56:386,26–27 = LW 25:376–77: here in the scholion on Rom. 8:28; trans. alt.).

263. WA 57/1:198,23.

264. Cf. n. 266.

> Therefore, even though these words are not immediately sweet to them, nevertheless, by *antiperistasis*, that is, the collocation of opposites, or, as I would say, theologically, in a hidden way, they are comforting. And yet no words are more effective than these for terrifying, humbling, and destroying pride. But it is impossible that those who are afraid and suffer for the word of God are reprobates or displeasing to God, since it is impossible for God to lie. He says as much in the last chapter of Isaiah: "Upon whom does my Spirit rest but the humble and quiet and those who tremble at my word?" To these Christ also says: "Do not be afraid, little flock, for it is your Father's good pleasure to give you the kingdom." He surely would not have said that unless he had noticed them thinking about the opposite, namely, fear and self-reprobation. And Isaiah 40 [35:4] says: "Take courage, you who are fainthearted: behold your God." And everywhere in the Scriptures, people like this, who tremble at God's word, are consoled and commended. Therefore, those who are overly afraid of not having been elected should rejoice and give thanks that they are afraid, for God's word has done its work in them by creating the fear and terror of God. And *in this way*, they should turn away from their foreknowledge of the terrifying God to the truth of the promising God, and they will be saved.[265]

This text appears in a remarkable twilight. On the one hand, scriptural words are quoted, which according to Luther's later understanding, are promises (that is, gospel in the proper sense). On the other hand, frightened people should not rejoice in them but in their fear ("They should rejoice"), for it is just this fear that offers them the best sign, the pledge of God's grace.[266] This thought, splendidly represented by the concept of *antiperistasis* (= "mutual replacement"[267]),

---

265. WA 57/1:199,6–21 (= WA 56:387,2–26 = LW 25:377–78; trans. alt; author's emphasis). The three degrees of election mentioned in 56:388 probably correspond to the three "levels of faith" that we know from the *Sermon on John 4* (1:87–88; see sec. E 1). If, in the first text, the highest degree of "election" is "resignation," then this points in the same direction as the statement in the second text, that 1 Cor. 13:7 describes "perfect faith" (or "absolute faith"—that is, "faith beyond words").

266. "But those who fear and tremble at these words have the best and most favorable sign" (on Rom. 8:28: WA 56:387,6–7 = LW 25:377; trans. alt.; similarly, ll. 17–18). See 56:423,23–33 = 25:415 (on Rom. 10:14). From the Psalms lectures, see 3:340,13–14 = 10:283: "For God disciplines all whom he loves. Therefore, every trial (*tentatio*) is the sign of a loving God. Therefore, it especially produces hope, Rom. 5[:4]" (on Ps. 60:8).

267. Luther uses a concept here from Aristotle's *Physics*. Aristotle had discussed it in his explanation of movement but rejected it (8:267a; I. Bekker 3:142–43). W. D. Ross (*Aristotle's Physics*

probably taken over from Gerson,[268] is a clear and powerful expression of the theology of the cross: *nothingness is the placeholder for comfort.*

The two sides, which at first glance seem to be contradictory, are inextricably intertwined for Luther. It is the promise of God itself that says that nothingness is the placeholder for salvation: "God, who cannot lie, has said: 'the sacrifice acceptable to God is a broken spirit,' that is, a despairing spirit; 'a contrite and humble heart, God, you will not despise'"[269] (Ps. 51:17). The reality of God's promise[270] is concretely experienced only as suffering.[271] By rejoicing in their suffering, the faithful take God at his word and thus *per antiperistasim* attain salvation: "And so by turning from the foreknowledge of the terrifying God to the truth of the promising God, they will be saved." With THEY WILL BE SAVED, Luther takes up Mark 16:16.[272] Why these words can be interpreted here from Psalm 51:17 and what such an interpretation means for the understanding of the word in the early Luther will only become clear in the second part of this chapter, which presents the relationship between *promissio* and *humilitas*, promise and humility, in a more extensive context.

Before that, however, we will try to examine the subject matter of this section ("Word and Christ") in a larger context in terms of its concrete setting in life (*Sitz im Leben*). This is found in a specific form of the "sacramental meditation on Scripture" and of the understanding of the Mass. This presentation will mark the intersection of the different perspectives from which we have so far viewed Luther's understanding of the word. What follows therefore comes in the middle of the first part of our investigation and forms an "intermediate chapter."

A Revised Text with Introduction and Commentary, 1955) understands it as "mutual replacement." It is likely to have reached Luther as a theological concept via Gerson (see n. 267).

268. Cf. G. Metzger, *Gelebter Glaube*, 143–44, esp. notes 36–37. Metzger tries to set Luther apart from Gerson (144).

269. WA 56:387,22–24 = LW 25:377–78; trans. alt. (preparation of the *Dictata* text cf. n. 265). Cf. Biel, Lect. 17 C (1:142): "We offer . . . Therefore" (Ps. 51:17 follows).

270. Luther introduces a divine speech ("who says"). Accordingly, instead of the words in the quote "to God" we should read "to me," and instead of "you will not despise," we should read "I will not despise."

271. Cf. WA 56:387,24 = LW 25:378: "Moreover, he [David] himself knows what it is to have a 'broken' spirit" (trans. alt.).

272. That Mark 16:16 is specifically meant and not Rom. 10:13 is clear from the use of Mark 16:16 in the *Dictata* (on this, see section I 1 p. 123: "The Fulfillment of the Promise in Judgment").

Sacramental Meditation on Scripture and the Understanding of the Mass

1. The Sacramental Meditation on Scripture[273]

IN HIS INTERPRETATION of Romans 6:3–4, Luther uses the terms *sacramentum* and *exemplum* (*sacrament* and *example*). Here we have a memorable schema, a concise formula, where the two terms themselves remain the same from 1509 to 1543,[274] but their content and function change with the upheaval of the Reformation. This is completely overlooked, for instance, by E. Iserloh.[275] This is another instance of where it is important not to allow a formal continuum to obscure material shifts. Moreover, we can only speak of a formal continuum because Luther does not strictly adhere to the conceptual shift that marks the material break, although he was under no necessity to do so. We will come back to this shift presently.

The *Brief Instruction on What to Look for and Expect in the Gospels* (1522), which opens the Wartburg Postil, replaces *sacramentum* with *donum* (Christ "as a gift and present"):

> The chief article and foundation of the gospel is that before you take Christ as an example, you recognize and receive him as a gift, as a present that God has given you and that is your own. This means that when you see or hear of Christ doing or suffering something that you do not doubt that Christ himself, with his deeds and suffering, belongs to you.

---

273. We select this heading to describe what is to be presented here on the basis of Luther's own formulations in the Christmas sermon of 1519 (WA 9:439–42): WA 9:440,10–11; 442,23–25; 442,31–33. For the Christmas sermon in English, see: "The Gospel as Sacrament: *Luther's Sermon on Christmas Day 1519*" in Phillip Cary, *The Meaning of Protestant Theology*, Appendix 2, 349–54. The counterpart to what follows comes in chap. 8 ("Promise and Meditation"), in the second part of the book, and should be everywhere compared with what is said here.

274. WA TR 5:216 (no. 5526). Cf. n. 284.

275. Iserloh, "Sacramentum et Exemplum—Ein augustinisches Thema lutherischer Theologie," in *Reformata Reformanda* 1, Festgabe für H. Jedin (1965), 247–64 (= "Luthers Stellung in der theologischen Tradition," *Wandlungen des Lutherbildes* [1966], 34–46, and again: "Luther und die Mystik" [1967], 75–83). Cf. n. 284.

> On this you may depend as surely as if you had done it yourself; indeed, as if you were Christ himself . . . whereby the heart and conscience become happy.[276]

Luther says this so that "you do not make Christ into a Moses, as if Christ did nothing more than teach and provide examples as the other saints do, as if the gospel were simply a textbook of teachings or laws."[277]

Christ as a gift creates faith, while Christ as an example models works of love:

> Christ as a gift nourishes your faith and makes you a Christian. But Christ as an example exercises your works of love. However, these do not make you a Christian but proceed from you once you have been made a Christian. As widely as a gift differs from an example, so widely does faith differ from works, for faith has nothing of its own, only the life and works of Christ. Works however have something of your own in them, yet they do not belong to you but to your neighbor.[278]

Seen from this perspective, The Freedom of a Christian, *with its two parts, appears as a reformational recasting of what the early Luther had understood by the two concepts* sacramentum *and* exemplum.

Finally, the *Brief Instruction* clearly shows that *promissio*, understood as the specific way in which Christ gives himself to me, is a constitutive part of the sacrament in the new sense of gift (*donum*). It is "the sermon or gospel through which he comes to you, or you are brought to him[279] . . . So you see that the gospel is really not a book of laws and commandments that requires us to do something, but a book of divine promises in which God pledges, offers, and gives us all his goods and blessings in Christ."[280]

This will be our criterion for the following critical examination of Luther's early texts.

---

276. WA 10/1.1:11,12–18,22 = LW 35:119. Christ as "gift": 10/1.1:11,14; 12,7–8; 12,17; 12,20 = 35:119–21.

277. WA 10/1.1:10,20–11,1 = LW 35:119.

278. WA 10/1.1:12,17–13,2 = LW 35:120 (trans. alt.).

279. WA 10/1.1:13,21–22 = LW 35:121 (trans. alt.).

280. WA 10/1.1:13,3–6 = LW 35:120 (trans. alt.). Cf. the parallel passages from the preface to the September Testament and from the freedom tractate quoted above and documented in nn. 226 and 227.

1.1. Marginal Notes on Augustine's *De trinitate* Book 4 (1509)

Luther tries to briefly summarize Augustine's difficult and quite extensive train of thought in *On the Trinity* 4.3.5–6 as follows:

> The crucifixion of Christ is a sacrament, because it signifies the cross of penitence on which the soul dies to sin, but it is an example because it incites us truly to offer our body to death or the cross.[281]

This statement has grown so directly out of the Augustinian text in terms of its train of thought and conceptuality that it cannot be distinguished from it in any way. So we have every right to first interpret it in the sense of Augustine.

As far as we know, Augustine *only*[282] uses the twin terms *sacramentum* and *exemplum* in *De trinitate* 4 (and so we can *not* speak of an "Augustinian *schema*" in Luther's theology![283]). Luther was so impressed with the way that Augustine clearly defined these terms in relation to each other that he never again forgot them and often referred to them, even expressly stating their source and context.[284] But they occur separately.

---

281. WA 9:18,19–23.

282. The additional text from Augustine (*De consensu evangelistarum* [= *The Harmony of the Gospels*] bk. 1 chaps. 53 and 54: MPL 34:1069–70), noted in WA 39/1:463,8–9 = LW 73:146 n. 80 (Argument 15 of the *Second Antinomian Disputation*), cannot be considered as a parallel to *De trinitate* 4. Both terms do indeed occur in a single section, but they are not related to each other.

283. Against Iserloh: see nn. 275 and 284. Iserloh speaks throughout of an "Augustinian *schema*" or an "Augustinian *theme*."

284. WA 56:321,23–322,9 = LW 25:309–10 (on Rom. 6:3); 57/3:223,10–14 = 29:225 (on Heb. 10:19); 1:309,18–21 (*Asterisci*); 2:501,34–37 (*Galatians Commentary* of 1519 on 2:19); 39/1:463,8–9 = 73:146 (*Second Antinomian Disputation*) and especially theses 51 and 52 of the *Fifth Antinomian Disputation*: "This most splendid thought is not ours, much less theirs, but Augustine's" (39/1:356,37–38 = 73:66). "He says that Christ with his single [death] harmonizes with our double [death] and makes a perfect number" (39/1:357,1–2 = 73:66). That Luther was unaware that he was criticizing what Augustine was saying in his train of thought is evident from the highly instructive late table talk (TR 5:216,26–31 [no. 5526]), which appeals to Augustine against Augustine. We quote it here as the counterposition to his early understanding; its content is in full agreement with the *Brief Instruction* (see above): "Augustine distinguishes the suffering of Christ thus: He says it is a double: a sacrament and an example. In the same way, he calls our suffering a single since we can only suffer the example; but the suffering of Christ he calls a double since it is a sacrament of redemption as well as an example. We must be conformed to the example of Christ, but we cannot be the sacrament of redemption, for we are too insignificant for that."

Sacrament is the technical term of biblical interpretation and virtually interchangeable with *mystery* and *figure*.[285] The serpent raised on the pole in the wilderness, for instance, means, as a *sacramentum* (that is, in its sense or significance), Christ on the cross and together with him at the same time—also as a sacrament—every Christian who dies to their sin.[286] It is therefore the same interpretative bracket that forces the Old Testament and Christ, Christ and us, as well as us and the Old Testament together,[287] even if in the things and events to be compared, only a trace of a common third thing, a certain connecting

---

Iserloh failed to recognize the fact that Luther does not simply draw on Augustine but, in his reformational period, also materially contradicts him. Therefore, the picture he sketches of the function of the two terms in Luther's theology is decidedly wrong, because it is unhistorical. He is "impressed with how Luther held on to the Augustinian theme of *sacramentum-exemplum*" (*Reformata Reformanda* 1,264 = "Luthers Stellung in der theologischen Tradition . . .," 46). But Iserloh can only arrive at this conclusion by dismissing the table talk just quoted, which of course contradicts his thesis, with the remark: "We can only assume that the Protestant copyist, no longer familiar with the theological tradition, has not fully and reliably recorded these rather difficult ideas" (*Reformata Reformanda* 1,264. In *Luther und die Mystik*, this text that proved especially troubling to Iserloh no longer appears). And yet it is just this table talk that brilliantly formulates the real point of Luther's conception, which can easily be demonstrated from all the later material.

285. Cf. G. Ebeling, *Evangelienauslegung*, 120–21, esp. the text cited on p.120, n. 49. However, what Ebeling says (p.121) about the *res* present in the *signum* must surely be corrected with U. Duchrow, *Sprachverständnis und biblisches Hören bei Augustin*, 157 (see there esp. n. 47). As an example of this use of *sacramentum* in Luther, cf. the Genesis scholia 1519–1521: "Lot's wife has warned us by means of a great *sacrament* so that we who have once entered on the way of the Lord may not slip back again to the elementary principles" (WA 9:359,34–35).

286. "Our old self would not have been crucified at the same time, as the same apostle says elsewhere, unless the figure of our sin had hung on that death of the Lord, so that the body might be purged of sin, and that we might serve sin no longer (Rom. 6:6). Also Moses in the desert lifted up the serpent on a tree as a figure of the sin and death of the old self (Num. 21:9). For by the serpent's persuasion humanity fell into the condemnation of death. Therefore, it was only fitting that the serpent was lifted up on a tree as a sign of its own death, for the death of the Lord on a tree hung on that figure. And who would be aghast if it were said, 'Cursed is the serpent that hangs on a tree'? And yet the serpent in prefiguring the death of the Lord's flesh did in fact hang on a tree, and the Lord himself bore witness to this sacrament saying" (John 3:14 follows): Augustine, *Commentary on Galatians* (on 3:13); MPL 35:2120. See on this Luther: WA 57/3:75,9–16 (Gloss on Heb. 12:3).

287. For Luther, cf. here the scholion on Heb. 10:19: "That way or entrance of the priest in former days was old and dead *signifying* this new and living way and entrance of Christ. Thus he fulfilled the figure and removed the shadow. But all this, at the same time the fullness and figure of the truth (for the apostle beautifully unites them both at the same time and discusses them with the same words), further *signifies and is the sacrament* of imitating Christ, that is, his flesh, which he assumed; it signifies the weakness of our flesh, the weakness that we assumed through sin and that causes us to walk in the old and dead way, that is, following the lusts of the flesh" (WA 57/3:222:21–28 = LW 29:224–25; trans. alt.; author's emphasis). It is by no means an accident

resemblance,[288] can be discovered. The term "*sacramentum*" thus initially means nothing other than a "meaning" or "significance":[289] that which a given object reveals, shows, and signifies beyond itself.[290] That *sacramentum* means "significance" follows quite unmistakably from the fact that, both in Augustine and in Luther's marginal note, it is linked with the verb *signify*.

The concept sacrament covers, so to speak, the path from the sign (*signum*) to the thing itself (*res*), connecting both. And *thus* the sign also effects (*facere*) what it signifies (*significare*). *Thus* there is no opposition between "*facere*" and "*significare*," neither in Augustine nor in the early Luther.[291] Because of the similarity of the two events centered in the notion of dying, the crucifixion of Christ as a *signum* is the way to our penitence, the *res*. In this respect, it holds "that the death of Christ brings about the soul's death to sin." This is how Luther put it in a new attempt to rhyme together Christ's destiny and ours according to the ratio 1:2.[292] The sacrament with its inner significance addresses a relationship that

---

that the interpretation that follows runs up to *De Trinitate* 4.3 (57/3:223,10–14 = 29:225). The scholion on Heb. 10:19 is specifically discussed below; see chap. 5, n. 123.

288. Cf. from sec. 9 of Letter 98 (CSEL 34:2,531,3–5 [= MPL 33:363–64]): "If the sacraments did not have a likeness to those things of which they are sacraments, they would not be sacraments at all."

289. We should note the parallelism of "signification" and "sacrament" in the text quoted in n. 286.

290. Cf. *On Christian Doctrine* 2.1.1: "A sign is a thing (i.e. an object before us) that causes us to think of something beyond the impression the thing itself makes upon the senses" (*CCL* 32:32 [= MPL 34:35]); cited from Lombard as IV/d.1/c.3 [Bonaventure 4:8]) and Sermon 272: "They are called sacraments because in them one thing is seen, another is understood" (MPL 38:1247). *From Augustine's definition of the sign, the tag "One thing is seen, another is understood" characterizes not only the institutional sacrament* (to which the last quoted passage refers, as well as the text quoted in n. 288), *but also the understanding of sacrament where it is used in the interpretation of Scripture.*

291. Therefore, E. Iserloh, *Reformata Reformanda*, 250–51, wrongly dismisses E. Bizer's interpretation ("Die Entdeckung des Sakraments durch Luther," *EvTh* 17 [1957]: 64–90, here 66). For more on the interweaving of *significare* and *facere*, see pp. 89–91 but esp. chaps. 8 and 9. This interweaving is constitutive of "archetypal Christology."

292. Following Augustine's sentence: "Therefore, the one death of our Savior was our salvation from two deaths" (MPL 42:892), Luther notes (WA 9:18,25–30):

> "This single can also be compared to the double in another way:
>
> In order that Christ's death may redeem the soul from death, he devoured death by his death.
>
> In order that Christ's death may bring about the soul's death to sin, let us be crucified to the world and the world to us."

M. Elze, who in his essay "Das Verständnis der Passion Jesu im ausgehenden Mittelalter und bei Luther," in *Geist und Geschichte*, Festgabe für H. Rückert (*AKG* 38 [1966]: 127–51), investigates

must have already existed beforehand and thus includes the same presupposition as tropology,[293] of which it is one aspect.

If the *sacramentum* is the inside of the tropology, the *exemplum* is its outside; if the one refers to the inner self, the other refers to the outer self.[294] The fact that the exhortation is seen as a function of the *exemplum* does not exclude the latter from having a significative aspect, just as the significative function of the *sacramentum* can also lie entirely in its effect as an exhortation.

1.2. The First Psalms Lectures

The pair of terms is not explicitly encountered here;[295] however, their material references, which appear in the sense of the marginal note discussed already, often come to the fore. By looking at them, we gain a more concrete picture of what the early Luther meant by *sacramentum* and *exemplum*.

Both are often included in tropology without differentiation:

> Christ's literal shame and blushing teaches us to be ashamed tropologically. For just as he died that we might die morally, so too he was put to shame that we might be put to shame morally. But it is a moral shame when someone is displeased with themselves and does not rely

---

carefully the two marginal notes (148–50), plays the second off against the first—that is, gives the effective aspect priority over the significative: "Christ's death does not 'denote' a corresponding human behavior nor does it give an 'example' of it, but itself exerts an effect on humans and in humans . . . But it is this understanding that reappears in Luther wherever he later remembers the Augustinian terms *sacramentum-exemplum*, and which he then always attributes to them" (150). But already for Augustine, the significative and effective aspects are intertwined (MPL 42:891): "Therefore, our Savior applied his single death to this our double death, and he uses his one resurrection to *effect* both our resurrections, in the sacrament and the example . . . For that expression was given to the sacrament of our inner self to *signify* the death of our soul" (author's emphasis). Luther thinks the same way, as can be seen even more clearly from the following (cf. esp. the understanding of the idea of cause and movement in the *Sermon on the Assumption of the Blessed Virgin Mary*, see pp. 89–91).

293. Cf. pp. 64–66.

294. Cf. WA 9:18,18 and the Augustine text.

295. In two passages (on Ps. 68:4 in WA 3:392,35–393,5 = LW 10:326–27 and on Ps. 69:1 in 3:418,20–29 = 10:354), Luther refers to *De Trinitate* 4.3 on the basis of the Latin Vulgate but without mentioning the keywords *sacramentum* and *exemplum*: "Thus in short, the single going down of the Lord (according to Augustine) harmonizes with our double: and by his one single defeat and ascent, he overcame our double at the same time. For our going down is both in sin and death. But Christ's is only in death and not in sin" (3:392,35–38 = 10:326; trans. alt.; the point Luther makes does not come out in the English Bible). "It should be noted however that Christ always answers to our double with his single, according to blessed Augustine (bk. 4, chap. 3). For he was not in misery spiritually but only literally" (3:418,20–22 = 10:354; trans. alt.).

> on their moral sense and prudence or goodness, like the heretics and the presumptuous.[296]

The story of Jesus ("Christ's literal shame") is doctrine ("it teaches"). So it points to and aims at our story; his death signifies and effects our penitence. But going from his death to our penitence means jumping from one level to another. Luther is well aware of this transposition, this break in the modality of the conformity, and marks it with a *similiter* (similarly): "Judgment was pronounced on us in the cross of Christ, for just as he died and was made an outcast of the people, so we too must bear a similar judgment with him, be crucified and die spiritually, as the apostle explains in Romans 6[:4–5] and 8[:10–11]."[297] Christ's deeds and sufferings only bear fruit if they are reenacted "spiritually" and *in this way* repeated. When Luther later emphatically rejects wanting to become like Christ in the way in which he is uniquely our salvation once and for all—"we cannot be the sacrament of redemption, for we are too insignificant for that"[298]—he becomes critical of his earlier understanding. The *interpretation of Psalm 69* in his first Psalms lectures is the best place to see this.

Here Romans 15:3–4 is primarily understood soteriologically and not, as then in the second part of the freedom tractate,[299] only ethically. That is, *sacramentum* and *exemplum* (in the later sense) are intertwined here without differentiation:

> The apostle's statement in Romans 15[:3] fittingly explains the whole psalm, as it were, tropologically. He argues from the letter to the tropology thus: "Christ did not please himself, but [as it is written:] 'the reproaches of those who reproached you fell on me.'" So too, we should not please ourselves but rather displease ourselves. And the reproaches that we and others have uttered against God should fall on us and thus humble us so that we bear the infirmities of the weak as if

296. WA 3:445,35–446,1 = LW 10:390 (on Ps. 70:3) (trans. alt.).

297. WA 3:463,17–20 = LW 10:405 (on Ps. 72:2) (trans. alt.).

298. WA TR 5:216,26–31 (no. 5526); cf. n. 284.

299. §§26–30 (WA 7:34–38 [German]) or WA 7:64,13–73,12 = LW 31:364–77 [Latin]. Interestingly, here Rom. 15 is not specifically taken up but rather Phil. 2. Luther noted the context of the two passages already in the Romans lectures: 56:519,10–14,25–6 = 25:515 (Scholion on 15:3; cf. the gloss: 56:136,12–13 = 25:119) and 56:114,18–20 = 25:509 (Scholion on 15:1). Also, for the understanding of these passages, we cannot yet assume the distinction between faith and love, and again between soteriology and ethics, which is fundamental in 1520.

> they were our own. Just as Christ bore them physically, we should bear them morally or affectually. And to prove that this conclusion from the letter to the tropology is valid, he writes: "Whatever was written [in former days] was written for our instruction (that is, tropologically)."[300]

This text presents us with *the christological side of that internal sacrament of contrition as described above from Psalm 77.*[301] The Christ event is understood tropologically—that is, seen in such a way that we do and suffer the same as Christ—but now "through our affects and meditation."[302] This meditation is therefore highly effective[303] because it makes us ready for and receptive to God's mercy: "Therefore, since we do not have real sufferings and afflictions in our time, it is extremely necessary that we at least bring these emotional ones (*affectuales*) upon us, so that we might be the kind of people on whom God would have mercy and whom he would save. So let us be our own tyrants, tormentors, heretics, and rouse these feelings within us."[304]

It is not the promise of grace but the affective and effective dying of sin, understood as the sign of grace,[305] that is the pivotal point of our relationship with God. Luther is still operating here entirely with the *affectus-effectus* schema,

300. WA 3:440,25–33 = LW 10:383–84.

301. See pp. 29–35.

302. In a parallel train of thought to the text quoted above, it says: "'Christ did not please himself' [Rom. 15:3], wishing that we too would do the same tropologically, namely, assume the sins of all through our affects and meditation" (WA 3:432,18–20 = LW 10:372; trans. alt.). Reflection on the tropology then follows again: "Now that we should accept this authority tropologically, listen to these great words, 'Whatever was written was written for our instruction' [Rom. 15:4], that is, moral teaching. Therefore, even the things said here literally of Christ are for our moral instruction" (3:432,22–25 = 10:372–73; trans. alt.). Cf. the marginal gloss on Ps. 60:1 (FOR OUR INSTRUCTION)—that is, moral instruction. "For the moral sense is called teaching (*doctrina*) in Scripture. Rom. 15: 'Whatever was written was written for our teaching (*doctrinam*).' And therefore, the tropological is the ultimate and principally intended sense of Scripture; hence 'I am teaching you useful things' (i.e. Isa. 48:17)" (3:335,19–22).

303. Cf. WA 3:431,30–33 = LW 10:371: "Hezekiah had a most devout and efficacious meditation of this kind when he said [Isa. 38:10]: 'I said, in the midst of my days I shall go to the gates of hell,' although he never actually entered them."

304. WA 3:432,26–30 = LW 10:373; trans. alt. (Luther gives special emphasis to this whole text).

305. WA 3:433,2–4; quoted in main text at n. 308). Cf. n. 266.

which is characteristic of late medieval passion piety.[306] Admittedly, for Luther the imitation of Christ is not about a superficial compassion—that is, one that does not touch the ground of our own existence— nor about the external imitation of Jesus's deeds but about becoming inwardly conformed to the archetypical Christ event. This means a fundamental change to our existence. However, this particular form of the *imitatio* piety is not characteristic of Luther's reformational theology, but agrees in substance with the tradition enshrined in the following verses attributed to Tauler:

Whoever wants to embrace
this child with kisses of joy,
must first suffer with him
great pain and much torture.

Then they must also die with him
and rise spiritually,
to obtain eternal life,
just as he did.[307]

It is precisely this spiritual dromenon sung here that Luther describes in his interpretation of Psalm 69:

> Therefore, if you are looking for a sign of God's grace and whether Christ himself is in you, behold, no sign will be given you except the sign of the prophet Jonah. If therefore you have been in hell for three

306. M. Elze (*Das Verständnis der Passion Jesu im ausgehenden Mittelalter und bei Luther* part 1, 127–34) has presented this schema. Cf. further Altenstaig, s.v. "sacrificium": "Either it happens by an inner act in the spirit, or by an outer act: through our *affects* . . . and *effects*" (*Vocabularius Theologiae*, 1517, Fol. 234^v; author's emphasis). Luther himself can use the twin terms *affectus-exemplum* instead of *sacramentum-exemplum*: "To bear the image of Christ is to live according to the affects and example of Christ" (Heb., scholion on 9:23; WA 57/3:214,21 = LW 29:216).

307. The text of these two German strophes is only available in a collection of songs from the beginning of the seventeenth century (E. Becker, "Untersuchungen zu dem Tauler zugeschriebenen Lied: *Es kumpt ein Schiff geladen*" [*A Ship Is Coming Laden*] in *Johannes Tauler—Ein deutscher Mystiker*, Gedenkschrift zum 600. Todestag, ed. E. Filthaut, 77–92, here 79. The question of whether there is a literary connection with Tauler can be left open. But the factual similarity is obvious. Cf. the words from Luther's well-known sermon on 2 Cor. 3:6 (see sec. D 1): "If ever you wish to come to the new, you must first suffer the old, be afraid and fear [God] in your humility" (F. Vetter, 395,26–27); see further, Vetter, 70,15–34; 71,7–8; 163,9–12; 230,24–30; 229,5–27.

> days, it is a sign that Christ is with you and that you are with Christ.[308] This selfsame Jonah said (Jonah 2:3): "I cried out to you from the belly of hell." And so all the saints first die with the Lord and descend with him into hell with their emotions so that at length they rise and ascend with him into heaven and send the Spirit's gifts to others. But I say all this tropologically. For they die, as far as the desire and purpose to commit sin are concerned. Similarly, they descend into hell as far as the attitude toward its punishments is concerned. And so all the prayers of the psalms, which are uttered in the person of Christ who is in hell, are also uttered in the person of the saints who are descending into hell with their hearts and feelings.[309]

> In short: "Whoever does not die with Christ and descend into hell, will also never rise with him and ascend."[310]

The Christ event is repeated in a tropological refraction by an existential dromenon.[311] The individual experiences Christ's descent into hell and his ascent

---

308. WA 3:433,2–4 = LW 10:373.

309. WA 3:431,39–432,7 = LW 10:372 (trans. alt.).

310. WA 3:432,8–9 = LW 10:372 (trans. alt.). Cf. from the meditations of Pseudo-Anselm, which were well known to Luther (see WA 9:106): "Conform also your servant to your life-giving death, working in me that I may die to sin according to the flesh, but live to righteousness according to the spirit" (MPL 158:759).

311. Here and in the following, we refer to WA 3:433,24–434,1 = LW 10:374 (trans. alt.): "Therefore, draw the conclusion. If you are not affected in this way, if you are not already condemned and burning in hell, or already dying, you cannot worthily say such prayers, nor can you presume that you are perfect. For the more clearly and intensely you can assume this feeling, the more you will progress, and conversely the colder you are, the more you will fail. Therefore, you have here the best reason for being humbled, for when you are not in hell or death, you can confidently fear God's wrath and not yet expect his mercy, for you are not yet fit and worthy for him to have mercy on you. *Thus, we are told in the* Lives of the Fathers *that no one can finish a single day unless they regard it as their last.* So, let us add: No one will fill up even a single hour or moment worthily unless they regard it affectively as their last. For then they will be humbled and afraid. And in this way God will give them his grace, and his Spirit will rest upon them ... But this must be done not only with the feeling of fear but also with the feeling of hope and love, so that just as no one can pray the prayers of affliction worthily unless, as I said above, they enter into death and hell, so, conversely, no one can rejoice and sing praises worthily unless they ascend into heaven with the feeling of hope and, as intensely as possible, actually consider themselves already in the midst of the angels and saints." Cf. "Through meditation, they descend in one and the same person of Christ from God to humanity, and ascend from humanity to God,

into heaven in their own person as a dialectic of fear and hope. In this dialectic, the whole history of salvation is condensed each time anew into a single point, the eternal now. For not only is the death of Jesus perceived in penitence and humiliation, but at the same time, according to an old monastic tradition,[312] the last judgment is also said to occur at every moment.[313] That is the extent to which the imitation piety of the early Luther adheres to the traditional principle drawn from Romans 15:4: "Every action of Christ is for our instruction." The exact words of course only occur in the Romans lectures.[314]

---

just as the angels ascend on Jacob's ladder in Genesis 28[:12]": 3,181,36–182,1 = 10:153 in the context of 3:181,28–182,6 = 10:153 (Interpretation of Ps. 33:2: PRAISE THE LORD WITH THE HARP) and further 3:319,28–320,13 = 10:265–66 (on Ps. 57:8), as well as 3:611,29–32; 614,1–615,25 = 11:102–5 (on Ps. 81:1). On 3:181,36–182,1 = 10:153, cf. the *Glossa ordinaria* on Ps. 50:23 (3.157A): "And this is the way to God: Jacob's ladder, on which the angels, that is, the faithful, ascend to the praise of God, and descend to the praise of humanity."

312. Luther himself refers to the *Lives of the Fathers* in line 31 (italicized in n. 311). Cf. from the *Life of St. Pachomius*: "Above all, let us keep in mind the last day, and fear the suffering of eternal pain every moment" (*Vitae Patrum* 1; MPL 73:265). Cf. p. 32, esp. n. 60.

313. Cf. WA 3: 433,31–35 = WA 10:374; see pp. 30–34.

314. On the significance of Rom. 15:3–4 for the Psalms lectures, see pp. 81–83. In the Romans lectures, the marginal gloss on 15:4 reads as follows: "[Paul] is contending against the hidden objection of his readers, namely, 'What is that to us? This is speaking about Christ, not us.' Paul answers that what is said about Christ is also 'written for our instruction' that we might imitate him. And so we must understand what is said about Christ not only speculatively but also as an example for us. When understood in this way, we derive a remarkable insight from this passage, that *every action of Christ is for our instruction*" (WA 56:137,17–22 = LW 25:119–20; trans. alt.; author's emphasis). Luther adds to this axiom in his dictation: "Therefore, a narrative or story about him is always teaching for us, because he is the image of all things" (57/1:116,26–27). Luther glossed between the lines: "FOR WHATEVER THINGS WERE WRITTEN about Christ and anyone else WERE WRITTEN FOR OUR INSTRUCTION by understanding the moral instruction as an example" (56:137,1–4 = 25:119–20; trans. alt.) or (57/1:116,9–10) "FOR OUR INSTRUCTION moral instruction for the imitation of Christ." When Luther says, "Every action of Christ is for our instruction," he is not freely following Gregory (in Ezek. 2:2,6: MPL 76:952 [!]—thus J. Ficker 57/1:116 on 2:26–27; see, however, the *Heidelberg Disputation*: 1:364,35–36 = 31:57, where Luther mistakenly attributes it to Gregory) but is literally following Lyra, according to whom (on Rom. 15:4; 6:30F): "The things in sacred scripture are chiefly about Christ, whose action is for our benefit." Likewise, Dionysius the Carthusian comments on Rom. 15:4 (Fol. 33D): "Christ's action is for our instruction"; see also Ludolph of Saxony in the Prologue to his *Vita Christi*: "Therefore, his entire life on earth . . . was a teaching about morals (*disciplina morum*) . . . he became human to teach humans how to live . . . for every action of Christ is for our instruction" (Augsburg 1729); 4:1. We must at least mention here that Lyra interestingly enough lifts out of Rom. 15:4 a "fourfold pattern for interpreting Scripture that comes to us from Scripture" (6:30F); this, in a certain way, anticipates the schema that A.

1.3. Two Sermons from the Time of the First Psalms Lectures

The actions and sufferings of Jesus, his vitality, have a formative effect on those who open themselves to it in meditation "with their affects and understanding"[315] (that is, with their whole existence). Luther describes exactly how this happens in the sermon he preached presumably no later than 1515, which is printed in WA 1:340–45 as *Sermo II. De Passione* (*Sermon 2 on the Passion*), as well as in the sermon *De assumptione BMV* (*Sermon on the Assumption of the Blessed Virgin Mary*; WA 4:645–50), for which a dating to the time of the first Psalms lectures also seems possible.[316]

To explore more deeply the understanding of the word as expressed in the *sacramentum-exemplum* schema, we turn to *Sermon 2 on the Passion* (on Ps. 45:2a), particularly the following passage:[317]

> Behold, God has completed all these things in one abbreviated word so that it may truly be a word that abbreviates and completes for us, because all these things are not painted or written here with dead letters and figures as in books, but with the smallest works and real signs. For so many letters here indicate the individual virtues that the Lord suffers: blows, [cruel] words, and drops [of blood]. For in each of them, his humility, gentleness, love, and patience are revealed to you as a sign or

---

Hyperius (see A. Weissgerber, *RGG*, 3rd ed., 3:502–3) then drew up for preaching, a schema that was also based on Rom. 15:4 (and 2 Tim. 3:16).

315. On this pair of terms, see G. Metzger, *Gelebter Glaube*, 69–80.

316. WA 4:645 dates it to 1517; E. Vogelsang ("Zur Datierung der frühesten Lutherpredigten," *ZKG* 50 (1931): 112–45, here 132 = *BoA* 5:428, note on I.16), without explanation, dates it to 1520. On the other hand, M. Elze (*Das Verständnis der Passion Jesu*, 145, n. 87) rightly moves the sermon closer to *Sermon 2 on the Passion*, which in turn must have originated anyway before 1518 (with Elze, *Das Verständnis der Passion Jesu*, 140) and is possibly even the "allegorical or tropological interpretation" of Ps. 45:2 that is referred to in the sermon on this text for St. Barbara's Day (1514?; see n. 340): WA 4:644,30–31. The sermon *On the Assumption of the Blessed Virgin Mary*, on the one hand, touches on the Romans lectures (Scholion on Rom. 5:2), the marginal note on Tauler (1516) quoted in n. 202, the interpretation of the Lord's Prayer of 1517 (9:150,15–27), and even on the *Heidelberg Disputation* (see n. 319), but on the other hand, it also touches on the first Psalms lectures. Cf., for instance, 3:566,28–36 (on Ps. 78). Since the marginal gloss on Ps. 119:2 most likely picks up the sermon rather than prepares for it (see n. 328), we can probably date it to August 15, 1514.

317. WA 1:341,14–30 (cf. 4:646,28–32: cited in n. 333). On this sermon as a whole, see the careful analysis by Elze (*Das Verständnis der Passion Jesu*, 136–40); the passage we have in mind above is not discussed there.

> letter or entire word. Thus distinguish each one individually and learn really to read in it what it signifies that he sweats blood (to say nothing for now about understanding his teachings and prophecies). Surely it signifies his supreme love for you, his supreme humility, patience, mercy, righteousness, peace, and salvation for your sake. What does it signify that he is struck by a blow? Surely his supreme love, patience, and humility. What does the blood on the whips, thorns, and nails signify? Surely his supreme love. And so we could go on through each of the other virtues. But what does it signify for your understanding, if not that you also may suffer similar things in flesh and spirit, as it is appointed? Therefore, as I said, let us open our spiritual eyes and choose this beautiful form of all the virtues in Christ: for they are all depicted and presented in sufficiently clear, living, distinct letters and signs, and are known to us.

The incarnate Word that Luther sees in Romans 9:28 ("the word that abbreviates and completes"),[318] following the tradition, is not captured in the dead letters and images of books but appears alive and vivid before our eyes as the man Jesus, as a "word" that can really be read[319]—that is, as a clearly distinct vitality, one that we can empathize with, whose moving expression we can reproduce in spirit and flesh, according to the inner and outer self, and whose significance we can understand ("What does it signify for the understanding, if not that you too may suffer similar things in flesh and spirit, as it is appointed?"). The complex form of the "Word," as a beautiful form of all the virtues, appears fragmented ("distinguish each one"!) into small independent units of action and suffering, monads of Jesus's vitality, so to speak, which the viewer, following the traditional technique of meditation,[320] contemplates one by one and so perceives them as "individual virtues."

---

318. See chap. 1 C, esp. n. 83.

319. Cf. what Luther writes to Staupitz on May 30, 1518, in his letter of dedication accompanying the *Explanations* (*Resolutionen*): "The commandments of God become sweet when they are read not only in books but also in the wounds of the sweetest Savior" (WA 1:525,21–23 = LW 48:66) and what he had formulated just before in the proof of thesis 27 of the *Heidelberg Disputation*: 1:364,30–38, esp. 31–33,35–36 = 31:56–57: "The works that Christ does are the fulfillment of God's commandments given to us through faith. When we consider them, we are moved to imitate them . . . As St. Gregory says: 'Every action of Christ is for our instruction, indeed, a stimulus to get us moving'" (trans. alt.).

320. In the following (WA 1:341,35–36), Luther himself refers to the pertinent literature: "Notice this fruit can be found elsewhere, in the rose garden and other places." On the reference

The *Christmas sermon of 1519*, even though still cast in the schema of *sacramentum-exemplum*, now formulates without delay "the distinction between the gospel and human stories," employing a fundamental determination.[321] So when it says that "the histories of Livy depict certain images or likenesses of the virtues, which they cannot produce in other people, but the gospel truly depicts images of the virtues so that at the same time it is an instrument by which God changes and renews us,"[322] we have to see this as the fruit of many years of effort to solve the problem. For what we observed in the early passion sermon is meant to be nothing more than a precise answer to the question of the *proprium* or uniqueness of the gospel, which sets it apart from human histories or stories."[323, 324]

The *Sermon on the Assumption of the Blessed Virgin Mary* shows that Luther had already asked himself this question in his early days, not only indirectly but also explicitly. But while it addresses the same problems as the *Christmas sermon of 1519*, here the gospel, understood as the *story* of Christ, is not set apart from human histories but understood as the *word* of Christ, is contrasted with secular speech. And so in its function, the gospel is not specifically contrasted with historical writing but with rhetoric in general:

> The rhetoricians of the age hold that it is the duty of a good orator to instruct, to delight, and to persuade, which no one has ever done except in a carnal way. But Christ alone instructs, delights, and moves those who pay attention to him, to what he says through his most holy life. Others, if they are moved by a human mouth, are moved only for a time, and not by gratuitous love but selfish affection. But here they are moved solely by the affection of Christ, effectually and eternally.[325]

---

to Mombaer's *Rose Garden of Spiritual Exercises*, see M. Elze (*Das Verständnis der Passion Jesu*, 136, and esp. the passages mentioned there in n. 34).

321. WA 9:439,19–21.

322. WA 9:440,13–16.

323. WA 9:442,27.

324. The difference between this sermon and the earlier comparable statements will have to be determined in the second half of this book (see chap. 8, pp. 323–327). Here we only need to call attention to the problem's historical context from the vantage point of the earlier texts.

325. WA 4:646,32–38.

The three duties of the orator (or of the oration), instructing, delighting, and persuading (= moving[326]),[327] which Luther would have been familiar with from his studies in the arts faculty, also characterize Jesus's speech throughout "his most holy life."[328] But oratory is effective only "for a time," Jesus's speech "for eternity"; the former is effective on the basis of the listener's own affects, the latter on the basis of donated love. But is this distinction justifiable, theologically? Is Luther here really describing anything more than the historical impact of the man Jesus? Does his life move us—even if it is understood analogously to the Aristotelian predication of God as the "first mover" (*primum mobile*) and to Christ the orator as the one who can move others (*ens mobile*)[329]—in a fundamentally different way than a secular oration, which moves people by presenting them with real facts?[330, 331] How does our fusion[332] with the manifold vitality (his actions and sufferings) that springs inexhaustibly from Jesus's vivid life,[333]

326. See Luther's own view by comparing l.33 with l.34 and with ll.36–37.

327. Quintilian 12,10,59: see H. Lausberg, *Handbuch der literarischen Rhetorik* (1960), §257; on the concept of "duty" (*officium*), cf. §1078 and §61. Luther expressly attests to his knowledge of Quintilian: WA Br 1:562–63; ll.9–12.

328. Luther mentions the same requirements of rhetoric in the marginal gloss on Ps. 119:28 (STRENGTHEN ME BY YOUR WORD) that come from the time of the lectures, probably around the turn of 1514/1515. Here in the glossed part of the verse, they are initially applied to only the *words* of Christ: "For the words of Christ have power not only to instruct but also to rouse [to move]" (WA 4:284,32–33), but then they are also used in the comprehensive sense of our sermon: "(Christ) not only instructs but also influences people. There are three things that a good speaker does: teaches, delights, and persuades" (WA 4:284,36–39). If we may assume that this text presupposes rather than prepares for our sermon (since the characterizations of rhetoric appear less necessary in the text than in the sermon), then it provides us with the *terminus ad quem* for its dating (cf. n. 316).

329. Christ is a "mobile being. Indeed, just as in the world the first mover is moved most of all in itself, and is the cause of movement in all others, so Christ, who according to his humanity is always restless and working even to the point of death, also causes all his own to be moved by a similar movement" (WA 4:645,17–20).

330. S. H. Lausberg, *Handbuch*, §257, 3a.

331. "It is impossible for the soul not to receive the flame of a noble desire as it gazes fixedly at the wounds of Christ. And again: 'My soul in the clefts of the rock, in the crevices of the cliff,' that is, in the stripes and wounds of Christ. There it has its life, and from there the impulse of the good life, the light of true reason, and the ardor of holy desire flow into it" (WA 4:646,10–14). Cf. WA 3:645,24–33 = LW 11:140–41 (on Ps. 84:3) and on this, see pp. 107–111.

332. "They must be conformed to the image of God's Son and suffer with him, endure with him, and work together with him" (WA 4:645,21–22).

333. "Christ, according to his humanity, is . . . the fount, head, cause, and origin of the laborious life. (The theme of the sermon is the assignment of the active life [*vita activa* = laborious

which psychologically could be described quite plausibly as imitation,[334] lead to the peace of God, the certainty of God, that Luther is aiming at with the end (the short second part) of his sermon?[335]

Already in the first part, he speaks of the "great miracle, that the soul has rest in its restlessness, peace in its work, and sweetness in its suffering, because it delights to be moved, to labor, and to suffer."[336] In doing so, however, Luther does not refer to Christ according to his divinity but sticks entirely to his lively humanity. Nor does he show that, and how, his divinity appears in it.[337] The peace comes about by means of an interaction between the living image of Jesus and the soul:

> There is rest and peace because the soul has its eyes fixed on Christ and delights in the love that it sees shown to it. And so it is that Christ's work is its peace and joy. But there is work for the soul, because it is armed and moved by the same thought (an allusion to 1 Pet. 4:1!), that it also needs to work and suffer. And so it is that the soul's own work and suffering become its peace and joy in Christ, who rests for himself and is well-pleased with its conformity to him. Thus Christ and the

life] and the contemplative life [*vita contemplativa* = the quiet life], embodied by Martha and Mary respectively, to a human being [WA 4:649,11–12] where the former corresponds to Christ according to his humanity [4:645,11–650,3] and the latter to Christ according to his divinity [4:650,5–15]) . . . Behold, there is nothing to be seen in the humanity of Christ except restlessness, toils, sufferings, exhaustion, prayers, watches, fasting, reproaches, preaching, mocking, right up until his end" (4:645,12–13, 14–17). Cf. 4:646,38–647,1. The actions and suffering of Jesus mentioned here individually are "the living scriptures, the living law, the living doctrine, indeed, the very life of Christ itself. For this is common to all. There is no need for Greek, Latin, or Hebrew. For any uneducated person can read here what to do and what not to do, what to endure and what not to endure, and they can read it in such a way that they are moved to imitate it and become like Christ whom they read about and see" (4:646,28–32. Cf. pp 87–89).

334. "But that mode of moving us is not forced but voluntary, so that when the soul looks at Christ's works, labors, sufferings etc., it is immediately stirred to do and suffer similar things itself, and all this with a willing spirit, for no other reason than because it is moved by a sweet affection for Christ, and wants to do good and suffer ill because of his love. Since the soul sees its Lord doing such things out of love for it, because it sees Christ praying for its salvation, it immediately feels a flame and is moved by his prayer and says to itself: This is what you should be praying for too, and also for others in a similar way" (WA 4:645,22–29). The obvious question that Luther asks and tries to answer is this: "What if I do not always find in Christ a likeness of what lies before me?": 4:647,11–18.

335. WA 4:650,5–15.

336. WA 4:646,15–17.

337. Cf., on the other hand, the *Sermon on John 11* from Lent 1518: WA 1:273–77, esp. 274,28–275,37.

> holy soul interact when Christ calms it with his love, moves it with his works, and moves in it with his holy affection.[338]

But if it is Christ's humanity that gives certainty, then the second part of the sermon makes no sense because, according to it, the certainty comes from his divinity.[339] In any case, the answer Luther gives here to the problem of the two natures doctrine is unsatisfactory. Obviously, with the claim that the man Jesus has an immediate effect on the soul, the christological and trinitarian formulas, to which Luther certainly adheres,[340] lose their function and are no longer necessary. In this sense, historians who align themselves with Luther's reformational theology can only agree with Stephan Roth, who probably under the influence of Luther's later statements, said about this sermon: "If you apply reason and sound judgment in reading it, it is incorrect."[341]

1.4. The Romans Lectures

a) Already for the marginal notes to Augustine's *De trinitate* 4, *significare* (to signify) included *facere* (to make); likewise, the *Sermon on the Assumption of the Blessed Virgin Mary* described the significance of Christ as the cause of every movement of our existence shaped like Christ's action and suffering. The effective aspect is now especially emphasized in the Romans lectures *on 4:25*, in a text containing a tradition already known to Luther[342] that clearly articulates the sacrament (= mystery) of the death and resurrection of Christ.

> The death of Christ is the death of sin and his resurrection the life of righteousness, because by his death he has made satisfaction for sin, and by his resurrection has brought us righteousness. And so his

338. WA 4:646,17–24.

339. "Just as the cross comes from Christ's humanity, so too peace comes from his divinity" (WA 4: 650,13–14).

340. Cf. the *Sermon on St. Barbara Day 1514* (or earlier). According to the Augustinian speculation on the Trinity taken up here (see esp. WA 4:643–44), it cannot be dated later than the first Psalms lectures: WA 4:644,5ff.

341. WA 4:645, note on line l. Cf. 4:589.

342. Luther had read a longer quote in Biel's commentary on the Mass (Lect. 39 I, 2:92–93) from Innocent III, *De celebratione Missae* [*On the Celebration of the Mass*], from which we see that Christ's death and resurrection were understood as a sacrament (= mystery) in light of Rom. 4:25 and as an example in light of 1 Pet. 2:21. The quote is also included in the corpus of canon law *Corpus Juris Canonici* (Richter-Friedberg 2, 638; documented in Oberman/Courtenay 2, 92, n. 4) and so was in the general theological consciousness.

> death not only signifies but also causes the forgiveness of sin as a most sufficient satisfaction. And his resurrection is not only the sacrament of our righteousness but also effects it in us, if we believe it, and is its cause. We will speak in greater detail about these matters later (i.e. in the interpretation of Romans 6:3–4).[343] The scholastic theologians call this whole thing one exchange: the expulsion of sin and the infusion of grace.[344]

This text again makes it clear that "sacrament" means the same thing as "significance." But Luther stresses here more emphatically than before that this signifying is an action.[345] The reason for this was perhaps the *Glossa ordinaria*, which in Romans 4:25 also emphasizes both the significative and effective aspects of the Christ event in relation to us.[346] In any case, it is striking how vigorously Luther distances himself from a one-sided significative understanding of the Christ event. Here we can see concretely the progress that he later speaks of in a table talk: "When I was a monk, I was a master of allegories. I used to allegorize everything. But after I went through the Epistle to the Romans, I came to some knowledge of Christ. There I saw that allegories were not what Christ signified but what Christ was."[347] But Luther seems to have indicated the main point of his scholion in its final sentence. The fact that the "infusion of grace" and the "expulsion of sin" coincide and happen simultaneously means in the context of

---

343. That this reference is correct is proven by the explicit statement "as below in chap. 6" in the marginal gloss on Rom. 5:10, which in turn is clearly a parallel text to the scholion on 4:25 (see n. 345).

344. WA 56:296,17–24 = LW 25:284 (trans. alt.).

345. Cf. also the identical marginal gloss on Rom. 5:10 (WA 56:51,20–24 = LW 25:45): "The resurrection and life of Christ is not only a sacrament, but also the cause, that is, the efficacious sacrament of our spiritual resurrection and life, for it causes those who believe in him to rise again and live, as we read below (Rom. 10:9), 'If you confess that Jesus is Lord and believe in your heart that God raised him from the dead, you will be saved,' for in his death we die spiritually, as we read below in 6:3–11" (trans. alt.).

346. "The death of Christ marks the destruction of the old life, and his resurrection is the mark of the new life. This new life begins with justification and is completed in immortality. Christ's death and resurrection are the same by virtue of what they produce in us: because they have freed us from our sins and from the yoke of the devil. But they are different by virtue of what they signify: because his death marks the fact that we die to the old life, his resurrection that we walk in newness of life, and so finally into the newness of immortality. So just as Christ is risen already, we will rise again" (6.12A). Luther's scholion on Rom. 4:25 is not in opposition to the *Glossa ordinaria*, as J. Ficker notes in WA 56:296 on l.19.

347. WA TR 1:136,14–17 (no. 335; summer 1532; *VD.*): O. Scheel, 98 (Document no. 251). We should note of course the "some."

the lectures[348] that we only perceive the significance and power of Christ's death and resurrection through penitence. But there is no mention of the fact that what Christ's death and resurrection are and mean is given to us in the word—and only in the word.

b) The glosses and scholia on Romans 6:3–4 take us no further. At the beginning of the scholion on 6:3, the text from *De trinitate* 4, which Luther had summarized in schematic fashion in those marginal notes, is widely quoted. In the sense of Augustine,[349] it is said that "in this passage the apostle is speaking of the death and resurrection of Christ with reference to the sacrament, but not with reference to the example,"[350] thus in relation to our inner self. Christ died and rose "bodily for himself" and "sacramentally for us,"[351]—that is, to effectively signify this to us,[352] to conform us to his destiny[353] (from here "sacrament" is defined as the logos or medium of an analogous event; it is the abstract third thing that brackets history with existence, his history or the account of it with our existence!): "To the spiritual self, everything should appear in the opinion

348. See the passages mentioned in n. 35 and n. 251.

349. WA 56:321,28–322,1.

350. WA 56:322,7–9 = LW 25:310. Cf. 56:323,7–9 = 25:310.

351. The line gloss at Rom. 6:9: WA 56:58,19–59,1 = LW 25:52.

352. Cf. from the *Sermon on St. Andrew's Day* (Nov. 30) 1516, which is especially characteristic of the time of the Romans lectures: "Those (i.e. who adore the cross like Andrew; see n. 211) are they who desire . . . that their love of things is crucified quickly and completely, for *this is what is signified by the crucifixion of Christ in all his nakedness, who bore in himself a figure of the old self* and its affections and of the old boat that had to be left behind (Matt. 4:20 is the sermon text!). For by leaving behind the mortal life of his body, he taught that our love of all things transient had to be relinquished, which, as I said, is also signified by his nakedness" (WA 1:102,30–34; author's emphasis). See in addition the following from the *First Sermon on the Fifth Commandment* at almost the same time (see WA 1:461, n. 1): "What do you think *Christ's suffering and death signify*, if not *the death of the old self* and of the whole Adam? Although it may not die immediately, the old self must be afflicted with so many strokes, blows, scourges, thorns, and finally pierced and wounded with nails, until at last it expires with bowed head. The head itself is the tinder, the inmost root of anger and lust, which is not killed until at length it is broken by many adversities and finally yields to death. *The same thing is signified* by the fact that in former times, all the children of Israel died in the wilderness except Joshua and Caleb, and only the next generation entered the promised land, which *represented the second circumcision in the spirit*. God did this to keep Israel away not only from temporal but also spiritual things" (1:468,25–34; author's emphasis). Note that an Old Testament event can have the same "significance" (*significatio*) as Jesus's death on the cross (see pp. 78–80; esp. n. 286 and n. 287)!

353. Luther takes up the Augustinian term *singing together* (*concinere*) and understands it quite concretely as "singing before" (*praecinere*) and "responding" (*respondere*), a conception that "obviously comes from monastic worship" (E. Bizer, *Fides*, 26). [The image is that of two choirs singing antiphonally with one leading and the other responding. Trans.]

of others and of itself in the same way as Christ appeared dead and buried in the eyes of the Jews. For he is our precentor and sings before us in order that we may respond to him in everything."[354]

1.5. Marginal Note on Tauler's Sermons

It is not enough to set Luther apart from the tradition by emphasizing that tropological interpretation was not an acceptable method to him and that he understood our correspondence to Christ's death in penitence solely as the work of God, not as something brought about by our own will but solely as a gift. This is true of course and must be asserted against many late medieval voices, such as those of Ludolf of Saxony[355] and Mauburnus. But does the *sola gratia* have to be understood in a reformational sense? Did not Augustine, at the latest with his anti-Pelagian writings, have nothing but 1 Corinthians 4:7 in mind? Is it really the *sola gratia* and not his particular concept of the word that sets Luther apart from everyone before him?

Tauler's sermons, for example, make it clear that it is possible to practice a meditation piety free from any synergism[356] that is not yet faith in the word in the reformational sense. Certainly, there are also significant differences between the pre-reformational Luther and Tauler. And yet at the point of interest here, we can see both positions together in relation to Luther's reformational theology of the word.

In the sermon on Luke 10:23 (BLESSED ARE THE EYES THAT SEE WHAT YOU SEE), Tauler turns against those who, when contemplating the suffering of Christ, focus solely on historical facts but disregard their own existence and thus perform only an external act of piety, only a work that is more interested in the method than in the object of meditation: "They say, 'Lord God, I think every day about the suffering of our Lord, how he stood before Pilate and before Herod, and about the column where he was scourged and so on and so

354. WA 56:324,5–8 = LW 25:311–12 (trans. alt.). The *Sermon on the Passion* (1518) seems like an explanation of this sentence (sermon: WA 1:336–39,14); see esp. 1:337,21–31; 338,35–339,8.

355. But even here we might need to be more careful in view of the prayers that conclude each meditation and refrain from the sort of blanket condemnation of them (as a "work"!) that we find, for example, in G. Ebeling (*Evangelienauslegung*, 230–32; cf. 291–92) and W. Jetter (*Die Taufe beim jungen Luther*, 139, 145).

356. Cf. B. Hägglund, "Voraussetzungen der Rechtfertigungslehre Luthers in der spätmittelalterlichen Theologie," *LR* 11 (1961): 33–39. For a summary of this, see "Luther und die Mystik," *Vorträge des 3. Intern. Kongresses für Lutherforschung* (1967), 93: "According to Tauler, everything that belongs to our redemption is exclusively God's work . . . Redemption only comes about when all human work is destroyed."

forth.'"[357] But that is only a blind remembrance of Christ's suffering that cannot produce any fruit in them: "For they all remain as they are."[358] Self-knowledge and the transformation of one's whole life can only come from Christ's passion.

> Dear child, this is how you should practice and ponder the holy passion of our Lord, that it may bring forth living fruit in you.[359] . . . Submit yourself to the cross, wherever it comes from, whether it be outside or inside. Bow your proud heart under its thorny crown and follow your crucified God with a submissive heart, and truly belittle yourself in all ways, both inwardly and outwardly, for your great God was thus belittled and condemned by his creatures and was crucified and died. Therefore, with patient suffering and with all humility, train yourself in the way of his suffering and engrave it on your heart."[360]

Luther keeps to this sermon when he continues:

> Take note: to remember the passion of Christ literally as presented in Scripture produces nothing, but to remember it spiritually is life.[361]

Luther can only formulate this alternative of Scripture or history and existence because he does not yet understand that the Christ event is encountered here and now in the words of the promise "for you . . . for the forgiveness of sins." The "literally" ("*verbaliter*" = "*literaliter*"), in which the alternative would be overcome, should not be seen included here in the "spiritually" ("*spiritualiter*"). We experience Christ's suffering *spiritualiter* (= "*sacramentaliter*") when we experience it as our own cross and suffering,[362] which God sends us without it being sought (see Tauler: "the cross, wherever it comes from"!). As an experience of existence, therefore, it signifies life, it produces fruit. Of course, it must be "preached," but it goes right through the word, as it were, and does not become attached to it. Thus we receive salvation and life, not only—that is to say, not at all—through the word but also through experience. So, too, Luther's understanding of the

357. F. Vetter, 199,6–7.

358. Vetter, 199,25 (in the context of ll.22–28).

359. Vetter, 199,29–30.

360. Vetter, 199,14–21.

361. WA 9:103,28–30.

362. See pp. 62–63.

Lord's Supper is no different, as the second part of this intermediate chapter will show, from what we find in Tauler, who says with 1 Corinthians 11:26 in mind: "The proclamation (in connection with the eating and drinking of the body and blood of Christ) is not with words nor with remembrance, but through dying and being annihilated by the power of his death."[363]

It has become clear that tropology in the schema of fact and significance does not need the word to grasp the fact in its lived significance; that is, in tropology, the "word" is understood as the significance of its existence and not as a preached promise. That the contrast thus emphasized is not a construction of the interpreter but actually exists is shown by the difference between the two versions of the interpretation of the fourth petition of the Lord's Prayer, one from the spring of 1517 and the other, to be treated later (chap. 9 B), from the spring of 1519.[364]

1.6. The Interpretation of the Fourth Petition of the Lord's Prayer (Spring 1517[365])

This interpretation, which prepares for the passion sermon on BEHOLD THE MAN (John 19:5) of 1518,[366] speaks at length about the food of the soul. Traditionally, according to Matthew 4:4,[367] this consists of "hearing and contemplating the divine word."[368] What does this mean? Luther says that the sole task of the word is to present the reader or hearer of "a gospel"[369]—that is, a portion of text from the gospels, with a scene from the life of Jesus—, drawn mainly

---

363. In the sermon WHOEVER EATS MY FLESH; F. Vetter, 314,36–315,2.

364. See the account of E. Bizer, *Fides*, 131–47. The mentioned difference is one of the strongest reasons in favor of Bizer's overall view in *Fides ex auditu*.

365. WA 9:141–52; on the dating: 2:74. Although transcribed, translated, and lightly edited by *Agricola* (9:124,14–19; cf. 2:74), the text may be taken as *Luther's*, provided it does not contradict his other statements of this time.

366. The connection with this sermon (WA 1:336–40) arises not only from the general agreement with it in terms of content but also especially from the explicit linkage between the sacramental meditation on Scripture and the preparation for the reception of the Sacrament of the Altar, which can be observed on two occasions. Cf. 9:146,17–147,26 (1517) with 1:334,3–11 (*Sermon on Worthy Preparation*, 1518). When Luther says that "this remembrance however requires another sermon" (*Sermon on Worthy Preparation*, ll.10–11), he may well have in mind precisely the passion sermon on John 19:5 (cf. also 1:335).

367. WA 9:143,10–12. Cf. the interpretation of the fourth petition of the Lord's Prayer in Biel's commentary on the Mass, Lection 71G (3179–80). This section shows the depth of understanding of the "word" that the tradition had before Luther.

368. Cf. WA 9:143,14.

369. Cf. WA 9:145,8.

from the Christmas and passion stories[370]—and to do it as vividly as possible. In the spirit of the late medieval meditation books,[371] which Luther also eagerly read, it takes the life and suffering of Jesus from the past and presents it to the listeners, but that now means immediately to the contemplators.[372] For what is presented to them has a direct effect on their imagination and it is now the imagination itself that presents it (that is, reproduces it). In this way, the vitality inherent in the image merges with its effect, the ideas of the human imagination. But these in turn are not simply experienced and received by it but at the same time spring from it anew—that is, from its own activity. For the human will focuses intently on what it encounters, which in turn arouses it, "fires" it "up," and "stimulates" it.[373]

But the will can do no more than stimulate us to attune ourselves to the life and suffering of Jesus presented to us, to match our emotions with his, to "share" them,[374] and thus to sympathize with *another* person, to empathize with a basically *alien* vitality—for this "literal" and "historical"[375] understanding is

370. Since Luther presents his interpretation of the Lord's Prayer in Lent (cf. WA 9:142,24–26), he can only have the passion story in mind in our text. In other ways, too, the sacramental meditation on Scripture, as the interpreted texts show, usually only refers to it. But the meditation also includes the story of the nativity and the circumcision, indeed, according to the *Sermon on the Assumption of the Blessed Mary* (see pp. 89–92, the whole life and suffering of Jesus. The following section from the *Sermon on the Feast of the Assumption of Mary* (Aug. 15, 1516) may be understood as a *meditation on the nativity story*. The meditator here does not look like Jesus but Mary: "We too should rejoice for her and for ourselves, because the Lord has done great things for her, and because he has done great things for her, he has done great things for us; for she has nothing that we do not have also. She carries the Son of God in her lap and we in the womb of our heart. The mother herself is physical, but he said, 'Whoever does the will of my Father is my mother, brother, and sister.' He was nursed at the breasts of the Virgin; we nurse him with our pure and holy meditations. She embraces him with her holy arms; we embrace him with our fervent affections of love and with our desires: the beloved himself lingers between the breasts, both hers and ours" (1:78,39–79,6; see Bernard on Song of Songs, Sermon 43, par. 3 [*Opera* 2, 43–44]). The circumcision of Jesus is meditated on sacramentally in the sermon of Jan. 1, 1517 (see esp. WA 1:120,35–121,30).

371. On that, see M. Elze, "Züge spätmittelalterlicher Frömmigkeit in Luthers Theologie," *ZTK* 62 (1965): 381–402. Cf. G. Metzger, *Gelebter Glaube*, 56, n. 7.

372. Cf. from the pseudo-Anselmian meditations read by Luther (WA 9:106), "My soul, . . . contemplate very carefully this memorable, living man, whom you gaze at in the mirror of the gospel sermon as if you were looking at him here and now" (MPL 158:755).

373. WA 9:143,24–25.

374. That "we share in his sorrow, grief, misery, persecution, poverty, affliction, distress, his wounds, his drops of blood, and contemplate all his members . . . this is what it means 'to eat Christ'" (WA 9:147,17–20).

375. See the marginal note on Tauler, pp. 95–97.

missing from our final inner involvement when we try to understand it; our own self is not affected emotionally. But when the life and suffering of Jesus are viewed and considered correctly, and our affects are in sync with his, they immediately undergo a turn from object to subject and so are directed toward us as we contemplate them,[376] leading us to self-knowledge. Only this turn brings about the true Christlikeness.[377] But when Luther here describes a change and exchange,[378] he means less the idea of substitution than that of "sacrament," even if the word itself does not appear here. Christ's significance for us is nothing but his effect on us and in us, in the sense of the process of understanding described, which is most aptly called *devotion*.[379]

The individual aspects of devotion, which we have presented separately and in a factual sequence to grasp exactly what Luther meant, are already intertwined in his interpretation from the outset, since they are less a description than a practical exercise in devotion. Yet even this exercise does not proceed step by step, but the ideas and examples are repeated.

As evidence of its anticipated general characterization, we have compiled several striking and impressive formulations descriptive of this devotion that keep recurring, though modified each time, and may be considered typical of the whole. The "food of the soul is in the words, works, life, suffering, death, bloodshed, crowning and scourging of Christ, our dear God."[380] This is realistically depicted in a series of tiny images: "Even every little drop of Christ's rose-colored blood, every little thorn that pierced through his tender head and skull, every slap on his cheeks, every act of mockery and ridicule, which they inflicted on our

---

376. "Thus we find ourselves thinking that we are the ones for whose sake he did all this" (WA 9:143,35–36). Therefore, part of our sorrow etc. (see n. 374) is thinking about "why did he suffer this" (9:147,19–20).

377. WA 9:145,14.

378. "The righteous do not live in a multitude of works but in faith, and this faith is thus active. When I find in myself nothing else but wretchedness and poverty, sin . . . I console myself with the fact that Christ is rich, powerful, and without sin, and believe that his good work, agony, shed blood, and death . . . have become mine . . . we need to hold on to him and climb into heaven on his back and in his skin, for he is the way" (WA 9:144,16–27). Here Luther is clearly speaking of the "change and exchange" (*Wechsel und Tausch*) between Christ and us. But we must pay attention to how this happens and how we can be sure of it. Cf. esp. n. 374. The words "to take on Christ in his life, works, suffering and death" mean in fact that "we share in his sorrow, grief, misery, persecution, poverty, affliction, and distress" (9:147,16–18; see n. 374). On this purely negative way of defining "change and exchange," cf. chap. 1, n. 90, and pp. 151–153.

379. *Andacht*: for the definition of this term, see L. Richter s.v. "Andacht" in *RGG*, 3rd ed., 1:360–62. Cf. Grimm, *Dt Wb*, s.v. "Andacht": "A collection of thoughts on a topic; an inner memory" (1:303).

380. WA 9:143,22–23.

dear Christ in many and various ways, and every noble tear that he wept, is a dish from which the soul's food is prepared."[381] Each of these linguistic "devotional pictures" call to mind a section of the passion story. Each one is a station of the cross, so to speak, and stands for "a[382] gospel—as for example, when Christ left his disciples and went up on a mountainside by himself to spend the whole night in prayer,"[383] or "when Christ was cruelly bound to a pillar by Pilate and mercilessly scourged until there was almost nothing left of his body, collapsing to the ground from torture and weakness, with no one to comfort him."[384] "But the food of the soul is that which it takes to heart, which it desires and does not cease desiring until it has it. For the pleasure it takes in the thing it loves is called its food."[385]

We see how precisely Luther thinks about the acceptance (*Annahme*) and reception (*Aufnahme*)[386] of what is presented through its reproduction in the intentional act ("when it takes to heart[387] what it desires"). But the intentional "acceptance" of Jesus's suffering is not enough; the sacramental side must follow.[388] The image that has entered the heart does not cease to exist, but it is just

---

381. WA 9:143,27–32.

382. In agreement with the late medieval books of meditation, Luther holds "that we do not need to have the entire suffering, life, or work of Christ before us every day to contemplate it, but every day we should meditate on a part of it: now how he is led out, now how he is crowned, mocked, ridiculed etc. (WA 9:146,31–33). Also, according to the sermon of Jan. 1, 1517, which meditates sacramentally on the circumcision of Jesus (see n. 370), it is sufficient to attend to a part of Jesus's life: "His (i.e. Christ's) example or a part of his example should be taken to heart. For no one can have the whole Christ in this life, but we all participate in him" (1:120,39–121,1).

383. WA 9:145,8–10.

384. WA 9:145,15–18.

385. WA 9:142,35–7.

386. Cf. the formulation: "*accept* (*annemen*) Christ in his life, works, suffering and death" (WA 9:147,16–17; author's emphasis).

387. This verb (*take to heart*) tellingly turns up several times (*in sich bilden*: WA 9:142,36; *einbilden*: 9:143,24; *in das Herz bilden* = to imprint on the heart: 9:145,7–8; 146,25–26).

388. Cf. WA 4:271,10–15 = LW 11:406 (on Ps. 116:13): "We should all take the cup of the Lord, though some do so only intentionally (*intentionaliter*), that is, in remembrance; others do so spiritually (*spiritualiter*), that is, by crucifying the flesh with its desires, that is [*sacramentaliter*] as through the sacrament signified by Christ's sufferings, according to the apostle; still others take the cup following Christ's example [*exemplariter*], like the martyrs, who suffered similar things to Christ" (trans. alt.; author's emphasis). To begin with, it is striking that Luther here speaks of three possible ways in which different people can "take the cup of the Lord," whereas otherwise, in connection with *sacramentum-exemplum*, he only speaks of a single person in a double way (*homo interior-homo exterior*). However, we must not use the formulation of this one passage to reinterpret all the other texts relating to our topic. This passage here interests

there that it becomes most active. It is impossible "for the soul to remain still once it has been moved in this way, for when a little drop of (Christ's) blood stirs the soul, it begins to act freely."[389] This work wrought by the image is called penitence. With it, however, the life and suffering of Jesus are no longer only perceived and understood historically—noetically, aesthetically—but existentially (spiritually), in self-knowledge, and thus act as a "sacrament": "The blood of Christ has to work in you to warm you up so that you come to true remorse of heart . . . Then the heart melts at once and says: 'Behold, I'm a real scumbag! What have I done?' And it begins to hate itself and love God."[390] The following sentence sounds like a brief and concise summary of what the sacramental meditation on Scripture is meant to achieve: "Thus we have to suck what is ours from the wounds of Christ, especially penitence."[391]

What does all this mean for the understanding of the *word*? It means that it has no other function than to lead the hearer and reader into devotional contemplation. However, what is effective in the proper sense is not the word but the devotion—that is, a process of understanding in which the oral and binding word plays no constitutive role.

This[392] means that it was not the sacramental meditation on Scripture that brought about the reformational understanding of the promise (and so of word

---

us because, apart from 3:319,38–320,4 = 10:265, it is the only one in which Luther not only differentiates the tropological reference into *sacramentaliter* and *exemplariter* but goes even further and includes *intentionaliter*.

389. WA 9:145,25–26. Parallel to this: "It is useless (i.e. impossible; cf. 9:138 n. 2) for the soul to rest when Christ's work or suffering warms it up" (9:144,2–3) and: "When the soul takes to heart one of these (i.e. the words, works, or scourging of Christ: see pp. 99–101, it is stretched and freshened up, fired up and stimulated to devotion, love, chastity, penitence, piety, and the like" (WA 9:143,23–25). Attention should be given to the verbs *stir, warm up, freshen up, fire up*, and *stimulate*.

390. WA 9:145,34–37. The insight into one's own depravity that comes from looking at Jesus is expressed in lament and confession: "Behold, I . . ." Cf. 9:145, 10–13, 18–24, 32–33.

391. WA 9:145,31–32. See from the pseudo-Anselmian meditations read by Luther (9:106): "Grant, I pray, that some likeness of the thorns of your head may also appear in me, and that both the remorse of salutary penitence and the compassion for another's afflictions may fill my mind" (MPL 158:759).

392. In our presentation, we have disregarded a text which, according to the dating of the WA (1:74, n. 2: Aug. 10, 1516), belongs to the period that we have investigated here: 1:76,39–77,15. This text assumes a precise knowledge of the letter to the Hebrews (Christ as "the author of hope, as the apostle says" [1:76,39–40] refers not to 1 Pet. 2:21 [so WA] but to Heb. 2:10 [THE AUTHOR OF SALVATION], 5:9 [CAUSE OF SALVATION], and 12:2 [THE AUTHOR OF FAITH]) and is best understood in the context of the Hebrews lectures. For the sharp distinction between *sacramentum* and *exemplum*, see the scholion on Heb. 2:3 (WA 57/3:113,21–114,20 = LW 29:123–24), and for the strong emphasis on "help" (77,3) and "confidence" (77,11–12,

and sacrament). But this does not mean that some of its aspects could not still regain a place in it. We only have to think how often the later Luther uses the expression "to take to heart" (*einbilden = sich einprägen*: "to imprint or impress on the heart") in speaking about the word as a promise[393] and what he says about the way that faith is formed by the word. So the question is, *What* are we to take to heart to be saved? *What* is it that really gives us certainty? Is it a vivid, pictorial impression that immediately imprints itself on the soul, whereby the image before me only proves to be true when it is reenacted and when it has an affect on me, which concretely means only when it produces contrition?[394] Or is it a preached word that by its very nature is spoken to me by another and that makes a binding commitment to me?

These alternative questions bring out the difference between the interpretation of the fourth petition of the Lord's Prayer of 1517 and that of 1519 [which in this investigation is called an "exposition" to differentiate it from the 1517 "interpretation"]. It is therefore a question that the contradictory story of Luther's theology itself poses but one that can be answered unequivocally from Luther's reformational theology. What Luther advocates in 1517 is the position of Karlstadt—the very position that he later opposes.[395]

2. The Understanding of the Mass

Just as the understanding of Christ as a gift in the word, according to the *Brief Instruction* at the beginning of the Wartburg Postil, corresponds directly to the understanding of the sacrament in *The Babylonian Captivity of the Church*, so for

---

14), which cannot be explained by the theme of the sermon alone (1:74,11–15), see esp. the final section of the scholion on Heb. 10:19 (57/3:223,24–224,15 = 29:225–26: on this, see chap. 5, n. 123), and for the motif in 77,1–2, see the scholion on Heb. 2:10 (57/3:124,4–125,13 = 29:131–32: on this, see chap. 9A).

393. Cf., for example, WA 2:715,13–17 = LW 35:11 (*Sermon on the Sacrament of Penance*, 1519); WA 7:23,8 (*The Freedom of a Christian*, §7); on the topic, see pp. 320–323. Numerous passages have been compiled by Jacob and Wilhelm Grimm, *Deutsches Wörterbuch*, s.v. "Einbilden" (3:150). Regarding Grimm's statement:"The mystics may have introduced the term, later it was often used by Luther, but is not in the *Lutherbibel*," it should be added that the word probably became important to Luther from Tauler, in whose writings the verb, but especially the noun *image*, occur very frequently,and are almost key terms (cf., e.g., the text quoted and documented at n. 360).

394. Cf. WA 9:146,2–5: "It is a sure argument and sign of the grace of Christ when the hatred and indignation over sin and the love of righteousness increase, grow, and multiply. Whoever does not feel this sign within them surely has a dead stomach for they cannot digest this food."

395. See pp. 213–214. See chap. 8 for a discussion on how (pre-reformational) meditation piety and (reformational) *promissio* theology are related to each other.

the early Luther participation in the Mass has the same effect as the sacramental meditation on Scripture—namely, conformity with Christ in our self-knowledge, penitence, and co-sacrifice. *It is the notion of sacrifice, understood tropologically, that plays a decisive role in Luther's interest in the Mass.* From this we also understand why Luther can put the Mass and the gospel on an equal footing: the Mass shows and effects the co-sacrifice of the faithful with Christ—in fact this is what it essentially is—while the gospel brings judgment and so, like the Mass, brings about mortification. The covenant (*testamentum, pactum*) with Christ is aimed at this via the mediating concept of the covenant sacrifice.[396] It is especially important for our question about the story of the *promissio* concept to note the significant difference here between the latter view and *The Babylonian Captivity*, where the concept of "testament" (*testamentum*) is used to speak about "inheritance," "gift," and "distribution." And if the gospel continues to be preferred to the Mass,[397] as is the case with the early Luther, it is obviously because it is an even sharper "knife" for the "slaughtering" of the faithful[398] than the idea of the sacrifice of the Mass.

This summarizes what must now be shown in detail.

2.1. The First Psalms Lectures

Luther operates within the traditional horizon defined by the *Glossa ordinaria* (on 1 Cor. 11:24–25) as follows: "There are three things in this sacrament. The first is the sacrament alone: the visible species of bread and wine. The second is the sacrament and the thing it signifies (*res*): Christ's own flesh and blood.

396. WA 3:282,4–16 = LW 10:232 (Scholion on Ps. 50:5): "WHO ORDER HIS TESTAMENT/COVENANT ABOVE SACRIFICES. First (that is, those who make a pact with Christ instead of a sacrifice: this is how the Hebrew text reads) they receive his law that they may worship him with a sacrifice. Whence the sacrifice is the end (i.e. goal, intention, meaning) of the law and the gospel: for what else does the gospel do but slaughter and kill us according to the flesh and thus offer us to God as living sacrifices according to the Spirit?" (Then Rom. 12:1 and 1 Pet. 2:5 follow) . . . "Second, 'above sacrifices,' that is, the testament/covenant is more perfect and more worthy than the sacrifices of the law, and more than them. However, 'they order it' because they offer themselves first and then others and they do it according to the word of God. For this is what the order of love demands: that first we make a pact and testament with the Lord to sacrifice ourselves, then others also" (trans. alt.). Cf. 3:282,23–283,20. By referring to this text and highlighting its significance for the understanding of the Mass, we are already touching on the understanding of the promise in the *Dictata* (first Psalms lectures), which we still need to give special attention to; see the sections H–L.

397. See pp. 114–115.

398. See pp. 107–109.

The third is the thing it signifies and not the sacrament: the mystical flesh of Christ."[399]

These determinations, which Luther at any rate was familiar with from Biel's commentary on the Mass,[400] also shape his own understanding. According to this, Christ distinguishes himself from the "the thing signified by the sacrament" (*res sacramenti*), which we describe as the church.[401] Here change and real presence—"the true Christ is on the altar"[402]—are presupposed as unshakeable foundations;[403] but Luther has no particular interest in them. His attention is focused rather on the *res* of the sacrament, what it signifies: "We should consider the thing signified by the sacrament more than sacrament itself."[404]

---

399. 650E. See also in Peter Lombard: IV/d.8/c.7.

400. "There are three things in this sacrament: 1) the visible form of bread and wine, 2) the truth of Christ's body and blood, and 3) the spiritual power of the unity and love of the people communing. The first is the sacrament alone. The second is the sacrament and the thing it signifies (*res*). The third is only the thing it signifies" (Lect. 35 Q, 2:31). Cf. Lect. 35 N, 2:29; Lect. 36 G, 2:46–47; Lect. 37 L, 2:68; Lect. 55 F, 2:350; Lect. 55 N, 2:358.

401. "A 'sacrifice of righteousness' before God is not possible unless it is spiritual, rational, living, which is Christ in the sacrament with the thing signified by the sacrament (i.e. the church and Christ himself)": marginal gloss on Ps. 4:5 (WA 55/1:20,30–31; 22,7). The distinction between "the sacrament of Christ's body" and the "thing signified by the sacrament" (= "the people of Christ"), which (according to Hirsch/Rückert on Heb. 5:1) goes back to Augustine in *Tractate on John* 26:15 (MPL 35:1614) and was kept alive in the Middle Ages by Peter Lombard (IV/d.8/c.6–7.), is also found in the Hebrews lectures (on 5:1: WA 57/3:167,25–168,11 = LW 29:170) and in the Lord's Supper sermon (on this, see chap. 6 A). Additionally, see on the distinction between *sacramentum* and *res sacramenti* the rich material on the history of the tradition offered in WA 55/1:21,40–47; 23,17–38 and also the contrast between "sacramental" (*sacramentaliter*) and "spiritual" (*spiritualiter*), which we find repeatedly in Biel's commentary on the Mass (e.g. Lect. 29 B; 1, 290: "The priest offers" the eucharistic sacrifice "to the supreme Father, truly and sacramentally, while the people present offer it spiritually").

402. WA 3:460,32 (Marginal gloss on Ps. 72:16). See the line gloss: "Christ himself WILL BE the sacramental GRAIN of the eucharistic bread on the altar" (3:460,17–18) and the scholion: "Christ in the sacrifice of the mass is the heavenly grain and bread in the sacramental species" (WA 3:470,30–32 = LW 10:413–14) and further (in the interpretation of FIRMAMENTUM = PILLAR, which the Septuagint offers instead of FRUMENTUM = GRAIN): "And Christ in this sacrament is the one and only pillar of the whole Christian faith and religion. Remove this sacrament, says Bonaventure, and paganism and idolatry will be mingled with true faith throughout the whole church" (3:470,33–471,2 = 10:414; trans. alt.).

403. See Luther's interpretation of FIRMAMENTUM quoted in n. 402.

404. WA 4:244,14–15 = LW 11:379 (on Ps. 111:5) (trans. alt.). See 4:234,33–38 = 11:368–69 (on Ps. 110:4): "He [i.e. Melchizedek] offered bread and wine only sacramentally, but Christ did it sacramentally and spiritually at the same time. For sacramental bread and wine are the species of the sacrament of bread and wine. But spiritual bread and wine is Christ himself, the

a) What this *res* is for Luther is shown by the interpretation of *Psalm 50:14,23*:

The "sacrifice of praise" of these verses has its settled place in the liturgy of the Mass (in the prayer of the canon: AND ALL HERE PRESENT . . .).[405] So it is understandable that Lyra[406] and Paul of Burgos,[407] for example, refer it to the Eucharist. Luther takes up this reference in the scholion on verse 14 and even identifies the "sacrifice of praise" with the "the thing (*res*) itself of the sacrament,"[408] but to avoid the misunderstanding that the sacrifice was limited to the time and place of the celebration of the Mass, he insists, appealing to Augustine, that it is to be lived as an act of total surrender in continual worship.[409]

With this, Luther has brought us to the center of his thinking about the Mass, which is nothing other than the radically conceived notion of the *opus operantis*, the work of the doer, the work of the one who offers the sacrifice of the Mass. This is shown very clearly in the marginal gloss on verse 23:

> Although the sacrifice of the altar is truly what is here called praise, in which the prayers and praises of all are offered, yet it is not for all, but only for those who also offer themselves in and with it in its effect and in the *re sacramenti* (i.e. in the essence of the sacrament).[410] For

head, and the whole church. Thus, the apostle says in 1 Cor. 10[:17]: 'We who are many are one bread and one body'" (trans. alt.).

405. See Biel, Lect. 29 F (written out by Altenstaig: s.v. "sacrificium" Fol. 224[v]), 1:293.

406. On v. 14: 3:157F.G. (cf. Luther's line gloss on the same verse: WA 3:279,1–2) and on v.23: 3:157B.

407. On v. 23 (Additio 2): 3:157C.

408. WA 3:283,21–23 = LW 10:234 [Although the LW translates "res" as "reality," we have retained "thing" for consistency; trans. note.]

409. WA 3:283,23–27 = LW 10:234 (trans. alt.): "For in it (i.e. in the sacrament, or in the sacrifice of the altar) the sacrifice of praise is always offered, of which he [the psalmist] is speaking here, but not only in it. Indeed, the sacrifice of praise is the daily sacrifice that never ceases to be offered. For God wants us ourselves and not our sacrifices, except as a sign or sacrament of the sacrifice that we are" (i.e. the individual works ["our sacrifices"] that we do can only be a sign and pointer ["sacrament"] to the total sacrifice that basically determines our life ["what we are"]; cf. 3:282,23–283,20 = 10:233–34 and section E: "The Word as Total Demand," which is based especially on the interpretation of the scholion on Rom. 10:10). "Also Blessed Augustine explains such a sacrifice." See Augustine on the vv.14–16,23 (MPL 36:578–80, 84).

410. Cf. the line gloss on Ps. 4:7: "BY THE FRUIT, i.e. by what the sacrament signifies (*re sacramenti*) or by its effect" (WA 55/1:24,4–5 = WA 3:39,6–7). And, on this, see Biel's definition in Coll. IV/d 4/q 2/a 1 not. 3 (C) given by Luther in 55/1:21,41ff.

> it is not enough for us that the sacrifice is pleasing to God in and of itself, rather than because of us who offer it. Because it was not given to us that it should only be pleasing to God because of itself (*ex se*) but rather entirely because of us (*ex nobis*). Otherwise, it would no longer be a sacrifice. Therefore, in vain do they build, furnish, and multiply churches and institute masses if they do not also sacrifice themselves in the sacrifice of praise and confession. This confession comprises words and deeds and the mind.[411]

Inasmuch as Luther does not understand the *opus operantis* as a single pious work but as the basic attitude or disposition of the whole person, he moves away from the tradition. On the other hand, however, he still remains firmly attached to it with his fundamental adherence to the *opus operantis*.[412] For even the radically understood *opus operantis* is not yet faith in the reformational sense, which depends solely on the promise, and does not first give itself but takes what is offered ("Take and eat"). When Luther later understands the relationship of the *opus operatum* to the *opus operantis* as substantially that of promise and faith and stubbornly insists on the *opus operatum* in the sense of the promise, it means nothing else than that the efficacy of the sacrament "does not depend on the worthiness or unworthiness of the minister who offers it, or of the person who receives it" as attested by the Wittenberg Concord (1536).[413] Then too the idea of sacrifice occurs in a different context.[414] The sacrifice with heart, mouth, and hands, which for *The Babylonian Captivity follows* the sacrament comprising word and faith, is for the first Psalms lectures the *substance* of the sacrament *itself*.[415] The

---

411. WA 3:280,29–37.

412. Cf. Biel, Lect. 29 D (1:291–92): "Therefore, faith is required of those present at the altar so that the sacrifice of oblation, through which they are received into the unity of the sacrament, may benefit them . . . For faith working through love purifies the hearts of those who participate so that they too may be offered up spiritually in that oblation, which, because of their purity of heart, represents the purity of the mystical body, as we have it in Acts 15: 'Purifying their hearts by faith' . . . But since these two things exist in those who hear the mass, namely, faith and devotion, they lay hold of the fruit of this sacrament of divine grace, sometimes offering it more bountifully than the priest."

413. *BSLK* 65,37–38.

414. Here it becomes clear at a specific point that to determine the relationship between Luther's early theology and his reformational theology, we should not compare individual motifs per se but only their entire material contexts.

415. The other important difference, which lies in the concept of "testament" (sacrifice—inheritance), has already been pointed out (see pp. 102–103).

salient difference that emerges here is of the greatest importance for differentiating between Roman Catholic theology and Protestant theology.[416]

b) The notion of sacrifice also guides the interpretation of *Psalm 84:3*. But unlike his interpretation of Psalm 50:14,23, here Luther does not even include a reference to the institutional sacrament, even though the word ALTARS[417] would suggest it. Rather, he immediately interprets the verse in the sense of sacramental meditation on Scripture.

A "memorial" and "model" must be made from "the works of humility and the example of Christ and the saints"[418] in order that we can arrive at "remorse" and the "works of penitence" by meditating on them[419]—for remorse or penitence is the aim of the whole interpretation.

Memorial, drawn from 1 Corinthians 11:24–25 and Leviticus 22:19, is one of the terms that Luther uses to speak about the sacrament (or sacrifice) of the altar[420] but in another way than that used in the tradition that shaped

---

416. This is the real point of difference between the Mass and Lord's Supper: see E. Bizer, "Römisch-katholische Messe und evangelisches Abendmahl" in *Ecclesia semper reformanda*, Sonderheft der EvTh zum 50. Geburtstag von Ernst Wolf (1952), 17–40. [This difference also has implications for modern ecumenical discussion; trans. note.]

417. Cf. the *Glossa interlinearis* (3.210): "ALTARS the sacraments of the church."

418. WA 3:645,3–4 = LW 11:139.

419. WA 3:645,32–33 = LW 11:140. Here Luther formulates not only the *summary sentence* of the section 3:645:1–34 ("Blessed are those who continually meditate on them and are contrite and do the works of penitence") but of his entire interpretation of Ps. 84:3a (cf. 3:645,32–33 = 11:140 with 3:644,32–39 = 11:139; on the interweaving of the praise of God and the confession of sins, see pp. 116–118 and p. 159). This is also confirmed in retrospect from the following interpretation of v. 3b (3:645,34–648,3), which Luther puts under the same title as that of v. 3a (3:646,36–37 = 11:142): "Cross, winepress, nest, altar, all these are the same"). For his interpretation of 3a, Luther expressly refers to Bernard's Sermon 43 on the Song of Songs (WA 3:645,31–32 = LW 11:140–41: "Just as blessed Bernard discusses in relation to the bundle of myrrh"), which he considers together with Sermon 61 on the Song of Songs (cf. 3:645,29–31,32 = 11:140–41 with Sermon 61 on Canticles 2:14, "MY DOVE IN THE CLEFTS OF THE ROCK because she dwells in the wounds of Christ through wholehearted devotion and lingers there through constant meditation" [*Opera* 2, 152], and M. Elze, "Züge spätmittelalterlicher Frömmigkeit in Luthers Theologie," *ZTK* 62 [1965]: 381–402, here 396–98). We do not, however, have to infer from this coupling of two sermons an indirect tradition (so Elze, 398); it could just as well be all Luther's own work. The *shift* that the Bernardine motif undergoes when it is taken up by Luther is very typical of his early theology: If Bernard finds that Canticles 2:14 (MY DOVE IN THE CLEFTS OF THE ROCK) speaks especially about the security of faith (in Sermon 61, *Opera* 2, 148–55, also in Sermon 43 *Opera* 2, 41–44, comfort is the most important thing), Luther will immediately say that it and Bernard's interpretation refer to the cross that is given to believers (see 3:645,32–33 = 11:141 and the complete interpretation of v. 3b). Cf. pp. 163–164.

420. Cf. the line gloss on Ps. 22:27, "THEY SHALL REMEMBER i.e., they shall perform this very memorial of my passion, namely, the sacrifice of the altar" (WA 3:138,19–20), and from the

him.[421] If it is not the Mass that appears here as a "memorial" but "the works of Christ and the saints, done in humility, lowliness, poverty, dejection, and affliction . . . when they become examples and are taken as examples and are set forth for imitation,"[422] then for Luther the term is not being used improperly. On the other hand, the Mass is not simply replaced by penitential meditation but interpreted.[423] That is, the event of the Mass, understood as a sacrificial act, is meditated on and understood as having the same tropological significance as the passion story, whether painted, read, or heard. *This* consonance of functions, and not Luther's preference for the "word" arising naturally from his reformed soul,[424] makes it clear why Luther in his interpretation of FOOD in Psalm 111:5, which traditionally[425] referred to the Eucharist, can draw a strict parallel between "evangelical" and "sacramental" food and emphasize that "the sacrament and the gospel are to be consumed at the same time, and that each is a memorial of Christ, so that 'as often as you eat it, you proclaim the Lord's death.' Thus here we have the gospel with the sacrament."[426] Word and sacrament unanimously

---

scholion on Ps. 72:16, the Sacrament of the Altar "is memorable wheat, for it was instituted in memory of the Lord's suffering. Therefore, it is called a memorial of the Lord" (WA 3:471,3–4 = LW 10:414; trans. alt.). See the glosses on Ps. 111:4: "HE HAS MADE A REMEMBRANCE a memorial, namely, the Eucharist" (in the margin: "whence it says: 'As often as you do this, you do it in remembrance of me'"; 4:236,29–30) OF HIS STRANGE WORKS which he did and suffered in his life for us" (4:236,17–18; cf. WA 3:549,22–25 = LW 11:37 [summary of Ps. 77] and 3:320,9 = 10:265). Cf. further the Hebrews lectures (on 9:2): 57/3:199,10–18 = 29:201.

421. See Lyra in his general remarks following his detailed interpretation of Heb. 9 (6:151H) and on 1 Cor. 11:24–25 (6:50H) as well as Biel, Lect. 16 A (1:129): "Note that the sacrifice is that memorial of our Lord's suffering, according to the passage in 1 Cor. 11"; Lect. 53 U (2:331). See J. Ficker (WA 57/3:199 on l. 17), who for Biel's understanding still refers to passages in his sermons.

422. WA 3:645,24–27 = LW 11:140.

423. One thinks of Ignatius Loyola, who when he attended Mass, did not pay attention to the words and actions but immersed himself in the passion story using the book of meditations that he brought with him (see H. Boehmer, *Loyola und die deutsche Mystik*, 1921, 20–21)!

424. A. Brandenburg detects in Luther's work an "original flair for proclamation" and holds that Luther was "a born preacher" (*Gericht und Evangelium. Zur Worttheologie in Luthers erster Psalmenvorlesung*, 1820). However, there is no historical basis for this assertion. Another view says that if it is not Luther's innate gift for preaching, then "the primacy of the word, its understanding as a means of grace equal to and even superior to the sacraments, goes back to the original elements of Luther's theology that cannot be completely explained": this is the opinion of W. Jetter, *Die Taufe beim jungen Luther*, 339. Cf. K. Holl, "Die Entstehung von Luthers Kirchenbegriff," *Aufsätze*, 1, 292–93.

425. See especially Lyra (3:252H–53G) and Paul von Burgos and Matthias Döring (3:253G–254E). Cf. "The Council of Trent, Decree on the Eucharist," chap. 1 (*Denz. Enchiridion*, 875).

426. WA 4:236,33–36 (cf. l. 21: "FOOD sacramental and spiritual"). In the same sense, it says in the scholion on v. 4: "However, this food and remembrance is twofold: sacramental and

teach the same thing: "the crucifixion of the flesh." This is clarified by Luther's interpretation of *Psalm 84:3b* (keyword: *ALTARS*) with the sharpness of an ideal type. It is this to which we must now finally give attention.

The marginal gloss refers the keyword to Scripture, or more precisely, because of the plural *ALTARS*, to the Scriptures, and so to the individual passages in Scripture, all of which work judgment in the way known to us already:[427] "The Scriptures are the altars of Christ on which we are to offer and surrender ourselves in obedience to him, to be slain and offered up with the Lord . . . The Scriptures, I say, are the greatest altars, which teach about the crucifixion of the flesh."[428]

The question "Why did the psalmist speak of many altars?" receives a new answer from the scholion that still encompasses the gloss: "Because there are many crosses and sufferings and afflictions of the saints."[429] And the difference in heading between Psalm 8 (FOR THE WINEPRESS: Christ in the winepress) and Psalm 84 (FOR THE WINEPRESSES: Christians in the winepress),[430] reflecting the shift in number from singular to plural, yields an important

---

spiritual. The preaching of Christ and the gospel is itself spiritual" (WA 4:243,18–19 = LW 11:378). On the parallelism between Mass and gospel, cf. further WA 3:58,17 (= 55/2:82,20–21) = LW 10:70; WA 3:372,34–35 = LW 10:314; WA 4:417,4; 451,20–21; 4:453,22–23; 4:454,20.

427. See, for example, section D ("The External Word: Public Judgment").

428. WA 3:640,35–38.

429. WA 3:647,21–22 = LW 11:143.

430. WA 3:647,22–23. The Latin title FOR THE WINEPRESS (Ps. 8) means, as Luther says: "for the suffering and death of Christ, i.e., for his crucifixion" (WA 55/1:58,10–11 = WA 3:79,16–17), and FOR THE WINEPRESSES (Ps. 84) means "for the saints and their sufferings" (3:640,1). But already the heading of Ps. 81 contains the words FOR THE WINEPRESSES. The explanation given there prepares for the interpretation of ALTARS in the scholion on Ps. 84:3: "The winepress in Ps. 8 is explained as standing for the suffering of Christ. So now, according to Augustine, in this passage it is explained mystically as standing for the sufferings and afflictions of the saints . . . But the winepress is also any cross of penitence, since we are all called to take up the cross of the Lord and follow him, otherwise we will not be worthy of him" (3:610,29–34). If Paul preaches nothing else than "Christ crucified," he is thinking here, according to Luther, "not only of the cross that he carried but also of the cross that we are called to carry" (3:613,13–16). And so "winepress" in this context is the right word, for "the word of the cross squeezes and squashes our flesh" (3:613,24–25). God exhorts us "and makes us remember our misery . . . so that we may always be of the mind to repent and tread the winepress of salvation" (3:617,21–23). As the earliest text on this matter, see the remark in Faber's *Psalterium* in WA 4:476,22–31. *Given its vividness, it is hardly surprising that the interpretive motif "Christ in the winepress" also became concretized as an image and thus appeared in medieval art.* In the late Middle Ages, it became a devotional image that was immensely characteristic of the passion piety of the time: we only have to think of the single page woodcut reproduced, for example, in *RGG*, 3rd ed., vol. 4, Table 57 (illus. 4), from which we can also explain the interplay between the passion meditation and the piety surrounding the sacrifice of the Mass, which can be seen in the early Luther. (For an article that is fully informed by the questions of art history, see A. Thomas, "Christus in der Kelter," *RDK* 3 [1954], 673–87.)

explanation for the plural ALTARS: "It is now clear that our altar is duplex: *first*, literally, the body of Christ, and *second*, tropologically, all the sufferings of the saints that are the mystical cross of Christ."[431]

Luther then briefly summarizes what he had previously explained in broad terms:

> Our *first* altar is Christ, himself the priest and victim and our altar, on which we are placed and offered to God the Father, and in whom we offer all our sacrifices. And he himself in his body offered us to God, mortified in the flesh but made alive in the spirit. But if he offered us in his body, then his body is our altar since the offering can only be made on an altar. His cross was his altar on which he himself was offered for us, offering us in himself.
>
> The *second* altar is the mystical cross of Christ, on which all must be offered. Because "whoever does not take up their cross and follow me is not worthy of me." For as he was offered on the cross, so too we in like manner must be offered to God on the cross . . . and we are offered on it and in them (that is, on the cross and in the sufferings of Christ, which are those base and worthless things in the world: humility, reproach, refuse, perplexity etc. which the apostle lists in detail in 2 Corinthians 6). So just as Christ was offered on the cross, so too we are offered in them: they are our crosses, our sufferings, and our altars, on which we present our bodies as a living sacrifice. If Christ is the priest, then he is the altars, and therefore he slaughters the victim. The altars are the crosses, the word of God the knives with which he slays.[432]

Here, too, Luther does not ask about the basis of our surrender and self-sacrifice.[432a] Of course, the emphasis is placed on Christ. But what grows

431. WA 3:647,23–25 = LW 11:143.

432. WA 3: 646,13–31 = LW 11:141–42 (trans. alt.).

432a. At one point (in the scholion on Ps. 111:4: HE HAS MADE A REMEMBRANCE OF HIS WONDERFUL WORKS; WA 4:243,7–16 = LW 11:377–78. Cf. 3:544,7–13 = 11:511:29–30, on Ps. 77:15 in reference to v. 11), the Mass is understood in such a way that it is a reminder that Christ's passion is not an *exemplary* but an *archetypal* event. By his death, Christ has killed death so that now death is life and suffering is pleasure. Here we catch a glimpse of the strange way in which God deals with his people: "For thus 'the Lord has dealt with his saints in a strange way.' But these strange works were done radically and causally in the sufferings of Christ, to whose example all must be conformed. Therefore, the Sacrament of the Eucharist is the mark of his suffering, that is, the remembrance of his strange works" (ll. 13–16). The Christology underpinning this is discussed in chap. 9 A: see p. 348 and p. 369.

out of his suffering is not first and foremost a gift but an immediate task, not a promise but a demand. In the Mass, understood as the "memorial" of his suffering, Christ meets us as the one whose works help us, "when they become examples and are taken as examples and are set forth for imitation."[433] But, according to Luther, we also see sacrifice and surrender in the life of every saint or bishop "whose example is adopted for imitation."[434] If, however, the idea of sacrifice is the guiding principle for understanding the Lord's Supper, then Christ and the saints, Christ and the church, become so closely intertwined that they are practically indistinguishable. But then the Lord's Supper, as the place of the *reconstitution* of our baptismal faith through the reception of the gift, has become a celebration and *representation* of the surrender that takes place in the Christian life and the life of the church.

2.2. The Sermon on the Decalogue of September 21, 1516

Luther's first thematic statement on the Mass that has come down to us[435] is his interpretation of the third commandment of September 21, 1516, which belongs

---

433. WA 3:645,26–27 = LW 11:140 (see p. 107).

434. WA 3:647,38–40 = LW 11:144 (cf. ll.26–37); this text is especially highlighted by Luther.

435. a) The *Sermon on the Lord's Supper* mentioned by Luther in WA 3:58,16 (= 55/2:82,19–20) = LW 10:70 (Sermon on Ps. 4:7) is unfortunately lost to us. It must have been delivered in 1516 at the latest, which we know from the passage mentioned belongs to the parts of the first Psalms lectures that were revised in the fall of 1516 (see chap. 2, n. 1).

b) H. Boehmer (*Luthers erste Vorlesung*, 38–41), E. Vogelsang (*BoA* 5:40), and R. Schwarz (*Fides, spes und caritas*, 76, n. 1) also include in this revision of the fall of 1516 the *Interpretation of Psalm 23*, given in WA 31/1:464–71, which is important for Luther's understanding of the Lord's Supper. (We can disregard here 31/1:471,16–480 [the interpretations of Psalms 24 and 25].) But unfortunately, the date of origin of this interpretation cannot be determined exactly (see chap. 5, n. 43) so that we cannot rely on it for a description of his early understanding of the Lord's Supper. But if it were to be placed before the Hebrews lectures, we could get an idea of how it might look from chap. 5 (pp. 236–237).

c) The dating of Luther's *Randbemerkungen zu Gabriel Biels Collectorium in quattuor libros sententiarum* must also be briefly discussed here, since their editor, H. Degering, sees these marginal notes dating to 1515/16 (7–12). In view of their *terminus ad quem*, they can only be dated from their content. However, Luther did not say prior to the Hebrews lectures that because the scholastics "do not pay attention to the fact that the spoken word in the sacraments is the word of God himself" (18), they do not speak of "faith in the sacrament" (18) and that therefore they lack "an understanding (*scientiam*) of the promises and the knowledge (*notitiam*) of faith" (19). There is no evidence of an earlier date in the statements that can be dated with certainty. The sermon presented in what follows specifically contradicts these remarks but fits perfectly within the framework of the Romans lectures; the dating adopted by the WA (see n. 436) is therefore supported by its content.

to his series of sermons on the Ten Commandments.[436] Here he emphasizes[437] that sanctifying the holy day (the day of rest) requires five things: hearing the Mass, hearing God's word, praying, offering sacrifices,[438] and repenting of sin.

All of this should not be done "literally," as works of external holiness, but "spiritually," with the heart.[439] For as the previous sermon explained right at the beginning of the interpretation of the third commandment—as a basic principle, as it were—this commandment does not demand work but simply that we keep still ("pure rest"), to prepare "us for God like pure matter."[440] "For we are good, not by working, but by being worked on, when we suffer God's actions and are ourselves at rest."[441] This principle, clearly expressed in the thoughts and concepts of mysticism, must be kept in mind as we turn to the section on hearing the Mass and its connection with hearing God's word, praying, and repenting of sin.

a) Hearing the Mass

Luther's remarks on hearing the Mass are witness to an unbroken ecclesial positivism (an uncritical acceptance of church teaching) and at the same time a spiritualistic sacramental piety that has basically no interest in external things. What

---

The above-mentioned marginal notes (*Randbemerkungen*) most likely did not appear until 1520, with the preparation of the treatise on *The Babylonian Captivity of the Church*, perhaps even especially in connection with the drafting of its baptismal section. This thesis is explained in more detail in chap. 7.

436. On this dating, see WA 1:443, n. 1, and WA 1:85, n. 2.

437. "There are five things to be done to sanctify the holy day, as drawn from the decree: to hear mass, to hear God's word, to pray, to sacrifice for the benefit of others, and to be contrite for one's sins" (WA 1:443,8–10).

438. Luther himself explains briefly and succinctly what is meant by this in WA 1:446,7–10.

439. WA 1:443,3–4.

440. WA 1:436,16–17, 18–20. Similarly, already in the *Dictata* (on Ps. 118:27): 4:277,29–31. [Note: "as pure matter" = "as purely receptive material," trans.]

441. WA 1:437,21–22. Cf. 1:470,36–37: The third commandment is all about "God's noblest and greatest work that he does as we hear, teach, and meditate on his word inwardly in the Spirit. Outwardly we are at rest, but inwardly God is busy at work and extremely active." See further 1:471,4–9: "Furthermore, to sanctify our rest is to present ourselves to God as inactive, receptive (passible), so that God alone is at work in us: here patience and hope are needed, for here we enter into the darkness where humans do not work but are strangely led on the path of submission where they receive from God. Therefore, as often as you submit, you cease to work, you do no work but rest, and God works on you and in you, but you do not know what he is doing, because you are passive ("you suffer") and nothing more than inert material (*nuda materia*) for God to work on. Hence he says: 'Be still and know that I am God' [Ps. 46:10]."

Luther himself was later to stubbornly insist on, he here resolutely rejects—namely, reciting the canon of the Mass aloud.[442]

AA) Ecclesial Positivism[443]

Against certain interpreters of the canon of the Mass who want to have it read aloud, Luther asserts that it is necessary for "the canon of the mass, which alone is properly the mass, to be read with subdued voice so that it is not heard." The Mass is not meant to be heard but seen! Whoever wants to have it read aloud for the sake of the gospel should remember that "the command concerning the word of God (that it should be spoken) is one thing, and that concerning the mass another."

The prevailing ecclesial custom is, in accordance with the nominalist view, always a "command" and must therefore be applied unconditionally. Therefore, the canon is to be prayed silently. Also the distinction between the "command concerning the word of God" and that "concerning the mass" must be observed. The thinking stemming from God's ordained power (*potentia ordinata*) remains a fundamental force of Luther's theology also later on. But here, there is still no critical principle for singling out one command among the many and giving it priority. So what we observed in the interpretation of Romans 3:20,22 in the lectures also applies here;[444] namely, that if there is no concentration on one single thing, the idea of the *potentia ordinata* loses its power to guarantee certainty.[445]

---

442. Of course, later the whole canon will be reduced to the words of institution alone and specifically the gifting words [take and eat . . . take and drink . . . this is my body . . . this is my blood], which are to be spoken aloud to the congregation. To that extent, Luther does not exactly advocate here what he then later rejects.

443. We follow the text in WA 1:443,11–17: "Here they interpret the canon in an exceedingly foolish way, wishing to have the mass read with a loud voice because it was commanded to be heard not seen, as if it were not rather commanded that the canon of the mass, which alone is properly the mass, be read with subdued voice so that it is not heard . . . If they want it read louder for the sake of the gospel, why do they not consider carefully that the command concerning the word of God is one thing and that concerning the mass another?"

444. See sec. D 2.

445. But the command already has its meaning in itself, for it brings about obedience, even if blind obedience, and with it the humility that is absolutely constitutive of salvation. Shortly thereafter, in the same sermon, Luther adopts the same stance that he took in assessing the problem of the Mass said in secret when he now comes to the question of whether the Mass can be heard anywhere: "No one is permitted in this very matter to follow their own judgment, their own opinion, or their own devotion, but they must follow the authority of the church and take captive their reason to make it obedient to Christ . . . The church cannot err, but an individual can err in their devotion." We should obey the one that stands against us, as in the well-known reference to the person who must come to terms with their accuser while on the way to court

ab) Spiritualism

Second, the idea of God's ordained power cannot deliver certainty if, in the performance of the Mass, the external thing and its inner significance are not necessarily connected but break apart into two things that are basically only arbitrarily related to one other.

The fact that everywhere in the church, as Luther explains,[446] only the priest hears the whole Mass, including that which remains *inaudible* to everyone else, means that Christ, the true priest, in addition to what he does "in the church through the external sacraments and visible ceremonies," works *in an invisible way* for us with God.[447] The pinnacle of the Mass, the canon, merely because it remains inaudible, becomes the "great sacrament" for the invisible work of the heavenly Christ; that is, it becomes the mere pointer to a deeper significance, to a *res*, which is not bound to its *signum* as such.[448] Therefore, the center of the Mass, although eagerly retained in its external form, as decreed by God's ordained power, is inwardly emptied because, understood allegorically, it vanishes into a sign, which only has a broken, purely accidental relationship to the

---

in Matt. 5:25, which is already familiar to us (WA 1:444,14–28). Also, here it should be said that the idea of a fixed place that excludes the vagrantism of a wayward and errant piety remains a fundamental emphasis of Luther's theology, especially of his doctrine of the Lord's Supper (see pp. 280–281). But later he is positively disposed to the help that an assertoric promise (the preaching of the gospel) can give to the conscience that is wandering to and fro, unable to find a firm footing. On the other hand, in his pre-reformational period, Luther was initially concerned only with his obedience as such and with the humility that it demonstrated in him (cf. section D 2).

446. "But let them cease these vain dreams, since throughout the whole church no one but the priest alone may hear the whole mass, that is to say, in that great sacrament, because (and this surely is the deep meaning here) Christ is the true priest, even though he does much in the church through the external sacraments and visible ceremonies, in which the faithful sing and work with him, as the clergy do now with the priest in song, prayer, and the responses. Yet Christ does most things for us invisibly with God, which the people and the church do not even see or understand" (WA 1:443,17–23).

447. Biel (Lect. 15 D; 1:122) puts it differently: "The canon is called secret . . . on the basis of its double meaning: namely, in Christ and in the celebrant. In Christ, because it represents this secret by which Christ was concealed and hides himself from the crowds . . . But in the priest, it signifies the silence of the mind, by which the devotion of the heart, without the noise and confusion of words, is directed to God, who listens to the heart, not the voice." The fact that the silence of the canon can be interpreted in such different ways by Luther and Biel is testament to the arbitrariness and contingency of these interpretations.

448. Cf. Hugo of St. Victor 2:8,7 (quoted in Biel, Lect. 39 K; 2:93–94): "The sacrament is both a sign and an image of our invisible and spiritual participation in Jesus, which is brought about inwardly in the heart through faith and love." The starting point and point of reference are different here than in our Luther text, but the hermeneutic of signification is the same in both cases.

thing it signifies. We can see that at the end of 1516, Luther is still a long way from the position he adopted later. The picture does not change either when we now turn to Luther's remarks on the second point regarding the sanctification of the holy day.

b) Hearing God's Word

After Luther assigned the Mass itself a basically irrelevant role, it is not surprising that he considers hearing God's word to be more necessary than hearing the Mass, which according to the will of Christ (1 Cor. 11:25) and Paul (1 Cor. 11:26), is to be celebrated precisely for the sake of the proclamation of the gospel.[449] But after what Luther has said in the first point about the distinctiveness of the Mass, there can be no talk here of a coincidence of the Mass and the proclamation of the gospel in the sense in which he later advocates when he says that the center of the Mass (namely, the words of institution), understood as a promise, are the proclamation of the gospel and that *therefore* the proclamation of the gospel, understood as a promise, is determinative of the sacrament. Luther's only concern here is that no Mass should be held without preaching[450]—and not the preaching of "human matters and the teachings of the law and the philosophers" but the "gospel, that is (according to 1 Cor. 11:25), the remembrance of Christ".[451] What Luther means by this preaching of Christ he explained very clearly six months later in his explanation of the fourth petition of the Lord's Prayer:[452] the word here is not understood as a proclamation but as a basically accidental means to assist the faithful to immerse themselves devotionally in the image of the suffering and dying Christ.

Orality, the public preaching of the word is just as important or unimportant as the external celebration of the Mass. In both cases, the external form—the silent canon in the case of the Mass, or what is contained in the words of the sermon—must first be converted into its inner significance: *signum* and *res* are separated and only connected to each other through the path of interpretation, the sacrament. The *res* behind the silent canon is Christ's invisible work for us with God; the *res* behind the preaching of Christ is the knowledge and confession of one's own sin, the contrition, which is awakened by the contemplation of the crucified one.

---

449. WA 1:444,33–8.

450. WA 1:444,38: "Therefore, it is not permissible to perform the mass without the gospel."

451. WA 1:445,21–22. Cf. from the interpretation of the penitential psalm [Ps. 101] in 1:204,12–17. On the concept of "remembrance" (*memoria*), see pp. 107–109.

452. See pp. 97–102.

According to our text, Luther then quite logically also sees the hearing of God's word once more surpassed, this time by a purely interior event that no longer has any connection to the oral word but is a bare spiritual prayer.[453]

c) Contrition for Sin

This last point is about what is of "the greatest and first importance, namely, to be reconciled to God through the examination of the conscience and contrition for sins."[454]

The "truest contrition, which is living and effectual" and which should spring more from love than hate, consists of two things: hate and contempt for oneself and love and praise for God.[455] "These two things, namely, God's good and our evil, are the very ladder to God, on which we descend into ourselves and ascend into God."[456] Both of these should be heard from the gospel and then

---

453. The third point Luther dealt with was *prayer.* Here he was faced with two alternatives: either outward, mindless babble or inward prayer. However, he does not yet consider that our entire prayer life can be embraced by vocal prayer—that is, that it can also include "inward" mental prayer, prayed with the heart, and that even the prayer of the heart can be included in the externality of the word. Vocal prayer at this stage is merely the occasion for and introduction to spiritual prayer, as we see from WA 1:445,37–38: "For prayer is an ascent of the mind into God ('a definition common in the Middle Ages going back to John of Damascus'; J. Ficker on 56:467,26–27; cf. G. Metzger, *Gelebter Glaube*, 63, n. 33): words are the ladder, but the voice is only the preparation of the ladder" (cf. the simultaneous marginal note on Tauler, who writes: "Thus prayer learned by heart has no other use than to prompt us to this noble devotion" [Vetter 20,9]: "Vocal prayer should be omitted where mental prayer has already begun [9:99,35]). For the understanding of true prayer, the *oratio spiritualis*, Luther refers (1:446,6) to the fifth point, which (according to the formulation of 443,10) is about "being contrite for our sins." Its presentation can be viewed as a whole, but in any case, some parts of it may be seen as a substantive development of the third point.

The five conditions of true prayer (WA 4:624) of the Rogate sermon of 1520, which are entirely based on the reformational concept of the promise, stand in sharp contradiction to the understanding of prayer expressed in this sermon of 1516: see chap. 10.

454. WA 1:446,11–12.

455. WA 1:446,13–14, 21–23.

456. WA 1:447,9–11. It goes on immediately to say (still l.11), "as pictured in Gen. 28"; Ps. 50:23 ("the sacrifice of praise") is then quoted, which the *Glossa ordinaria* (3.157A; see the end of n. 311) interprets thus: "This is the way to God, Jacob's ladder, on which the angels, that is, the faithful, ascend to the praise of God, and descend to the praise of humanity." Our passage (1:447:9–11) means the same as that well-known sentence from the scholion on Rom. 3:5 (WA 56:229,21–22 = LW 25:213): "By going out of himself, God causes us to enter into ourselves, and through his knowledge also gives us knowledge of ourselves" (trans. alt.). It should be noted that, according to these two texts, now the human being and now God appears as the subject in

moved into the heart.[457] They are the sacrifices we offer to God, but in line with the basic principle enunciated at the beginning of the interpretation of the third commandment,[458] not as a work that we do, but as a work that God does: "the sacrifices of praise and confession."[459]

The event that is operative in the praise of God and at the same time[460] in the confession of sins is nothing other than the double movement of justification that is already known to us[461] and that we will encounter in the following from the angle of the promise,[462] which Luther here, so to speak, places in a relationship of varying intensity to the celebration of the Mass, to the hearing of the sermon, and to prayer. However, there is no direct and necessary connection between the celebration of the Mass and justification in praise and confession as the actual event of salvation, apart from the idea of sacrifice, which is not even mentioned here, except in the last point (c). Justification here does not have its proper setting in life (*Sitz im Leben*) in the divine service (*Gottesdienst*)—that is, in the preached promise of the forgiveness of sins, in the oral and public word—but in spiritual prayer, which certainly does not mean quietism but is lived out extremely dynamically in mortification.

---

the same event. In the double confession of God's righteousness and our unrighteousness, God and humans are one (see pp. 52–53).

457. WA 1:447,8–9.

458. See p. 112.

459. WA 1:447,11–16. It is very instructive how Luther understands praise from Ps. 50:23 and confession from Ps. 51:17: "There are also those two sacrifices of praise and confession, of which it says: the sacrifice of praise honors me, and because that is an ascent to God (cf. die *Glossa ordinaria* quoted in n. 456), it follows (v. 23): and that is the path by which I will show them the salvation of God, that is, I will reveal to them eternal salvation. Concerning the second sacrifice it says: Sacrifice to God is a broken spirit, a contrite and humbled heart, O God, you will not despise." Luther tries throughout to emphasize the double aspect of the praise of God and the confession of sin—also in relation to the Lord's Prayer; see from his sermon of Oct. 12, 1516 (according to 1:89, n. 2): "Built into the name, 'Father,' is that ladder of double confession by which the heart is addressed and directed to its most certain contrition, so that it may be fit to pray the following petitions" (1:90,23–25).

460. WA 1:447,16: "These two must be offered together." Cf. also from the scholion on Heb. 3:1: "The confession of sins and of praise is one and the same confession" (WA 57/3:137,16–17 = LW 29:144; cf. 57/3:138,1–4 = 29:144). "The term *confessio* as used by the young Luther" ("Der confessio-Begriff des jungen Luther") is by no means as original as E. Vogelsang's essay of the same name (*Lutherjahrbuch* 12 [1930], 91–108) suggests. One need only note what, for example, J. Altenstaig can say under "confiteri" (Fol. 47^{v}).

461. See pp. 52–53.

462. See pp. 128–130.

This sermon appears again in an extremely brief summary in the spring of 1517 in the *Instruction for the Confession of Sins*,[463] where Luther again gives his interpretation of the third commandment. He says it is fulfilled "by keeping the first and second commandments, that is, by making ourselves fit for grace and offering ourselves as material for God to work on. This happens by praying, hearing the mass and God's word, remembering Christ's suffering, and lamenting our sins. This is what it is to commune spiritually, wholly by God's grace through Jesus Christ."[464] The German version also emphasizes that "this commandment demands a soul poor in spirit, *which offers its non-being before God*, so that it may be God and in its nothingness receive his work and his name."[465] Luther preaches at the same time on the fourth petition of the Lord's Prayer in this sense and defines "preparation" for the Mass as "sacramental meditation on Scripture." This for him is the only right way in which the death of the Lord is "remembered" and he is "proclaimed."[466]

From a few fragmentary utterances in the first Psalms lectures and a single reasonably complete statement on the subject in the sermon of September 21, 1516—nothing more by way of documents on Luther's understanding of the Mass before the Hebrews lectures has come down to us[467]—we have a picture with very specific contours. Above all, it shows that Luther does not see the "sacrament," understood in the sense of the radically conceived *opus operantis*, in tension with the "word." For both are unimportant as external events and thus are understood figuratively. Both stand equally in service of the idea of sacrifice—that is, in service of penitence—understood as the surrender and sacrifice of oneself. The inner and outer life, prayer and ethics, God and the world, all find their unity in it.

Thus the thesis that Luther came to his reformational understanding of the word before he arrived at his new understanding of the sacrament is

463. WA 1:257–65. With Th. Brieger, "Kritische Erörterungen zur neuen Luther-Ausgabe," *ZKG* 11 (1890): 101–54, here 130, 148, we consider 1:264,9–265,11 as an appendix, which was added in 1518 to the "Instruction" that appeared a year earlier. See chap. 5, n. 13.

464. WA 1:263,10–14.

465. WA 1:254,26–28 (author's emphasis).

466. WA 9:146,11–30. Cf. what is said on pp. 97–102 and by E. Bizer, "Die Entdeckung des Sakraments durch Luther," *EvTh* 17 (1957): 64–90, here 76–78, esp. the conclusion: The Lord's Supper in 1517 is still "entirely a means of devotion and is fulfilled wherever people are aroused to devotion by the word" (78–79; cf. *Fides ex auditu*, 136).

467. We are disregarding here Luther's later retrospections (easily accessible in O. Scheel, *Dokumente*; s.v. "Messe" and "Messedienst"). Their negative slant provides no answer to our question and their value is only as evidence of Luther's reformational understanding.

untenable[468] for the following three reasons: 1) in Luther's later theology, word and sacrament are inextricably intertwined; 2) with the radical changes brought about by the Reformation, a new understanding of word and sacrament emerged at the same time through their mutual interpenetration[469]; and 3) even in his early period, Luther had a unified conception of word and sacrament. So for these reasons, Luther's reformational understanding of the sacrament predates his new conception of the word, not only in time but also especially in terms of its content.[470]

2. Promise—Faith

From what has been said so far, it follows that, for the early Luther, faith is not created by an oral and binding word of salvation but is only kept in motion by way of negation, thus without any real basis and without any certainty. But does this view not have to change if we look at the numerous passages, especially in the first Psalms lectures, where Luther insists that with the sending of Jesus, God has spoken his "abbreviated and completed word" (Isa. 10:22–23 = Rom. 9:28) "in the midst of the years" (Hab. 3:2)[471] and so has fulfilled his promises to the fathers of the old covenant and thereby demonstrated his faithfulness (*fides*), to which we can now respond in faith (*fides*), where faith is understood as the tropological fulfillment of the promise? In short, we are asking how we are to understand the well-known marginal gloss on Romans 4:14, "*faith and the promise are correlative*" (*fides et promissio sunt relativa*),[472] and at the same time how the famous

468. Against W. Jetter, *Die Taufe beim jungen Luther*, 191, who maintains that "*the priority of the word over the sacrament* was, as far as we can tell, *the starting point of Luther's general doctrine of the sacraments from the very beginning*."

469. The second part of our investigation will show this.

470. We have a different understanding to Ebeling of the view of word and sacrament that Luther has been advocating with increasing consistency from the time of the Hebrews lectures onward. Contra Ebeling, this is not "simply the clarification of his basic position" (Luther, 2: *Theologie*, *RGG*, 3rd ed., 4:502) "that Luther had previously reached and that still had to be developed on the basis of the church's teaching about the means of grace with which Luther's position was at variance" (503). Since we cannot prove the necessary connection between Luther's "basic position" and its "development" (to use Ebeling's terms), which Ebeling obviously assumes—which is the negative finding of this whole intermediate chapter—neither do we have "the right to call Luther's basic theological insight (i.e. his early doctrine of justification) a reformational turn that required and enabled him to take the step to the reformational event itself" (503). Cf. Ebeling, *Luther. An Introduction to His Thought*, 70–71, 73–74.

471. Cf. chap. 1 C, esp, nn. 82 and 83.

472. WA 56:45,15 = LW 25:39 (trans. alt). Cf. H. Bornkamm, *ARG* 53 (1962): 1–60, here 6, n. 29.

scholion on Romans 1:17,[473] whose meaning is disputed,[474] is to be understood in the context of Luther's first Psalms lectures and his Romans lectures.

H) The Fulfillment of the Promise in Christ[475] [Rom. 3:3; Ps. 85]

1. Luther sees two possible interpretations of the ambivalence of *FIDES* in *Romans 3:3* (WILL THEIR UNBELIEF NULLIFY THE FAITHFULNESS OF GOD?): one with reference to the faithfulness of God,[476] the other with reference to the faith of human beings.[477] Yet there is no real difference between these two possibilities; they do not contradict each other but even correspond. "For whatever is said concerning the objective truth of faith in a literal sense, the same is also understood in a moral sense concerning our faith in this truth." Luther then formulates it in his dictated lectures thus: "For whatever is said concerning the truth of God, since it is the object and correlative of faith, the same is also understood in a moral sense concerning our faith in this same truth."[478] The fact that "belief in God" itself is the "fulfillment of the promise,"[479] is due to its correlate, that to which it is directed: the faithfulness of God, which is identical with his fulfilled promise. "That is, Christ, according to that verse of Psalm 85: 'Truth has sprung up from the earth,' that is, the promised Christ has come forth from the Virgin."[480]

---

473. WA 56:171,26–172,15. The text is of interest to us in this context, not for what it says about "righteousness" but specifically for what it says about the understanding of the word. Above all, it raises the question, "In what sense does Luther here use Mark 16:16?" But since this cannot be determined exactly from the scholion itself, we will approach it by way of the interpretation of Ps. 51: see sec. I (p. 123).

474. Cf. Bornkamm, 1–2.

475. Besides the texts dealt with below, see the line gloss on Ps. 100:5: "HIS TRUTH is the demonstration of his promised mercy, or as the Hebrew says, 'his faithfulness.' For faithfulness is itself the grace and mercy once promised, because by it we are justified and saved. For in the faithfulness of Christ, all the things that were once promised are given to us" (WA 4:127,17–20). See also the scholion on Ps. 119:90 (WA 4:350,25–31 = LW 11:477), and the scholion on Ps. 119:160 (4:379,25–380,3 = 11:517).

476. WA 56:224,15–20 = 57/1:146,19–147,3 = LW 25:209.

477. WA 56:224,20–23,25–225,1 = WA 57/1:147,3–15. The double sense of *fides* was noted already by Augustine (*Concerning the Spirit and the Letter* 31:54; CSEL 60:211): "According to this faith, by which we believe, we are faithful to God; but according to that other faith, by which he does what he promises, God himself is also faithful to us."

478. WA 56:224,23–25 (supplement). WA 57/1:147,15–18 = LW 25:209.

479. WA 56:224,21–22 (WA= 57/1:147,3–4) = LW 25:209.

480. WA 57/1:146,17–19 (= WA 56:224,13–15) = LW 25:209 (trans. alt.).

Even if Luther himself had not pointed this out to us, we would still have to have gone back to the interpretation of Psalm 85 in the *Dictata* to understand the scholion on Romans 3:3. For there is no other passage in the early texts where Luther gives the same thematic attention to this matter.[481]

2. According to *Psalm 85:10–11*, "mercy" (*misericordia*) and "truth" (*veritas*), the grace of God[482] and the fulfillment of his promise,[483] have met in the person of Christ.[484] Luther understands both terms, as he explains using the exact words of Lyra, in the sense of salvation history and the incarnation.[485] The "truth" understood as fulfillment has two aspects: in terms of salvation history in relation to the promise, it is faithfulness, while ontologically, in relation to the "figure" or "shadow," it is reality.[486]

Luther now derives the following double aspect from these two terms: what God promises and that he even makes a promise at all and binds himself to it, he does out of "mercy"—"for us."[487] That he keeps his promise and delivers on it demonstrates his "truthfulness"—"for himself."[488] For the fact that God in his promise makes himself a debtor by no means puts him at our disposal. God

---

481. That Ps. 85:10–11 remains important is evident from the reference to this text, for example, in the *Sermon on Prayer and Procession During Rogation Days* (1519), sec. 4 (WA 2:176,21–177,11 = LW 42:88–89).

482. WA 4:2,20.

483. WA 4:2,20.

484. WA 4:2,20–21. The "truth" is the faithfulness with which God stands by his promises (e.g., 3:167,3–4 [on Ps. 31:23]; 3:226,7–8 [on Ps. 40:10]). Since he honors and fulfills them in Christ, Christ is God's faithfulness in person (e.g., 3:167,34: "Christ is his truth and faithfulness" [on Ps. 31:23]; 3:226,10–11 [on Ps. 40:10]).

485. "Lyra explains it well when he says (and this is especially emphasized by Luther): 'Mercy and truth have met each other,' that is, they have come together in one person. For by God's mercy, the Word took on flesh to fulfil the truth of the promise made to the fathers of the Old Testament concerning the incarnation of God's Son" (WA 4:13,9–13 = LW 11:165 [trans. alt.] = Lyra on Ps. 85:10: 3:212C). Cf. 4:13,27–28 = 11:166: "Mercy and truth have met each other, revealed in one deed and work." Cf. the gloss at 4:2,22–23.

486. "Here it should be noted that truth is (1) sometimes contrasted with what is false and lying and (2) sometimes contrasted with the shadow and the figure" (WA 4:12,35–37 = LW 11:164–65 (trans. alt.); cf. the explanation in 4:12,37–13,9). For the interesting interweaving of salvation-historical and ontological thinking in the first Psalms lectures, cf. especially the scholion on Ps. 64:9: 3:368,18–35 = 10:311 (cf. chap. 1, n. 75) and the marginal gloss on Ps. 66:5: 3:375,25–33.

487. WA 4:2,38–41 (no LW trans.); 4:13,13–15, 17–18 = LW 11:165. Cf. 4:13,32–33 = 11:166.

488. WA 4:2,38–41: 4:13,15–17,18 = LW 11:165; cf. 4:13,32–33: "Divine goodness is merciful in one affection and true in another; merciful for our sake, but true for its own sake."

owes the fulfillment to himself, not to us, to his promise, not to our merit.[489] "The fact that Christ came and was born was sheer promise and not merit. And by this very fact we are now justified, namely, by his coming. It is not that we first became righteous and deserving, and that God then showed that he was faithful by sending him."[490]

But the promise that was fulfilled in salvation history and the incarnation now needs to be grasped, "for although Christ's coming is for all, not all received him . . . he was promised to all and offered to all, but not all are thereby justified."[491] Basically, this problem of communicating and appropriating the fulfilled promise comes up at the end of the interpretation:

> As for the tropology of the Psalm, I believe that it is readily apparent from what has often been said. For whatever is said of his first coming into the flesh is understood at the same time to refer to his spiritual coming. Indeed, his coming into the flesh is determined and comes about because of that spiritual coming. Otherwise, it would have been of no use. Hence, also these words "mercy and truth" cannot be affirmed of Christ except because of his second advent, and for that reason this is chiefly intended. For what good would it do for God to become human, if it were not that by believing, we might be saved? Therefore, Christ is not called our Righteousness, Peace, Mercy, and Salvation in his person except in an effectual sense. But it is faith in Christ by which we are justified and granted peace, and it is by that faith that Christ reigns in us.[492]

But even with the emphasis on the effective character of the tropology, its shape is not yet precisely delineated. Has Christ already become for Luther here a concrete oral word of promise that is fulfilled by creating faith? With his interpretation of the term *righteousness*, Luther at least points us in the direction in which we should look for the answer to this question.

---

489. Luther's formulation, "(God) made himself a debtor by promising and not by receiving anything—and what did he make himself a debtor of by his promise if not sheer grace and mercy?" (WA 4:13,25–7 = LW 11:166), probably follows Augustine's exposition of Ps. 84 (*Enarrationes in Psalmos 83*): "The Lord made himself a debtor, not by receiving, but by promising; it is not said to him: 'Hand over what you received,' but, 'hand over what you promised'" (*CCL* 39:1160 [= MPL 37:1068]).

490. WA 4:17,22–25 = LW 11:171 (trans. alt.); cf. WA 4:17,36.

491. WA 4:17,27–31 = LW 11:172 (trans. alt.).

492. WA 4:19,31–39 = LW 11:174 (trans. alt.).

Verse 12 (TRUTH HAS SPRUNG UP FROM THE EARTH, AND RIGHTEOUSNESS HAS LOOKED DOWN FROM HEAVEN) contrasts "truth" and "righteousness." For Luther, this expresses the tension between the origin and goal of faith and the movement arising from it: "truth" pushes, "righteousness" pulls. "And thus through truth he comes to us, and through righteousness we come to him."[493] With the promise, God's "truth," which is fulfilled in the history of salvation-incarnational sense, we are not yet given the final "righteousness." Only those who seek and accept the "truth" are justified.[494] But what exactly does this seeking and accepting of God's truth mean for the early Luther? This can no longer be known from the interpretation of Psalm 85 and Romans 3:3 but must be found in the immediately following interpretation of Romans 3:4–5, in which Luther takes up his interpretation of Psalm 51:4 from the first Psalms lectures. Only in this passage do we find one of the two aspects of the understanding of the promise that is decisive and typical of the early Luther and that must be understood as an authentic interpretation or culmination of his statements about salvation history and the incarnation. But the following section will show that this culmination is in fact a turn, not a real climax, and that, for the decisive area of tropology, we have to speak rather of the "fulfillment of the promise in judgment."

I) The Fulfillment of the Promise in Judgment[495] [Ps. 51; Rom. 3:4–5]

1. When we look back from *The Babylonian Captivity* to the interpretation of Psalm 51 in the *Dictata*, there can be no doubt that it is precisely the notion of promise that allows us to determine the reformational turn in Luther's theology with the utmost clarity and specificity.

In *The Babylonian Captivity*, Luther relies on three "promises." Two of them, the words of distribution in the Lord's Supper and the words about the binding and loosing of sins (Matt. 16:19; 18:18; John 20:23), are clearly not taken up

493. WA 4:17,38–39 (cf. the context: ll. 33–39) = LW 11:171.

494. WA 4:17,42–18,4 = LW 11:171.

495. For this heading, see specifically the scholion on Ps. 111:7 (THE WORKS OF HIS HANDS ARE TRUTH AND JUDGMENT): "'Truth' is every good thing by which the spirit is saved, for it cannot be saved by carnal things, which are a shadow, but only by the truth, which is eternal. And these good things are therefore called 'truth' because, having been once promised, they are now given, and because they are not written and temporal. But '*judgment*' is every condemnation and crucifixion of the old self, which is likewise *truth*, that is, the *fulfillment of the promise*" (WA 4:245,31–36 = LW 11:381; trans. alt.; author's emphasis). See the Romans lectures (on 3:5): 56:231,6–19, esp. 14–15 = 25:215: "It was foretold that the kingdom of Christ would be in the form of this humility and judgment."

anywhere before the Hebrews lectures.[496] This is in contrast to the words about baptism in Mark 16:16, which in the early texts appear in a few places, the most important of which is the interpretation of Psalm 51.[497]

First, we need to point out the continuity in Luther's theology. As in 1520, Mark 16:16 is understood here in line with the nominalist tradition[498] as a declaration of God's will. Luther remarks, "He made a testament (*testamentum*) and a pact (*pactum*) with us so that whoever believes and is baptized will be saved... In this pact, God is true and faithful and saves as he promised."[499] With Mark 16:16, God in his sovereignty ties himself down "freely"—"that is, by his election

496. a) We only come across Matt. 18:18 a single time, and that is as the text for the sermon on the Feast of St. Peter in Chains (Aug. 1), 1516. But nowhere in the fragment of this sermon preserved for (WA 1:69) is there any mention of the keyword about binding and losing. Further, we find it again in the sermon for Candlemas in WA 1:130–32 (= WA 4:636–39). Löscher dates this text in one place to 1517 (supported also by E. Vogelsang, *ZKG* 50 [1931]: 112–45, here 134), and in another to 1518 (see 1:130, n. 1). But we can say for certain that it belongs to the year 1518 when Luther was drafting the *Explanations of the Ninety-Five Theses* because it specifically bears their stamp. The reference to precisely Matt. 16:19 (1:131,5–19) is unexpected in view of the text (Mal. 3:1–4) and only makes sense if he was preoccupied elsewhere with the sacrament of penance: see "Explanation" 7 and 38. Further, WA 1:131,2–4 should be compared with "Explanation" 58 (LW 31:212) and WA 1:131,33–37 with "Explanation" 15 (LW 31:125).

b) The formula of distribution of the Lord's Supper is only adduced in WA 56:385,28–31 (= 57/1:198,2–4) = LW 25:376 as proof that not all people are elected ("'for many'—he does not say 'for all'": l.30). The fact that these are the gifting words of the sacrament is not important for Luther at this time.

497. We will include the other two passages of the *Dictata* (WA 4:92,26–27 = LW 11:243 and 4:193,12–13) in our presentation immediately. WA 1:43,1–2 and 3:75,30–31 take up Mark 16:16 in a different respect. It is interesting that Luther uses this text in his early Erfurt sermon on John 3:16 (4:601,7–25), which reveals a theological understanding that is given up already in his Psalms lectures. In the Romans lectures, he refers to Mark 16:16 in the scholion on 1:17 (56:171:26–172,15 = 25:151–52; cf. 57/1:14,1–5) and on 1:29 (56:186,22–25 = 25:168).

498. According to Biel (IV/d 1/q 2/a 1 [A]), God instituted the sacraments freely, of his own accord, and not out of compulsion. (Cf. the concluding sentence of Lect. 59 S in the commentary on the Mass [2:447]: "God is our debtor by his own merciful will, not by reason of necessity"). According to the ordinance of Christ, "unless one is born again... John 3:5" (= Mark 16:16: see IV/d 1/q 4/a 3 [H] and IV/d 4/q 1/a 2 [F]), no one can be saved without the sacrament (and faith: see IV/d 4/q 1/a 2 [F]). For the earlier Franciscan voluntarist tradition, see Bonaventure: "The institution of Baptism, where Christ said: whoever believes," gives an "effectual and infallible ordinance for the reception of grace" (III/d 40/dub 3; 3:895 b). "For the Lord made a pact when he said in the last chapter of Mark: whoever believes..." (IV/d 3/a 1/q 3; 4:69 b). See H. A. Oberman, *ZKG* 78 (1967): 232–52, here 243.

499. WA 3:289,3–5. Also in the line gloss on Ps. 105:8, Mark 16:16 appears as the words of divine institution. They must be recognized and accepted as the declaration of God's will: "HE COMMANDED, God ordained that these words are taken as a command, so that whoever believes will be saved" (WA 4:193,12–13; cf. the context of ll.10–22).

of predestination."[500] He will not go back on what he determined and instituted, for he cannot deny himself (2 Tim. 2:13).[501]

With our comparison, however, we must pay close attention to a shift that is not just an insignificant nuance but a profound difference.

According to *The Babylonian Captivity*, the content of faith, which Mark 16:16a speaks of in the preceding relative clause, arises from the statement of the main clause: the promise of salvation is to be believed, and those who believe God's promise of salvation are saved.[502] Those reached by his word and sacrament belong to God's elect, as Luther now expressly tells those listening to his sermon.[503]

For the interpretation of Psalm 51, on the other hand, God's promise of salvation is identical with his verdict of judgment, which is the sole determinant of faith: those who judge themselves and thus agree with God's judgment on them will be saved.[504]

---

500. WA 4:92,26–27 = LW 11:243 (scholion on Ps. 94:1: God acts "'freely,' that is, through the election of predestination, not through the succession of birth or of any pact, but 'whoever believes will be saved'" [trans. alt.]).

501. Cf. WA 3:291,18 = LW10:240: "God cannot deny himself" (on the context 3:291,14–21, see pp. 124–127) with 6:528,28 = 36:60 (here, in *The Babylonian Captivity*, expressly taking up 2 Tim. 2:13), and compare both with Lect. 59 S of Biel's commentary on the Mass: "Although the promise itself is contingent, as is also predestination, and although what God has promised he is able not to have promised, and although he is able not to save those he has predestined in the divided sense, since he is able not to have predestined them, nevertheless, he is not able not to keep his promise in the composite sense. Hence 2 Tim. 2[:13]: GOD CANNOT DENY HIMSELF" (2:446–47).

502. Luther begins the programmatic account of his understanding of baptism with Mark 16:16 (WA 6:527,33–34 = LW 36:58). He expressly refers to this passage again in 6:533,29–534,2 = 36:67 and 6:543,31–33 = 36:82. Cf. here esp. l. 33: "believing that they would obtain salvation."

503. Probably in 1520 (cf. WA 4:706, n. 1), Luther preaches: "Do not doubt then, my friends, that if you have received the sacrament, you are ready either for life or death, as your Lord God pleases, and that you are truly blessed and holy on account of the power of the one who promises this and who therefore makes himself the pledge of your blessedness. You could not dishonor God anymore (who for you is the truest and most reliable of all) than by doubting that you are numbered among the saints. *Unless you were numbered among the saints, he would not have offered you his word and sacrament.* But 'whoever does not believe will be condemned'" (4:712,42–713,7; author's emphasis). On the use of Mark 16:16 as a preached promise of salvation, see the first reformational text—namely, the "Explanation" of thesis 38 of the *Theses on Indulgences* (1518): 1:595,1–4 = 31:193. On that, see pp. 223–225.

504. We cannot relativize this statement by pointing to the wording of the psalm that Luther interpreted. Why, then, does he quote Mark 16:16 just here? Obviously, he wants this text to be understood in the context of Ps. 51.

"It is true that we always stand in our sin before him, so that he, according to the pact and testament he made with us, may be our justifier. Hence the Hebrew literally says: 'Against you, you only, have I sinned. Therefore, you are justified in your word,' that is, according to your pact. Consequently, those who do not sin or do not confess their sin are not justified by God in accordance with his pact, for since 'they do not believe etc.,' God cannot justify them."[505] God wills to give his grace only to the humble (1 Pet. 5:5).[506] This will enshrines the true soteriological center of salvation history (*Heilsgeschichte*).[507] God has commanded all people to recognize and confess their sin.[508] Luther interpreted Mark 16:16 from Galatians 3:22 (or Rom. 11:32), putting all the emphasis on the first half of the Pauline verse with its focus on sin.[509] However, ultimately the decisive sentence, which guides the early Luther's understanding of the promise, is a passage that we know already is significant for him from the "internal sacrament, and that is 1 Corinthians 11:31":[510]

> Therefore, sin must always be feared, and we must always be accused and judged in the presence of God. If we judge ourselves, we will certainly not be judged by the Lord; for we will not be judged twice for the same thing. God cannot condemn us if we have already judged ourselves and judged ourselves by his own words. For God cannot deny himself. But he has judged him [David] to be a sinner, and yet David has already done the same thing himself. Therefore, God cannot be against him, since

505. WA 3:289,6–10 = LW 10:237 (trans. alt.). For the consequences of this idea of the pact, see the *Operationes in Psalmos* on Ps. 22:25: 5:663–64, esp. 663,27–35; 664,18–19 ("Remember the pact you entered into: you promised to justify God and to condemn yourself continually—do this and you will be saved").

506. Cf. the scholion on Ps. 84:11, "This is truth, to be humbled and know yourself. Then he will give you grace and glory, for he gives his glory to the humble, and exalts the humble and lowly" (WA 3:651,35–37 = LW 11:149; trans. alt.), and the marginal gloss at Rom. 11:10, "God has determined to do good to the humble, that is, his elect" (56:109,19–20 = 25:98; trans. alt.).

507. The "truth," still hidden in the old covenant but now revealed (Rom. 3:21): WA 3:285,7–9, means "not the shadow of the law in its righteousness but the truth of your righteousness, which is humility and confession of sin, accusation of self" (WA 3:285,5–7; on Ps. 51:6). Cf. n. 495.

508. Cf. the line gloss on v. 4 (WA 3:284, 24–25): "IN YOUR WORDS, in which you promised your righteousness and decreed that all people are in sin" (note the parallelism of both parts of the sentence!).

509. Cf. Gal. 3:22 in the Latin text with the line gloss quoted in n. 508. The marginal gloss on Rom. 11:32 refers back explicitly to Ps. 51:4 (Against you, and you only, have I sinned): WA 56:115,16 (cf. 56:115,6–8) = LW 25:102.

510. Cf. p. 32.

> David has judged himself in this way. Otherwise, God would be against the very person who was conformed to him in judgment. Therefore, God must recognize and approve David's own judgment against himself.[511]

Here an old tradition of monasticism[512] is closely linked with the idea of God's pact, which is so important for nominalism. This alone puts faith and grace in a very specific relationship to each other:[513] *Whoever believes, that is, whoever judges themselves, will be saved, that is, will no longer be judged.*[514] But you are no longer judged, not because you judge yourself but because God, according

511. WA 3:291,14–21 = LW 10:240; trans. alt. (cf. whole interpretation of Ps. 51, but esp. 3:289,34–37 = 10:237–38; 291,27–28 = 10:240). The matter addressed here has fundamental validity: "This insight is useful not only for this verse or this psalm but for all the psalms" (3:291,39–292,10 = 10:241). Cf. on the use of 1 Cor. 11:31 the scholion on Ps. 72:4: WA 3:465,31–35.

Dionysius the Carthusian (Fol. 53 F) interprets 1 Cor. 11:31 like Luther: "Then he shows how we can avoid God's wrath and judgment. IF WE JUDGED OURSELVES, that is, if we considered, reproved, and punished our sins, saying: Against you, you only have I sinned . . . WE WOULD NOT BE JUDGED . . . concerning which John says that whoever believes in the Son is not judged, i.e., we are not condemned . . . The Lord will not judge us twice for the same thing." See the corresponding use of 1 Cor. 11:31 in Gerson's sermon on Mark 1:15 (REPENT AND BELIEVE THE GOSPEL); *Opera* 2:40, in Biel, Lect. 72 G (3:191); and in Cajetan's tractate: *Whether for a fruitful reception of absolution in the sacrament of penance, we must have that faith by which penitents believe with full certainty that they are absolved by God* (*Opuscula* 1575, 110, 56ff.) of Sept. 26, 1518. *Cajetan therefore in his polemic against Luther's newly discovered theology of the word with its power to give certainty* (see chap. 4), *relies on the very passage that Luther's own early theology had latched onto in a special way!*

512. Cf. p. 32. Augustine's interpretation of Ps. 85:11 should also be considered: "TRUTH HAS SPRUNG UP FROM THE EARTH in the confession of sins; AND RIGHTEOUSNESS LOOKS DOWN FROM THE SKY so that this publican could go home justified . . . What RIGHTEOUSNESS LOOKS DOWN FROM THE SKY? The righteousness of God that says, as it were: Let us spare this person, for they did not spare themselves; let us forgive them, for they acknowledge [their sins]" (*CCL* 29:1174 [= MPL 37:1079]).

513. WA 3:289,1–3: "Even faith and grace, by which we are justified today, would not justify us by themselves unless God had made a pact. For it is precisely for that reason that . . ." (then follows the text quoted above and documented in n. 499).

514. Cf. the "Explanation" of thesis 5 of the *Theses on Indulgences*: "The cross and the mortification of our passions," according to 1 Cor. 11:31, are "commanded by Christ and are of the essence of spiritual penance and wholly *necessary for salvation*" (WA 1:534,31–35 = LW 31:90; trans. alt.; author's emphasis. Cf. the parallel statements in Luther's *Asterisci*: 1:284-85, esp. 285,5–7). Concerning thesis 4 of the *Heidelberg Disputation*, Luther says: "This ugliness in us however comes about either because of God's punishment or our own self-accusation, as 1 Cor. 11[:31] says . . . In this way therefore the ugly works that God produces in us, that is, works that are humble and devout, are truly immortal for humility and fear of God are our entire merit" (1:357,12–17 = 31:44; trans. alt.). Cf. thesis 12 of the same disputation: "God pardons us only as much as we accuse ourselves" (1:359,29–30 = 31:48; trans. alt.).

to his pact, no longer judges those who judge themselves—just as, for Biel, you do not enter into eternal life because you keep the commandments but because God, in faithfulness to his pact, cannot and will not leave those who keep them go unrewarded.[515]

2. The notion of the promise in Luther's interpretation of Psalm 51, which clearly differs from that of his reformational view, continues to influence his interpretation of *Romans 3:4–5*. First Corinthians 11:31 is nowhere specifically quoted here; but Mark 16:16 appears again in the same relation to the confession of sins: "Thus also God's justification in his words is rather our justification; and his judgment or condemnation is rather ours according to the saying, 'Whoever does not believe will be condemned.'"[516]

The promise of salvation is fulfilled in negative reflection on oneself: in the confession of sins and self-accusation, not by immediately believing in the *promise*: "We believe from the heart that we are sinners, that we act, speak, and live wickedly, and that we are in error, and so we accuse, judge, condemn, and hate ourselves. 'Whoever does these things shall never be moved' (Ps. 15:5)."[517]

Against the background of the interpretation of Psalm 51, we can also recognize its special pact theology in that formula that includes the whole complex interpretation of Romans 3:4–5: "*When God is justified, he justifies, and when he*

515. Cf. Lect. 59 R (2:444–45) especially: "For God's part, since he made a promise, justice demands that he pay up. For it is only just that he keep his promise. Hence the laborer is told: TAKE WHAT IS YOURS [Matt. 20:14]. Not to pay up would be unjust of him. But this justice is not a natural act but arises from the immensely generous promise of God who willingly made himself a debtor and obligated himself of his own free will to pay so great a reward for such work. And so there the worthiness arises from the faithfulness of the promiser, for since he stands by that promise of his master, to pay up is the only just thing to do, while not to pay would be unjust, although that justice depends solely on the immensely generous will of God, who promises such great rewards" (2:445). And see (2:446–47) especially: "For although, by the nature of things, God cannot be a debtor to any creature, yet by the nature of his immutable faithfulness and his generous and voluntary promise, he is free to make himself a debtor to his creation. By the same token, since he stands by his promise to give eternal life to those who keep his commands, he could not without injustice withdraw the rewards promised to them. For although he is wholly a debtor to no one and is able not to give an eternal reward to his creatures, just as he can also put off destroying them, nevertheless, since he stands by his promise and ordinance to give them life, he cannot destroy them, nor can he not give them the life he promised. For this ordinance and promise is nothing but an act of the divine will by which he wills to give them life at some point. Therefore, that will, since it is immutable, is not compatible with the will not to pay them their due" (2:446). See Lect. 47 X (2:227–28).

516. WA 56:213,13–15 = LW 25:198; trans. alt. (Mark 16:16a belongs to the first part of the statement about justification and corresponds to the second about judgment and condemnation). Cf., however, n. 503.

517. WA 56:233,17–19 = LW 25:218 (trans. alt.). Cf. 56:228,21–22 = 25:213: "Who can receive grace and righteousness except those who confess that they have sin?" (trans. alt.)

justifies, he is justified."[518] We encountered this formula and its closest context[519] in the first part of this chapter in connection with the "word and God"[520] and, by way of the scholion on Romans 6:17,[521] in connection with the Christ event understood as a word of judgment.[522] Now we see how, for Luther, our correspondence to the Word in his humiliation is expressly sanctioned by divine decree.[523]

Against the background of the prehistory of the interpretation of Romans 3:4–5 in the first Psalms lectures, the dialectic of the active and passive justification of God is thus identical with the double-sidedness of God's pact as formulated in Mark 16:16. This dominical word, which according to *The Babylonian Captivity* can be taken homiletically as the baptismal promise, is only interpreted in the sense of Luther's early theology when seen in the light of 1 Corinthians 11:31. That is, for early Luther, *the promise of salvation is realized specifically in the confession of sins and the judgment of self.* This is the center of Luther's monastic existence and at the same time of his early theology. It is understandable that the professor of biblical theology is particularly preoccupied with the texts that he uses almost hourly as a friar: especially therefore with Psalm 51, which is prayed at the end of every canonical hour.[524] Psalm 51:4 is quoted in Romans 3:4. Thus the remarkable interest that Luther takes in this text in his Romans lectures is not all that surprising given that he tries to interpret it again and again in a whole series of scholia.

The *plea* for righteousness arises from the confession of sins.[525] This is the main theme of the interpretation of Romans 4:7, and it can be shown that this also has its background in the theology of the pact.[526]

---

518. WA 56:227,7–8 (= 57/1:149,10–11) = LW 25:211 (trans. alt.). The formula prepares for, for example, 56:212,26–33 = 25:198; 56:213,4–5 = 25:198; 56:213,13–15 = 25:199; 56:215,5–9 = 25:200; 56:218,7–219,11 = 25:204; 56:220,9–221,3 = 25:205 (cf. 56:221,15–19 = 25:206 and 56:222,5–6 = 25:206–7); 56:221,27–36 = 25:206; 56:225,25–226,1,4–6 = 25:210.

519. WA 56:226,23–227,16 = LW 25:211–12 (cf. 56:224,23–25 = 25:209 (on this, see pp. 119–121 and 56:227,18–228,2 = 25:211–12).

520. See pp. 52–53.

521. Cf. n. 25.

522. See pp. 21–22 and pp. 26–27.

523. Cf. pp. 74–75.

524. H. A. Köstlin, *RE*, 3rd ed., 13:88,4–5 (s.v. "Miserere"). Cf. chap. 3 A 1.

525. Cf. WA 56:221,29–33 = LW 25:206: "When I acknowledge that I cannot be righteous before God . . . then I begin to ask for righteousness from him. And so the acknowledgment of my sin compelled me to ask that God might be justified in me (i.e. that I might believe in him and that he would therefore justify me)."

526. See section L ("Promise and Supplication").

In the last two sections, we have considered two aspects of the promise one *after* the other: first, its salvation-historical and incarnational aspect (H) and then its tropological aspect (I). However, these two aspects are *intertwined* in the scholion on Romans 9:28. The dialectic of negation and fulfillment that Luther develops here within the correlation of word and faith has exemplary significance for the entire period of the Romans lectures.

K) The Word That Completes and Abbreviates [Romans 9:28]

In Romans 9:28, Luther is faced with a striking double determination of the word ("it abbreviates and completes"), which was of fundamental importance to the exegetical tradition and to Luther himself, at the time of his exegesis of the psalms, for his understanding of "word and Christ."[527] In fact, it became a crystallization point for his whole theology, which was governed by the idea of negation (*via negationis*).

According to the *Glossa ordinaria*, the "word that abbreviates and completes" excludes the "boasting of works" "and abbreviates all legal matters into the one Christ . . . so that God might save by grace through the abridgment of faith: not by countless works."[528] If the emphasis here is on exclusion rather than compression,[529] then with Luther it is the reverse, and compression is foremost rather than exclusion. In fact, he emphasizes the compression in a fundamental expansion that goes beyond the problem of the law.

The one word is divided into two determinations: "it is completed because it announces divine and invisible things" and is "abbreviated . . . because it is cut off from everything visible and figurative."[530] At first glance, these two determinations appear to have different meanings. Luther says, "These two refer to different things: 'completed' to the end point but 'abbreviated' to the starting point."[531]

527. Cf. n. 529 and n. 539 and see pp. 16–18 (esp. n. 83) and p. 88.

528. 6:22E.

529. The *Glossa interlinearis* probably formulates it in the same sense: "The abbreviated word is love, on which depend the law and the prophets." Likewise, for Lyra the same is true of the "WORD THAT COMPLETES, namely, the gospel: because it is the perfection (*sic*!) of the law" and of the word that "ABBREVIATES because it cuts off all legal matters: which have no place in the new law" (6:22G).

530. WA 57/1:206,7–10.

531. WA 57: 206,13–14. Luther had already tried to do the same thing in the first Psalms lectures in the addendum to the interpretation of Ps. 74: "'End' is twofold; it has two senses, that of destruction (*consumptio*) and that of completion (*consummatio*). This can agree with philosophical thinking about the end 'by which' (*de fino quo*) and 'for the sake of which' (*gratia cuius*). The end 'by which' is that of destruction and cessation, while the end 'for the sake of which' is that of attainment and acquisition" (WA 3:506,23–26 = LW 10:450; trans. alt.). "Therefore, Christ

But since the "to which" is no more than the negation of the "from which," they collapse contentwise into a single back and forth movement (think of the scholion on Rom. 12:2![532]), which of course can only be represented conceptually by separating their two opposing aspects. But these two, the "abbreviation" and the "completion" hold true at the same time: "*When the word is completed, it is abbreviated, and conversely, when it is abbreviated, it is completed.*"[533] These two aspects are so intertwined that the question, which of them is basically the more determinative, seems to be left in abeyance. But the dialectic cannot hide the fact that it ultimately lives by its negation, in its abbreviation, its separation from all visible things, and in its denial and radical exclusion.[534]

To be sure, it is said that the word is abbreviated and abbreviating, "because it is a 'completed,' that is, a finished word."[535] But what does this explanation mean if, immediately afterward, this completion is again determined solely by what has been negated?[536]

We must not underestimate the enormous power of negation: it cuts off wrong paths and detours, does away with the law in its fragmentation, and leads through abstraction from the manifold to a concentration on the one (see the section on "God and the Word"[537] and the interpretation of Psalm 45 in the *Dictata*[538]).[539] Without doubt, *this understanding of the positive role of negation,*

is called the end . . . because he completes and destroys." And, similarly, "faith in him is, like himself, the word that completes and abbreviates" (WA 3:507,12–15 = LW 3:451; trans. alt.).

532. See sec. A.

533. WA 56:407,24–25 = LW 25:397 (author's emphasis); cf. WA 56:410,12–19 = LW 25:400.

534. WA 56:406,27–31 = LW 25:396; 56:407:13–16 = 25:397.

535. WA 56:407,16–17 = LW 25:397 (trans. alt.).

536. WA 56:407,18–24 = LW 25:397. On the fact that "God alone" (l. 24) is also only a negative determination, see pp. 54–55.

537. See pp. 56–57.

538. See chap. 1 C, esp. n. 83.

539. This idea, common in the first Psalms lectures, is mostly connected with STRAIGHT (RECTUM), STRAIGHTNESS (RECTITUDO), etc.: "'To direct' is to lead by a straight path and a short way, not by a circuitous and roundabout way. But this does not happen except in the truth and faith of Christ, as Isa. 10[:23] says: 'for the Lord will execute his word upon the earth, a word that abbreviates and completes,' that is, a word of faith, which is finished and brief. The Law of Moses, like human laws, did not lead to the truth but to a roundabout path of figures and of endless ceremonies, as symbolized by the fact that the people of Israel wandered in the wilderness for forty years" (Gloss on Ps. 25:5, WA 3:143,23–29). "I have directed my steps, i.e., I have walked by a straight path and a short way, not in the long circuitous way of the letter, but in the abbreviated way of the spirit" (Gloss on Ps. 59:4: 3:326,35–37 and its scholion: 3:333,1–3, 9–13). See 3:150,3; 3:178,32–33; 3:383,14–15; 3:567,11–15; and esp. the

as we see it in the interpretation of Romans 9:28, is an extremely important aspect of the prehistory of the reformational exclusive particle. Negation will later be an indispensable part of the unambiguity of the word, but it cannot create this on its own. For while an affirmation without a negation would be blind because it would be caught in the confusion of the ambiguous, a negation without a real affirmation is empty because it is always being referred back to itself.

This is also evident in the understanding of time that Luther briefly develops for the word in the interplay of *abbreviatio* and *consummatio* and corresponding to this in the following brilliant sequence: "The word of the gospel is completed, because it gives what it signifies, namely, grace. Therefore, it is also abbreviated, because it does not defer what it signifies, but instead cuts itself off from everything that prolongs and impedes its reception."[540]

What is signified by the word is not far removed from it[541] but is given with it (it "gives what it signifies"); the word does not draw out or delay its fulfillment ("it does not defer it") but brings it about itself. The Augustinian path from *signum* to *res* thus seems compressed into a single point and Luther's later theology of the word, with its stress on the gift of salvation in the present, is already clearly anticipated.

Certainly, this closing of the intervals (between *signum* and *res*) and its compression into the moment, which is nothing but the expression of the exclusive determination in the understanding of time,[542] points to Luther's later position, which is clearly confirmed by his explicit recourse to this interpretation in an important passage in both the *Treatise on the New Testament*[543] and *The Freedom*

---

marginal gloss on Ps. 51:10 (AND A RIGHT SPIRIT): "For he leads me to salvation by short way and an abbreviated word and directs me by a straight path, whereas the law goes around in circles. But the exalted Christ drew everything to himself, for he is the center of all things, and by his hold on them, all things are held together at their circumference, and he is the one who fills all in all" (3:285,33–37; cf. chap. 1, n. 75). For the time after the origin of the scholion on Rom. 9:28, we need to remember the sermon on the Fourth Sunday of Advent (Dec. 21) 1516: 1:110,13,21–24.

540. WA 56:408,13–16 = LW 25:398; compare ll. 6–9 in the Latin text for the antithesis.

541. WA 56:408,7 = LW 25:398 (trans. alt.).

542. To understand Luther's later theology, we must also keep sight of the fact that the exclusive particle not only means "without works" but, understood as "by the word alone," it also includes or expresses a very specific relationship to time. This aspect of the exclusive particle is mostly overlooked. Moreover, the decisive factor in the reformational concept of the word is precisely a specific understanding of time. Nevertheless, for Luther at this stage, this can only be specified negatively with the help of the exclusive particle coming from negative theology but not positively (as in the sense of 2 Cor. 6:2) as in the reformational Luther.

543. In the final section (39): "So we see that Christ burdened his church with very few laws and works but raised it to faith with many promises. Yet now, alas, everything is turned completely

of a Christian.[544] But here in our scholion on Romans we must carefully note the following:

(a) that and how it is not first and not only the word that abbreviates and perpetuates, empties and fulfills, and
(b) that and how the negation, which is basically the only thing valid, cannot accept the stated presence, the moment, but must take it back into itself again, and thus must again withdraw and condition its affirmation.

a) The interplay of *abbreviatio* and *consummatio* takes place—through faith ("*fit per fidem*").[545] "Faith is the completion, the abbreviation, and the short way of salvation. Indeed, the abbreviated word is nothing but faith. How can we prove this? Because the abbreviated word is such for no one, except for those who understand it to be such. But it is only understood by faith. Therefore faith is life, and the living word abbreviated."[546]

This clearly says that the word does not establish faith by preestablishing it in an irreversible relation. Rather, word and faith are mutually established at the same time, with neither one coming before the other (just like *abbreviatio* and *consummatio* within the word or faith). The word does not interpret itself; it is dependent on faith that understands it, is conditioned by it, and is delivered over to it. But the relationship that now seems to have become one-sided can be reversed immediately: "The word of faith takes more than it is taken, because it takes captive the thoughts of humans."[547]

Word and faith constantly reverse their relationship, exchange places with each other, and thus appear to be of the same origin. Here we recognize that unity-creating correlation, which was expressed in the Christmas sermon of 1514

---

upside down. We are driven by many long and burdensome laws and works to become righteous; yet nothing will come of it. But Christ's burden is light and soon produces an abundant righteousness, which consists in faith and trust and fulfils what Isa. 10[:22] says: 'A short completion will bring a flood, full of righteousness.' That is, *faith*, which is a *short thing*, comprises neither laws nor works. Indeed, faith cuts off all laws and works and fulfills all laws and works. Therefore, nothing but righteousness flows forth from it. For faith is so perfect that, without any effort or law, it makes everything we do acceptable and well pleasing to God . . . therefore, let us only attend to the divine promise and faith" (WA 6:378,1–15 = LW 35:111; trans. alt.; author's emphasis).

544. §7 (WA 7:23,7–23 = 7:52,12–19) (German); cf. LW 31:347–48 (Latin).

545. WA 56:408,17 = LW 25:398.

546. WA 56:409,4–8 = LW 25:399 (trans. alt.).

547. Gloss on Rom. 9:28: WA 56:96,22–23 = LW 25:85.

in the Aristotelian schema of form and matter. However, this correlation of word and faith, at least as it appears in Luther's early theology, cannot bring out the fact that the word comes before faith.

b) Not only do word and faith as such exchange places but so do the aspects that determine them, the *abbreviatio* and *consummatio*: "But for those who also abbreviate and complete themselves, this word is completed and abbreviated for their righteousness."[548]

Clearly, the word can be represented by faith because of faith's *abbreviation*, because of its lived negation, which now once again objectively presupposes the word: "The word of Christ cannot be accepted unless it is denied and cut off from everything, that is, also from the captive intellect and from every thought brought into humble submission to it."[549] *In this way*, faith itself is "life, and the living word abbreviated."[550]

But finally, faith also lives from negation as the *completed* word: "For 'it is the substance of the things hoped for,' that is, the possession and use of the future things that are eternal, but not of the present things, from which it cut us off (*abbreviat*)."[551] The statement "the possession and use of the future things that are eternal," which initially appears as an affirmation, is immediately determined again but, as we have seen throughout the lectures, only with reference back to what has been negated ("but not . . ."). Being thus "fulfilled," faith (as "love" in the sense of the scholion on Rom. 5:5[552] and as "hope" in the sense of the interpretation of Rom. 8:24[553]) can be nothing but an empty movement,[554] because it

548. WA 56:407,8–9 = LW 25:397 (trans. alt.).

549. WA 56:408,23–25 = LW 25:398 (trans. alt.). See 56:407,11–13 = 25:397: "All who believe this word are righteous. But they do not believe unless they take their intellect captive to the invisible things and cut themselves off from the sight of all visible things" (trans. alt.).

550. WA 56:409,7–8 = LW 25:399.

551. WA 56:409,11–12 (trans. alt.) = LW 25:399 (trans. alt.).

552. "It is called '*God's love*' because by it we love God alone, where nothing is visible, nothing experiential, either inwardly or outwardly, in which to trust or to love or fear; but it is carried away beyond all things into the invisible God, who cannot be experienced or comprehended, that is, into the midst of the inner darkness, *not knowing what it loves, but only knowing what it does not love, and turning away from everything that it has ever known and experienced*" (WA 56:307,4–9 = LW 25:294; trans. alt.; author's emphasis).

553. See chap. 1, n. 73.

554. Cf. the description of faith, hope, and love in the Epiphany sermon of 1517 (WA 1:123,24ff., esp. 123,36–124,4): "Love also takes away from us God and all that exists, reducing us to the pure nothingness from which we were created, and this with joy and eager desire. For this is the myrrh, pure and choice, to resign ourselves to pure nothingness, as it was before we existed, and to desire neither God nor anything outside of God, but only to be willingly brought back to our beginning, that is, to nothingness, at the pleasure of God. For just as we were nothing,

only tries to win itself from what has been negated against it, but this means that it is "grounded" in the negation.[555] In fact, the predication of the word asserting that salvation is a present reality (it "gives what it signifies") is withdrawn again. For the word gives the grace that it signifies, in that faith, or more precisely, the lived negation, activates and confirms it. To be sure, the gift here is not simply realized by its own doing, because the lived negation is indeed understood as coming from God.[556] But the inclusion of the word in a mutually interconnected and conditioned dialectic means it surrenders to it. The one seemingly fixed place, and the time seemingly compressed into a moment of salvation, are spread out in a relentless back-and-forth movement, in which there is no certainty and which has its affirmation in pure negation and its fulfillment in emptiness.

L) Promise and Supplication [Biel: Lect. 59; Ps. 115:1 (Vulg. Ps. 113:9); Rom. 4:7]

In the Romans lectures, the two series of scholia on 3:4–5 and 4:7 are particularly striking, if only because of their sheer size. In ever-new attempts, Luther tries here to fathom texts in which he obviously has a passionate interest.

As we have seen, the correct approach to the first series comes from the interpretation of Psalm 85 and Psalm 51, while that to the second, which must now be proved, comes from the interpretation of Psalm 115:1. In terms of content, this means that just as the key to understanding the interpretation of Romans 3:4–5 lies in Luther's interpretation of the pact in Mark 16:16 through 1 Corinthians 11:31 (on Ps. 51), so the words of Luke 11:9–10, which are also to be understood as a pact, can be seen, by way of the interpretation of Psalm 115:1, as the secret center of the scholia on Romans 4:7: God gives his grace by definition only to those who ask.

---

and desired nothing before we were created, except to be solely in the knowledge of God, so we must return there, so that we in like manner might know nothing, desire nothing, and be nothing. This is *the short way, the way of the cross*, by which we may arrive at life most shortly, which we can never reach by our own works but will only end up being led astray more and more (author's emphasis).

555. This is also shown in its own way by the interesting little passage WA 56:407,3–7 = LW 25:396-7, where it says that the word is interposed between the visible things and the future (invisible) things. But the word does not deliver the future things, except (as the abbreviating word) by negating the visible things by way of faith.

556. It is characteristic that our own action is understood as suffering passively (in the sense of submitting to something, allowing it, undergoing it, or experiencing it): cf. WA 56:407,12–13 (*sese praecidere*) = LW 25:397 (to cut ourselves off) with WA 56:408,26 (*verbo capi*) = LW 25:398 (to be taken captive by the word).

1. The scholion on Psalm 115:1 (= Vulg. Ps. 113:9), NOT TO US, O LORD, NOT TO US, shows like no other passage Luther's strong tie to the nominalist pact theology and its doctrine of justification.

Lection 59 of Biel's commentary on the Mass presents us with a text that Luther was immediately familiar with and that represents precisely this theology. Here the canon prayer TO US (SINNERS) ALSO and especially its form of address that calls God NOT A WEIGHER OF MERIT, BUT A BESTOWER OF PARDON is interpreted.

"Not presuming on our own righteousness," we must put our trust in God's mercy, accuse ourselves (THE RIGHTEOUS ARE FIRST ACCUSERS OF THEMSELVES: Prov. 18:17), confess with the centurion LORD, I AM NOT WORTHY TO HAVE YOU COME UNDER MY ROOF (Matt. 8:8), and pray with the tax collector GOD, BE MERCIFUL TO ME A SINNER (Luke 18:13). "These examples show that those who ask for things that pertain to salvation are graciously heard by God, and all the more so the more they humble themselves and condemn their sins by true confession." Thus, "by true and humble obedience," we are God's household.[557]

But although with the address NOT A WEIGHER OF MERIT we confess that ALL OUR RIGHTEOUS DEEDS ARE LIKE A POLLUTED GARMENT (Isa. 64:6) and from the BESTOWER OF PARDON we are to expect everything: "All our sufficiency is from you,"[558] nevertheless sin, judgment, and grace are not understood radically but placed in a quantitative relation to each other. God is therefore NOT A WEIGHER OF MERIT, "because he does not reward us exactly according to our merit but out of his generosity gives us much more. "So then . . . he always rewards us more than we deserve and punishes us less than we deserve. Therefore, our text does not deny the weighing or awarding of merit pure and simple, but a weighing that rewards people exactly according to what they deserve."[559]

God does not submit to any law of retaliation with regard to the sinner; his judgment and grace are incommensurate with our actions: THEY ARE NOT WORTHY OF COMPARISON . . . (Rom. 8:18).[560] God only really acts commensurately—that is, in direct correspondence—with the rule that he himself established, that "no one will be *glorified* in their homeland unless they have first received grace on the way."[561] For he only accepts from people what he himself

557. B (2:429).

558. I (2:438); for the last expression, see 2 Cor. 3:5.

559. K (2:439).

560. I (2:438); cf. Q (2:444).

561. O (2:442). Cf. S (2:446), where the connection between *gratificatio* and *glorificatio* is seen in the love given by God: "The grace given on the way is not really distinguished from the love

has given them; it would be Pelagian to assert that "humans can obtain eternal happiness (beatitude) by their natural powers."[562]

Considered "internally," in and of itself, thus apart from grace, our work has no claim to eternal reward.[563] Only the matchless "gift of God," the grace that works together with our free will in such a way as to steer it like a rider their horse,[564] creates the merit that according to the testimony of Scripture, is necessary for salvation.[565] But even this meritorious work accomplished on the basis of the *gratia gratum faciens* (the grace that makes us pleasing to God)[566] cannot alone guarantee, because of the nature of the act, the allocation of a reward that fully corresponds to it:[567] "But the work is worthy only because of God's gratuitous acceptance of it, and thus his willingness to obligate himself to the worker,"[568] and therefore only "because of the pactal agreement[569] or convention, or even simply because of his promise to accept it."[570]

---

of the homeland, except perhaps as a part from the whole, for grace is the love that remains in the homeland when faith and hope have run their course. FOR LOVE NEVER ENDS, as the apostle says in 1 Cor. 13[:8]. And glory itself is but grace perfected."

562. E (2:432).

563. O (2:442); cf. L (2:439) and Q (2:444). "Inwardly" is a technical term that we will come across again in an important passage in Luther (at the beginning of scholion on Rom. 4:7). For Biel, it is certain that our works can also be considered "according to themselves, as done by us through our active, natural strength, which we received with our first nature, in which we freely received the ability to do either good or evil works," which is proven by scriptural texts (L; 2:439). For Luther, on the other hand, as far as who we are and what we do are concerned, we are only ever sinners (see pp. 146–153).

564. L (2:439); cf. E (2:432): "We have received the grace by which we can do meritorious deeds from God alone, the creator."

565. From many passages (K; 2:438–39), Biel draws the compelling conclusion: "But otherwise temporal things do not work eternal things except by way of merit" (Ibid: K; II, 439).

566. The *gratia gratum faciens* produces "the worthiness of the worker" (O; 2:442). See T (2:447): "Sinners deserve nothing from God on the basis of merit (*de condigno*) because they are not friends but enemies of God" (N; 2:441). God first accepts the person and only then looks at their works: see the passage quoted in n. 621.

567. Q (2:444).

568. N (2:441): "However, the "only" by no means excludes what Biel means by the "partly–partly" ("*vel–vel*") of the text quoted in n. 570.

569. Cf. further (in the same section N; 2:441): "But this agreement in God is nothing but his divine will that willed from eternity that the act thus elicited or commanded should be worthy of such a reward (*meritum condignum*), either ("partly") because of the nature of the act, or because of his pact and promise by which he willed to be the one who should pay such a reward and thus the workers themself." Cf. Coll. II/d 27/q un/a 1/nota 3 (C).

570. N (2:440).

The following sentence, which we can now finally understand as defining condign merit (*meritum de condigno*), brings together all the aspects that have been highlighted: "If we consider the worth of a meritorious work on the basis of grace, coefficient with free will, and on the basis of the movement of the Holy Spirit, as well as on the basis of God's decree and promise of a beatific reward, then we can say that our works elicited by grace are condignly meritorious of a beatific reward."[571] That is, God himself establishes, effects, and guarantees the beginning, middle, and end of the process of salvation.[572]

In contrast to the "condign reward" (*praemium de condigno*), the *congruent* reward (*praemium de congruo*) is given for the actions of the enemies of God, sinners, and so for the actions of people who are determined, not by the grace that makes them pleasing to God (*gratia gratum faciens*) but only by their natural ability and endowment that God freely gives to everyone (*gratia gratis data*).[573] Thus "a good work of the kind done by an enemy (if it is accepted that an enemy should be repaid at all for doing something good) as a good natural impulse of the sinner's soul by which they do what lies within them . . . is a reward of grace based on the kindness and liberality of the giver (*de congruo*)."[574]

The fact that this merit receives its reward, the infusion of "justifying grace" (= "the grace that makes us acceptable to God"),[575] congruently means that it is not paid as a debt of justice, a debt that God owes,[576] but is given out of sheer generosity.[577] That is, God is under no obligation to the person of the sinner. In fact, by infusing the sinner with grace, God strictly acts improperly. Admittedly,

---

571. R (2:444).

572. Cf. R (2:445): "Equality [of work and reward] *comes from the first mover*, the *Holy Spirit*, who moves the will by his grace. But this is an infinite good, by reason of which the meritorious work is equal to the objective reward, which is the triune God, of whom GEN. 15 says: I AM YOUR VERY GREAT REWARD. Hence the Holy Spirit is the pledge of our inheritance, 2 Cor. 1[:22]. However, there is also equality *on the part of the second mover*, which is *grace* with respect to the formal reward, which is the vision and enjoyment of God, and this in power, though not in act, like the seed of a tree, in which is the power of the whole tree. The work is also done by grace as if by God, and the work shares in the divine nature. For we are adopted by grace as children, to whom the inheritance is due by the very right of adoption that Paul speaks of in that passage in ROM. [8:17]: IF CHILDREN, THEN HIERS. *Because of God's promise, it is only just and right for him to deliver on it*" (author's emphasis).

573. Cf. T (2:447): "No gift of grace freely given (*gratia gratis data*) can be compared to the grace that makes us pleasing to God (*gratia gratum faciens*)."

574. N (2:441).

575. N (2:441); P (2:444): cf. the statement quoted in n. 582; T (2:447).

576. N (2:441); P (2:443).

577. N (2:442); cf. P (2:443): "With a very generous recompenser, no good goes unrewarded."

it is true that God "ordained from eternity to give grace to those who do what lies within them."[578] But it would be wrong to conclude from this that there is now no such thing as improperness of behavior.[579]

Now that we have finally clarified what it means "to do what lies within you" (*facere quod in se*), let us return to the subject matter at the start of the lection: the confession of sins.

It is no coincidence that Biel cites precisely the humiliation of a sinner, King Ahab, as an example of what humans can do of their own accord.[580] As a general definition, it is true that "people do what lies within them, who, enlightened by the light of natural reason or of faith or both, know the depravity of their sin and, intending to rise from it, desire divine help by which they can be cleansed from sin and cling to God their creator."[581] Therefore, "to do what lies within you" ultimately involves the question of God,[582] which is expressed in the humble confession of sin and the fervent plea for purification from it. "For God determined to infuse grace into those who do these things."[583]

In a nutshell, Biel's doctrine of justification can be outlined as follows: "*Just as God has ordained to reward out of grace those who keep his commandments, so he has ordained from eternity to give grace to those who do what lies within them.*"[584] This is the point in tradition history at which Luther's scholion on Psalm 115:1 (Vulg. Ps. 113:9) connects directly with Biel's theology.

2. The first part of the *scholion on Psalm 115:1* clearly refers back to the interpretation of Psalm 85:11 and so initially comes under the topic of the "fulfillment of the promise in Christ":

---

578. T (2:447); cf. from P (2:444) the text referenced in n. 583 and "The Lord gives his grace to sinners who do what lies within them, which he would not do unless they did what lies within them" (2:443).

579. Biel knows the proposition that "just as God has ordained that he would reward out of grace those who keep the commandments, so he has ordained from eternity to give grace to those who do what lies within them." However, he refuses to conclude from this (T, 2:447) that "therefore, just as those who keep the commandments justly merit glory, so those who do what lies within them justly merit grace."

580. P (2:443).

581. P (2:443). The quote is a summary of Biel from a previously quoted section from the *Summa* of Alexander of Hales, which ends with the words "Fear . . . and . . . hope . . . this is to do what lies within you."

582. Cf. Coll. III/d 27/q un/a 3/dub 2/prop 2 (Q): "The most perfect way of doing what lies within you is to seek God."

583. P (2:444). Cf. P (2:443): "God gives his grace to those who do these things, and he does so out of necessity, not the necessity of compulsion (cf. n. 576) but that of immutability."

584. T (2:447); cf. n. 579.

> Just as the advent of Christ in the flesh was given out of the pure mercy of the God who promised him and was neither granted by the merits of our human nature nor denied by our misdeeds, nevertheless, it was necessary that the preparation and disposition for receiving him were made, as was done in the whole of the Old Testament through the lineage of Christ. The fact that God promised his Son was his mercy, but that he gave him was his truth and faithfulness, as we read in the final verse of Micah [7:20]: "You will give truth to Jacob and mercy to Abraham, as you swore to our fathers from the days of old." He does not say "as we deserved," but "as you swore." Hence the fact that God made himself our debtor is because of the promise of him who is merciful, not because of the worth of our deserving human nature.[585]

The problem that opens up here of the appropriation of the promise of salvation fulfilled with the incarnation of Christ, which we have already come across in the interpretation of Psalm 85, found a solution in the *judgment doxology* in the interpretation of Psalm 51 (and Rom. 3:4–5). Here we will now find that the *prayer of supplication* offers a second solution.

For Luther's early theology, the judgment doxology and the prayer of supplication (together with their inner dialectical switch to salvation and answered prayer[586]) are the only two concrete basic forms[587] in which God and humans meet.

We have already seen how the notion of promise fits into the first form. How it intertwines with the second becomes clear from the scholion, the beginning of which was just quoted above and which Luther brings to a close with the following paragraphs:

> He required nothing but preparation so that we might be able to receive that gift, just as if a prince or king of the land promised his robber or murderer one hundred florins, as long as he was ready to wait for him at the appointed time and place. Here it is clear that the king is that debtor of his own free promise and mercy, without any merit on the part of the robber or murderer, nor would he deny him what he had promised because of his lack of merit.

585. WA 4:261,25–34 = LW 11:396 (trans. alt.).

586. See esp. sec. C.

587. A form, in the sense of form criticism (*Formgeschichte*), is understood to be a concrete and always unmistakable statement and manifestation of life, in which the form of speech and its circumstances are interwoven as constitutive elements.

So also, Christ's spiritual advent is by grace and his future advent will be by glory, for it is not because of our merits but the sheer promise of our merciful God.

For he promised regarding his spiritual advent: "Ask, and you will receive; seek, and you will find; knock, and it will be opened to you. For everyone who asks receives, etc." [Luke 11:9–10] Hence, the [scholastic] doctors rightly say that God infallibly gives grace to those who do what is in them. And although they cannot prepare themselves for the grace that is merited (*de condigno*) because it is incomparable, yet they can prepare themselves for the grace that is unmerited (*de congruo*), on account of God's promise and his covenant (*pactum*) of mercy.

Thus he promised regarding his future advent, "that we should live just, sober and godly lives in this world, looking for the blessed hope" [Titus 2:12–13]. For no matter how holy a life we may have lived here, hardly any disposition and preparation for the future glory will be revealed in us at the end, so much so that the apostle says [Rom. 8:18]: "The sufferings of this present time are not worthy (not condign) etc." But they can make us fit (can be congruent).

Therefore, God bestows everything on us freely and only on account of the promise of his mercy, although he wants us to be prepared for this as much as it lies within us. Hence, just as the law was a figure and preparation of the people for receiving Christ, so our doing, as much as it lies within us, disposes us to grace. And the whole time of grace is a preparation for the future glory and the second advent. Therefore, he commands us to watch, be prepared, and wait for him etc.[588]

As can be seen on the background of the Biel text analyzed above, Luther takes up the nominalist tradition here. The fact he does this approvingly seems particularly remarkable in view of his otherwise strong opinion against Biel.[589]

At first glance, it seems our text clearly has two parts: Like the story of the old covenant to the "advent of Christ in the flesh," so now, after the incarnation,

---

588. WA 4:261,34–262,17 = LW 11:396–97 (trans. alt.); in Luther this follows on directly from 4:261,25–34 [see n. 585] to form a single section).

589. See on that Leif Grane's careful work, *Contra Gabrielem—Luthers Auseinandersetzung mit Gabriel Biel in der Disputatio Contra Scholasticam Theologiam 1517* (1962), in which our text is also treated (296–301). Independently of Grane, we have arrived at the same interpretation at important points. But with the aid of tradition history, we need to determine the place of the whole in the context of our research question in a more differentiated way.

the process of an individual's salvation[590] runs to the "spiritual advent of Christ," to *grace*, and from grace to the "future advent of Christ," to *glory*. Grace and glory can only be reached because of God's eternal decree, which Luther sees described in Luke 11:9–10 in relation to grace and in Titus 2:12–13 in relation to glory. This twofold nature of the process of salvation corresponding to God's two eternal decrees is traditional.[591]

Also with the tradition, Luther sees that the attitude ("preparation," "disposition") to the promise is contained in the "*facere quod in se*" ("do what lies within you"). But the distinctiveness of his early theology only becomes apparent when we look at the content of these words. From all the traditional understandings of the *facere quod in se*, he only takes up the one that is factually original,[592] which speaks of seeking and asking God. The fact that he understands it exclusively in this way gives it special significance.[593]

This makes Luther think that a more appropriate expression of this understanding in relation to God's promise can be found in Luke 11:9–10.[594] This verse is also alluded to elsewhere in connection with the *facere quod in se*—for example, in the scholion on Psalm 119:41: "Anyone receives God's grace as a free gift, no matter how fitly (*congrue*) they dispose themselves. For it is given not on

590. This parallelism at the beginning (WA 4:261,25–29) and end (4:262,13–15) of our text also occurs elsewhere. Cf. the scholion on Ps. 119:41: "Just as the human race received Christ, not as its own justice but as the mercy of God, no matter how appropriately (*congrue*) it disposed itself, so everyone receives God's grace freely, no matter how appropriately they have disposed themselves" (WA 4:329,31–34 = LW 11:448–49; trans. alt.). See also the scholion on v. 17 of the same psalm: "Although those who served the law literally did not merit anything condignly on the basis of worth (*de condigno*), yet since the law was a dispensation and pedagogue until Christ came, as faith in Christ is until the future glory, what they did merit was merited congruently (*de congruo*), on the basis of God's pact and promise, and of faith, which was to be transferred to faith in another" (4:312,38–41 = 11:424; trans. alt.).

591. Cf. the quote that conclusively summed up Biel's doctrine of justification (the text is given at n. 584).

592. See pp. 138–139.

593. However, the scholion on Ps. 119:168 shows that this exclusivity is not maintained everywhere, as we see from the following: "Those who do not first obey the commandments with works do not acknowledge or care for the promises either, for the commandments prepare the soul to hope for the things promised, and without the commandments there is no hope, which requires some merits beforehand" (WA 4:389,36–39 = LW 11:531; trans. alt.).

594. In Biel, these words also appear in connection with the *facere quod in se*: Coll. III/d 27/q un/a 3/dub/ 2/prop 2. This passage was familiar to Luther, as we see from thesis 28 of the *Disputation Against Scholastic Theology* (WA 1:225 = LW 31:11; E. Vogelsang's note gives the quotation in Biel: 5:321 on ll.5ff.). Biel quotes the logion under Luke 11 as does Luther also in WA 2:175,24–25 (1519), which is why we have not taken over the biblical reference from the WA (4:262,2–3: Matt. 7:7–8).

the basis of my preparation but on the basis of the divine covenant (pact), since God promised that he would come by means of this provision, if he were awaited and requested to do so."[595]

The motif of the Aristotelian concept of motion turned into history, which we are familiar with from the Christmas sermon of 1514, is now inextricably linked to the request, understood as an appropriate attitude and counterpart to the promissio:[596]

> And Christ continually gives to all who are progressing, not according to merit but mercy, the mercy by which he made a covenant with us to give freely to us who ask and beg. But he gives much more to beginners. And, as has often been said, to make progress is nothing but always to begin. But to begin without making progress is to fail. This is clear from every movement and act of the whole creation (on Ps. 119:88).[597]

From the fundamental homogeneity of this movement of asking, the dialectic of which is formulated with the sentence "to make progress is nothing but always to begin," the complete structural equality of its orientation toward grace and toward glory, which is a striking feature of our guiding text, becomes understandable.

---

595. WA 4:329,33–36 = LW 11:449 (trans. alt.). See the line gloss on Ps. 143:1, "LORD, HEAR MY PRAYER . . . IN YOUR TRUTHFULNESS that is, through your promised faithfulness, by which you promised mercy to the penitent and those who ask, not because of their merit" (WA 4:443,5,8–9), and the marginal gloss on IN YOUR TRUTHFULNESS, "the Hebrew has, 'in your faithfulness,' i.e., by the faithful fulfilment of your promise, that you may be found true and just—by delivering on your promised truthfulness, not as a debt owing to me on my account but as a debt owing to you on account of your pact" (WA 4:443,29–31). There is an explicit reference to Luke 11 in the scholion on Ps. 119:147, which comes very close to Luther's later understanding of promise: "Since he promised, 'whoever asks receives and whoever seeks finds,' therefore without saying anything about our merits, and trusting completely in the mercy of him who promises, we are very bold to take him at his word in order that we may receive what he promises" (WA 4:375,33–5 = LW 11:512; trans. alt.).

596. Grane (*Contra Gabrielem*, 299–301) overlooks the philosophical character and thus the dubiousness of this motif.

597. WA 4:350,12–16 = LW 11:477 (trans. alt.). See the scholion on Ps. 119:20: "Therefore, to want to remain always with the tendency and desire to progress—that is true humility" (WA 4:315,34–35 = LW 11:428; trans. alt.) and the scholion on Ps. 119:76: "Those who are progressing are always beginning in relation to what they do not yet have . . . Here nothing is ever sought except the gospel and grace" (WA 4:344,12–15 = LW 11:469; trans. alt.; Luther emphasized this especially).

With the finding of this structural equality, that first impression of the twofold nature of the process of salvation is corrected. At the same time, there is a difference to Biel, for whom human activity before and because of the *gratia gratum faciens* (the grace that makes us pleasing to God) always has different values.[598] But even here, despite all their differences, we must not overlook what they have in common: Biel also emphasizes that even the things accomplished on the basis of grace bear no comparison with glory: THEY ARE NOT WORTHY TO BE COMPARED . . . (Rom. 8:18),[599] even if, unlike Luther in our text, he does not draw the conceptual (and thus of course factual) consequences of calling these things "hardly a disposition or preparation" but merely activities that are "well-suited" and that make us fit to receive what God gives us in his grace.

Compared to Biel, we thus recognize two characteristic features in Luther: First, he understands the *facere quod in se* exclusively as seeking and asking God, and second, he understands this movement of existence as a permanent dialectic. The fundamental homogeneity of this movement implies the uniformity of the process of salvation on the way (*in via*). Here Luther actually rejects its twofold nature found in the tradition, even if not always consistently,[600] and instead asserts a single movement that always begins anew. Hence, he can say that "the whole time of grace is a preparation," and that "to make progress is nothing but always to begin."[601]

But despite these differences, our guiding text belongs on the side of Biel when it is considered in the light of *The Babylonian Captivity*. Because the consequence of Luther's characteristically human attitude to the promise is its fundamental uncertainty of salvation, and its constant wavering between fear and hope, exactly as in Biel. However, Luther has clearly distanced himself from Biel through his radical Augustinian doctrine of sin and grace, especially in the matter of "seeking God"![602]

---

598. Cf. pp. 136–139.

599. Cf. Lect. 59 Q; 2:444 (cf.1 [2:43] and Coll. II/d 27/q un/a 2/concl. 1 [F]) with WA 4:262,7–13 and 4:344,1–4 (Scholion on Ps. 119:76): "All this (i.e. rewards and eternal life) however comes not from our merits but from God's promises. Therefore, he calls that mercy, which is given because of his pact and promise, but only if the pact and its testimonies are kept. For our sufferings or rewards are not worthy to be compared with the future glory etc."

600. Cf. n. 599.

601. Some ambiguities of course remain. For instance, Luther distinguishes between grace and glory but not between the attitude ("preparation," "disposition") to both (we still find him making the same distinction as in our text—compare WA 4:262,14–15 with 15–16—in a sermon of 1516: WA 1:68,22–25). Should he, then, not make both of them identical?

602. Cf. thesis 28 of the *Disputation Against Scholastic Theology* (1517): WA 1:225 = LW 31:11.

For the overall topic of our work, it is now important to consider why the notion of promise as such did not yet have to lead to the reformational understanding of the word.

In the divine pact, God's promise is related to a particular human attitude, just as in legal norms, the legal consequence is related to the facts of the case. As an eternal decree, the divine pact—analogous to the legal norm that applies by virtue of the will of the lawgiver, even before its application and without it—precedes the implementation of a particular human attitude, understood as a temporal event, and thus, in its abstraction from time, is its basis. But if a person tries to live up to the promise in a concrete way, then they find themselves caught between the definitive decree *before* time and its definitive execution *after* time. Neither reaches them concretely *in* time; what remains is the *Anfechtung* of predestination as well as the uncertainty they feel in view of the last judgment. Because the *promissio* is not also encountered definitively as an oral promise in time, it is only experienced as a demand for a certain human attitude and as an object of hope. Luther says here that you only really become aware of it in time with your attitude to it. It itself remains the abstract condition of your response to it, but this alone remains its concrete reality, which the interpretation of Romans 4:7 will then present in the schema of *res-spes*.

The idea of the *promissio* in Luther's early theology did not solidify into an all-determining basic form, as it later did, because it had not yet found its *Sitz im Leben*, or setting in life. Only when seen from the perspective of the sacrament can the promise for Luther become the form of *proclamation*, the performative word of the sermon, that gives what it promises.[603] But according to its nominalist origins, the promise is not a proclamation that gives what it promises but is understood primarily as a divine decree, in the doctrine of justification and in the doctrine of the sacraments as well as in the intersection of both.[604] Its essentially reformational character therefore lies in its concrete locatedness in a specific *Sitz im Leben*, and so in its temporal character as an oral word of promise, which in its unambiguity creates certainty by removing the *Anfechtung* of predestination and at the same time the uncertainty associated with the last judgment.[605]

603. The difference between the promise proclaimed and given ("*exekutiv*") in the sermon and that legislated ("*legislatorisch*") in a divine decree is the difference between Luther's reformational theology of promise and the nominalist theology of promise and pact. The matter that has only been briefly addressed here will become clearer in the second part of our investigation. Cf. esp. chap. 7.

604. The legislative understanding of the promise (especially, e.g, Mark 16:16, with its words of institution for baptism) still persists, even if, as in Biel (see on this W. Jetter, *Die Taufe beim jungen Luther*, 85,87,93) the necessity of its "promulgation" is emphasized. What is proclaimed, then, is the command to perform a symbolic act or to let it happen by itself.

605. See n. 503.

3. The key to understanding the interpretation of *Romans 4:7* lies in recognizing that this whole difficult text is nothing more than an unfolding of the particular understanding of the promise that we encountered in the scholion on Psalm 115:1 (Vulg. Ps. 113:9).

Luther's remarks stand out significantly from the text he has interpreted, which in itself could very well lead to his later understanding of the promise.[606] They thus reveal precisely his own view to us, which is that in Romans 4:7, Paul, with the help of the makarism from Psalm 32:1–2 ("Blessed are those . . ."),[607] interprets the present promise of righteousness (Gen. 15:6 = Rom. 4:3,6) as the forgiveness of sins that has been bindingly promised and proclaimed. But Luther now turns the promise into a prayer of supplication, meaning that it is not given to us unless we ask for it. Therefore, forgiveness cannot be believed to have happened, but it is something that is only always expected. Of course, the origin and goal of this expectation lie in a promise, but this promise is nowhere heard concretely; it is never tied to a specific location, and so it is unable to convey the certainty that it carries within it.[608]

The whole interpretation is embodied in its first guiding principle:

> *Saints are always sinners inwardly (*intrinsece*),*
> *therefore, they are always justified outwardly (*extrinsece*).*[609]

What is immediately noticeable here is the two-part scheme of the statement, which is also constantly repeated in the parallel texts.[610] It is not apparent

606. We only have to think of the interpretation of Ps. 32:1–2 in Luther's *Sermon on the Sacrament of Baptism*, 1519, §12: WA 2:732, esp. ll.15–24 = LW 35:36: "As the prophet says in Psalm 32, 'Blessed are those whose transgression is forgiven; blessed are those to whom the Lord imputes no iniquity.' This faith is the most necessary of things, for it is the ground of all comfort. Those that do not have such faith must despair of their sins, for the sin that remains after Baptism makes it impossible for any of our good works to be pure before God. That is why we must stick boldly and fearlessly to our Baptism and hold onto it against all sin and terrors of conscience, humbly saying, 'I know very well that I cannot do a single thing that is pure. But I am baptized, and through my Baptism God, who cannot lie, has bound himself to me. He will not count my sin against me but will kill it and blot it out'" (trans. alt.). See pp. 294–295.

607. Luther's interpretation of this verse in the *Dictata* prepared the way for the scholion on Rom. 4:7 (cf. esp. WA 3:171,26–27; 172,2–4,35–36; 173,1 [*tunc mox*: then immediately!], 30–32).

608. WA 56:272,18 = LW 25:260: "the sure promise of God."

609. WA 56:268,27–28 = LW 25:257 (trans. alt.).

610. Luther tries to articulate a single fact in ever-new ways. When analyzing the guiding principle, two textual units in particular must be kept in mind, which run parallel to it in their thought progression and formulation:

at first glance, however, that the two parts are not antithetical to one another but rather integrate one other to form a synthesis. The *two-part nature of the guiding principle reflects the two-sidedness of the divine pact*: The first part describes the human condition corresponding to the promise ("they are sinners" means "recognizing and confessing that they are sinners").[611] The promise itself is characterized in the second part, at least according to its function.[612] However, this happens in such a way that it in turn refers back to the human attitude and appears conditioned by it ("therefore"). It should be added immediately, however, that this condition is entirely reversible: "We are righteous only because God reckons us to be such . . . *Therefore*, inwardly and of ourselves we are always unrighteous."[613] Thus the "therefore" marks the pivotal point in the structure of the *pactum*. Its two sides refer to each other, demand and condition each other, and depend on each other; in short, they are relatives.[614]

---

a) "For since the saints are always conscious of their sin and pray fervently for righteousness from God in accordance with his mercy, they are always reckoned as righteous by God. Thus in their own eyes, and in truth, they are unrighteous. But to God they are reckoned as righteous on account of their confession of sin. They are sinners in fact, but righteous by the reckoning of a merciful God. Without knowing it, they are righteous; knowing it, they are unrighteous; they are sinners in fact, but righteous in hope" (WA 56:269,25–30 = LW 25:258; trans. alt.).
b) "Now are these persons perfectly righteous? No. But at one and the same time they are sinners and righteous (*simul iustus et peccator*). They are sinners in fact, but righteous by God's reckoning and sure promise that he would continue to deliver them from sin until he has completely cured them. And so they are completely healthy in hope, but sinners in fact. They have the beginnings of righteousness, and so always continue more and more to seek it, while realizing that they are always unrighteous" (WA 56:272,16–21 = LW 25:260 [trans. alt.]; cf. WA 56:271,27–272,2).

Besides these two parallel texts, we should compare especially the Disputation *De viribus et voluntate hominis sine gratia* of Sept. 1516 (1:142), which, in corollary 3 of thesis 2 (1:148,35–149,18), takes up the texts of the lectures cited above almost word for word (see esp. 1:149,8–10).

611. Cf. WA 56:276,3–9 = LW 25:263.

612. The logical subject here is therefore God, who declares us righteous.

613. WA 56:269,8–10 = LW 25:257 (trans. alt.; author's emphasis).

614. WA 56:269,7–8 = LW 25:257 ("according to the law of mutual relationship"), 269,13 = 257 ("by the force and necessity of this relationship"); cf. 56:45,15–16 = 25:38 (Marginal gloss on Rom. 4:14: see p. 119); 56:292,29–30 = 25:279 (Scholion on Rom. 4:14). See the definition given by Altenstaig in his dictionary: "A RELATIVE is said to refer to something else. And terms are relatives which by the nature of language signify one thing and with it connote another, so that what they signify cannot be verified unless what they connote is understood, just as the word father signifies a father but at the same time connotes a son. It can never be written that a father is verifiably the father of someone, unless a son (or daughter) is understood, who is different from the father" (Fol. 216[v]); cf. also Luther's almost identical marginal note on

"Intrinsically" here, as well as in Biel, defines our actions and abilities when considered apart from God's promise and his reckoning.[615] The definition of its correlate "extrinsically" (= "how we are with God and by his reckoning"[616]), which in the context given here is Luther's own coinage and as such only appears in the Romans lectures,[617] is immediately given in Biel as "by gratuitous divine acceptance."[618] The pair of terms "*intrinsece-extrinsece*" is identical with that of "*in re-in spe*,"[619] a formula familiar to us from the tradition.[620]

But what makes the guiding principle unmistakably a statement of the early Luther is the "*semper*" that we have known since the Christmas sermon of 1514. The fact that it occurs in both parts points to the homogeneity of the movement of both relatives, which in their simultaneity thus merge into a single unified event.[621]

However, the *chronological uniformity* that emerges with the "*semper*" expresses nothing but that *material co-originality* of the determinations

---

Lombard, only specifically in relation to the doctrine of the Trinity: WA 9:38,28–37. [Trans. note: Aristotle teaches that "all relatives, if properly defined, have correlatives" (Categories, ch. 7). Noted in LW 25:257 n. 5].

615. Cf. Luther's explanation: "I mean intrinsically, that is, how we are in ourselves, in our eyes, in our estimation" (WA 56:268,31–32 = LW 25:257; trans. alt.) with Biel's theses: "Our work, considered according to its own intrinsic goodness, which it has precisely by itself and its own eliciting will circumscribed by grace, is not the merit of beatitude, neither congruent nor condign" (Lect. 59 O; 2:442) and "By comparing works according to themselves and the intrinsic goodness they have by virtue of the divine will calling them to the beatific reward of heaven, it is clear that even the good works done by grace are by no means condignly worthy of this beatific reward" (Lect. 59 Q; 2:444. Cf. Coll II/d 27/q un/a 2/concl. 1 [F]).

616. WA 56:268,32–269,1 = LW 25:257.

617. See sec. F ("Word and God"). In addition to what was said there, the concept of promise must also be expressly included here in the treatment of the scholion on Rom. 4:7 and the God—human dialectic portrayed against the background of the nominalist doctrine of justification.

618. See the proof passage in n. 568.

619. See n. 610.

620. Cf., for example, Biel Lect. 19 E (1:166): "Those born of the earth ARE FULL OF GLORY not in reality and by possession, but in hope and by promise."

621. But even here in the interpretation of Rom. 4:7, the break with the tradition is not yet complete. The section on the righteousness of the saints (WA 56:276,20–277,3 = LW 25:263–64) shows again the traditional two-tier approach: "First they were reckoned [as righteous] because of their humble groaning of faith, then their works were also reckoned and approved" (56:276,33–35 = 25:264; trans. alt.). Luther clarifies this from Gen. 4:4: 56:276,35–277,2 = 25:264; see the scholion on Rom. 4:6: "God does not accept a person because of their works, but their works because of the person; first the person, then the works. As it is written: 'The Lord had regard for Abel (first) and (afterwards) for his offering'" (56:268,4–7 = 25:256; trans. alt.). Right up to the two additions to the biblical text, Luther agrees with Biel: "For the Lord does not accept anything from anyone as worthy of reward unless he has first accepted them as persons." For God first had regard for Abel, and then for his offering" (Coll. IV/d 16/q 2/a 3/dub 4/prop 1 [K]).

contained in the two parts of the guiding principle. This is shown by the fact that the sequence in which they follow each other and the relationship that they have to each other are reversible (*therefore*). *Thus we can understand why Luther uses a double "semper" in the same sense as a single "simul": "simul peccator et iustus,"* sinner and righteous at the same time.[622]

From the standpoint of the reformational sense of the promise, we can only understand the dialectic formulated in our guiding principle if we see what it excludes. And what it excludes is the Aristotelian idea of permanence, which prevents the finality of the promise and thus the certainty of faith from being expressed in a concrete way. For the early Luther, the very thing that the promise in its finality must not become is temporal and verbal, because of the *duration* of its dialectical movement, which then also quite logically appears as willed by God's eternal decree: "God *(has) decreed* to impute sin to everyone except to those who are groaning, and fearing, and *constantly* imploring his mercy."[623]

This guiding principle further shows that, as in the tradition, Luther's attitude to the promise is still hamstrung by the notion of its conditionality. This is not even overcome by the fact that it is understood as "indisposition,"[624] as knowledge and confession of sin and as sighing and pleading for mercy, in short, as confession of sin and supplication.[625] Luther certainly has a different anthropology and a different understanding of sin and grace to that of Biel, for example,[626] but it is by no means the reformational faith in the word.[627] Or

---

622. See n. 610b.

623. WA 56:281,18–19 = LW 25:268 (author's emphasis; trans. alt.; note the context: 56:281,4–21). *This text alone would suffice to show that the interpretation of Ps. 115:1 [= 113:9; Vulgate] is inextricably bound up with that of Rom. 4:7.*

624. Cf. thesis 30 and its corresponding thesis 25 from the *Disputation Against Scholastic Theology* (WA 1:225 = LW 31:10–11).

625. See, besides the text mentioned in n. 610 a), WA 56:271,21–22 = LW 25:259, "God forgives through his non-imputation out of mercy for all who acknowledge and confess and hate their sin and ask to be healed from it" (trans. alt.), and 56:284,12–14 = 25:271, "Sin is covered . . . through God's non-imputation of it because of humility and the groaning of faith for him" (trans. alt.). See further 56:287,19–24 = 25:274-75; 56:236,27–28 = 25:222 (on Rom. 3:10); 56:247,14–17 = 25:233 (scholion on Rom. 3:17–18); the scholion on Rom. 3:21 (56:256–61 = 25:243–48), which provides a parallel to the interpretation of Rom. 4:7; 56:428,6–13 (scholion on Rom. 10:19–20); and 56:503,20–21–504,3 = 25:497–98 (scholion on Rom. 14:1).

626. To see this, we only need compare with Biel Luther's interpretation of Rom. 4:7, esp. WA 56:273,3–276,19 = LW 25:261–63 and, for the wider context, his theses from the *Disputation Against Scholastic Theology* (1:224–28 = 31:9–16) that are already emerging specifically in this section.

627. What Luther wants to assert against scholastic theology (cf. the first three theses of the disputation: WA 1:224 = LW 31:9 and the "epilogue", 1:228,34–36 = 31:16 [which in substance is the usual "Declaration" (*Protestatio*) that Luther also uses as a preface to his *Explanations of the Theses on Indulgences*, 1:529,30–530,12 = 31:83]) and what is asserted is nothing but

does it make no difference if we only ever long for the promise, without it ever becoming concrete in its finality; again, does it make no difference if it always remains in limbo, without us ever receiving it as a proffered gift and rejoicing in it, or better, rejoicing in its giver?

It is significant that Luther, in his interpretation of Romans 4:7, can only present the alternative of either "trusting" with a false sense of security that we are justified by the church's sacrament, especially the sacrament of penance, or knowing that we always remain in need of justification and are always to "humbly seek God's healing grace by yearning for it and recognizing ourselves as sinners."[628]

In view of the controversy among scholars about the understanding of the "*propter*"[629] ("because of"), it should be emphasized again that our attitude to and preparation for the promise—that is, our confession of sins and our sighing and pleading for grace—does not unilaterally condition the God–human relationship. The statement that we are "righteous because of our confession of sins and plea for grace" is only valid since we are "righteous because of the reckoning and sure promise of God."[630] But at the same time, God's reckoning and promise in turn only find their concrete reality in our confession of sins and supplication and do not themselves make our faith sure and certain, which means we are still left in doubt.

The only possible hope is one that moves in a circle of uncertainty: on the one hand, it comes "by the sufferings that destroy merits";[631] on the other hand, "by God's reckoning and sure promise to free us from sin"[632]—a "sure promise," yes, but one that is never made verbally and one that you are not

---

his affirmation of Augustine's anti-Pelagian writings. But it cannot be demonstrated that this affirmation already carries within it the reformational understanding of the word.

628. WA 56:276,11–14, 8–9; trans. alt. (the form of the verbs in the Luther text has been changed).

629. Cf. Bornkamm's statement (*ARG*, 1962, 1–60, here 16–18) against Bizer (*Fides*, 47) and Bizer's response (Afterword to 3rd ed., 199–201).

630. Cf. the texts mentioned in n. 610 a) and b) with each other. The double determination "righteous because of the confession of sins" and "righteous because of the promise" remains well within the nominalist doctrine of justification: cf. n. 570.

631. Thesis 25 of the *Disputation Against Scholastic Theology*: WA 1:225 = LW 31:10. "Hope does not grow out of merits, but out of the sufferings that destroy merits" (The thesis is the result of a struggle with Lombard over the correct understanding of Rom. 5:3–4: see the passages noted by E. Vogelsang in *BoA* 5:322, line 11).

632. See n. 610 b). From this text, it is also clear that "by [God's] reckoning" is identical with "in hope" (see also pp. 147–149. "*Promissio*" here is "*Versprechen*," which is "a promise that looks to the future ("to free us": WA 56:271,31 = LW 25:260; cf. 56:272,18–19 = 25:260 in the context of 56:272,3–273,2 = 25:260–61), but not, as later, "*Zuspruch*," which is a promise given in the

supposed to know anything about. "Indeed, people do not know when they are righteous, because they are righteous only by God's reckoning, which nobody knows anything about; all they know is that they have to keep seeking it and hoping for it."[633]

As a result, Luther ends up again with the traditional doctrine of justification.[634] Or is the "royal way" recommended by Luther between security and despair, which leads to ever-new requests for grace without the enabling power that comes from a concrete promise[635]—is it, when measured against the reformational understanding of the word, something different to the Staupitzian vacillation between security and "disordered fear"[636]?[637]

In the general part of this chapter, the sections "Word and God" and "Word and Christ" could follow each other because Luther himself interprets the determination "outside of us in God" as "outside of us in Christ."[638] The same can also be observed especially in connection with the notion of promise.

In the course of his interpretation of Romans 4:7, Luther expressly goes back to his first guiding principle, which we continue to adhere to, in order to show its christological side: "I said that all our good is outside of us, which is Christ, as the apostle says (1 Cor. 1:30): 'God made him our wisdom, our righteousness, and sanctification, and redemption.'"[639] But it should also be noted here again *how* Luther defines the access that Christ opens up for us or *by what means* the "external righteousness of Christ"[640] actually comes to us. "All

---

present. "The content of the promise [*Verheißung*] or of faith here is the future complete deliverance of believers from their sins" (E. Bizer, *Fides*, 48).

633. WA 56:268,21–23 = LW 25:256–57 (trans. alt.). Cf. the text quoted in n. 610 a): "Unknowingly" stands in parallel with "in hope" and "by the reckoning of a merciful God."

634. Cf. p. 144.

635. WA 56:283,7–12 = LW 25:270. Cf. 56:281,4–21 = 25:268. Cf. the *Fragmentum Lektionum Lutheri* printed in 1:347–49, which is closely related to the series of scholia on Rom. 4:7 and therefore probably does not belong to "the first quarter of the year 1518" (WA 1:346).

636. Cf. E. Wolf, *Staupitz und Luther*, 62.

637. G. Ebeling is of a different opinion: "Basically, even if it is not always sufficiently clear in its formulation, faith between presumption and despair is to be understood not, as in Scholasticism, as a hovering in uncertainty, but as the certainty of salvation. For faith, which always includes the fear of God, clings to the certainty of the divine promise amid the trials and attacks (*Anfechtung*) that accompany it" (Luther 2, *Theologie*, *RGG* 3rd ed., 4:501–2).

638. WA 1:139,35 = LW 51:28. Cf. p. 51 and p. 58.

639. WA 56:279,22–24 = LW 25:267. Cf. 56:279,22–23 = 25:267 with 56:280,2–3 = 56:267.

640. Scholion on Rom. 1:1 (WA 56:159,2 = LW 25:137; trans. alt.), which in its first part (56:157,2–159,24 = 25:135–38) is a "summary" of the interpretation of the whole letter (cf.

things (i.e. wisdom, righteousness . . .) are in us only through faith and hope in him."[641] In what follows, faith in Christ is again described as "always seeking," "always desiring," as a confession to being poor and empty inside but as having full sufficiency and righteousness outside.[642] This confession connects Christians with the "good word, that is, the sweet and comforting word" that the prophet utters from his heart (Ps. 45:1).[643] But "what is it, this saying, 'You are the most handsome of men' (v. 2a)? It means that Christ alone is beautiful and all humans are ugly."[644] If we take the passion sermon on the same text (Ps. 45:1) that we are familiar with already,[645] then it becomes clear on a broader horizon that the "good word" specifically means the image of the crucified, which comes into its own through our sacramental meditation on Scripture in penitence.[646] It is in this context that the idea of "exchange" must also be understood, with which the christological part finishes: "We are his kingdom, but the beauty in us is not ours but his, and with it he covers our ugliness."[647] We are already familiar with this idea from the tropological concluding part of the Christmas Sermon of 1514. There it was understood as the humiliation of ourself corresponding to the Christ event (Phil 2:7; John 1:14), the movement of penitence.[648] That the same is meant in the interpretation of Romans 4:7 is shown by the text immediately following the christological section.[649] Its intention is evident from the sentence

---

56:157,2 = 25:135). To understand the interpretation of Rom. 4:7 especially, this summary passage should always be kept in mind.

641. WA 56:279,24–25 = LW 25:267. Cf. 56:280,3–4 = 25:267.

642. WA 56:279,25–32 = LW 25:267 (trans. alt.).

643. WA 56:280,4–5 = LW 25:267: "Thus (cf. ll. 2–4) in Ps. 45:1 the prophet testifies that his heart is uttering a good word, that is, a sweet and comforting word" (trans. alt.).

644. WA 56:280,5–7 = LW 25:267 (trans. alt.).

645. Cf. pp. 87–89. The dating to 1515 (see n. 316) is of course not entirely certain.

646. Also the passage parallel to our section (WA 56:279,22–280,9 = LW 25:267)—namely, 56:278,1–10 = 25:265 (cf. esp.: "It [i.e. sin] is covered . . . through Christ who dwells in us . . . *the soul throws itself on Christ's humanity* and is covered by his righteousness," 56:278,1–5 = 25:265; author's emphasis; trans. alt.) is best understood against the background of the explanation given above concerning the sacramental meditation on Scripture (see esp. pp. 89–92).

647. WA 56:280,8–9 = LW 25:267. As an explanation of this, we can compare the letter to Spenlein (Apr. 8, 1516), which is one of the most beautiful testimonies of the early period: WA Br 1:33–36, ll.24–36 = LW 48:11–14.

648. Cf. chap. 1, n. 90.

649. WA 56:280,10–281,21 = LW 25:267–68.

already mentioned earlier: "God (has) decreed to impute sin to everyone except to those who are groaning, and fearing, and constantly imploring his mercy."[650]

Summary: In the last quoted text, the early Luther's notion of promise is presented in one of its two aspects with exemplary clarity. It is based on Luke 11:9–10[651] and takes the form[652] of the *prayer of supplication*.

Its other aspect was particularly evident in the interpretation of Mark 16:16 through the eyes of 1 Corinthians 11:31.[653] It is the idea that the promise of salvation is realized specifically in the form of the *confession of sins*.[654]

650. WA 56:281,18–19 = LW 25:268 (trans. alt.). Cf. p. 148. Cf. the sermon of Feb. 15, 1517, which stresses "that grace must be thirsted for, sought after, and received with the sighing and constant groaning of the yoke, and that we should never presume that a person has begun, for as scripture says, 'when a person has finished, then they will begin' [Ecclus. 18:7]" (WA 1:136,9–12).

651. Cf. Luther's interpretation of Ps. 115:1 [= 113:9; Vulgate]; on that, see pp. 139–145, esp. p. 142.

652. Cf. n. 587.

653. See sec. I p. 118 ("The Fulfillment of the Promise in Judgment").

654. That these two forms belong together, see p. 171.

CHAPTER 3

The Interpretation of the Seven Penitential Psalms (1517)

IF WE REVIEW the main chapter of the first part of this investigation, we see that the thrust of the Christmas sermon of 1514, especially its tropological conclusion, also determines the texts from the time of the Romans lectures. "Faith," corresponding to the "word," is understood as the motion of penitence in total self-surrender, in the confession of sins and supplication, but not, as in *The Babylonian Captivity*, as a creature of the audible and public promise—that is, the preached promise of the forgiveness of sins. The special term *promissio* does not go beyond this general understanding of the word but fits seamlessly into it. Because at this time it does not yet have any independent significance, or even a significance that is fundamental for the whole of Luther's theology, we could only present it properly in a broader context.

Like the exposition, we also let Luther himself provide the conclusion of the first part of our investigation in a complete textual context, such as we have in the German *Interpretation of the Seven Penitential Psalms*.[1] This authentic compendium[2] of his early theology appeared in the spring of 1517.

---

1. WA 1:154–220. The *Interpretation of the Seven Penitential Psalms (Bußpsalmen)* has the advantage over the simultaneous interpretation of the Lord's Prayer, which is also highly characteristic of Luther's early theology, in that it was published by Luther himself.

2. See pp. 158–159.

A 1.

It is no coincidence that Luther, in this his first publication,[3] which at the time[4] he was very satisfied with,[5] deals precisely with the penitential psalms.[6] They played a special role in monastic life, with Psalm 51 being prayed at the end of every canonical hour.[7] We need to remember that the professor of biblical theology was himself a friar. So from the outset, Luther has no scholarly interest in the psalms, including the penitential psalms, or even any other part of Scripture for that matter, purely for its own sake but only if it is connected with the life of faith. Rather, they interest him because he sees them as an expression and seedbed of living piety,[8] so that, as Luther emphasized when revising his interpretation of the psalms in the autumn of 1516, it is not the interpreter that interprets

3. WA 1:154. Luther's edition of the Psalter of 1513 (see on that the article "*Psalterdruck*" by G. Ebeling, *ZThK* 50 [1953]:43–99) was only for internal use by his students but not intended for a wider public.

4. However, his interpretation of the *Seven Penitential Psalms* appeared again in 1525 (WA 18:467–530 = LW 14:137–205) but in a revised form, since "the Gospel has reached high noon and is shining brightly, and I also have made some progress in the meantime" (Preface: 18:479,11–12 = 14:140). The difference between the two versions is noticeable (cf. K. Aland, *Der Weg zur Reformation*, 1965, 85–102), but it is more a *pointer* (cf., e.g., p. 158) to an intervening theological turn than its immediate *proof.* For Luther in 1525 finds "nothing objectionable" with his first edition seen as a whole (Preface: WA 18:479, 4–5). That can only mean that he read it in the light of his reformational understanding of the word and so presupposed the very thing that in 1517 was not yet implied. Not everything that remained in 1525, therefore, can be considered Luther's view at the time (see only the interpretation of Ps. 51:8; on that, see pp. 163–164. *For Luther's reformational understanding and so for a proper comparison of the reformational texts with the early texts, it is essential that we use actual revisions, such as the lectures on Ps. 51 of 1532* (WA 40/2:313–470 = LW 12:303–410), *which we draw on in what follows.* [Note that the translation of Luther's interpretation of the *Seven Penitential Psalms* in LW 14 is not based on the original 1517 edition in WA 18 but on the 1525 revision. Hence the referencing will not follow the usual convention of WA 18 = LW 14 (even if the text is unaltered), but after the WA 18 reference the footnote will read: cf. LW 14.]

5. Luther writes to Lang on Mar. 1, 1517, at Erfurt: "I have translated the Psalms and explained them in German; even if they should please no one else, nonetheless they please me exceedingly well" (WA Br 1:90,12–13 = LW 48:40): WA 1:154.

6. On the definition of the term (the number seven, etc.) see A. Hauck, *RE* 3, 3:592 (s.v. "*Bußpsalmen*") and E. Hertzsch under the same keyword in *RGG*, 3rd ed., 1:1538–39.

7. See chap. 2, n. 524.

8. Very instructive on this is G. Metzger, *Gelebter Glaube*, 1964, 54–68 ("The interest in the affects of Scripture against the background of the monastic cultivation of the affects"). Cf. M. Elze, *Züge spätmittelalterlicher Frömmigkeit in Luthers Theologie*, *ZThK* 62 (1965): 381–402, here 382. On the study of Scripture in general, cf. the instruction given in WA Br 1:396–97 (see esp. ll. 20–25) that probably comes from the years 1517/18.

Scripture but Scripture that interprets the interpreter. Scripture thus takes care of its own interpretation and is its own interpreter.[9]

Those who pray find themselves so immersed in the words of the psalter that by repeating them, they make these words the expression of their own piety. The generic "I" of the psalms[10] is exemplified in Christ; they speak in his person. ("Person" here is not to be understood in the developed christological or trinitarian sense but in the original sense of *prosopographic exegesis*, which Christianity inherited from Hellenistic Judaism. This form of exegesis remained independent in the tradition and was handed down to Luther via Augustine, especially via his interpretation of the psalms.[11]) The fact that Christ speaks in them is ultimately what establishes them as subjects that are able to interpret their interpreters. But Christ does not speak in them and from them *to us* but *for* us, in our place, so that we have to confess ourselves as sinners in and with his words here in the penitential psalms. As he had already done in the *Dictata* for many psalms, taking up an old tradition of interpretation,[12] Luther explains programmatically,[13] before beginning his interpretation of the first penitential psalm (Ps. 6), that "these words were spoken by a sinner, but yet *through Christ* in the person of the sinner."[14] Thus Christians appear directly conformed to Christ. This was already expressed in the adscription of the interpretation ("To all the dear limbs of Christ"[15]). But Luther says very clearly in the fundamental remark that prefaces his explanation of the third penitential psalm (Ps. 38): "*Christ prays these Psalms in his suffering and penitence*, which he had to undergo for our sin. This indeed is the true rule that we follow: whoever hears all the psalms as spoken by the mouth of Christ, and then repeats them after him, as children repeat the prayer of their father, cannot pray them after him *unless they are conformed to*

9. WA 3:20,15–21,8 = LW 10:18–19. In terms of its content, Scripture interprets itself as a word of judgment requiring the humiliation of the exegete and hearer: see pp. 21–22 (Scholion on Rom. 6:17) and esp. the texts cited there in n. 2. Also here, nothing would be gained by pointing to the constant basic structure that links Luther's early understanding with his later thought.

10. WA 1:159,36 (on Ps. 6): "This Psalm is common to all and excludes no one" Cf. 1:175,21–22 and 1:212,12–13.

11. Cf. C. Andresen, "Zur Entstehung und Geschichte des trinitarischen Personbegriffes," *ZNW* 52 (1961):1–39.

12. Especially in the summaries (cf. Ebeling, *Luthers Psalterdruck*, 57–58) and each of the first marginal glosses (cf., e.g., the passages mentioned in n. 14 and n. 16 from the first Psalms lectures).

13. WA 1:159,15.

14. WA 1:159,32–33 (author's emphasis). Cf. 3:68,28–37.

15. WA 1:158,1.

him in penitence and suffering."[16] With these words we are again in the horizon of the sacramental meditation on Scripture, which expressly presupposes the interpretation of the penitential psalms. Of course, it is not yet developed; but that happens, as we know, at about the same time as Luther interprets the fourth petition of the Lord's Prayer.[17]

In 1525, while revising his earlier interpretation of the penitential psalms,[18] Luther consistently deleted the three places in which he had said in 1517 that the relationship of Christians to Christ is not mediated through the word but is immediate, through an existential reenactment.[19] Instead, he now inserted into his interpretation at various places the formula "through word and Spirit," which can easily be understood from the writings of these years.[20] He probably does both for the same reason that later makes him say in a table talk: "We must conform to the example of Christ, but we cannot be the sacrament of redemption, for we are too insignificant for that."[21]

A 2.

What is it exactly that gives us the right to view Luther's interpretation of the seven penitential psalms as an authentic compendium[22] of his early theology? The answer to that lies in his "confession" in the epilogue to this writing,[23] where he says that "his only desire is to keep harping away on *one* string and singing just *one* little song.[24] All he wants to do is to vary a single theme, thereby reflecting that "*all the Psalms, all Scripture* . . . praise God's work alone, but condemn all

16. WA 1:175,17–21 (author's emphasis). Cf. WA 3:211,15–212,26.

17. Cf. pp. 97–102.

18. Cf. n. 4.

19. Luther avoids the adscription "To all the dear limbs of Christ" (WA 18:479) and strikes "through Christ" in the text quoted in n. 14 (WA 18:480,19; cf. LW 14:141) and the whole passage attested in n. 16. This is the more conspicuous as the entire preliminary remark on Ps. 38 is not omitted (WA 18:492,13–14; cf. LW 14:156).

20. WA 18:489,24 (cf. 1:172,1ff. = LW 14:152); 18:513,29 (cf. 1:202,10–14 = 14:184); 18:513,22–23 (cf. 1:202,3–5 = 14:184) and 18:519,23–24 (cf. WA 1:209,18–23 = 14:184; on that, see p. 165).

21. No. 5526 (WA TR 5:216,29–31): 1542/43. Cf. chap. 2, n. 284.

22. See p. 155.

23. The section concluding the interpretation (WA 1:219,21–220,23; cf. LW 14:204–5) may be regarded as such, even though it is not separated from the foregoing by a special heading. See LW 14:204, where he says: "As for me, I confess: . . ."

24. WA 1:219,23–24, 25–26 (author's emphasis); cf. LW 14:204.

human work . . . for *it is all the one voice.*"[25] This is how Luther himself emphatically answers the difficult question about the unity of his early theology and its understanding of the word.

To lift up and present this understanding of the word from the interpretation of the penitential psalms to complete the first part of our investigation is more difficult than analyzing the Christmas sermon of 1514 because here the unity of the subject matter does not lie in the logical consistency of a single unified train of thought but in the constant repetition of the "one little song." Accordingly, our presentation cannot follow the text linearly and show how its train of thought progresses but must discursively consider the one topic that keeps being repeated with variations.

In doing this, we will again encounter the individual aspects from which we have developed our understanding of the word at the time of the Romans lectures. What Luther had tried to sort out in the lectures in ever-new attempts—we only have to think of the interpretation of Romans 3:4–5 and 4:7!—is presented here in a balanced and clarified way. What we have before us in this writing is not a first attempt but a conclusion. It is the popular and edifying devotional compendium of the theology of the Romans lectures, which was linked with the theses of the *Disputation Against Scholastic Theology*[26]—which themselves had been prepared in the Romans lectures—as an academic and polemical counterpart in September of the same year.

B I. Confession of Sins—Forgiveness of Sins

The praise of God and his righteousness are inextricably intertwined with the confession of our own depravity. The person praying recognizes and confesses that "praise and honor are yours alone and that therefore righteousness is yours alone, and so too wisdom etc. For no one can honor and praise you without rebuking and dishonoring themselves."[27] It is just another way of expressing the same double movement when the beatitude of Psalm 32:1–2 (= Rom. 4:7) is described in a purely negative way as existing precisely in and with the confession of sins: "Blessed are those to whom God imputes no sin . . . These are they who constantly impute manifold sins and transgressions to themselves."[28] In the background is clearly the notion of the promise of judgment connected with 1

25. WA 1:212,9–12 (from the preliminary remark on the interpretation of Ps. 144; author's emphasis).

26. WA 1:221–28 = LW 31:9–16.

27. WA 1:193,5–7; cf. LW 14:173 (on Ps. 51:15b; trans. alt.)

28. WA 1:167,26–28; cf. LW 14:148 (see parallel WA 1:167,18–20); cf. ll. 22–24.

Corinthians 11:31 ("If we judged ourselves, we would not be judged").[29] It is expressed in the legal principle "Whoever is unmerciful to themselves, to them God is merciful."[30] This leads to prayer and confession: "Therefore, I fear your wrath and am full of remorse in order to forestall your judgment,"[31] and again, "You are gracious, and so willingly hear the true acknowledgment and humble confession of my sins, so that you may also *immediately* comfort me and lift me up, *as soon as* I resolve to humble myself. As soon as I recognize that I am a sinner and lament my sin to you, then I am immediately righteous and pleasing in your sight."[32] Like David says in the psalm, "*I will declare my guilt; then the Lord will declare my reward*, as he did to Mary Magdalene in the house of Simon the Leper."[33] It is precisely this text that clearly shows the difference between the pre-reformational and reformational understanding of the promise. The story of Mary Magdalene (Luke 7:36–50) is seen by the Middle Ages as a great example in a special way.[34] For Luther, on the other hand, it is the unconditional

---

29. See chap. 2, sec. 1 ("The Fulfillment of the Promise in Judgment").

30. WA 1:211,12–13; cf. LW 14:194 (on Ps. 130:8).

31. WA 1:200,6–7 (on Ps. 102:10b). The passage continues: "For such is your nature that those whom you exalt you humble, and those whom you build up you break down" (ll. 7–8).

32. WA 1:170,13–16; cf. LW 14:150 (on Ps. 32:5; author's emphasis). Cf. the interpretation of the Decalogue: "We confess [our sins] . . . and by this humility we deserve to be forgiven . . . However, those who confess are forgiven because God gives grace to the humble" (WA 1:429,18–22). Cf. above pp. 125–126.

33. WA 1:170,21–23 (on Ps. 32:5; author's emphasis). Immediately before (ll. 19–21) it reads: "I will rebuke myself that God may praise me; I will shame myself that God may honor me; I will accuse myself that God may pardon me; I will speak against myself that God may speak for me." This thought is also determinative of the almost simultaneous interpretation of the Lord's Prayer (see chap. 10, n .95). Luther had likewise preached in the same way on Jan. 1, 1517: "But those overcome by shame need only mourn and confess the loss they incurred, and *immediately* their sin is forgiven, as is clear from David, who as soon as he had said, 'I have sinned against the Lord,' heard from Nathan the prophet, 'And the Lord has taken away your sin.' Hence David said, 'I will confess against myself my transgressions to the Lord,' and you forgave the guilt of my sin" (Ps. 32:5: WA 1:120,29–34; author's emphasis; cf. LW 14:150–51). See, *on the other hand*, the interpretation of Ps. 51:8 of 1532: "As David heard, 'the Lord has taken away your sin.' If this word had not come, his broken bones, his fear and despair would have remained. But the word of divine promise must be there, it must be heard" (40/2:415,6–8). See also the sermon of Jan. 6, 1517: "'God, be merciful to me, a sinner.' This saying is well known, but rarely tested with the heart. For if you said these words with true feeling, *by that very act alone* all your sins would be forgiven. Thus, the publican's sins [Luke 18:13] were forgiven through the same word" (1:124,39–42; author's emphasis). See again, o*n the other hand*, the interpretation of Ps. 51:6 of 1532: "'Be merciful to me, a sinner.' And unless they (i.e. the saints) already had a merciful God and the forgiveness of sins, they could not have uttered these words" (WA 40/2:396,8–9).

34. That is shown by Wiltrud von der Fünten ("Maria Magdalena in der Lyrik des Mittelalters," *Wirkendes Wort*, vol. 3, Düsseldorf, 1966, Part 3: Mary Magdalene as example, 166–215). Mary

promise of the forgiveness of sins that later becomes crucially important, not Mary's example. What makes it important is that this promise of forgiveness is assertoric and therefore undialectical, not coinciding with the confession of sins but understood as a proclamation that creates the very reality it promises (thus Luke 7:48,50 are the important verses, not 47).[35] The interim solution, which we first come across in the *Explanations of the Theses on Indulgences*,[36] is still held by Luther in 1518/19 in his exposition of the fifth petition of the Lord's Prayer:[37] As is typical of his early theology,[38] actual forgiveness is said to take place in secret, while public forgiveness can be added as a reassuring declaration of the actual

---

Magdalene is the model of compassion in the late Middle Ages; sinful people identified themselves with her; her figure stands for them.

35. Cf. Luther's first Mass sermon of the early summer of 1518, which directly reflects the reformational turn in his theology (see chap. 4, n. 19): "Christ said to the sinful woman: 'Your sins are forgiven,' I absolve you, 'go in peace,' because you believe . . . I promise you that you are absolved, be of good cheer, and never doubt this word . . . Thus our salvation is in the word and yet not in the word, but since Christ is bound to the word, you must not waver. The sacrament is a rock founded on Christ, but Satan will suggest to the dying person: You are not contrite enough, nor have you made sufficient satisfaction. And with many other such snares, he will try to dislodge them from the foundation of their faith. But they boldly say back to Satan: I am absolved; if I have done nothing, I commit myself to God. And just as Christ does not die, no one who believes in him perish. Christ would have to die a thousand times before any such person was lost. Those who say otherwise are his bungling preachers. Let the dying put their trust in Christ through the judgment of the priest" (WA 4:658,21–34). On the characterization of the promise in the reformational sense given above, see further the *Sermon on the Sacrament of Penance* (1519): "[There are three things in the holy sacrament of penance:] The first is the absolution, the word of the priest, which shows, tells, and proclaims to you that you are free and that your sins are forgiven before God, according to and by virtue of the above words of Christ spoken to St. Peter. The second is grace, the forgiveness of sins, the peace and comfort of the conscience, as the words declare . . . The third is faith, which firmly believes that the absolution and the word of the priest is true by the power of Christ's words, 'Whatever you loose . . . shall be loosed,'" etc. (WA 2:715,22–30 = LW 35:11; trans. alt.).

36. Especially in the "Explanation" of thesis 7 (WA 1:539–45 = LW 31:98–107; on the "Explanation" of thesis 7, see E. Bizer, *Fides*, 108–14 and chap. 4 A). Here, too, Luther expressly refers to the story of Mary Magdalene: 1:541,24–29 = 31:101.

37. "The first forgiveness is bitter and difficult for us but is the noblest and dearest of all. The second is easier, but that much smaller. The Lord Christ shows both to us in Mary Magdalene. The first was when he turned his back to her and said to Simon: her many sins are forgiven her. But she still lacked peace. The second was when he turned toward her and said: your sins are forgiven. Then she went in peace and had peace. Therefore, the first makes you clean; the second gives you peace. The first works and brings; the second rests and receives. There is an immeasurable difference between the two. The first is only in faith and merits much; the second is in feeling and receives the reward. The first is used with the advanced; the second with the weak and with beginners" (WA 2:117,15–25 = LW 42:64; trans. alt.; cf. 2:116,28–34 = 42:63).

38. See chap. 2, sec. C ("The Inner Word: Hidden Grace").

forgiveness that has previously taken place, but it does not have to be.[39] *These three stages in the history of the interpretation of a single text clearly show how difficult it was for Luther to arrive at his reformational understanding of the word. It is therefore by no means a matter of simply positing that this later understanding is already implied in the early texts.*

We must now show more precisely that the linguistic and material difference between the confession of sins and the forgiveness of sins, which Luther later strongly emphasized[40] and which is also evident in the psalms themselves, considered from a form-critical perspective,[41] is not yet present in his interpretation of the penitential psalms.

In Psalm 32:5b[42] ("I said"), the praying person first speaks of their confession and then of the turning point that occurred with their forgiveness.[43] Luther here does not yet see this turn as a new start (think of his later saying, "then comes the other word"[44]) but as something given immediately with the confession of sins: "You have remitted them, *because* I have reckoned them to my account and confessed the disobedience of my sin."[45] Likewise in Psalm 6, Luther had disregarded the contrast between the psalmist's pleas and laments and his sudden and sure certainty of being heard ("God has heard . . .": v. 8[46]), and in doing so, he ignored the past tense altogether, which is especially noticeable

39. Otherwise, E. Bizer, *Fides*, 145.

40. Cf. Luther's interpretation of Ps. 51:8 (1532): "We teach that this is the doctrine of justification, that justification is given only to those who believe the word. When you hear the absolution, *you must distinguish* between your contrition, which is without solid ground and so very feeble, and the word of absolution, which by comparison is like heaven, or God himself. You can be certain that your contrition counts for nothing, but under no circumstances should you doubt the absolution. What the minister says should be considered as having been spoken by God himself . . . [Say to yourself:] this applies to me. God has given me ears to hear and proclaims to me: 'I absolve you.' I believe it because it is true" (WA 40/2:412,5–9, author's emphasis, 414,1–2; cf. further n. 56).

41. Cf. J. Begrich, *Das priesterliche Heilsorakel*, *ZAW* no. 52 (1934): 81–92.

42. According to Luther's numbering, 32:6.

43. Cf. besides Ps. 6:8/9, whose interpretation by Luther is dealt with in the following, Ps. 22:21/22 (cf. v. 24) and Ps. 28:5/6.

44. *The Freedom of a Christian*, §9; WA 7:24,9–10 [German]; cf. LW 31:348 [Latin].

45. WA 1:170,25–26 (author's emphasis). On the "because" (*propter*) and its background in the theology of the pact (covenant), see pp. 147, 149–151.

46. According to Luther's numbering, vv. 9b,10. [The words "God has heard" are Luther's and not found in the English Bible.]

given his otherwise careful attention to exegetical details.[47] There is no mention at all about the psalmist's prayer having been answered but only about the fact that God "gladly hears those who cry out and lament their sin, but not the smug and secure" and that therefore the godly "live a good life" . . . "in a groaning and sorrowful spirit."[48] In 1531/32, on the other hand, Luther writes regarding Psalm 6: "But in the end, the Psalmist indicates that such a prayer will be answered, as a comforting example and encouragement to all who are suffering such affliction (*Anfechtung*), *that they should not remain inside themselves*."[49]

B 2. The Secret Whisper—The Forgiveness of Sins

Psalm 51:8a[50] (LET ME HEAR JOY AND COMFORT) is the plea that "I may hear your secret whisper: your sins are forgiven. No one is aware of hearing it, no one sees it, no one understands it. But it can be heard, and hearing it gives one a bold and cheerful conscience and confidence toward God."[51]

The primacy of the inner word,[52] known to us from the Christmas sermon of 1514 and from many places in the first Psalms lectures, still prevails, as we see, in 1517. Luther here goes back directly to his gloss in the *Dictata*: "TO MY inner HEARING, that is, to my conscience made restless by sin and vexation, YOU WILL GIVE by the inspiration of your grace JOY AND GLADNESS,"[53] which

47. Thus, for example, in Ps. 32:7/8 (according to Luther's numbering, 9/10), Luther makes a point of stressing the transition from the plea to God's answer ("Now God answers": WA 1:171,21–22) but of course without any mention of its concrete mediation through the word. [This transition does not come out in the English Bibles, trans.]

48. WA 1:165,10–13; cf. LW 14:145. See also the two whole sections 1:165,5–28; cf. 14:145–46. Luther also ignores the past tense in the Latin Vulgate of Ps. 102:18 [the equivalent text in the English Bible, Ps. 102:17, is cast in the future tense and so does not demonstrate Luther's point, trans.]. This paraphrase in the present tense immediately turns, against the intention of the Latin text, away from the fact that the psalmist's prayer was heard and focuses instead on those who need, or supposedly do not need, God to hear them (1:202:15–29).

49. *Summarien über die Psalmen und Ursachen des Dolmetschens* [*Summaries of the Psalms and the Reasons for Luther's Interpretations*]: WA 38:20,8–10 (author's emphasis).

50. According to Luther's numbering, 51:9a.

51. WA 1:190,1–4; cf. LW 14:170. Luther himself refers to this passage in his interpretation of Ps. 143:10 (according to the English Bible: v. 8): "LET ME HEAR EARLY OF YOUR MERCY. That is, as stated in the fourth penitential Psalm (51:8), let me hear joy and comfort, let me hear of your grace that says in my heart, your sins are forgiven. Thus God speaks peace in the heart of his people" (WA 1:216,35–38; cf. LW 14:201).

52. See B 1 above and chap. 2 C ("The Inner Word: Hidden Grace").

53. WA 3:285,15–16.

in turn must be seen together with the interpretation of Psalm 85:8: I WILL HEAR WHAT GOD THE LORD WILL SPEAK IN ME.[54] In the spiritualism referred to here, "the *internal* work of God" can only be contrasted with "the external work of humans"[55] but not with the external oral word, which is what everything will depend on in the interpretation of the same verse in 1532.[56]

Nevertheless, compared to the *Dictata* gloss, Luther's use of Matthew 9:2 to understand the "secret whisper" is striking. He says the whisper is "your sins are forgiven." Here he takes up his scholion on Romans 8:16,[57] in which he quotes Bernard in support: "This is the testimony that the Holy Spirit gives in our heart, saying, your sins are forgiven."[58] But he stops just short of the main point of the quote and goes on again with his own commentary to make it clear that we can only be certain of forgiveness through "humility" and "remorse."[59] It is only since the *Explanations of the Theses on Indulgences* (Latin: *Resolutiones*)

---

54. In the *Dictata* (on Ps. 112:7: WA 4:253,23–26 = LW 11:389; see chap. 2, n. 46), Luther himself deliberately put these two passages together. On his understanding of Ps. 85:8, see chap. 1, nn. 39 and 43.

55. WA 1:190,7–12 (on Ps. 51:8a [author's emphasis]; according to Luther's numbering, v. 9b).

56. "You must make the spoken word your own. It fights against those who hate the external word . . . We treat confession and the sacraments in such a way that we urge the word itself. In confession, we are not concerned about contrition but concentrate on the word etc. Thus we are called back from our deeds to listen to it. So too in Baptism, you find that the hearing of the word brings joy. Again, in confession and the sacrament, we hear the words 'given for you' and so are called back to divine consolation. The main part of confession and the sacrament should be the hearing of the word itself. The pope, on the other hand, obscures the absolution and the words [of institution] in the sacrament" (WA 40/2:411,1–2, 4–10; cf. LW 12:369–70). "Therefore, the Psalm teaches us the true way to calm our heart, which is none other than to hear the word either from a brother or from listening to a sermon" (40/2:414,3–5). See the whole interpretation of the verse: 40/2:408,11–418,4; cf. LW 12:367–74.

57. Before that, compare the gloss on Ps. 143:8: "LET ME HEAR, i.e., let me hear and feel by inner inspiration . . . YOUR MERCY, that is, that my sins are forgiven through it" (WA 4:444,17–19).

58. WA 56:370,10–11 = LW 25:360 = MPL 183:384 A (*Sermon for the Feast of the Annunciation of the Blessed Virgin*); already referenced by J. Ficker in 56:369 at I.28.

59. Luther speaks first (WA 56:370,7–8, 12–14 = LW 25:360) of the need for each of us to have a faith that is sure and certain, in the spirit of Bernard (*Sermones Super Cantica Canticorum*, MPL 183:384 A and B), but this is all but withdrawn again when he says: "However, it is our humility and remorse in good works that makes them pleasing to God" (56:370,20 = 25:360, trans. alt. The same sentiment is found in the letter to Spalatin of Feb. 15, 1518: WA Br 1:144–47; ll. 12–51). What Luther says in 56:370,24–29 = 25:360 cannot deny the correctness of this interpretation, for in the marginal gloss on Rom. 8:38 (56:86,19–24 = 25:78), he takes back again what he says in 56:370,24–29 = 25:360.

and the Hebrews lectures[60] that Luther knows that the certainty of forgiveness comes through the concrete oral promise.

Before that, the new understanding of the promise seems to be heralded in only a single place, in the German *Interpretation of the Penitential Psalms*, specifically Psalm 130:5: "AND ON HIS WORD I HAVE RELIED, that is, on his pledge and promise.[61] This is now the nature of the new and inner self, that it constantly waits, hopes, trusts, and faithfully believes in God. Therefore, God does not forsake it, for he has promised grace and help to all who trust in him, rely on him, and wait for him. The same word and promise of God is all that there is to support the new self that lives not by bread alone but by the very word of God (Matt 4:4)."[62] Here, too, Luther again follows his *Dictata* gloss: "MY SOUL HAS WAITED ON HIS WORD his *promissio*."[63] But the marginal gloss shows that "*promissio*" here is not yet meant in a present sense, as a legally binding promise with immediate effect, but in a purely future sense: "No one waits except the one who has not yet received what is promised."[64] This is how "promise" seems to be understood also in the German interpretation, as suggested by the immediate context of the passage cited. Here the "word and promise of God," "his promise and pledge," certainly give no certainty but are perceived only in fear and hope.[65]

B 3.

The *christological features* that appear in the interpretation of the individual passages[66] do not change the picture. Even the significance of Christ can only be spoken of negatively. Righteousness, which is Christ (1 Cor. 1:30), produces in us nothing but an acknowledgement and confession that we are

---

60. Cf. there esp. the scholia on Heb. 5:1 (WA 57/3:169–171 = LW 29:171–73) and 9:24 (57/3:215–216,19 = 29:217–18.

61. In 1525 this sentence is added here: "For to hope and wait without the word of God is tempting God" (WA 18:519,23–24 = LW 14:192).

62. WA 1:209,17–23; cf. LW 14:192. Although Grimm's dictionary, *Dt Wb*, s.v. *enthalt* (3:549) does not specify the meaning of the word (*Halt, Stütze*, or *Inhalt*?) for our passage, it can be unambiguously determined from Luther's other linguistic usage at this time, where it is understood as "support." See the first Mass sermon of 1518, "This is our comfort and our life's support" (WA 4:656,8), and the *Exposition of the Lord's Prayer* of 1519, "Humility alone supports (= *erhält, hält, stützt*) even those who live by grace" (WA 2:122,14–15 = LW 42:70, trans. alt.).

63. WA 4:419,10–11.

64. WA 4:419,23–24.

65. The interpretation of Ps. 130:5c has as its parallel that of v. 5a and v. 5b (WA 1:208–9; cf. LW 14:191–92): See below B 4: "Fear and hope."

66. On the Christology of the preliminary remarks, cf. A 1.

sinners: "A holy person . . . does not stand on their own holiness but on the rock of your righteousness, which is Christ, and on this rock are founded all who are their own accusers, punishers, and judges"[67] (on Ps. 32:8 = 32:5). As in the Romans lectures, the affirmation is immediately interpreted by the negation.

This is consonant with the fact that the conformity of the person who recognizes their sin with Christ, who was struck by God, is based on a linguistic event (God's "wrathful words"[68]): "God's arrows and his wrathful words make the sin in my heart actual . . . Where this is the case, things are right with us; for the same thing happened to Christ" (on Ps. 38:3).[69] However, this conformity with the exalted, justified Christ can only be asserted where grace is simultaneous with the confession of sins—a simultaneity that Luther presents here, as already in the Romans lectures,[70] in the schema of the communication of attributes (*communicatio idiomatum*): "It must be true that those praying here are full of sin, since they confess their sin, as the text says, and yet it must also be true that those who pray are without sin, and so, just as Christ was truly alive and dead at the same time, so too those who are full of sin and without sin at the same time must be true Christians" (on Ps. 38:4).[71] This schema, however, does not allow the linguistic and factual difference between the confession of sin and the promise of grace to emerge.

The interpretation of Psalm 51:4[72] is of particular interest to Luther in the Romans lectures because of its importance. According to the interpretation of Romans 3:4–5, the WORDS of the psalm verse are the words of judgment that must be revealed if there is to be a recognition and confession of sin.[73] Here they also appear from a christological perspective, in a fundamental and comprehensive statement based on Luke 24:45–47: "All Scripture and God's word point to the suffering of Christ, as he himself testifies in the last chapter of Luke: Scripture contains nothing but the promised grace and forgiveness of sins through the suffering of Christ, so that whoever believes in him . . . will be saved."[74]

---

67. WA 1:171,4–6; cf. LW 14:151.

68. Cf. chap. 2 D ("The External Word: Public Judgment").

69. WA 1:176,23,26–27; cf. LW 14:157.

70. Cf. chap. 2, n. 242.

71. WA 1:177,11–14; cf. LW 14:158.

72. According to Luther's numbering, v. 5.

73. WA 56:229,24–25,28–32; 230,13–15 = LW 25:214.

74. WA 1:187,29–32; cf. LW 14:168; the conclusion is based on Mark 16:16 and Rom. 10:11.

The way that Luther now turns this summary statement around is significant.[75] Unbelief here is not applied to those who reject the word announcing the *forgiveness* sins but to those who refuse to be sinners: "This truth and the faith and suffering of Christ is opposed by all those who do not want to be sinners."[76] The word that *reveals* our sins is the only content of Scripture, even of its promises, "thus God promised in all his words that Christ would die because of *sin. Therefore*, anyone who will not consider themselves, or be considered, a sinner tries to make God a liar and themselves the truth."[77] Luther's reversal of the intention of Luke 24 in this way may be justified in view of the interpretation of the text (Ps. 51:4 = Rom. 3:4). However, it is instructive of Luther's own theology that he makes this reversal everywhere, even in texts that do not permit it, as for example in Romans 8:31 (on Ps. 130:4: BUT WITH YOU ALONE THERE IS FORGIVENESS), where Paul says, "Thus God is *for* us, who will be against us?" And yet even here, Luther turns around and asks, "*But then*, who will be for us when God is *against* us?"[78]

Finally, here too, in Psalm 102:13, that formula, "the Word became flesh in order that the flesh may become the Word," which Luther had developed in the conclusion of his Christmas sermon of 1514, is again discernable: "[I cannot come to you. Therefore, Lord, arise, come to me, and take me to yourself.] The arising refers to the very sweet and gracious coming of God into the flesh, for he came to us in order that he might raise us to himself."[79] This happens only because God's incarnation becomes for us his word of judgment: "AND WE HAVE SEEN HIS GLORY (Ps. 102:16; cf. John 1:14). It has now come about through God's gracious incarnation that the unknown God has become known, and that all honor is his alone, and that no one is righteous, good, wise, strong, holy, and true but God alone. But before that, God was not honored, for humans considered themselves wise, righteous, good etc. and so God's honor was ascribed to them instead."[80]

B 4.

Fear and hope is the immediate anthropological outcome of the intertwining of the confession of sins and the forgiveness of sins where no verbal distinction is made between them.

75. "We cannot even list here all the words that are contradicted by the proud, if we want to put them all in one heap and name them" (WA 1:187,27–29; cf. LW 14:168).

76. WA 1:187,33–34; cf. LW 14:168.

77. WA 1:187,35–38; cf. LW 14:168 (author's emphasis). Cf. the scholion on Ps. 51:4: WA 3:288,1–3,8–36 = LW 10:236.

78. WA 1:208,3–4; cf. LW 14:191 (author's emphasis).

79. WA 1:200,33–201,2; cf. LW 14:183.

80. WA 1:202,9–14.

[Up to this point the psalmist has described] "fear, the cross of the old self," and "hope, the life of the new." Luther goes on to say:

> These two things are taught in all the psalms, indeed in all of Holy Scripture, for God works so strangely in his children[81] that he saves them equally through things that are contradictory and opposed, for hope and despair are against each other. Accordingly, they must hope in despair, for fear is nothing but the beginning of despair, and hope is the beginning of salvation. These two opposite things must be in us and therefore there must be two opposite selves in us, the old and the new. The old must fear, despair, and perish; the new must hope, endure, and be raised up. Both of these exist in one person, indeed in one work at the same time. Just like a carver, by chiseling away the wood that is not needed for the image improves its shape, so the fear that cuts the old Adam down produces the hope that forms the new self.[82]

The formation of the new self is described here again[83] with the Aristotelian model of the "artisan," and where at the same time we see Tauler's principle that "the greater the unbecoming (*entwerdendes*), the greater the becoming (*gewerdendes*)"[84] also brought to bear.[85] This description uses formulations that Luther had used on the title page of the partial edition of his *German Theology* (*Theologia*

81. Luther cites here Ps. 68:35: GOD WORKS STRANGELY (*MIRABILIS*) IN HIS SAINTS. Cf. Ps. 4:3.

82. WA 1:208,15–30; cf. LW 14:191 (on Ps. 130:5).

83. See pp. 28–29 (esp. nn. 35 and 36).

84. See chap. 2, n. 251.

85. Also the idea of "*resignation*" is strongly emphasized. In expounding Ps. 51:19, where he takes up the scholion on Rom. 10:10 (on that, see pp. 45–47) almost word for word, Luther writes: "The person who offers a sacrifice of righteousness gives God his due. But we owe God more than we have. Therefore, we can pay him in no other way than by handing over all that we have and all that we are, while at the same time humbly acknowledging our sin and confessing his righteousness: that he is just in whatever way his divine will deals with us. This attitude and resignation is the highest righteousness that we can possess" (WA 1:194,7–13; cf. LW 14:175). And in looking back to Ps. 51:19, he says in connection with Ps. 143:4, entirely in the sense of Tauler, that a sacrifice pleasing to God is offered "when a soul is without comfort from any creatures and is even forsaken and persecuted by itself, so that it looks for nothing but the sheer pure grace of God" (WA 1:214,24–26; cf. LW 14:198). Cf. WA 1:217,10–11; LW 14:201 (trans. alt.): "Humans must become blind and surrender themselves to God in true faith. But faith sees nothing, for it is the dark way" (on Ps. 143:8).

deutsch) that appeared in December 1516 to list the contents of this writing[86]: "With us, the situation is that Adam must get out and Christ must come in; Adam must become nothing, and Christ alone must remain and rule."[87]

Like Adam and Christ, and the old and the new self, "fear and hope go hand in hand."[88] In a similar way, in the contemporaneous sermon on the stilling of the storm (Matt. 8), Luther can formulate this in a chain of inferences as an order of salvation (*ordo salutis*): "Just as God's judgment produces fear, so fear produces crying, but crying obtains grace."[89] Of course, the individual phases here do not become detached; the moments of this *ordo salutis* appear simultaneously, for "since the old self lives, fear, which is its cross and death, must not cease and God's judgment must not be forgotten. And whoever lives without the cross, without fear, and without God's judgment does not live rightly."[90]

The path of fear and hope is not taken with a certainty that is guaranteed by the word of salvation and based on it alone, because according to an almost formulaic sentence,[91] "This same good thing is not apparent but concealed under the cross, annihilated, and hidden in God."[92] But how are we to know that it is

---

86. "A noble little book of great spiritual value on the right distinction and understanding of the old and the new self, of Adam's child and God's child, and of how Adam in us must die and Christ arise" (WA 1:153; cf. 1:152).

87. WA 1:186,25–26; cf. LW 14:167 (on Ps. 51:2; according to Luther's numbering v. 3); cf. 1:160,14–17; cf. 14:141; 1:188,18–22; cf. 14:169; and 1:194,37–39; cf. 14:175. Cf. interpretation of the Lord's Prayer of 1517: "Since Christ must come in . . . Adam must get out" (WA 9:147,38–39 in the context of ll. 27–39).

88. WA 1:207,31; cf. LW 14:190 (on Ps. 130:3).

89. WA 1:207,31–33; cf. LW 14:190 (on Ps. 130:3); cf. the parallel formulation in 207,24–26. In the sermon on the stilling of the storm of Feb. 1517, he says: "Anyone for whom Christ does not sleep does not perish, anyone who does not perish does not cry out, anyone who does not cry out is not heard, anyone who is not heard receives nothing, anyone who receives nothing has nothing, and anyone who has nothing will perish" (1:129,23–25 = 51:25). See Augustine on Ps. 50:15: "To that end, I allowed a day of trouble to come upon you, for if perhaps you had not been afflicted, you might not have called on me, but because you are in trouble, you call on me, and when you call on me, I will deliver you, and when I deliver you, you will glorify me and therefore you will no longer depart from me" (MPL 36:578).

90. WA 1:207,33–36; cf. LW 14:190 (on Ps. 130:3).

91. See esp. pp. 54–56.

92. WA 1:183,29–30; cf. LW 14:162 (on Ps. 38:20). See the slightly earlier interpretation of the Decalogue: When humans see their lostness, "it gives rise to groanings, self-hatred, and a longing and pleading for those things. Then God gives his grace to the humble, which he later takes away again and hides in order to add something even greater, but always hiding the opposite under its opposite. Therefore, this is the wisdom that is drawn out of the things that are concealed and found in the things that are hidden" (WA 1:487,10–14).

"his goodness and friendship" that God "has hidden and gives under his wrath and chastisement,"[93] and that therefore "all God's chastisements are friendly and meant to be a blessed comfort in disguise"?[94] How are we to know this for sure if Luther himself says earlier that "when God attacks us, our nature is so weak and despondent that we do not know whether he is attacking us out of wrath or grace"?[95]

The absence of the word that gives certainty does not mean that (on Ps. 51:10) Luther could not speak of the "upright spirit" and "good will," which is "directed straight to God and that seeks God alone"[96] and which is "poured into the innermost part of our heart by God."[97] But this is still nothing more than Augustinian.

Only the disposition—that is, the humility produced by the acceptance of the word of judgment (admittedly, produced entirely by God!)—receives God's wisdom. This is not shown in the word but is revealed to the humble "in its inner truth and hidden depths"; on the other hand, "the proud only see its outward appearance."[98] Luther says clearly enough that salvation has no verbal form and so is not to be found in the word of promise: "The inner and hidden part of this wisdom is nothing but knowing oneself thoroughly, and therefore hating oneself, seeking all righteousness not in oneself but in God alone, always being dissatisfied with oneself and yearning for God, that is, humbly loving God and looking away from oneself."[99]

B 5.

The beginning of the interpretation of the final penitential psalm (Ps. 143), HEAR MY PRAYER, O GOD, points to Luther's early understanding of *law and gospel*: "The life of a saint is more a taking from God than a giving; more a desiring than a having; more a becoming righteous than a being righteous. Thus St. Augustine says that faith acquires what the law requires. Therefore, asking, desiring, and seeking is the true essence of the inner self."[100]

---

93. WA 1:160,30–31; cf. LW 14:142 (on Ps. 6:3).

94. WA 1:160,27–28; cf. LW 14:142.

95. WA 1:159,25–27; cf. LW 14:140 (Preliminary remarks on the interpretation of Ps. 6).

96. WA 1:191,4; cf. LW 14:172 (on Ps. 51).

97. WA 1:191,5–6; cf. LW 14:172.

98. WA 1:188,32–34; cf. LW 14:169 (on Ps. 51:6). Cf. above p. 163.

99. WA 1:189,4–8; LW 14:169 (on Ps. 51:6). Notice also here the subtle but significant difference to the interpretation of 1532 (on the same verse): "This wisdom is hidden so that, even if it is preached and taught, it still remains hidden, *because human reason cannot grasp it*; as he [the psalmist] says, he sins in all that he does" (WA 40/2:393,6–8; cf. LW 12:357). Cf. pp. 57–58, esp. n. 190.

100. WA 1:212,19–22; cf. LW 14:196.

The words of Augustine quoted here, "What the law of works commands by threatening, the law of faith obtains by believing," introduce the section in his *On the Spirit and the Letter*[101] that Luther takes up with its conclusion: "Therefore, ask and desire"; "And so by the law of works, God says, do what I command! But by the law of faith, we say to God, *give* what you command! Therefore, the law commands in order to remind faith what to do. That is, faith is commanded to ask, even if it is not yet able to do it, in order that it may at least know that it needs to *ask*."[102]

The significance of this passage for Luther's theology of the years 1515–1517 can hardly be overestimated. In the Romans lectures, it is determinative for the great scholia on 3:21[103] and 3:27,[104] which in turn are parallel texts for the interpretation of 4:7.[105] It strengthens Luther in his view that "the true essence of the inner self" lies solely in "asking, desiring, and seeking." The asking arises from the confession of sins: "Therefore, they are holy because (a) they lament to you their evil and (b) they ask for grace."[106] But, at the same time, it is faith that obtains what the law demands, through asking, desiring, and seeking it.

From this we can conclude and summarize Luther's repeated[107] developed understanding that *the law produces the confession of sins, the gospel the supplication or request.*

---

101. 13:22 (CSEL 60:175 = MPL 44:214).

102. 13:22 (CSEL 60:175 = MPL 44:214; author's emphasis); cf. LW 25:243.

103. WA 56:256,25–261,9 = LW 25:243–48. The subject of the interpretation is set by the scriptural passages mentioned in the first section (56:256,25–28 = 25:243), but the interpretation itself is objectively carried out by the quotations compiled from *Concerning the Spirit and the Letter* in the second section (56:256,29–257,9 = 25:243–44). Of these, it is especially chap. 13,22 in the following text (56:257,15ff = 25:244) that is most important, because it interprets the "law of faith" as a "humble prayer" or request (cf. 56:257,3–4 = 25:243).

104. WA 56:263,31–267,7 = LW 25:251–54 (the key text is the section 56:264,5–15 = 25:251, which is crystallized around Augustine's *Concerning the Spirit and the Letter*, chap. 13,22).

105. Cf. chap. 2, n. 625.

106. WA 1:170,31–32; cf. LW 14:151; the same again in ll.33–34: They "fear your judgment and know (a) that their holiness is nothing in your sight but (b) wait humbly for your grace" (on Ps. 32:6; (a) and (b) have been inserted by the author). Cf. chap. 2, n. 525.

107. The texts to which we refer in the following are

a) the scholia on Rom. 3:21 and 3:27 (see nn.103 and 104); the scholia on Rom. 7:6 and 10:15 (see chap. 2, n. 30);
b) the Advent sermons of 1516 (WA 1:104–6; 107–9; 109–111; 111–15 = LW 51:17–23);
c) the scholion on Gal. 1:11 (WA 57/2:59,17–60,22), which clearly takes up the texts mentioned in a) and b), and the *Heidelberg Disputation* (WA 1:350–74 = LW 31:39–70), in which the final form of Luther's early theology is clearly formulated.

This is the only way to understand why law and gospel appear clearly separate, on the one hand, while on the other—and this is the predominant impression—they merge smoothly into each other:

> The law makes sin known, so that once it is recognized, grace may be sought and obtained. Thus, God gives grace to the humble and those who humble themselves are exalted. The law humbles, grace exalts. The law produces fear and wrath; grace produces hope and mercy. For through the law we acquire a knowledge of sin, and through a knowledge of sin, humility, and through humility, grace. Thus God's alien work finally brings about his proper work, in that he makes people sinners in order to make them righteous.[108]

The transition from the law to grace takes place in an immanent dialectic and does not appear as "the other word" in an assertoric orality[109] that clearly proclaims the difference between law and grace. Christ does not become the "voice" but remains a "word, albeit a hidden word, because he will teach you inwardly."[110] We are called to make ourselves certain of this inner word—even if it is expressed in the invitational call of Matthew 11:28 or in the words of the forgiveness of sins in Matthew 9:2[111]—by means of cross and humiliation[112] ("for to come to Christ and leave yourself is a great cross"[113]). We are thus formed into the image of the

108. Proof of thesis 16 of the *Heidelberg Disputation*: WA 1:360,37–361,5 = LW 31:50–51 (trans. alt.). See the interpretation of the Decalogue (1516): WA 1:429,36–430,2 and the proof texts quoted in n. 89 (*ordo salutis*).

109. An intermediate step in the understanding of "law and gospel" between the *Heidelberg Disputation* and the *Freedom Tractate* can be seen in the *Exposition of the Lord's Prayer* of 1519: see WA 2:93,30–34 = LW 42:35; 2:95,16–18 = 42:37 and 2:99,13–23 = 42:42.

110. Sermon for 3 Advent 1516 on John 1:23 (I AM THE VOICE OF ONE CRYING IN THE WILDERNESS): WA 1:109,4–5 in the context of ll. 3–5. Cf.: "Thus he calls himself the voice of one crying, i.e., a voice calling out loudly, to distinguish it from the word that is Christ and very much hidden" (WA 1:108,10–12); on both, see chap. 1, nn. 43 and 39, in the context of B 2.

111. Sermon for 2 Advent 1516 on Matt. 11:5 (THE POOR HAVE THE GOOD NEWS PREACHED TO THEM): WA 1:105,19–22. Cf. the approximately simultaneous scholion on Gal 1:11 (57/2:59–60).

112. WA 1:105,26: "By clinging to Christ and being conformed to him through faith." Particular attention should be paid to this closer definition of how we are to make ourselves certain (with E. Bizer, *Fides*, 149): cf. n. 113.

113. Sermon on St. Matthew's Day (Feb. 24, 1517): WA 1:141,11. This sermon clearly shows that Matt. 11:28 has a completely different function in the texts considered here (cf. n. 111) than in the scholion on 5:1 of the Hebrews lectures (for that, see chap. 5): At first it appears

crucified Christ, which is vividly set before our eyes: "Behold, the Lamb of God, who takes away the sins of the world";[114] "behold, here is Christ and his Spirit."[115] By being thus formed into him,[116] we leave behind our own form and take on the form of the humbled and humiliated Jesus, as the 1514 *Sermon on the Prologue of John* had already explained.

With *The Babylonian Captivity of the Church* in mind, we asked about Luther's earlier view of the promise and faith and put it in the framework of his general understanding of the word prior to the Hebrews lectures. The special concept of *promissio* fits seamlessly into this framework, showing that it is not yet understood as a promise that gives certainty but is only seen in connection with the confession of sins and the prayer of supplication.

---

as a comforting promise (1:140,27–34), *but then is immediately revealed again as a guide to the verification of the cross of Christ through our own reenactment of it* (1:141,7–37).

114. WA 56:424,15–16 = LW 25:416 (this is the culmination of the scholion on Rom. 10:15).

115. WA 56:338,30 = LW 25:327 (this is the culmination of the scholion on Rom. 7:6).

116. See the section "Sacramental Meditation on Scripture," esp. pp. 87–92, and E. Bizer (*Fides*, 148–49) on the *Sermon on the Assumption of the Blessed Virgin Mary* (cf. pp. 89–92): "Here the difference between law and gospel is that the law apparently only remains 'teaching,' but that the image of Jesus is able to ignite the will in a completely different way so that we freely take on his labors in voluntary obedience, and this is precisely the grace that is given to it." This finding can be compared with what has been said about Rom. 7:6 (*Fides*, 44) via the proof texts quoted in nn. 114 and 115.

Part 2

Structure of the Presentation

IN HIS SERMON on Genesis 9:9 of November 1519,[1] the keyword *PACTUM* prompts Luther to make an excursus into the meaning of the "promise" from Adam to David. He begins with a general note: "Observe the words used in the Scriptures: covenant, pact, promise, testament, sign of the covenant, testimony, cup of the new and eternal testament."[2] He then draws the important conclusion: "Christians have the word of the gospel, Baptism, and the Eucharist. If you wish, you could add to them the promise (or we could read 'prayer') and the meditation on the teaching of Scripture. On the other hand, matrimony, unction, and confirmation are not sacramental signs and have no promise attached to them. The order is immaterial."[3] The importance of this summary lies in the fact that it is the first document to give the overall conception of the treatise *The*

1. WA 9:348–49. The list of promises compiled here is incorporated into *The Babylonian Captivity of the Church* (see chap. 6, n. 118, for a list that is more differentiated from a literary critical perspective). On its dating, see 9:322–23. Cf. W. Maurer (Melanchthon 2, 150), who holds that the sermon "was probably given in November 1519 . . . but is no longer available to us in the original transcript but only in a supplementary revision and in this form it is closely related to the Easter sermon of April 8." Maurer continues, "I do not shy away from the assumption that it was Melanchthon who made this revision," which of course cannot be conclusively proven.

2. WA 9:348,9–10. See also 357,4–6 (on Gen. 17): "We must observe in the scriptures the terms testament, covenant, pact etc. For they strengthen God's promise. Every pact (covenant), as the apostle says (probably in the Epistle to the Hebrews) is completed among the Hebrews through the death of the testator." It seems to me that the Genesis sermons prepared for the sermon *Concerning the Testament of Christ* of Apr. 8, 1520, rather than being edited later by Melanchthon in the places in question (see n. 1).

3. WA 9:349,2–5. The conjecture that has been made is required by what is said in the otherwise almost identical passage in Melanchthon's *Capita* (for its relationship to Luther's Genesis sermons, we can now compare the perceptive excursus of Maurer, Melanchthon 2, 148–51 with 113–19): "These, properly speaking, are sacraments, which are signs of the divine promises. And so, in the New Testament the sacraments are, properly speaking, Baptism, Absolution, and the Lord's Supper. For these have promises attached to them. The order is immaterial. Perhaps there is good reason to add prayer and the meditation on Scripture (*doctrina divina*) to the list of sacraments" (CR 21:41–44). Moreover, *promise*is a generic term for the whole series (WA 9:349,2–5) and therefore meaningless in the passage in question. Maurer, Melanchthon 2, 150, n. 157, confirms this assumption. On the close cooperation between Luther and Melanchthon on just this matter of the sacraments, see Luther's letter to Spalatin of Dec. 18, 1519 (see n. 6): ll. 34–35 in the context of ll. 26–42; Br. 1:595.

Babylonian Captivity of the Church of 1520. To understand it is the aim of this whole investigation into the meaning of the "word" in early Luther.[4]

On December 18, 1519, Luther writes to Spalatin about the sermons he had just[5] published on penance, baptism, and the Lord's Supper:

> Neither you nor anyone else should hope for or expect any treatise from me on the other sacraments until I am shown where I can prove them [in Scripture]. For I cannot think of any sacrament that is not a sacrament already. For there is no sacrament unless it has been expressly given by a divine promise for the exercise of faith, since we cannot deal with God without the word of the promiser and the faith of the receiver. You will hear about those seven sacraments another time.[6]

Our understanding of the sacrament is further clarified by a series of disputations that immediately prepare for *The Babylonian Captivity* and so must belong to the first half of the year 1520.[7] Thus the principal themes of the treatise, according to the two passages mentioned, appear again in Luther's explanation of the first thesis of the *Disputation Concerning Infused and Acquired Faith* held February 3[8] ("Infused faith is absolutely necessary for approaching the sacrament"):

> Wherever we have the word of God promising us something, there faith on the part of humans is necessary who believe that this promise is true and will be fulfilled so surely and firmly, that they would rather deny all sense, all reason, all knowledge, all contradiction, even all creation rather than not believe the word of God. For whoever does not believe the word of God makes God a liar, denies his truth, and sins against the first commandment. But in every sacrament, God's word promises us something, such as, "I baptize you in the name of the Father etc.," "I immerse you with all your sins," likewise, "I absolve you etc.," "I forgive

4. For the research question and method, see pp. xxxv–xxxix.

5. For a more precise dating, see *BoA* I:174.

6. WA Br 1:594–95; ll.19–25; see LW 35:5.

7. Apart from the two disputations named below, we can mention here the theses of the *Disputation on Circumcision* (WA 8:30–31), the theses of the *Circular Disputation on the Signs of Grace* (WA 6:470–71), and the theses of the *Disputation concerning the Baptism of the Law, of John, and of Christ, performed according to the Law* (WA 6:472–73).

8. WA 6:84–98.

you all your sins etc." Therefore, in every sacrament, it is necessary to have a most certain faith in the promise of God.[9]

A short and concise outline of *The Babylonian Captivity* is finally presented in the *Theses of the Disputation on Distinction 2, Book 4 of the Sentences.*[10] This expressly proves that Luther's examination of scholastic sacramental theology (or, more precisely, as can be seen from the baptismal section of *The Babylonian Captivity,*[11] Luther's examination of the fourth book of Gabriel Biel's *Collectorium*, as attested by the marginal notes in Luther's own personal copy) goes beyond that of penance. Consider the following theses:

"3. We hold that the sacraments of the new law consist of a promise of God and a visible sign.
4. There are as many sacraments of the new law as there are promises and their associated signs.
5. Baptism, the Eucharist, and penance are properly the three sacraments of the new law.
6. The rest seem to have been first instituted and called sacraments of the new law by the church and usage.
7. There is no obstacle to saying that there are as many sacraments as there are articles of faith, if you remove the visible sign.
8. In fact, there are almost as many sacraments as there are words of God, and these sacraments arouse faith even if the sign is missing."

Together with that summary of November 1519, these theses, which cannot be precisely dated, formulate for the first time the *overall* understanding of the "reformational"[12] doctrine of the word and determine the structure of the tractate *The Babylonian Captivity* right up to its conclusion. It could in fact be headed "concerning promises in general."[13] According to this conclusion, we could number "among the sacraments all those things to which a divine promise has been given,"[14] especially prayer. Accordingly, in what follows we will present Luther's understanding of penance, the Lord's Supper, baptism, meditation on

9. WA 6:88,31–89,8.

10. WA 9:312–13.

11. See chap. 7.

12. See pp. xxxv–xxxix, esp. the essay mentioned there in n. 1.

13. WA 6:571,35–572,9 = LW 36:123–24.

14. WA 6:571,35–36 = LW 36:123 (trans. alt.).

Scripture (*divina doctrina*), and prayer. With that, we will have then described the specific forms of his reformational concept of promise (and at the same time the marks of the church![15]).

Except for chapter 5, the substance of which continues in chapter 6,[16] each chapter will be self-contained and lead to the reformational understanding of the promise in its entirety. In addition to chapter 5 (the reformational turn), chapter 9 (the new Christology) has a special place since the topic discussed there has implications for all chapters. The order of the chapters gives an indication of the chronological order in which the organizing center of Luther's reformational theology was expanded.

15. On the marks of the church (*notae ecclesiae*), see *On the Councils and the Church* (1539): WA 50:628,29–642,32 = LW 41:148–65; "Against Hanswurst" (1541): WA 51:484 = LW 41:194–98.

16. Cf. p. 255.

CHAPTER 4

The Reformational Turn and the Reconfiguration of the Sacrament of Penance

(The Promise of Absolution—Faith)

THE FIRST AND at the same time decisive phase in the discovery and development of the reformational understanding of the promise lies in the indulgence controversy—that is, in the conflict between Luther's early theology, presented in the first part of this investigation, and the traditions of sacramental theology, especially those relating to the sacrament of penance, that Luther inherited and that are inherently contradictory and full of tensions. At the beginning of the indulgence controversy, there is yet no sign of "the reformational turn in Luther's theology."[1] Luther begins the discussion based on the theology presented in the first part of this investigation. We see this clearly from the sermon on the story of Zacchaeus, preached on October 31, 1517,[2] which in view of the Festival of All Saints the next day with its great pomp of indulgences,[3] Luther concludes with a statement on the matter of indulgences, which he loosely tacks on to the main part of the sermon.

Luther initially accepts the Lombardian and Thomistic definition "that there are three parts to penance":[4] contrition, confession, and satisfaction. As in the *Sermon on Indulgences and Grace*, Luther's first German publication on the matter of indulgences,[5] it is striking that he speaks only of the *materia* of the

1. See above "Structure of Presentation," n. 12.

2. WA 1:94–99 (Statement on the question of indulgences: 98,12–99,28). For the dating, cf. K. Bauer, "Das Entstehungsjahr von Luthers *Sermo de Indulgentiis pridie Dedicationis*," *ZKG* 43 (1924): 174–79, who argues in favor of fixing the date at 1517. E. Vogelsang ("Zur Datierung der frühesten Lutherpredigten," *ZKG* 50 (1931): 112–45, here 121) simply follows the WA—that is, the editor Knaake, who dates the sermon to 1516 (1:94, n. 2)—without even considering the arguments of Bauer.

3. WA 1:98,18: "This great pomp of indulgences is near at hand."

4. WA 1:98,23 and 1:243,4–7 = AL 1:60 (*A Sermon on Indulgences and Grace*; see n. 5): "Some new teachers, such as the Master of the Sentences, St. Thomas [Aquinas], and their disciples, divide penance [*puß*] into three parts: contrition, confession, and satisfaction." See Peter Lombard: IV/d.16/c.1 and Thomas Aquinas: *ST* III/q.90/a.1. [*Puß* (= *Buße*) or *poenitentia* has three meanings in English: the sacrament of penance, penitence, and repentance; trans. note.]

5. WA 1:239–46 = AL 1:57–65.

sacrament and passes over the *forma*; that is, he says nothing about the words of absolution, which will later be for him the ground and center of its conception. However, Luther now prefers a two-part division rather than the three-part: "Penance has two parts: the sign (*signum*) and the thing itself (*res*),"[6] as in the hermeneutical schema of Augustine. "The *res* comprises the interior and only true penance of the heart, of which Christ speaks when he says: 'Do penance . . . The *signum* comprises the exterior penance, which is frequently fictive, although the interior penance is often feigned also."[7] All the weight is put on inner penance. This is stated in even more detail in the sermon:

> Interior penance is true contrition, true confession, true satisfaction in the spirit. When penitents are truly and rightly displeased with themselves in all they have done and are effectually converted to God, and clearly acknowledge their guilt and confess it to God in their heart, then by hating themselves, they punish and put themselves to death internally. In this way, they make satisfaction to God. In fact, those who are truly penitent would wish, if it were possible, that all creation would see their sin and hate it and they are ready to be trampled on by all.[8]

This statement against indulgences culminates in the remark that true penitents "do not seek indulgences and the remission of penalties . . . they do not ask for indulgences but crosses."[9] With this, Luther himself gives a succinct summary of his early penitential theology, indeed, of his early theology in general. We also find his early theology in the *Treatise on Indulgences*,[10] which is probably to be understood as a preparation for the disputation on *The Ninety-Five Theses*, which was never held. In view of his otherwise thorough discussion, the fact that Luther says nothing about the priestly words of absolution, either in these

---

6. WA 1:98,23–24.

7. WA 1:98,24–7. [Luther is quoting the standard Vulgate rendering of Matt. 4:17 (*Poenitentiam agite*), which is translated as "repent" in most English versions of the Bible. However, the translation that best renders Luther's understanding of Jesus's words at this time is "do penance"; trans. note.]

8. WA 1:99,1–7.

9. WA 1:99,7–8,12.

10. WA 1:65–9 (*Tractatus de indulgentiis*). On the literary character of this text along with its temporal and material classification, see the investigation by J. Wicks, S. J., "Martin Luther's Treatise on Indulgences," *Theological Studies* 28 (1967): 481–518. An English translation with commentary is given in Wicks, *Man Yearning for Grace* (Corpus Books, 1968), based on the superior text in WA Br 12:5–10 = LW 71 (forthcoming).

two texts or in the *Sermon on Indulgences and Grace*, is surely no accident. This also lends special significance to the striking finding that prior to working on the *Explanations of the Theses on Indulgences*, Luther had never once dealt with Matthew 16:19 (or Matt. 18:18; John 20:23). That is, he says nothing about this key text from 1509 until the end of 1517 or the beginning of 1518. Indeed, for the same reason that lets him pass over even the gifting words of the Lord's Supper,[11] he sees the "infusion of grace" as an inner change from God's judgment to God's righteousness,[12] as "an interior illumination of the mind and a kindling of the will,"[13] but nowhere, as later, does he see this grace as bound to the *promissio*, understood as an external, oral, and public promise.[14]

This concept of promise appears for the first time in the theses of the circular disputation *Pro veritate inquirenda et timoratis conscientiis consolandis* (*On Seeking Out Truth and Comforting Terrified Consciences*; from here on, the Latin title will be used in abbreviated form, *Pro veritate*) from the early summer of 1518.[15] This is a document of the first rank for the story of Luther's theology, yet until now it has gone almost unnoticed.[16] It clearly summarizes the result of the enormous intellectual effort that Luther expended on the "Explanations," and if *The Babylonian Captivity* is the benchmark of his reformational theology, then the *Pro veritate* theses deserve more attention than the *Heidelberg Disputation*,[17] which also grew out of the "Explanations" but yet in contrast to them, shows no sign of the reformational turn in Luther's theology at any point.

The groundwork for the *Pro veritate* theses is laid in the "Explanations" of theses 7 and 38 of the *Theses on Indulgences*, which are first taken up in the

11. Cf. chap. 2, n. 496.

12. Cf. chap. 2 C ("The Inner Word: Hidden Grace").

13. WA 1:66,9 (*Tractate on Indulgences*).

14. It is hard to understand how, in such a careful investigation as *Vorgeschichte der reformatorischen Bußtheologie* by R. Schwarz, this difference can be completely overlooked (304–5: "Luther means the same." Note also the lack of precision on p.15, where he calls the first Psalms lectures "reformational," but then goes on to distinguish them from "what is truly reformational").

15. WA 1:629–33 = LW 71 (forthcoming).

16. The text is so little known that it does not appear in any modern select edition of Luther's works. In connection with the question of the reformational turn, only K. Aland (*Der Weg zur Reformation*, 108), to the best of my knowledge, has referred to it. On the one hand, he strongly emphasizes its importance, but on the other he again limits it ("Here the new insight shines through in several places," 108). It is now included in *Luther deutsch. Die Werke Martin Luthers in neuer Auswahl für die Gegenwart*, ed. K. Aland, vol. 1: Die Anfänge, 1969. For the English translation, see LW 71 (forthcoming).

17. WA 1:350–74.

conclusion of the *Sermon on Penance* (*Sermo de Poenitentia*; before Easter 1518).[18] We must therefore turn to them first. We will then be able to conclude this chapter with a comprehensive presentation of the theses *Pro veritate*, which need to be considered together with a specific commentary on them found in a first Mass sermon of the same time[19] and, above all, together with the *Acta Augustana* (*Proceedings at Augsburg*).[20] With the theses *Pro veritate* and their defense in Augsburg before Cajetan, we reach the climax of the indulgence controversy. The battle over papal and scriptural authority[21] is only the aftermath. The famous *Sermon on Matthew 16:13–19* in Leipzig on June 29, 1519,[22] which Luther himself describes as a summary of the entire subject matter of the *Leipzig*

18. WA 1 (:319–24; on its dating, 1:317):323–324,23. This passage at the end of the sermon follows almost immediately after a discussion of interior contrition (cf. the *Treatise on Indulgences* [see n. 10], esp. 1:66,9–15, and the appendix to the *Sermon on Zacchaeus* [see n. 2], esp. 1:99,1–8), which contains penitential motifs from late medieval meditative piety (WA 1:319,27–320,39, esp. 1:319,27–31; see the "Explanation" of thesis 26 of the *Theses on Indulgences*, 1:576,10–26 = LW 31:160–61), in which traditions stemming specifically from Augustine (1:320,14: "Blessed Augustine, *Confessions*, Book 8") and Bernard (1:323,18–22; 1:323,2–3) (cf. "Explanation" of thesis 4 of the *Theses on Indulgences*: 1:534,5–10 = 31:89) are treated. We can see from the discussion that the influence of Augustine's *On the Spirit and the Letter* (cf. chap. 3 B 5 [on law and gospel]) was particularly significant for Luther's theology from 1515/16–1517/18: WA 1:321,30–322,7. The strong tension that exists between the final passage and the rest of the sermon becomes clear from the 1519 *Sermon on the Sacrament of Penance* (WA 2:709–23 = LW 35:9–22), the conception of which is based solely on the new starting point or organizing center evident in the final passage and no longer needs the other motifs of the 1518 *Sermon on Penance*.

19. WA 4:655–59. The *terminus a quo* for the dating of the sermon is the drawing up of the "Explanation" of theses 7 and 38 of the *Theses on Indulgences*, without which it is incomprehensible. For the *terminus ad quem*, we cannot go too far beyond May 30, 1518, since at one point it touches almost verbatim on the letter of dedication, accompanying the Explanations, addressed to Staupitz, which is tied to this day (WA 1:527,14–15): WA 4:658,40–659,5 = WA 1:525,24–526,9. Cf. E. Vogelsang, "Zur Datierung der frühesten Lutherpredigten," *ZKG* 50 (1931): 112–45, here 133.

20. WA 2:1–26.

21. Cf. the finding of G. Hennig, *Cajetan und Luther*, 81, that "the reformational Scripture principle has its *Sitz im Leben* in the reformational understanding of the sacrament and its constitutive word."

22. WA 2:241–49. "The gospel embraces all matters of the whole disputation" (2:246,23). See the letter to Spalatin of July 20, 1519: WA Br 1:420ff., ll. 130–32: "It is, however, the gospel that most clearly embraces the substance of both disputations; therefore, I am compelled to explain the sum of the whole disputation to all".

Disputation, as well as the *Sermon on the Sacrament of Penance* of 1519[23] and the treatise *The Babylonian Captivity*,[24] which he describes as a brief repetition of what he has already said "in treatises and disputations,"[25] do not take us beyond the *Pro veritate* theses and so do not warrant any special attention.[26,27,28]

A) Declaration ("Explanation" 7 and Scholion on Hebrews 7:12)

a) Explanation 7

Immediately following the "Explanation" of thesis 6, Luther tries in his "Explanation" of thesis 7 of the *Theses on Indulgences* (abbreviated to "Explanation" 7 in this section) to determine the relationship between divine forgiveness of the guilt of sin and priestly absolution. In doing so, he touches on a neuralgic point in the tradition and rightly says that "not even our adversaries themselves, with all their teachers, can show to this day *how* a priest forgives sins."[29]

The relationship described is more than a little problematic for Luther because, on the one hand, he wants to understand the declaration of absolution as an indication of the divine forgiveness that has already taken place,[30] but on

23. WA 2:709–23 = AL 1:181–202 = LW 35:3–22. Cf. the sermon of Oct. 30, 1519, on Matt. 9:1–8: WA 9:415–16.

24. WA 6:543–49 = LW 36:81–91 (The Sacrament of Penance).

25. WA 6:543,5–7 = LW 36:81. Possibly what is meant by "treatises" is especially the 1519 *Sermon on the Sacrament of Penance* (see n. 23) and by "disputations" especially the *Circular Disputation Pro veritate* (see n. 15).

26. Footnote missing in German original.

27. Footnote missing in German original.

28. Footnote missing in German original.

29. WA 1:544,35–36 = LW 31:106 (author's emphasis; trans. alt.). See the *Asterisci Lutheri adversus Obeliscos Eckii* of Mar. 1518 (WA 1:279), whose connection with the *Theses on Indulgences* Luther himself expressly emphasizes several times (1:287,1–2; 1:289,32; 1:290,32–33; 1:293,15; 1:296,33–34; 1:298,11–12; 1:301,18,29; 1:313,34–35): "How they (i.e. the keys) remit sins . . . is uncertain to all" (1:287,4–5; cf. 1:285,36–37).

30. Luther does indeed emphasize the hypothetical character of his assumption of the declarative understanding ("I did not put it forward from the heart but because of the way it is used by others": WA 1:287,3 [*Asterisci*] = WA 1:544,34–35 = LW 31:106 ["Explanation" 7]; "from the heart" = "with full conviction": see 1:297,30–31; 1:307,11), but at first, in "Explanation" 7 (cf. the *Asterisci*: 1:287,14–17), he is unable to find any other solution.

the other, against this understanding, he finds himself persuaded by the text of Matthew 16:19, according to which "God is understood to approve that which the priest looses [absolves] rather than the other way around."[31]

However, there is an objection to this correct insight that comes in the form of Luther's early theology of the cross, which he also uses here, especially with its exciting themes of lament and theophany in the psalms. The objection is that God himself must act first.[32] This leads Luther back again to the declarative understanding prevalent in nominalism, according to which God's forgiveness precedes the word spoken by the priest.[33]

First of all, we find again that notion of penance and grace known from the *Dictata* as the "internal sacrament":[34] "But then humans know so little about their justification that they think they are close to damnation, and do not think that this is an infusion of grace but rather the effusion of God's wrath upon them."[35] Surprisingly, however, this thinking does not stay with the early immanent dialectic, as strikingly demonstrated by the new interpretation of the story of Mary Magdalene (Luke 7) and that of David before Nathan (2 Sam. 12).[36] Luther now realizes that this dialectic offers no certainty: "As long as they remain in this wretched state where their conscience is confused, people have neither peace nor consolation, unless they flee to the power of the church and seek solace and remedy for their sins and afflictions uncovered by confession. For they will not be able to find peace by their own council or strength but, on the contrary, will finally be swallowed up in despair by their own melancholy."[37]

---

31. WA 1:539,22–23 = LW 31:98 (trans. alt.), in the context of 1:539,17–23 ("Explanation" 6). See WA 1:539,38–39; 540,4–5 = LW 31:98–99 ("Explanation" 7) and WA 1:288,6–10 (*Asterisci*): "He did not say: Whatever or how much I have bound in heaven will also be bound on earth but, on the contrary, whatever you have bound etc. These words signify rather that God confirms the things done by his servants on earth. Therefore, as I said, I have put thesis 6 [i.e. thesis 6 of the *Ninety-Five Theses* repeated in "Explanation" 6] forward, but not with full conviction, so that I can listen to what others have to say."

32. WA 1:540,8–30 = LW 31:99.

33. Cf. Biel, who says with reference to the "Master" [i.e., Peter Lombard, the "Master of the Sentences"]: "Priests forgive or retain sins when they judge and show the sins that have been forgiven or retained by God. Consequently, it follows from this that guilt is not forgiven through the sacrament of penance, but is forgiven by God through prior contrition before the sacrament is actually received, though not before it is received with prayer and a good intention" (IV/d.14/q.2/a.1/not. 2 [D]; likewise, IV/d.4/q.2/a2 concl. 4 [H]). Biel takes the first sentence word-for-word from Lombard's *Sentences* IV/d.18/c.6. See ibid. (c.1) the framing of the question.

34. Cf. chap. 2 C.

35. WA 1:540,30–32 = LW 31:100 (trans. alt).

36. WA 1:541,24–542,6 = LW 31:101–2. See chap. 3 B 1.

37. WA 1:540,34–38 = LW 31:100 (trans. alt.).

For the first time in Luther's theology, the priestly word of absolution, whose power is "imparted"[38] in Christ's word of promise in Matthew 16:19, receives a function that turns the dire need around and brings it to an end; it "causes"[39] and produces certainty, "provokes" and "arouses" it.[40] "Here the priest, seeing such humility and remorse, will presume to trust in the power that has been given to him most fully for rendering mercy and will loose [the sins of the penitent], and having loosed their sins, he will declare them absolved and thus give them peace of conscience."[41]

Certainty is found in the external word ("in the judgment of another"), not in one's inner experience.[42] This is the first clear reference ever to the reformational understanding of word and faith. It reads as follows:

> Those to be absolved must guard themselves very carefully against any doubt that God has forgiven their sins and that they can have peace

38. WA 1:543,16 = LW 31:104 ("conferred"); ll. 17–18 ("given") in the context of ll. 14–19. It is not quite clear to Luther at this point *how* Matt. 16:19 (or Matt. 18:18 and John 20:23) can be a "promise." Although the words "[their sins] are forgiven them," being in the third person dative case (Latin: forgiven to them), are not a promise spoken directly to the person (as in "I absolve you"), Luther nevertheless takes them that way: "With the words, 'their sins are forgiven them,' sinners are stirred to believe this forgiveness . . . and our faith is kindled with the words, 'they shall be loosed.'"How Luther imagines the relationship within the promise between the historical institution (cf. "if only people will believe that what Christ *has promised* is true"; WA 1:541,14–15 = LW 31:101; author's emphasis; trans. alt.) and the present effect (cf. 1:541,21–22 = 31:101: "unless you believe in Christ who *promises*"; author's emphasis; trans. alt.) is not revealed here. According to Biel, the two are so tightly intertwined that the present effect arises from "the *pactum* of God, who assists his sacrament to achieve the effect for which he instituted it" (IV/d 14/q 2/a 1/not. 2 [D]). See, with the necessary changes, the commentary on the Mass: Lect. 47 X (2:228).

39. "Therefore, I am not concerned whether the priest is the necessary cause or whether there is another cause of the forgiveness of sins, as long as it is certain that by some means the priest truly forgives sins and guilt" (WA 1:543,31–33 = LW 31:105; trans. alt.).

40. See nn. 38 and 177.

41. WA 1:540,38–41 = LW 31:100 (trans. alt.). Luther here is clearly dependent on traditional ideas. See Biel in his commentary on the Mass (Lect. 1 D; 1:12–13; author's emphasis): "God has given the church the power by which it can *distinguish* a case on account of which heaven is closed and *render judgment* by *declaring* this person worthy and that person unworthy. The *worthy grieve over their sins and confess them*, the unworthy do not grieve over their sins, no matter how much they confess them . . . And the authority to do this is called the power of the keys. This is twofold, namely, the authority *to examine* the case of the sinner who is making confession, and the authority *to judge* it accordingly. This twofold power or authority is called the keys. The first is the key of knowledge, the second the key of power." See further pp. 192–193, esp. n. 73.

42. Apart from the text that follows above, see WA 1:542,24–26 = LW 31:103: "We . . . cannot forgive ourselves the guilt of our sin, for no one should believe in themselves unless they want to make two confusions out of one" (trans. alt).

> of heart. For even if they are uncertain because their conscience is confused (as must regularly happen if our remorse is true), yet they are constrained to abide by the judgment of another, not because of the priest himself or his power, but because of the word of Christ who cannot lie when he says, "Whatever you loose on earth." For faith born of this word will bring peace of conscience, so long as the priest looses according to it. Whoever seeks peace in another way, for example, inwardly through experience, certainly seems to tempt God and to desire to have peace in fact, not in faith. For you will only have peace as long as you believe in the word of the one who promised: "Whatever you loose, etc . . ."[43] If you believe you have received it, you have it: you only have as much as you believe you have on account of Christ's promise.[44]

The fact that this word holds true by itself, of its own accord, and is not dependent on the credibility of the transmitter, so not on the *opus operantis* [the work of the worker = the priest doing the action], is clearly highlighted by the enormous number of examples where the efficacy of the sacrament is ex *opere operato* [derived from the action of the sacrament itself, not from the merit or holiness of the priest], as for instance in the case of the mock baptism of Gelasinus.[45]

Nevertheless, the reformational understanding of word and faith, in the strict sense, is not yet evident here, for the external word does not bring about actual justification but presupposes it and, as a judgment, only "decides" about

43. WA 1:540,41–541,8 = LW 31:100 (trans. alt.). Cf. 1:542,15–18 = 31:102.

44. WA 1:543,8–9 = LW 31:104 (trans. alt).

45. WA 1:543,35–544,8 = LW 31:105. As in the *Sermon on Penance* (1:323,38–324,2) and in later statements (see, e.g., the interpretation of Matt. 18:20 of 1537: WA 47:301,28–303,7), Luther places the story, recorded in *The Paschal Chronicle* (MPG 92:684–85), of the mock baptism and martyrdom of Gelasinus ("We read among the deeds of the martyrs that there was a certain actor who desired to be baptized as a joke to ridicule baptism, but since he was converted while being baptized, he was truly baptized by his heathen companions and immediately crowned by them with martyrdom)," alongside the story of St. Athanasius as a boy ("He baptized boys whom the Bishop of Alexandria afterwards declared baptized"). Luther's conclusion that "therefore we are justified by faith, and by faith we also receive peace, not by works, neither by penances, nor by confessions" (ll. 7–8) is not surprising and is not a contradiction of his assertion that the word is effective *ex opere operato* (which for Luther means *ex verbo dicto*, because the word is spoken) but its consequence: "The word of Christ and faith in the word are such great things" (WA 1:543,40–544,1 = LW 31:105; trans. alt.). These words are put even more precisely in the *Sermon on Penance* (see n. 18): "Faith is such a great thing and the word of Christ so powerful" (1:323,34–35).

it[46]—that is, whether there is evidence of it in the contrition of the penitent ("the priest *seeing* such humility and remorse"). But in relation to what is made certain, it must be considered as the grace and gift of God, because it works *faith* in forgiveness. With this, Luther arrives at an ambivalent concept of grace, which he puts succinctly and concisely as follows: "God's forgiveness (by infusion) effects grace, but the priest's forgiveness (by the word) brings about peace, which is both the grace and gift of God, since it is faith in God's actual forgiveness and grace."[47] Insofar as the priestly word bestows the grace of peace,[48] Luther can say: "*This* (i.e. grace = peace) . . . is what our teachers say is effectually conferred by the sacraments of the church."[49]

The efficacy of the priestly word therefore only applies to making forgiveness certain, not to forgiveness itself. In regard to the latter, it only has a declarative meaning: "Therefore, Peter does not loose before Christ but declares and shows Christ's loosing."[50] In sum, the priestly absolution does not absolve sins but only declares and shows that our sins have already been absolved.

But this distinction between actual forgiveness (in heaven) and the word that decides about it and makes it certain (on earth) is already beginning to be abolished: "As long as it is uncertain to us, it is not forgiveness, since it is not yet forgiveness *for us*."[51] The difference in understanding to that of Romans 8:16,[52] which we know from the lectures and the interpretation of the penitential psalms, is palpable: The "testimony of the Spirit" now comes directly from the word of Christ in Matthew 16:19, which is used and claimed with the priestly declaration of absolution, and remains bound to it. The Spirit of God is the word of Christ that creates certainty:[53]

---

46. On "judgment" as the finding of the priest, see esp. the scholion on Heb. 7:12 and on that see pp. 192–195. Cf. n. 41.

47. WA 1:542,7–9 = LW 31:102 (trans. alt.).

48. Luther finds this keyword for the "certainty of forgiveness" esp. in the story of Mary Magdalene (Luke 7:50: "Go in peace"!): WA 1:541,29 = LW 31:101.

49. WA 1:542,9–10 = LW 31:102 (author's emphasis; trans. alt.). On the tradition in question, cf., for example, Thomas Aquinas *ST* III/q 62/a 1–6. See the continuation, "but not the first justification itself, which must be present in adults before the sacrament" (ll. 10–11).

50. WA 1:542,14–15 = LW 31:102 (trans. alt.)—formulated in the light of Matt. 16:19 and the problem highlighted on pp. 185–186.

51. WA 1:541,22–23 = LW 31:101 (trans. alt.; author's emphasis).

52. See pp. 163–164. See the scholion on Heb. 5:1 and on that see pp. 233–234.

53. Thus the connection of the following passage (WA 1:543,20–26 = LW 31:104; trans. alt.) with the immediately preceding sentences of the same section (see n. 38) is deliberate.

> Christ knew that the conscience, already justified by grace, would by its own anxiety cast out grace if it had not been aided by faith concerning the presence of grace in the ministry of the priest. Indeed, sin would have remained if the sinner had not believed it was forgiven. For even the forgiveness of sins and the gift of grace are not sufficient; we must also believe that we are forgiven.[54] This is the testimony the Spirit of God gives to our spirit, that we are children of God, for to be a child of God is something so deeply hidden (for children may even appear to themselves to be enemies of God) that unless we believe that we are children of God it could not be so.

The peculiar sequence of actual justification (without the oral word of salvation) and the confirmation of its certainty by the word of absolution—which is understood as declarative with regard to the justification that has taken place but effective with regard to the confirmation that follows—is made clear again in the polemical conclusion of the "Explanation" directed against Wimpina.[55]

In his countertheses, Wimpina had criticized something that is easily understandable from his Thomistic point of view, as Cajetan also did later—namely, the declarative understanding of the word of absolution expressed in thesis 6 of Luther's *Theses on Indulgences*.[56] He says against Luther: "Not only 'by confirming and declaring,' as the priests and Levites of the old law used to do with lepers, but also by doing that very thing ministerially, instrumentally, and dispositively through the sacrament."[57] Luther does not accept this objection but persists in his own view: "The priest of the new law only declares and confirms the loosing of God (that is, shows it) and by this showing of it and by his judgment, he calms the troubled conscience of the sinner, who is bound to believe his

---

54. This statement was expressly condemned by the Bull *Exsurge Domine* (of June 15, 1520) (Denzinger, 750). Compare, on the other hand, the argument of Seripando, the papal legate, at the Council of Trent with Augustine's statement from *On Christian Doctrine* 1.18 on the dominical words concerning the keys: "That whoever in the church does not believe that their sins have been forgiven them, they are not forgiven them" (MPL 34:25). However, his argument failed to persuade the council fathers (H. Jedin, *Geschichte des Konzils von Trient*, 2:325).

55. WA 1:544,9–545,8 = LW 31:105–7.

56. See his tractate *Utrum sacramentalis absolutionis effectus sit remissio culpae* of Oct, 1, 1518 (*Opuscula* 1575,111). Cf. G. Hennig, *Cajetan und Luther*, 57,59–60.

57. W. Köhler, *Dokumente zum Ablaßstreit*, 129,27–30. Luther also refers in WA 1:544,26–27 = LW 31:106 to the text printed in Köhler, *Dokumente*, 2:32–34. Also Prierias, likewise a Thomist, raises the same objection as Wimpina: WA 1:659,3 (Luther's *Ad dialogum Silvestri Prieratis de potestate papae responsio* of Aug. 1518). On Wimpina's text, cf. directly Thomas Aquinas *ST* Suppl. q 18/a 1.

judgment and receive peace."[58] The word seems to presuppose actual justification and with it faith as well: "If it is necessary for those approaching [the sacrament of penance] to believe, then it is not the sacrament itself, but faith in the sacrament that justifies . . . since it is impossible for the sacrament to be given beneficially unless it is to those who *already* believe and are righteous and worthy."[59]

Thus the ambivalent concept of grace means an ambivalent concept of faith. On the one hand, faith as "purity of heart" (Acts 15:9),[60] the effect of actual justification, presupposes the word of absolution; on the other hand, however, the word of absolution follows it, and it is only now created as certain faith.

These two valencies of the notion of faith (which Luther still uses in thinking about the traditional distinction between divine forgiveness and the priestly word), which can be expressed as "we are justified by faith, and by faith we also receive peace,"[61] first coincide in the theses *Pro veritate.* They make it clear that faith comes from the word alone and is no longer presupposed by it. Accordingly, actual justification is shifted into the word of absolution so much that it means the same as being made certain of justification. The word no longer *decides* about it (the abandonment of this traditional aspect is the decisive theological step, but because it clearly reflected Luther's thought about the word and justification, it was consequently rejected at Trent![62]) but *brings it about.* This determines the relationship between them in Matthew 16:19, which is dealt with in "Explanation" 7 with its identification of divine justification with the human word of absolution. Thus an insight that Luther came across at one point already in "Explanation" 7 is consistently and logically retained: "As long as we are uncertain, it is not forgiveness, because it is not yet forgiveness for us."[63]

---

58. WA 1:545,1–4 = LW 31:107 (trans. alt.).

59. WA 1:544,40–41 = LW 31:107 (cf. below pp. 234–235), 1:544:39–40 = 31:107 (author's emphasis; trans. alt.).

60. WA 1:544,32–33 = LW 31:106 (on "purity of heart" cf. the scholion on Heb. 5:1 and on that see pp. 234–235). If we compare the wording of 1:544,29–31 with that of ll. 32–33, there seems to be an incongruity. But how the sentence that Christ *works* the "justifications in the Spirit" and "purity of heart" *through* the priest is to be understood can be seen unmistakably from 1:545,4–6 = 31:107, which is the immediate continuation of 1:545,1–4 (n. 58), and from the use of "to work" (l. 6) in the context of 1:545,4–6 = LW 31:107, as well as from the scholion on Heb. 7:12, which will be treated presently (pp. 192–195).

61. WA 1:544,7–8 = LW 31:105.

62. Canon 9 *Concerning the Sacrament of Penance*: "If anyone says that the sacramental absolution of the priest is not a judicial act . . . or says that the confession of the penitent is not necessary for the priest to be able to absolve them, let them be anathema" (Denzinger, 919; cf. 902, esp., "a judicial act in which a verdict is delivered by the priest as by a judge").

63. See n. 51.

Luther recognizes in "Explanation" 7 that the distinctions made in the traditional description of the power of the keys[64] obscure the certainty of divine forgiveness precisely because they destroy its unambiguity through a never-ending regress from authority to authority.[65] So he puts forward the objection "We know of only *one* type of keys, namely, those which are given to earth."[66] But, apart from the traditional distinction between divine forgiveness and the word of the priest, the one thing that prevents us from asserting here their anticipated unity—as we have it, for example, in the treatise *On the Keys* (1530)[67]—is the theology of the cross, which in the form in which it has been presented so far, has no place for the external word of salvation. Its inner dialectic of judgment and grace still remains. But the theology of the cross is no longer the only valid theology in the church. Its sole validity is abolished when the external word appears for the first time as the means *of bringing about the certainty* of grace, which was previously an unsolved problem.

If what is "reformational" is defined by *The Babylonian Captivity*, then "Explanation" 7 marks the beginning of the reformational turn in Luther's theology. To be sure, it is only the beginning, because the word is still not seen as a proper means of grace.

This finding is confirmed by a scholion in the Hebrews lectures, which we will now examine.[68]

b) Scholion on Hebrews 7:12

The corollary embedded in the scholion on Hebrews 7:12 overlaps materially with "Explanation" 7, especially its concluding part. The corollary deals with Lombard's sentence: "The sacraments of the law did not justify, but the sacraments of the new law confer grace on all who put no obstacle in their way."[69]

---

64. WA 1:544,16–18 = LW 31:106: "He (i.e. Wimpina) introduces . . . another obscurity of words and draws another distinction between the keys, namely, between those of authority, superiority, and office" (trans. alt.). Cf. Wimpina: "Just as God has the keys of authority, and Christ the keys of superiority, so the Christian priest has the keys of office or the ministerial keys" (Köhler, *Dokumente*, 129,31–32).

65. Luther takes this regress to the point of absurdity with bold mockery. WA 1:544,18–24 = LW 31:106: "Perhaps they wish that whatever Christ shall loose with the keys of superiority in heaven (for on earth he himself does not loose) shall be loosed by God in a 'super heaven.' Then, in order that the pope may be God, some other higher God must be invented, who looses in the higher heaven whatever the pope has loosed with the keys of authority."

66. WA 1:544,25 = LW 31:106 (author's emphasis).

67. See pp. 210–211.

68. On the relationship of the scholion to the *Explanations*, see further pp. 231–232.

69. WA 57/3:191,20–22 = LW 29:192. This quote, introduced by Luther as "that commonly known saying of the Master and of the doctors who comment on it" (ll. 19–20), is nowhere to

The text (Heb. 7:12) prompts discussion about how the priestly action of the old covenant differs from that of the new. As Luther had said just before the corollary,[70] the one relates to the external states of purity and impurity; the other, to the purity and impurity of the conscience. Common to both, it seems, is the declarative function of the priest, who decides about purity and impurity by establishing either the one or the other and so distinguishes between them ("*discernit*"[71]) and then pronounces a corresponding judgment ("*iudicat*"[72]). Here the traditional doctrine of the twofold form of the key ("the knowledge to distinguish and the power to judge"[73]) comes into play.

This declarative understanding is now developed in the corollary.[74] Luther has to contradict Lombard's sentence in two ways, because Luther understands "justification" as a function of the sacrament or of the priest, in the sense of "declaring righteous." Thus on the one hand, the sacraments of the law also "justify," by "distinguishing."[75] On the other hand, the sacraments of the new law do not bestow grace since they also only "justify" by "distinguishing"—that is, by addressing and determining the said purity or impurity of the heart and

---

be found in Lombard. "Concerning the difference between the sacraments of the Old and New Testament," he says, "Augustine briefly explains this difference saying, 'the former only promise and signify salvation, but the latter give it" (Sent. IV/d 1/c 6; cf. Augustine *Enarratio* on Ps. 73, n. 2; MPL 36 (930–32), 931; cf. d 1/c 4. So what Luther quotes is a sentence from the history of interpretation of Lombard's *Sentences* ("the doctors who comment on it"). Cf., for example, Biel, IV/d 1/q 3/a 1 (C) and a 2 (D).

70. WA 57/3:191,8–17 = LW 29:192.

71. Cf. WA 57/3:191,12 ("*discernere*") and ll. 14–15 ("*distinguere*").

72. Cf. WA 57/3:191,10 ("*iudicare*").

73. Peter Lombard, *Sentences* IV/d.18/c.2, where he quotes the *Glossa ordinaria* on Matt. 16:19 (5.52E). See Thomas Aquinas, *ST* Suppl. Q.17/a.3: "The key is said to be twofold: the one is for judging the fitness of the person to be absolved and is called the knowledge to distinguish, the other pertains to the absolution itself and is called the power to judge." Lyra (on Matt. 16:19: 5.52F/G) puts it somewhat differently: "These two keys are not material but spiritual power. One is the power to distinguish sin from what is not sin, as in the old law where the priest used to judge between a leper and a non leper... The other key is the power to admit to the kingdom or exclude from it, depending on the true judgment rendered, since the unworthy ought to be excluded and the worthy received." Luther is familiar with this distinction, at least from Biel's commentary on the Mass (Lect. 1 D: see n. 41; cf. Lect. 75 A, 3:242).

74. WA 57/3:191,18–192,15 = LW 29:192–94. Cf. the scholion on Heb. 9:9: 57/3:205,18–206,5 = 29:206–7 (the quotation: IV/d 1/c 4).

75. WA 57/3,191,25–27 = LW 29:192. This of course means that they do not justify in the sense of "make righteous," so that in *this* way Luther can once again agree with Lombard. Cf. 57/3:205,25–206,4 = 29:207. (The text of the last sentence is in a mess, a fact that went unnoticed by the editor, J. Ficker. On the conjecture, see H. Bornkamm, *Luther and the Old Testament*, 183, n. 377.)

conscience as such.[76] Therefore, in receiving the sacrament, it is presupposed that we have a pure heart—that is, that we "draw near in the full certainty of faith."[77] This is also presupposed by "Explanation" 7[78] and the scholion on Hebrews 5:1.[79] For faith itself is already the grace that makes us righteous.[80] Luther had previously explained this in the scholion on Hebrews 7:1, in which he can have a fundamental discussion about his understanding of "the righteousness of God" without making any reference to the oral word (of salvation).[81] Therefore, such a word is not, as later, a constitutive part of actual justification. However, the faith that already exists does receive certainty about itself from the declarative word of the priest, and the scholion on 7:12 makes this even clearer than that on 7:1. Compared to the "secret whisper" in the interpretation of the penitential psalms, this is a decisive step forward.[82] Luther tries to keep his previous understanding of penance and justification but now adds as a second act the means of bringing about the certainty of justification through the oral word. This of course changes his previous understanding, which now begins to dissolve into a new one, as the analysis of "Explanation" 7 has shown.[83]

Without the thorough study of the institutional sacrament, especially that of penance, that we saw in "Explanation" 7, Luther would hardly have come to the view that he now presents succinctly and concisely in the corollary to Hebrews 7:12:

> In the sacraments of grace, we have the promise of Christ that states: "Whatever you loose on earth will also be loosed in heaven" etc. The old law did not have this promise; for humans were not clean in heaven

76. WA 57/3:192,2–5 = LW 29:193.

77. WA 57/3:191,23–24 = LW 29:192.

78. Cf. p. 191 (n. 59).

79. See chap. 5 A.

80. WA 57/3:191,24. "To justify" (*iustificare*) must be understood here as "to *make* righteous." Luther does not conceptually express the factual difference between "declaring righteous" and "making righteous."

81. WA 57/3:187,5–188,17 = LW 29:188–89. This fundamental excursus "on divine righteousness" (57/3:187,6 = 29:188) is prompted by the etymology of the name "Melchizedek" (Heb. 7:1; cf. v. 2) (57/3:187,4 = 29:188) and is not influenced by the train of thought of the text to be interpreted. For just this reason, it is particularly important as a document reflecting Luther's own theology.

82. See pp. 163–164.

83. See pp. 188–190, 191–192.

> because through the priesthood they were declared clean on earth, but they were only clean on earth. Therefore, the apostle calls Christ "the promise of a better testament" as the one who promises the forgiveness of sins and cleanness of heart through the word of his priest. Those who believe him are altogether righteous and clean before God.[84]

Through the priestly absolution that takes up the words about the keys in Matthew 16:19 (or Matt. 18:18), Christ himself guarantees the forgiveness of sins by promising it. In the context of the whole corollary, this promise is to be understood more exactly as the declaration certifying that the forgiveness of sins has already taken place (= justification); that is, the promise is to be understood as the *announcement* of forgiveness. Nonetheless, it is clear how what had previously been distinguished is beginning to be pulled together. It is now only a small but very important step to the understanding that sinners are not *informed about* the forgiveness that has already taken place in them (in the judgment), but that along with the certainty of forgiveness, forgiveness itself is *given to* them; that is, it actually happens. This step is taken in "Explanation" 38 (the abbreviation for the "Explanation" of thesis 38 of the *Theses on Indulgences*).

B) The Declaration Is Too Little ("Explanation" 38)

1. After "Explanation" 37 had still assumed the validity of the declarative understanding of the word and so had spoken of "forgiveness before the forgiveness, absolution before the absolution,"[85] the beginning of "Explanation" 38 with its clear abandonment of that understanding comes as a surprise: "The declaration is too little." It signifies contempt for the power of the keys entrusted to the church; in fact, it renders Christ's binding word "*irritum*"—invalid, indeterminate, futile—and makes everything "uncertain" for those absolved.[86] With this double objection, the reformational understanding of word and faith becomes clearly apparent. *Luther recognizes here the weakness of the declarative understanding of the word*[87] that works with the Augustinian distinction between *signum* and *res*. This discovery has far-reaching significance for the history of the

---

84. WA 57/3:192,8–15 = LW 29:193 (trans. alt.).

85. WA 1:593,30–34 = LW 31:191.

86. WA 1:594,5–12 = LW 31:191–92. See the reflection of the new insight in "Explanation" 58: 1:610,11–26 = 31:220 and with this text the scholion on Heb. 9:24 (on that, see chap. 5 C).

87. He thus draws the consequence of his exegetical observation regarding Matt. 16:19, which "Explanation" 6 already notes: WA 1:539,17–23 = LW 31:98 (see p. 186) and which he himself refers to in 1:594,6–7 = 31:191.

church and its theology, since with it the basis of the traditional doctrine of the sacraments is given up. According to Augustine's distinction, the *res* is not just connected with the *signum* but also separated from it. With such ambivalence, however, faith cannot be certain whether it really receives the thing itself, the reality (*res*), in and with the word.

It was precisely at this point that especially the Thomistic doctrine of the sacraments, with its strong emphasis on the efficacy of the sign, had already radically corrected the Augustinian view. However, it again limits and conditions the efficacy by requiring the right disposition of the giver and receiver. This becomes especially clear with regard to the sacrament of penance, whose *forma*, the word of absolution, necessarily needs its *materia* in order to constitute the sacrament together with it in a single event and to let God and humans come together in such a way that the oral word of God finds its point of contact previously created by God through "inner inspiration," "completes" it, but does not itself establish it.[88] This may also be the reason why even the Thomistic doctrine of the sacraments, despite its intention to emphasize the efficacy of the word of absolution, cannot do without the declaration, which indeed presupposes what is to be declared, finds what is to be judged, but merely establishes it.[89]

Luther, on the other hand, rejects the need for any disposition along with the declaration. This does not mean that he wanted to leave the word of absolution hanging. For this is not even possible, since it is already in itself—"I absolve you"— directed to the recipients and their situation in sin. This is why Luther also expressly states the reference to those "tormented by the terrors of conscience."[90] But this *reference* of the word does not become for him its *condition*,

88. Thomas Aquinas, *ST* III/q 84/a 1 Reply Obj. 2: "But in the sacrament of penance, as stated above (Reply Obj. 1), human actions take the place of the material element, and these actions proceed from internal inspiration. Hence the material element is applied not by the minister but by God working inwardly: but the minister furnishes the complement of the sacrament when he absolves the penitent."

89. Aquinas, *ST* III/q 84/a 3 Reply Obj. 5: "It is true in a sense that the words '*I absolve you*,' mean '*I declare you absolved*,' but this explanation (i.e. Lombard's: see n. 33) is incomplete. For the sacraments of the new law not only signify but also *do what they signify*... When the priest says, '*I absolve you*,' he shows the person has been absolved not only symbolically (*significative*) but also effectively (*effective*)."

90. "This faith (see the text referred to in n. 91, which comes immediately before this) is certainly tested especially in those who are tormented by the terrors of conscience and feel like despairing of themselves. But as for those who do not feel such wretchedness, I do not know whether the keys are a source of comfort to them or not, since only those who are sorry deserve to be comforted, not those inclined to believe in forgiveness only because, through lack of faith, they fear their sins may be retained" (WA 1:596,19–23 = LW 31:196). In contrast to his view in the Romans lectures, Luther no longer sees affliction (*Anfechtung*) as such as a "sign of grace" (cf., e.g., above pp. 72–75) but finds it only in the word of salvation that comes from outside.

which is why Luther says: "Therefore, it is not as necessary for the absolver to ask, 'Are you sorry?' as it is to ask, 'Do you believe that you can be absolved by me?'"[91] However, it would be a fatal mistake to think that Luther put faith in the place of contrition.[92] This, of course, is what he did earlier when he understood faith as divinely wrought contrition.[93] But now faith is, by definition, completely turned away from contrition of any kind and completely turned to the oral word of salvation. In sharp contradiction to the three truths of John Gerson that remain universally valid, Luther asserts "that people should *not* trust themselves to be in the state of salvation just because they can say that they are sorry for their sins, *but* rather they should pay much more attention to this, if they choose to go to the sacrament of absolution, that if they have received it, they will be absolved."[94] "Therefore, contrition is not as necessary as faith. For faith in the absolution obtains incomparably more than does the fervor of contrition."[95]

---

91. WA 1:596,17–18 = LW 31:195 (trans. alt.) (= WA 1:324,2–4; *Sermon on Penance*). Cf. 1:610,18–19 = 31:220 ("Explanation" 58): This forgiveness is understood "when sin is completely erased through contrition, rather through faith in the keys" (cf. 1:596,24–25). According to Biel, on the other hand, to exclude any possibility that the keys may err, the priest must inquire "whether the person confessing is remorseful or not" (IV/d 18/q 1/a 3/dub 2).

92. This misunderstanding comes out, for example, in W. Köhler's judgment quoted in n. 142.

93. See n. 210.

94. WA 1:596,1–5 = LW 31:195 (author's emphasis) (trans. alt.). W. Köhler, *Luther und die Kirchengeschichte*, 350–51 (to which *BoA* 1:106 refers), who did not find the correct point of reference in Gerson, sees it taken up *positively* by Luther here. That this is not the case is clear from the passage that Luther has in mind. At the end of the interpretation of the Decalogue in his *Tripartitum* (a collection of three treatises addressing the Ten Commandments, confession, and death), which he intended as a mirror for confession, Gerson emphasizes that God is "most ready to forgive us our offenses and grant us grace if only we would truly and sincerely apply to ourselves the three truths that follow. The *first* truth is: Lord, in one way or another, I have sinned against your goodness, which displeases me. I also repent because I have offended against you, you who are to be wholly venerated and worshipped, and because I have transgressed your commandment. The *second* truth is: Lord, I have a good intention and desire to guard against falling into sin and opportunities for sin as much as possible in the future, with your help. The *third* truth is: Lord, I have the good intention to make a complete confession of my sins at a time and place in accordance with your command and precept and that of Holy Mother Church. Whoever, in any place and at any time has sincerely uttered these truths from their heart, not falsely or deceptively, may be sure that they are in a state of grace and salvation and merit eternal life . . . We should note this and draw from it the salutary advice that every Christian should return to their heart twice every day, once in the evening and once in the morning, or at least on festival days, to examine their conscience to see whether they are capable of professing these three truths with a sincere heart. *If they can do this, they can be confident that they are within the state of salvation*" (*Opera*, 1489, vol. 2, 31 A; author's emphasis).

95. WA 1:595,22–23 = LW 31:194 (trans. alt.). Cf. the continuation of the passage, esp. ll. 27–28: "We must place our hope in Christ's word, not in our contrition."

"Imagine if (by some impossibility or contingency) someone is not or does not think they are sufficiently contrite and yet believes with absolute confidence the words of the one absolving them that they are absolved . . . It is this person's faith that causes them to be most truly absolved, because they believe the one who said, 'Whatever etc.'"[96]

This clearly shows that Luther, despite all his interest in faith, does not see it in any way dependent on the person before the word, but precisely because of this person and with reference to them, he argues exclusively for faith under the word and after the word (with which also the desire for the sacrament is understood anew[97]), and thus for faith that is determined precisely by the special promise and nothing else.

At the same time as denying the necessity of the disposition of the recipient, Luther denies the necessity of the disposition of the *dispenser* of the word of absolution. It is significant that he combines the objective empowerment conferred through priestly consecration—insofar as it goes beyond the obligation to use the power of the key—with the subjective disposition of the priest, which is traditionally to be distinguished from it, and rejects both together: "It makes no difference to me even if the bearer of the keys is unlearned or flippant. For the keys do not depend on the priest or his power[98] but on the word of him who said and does not lie: 'Whatever you loose etc.' For those who believe this word, the keys cannot err. The keys err only for those who do not believe that the absolution of the priest is valid."[99]

In this context, Luther refers to Augustine: "And this is what I understand it to mean when our teachers[100] say that the sacraments are effectual signs of grace,

96. WA 1:594,37–40 = LW 31:193 (trans. alt.). See the sentences in the conclusion of the *Sermon on Penance* (1:323,23–28, 32–34), which take up this text from "Explanation" 38 and which are condemned by the Bull *Exsurge Domine*: *Denz.*, 751–52.

97. "For this (referring to the preceding proof text in n. 94) is what it means to receive the sacrament by desire: it is the hearing of the word in faith, whether the word is actually present or just desired" (WA 1:596,5–6 = LW 31:195; trans. alt.; the desired "hearing" is the hearing of the word that is heard, not the unknown word; therefore, *post verbum*, after the word). Thus desire, understood as a provisional attitude and one aimed at a concrete churchly and sacramental fulfillment, has become an unsurpassable faith, which as faith in the *word*, is specifically determined from the outset by its ultimate fulfillment.

98. The fact that power (*potestas*) here means a "character" in itself and not the authority directly to use Christ's promise, which is so important for Luther, is shown not only by what follows in the text above but also unmistakably by WA 1:595,33–34 = LW 31:194: "It is neither the sacrament, nor the priest, but faith in the word of Christ through the priest and his office that justifies you."

99. WA 1:594,33–37 = LW 31:192–93 (trans. alt.).

100. Cf., for example, Thomas Aquinas, *ST* III/q 62/a1–6.

not simply because they are performed (as Blessed Augustine says) but because they are believed . . . Absolution is effectual, not simply because it is performed, regardless of who finally does it and whether they err or not, but because it is believed."[101] This is no relapse into an Augustinian spiritualism, as is clear from the interpretation of the Augustine passage[102] in the last sentence of the quote. Since Luther, unlike Augustine, now no longer splits *signum* and *res*, he is not interested in faith that looks behind the oral word (= *signum*) and beyond it[103] for immediate evidence of the *res*. Rather, his interest is first, negatively, that faith is independent of the disposition of the dispenser and then, positively, that it is dependent on the oral word and only on the word.

The orality of the word, which is the basis of its power, not its weakness, as Augustine and the early Luther thought,[104] is constituted concretely in time in a specific place. This place, in which God's "word speaks to you"[105] through human beings, even the most unworthy, is the sacrament. Luther says, "This is how I would understand what our scholastic teachers mean when they say that the sacraments of the church have been given to us to exercise and activate us.[106] That is, they have been given as inestimable gifts through which we have the chance to believe and be justified."[107] The sacraments give and preserve to faith this opportunity.[108] When Luther first discovered the opportunity for faith and thus faith itself (in its reformational understanding), he simultaneously understood the justifying word in its specific life setting (*Sitz im Leben*), and so in its concrete orality. *But his earlier understanding of the word thus underwent a profound transformation.* This is evident from the fact that Psalm 119:49 and 119:81

101. WA 1:595,5–8 = LW 31:193 (trans. alt.). Biel discusses the possible errors in the scholastic understanding of absolution in IV/d 18/q 1/a 3/dub 2 (N).

102. *Tractates on the Gospel of John*, tract. 80.3 (John 15:1–3): "For the word does it, not because it is said, but because it is believed" (CC 36,529 = MPL 35,1840). *Luther can only use the "it is said" (dicitur) if it is converted into "it is done" (fit)!*

103. See p. 8 and pp. 79–80.

104. See the *Sermon on the Prologue of John* of 1514; on that, see chap. 1.

105. WA 1:595, 39–40 = LW 31:195 (trans. alt).

106. The parallel passage in the *Acta Augustana* (WA 2:15,4–5 = LW 31:273) suggests that the reference to the tradition in "Explanation" 38 also refers to Lombard (Sent. IV/d.1/c.5): "They were instituted . . . for the sake of *exercise*: for since humans cannot be idle, a useful and salutary exercise is offered in the sacraments by which they may avoid being occupied with vain and harmful things." That Luther made something completely different of this explanation of why the sacraments were given to us is clear.

107. WA 1:595,36–38 = LW 31:194–95 (trans. alt.).

108. See further pp. 216–217.

now appear in a different context in "Explanation" 38 than in the *Dictata.*[109] But what is most amazing is the new use of Psalm 51:4. If the *Dictata* interpreted Mark 16:16 in the light of Psalm 51:4 (and 1 Cor. 11:31),[110] then conversely, "Explanation" 38 understands Psalm 51:4 (and 1 Cor. 11:31) in the context of Mark 16:16. The dominical word *here* has a meaning that corresponds exactly to *the word of absolution*[111]: "Even if you think you are not contrite enough (for you cannot and should not trust yourself), nevertheless, if you believe him who said: 'Whoever believes and is baptized will be saved,' I tell you, this faith in his word makes you truly baptized, whatever you may think about your contrition."[112] But Psalm 51:4 must now prove that it is "faith in the word of Christ spoken through the priest and his office that justifies you."[113] This clearly highlights the difference in theology here to the theology of justification in the first Psalms lectures and the Romans lectures.

2. In addition to the successful overcoming of the Augustinian hermeneutic of signification at a specific point, we should note the connection Luther makes in "Explanation" 38 between the "forgiveness of sins" and the "conferral of the goods of Christ." It emphasizes that "not only are such great *evils forgiven* but also such great *goods* are *given*, so that humans may be children of God, heirs of the kingdom, brothers and sisters of Christ, companions of the angels, and lords of the world."[114]

---

109. Cf. WA 1:595,27–31 = LW 31:194 in the context of the whole "Explanation" with 4:287,2–9 = 11:452–53 (Gloss on Ps. 119:49–50. Here it is about "the promise concerning eternal life" and "the hope of eternal life," but in "Explanation" 38 it is about special faith in the present, special oral word: see further below pp. 217ff and 4:291,26–292,1 = 11:471–72 (Gloss on Ps. 119:81: "MY SOUL HAS FAINTED with too much desire FOR YOUR SALVATION, i.e., a salvation which is spiritual and eternal. AND IN YOUR WORD the promise of the gospel I HAVE HOPED EXCEEDINGLY, because of this hope I hold all the good things of the world in contempt and suffer the evil things"). The scholion on Ps. 119:49–50 (4:332,15–33 = 11:452–53) seems at first sight to agree with the *promissio* theology of "Explanation" 38. But how the Luther of this time wanted the relationship between promise and hope to be understood can be seen from his Romans lectures on 4:7 (see esp. pp. 150–151). The passage Ps. 130:5, which is also quoted, represents a peculiarity in its earlier use (in the German interpretation of the penitential psalm): see p. 165.

110. See chap. 2, I ("The Fulfillment of the Promise in Judgment").

111. The *relationship* between penitence and baptism is not yet reflected on here in detail. For more, see pp. 223–225 and chap. 7.

112. WA 1:595,1–4 = LW 31:193 (trans. alt.).

113. WA 1:595,32–34 = LW 31:194.

114. WA 1:594,28–30 = LW 31:192 (trans. alt.; author's emphasis).

The meaning of this connection is evident already from "Explanation" 37. There Luther had described "participation in all the goods of Christ" in the same way as he will later speak of the "happy exchange" in the freedom tractate:

> By faith in Christ, a Christian is made one spirit and one body with Christ. For the two shall be one flesh. This is a great sacrament, referring to Christ and the church. Therefore, since the Spirit of Christ dwells within Christians, by means of which brothers and sisters become co-heirs, one body, and citizens of Christ, how is it possible for us not to be participants in all the goods of Christ? Christ himself has all that belongs to him from the same Spirit. So it happens through the inestimable riches of the mercies of God the Father, that Christians can be glorified with Christ and can with confidence claim all things in Christ. Righteousness, strength, patience, humility, and all the merits of Christ are theirs through the unity of the Spirit by faith in him. Conversely, all their sins are now no longer theirs, but through that same unity with Christ everything is swallowed up in him. And this is the confidence that Christians have and the joy of our conscience, that through faith our sins are no longer ours but Christ's, upon whom God placed the sins of all of us. And he takes away our sins, himself the Lamb of God, who takes away the sins of the world. In turn, all the righteousness of Christ becomes ours. For he places his hand upon us, and all is well with us. He spreads his cloak and covers us. Blessed be the Savior forever. Amen.[115]

The operative motif in this text, for which there are impressive parallel statements in the Hebrews lectures of the same time,[116] is already known from the earlier texts.[117] But if to this point the "exchange" was specifically defined solely by humiliation (*exinanitio*), in which the righteousness of Christ was given and received under its opposite,[118] then in "Explanation" 38 the place and mode of the giving and receiving now changes, even though the old understanding still

115. WA 1:593,14–29 = LW 31:190 (trans. alt.).

116. WA 57/3:129,21–25 = LW 29:136 (Scholion on 2:14); 57/3:147,18–148,2 = 29:152 (Scholion on 3:12); 57/3:151,9–18 = 29:155 (Scholion on 3:13); 57/3:153,8–10 = 29:157 (Scholion on 3:14); 57/3:156,20–157,4 = LW 29:160 (Scholion on 4:2); 57/3:187,17–188,3 = 29:188 (Scholion on 7:1; cf. above pp. 193–194 and n. 81.

117. See pp. 12–14, 18–20, 22, 27, 151–153.

118. See the passages quoted in n. 117.

lingers.[119] *The event of the "participation in the goods of Christ" is now seen analogously to the conferral of the forgiveness of sins through the oral, external word (but understood in a new way!)*: "Here I wish to think about our participation in the goods in the same way as I did before about the remission of guilt."[120]

Here we see the seam between the early and the reformational versions of that Christology, the history of which can be traced back to 1509 using the conceptual pair "sacrament and example" as a guide.[121] (After having played a role in the lectures to the Hebrews,[122] these terms are used, in parallel to the "Explanations," to distinguish between "remission of guilt" and "remission of penalty" in the *Asterisci*.[123]) In other words, here we see the *seam between the tropological* "pro me" *of Luther's early theology and the promissional* "pro me" *of his reformational theology*. That is to say, the meditation on Christ and the theology of the promise, which in the following years are mutually intertwined[124] and will only finally be merged in the freedom tractate ("God's pledge and promise . . . says . . . 'Come, believe in Christ, in whom I promise you all grace, righteousness, peace and freedom. If you believe, you have it; if you do not believe, you do not have it . . .'"[125]), are here connected for the first time. But now the theology

119. "Humans in their sin are so vexed and tormented by their conscience that in their mind they rather believe that they are participating in everything that is evil. Such people are certainly close to justification and have the beginnings of grace (cf. p. 186 and n. 35). Therefore, they should flee for refuge to the consolation of the keys that they may be calmed by the judgment of the priest, obtain peace, and gain the confidence that comes from participating in all the goods of Christ and the church. But if any do not believe, or doubt that this participation was brought about for them by the office of the priest, they are led astray, not by an error of the keys but by the error of their own faithlessness. They thereby inflict great damage on their soul and do great injury and irreverence to God and his word" (WA 1:595,10–18 = LW 31:193–94; trans. alt.). If the formulation "the participation *was brought about* for them by the office of the priest" expresses the new, effective understanding ("the declaration is too little"!), then the mention of the "*judgment* of the priest" that brings *peace* clearly calls to mind the declarative understanding of the word that we find in "Explanation" 7. Therefore, this intermediate stage still has an echo of the old understanding of "change" as an event that only happens under its opposite.

120. WA 1:594,14–15 = LW 31:192 (trans. alt.).

121. Cf. chap. 2: the sections on "The Sacramental Meditation on Scripture" and "The Understanding of the Mass."

122. Cf. the scholia on Heb. 2:3 (WA 57/3:113–14 = LW 29:123) and 10:19 (57/3:222–23 = 29:225) and the sermon in WA 1:76,39–77,15, which probably falls (see chap. 2, n. 392) in the time of the Hebrews lectures.

123. WA 1:308–9, esp. 309,13–21 (where ll. 16–21 should be compared with 307,22–27).

124. See chap. 8.

125. WA 7:24,10–14 (German); cf. LW 31:348–49 (Latin). On the final formula, see pp. 224–226. [Luther uses the term *Die gottlich vorheyschung und zusagung*, which has been translated as

of the promise is not determined by the meditation on Christ, but rather the latter is determined by the former ("Here I wish to think about our participation in the goods of Christ in the same way as I did before about the remission of guilt"). The connection is made at the earliest possible place: precisely where (completely independent of this connection: see sec. 1. on "Explanation" 38!) the reformational theology of the promise itself has its origin.

C) First Reformational Text (*Pro veritate* Theses)

1a) The theses *Pro veritate,* in contrast to the texts that prepare for them—especially the "Explanations" of theses 7 and 38 of the *Theses on Indulgences* [126]—present the reformational understanding without any trace of a transition. However, to present them in a way that does justice to their importance is difficult because, on the one hand, their factual elements correspond in detail to the medieval tradition, which Luther rejects yet has to take up when he deals with its problems. But, on the other hand, his view as a whole stands in sharp contradiction to the prevailing tradition. For decades, no one had recognized this more keenly than Cajetan. His recourse to Luther's "Explanation" 7 at their meeting in Augsburg[127] is no accident. The treatises he had studied to prepare himself for the hearing show this with the utmost clarity.[128] In them Cajetan discovered a "new and erroneous theology"[129] in Luther as the result of the cardinal's detailed and perceptive theological study, especially of the propositions of Luther's two "Explanations" just mentioned that come at the end of the *Sermon on Penance*[130] and in a more developed and clarified form in the theses *Pro veritate.* Above all, Cajetan does not criticize Luther's early theology of the cross and Christology, which were strongly championed in the "Explanation" of

---

"God's pledge and promise." However, the point the author is making is that when Luther uses this term, he is referring to both God's future promise (*vorheyschung*) and his present promise (*zusagung*). The latter, however, is his genuine reformational emphasis; trans. note.]

126. A hint, albeit unclear, of the connection between the set of theses and the "Explanations" is given in version B (see WA 1:629): "The author gives the proofs of these theses in his explanation of thesis 7 of the *Theses on Indulgences*" (1:633). The preparatory texts, in the broader sense, include above all the scholion on Heb. 5:1: see chap. 5 (pp. 232–239).

127. WA 2:7,35–38 = LW 31:261; 2:13,6–10 = 31:270. Compare this with Luther's letter to the elector of Nov. 1518: WA Br 1:237, ll. 55–58.

128. For this and the following, cf. G. Hennig, *Cajetan und Luther. Ein historischer Beitrag zur Begegnung von Thomismus und Reformation*, chap. 2 (41–82) and pp. 217–219, 220–221, 371–372.

129. WA 2:7,37 = LW 31:261; 2:13,10 = 31:270.

130. See n. 18.

thesis 58 of the "Explanations" of theses 7 and 38 of the *Theses on Indulgences*[131]—and, directly connected with it, in the *Heidelberg Disputation*.[132] Rather, what he criticizes is Luther's solution to the problem of certainty, which grows out of precisely his new understanding of the relationship between promise and faith. This corresponds to the fact that Cajetan's harshest criticism of Luther was aimed at the latter's understanding of certainty, which for Luther[133] was precisely the point that marked the difference between Christianity and heresy.[134]

Cajetan considers Luther's newly found solution to be "mistaken"[135]—but it is this solution that contained the very reason, according to Luther's own testimony, he "became a Christian" in the first place. On the other hand, in Luther's opinion, what Cajetan firmly adheres to is now "heretical." We can only call it a

131. WA 1:(605–14) 613,21–614,27 = LW 31:225–26; 1(350–74) 361,31–363,37 = 31:52–55: the theology of the cross. The *christological* understanding of "Explanation" 58, with its determination of the relationship between the "merits of Christ" and the "treasure of the church," only becomes the point of difference with Cajetan indirectly, via the question of the extent of the power of the pope (see Cajetan's preparatory treatise on the question "whether the church's indulgences come from the treasure of the merits of Christ and the saints" [*Opuscula*, 1575, 97–101] and the corresponding first part of Luther's written statement in Augsburg [WA 2:9,25–13,5 = LW 31:264–70]), in contrast to the question of *sacramental theology* (see above). This shows the still unconnected juxtaposition of Luther's Christology (see "Explanation" 58: 1:612,40–613,20 = 31:224–25; the *Heidelberg Disputation*: 1:364[1–38],23–38 = 31:[55]56–57; and the *Acta Augustana*: 2:12,7–13, 17–20 = 31:268–69) and his new understanding of the sacrament, which are only linked for the first time in "Explanation" 38: see pp. 200–203.

132. See, apart from the texts quoted in n. 183, Luther's letter to Karl von Miltitz of May 17, 1519, WA Br 1:402–3 (ll. 38–43), concerning Cajetan: "He tried to drive me away from the Christian faith in August; I doubt that he is a Catholic Christian. If there is any spare time, I will write to the Roman Pontiff, and the lords cardinals, and I will refute him, if he does not correct himself, in all the places in which he errs most shamefully. I grieve that the legates of the Apostolic See are people such as this who strive to do away with Christ."

133. WA 2:8,16–18 = LW 31:262.

134. During the meeting in Augsburg, on Oct. 14, 1518, Luther wrote to Karlstadt: "I will not become a heretic by contradicting the opinion that made me a Christian. I would rather die, be burnt, banished, or accursed etc" (WA Br 1:217, ll. 60–63).

135. WA 2:7,37 = LW 31:261; 2:13,10 = 31:270. See Cajetan's preparatory treatise of Sept. 26 on the question "whether for a fruitful reception of absolution in the sacrament of penance, we must have that faith by which penitents believe with full certainty that they are absolved by God," in which he originally concluded (since point 6 can only be added *after* the Augsburg meeting: see p. 372) that it must be stressed that the sacrament of penance is "effective in the recipient even without certain faith. *For this*, referring to Luther's insistence that *faith is necessary* to receive forgiveness, *is tantamount to founding a new church*" (*Opuscula*, 1575, 111a, 7–8; author's emphasis).

misunderstanding in that deep sense in which different assessments of the same thing by different people are fundamentally divided.

b) The peculiarity of the theses to be presented is not only seen in their contrast to Cajetan's way of thinking but above all in their contrast to Luther's own earlier theology. Also in relation to the latter, we must understand that, despite the close interweaving of individual motifs and at first glance common basic structures, the context of the theses as a whole is specifically new.[136]

In the understanding of the 1514 sermon on the Prologue to John and of the Romans lectures, God's *word* of judgment and our *faith* corresponding to it in the confession of sins, supplication, and the mortification of the flesh formed a single movement in the unity of their correlation. The obvious background of this understanding was the Aristotelian schema of form and matter and the concept of movement in permanence that was merged with it. But this view did not allow Luther to find a way out of his uncertainty. It did not let him grasp the finality and certainty of God's promise as something that was actually given, but he could only perceive it through the constant confession of sins and supplication. Therefore, matter (*materia*), is seen in a negative light as are the human capabilities—in contrast to Biel, for example—the understanding of sin and grace is correspondingly radical. But faith, in all its negativity and passivity, is a necessary condition of the word because even as *pure* matter, understood as *matter* of the form, faith is co-original with the word.

On the other hand—to anticipate a clear contrast in C 2 to what we have found here—in the reformational understanding of the relationship of word and faith, faith is not co-original with the word, but the word is the basis of faith and so comes first, while faith is the goal of the word and thus follows it; this relationship is irreversible. For now, the pure matter, contrition, understood as the effect of the word of judgment, is strictly distinguished from faith, because faith owes its origin specifically to the word of salvation, which relates to the pure matter but is not conditioned by it.

If, according to his early theology, judgment and grace, law and gospel, met in a single external form of the word, the word of judgment, which only became righteousness through an inner change or smooth transition from judgment, Luther now discovered the external independence and otherness of the word of salvation, which although strictly related to the word of judgment, was strictly distinguished from it ("Then comes the other word"[137]). In discovering the otherness of the word of salvation, he discovered the reformational distinction between

136. What follows is a concise summary of the first part of this work. For the explanation of individual aspects, see part 1.

137. WA 7:24,9–10 (German: *The Freedom of a Christian*; 1520); cf. LW 31:348 (Latin).

law and gospel. In direct correspondence to this, as already mentioned, faith, which is now seen as created by the oral public word of salvation, is distinguished from contrition and is itself no longer the confession of sins and supplication.

This oral and public word of salvation, which is distinguished from the word of judgment, is the basis of the certainty of faith. According to the Romans lectures (on 4:7), faith was uncertain because God's promise remained completely unreachable. Now, on the other hand, it can be grasped with certainty in the present promise of forgiveness. What this means will have to be made clear in C 2.

2. An analysis of the *Pro veritate* theses shows that in the main, they present the sacrament of penance in a new form that aims to clarify and determine nothing other than the relationship between the word that forgives sins and the certain faith that accompanies it.[138] This clarification is achieved through a polemical opposition to a priesthood that is not purely functional and a contrition that is not strictly distinguished from faith, and so is against the assertion of the necessity of "the worthiness of the one who distributes or receives it."[139] In line with this finding, the following presentation falls roughly into two parts—without wanting to separate what belongs together and without treating the word without its goal or even faith without its basis and content.

Analysis of the Theses

The theses 1–7 sharply formulate the recognition of the difference between the "remission of penalty" and the "remission of guilt," which briefly summarizes the result of the arduous theological work that went into the *Explanations of the Theses on Indulgences*. This distinction, the discovery of which marks Luther's turn from criticizing the system of indulgences to constructing a new theology,

138. To properly appreciate Luther's theological achievement and the deliverance it brought, we have to compare his simple and clear determination of the sacrament of penance as a relationship of promise (*promissio*) and faith (*fides*) with the dangerous and confusing notion of Gerson, who (*Opera*, 1489, vol. 2, 27 C) tries to show—without speaking about the word of absolution!—what in the sacrament of penance "is the *res* and what the *sacramentum*. It is said that just as in the Sacrament of the Eucharist, the species of bread and wine are the sacrament of a twofold thing, namely, of Christ's true body and of his mystical body, so here confession and satisfaction are the sacrament of contrition and the remission of sin. Hence, by virtue of contrition, they effect what they symbolize, namely, the remission of sin. And by understanding it this way, clearly contrition in its different forms is both the *res* and *sacramentum*: the *res*, namely, of confession and satisfaction, which are its sacraments, and the sacrament of the remission of sins, which is its *res*. From this the effect of penance is clear, namely, the remission of sins and the commutation of eternal punishment into temporal punishment, and consequently the bestowal of eternal life."

139. This formulation used for the summary, with reference to the Lord's Supper, comes from the *Wittenberg Concord* (1536; *BSLK* 65,37–38).

aims at a proper understanding of the "*remission of guilt*" (this point is not picked up, for example, by E. Iserloh—see note 143), which is then also the sole topic in what follows (theses 8–12; the distinction is only touched on once again, in thesis 29).

Immediately following the necessary opening (1–7) comes the central thesis of the whole series, which first appears as a double negation (8) and then positively (9) in its double structure:

"8. Remission of guilt depends *neither* on the *contrition* of the sinner, *nor* on the office or authority of the *priest*.

9. Rather, it depends on *faith*, which means faith in the *word* of Christ, who says, 'Whatever you loose etc.'" This thesis is now immediately reformulated—after an interpolation (thesis 10) explaining thesis 9, as signaled by its introductory "for." The interpolation consists of two traditional formulas that Luther frequently uses in the immediate vicinity of this text[140]—in such a way that the double negative is now summed up with a single negative:

"11. Christ did not want the salvation of humankind to fall to human hands or be left to the human will.

12. but, as it is written, 'God upholds all things by the word of his power,' and, 'he purifies their hearts by faith'" (Heb. 1:3; Acts 15:9).

The central thesis is developed in two parts corresponding to the double negation in 8.

1. The theses 13–22 appear mainly under the keyword *contrition* and are characterized more closely by the contrasting pairs "certainty and uncertainty" and "trust (dependability) and doubt." Together with the promise of Christ, they argue for the certainty of faith and its distinction from contrition.
2. This is also the aim of theses 23–50, but here the subject matter is moved under the keyword *priest*. The priesthood is to be understood in a purely functional way (23) because only the word of

140. "It is true that it is not the sacrament of faith that justifies but faith in the sacrament (that is, not because it is performed but because it is believed)." The explanation in parentheses is the altered quote from Augustine that we saw in "Explanation" 38 (see n. 102). The sentence that is explained appears already in "Explanation" 7 (see n. 59). Luther uses it for the first time as a "general (or very common) saying," in tight connection with the Augustinian quote in the *Asterisci* (WA 1:286,17–19; Mar. 1518; see 1:279), then in the 1518 *Sermon on Penance* (1:324,16–18), in *Pro veritate* (accordingly in the 1519 *Sermon on the Sacrament of Penance*: §6; 2:715,34–37), and finally, in the *Acta Augustana* (2:15,28–32). The two quotations are also connected in the scholion on 5:1 in the Hebrews lectures: see pp. 230, 232, 234.

> Christ (28–29) does God's work (24), which through the external word (30–33 define the relationship of word and Spirit) brings about faith and justification. This gets rid of the judicial function of the priest, which is very important to the absolution in the tradition and which focuses on what has already given (25–27). So word and faith do not depend on the condition of their recipient. Nor can they be overridden (36, 40) by canonical provisions ("the reservation or restriction of cases": 41,35–38) or by the priest's subjective unworthiness (39).

This is followed by theses on the basic problem of sacramental theology handed on by the tradition (see Peter Lombard, IV/d.1/c.6), which is the relationship between "the sacraments of the new law and those of the old law" (42–45). Luther tries to explain this in the sense of the central thesis. (45. But Luther does not maintain the difference between the Old and the New Testament as asserted here.[141])

Finally, the question of the difference between "venial and mortal sins" receives an answer (46–49): The priest's investigation and knowledge of such sins must not become the condition of absolution. Since all aspects of the theses *Pro veritate* recur in the *Sermon on the Sacrament of Penance* of 1519 (WA 2:709–23 = LW 35:3–22), this will be used in what follows because it solidifies them all.

a) The Word

Luther asserts the validity and infallibility of the sacrament of penance *ex opere operato* in the version *ex verbo dicto* more forcefully than ever before, something that people usually turn a blind eye to (on the Protestant side—in no small measure due to the influence of neo-Protestantism[142]—no less than on the Catholic side[143]). Luther articulates his view with the thesis "The power of the

141. Cf., for example, *Defense and Explanation of All the Articles*: WA 7:327,5–329,3 (esp. 7:327,13–15) = LW 32:17–19 (esp. 18); 1521, cf. chap. 7, n. 99.

142. According to W. Köhler, for example, Luther gave the sacrament of penance a new form in the following way (*Luther und die Kirchengeschichte*, 1900, 350): "He reduced the sacramental power of the priest to a minimum and put all the emphasis on the state of the heart of the receiving subject. *Faith* is the salient point for the efficacy of the sacrament."

143. Against E. Iserloh (*Luther zwischen Reform und Reformation*, 105), it has to be asserted (even more emphatically than H. Bornkamm does in his *Thesen und Thesenanschlag Luthers*, 48ff.) that Luther does not deepen the nominalist separation between the divine and the human but overcomes it. We do not do justice to Luther's negative attitude to the remission of punishment if we fail to mention that even when formulating the "crucial point" of the *Theses on Indulgences* (see Iserloh, ibid), which he indicated clearly enough with his circular disputation, at the same

keys produces a certain and infallible work through the word and mandate of God when the priest speaks the absolution" (thesis 24).

If we were to dispense with this thesis as quickly as possible as some want to do, simply because it adheres to the literal sense of the biblical text, we would forgo its proper understanding right at the crucial point.

Of course, the passage in mind here, Matthew 16:19,[144] is a text from the Bible. But it does not derive its importance from some abstract and general scriptural principle. Because for Luther this text from the very start is meant to be used—and this makes his understanding of Scripture a model of clarity—and can only be understood as a specific promise: "Your sin is forgiven; you have a gracious God. [Luther continues] this is a comforting statement, a wonderful word of God, to which he has bound himself: He will forgive my sins in heaven when the priest forgives them [on earth]."[145] Luther understands the divine pact found in the text of Matthew 16:19 *concretely* as a declaration of God's will; that is, he takes it performatively. Therefore, the text can never be separated from its use or misuse, even hypothetically (the criterion of which is the wording of the text itself, the logic of the grammar[146]). We get an idea of its enormous historical importance if we remember that the relationship between "Luther and the Pope" can be described as a dispute over precisely the use of Matthew 16:19.[147] Luther's fight against the papacy is nothing else than a fight for the proper use of this text against its obfuscation and misuse.

An important aspect of the enacted word [the concrete promise spoken by a priest to a confessor] is that it is actually enacted, as the idea of God's ordered power (*potentia dei ordinata*) is a major factor, if not *the* major factor of Luther's theology. However, this does not mean that the word is or can be established by

time as he rejects the remission of punishment in favor of the remission of guilt, he intertwines God's word and the priest's word in such a way that even a Thomistic instrumental understanding is far surpassed. Luther rightly says: "I do not believe that this opinion of mine lessens the power of the keys, of which I have been accused, but rather restores it from a false honor and tyrannical reverence to a place of worthy and loving esteem" (WA 1:596,24–26 = LW 31:196; "Explanation" 38). Cf. the *Asterisci*, 1:285,38–286,3; 306,34–307,4, and the answer to Prierias: 1:666,17–19.

144. Cf. the central thesis (9) and thesis 29 (John 20:23).

145. WA 2:249,17–19 = LW 51:59–60 (Sermon Preached at Leipzig on Matt. 16:13–19 [trans. alt.]; June 29, 1519; see n. 22). Cf. the *Sermon on the Sacrament of Penance* of 1519 (§10: 2:717 = 35:13–14) and the sermon for a first Mass mentioned above in n. 19, which expresses the promise of the forgiveness of sins in many variations.

146. Cf. merely the organizing center in "Explanation" 6 (WA 1:539,17–23 = LW 31:97–98) and the argument in *The Keys* of 1530 (cf. the text quoted below and proved in n. 151). The accusation is telling: "They follow a new dialectics (logic) rather than sound grammar" ("Explanation" 26: 1:577,37–38 = 31:163; trans. alt.).

147. Cf. Bizer, *Luther und der Papst* (Th Ex NF 69), 1958.

history. Since it is enacted, it does not need to be considered in a formal-historical way but only factually in relation to its content, for it is in the articulated word that God's will *is* determined and the certainty of faith *is* grounded. The fact that the promise of Matthew 16:19 is a divine mandate means that God not only reveals his will in the promise but also gives himself in it. He commits himself to it and in it in a very specific way but thus entrusts himself—precisely by handing himself over (*mandare*)—to its use and surrenders himself to it in order to lead us to certainty. He does this by thus emptying himself in the oral word, in which, however, he conversely—as it were through a communication of attributes (*communicatio idiomatum*)—fills it precisely with all his power.

God empties himself of his power in a human word. Luther now understands the *opus operatum* or objectivity of the word in terms of this radical abandonment of the Augustinian understanding of the sign![148] The *re*formational character of his theology comes out here at a specific point, where Luther returns[149] to the original point of a New Testament "sentence of holy law" with its double linguistic structure that creates its *unity*.[150] This is a move unheard of in church history! Writing on the keys in 1530, Luther says:

> Christ does not say, "You must know what I bind and loose in heaven." Who would and could know that? But this is what he says: "If you bind and loose on earth, I will bind and loose with you in heaven. If you use the keys, I will also. In fact, if you do it, it will be done, and there is no need for me to do it after you. What you bind and loose (I say), I will neither bind nor loose, but it will be bound or loosed without my doing so. It will be one and the same work, my work and yours, not two

148. This was still being tested in "Explanation" 7, where the priestly word of absolution was understood as declaratory.

149. Luther himself only intends to go back behind Scholasticism to the ancient church. See his question to Prierias (Aug. 1518): "Why did your Blessed Thomas not allow this understanding to remain with you, which the church Fathers, especially Chrysostom in his homilies on Hebrews, upheld, that with these words, Christ wished nothing more than that the faithful would have the binding and loosing of Peter in no other way than as if Christ himself had bound and loosed, that is, had ratified his binding and loosing on earth?" (WA 1:657,17–22).

150. Cf. E. Käsemann, "Sentences of Holy Law in the New Testament," in *New Testament Questions of Today*, 73: "The eschatological law of God, mediated through charismatics, is determined by the fact that on earth it is bound to the exclusive medium of the word and is only fulfilled in the proclamation of this word. That, conversely, lifts this word out of the sphere of mere information, and explains its . . . careful stylization . . . Everyone who listens to this word is thus judged or pardoned by it and at the same time always comes under the power of God operative within it" (trans. alt.). See below pp. 225–227, pp 303–304.

> different works. Your key and my key are one and the same key, not two different keys. If you do your work, mine has been done already. If you bind and loose, I have bound and loosed already.
>
> He commits and binds himself to our work. Indeed, he himself commands us to do his own work. Why then should we make it uncertain or reverse it, pretending that he must first bind and loose in heaven? As if his binding and loosing in heaven were different from our binding and loosing on earth, or as if he had different keys in heaven above from those that we have on earth below . . .
>
> But the idea that there are two kinds of keys originates in the mistaken idea that God's word is not God's word. Because it is spoken through human beings, some regard it as a human word. And God is thought of as high above in heaven and far, far away from such a word here on earth. So we stand there gaping toward heaven . . .
>
> Rely on the words of Christ and be assured that God has no other way to forgive sins than through the oral word, as he has commanded us. If you do not look for forgiveness in his word, you will stand there gaping, looking toward heaven in vain for grace, or (as the *Schwärmer* call it), inner forgiveness.[151]

This text, whose continuous history can be traced back to the "Explanations,"[152] offers an emphatic and unequivocal confirmation of thesis 24: "The promise is God's mandatary, his representative (*vicarius dei*)." In it, God defines himself, and at the same time defines us human beings.

Whoever hands it on by speaking it and making it heard is nothing but a servant (theses 23, 32, 33),[153] who hands out the goods entrusted to them. We can see that when the promise is taken seriously, a new understanding of the priesthood also appears. Apart from the power to hand on and offer the word, the priest has no power, no authority, and apart from handing on and offering

---

151. WA 30/2:(428–507) 497, 9–24,32–36; 498,26–30 = LW 40:365–66 (*The Keys*, 1530); trans. alt.

152. See n. 146 and Bizer, *Luther und der Papst*.

153. Cf. "Explanation" 38, "With respect to the keys, the pope is my servant and minster. As pope, he does not need the keys, but I do" (WA 1:596,32–33 = LW 31:196); *Sermon on the Sacrament of Penance* (§8), "Priests, bishops, and popes are only servants who hold before you the word of Christ . . . Moreover this is why the word is not to be honored for the sake of the priests, bishops, or pope; but priests, bishops, and pope are to be honored for the sake of the word, as those who bring to you the word and message of your God that you are loosed from your sins" (2:716,18–24 = 35:12); and *The Babylonian Captivity*: 6:543,28–544,13 = 36:82–83.

the word, the priest has no office,[154] because God himself comes in his word and vouches for its certainty himself—but nowhere else than in this very word.[155]

The word of God (thesis 24) is spoken by Christ (theses 9, 11, 15, 17, 21, 29, 32). What does this word say? As we have seen, Luther sets great store by one text, Matthew 16:19, but he sees it in a wider context. Whoever claims the authority to forgive sins—that is, uses Matthew 16:19 as "a servant of the word and representative (mandatary) of God"—is doing nothing other than Jesus did, according to Matthew 9:2 (thesis 28).[156] But the fact *that* the minister may and can do it, indeed must do it, requires express authorization (namely, the promise of Christ's word in Matthew 16:19). Conversely, of course, it becomes clear in such a context that this word of Christ is based on Jesus's actions and suffering. Hence Luther can turn it back to Jesus's death and in a series of inferences "demand" that "his blood, death, and resurrection must lie hidden in the keys of Christ, by which he has opened heaven for us, and that he distribute to poor sinners through the keys what he acquired through his blood."[157]

---

154. What Luther negates in the central thesis of *Pro veritate* ("not on account of the priest or his authority"; see "Explanation" 38: WA 1:594,33–34 = LW 31:192) is an aspect the priest's "character" as such and not his authority to directly use Christ's promise, which for Luther is of decisive importance. This is clear not only from the affirmation of the central thesis (9; cf. "Explanation" 38, 1:594,34–35,32 = 31:192) but especially from "Explanation" 38: 1:595,33–34 = 31:194 (see n. 98). See what *The Babylonian Captivity* says about ordination, esp., "it is the ministry of the word that makes the priest and the bishop" (6:566,9 = 36:115) and "the office of a priest is to preach, and if the priest does not preach, the priest is as much a priest as a picture of a person is the person" (6:566,5–6 = 36:115; trans. alt.).

155. The rejection of this view at Trent is illuminating: "If any one says that there is not in the New Testament a visible and external priesthood, or that there is not any power to consecrate and offer the true body and blood of the Lord, and to forgive and retain sins, but only an office and bare ministry of preaching the Gospel, or, that those who do not preach are not priests at all, let them be anathema" (Canon 1: Concerning the Sacrament of Order, *Denz.*, 961; cf. Canon 3: Concerning the Sacrament of Penance, *Denz.*, 913).

156. In the corresponding section of the *Sermon on the Sacrament of Penance* of 1519 (§21), Luther sees the present ministry of the word boldly claiming the *same* authority that Jesus exercised (WA 2:722,10–19 = LW 35:21; author's emphasis): "This is the authority of which Christ speaks in Matthew 9[:6–8], to the unbelieving scribes, 'That you may know that the Son of Man has authority on earth to forgive sins, he said to the paralytic, "Arise, take up your bed and go home." And he rose and went home. When the crowds saw it, they were afraid, and they glorified God, who had given such authority to human beings.' Now *this authority* to forgive sins *is nothing but* what a priest, indeed, if need be, any Christian, can say to another when they see them afflicted and troubled by their sins. They can joyously speak this verdict, 'Take heart, your sins are forgiven'" (trans. alt.).

157. WA 30/2:468,6–9 = LW 40:328 (*The Keys*, 1530; trans. alt.). Luther sees the christological shape of the promise definitively articulated most aptly in the gifting words [the words of distribution] of the Lord's Supper from *The Babylonian Captivity* onward. This Christ-shape of the

This specific correlation of the two verbs *acquire* and *distribute*, which are also found elsewhere[158] and thus used in a fixed terminological coinage, is nothing but a recognition and clarification of the problem of the relationship between the earthly Jesus and the kerygmatic Christ.

Luther acquired the intellectual and conceptual skills needed for such an understanding through painstaking theological work, mainly his work on the "Explanations," as he tried to determine the element of truth in the traditional idea of the "treasury of Christ's merits" administered by the church.[159] This attempt culminates with the written statement, submitted during the Augsburg hearing, on the first of the two objections raised by Cajetan, in which Luther, in an extremely perceptive argument, prepares the ground for that simple formula that appears later.

Luther claims for himself the very *Extravagante* of Clement VI's Papal Bull *Unigenitus* that Cajetan used against him, "since the text expressly states that Christ acquired this treasure for the church. This word 'acquired' clearly establishes and irrefutably proves that the merits of Christ by which he acquired the treasure is one thing, and the treasure itself that he acquired is another, for the cause is one thing and the effect another."[160] That is, the foundation [Jesus's death] laid under Pontius Pilate, which is expressed in its present effectiveness, is actually different from this effectiveness. And this difference between the

---

promise is clearly captured in texts around the time of the *Pro veritate* theses, for example, in the *Sermon for a First Mass*, recorded in WA 4:655–59 (see 655,2): "I give you this promise: You are absolved. Therefore, be confident and of good courage. Do not doubt it . . . So our salvation is in the word and not in the word, but since *Christ is bound to his word*, you have no reason to waver. The sacrament is a rock founded on Christ, but Satan will suggest to a dying person: You are not contrite enough, nor have you made sufficient satisfaction. And with many other such snares, he will try to dislodge them from the foundation of their faith. But they boldly say back to Satan: I am absolved; if I have done nothing, I commit myself to God. And just as Christ does not die, no one who believes in him will perish. Christ would have to die a thousand times before any such person was lost. Those who say otherwise are his bungling preachers. Let the dying put their trust in Christ through the judgment of the priest" (4:658,23–34; trans. alt.; author's emphasis).

158. There is complete agreement between the text quoted and Luther's *Against the Heavenly Prophets* (1525; WA 18:203,28–35 = LW 40:213–14) as we see from the following passage: "We deal with the forgiveness of sins in two ways. First, how it is won and acquired. Second, how it is distributed and given to us. Christ has acquired it on the cross, that is true. But he has not distributed it or given it on the cross. On the other hand, he has not acquired it in the supper or sacrament, but there he has distributed it and given it through the word, as also in the gospel, where it is preached. The acquisition of forgiveness happened once on the cross, but its distribution happens often" (trans. alt.).

159. Cf. "Explanation" 58 (WA 1:605–14 = LW 31:212–28) and "Explanations" 61 and 62 (WA 1:615–17 = LW 31:229–31).

160. WA 2:12,39–13,2 = LW 31:270 (trans. alt.). Cf. die *Asterisci*: 1:310,7–9.

action and suffering of Jesus ("the merits of Christ") and the "treasure" he thus acquired—that is, the resultant "power of the keys"—is clearly asserted. The effectiveness of the cause is recognized not in its unique authenticity [the death of Christ] but in its constant mediation through the word.

What is looming in the *Acta Augustana* is Luther's resolute rejection of the idea that Jesus's life and suffering are immediately accessible to Christians without mediation, a view that he himself had previously held with his meditative piety.[161] It is only this turn that enables Luther to later fight his own early theology in Karlstadt's position.[162]

Of course, it is difficult to see this turn in the making in the *Acta Augustana*. For Luther, there makes the distinction and correlation in terms of the remission of *penalty* and not, as in 1530, in terms of the remission of *guilt*. And the life-giving grace corresponding to it, on the other hand, is "distributed" according to the *Acta Augustana* in an immediacy of the Spirit reminiscent of the early meditative piety.

> Clearly then the merits of Christ must necessarily be understood in a twofold sense if the *Extravagante* is to be retained as authoritative. On the one hand, according to the literal and formal sense, the merits of Christ are a treasure of the life-giving Spirit and, since they are his very own, they are most properly distributed by the Holy Spirit alone to whomever he wills. On the other hand, according to the figurative sense, both effectively and literally, they stand for what is effected by the merits of Christ.[163]

But since the immediacy of the Spirit here is in contrast to the remission of penalty (that is, indulgences),[164] its connection to the oral word of the remission of guilt is not excluded. If, however, it had to be, then Luther would have invalidated his own previously disseminated *Pro veritate* theses (30–33).[165] Besides that, the connection between the "remission of sins" and the "conferral of the goods of

---

161. On Luther's meditative piety, see generally pp. 76–119 but specifically pp. 87–88, 89–92, 97–102.

162. Cf. the context of the passage from *Against the Heavenly Prophets* quoted in n. 158 with the text quoted below and referenced in n. 205. On Luther's earlier meditative piety, which had no place for the distributed word, see n. 161.

163. WA 2:12,23–27 = LW 31:269 (trans. alt.).

164. Cf. the entire context: WA 2:9,25–13,5, esp. 12,14–22 = LW 31:264–70, esp, 269.

165. Cf. below n. 173.

Christ" made in "Explanation" 38[166] would then be broken again and, not least, Luther's statement on the second point of contention at Augsburg[167] would be fundamentally contradicted.

This gives us an insight into a highly significant process in the history of theology. Its complexity shows in concrete terms how hard it was for Luther to correct the main point of his early theology and again how hard it was for him to arrive at his reformational theology of word and Spirit, for which the distinction between the acquisition and distribution of the forgiveness of sins, and between Jesus's death and Christ's word, is constitutive.[168,169]

By interpreting thesis 24, we have tried to determine Luther's understanding of the "work" of the word of absolution.

As explained in Matthew 16:19, with this work God binds himself to the will of Christ not to let the salvation of humans fall into their own hands or be left to their own devices (thesis 11). This will is done in word and faith. In the word, God's creative power upholds the world and its history, for God is powerful over all things. From this omnipotence and by it, humans receive in faith a clear and free conscience (thesis 12),[170] "so that they may be children of God, heirs of the kingdom, brothers and sisters of Christ, companions of the angels, and lords of the world" ("Explanation" 38).[171]

b) Faith

Because the word is *opus operatum* (the act done) in the radical way outlined, faith *cannot* be *opus operantis* (the act of the doer). For *faith subsists in the word.*

Luther had always and very clearly thought of the "personal union" of word and faith in the same formal way, and in numerous places, in the Hebrews lectures[172] but understood it in a completely different way in terms of its content. That is, he understood it in such a way that it either did not require the oral word as a constitutive element or did not require it at all. But the *Pro veritate*

166. See pp. 200–203.

167. See pp. 217–222.

168. Cf. the interpretation of the third article in the *Large Catechism*: *BSLK* 654:22–45 = *BC* 436.

169. Thus, Bizer's presentation (*Fides ex auditu*, 116–17) is partly taken up and partly corrected.

170. This thesis especially makes us think of the intention of the whole series (*Pro . . . timoratis conscientiis consolandis*: *On . . . comforting terrified consciences*).

171. See p. 200.

172. See the passages mentioned in n. 116.

theses (30–33) contradict the immediacy of the Spirit that this implies,[173] since they assert that the "ministration" of the word of absolution is instrumental in bringing about the Spirit-wrought faith that justifies. This means that the hiddenness of the "interior things" and "future things," which according to the first Psalms lectures and reflecting the Augustinian understanding of signs could at most be announced in the word but not given,[174] is now made public in a special oral word. According to the illuminating antithetical formulation of one of Luther's later table talks,[175] the word is no longer the sign of something that is absent but the sign of something that is present. Its externality, which the Romans lectures were able to speak of quite emphatically in their own special way,[176] is thus understood in the reformational sense.

Luther does not see the "opportunity to believe"[177] created by the word of absolution as a fundamental possibility, unlimited in its generality but defined in its particularity. For it is precisely this definiteness and specificity that makes the word unambiguous and creates in turn the certainty of faith. Faith, if it

---

173. "30. Just as the priest truly teaches, baptizes, and distributes communion, and yet these things are the work of the Spirit alone operating internally,

31. So also the priest truly forgives sins and absolves from guilt, and yet this is the work of the Spirit alone operating internally.

32. In all of this, when the priest ministers and brings the word of Christ, the priest at the same time exercises the faith by which the sinner is justified internally.

33. For nothing justifies except faith in Christ alone, for which the ministration of the word by the priest is necessary."

The starting point for determining this relationship between word and Spirit is likely to be John 20:23, quoted in thesis 29. The parallelism of the "justifications of the Spirit" (thesis 44) and "the word of the promiser" (thesis 45) should also be noted, whereas in "Explanation" 7 word and Spirit still appear as a sequence: the word follows as a sign giving believers the certainty that their justification has already taken place; see esp. WA 1:545,1–3 and section A above ("declaration"). Now the work of "the Spirit operating internally" takes place in, with, and under the oral promise, the external word. This also puts the saying from a sermon of Bernard that Luther has been working on since his Romans lectures (see p. 163) in a new context. In it, Bernard insists that the "for you" of the forgiveness of sins ("Your sins are forgiven *you*: WA 2:16,1 = LW 31:274) is the work of the Holy Spirit ("This is the testimony which the Holy Spirit produces in your heart": 2:16,1–2 = 31:274): see the *Acta Augustana* (2:15,35–16,3 = 31:274 in the broader context of 2:13,6–16,5 = 31:270–4). See what Luther says in "Explanation" 7 of the *Theses on Indulgences* in relation to the *Pro veritate* theses (see pp. 189–192) and in the scholion on Heb. 5:1 (on that, see pp. 233–234).

174. Cf., for example, WA 4:272,16–31 = LW 11:407 (on Ps. 116:10) and chap. 2 C ("The Inner Word: Hidden Grace").

175. See chap. 2, n. 198.

176. See chap. 2 F: "The Word and God."

177. See p. 199.

is to be certain, must remain bound to this place of the word, where the word is understood to be a specific word (such as a sermon). Faith is just as little a general possibility as is the word. When Luther says that the priest "exercises" faith with his ministration of the word (thesis 32), he does not mean that the priest is actualizing a latent possibility that lies hidden in the receiver of the word.[178] Rather, he exercises faith by "ministering" or bringing the word of forgiveness to people in their sin.[179] It is not a general ability or need that is being addressed but God's forgiveness that is being given to sinners. Thus they are called out of sin and "provoked"[180] *to* certain faith; that is, they are placed in forgiveness for the specific word. "Thus the word will keep you, and your sin must therefore be forgiven."[181] Certain faith is based on the specific word, understood as a completed work.

That we have correctly interpreted this is confirmed by Luther's statement on the second point of contention in Augsburg, the question of the certainty of faith.[182] This question is about nothing less than the sum and substance of salvation, where Christianity and heresy go their separate ways, as Luther explained to the reader with his publication of the *Acta Augustana*.[183]

---

178. WA 2:15,3–5 = LW 31:273 ("*actuatio*") is no objection to this in view of Luther's remarks in 2:13,20–22 = 31:271 (#3). Cf. the clear polemic of the "Explanation" of thesis 12 of the *Disputation Regarding Infused and Acquired Faith* held Feb. 3, 1520 (see WA 6:84), against "those who dream that it (i.e. faith) is a quality latent in the soul. But when the word of God says what is truth and the heart clings to it by faith, then the heart is imbued with the same truth of the word and is verified in this truth by the word of truth" (WA 6:94,9–12). Given Luther's reformational understanding of the word, the question must be asked whether Ebeling, when he speaks of the "word situation" to describe the "basic situation of human beings" (see esp. *Gott und Wort*, 1966), makes it clear that the concrete word of the sacrament is not limited to what is general and is by no means virtually, and always present as the basic determination of human beings hidden everywhere.

179. Thus thesis 32 asserts the simultaneity of "ministering the word" and "exercising faith." See the Sermon on Matt. 9:1–8 of Oct. 30, 1519: "Christ commands the paralytic, who does not yet believe sufficiently, to have faith and at the same time brings about his faith with the word. Therefore, whoever is going to absolve a sinner after the example of Christ must first proclaim the faith of sinners saying, 'have faith, my son'" (WA 9:416 [8–15], 11–15).

180. Cf. the phrase "provoke *to* faith in *The Babylonian Captivity* (WA 6:572,6 = LW 36:124; author's emphasis) and the remarkably frequent use of the word "provoke", in the same document in the discussion on the sacrament of penance (WA 6:543,17–18, 32,35; 544,7; 545,7 = LW 36:82–84).

181. WA 2:716,20–21 = LW 36:12 (*Sermon on the Sacrament of Penance*, 1519; §8).

182. WA 2:13,6–16,5. On that, see Bizer, *Fides ex auditu*, 117–23 (for a different view: Bornkamm, *ARG* 53 (1962): 1–60, here 31–34), and Hennig, *Cajetan und Luther*, 74–77 (cf. 49–61).

183. "My latter response, however, contains the whole summary of salvation. You are not a bad Christian because you do or do not know about the *Extravagante*. However, you are nothing

Like Cajetan in his criticism of "Explanation" 7 of the *Theses on Indulgences*, Luther in the main part of his argument proceeds from Matthew 16:19[184]—that is, from the *particularity* of word and faith that emerged for him in and with this particular word in Matthew 16. That this is the epitome of the entire statement is clear from the sixfold repetition of its formula,[185] which also expressly[186] articulates the point of the whole argument. According to this formula, faith is "not general faith, but special (or particular) faith concerning the present effect." This is aimed directly at Cajetan, who had put forward the opposite alternative with precisely this terminology during their discussion on the first day of the hearing.[187] Luther's response to Cajetan's criticism is every bit as sharp.

---

but a heretic if you deny faith in the words of Christ" (WA 2:18,14–16 = LW 31:278; trans. alt.). In the same sense, Luther answers the elector in a letter of Nov. 1518 (WA Br 1:236–46): "Nor am I therefore a bad Christian if I do not want indulgences . . .; but if I change this statement of faith, I will have denied Christ. This is how I understand it and will continue to understand it until a contrary statement has been proved by the Scriptures and the authorities adduced by me refuted. This has not yet been done, nor will it ever be done (God willing)" (ll. 80–85). "As I have consistently said, I am not about to resile from this point, not today, not ever" (ll. 59–60; cf. 71–77).

184. The center of the argument expands from this point (WA 2:13,31–15,27 = LW 31:271–74; the starting point of the expansion: 2:14,13 = 31:272), harks back to it in an interim conclusion (2:15[1–5],3–5 = 31:273), and then, after a further expansion (2:15,6–21 = 31:273–74), returns to it again in a final conclusion (2:15[21–27],26–27 = 31:274).

185. WA 2:14,15–19 = LW 31:272; 2:14,24–25 = 31:272; 2:15,1–3 = 31:273; 2:15,6–8 = 31:273; 2:15,21–24 = 31:274; cf. 2:13,29–30 = 31:271 ("in the present").

186. Cf., for example, "Here it is clear that . . ." (WA 2:14,15 = LW 31:272; trans. alt.).

187. Henning's otherwise excellent account overlooks the fact that Luther's contradiction is formulated using precisely the terminology that Cajetan had used in raising his objection in the first place.

In WA 2:14,15 = LW 31:272, the *illa* points to a referent outside the text, which is to be inferred thus: In his written defense, where he presents his position, Luther uses a term that has not previously been found in his own writings but which occurs in the treatise that Cajetan prepared for the hearing, "Whether for a fruitful reception of absolution in the sacrament of penance, we must have that faith by which penitents believe with full certainty that they are absolved by God" of Sept. 26, 1518 (*Opuscula*, Lugduni 1575, 109b–111a; see esp. 110a, 9ff., 24ff., 48ff., and 110b, 12ff., 60ff.). Hence it necessarily follows that it was at the oral hearing that Cajetan had determined the second disputed point in the alternative previously mentioned. The conversation on the first day of the hearing has therefore been able to be reconstructed at an important point beyond what Luther reports in WA 2:7,35–38 = LW 31:261.

To understand Cajetan's treatise, "Whether for a fruitful reception . . .," we should note that he refers not only to Luther's 1518 *Sermon on Penance* (Hennig, 46; cf. 49–56) but also particularly to "Explanation" 7 (cf., e.g., WA 1:543,17–19 = LW 31:104 with Cajetan's presentation in 110a, 9–15, where he says Luther's fanciful notion is based "on *the most certain efficacy of the specific words of Christ in the statement,* 'Whatever you loose . . . .' Accordingly, from such a certification of efficacy [Luther says] we are to deduce that confessing penitents must believe that

At the same time, in this situation, which is an eminent example of controversial theology—which highlights the differences between the Protestant church and the Roman Catholic church—Luther allows a formulation to be wrested from him in which his new, reformational, understanding is presented in an unsurpassably concise and clear manner.

According to the pre-reformational theology of the cross, the miraculousness of God's actions toward his saints (see Ps. 68:36, Vulgate; 68:35, English Bible)[188] lay precisely in the hiddenness of his help, not in his immediately accessible oral word of salvation.[189] The "special faith concerning the present effect" that corresponds to it would have threatened the purity and totality of a person's humiliation that is necessary for salvation. Now, on the other hand,[190] Luther sees true faith only where people can and should expect present help through the power and will of Christ.[191] This special faith expects the immediate turnaround of a concrete need, where the turnaround, the present effect, comes about solely by Christ's specific word (that is, a word spoken to the special need).[192] This word can and does transform the concrete situation of a person. "Thus Samuel's mother, Anna, when she believed the word of Eli, went her way and her face was no longer sad."[193]

---

they are absolved when the priest absolves them, regardless of whether the priest errs or not, . . . and that by saying 'whatever you loose' Christ gave him authority, and that by saying 'shall be loosed' the priest awakens faith regarding the effect of the word") and to "Explanation" 38 (cf. WA 1:595,27–35 = LW 31:194 with Cajetan's reference in 110a, 5–7).

188. Cf. the use of this psalm verse in the first Psalms lectures (WA 4:243,7–17 = LW 11:377–78; on Ps. 111:4), in the Romans lectures (56:269,21–22 = 25:258; 56:290,20–291,14 = 25:277–78, scholion on 4:7; 56:389,3–10 = 25:379, scholion on 9:2) and esp. in the Hebrews lectures (57/3:[127–134] 128,9–19: scholion on 2:14). In the *Operationes in Psalmos*, the early interpretation is revised (see chap. 9, n. 10). The intermediate link in the history of interpretation is found in "Explanation" 7, where Ps. 68:36 comes into the frame of the declarative understanding of the word (WA 1:543,27–30 = LW 31:104–5).

189. Cf. chap. 2, n. 266.

190. Cf., for example, the sermon on the calming of the storm pericope, already mentioned on p. 169 (Matt. 8:23–27), from Feb. 1, 1517 (WA 1:128–30 = LW 51:23–26), with the reference to Matt. 8:26 in the *Acta Augustana* (2:15,6–8 = 31:273). Here Luther sees the lack of faith rebuked. The sermon, on the other hand, extols precisely the salvation that comes from calling on Christ out of fear (1:130,2 = 51:25), asserts that help is already at work in it, but says absolutely nothing about the new beginning (Matt. 8:26). Instead, it affirms an *ordo salutis*, the elements of which are all intertwined as its formulation in the chain of inference indicates (1:129,23–27 = 51:25).

191. Cf. WA 2:14,14–18 = LW 31:272.

192. WA 2:14,24 = LW 31:272.

193. WA 2:15,19–20 = LW 31:273 (trans. alt.). See the *Treatise on Good Works* (WA 6:207,7–9 = LW 44:26; author's emphasis): "Samuel's mother, when she believed the priest Eli, *who promises her God's grace*, went home in peace and joy" (1 Sam. 1:17–18).

Luther thus discovered the turning point where the lament (or request) of the penitent turns into the answer and they are rescued. He found it in the word of God spoken by the priest. Even in the interpretation of the penitential psalms (1517), he had persistently ignored it and focused instead on the immanent dialectical change or smooth transition within the penitent from God's alien work (*opus alienum*) to his proper work (*opus proprium*).[194] *If this difference in the localization of the event of grace is not taken into account, if we do not realize that grace for Luther is bound to the word, the distinctive character of Luther's reformational theology is fundamentally misunderstood.*

What is distinctive about this view and the way it differs from Cajetan's understanding of the word can also be understood from another perspective. The dispute between Luther and Cajetan is not about the facticity of the word but about the modality of its efficacy. Cajetan also strongly emphasizes—in his criticism of the declaratory understanding of the word presented by Luther in "Explanation" 7, which of course along with "Explanation" 38 ("the declaration is too little") is already superseded[195]—that the word in absolution (as in the Eucharist) does what it says.[196] But it does it in a general way and *by itself*, not in a particular way here and *for me*—and if it does do it in a particular way (which of course would be "*in* me"), then again it is only "as far as the sacrament is concerned" and not "as far as the recipient is concerned." With this distinction,[197]

194. Cf. chap. 3 B I ("Confession of Sins—Forgiveness of Sins") and B 5 (on law and gospel) as well as the *ordo salutis* of the sermon mentioned in n. 190.

195. See pp. 194–200.

196. *Opuscula*, 1575,111 (Treatise on the Question: *Whether the remission of guilt is the effect of sacramental absolution*).

197. Cajetan has "in mind this distinction, namely, whether it concerns the sacraments or whether it concerns the recipient. Let him [Luther] say that faith is most certain and that also faith concerning the particular effect of the sacrament in me should be most certain, in so far as it concerns the sacrament; but in so far as it concerns me, the recipient, it is permissible to doubt its effect in me" ("Whether for a fruitful reception . . ."; *Opuscula* 1575, 110b, 11–15). The following passage from the *Operationes in Psalmos* refers exactly to this point in the dispute with Cajetan: "They find their distinctions in us, that the sacraments, so far as the authority and power of God working in them is concerned, produce a sure and certain effect of grace, but so far as the recipient is concerned, the effect is uncertain; and they assert that this doubt is godly" (WA 5:124,22–25; 1518/19). Likewise, the "Explanation" of thesis 1 of the *Disputation Regarding Infused and Acquired Faith* (1520) is aimed against the opinion "that no one can be certain of obtaining grace in the sacrament. They make this sort of distinction because they hold that, so far as the efficacy of the sacrament is concerned, the attainment of grace is certain, but so far as the recipient is concerned, it is uncertain, since we do not know whether we are worthy of hate or love. Nevertheless, they say that so far as the recipient is concerned, it is possible to have some certainty, namely, a moral and coarse certainty, that is, a certainty that is probable and likely, but not absolute and complete certainty, nor is this even necessary" (WA 6:88,23–29).

however, Cajetan tears apart what, for Luther, belongs together according to *God's* will. He fails to recognize that for Luther, the certainty of faith does not reflect a strong human will to believe but only the "presumption"[198] of an explicit divine promise corresponding to the declared will of God. What Luther emphasizes in opposition to Cajetan is nothing else than the literalness of the word, because he takes its content with radical seriousness. The word is not general but special because this word, which says "I forgive you," already speaks for me in itself, because it already addresses me in itself, because in defining itself it simultaneously defines me, anew, by imparting to me the forgiveness of sins, "as the words declare."[199] "Faith, however, does nothing but believe what God promises or says . . . *Therefore*, word and faith are necessarily simultaneous."[200]

According to Luther's reformational theology, the simultaneity of word and faith, in contrast to his earlier understanding,[201] lies in the fact that the word produces faith at the same time in an irreversible relation to the sinner's situation, which is to be understood temporally and materially. This means that faith is now unmistakably a creature of the oral word: "Without the word it is impossible to have faith," as it says in Isaiah 55:11.[202] Word and faith no longer appear to be of the same origin.[203] The "for me" is no longer obtained by means of a pictorial devotion in the sense of the early meditative piety—as a vivid, pictorial impression that immediately imprints itself on the soul, whereby the image before me only proves to be true in its reenactment and in its effect on me, specifically in

198. A formulation of the scholion on Heb. 5:1 reveals Luther's new starting point or organizing principle (cf. pp. 235–236): "Therefore, you are to approach [the sacrament] in the presumption of these words, and if you approach it this way, you will not be uncertain" (WA 57/3:[169–71] 171,7–8).

199. *Sermon on the Sacrament of Penance* (1519), §6 (WA 2:715 = LW 35:11). The definition of the sacrament of penance that Luther attempts here has three parts—sign, significance, and faith—and it is this definition, despite its Augustinian structure (cf. 2:715,26–27 = 35:11 with Peter Lombard's *Sentences* IV/d 1/c 2–4), that enables him to overcome the *Augustinian understanding of the sign* by tracing the *res* back again to the *signum*, via the saying "as the words declare" (ll. 25–26), since with the sign, which is the word ("I absolve you from your sins" = "You are absolved from your sins": §10; 2:717,8,17 = 35:13), God's work is done ("Your sins are also certainly absolved before God, before all the angels and all creatures": 2:717,8–9 = 35:13). See p. 210. *The main feature of Luther's doctrine of word and sacrament is its insistence on the actual wording of the biblical text*: see *The Babylonian Captivity* (e.g., 6:526,30 = 36:57) and the *Small Catechism* (*BSLK* [515–16] 516,1–2 = *BC* 359, but esp. *BSLK* 520,22–521,11 = *BC* 362–63).

200. WA 2:13,18–20 = LW 31:270–71 (author's emphasis; trans. alt.).

201. Cf. esp. the scholion on Rom. 9:28 (WA 56:406–10 = LW 25:396–400) and on that see pp. 130–135.

202. WA 2:13,20–22 = LW 31:271.

203. Cf. p. 205 and n. 201.

producing contrition.[204] Rather, in Luther's reformational theology, the "for me" comes solely from the literal "for you" of the proclaimed promise and also only remains in it.

> Christ on the cross with all his suffering and death is of no help, even if, as you teach, he is "recognized and meditated upon" with the utmost "passion, ardor, and heartfeltness." Something else must always be there. And what is that? The word, the word, the word! Hear that, you lying spirit. The word alone does it! Even if Christ were given and crucified a thousand times for us, it would all be in vain, if God's word were absent and not distributed and given to me with the words: this is for you; take it and have what is yours.[205]

Here, at the same time, Luther sharply asserts against his own earlier theology that faith is not *primarily* an existential stance or attitude, nor is it a more complete self-humiliation and contrition, not even if it is wrought exclusively by God, but comes solely from the promise and remains firmly grounded in it. Thus the promise also establishes a positive or certain basis for faith—all this of course in sharp negation to everything that is not this promise (*Pro veritate*, thesis 16).

Contrary to Luther's previous theology of the cross, the new understanding of the promise thus excludes also the disposition of indisposition,[206] which *Pro veritate*, taking up sentences from "Explanation" 38 of the *Theses on Indulgences*, formulates with numerous variations (theses 13–22, 25–28, 40).

To deny the necessity of any disposition, or generally to deny the existence of an obediential potency,[207] does not mean that the word of absolution is left in limbo. This is simply not possible because, as already shown, it is directed to the recipients and their situation, which is why Luther holds on to the reference

---

204. Cf., for example, the interpretation of the fourth petition of the Lord's Prayer of 1517 (WA 9:142,30–151,2); on that, see pp. 76–119, esp. 97–102.

205. WA 18:202,34–203,2 = LW 40:212–13 (*Against the Heavenly Prophets*, 1525; trans. alt.). Further (18:203,39–204,4 = 40:214): "If now I seek the forgiveness of sins, I should not run to the cross, for I will not find it distributed there. Nor should I hold to the knowledge and remembrance of Christ's suffering, as Karlstadt trifles, for I will not find it there either. But I should go to the sacrament or the gospel, for there I will find the word that distributes, donates, offers, and gives the forgiveness that was acquired for me on the cross" (trans. alt.). Cf. pp. 213–214.

206. Latin: the *dispositio* of the *indispositio*. Cf. theses 29 and 30 of the *Disputation Against Scholastic Theology*, 1517 (WA 1:225 = LW 31:11); on that, see p. 149.

207. Cf. the definition in K. Rahner and H. Vorgrimler, *Kleines Theologisches Wörterbuch* (Herder-Bücherei vol. 108/109, 6th ed., 1967, s.v. *potentia oboedientialis*).

to "those tormented by the terrors of conscience."[208] But for him this *reference* of the word is now no longer its *condition*, the addressee of the word is no longer its foundation, and sin is no longer linked etiologically with forgiveness. "Therefore, it is not as necessary to ask the person to be absolved, 'Are you sorry?' as it is to ask, 'Do you believe that you can be absolved by me?'"[209]

If, in the context of Luther's early theology, faith was indistinguishable from interior contrition,[210] it is now by definition completely turned away from any contrition because it is completely turned to the oral word of salvation.[211] Despite his interest in faith, Luther does not see it as dependent on us humans before the word (*ante verbum*) but rather, precisely for our sake and in relation to us, argues exclusively for faith under the word (*sub verbo*) and after the word (*post verbum*), and so for faith that is determined only by the special promise.

That to which faith is directed is in truth its ground; its object is its subject. This is seen in the phrase "believe in the word" (*credere in verbum*). It has the same sense as "faith in the word" (*fides verbi*), "faith in the absolution" (*fides absolutionis*), "faith in forgiveness" (*fides remissionis*), "faith in Christ" (*fides Christi*),[212] where the Latin genitive in each case, seen against the background of the tropological interpretation in the early texts, is to be understood not only objectively, but above all causatively or as a genitive of the author.[213]

The fact that the God who gives and the humans who receive agree in the word (see *Pro veritate*, thesis 45: "the word of the promiser—the faith of the receiver") is expressed in the same way as in the genitive of association "*fides verbi*"

---

208. See pp. 195–197.

209. WA 1:596,17–18 = LW 31:195 ("Explanation" 38): see pp. 196–197. *Pro veritate*, thesis 26.

210. See on that p. 182 and p. 183, n. 18.

211. Luther then shows how faith has completely shifted into the word as its basis. We see this very clearly in his treatment of the sacrament of penance in *The Babylonian Captivity* (WA 6:545,1–8 = LW 36:84; cf. 6:545,25–31 = 36:85). The decisive thing now is that law ("threat") and gospel ("promise") are no longer intertwined but sharply distinguished. Accordingly, "contrition" grounded in the threat and "consolation" grounded in the promise are also distinguished. Contrition no longer constitutes faith but is now its "inevitable *consequence*."

212. WA 1:594,35–36 = LW 31:193 (cf. l. 40 and 1:596,7–8 = 31:195); 1:595,3 = 31:193; 1:596,6,12 = 31:195; 1:595,23 = 31:194; 1:596,23 = 31:196; 1:594,40–41 = 31:193; 1:595,33 = 31:194 ("Explanation" 38); see in *Pro veritate* the central thesis (9). [In each of the compound genitives above, the genitive is best rendered with the preposition *in*. So, for example, the Latin "faith of the word" should be translated as "faith in the word."]

213. Cf. G. Ebeling, "Die Anfänge von Luthers Hermeneutik" (*ZThK* 48 [1951]: 172–230), here 228–29, and S. Raeder, *Das Hebräische bei Luther untersucht bis zum Ende der ersten Psalmenvorlesung*, esp. 36–42.

(faith in association with the word) in the *tantum-quantum* formula: "*tantum habes quantum credis*," "you only have as much as you believe."[214]

As a general statement, this formula occurs just as much in early texts[215] as in the 1520 tractates *The Babylonian Captivity* and *The Freedom of a Christian*. The difference between Luther's early theology and his reformational theology lies in the different way in which faith is understood. It follows directly from his discovery of the oral word of salvation, the basis and form of which he found in a new understanding of the sacrament of penance. It is the orally and audibly proclaimed promise of the forgiveness of sins, in which Matthew 16:19 is taken as a sentence of holy law, that gives certainty to the penitent.[216]

---

214. WA 1:595,5 = LW 31:193 ("Explanation" 38) in the context of ll. 1–5: "Even if you think you are not contrite enough (for you cannot and ought not trust yourself), nevertheless, if you believe him who said, 'He who believes and is baptized will be saved,' I tell you, this faith in the word of Christ makes you truly baptized, no matter how you feel about your contrition. Therefore, faith is everywhere necessary. You only have as much as you believe" (trans. alt.). See 1:543,8–9 = 31:104 ("Explanation" 7): "You only have as much as you believe, according to Christ's promise" (trans. alt.).

215. For the time of the first Psalms lectures, see the tropological conclusion of the *Sermon on the Prologue of John* of 1514: WA 1(:20–29),28,25–29,31, for that of the Romans lectures, see the scholion on 3:12 (WA 56:241,3–5 = LW 25:226–27) and on 8:24 (56:374,5–21 = 25:364), as well as the texts of the Hebrews lectures mentioned in n. 116.

216. *Like Matt. 16:19, Luther also understood the fifth petition of the Lord's Prayer as a sentence of holy law. It is "Christ's word, counsel, and promise"* (*Exposition of the Lord's Prayer*, 1518–1519; WA 2:118,17 = LW 42:65) *and his "command"* (2:118,14,38 = 42:65,66), *and they have become our legacy through his suffering and death.* Christ's "letter of indulgence reads thus: 'If you forgive those who sin against you, my Father will also forgive you; but if you do not forgive them, neither will my Father forgive you.' This letter, sealed with Christ's own wounds and confirmed by his death, was almost effaced and blotted out by the mighty cloudburst of Roman indulgences" (2:118,4–9 = 42:64–65; trans. alt.). Christ's testament contains the valid and sure promise of God, which is claimed in this way: "Would . . . that you would dismiss this guilt of ours and not enter into judgment with us, for no one is justified in your sight. Remember your promise that we are to sincerely forgive those who have sinned against us because you have promised forgiveness. It is not that through this forgiveness we are worthy of your forgiveness, but that you are truthful and graciously promised forgiveness to all who forgive their neighbors. We rely on your promise" (2:129,27–33 = 42:80; trans. alt.). For the nominalist roots of this concept of promise and its earlier form in Luther's theology, which even here is still evident (2:122,14–16 = 42:70), see chap. 2 I ("The Fulfillment of the Promise in Judgment").

It is strange that the following interpretation of the Lord's Prayer (*A Brief Form: How to Understand and Pray the Lord's Prayer*, 1519) shows no trace of this peculiar understanding of the petition. On the contrary: "This petition has an addendum and a condition, that we should first forgive those who have sinned against us; when that has happened, we can then say, 'Forgive us our sins" (WA 6:16,28–30 = WA 7:226,22–24; 1520). However, it appears again in the *Large Catechism*: *BSLK* 684–85 = *BC* 453. Here the forgiveness granted to the neighbor is set "as a sign

Only in this context can that famous saying "If you believe, you have it; if you do not believe, you do not have it" of the freedom tractate[217] also be properly understood. As a sentence of holy law, it is nothing other than a formula of blessing and curse, which is exactly what we have in Mark 16:16 (in the baptismal promise in *The Babylonian Captivity of the Church*[218]). The formula divides people into two categories in regard to their final destiny, the saved and the unsaved, corresponding to its two parts. The first part gives the saved the certainty of salvation, understood as the community of God and humans in the word, while the second part leaves the unsaved in no doubt about their condemnation.[219] Thus the eschatological wordtime of Christians[220] is given clear expression: "The sacrament of penance renews and points again to the Sacrament of Baptism when the priest says in the absolution, 'Behold, God has now forgiven your sin, as he promised you before in Baptism and has now commanded me to do by the power of the keys. Thus you are now returning to the work and essence of your Baptism. If you believe, you have it. If you doubt, you are lost.'"[221]

---

next to the promise that matches this petition in Luke 6[:37], 'Forgive, and you will be forgiven.' Therefore, Christ repeats it immediately after the Lord's Prayer, saying in Matt. 6[:14], 'For as you forgive others their sins, so your heavenly Father will also forgive you'" (*BSLK* 685,5–12 = *BC* 453, 96; trans. alt.). Hence, the fifth petition, which parallels these words, is therefore understood as a sentence of holy law. But Luther changed the relation of the antecedent (conditional) to the consequent (result) in a peculiar way so that the human and divine forgiveness are seen as being intertwined in a different way than the human and divine word of forgiveness in Matt. 16:19. The whole interpretation is primarily concerned with excluding the idea that comes readily to mind that God's forgiveness of us is conditional on our forgiveness of the neighbor. For Luther's understanding in detail, see the perceptive treatment by W. Joest, *Gesetz und Freiheit*, 121.

217. WA 7:24,13–14 (§9); cf. 7:23,16–17 (§7). Also, 7:23,17–19 (§7) and 7:24,14–17 (§9) (see already 7:23,19–22) correspond to each other as quotation and explanation.

218. Cf., however, "Explanation" 38 in the text quoted in n. 214. However, the *relationship* of penitence and baptism is not yet reflected here.

219. Cf. the "Explanation" of thesis 19 of the *Disputation on Infused and Acquired Faith* of Feb. 3, 1520: "The word and promise of God, as also the sacraments, are offered to all . . . For here Christ says to all: As you have believed, so be it done to you. That is to say, if you believe you will receive grace, you will have it, but if not, you will be condemned" (WA 6:97,28–29,34–36).

220. See my article, "Die reformatorische Wende in Luthers Theologie," *ZThK* 66 (1969): 115–50, here 147–48. [*Wordtime* is the English equivalent of the term *Wortzeit*, coined by the author to describe the time shaped and constituted by the word, specifically the word of baptism and the Lord's Supper; trans. note.]

221. WA 2:733,31–36 = LW 35:38 (*Sermon on the Sacrament of Baptism*, 1519; trans. alt.). Luther's claim that "If you believe" can be inferred from Mark 16:16 is also supported by the text quoted in n. 214. *The general formulation in the third person was characteristically*

This passage from the *Sermon on the Sacrament of Baptism* of 1519 is the first text[222] to show the way that the reformational understanding of the promise, stemming from a reconfiguration of the sacrament of *penance*, is impinging on the conception of *baptism* and to highlight the specifically reformational link between penance (repentance) and baptism. It is therefore also the first passage to depict the point of origin of the new reformational understanding of baptism[223] and as such is a good place to conclude our presentation on Luther's reconfiguration of the sacrament of penance.

At least in outline, it has become clear how not just the context of Luther's early theology but, even more, the whole network of traditional sacramental teaching is being torn apart and the reformational understanding of word and faith is now becoming visible.

With his stubborn insistence on Christ's specific *promissio* used in the oral promise and the faith that subsists in it, Luther brings the scholastic definition of the sacraments as "effectual signs of grace" (thesis 42)[224] to bear in a completely new way (thesis 45). This is not done by intensifying or deepening it but by a bold recourse to the New Testament, especially its sentences of holy law.

Three points have emerged that need highlighting. (1) The declarative understanding of the word, which Luther was still testing in "Explanation" 7, and with it the Augustinian distinction between *signum* and *res* has finally been overcome.[225]

---

transposed into the second person for the promise (see pp. 320–321), but the character of the saying was otherwise retained. Interestingly, Mark 16:16 still appears in the third person even in the Leipzig Sermon on Matt. 16:13–19 (where the text is in the second person) of June 29, 1519, there also in connection with the *tantum-quantum* (or *talis-qualis*) formula: "As one believes, so one has . . . if one believes it, one is saved, if not, one is condemned" (2:249,7–9 = 51:59; trans. alt).

222. Cf. nn. 214 and 218.

223. This thesis is the result of the analysis of the *Sermon on the Sacrament of Baptism*, as undertaken in chap. 7.

224. Cf., for example, Thomas Aquinas, *ST* III/q 62/a 1–6.

225. Cf. n. 199. It does not cast doubt on this statement but only confirms how unusual the effective or performative understanding of the word of absolution is for Luther when he himself can still speak favorably of the declarative understanding even in Aug. (1518), and so *after* he had drawn up "Explanation" 38 and *Pro veritate*: "But if grace alone grants contrition, what do the keys of the church do, if not declare or confirm the grace that already precedes them?" (WA 1:659, 21–23 in the context of ll. 17–36; *Against Prierias*). Accordingly, he also needs to speak again about the "*materia* of the sacrament of penance"—that is, "contrition" (1:659,25–28).

(2) The necessity of the disposition of the donor and recipient and thus the basic Aristotelian schema of *forma* and *materia*, form and matter, even in its highest sublimation[226] has been rejected. (3) The sufficiency of faith without Augustinian spiritualism has been affirmed because faith is maintained solely by means of the efficacy of the oral word of salvation:[227] "Faith and the word of Christ are the most true, the most certain, and the most sufficient."[228]

226. See pp. 205 and 221–223.

227. Cf. pp. 198–199; pp. 216–217 (n. 179); §9 of the *Sermon on the Sacrament of Penance*, where the sacrament of penance is defined entirely by the word of absolution (WA 2:717,1–2 = LW 35:13); and §15 of the same sermon ("The priest speaks a word, and the sacrament is there": 2:719,24–25 = 35:17), but esp. §12 of the same sermon ("to hear his sufficiently certain word in the sacrament": 2:718,12–13 = 35:15). The word is "sufficiently certain" because "there is no difference between the word of the priest, who is forgiving sins, and the word of God, although faith in the word is not given by the priest but by God. Hence the grace that takes away sin is not other than this faith in the word of God proclaimed by the priest" (WA 9:415,23–26; Sermon of Oct. 30, 1519, on Matt. 9:1–8). If we look back on the letter that Luther wrote two years earlier to the Archbishop of Mainz, it becomes clear what has changed in the meantime: "No one becomes secure in their salvation through any office of the bishop, although neither do they become secure through the infused grace of God. But the apostle commands us to always work out our salvation in fear and trembling" (Br 1:111; ll. 27–29).

228. WA 1:324,6–7 (*Sermon on Penance*, 1518).

CHAPTER 5

The Reformational Turn as Reflected in the Hebrews Lectures

THE RECONFIGURATION OF the sacrament of penance, presented in the last chapter as the reformational turn, is reflected in various scholia of the Hebrews lectures (on 5:1; 7:12; 9:14; 9:17; 9:24; 10:2–3; 10:5), all of which, except for the scholion on 5:1, come from the summer semester of 1518.

Since our *dating of the Hebrews lectures* differs from the commonly held opinion among Luther scholars (Easter 1517 to Easter 1518)[1], we need to explain here why it should be accepted.

"The manuscript of the Palatina has the year MDXVII at the end of the glosses on the otherwise completely blank page: it was probably under the printing of the text of the epistle that came below; and 1517 is repeated on the title page of the scholia."[2] Karlstadt mentions the lectures after the beginning of the winter semester of 1517.[3] Therefore, the only thing that is certain is that Luther lectured on the epistle in the winter semester of 1517/1518. Judging from what has been preserved of the lectures, it seems that they extended over two semesters. This can be confirmed by the Dessau transcript, which breaks off with the scholia on chapter 5 and so only contains about half the scholia of P, which probably amounts to about one semester's work.[4]

If we let the lectures begin after Easter 1517, then the scholion on 5:1, which in terms of its themes and motifs is undoubtedly closely related to the "Explanations" of theses 7 and 38 of the *Theses on Indulgences*, comes at the end of the summer semester, in October 1517, and thus stands in complete isolation for no comprehensible reason. For neither the above-mentioned *Zacchaeus*

---

1. E. Hirsch/H. Rückert, *Luthers Vorlesung über den Hebräerbrief* (1929), XXVI–XXVII; J. Ficker, WA 57/3, XIX; E. Vogelsang, *BoA* 5:344; H. Bornkamm, *RGG*, 3rd ed., 4:482 (Luther 1. Leben und Schriften); E. Bizer, *Fides ex auditu*, 75.

2. J. Ficker, WA 57/3:XVIII–XIX.

3. See the text in Hirsch/Rückert, XXIII, and on that see XXVI: Karlstadt's statement says "that Luther was reading the Epistle to the Hebrews at that time, November 1517." Ficker's interpretation of Karlstadt's remark ("halfway through the period of the lectures": WA 57/3:XIX) is not supported by it.

4. Cf. Ficker, WA 57/3:XIX.

sermon,[5] nor *The Ninety-Five Theses*, nor the *Tractate on Indulgences* associated with them,[6] suggest so much as a trace of the new insight that Luther expresses in the scholion on Hebrews 5:1.

On the other hand, it easily fits into the landscape of the texts that it belongs with, according to the dating of the lectures assumed here: at the end of the winter semester in March 1518. Ahead is the drafting of the "Explanations" of theses 7 and 38 of the *Theses on Indulgences*, which with their very specific interpretation of Matthew 16:19, already appear in the sermon for Candlemas (that is, on February 2).[7] But, on the other hand, they hardly arouse before January 20, at least the parts in which Luther expressly refers to the countertheses of Wimpina,[8] which Tetzel debated on January 20 in Frankfurt/Oder.[9] In the period before Easter (April 4), in March 1518, Luther preaches or writes the *Sermon on the Worthy Preparation of the Heart for the Reception of the Eucharist* [*Sermon on the Worthy Preparation*] as a counterpart to the *Sermon on Penance*. In a former sermon, he wants to bring to bear the insight he had gained from the sacrament of penance also for the understanding not of the Mass itself but of the preparation for the reception of the sacrament.[10] At the same time, he has to interpret Hebrews 4:16 in the lectures and for this purpose he includes

5. See pp. 181–182.

6. See p. 182.

7. WA 1 (130–32 = 4:636–39):131,5–19. The sermon dated by Löscher in one place to 1517 (supported also by E. Vogelsang, "Zur Datierung der frühesten Lutherpredigten" *ZKG* 50 [1931]: 112–45, here 134), but in another to 1518 (see WA 1:130), certainly belongs to the year 1518, the time that Luther was drafting the "Explanations," since they are specifically shaped by it. The reference to Matt. 16:19 (1:131,5–19), which is unexpected in view of the text (Mal. 3:1–4), only makes sense if the sacrament of penance is on his mind because he has had to deal with it elsewhere: see "Explanation" 7 and "Explanation" 38. Further, 1:131,2–4 should be compared with "Explanation" 58 and 1:131,33–37 with "Explanation" 15.

8. WA 1:544,9ff. = LW 31:105–7. Cf. 1:532,33ff. = 31:87–88 and 1:536,17–25 = 31:93.

9. S. N. Paulus, *Johann Tetzel* (1899), 171ff. (according to W. Köhler, *Dokumente zum Ablaßstreit*, 127).

10. WA 1:325–34 (*Sermo de digna praeparatione cordis pro suscipiendo sacramento eucharistiæ*). In terms of the subject matter, it makes sense to date the sermon (with 1:325) to the pre-Easter period, to which, for the same reason (cf. *Denz.*, 437), the *Sermon on Penance* (1:317–24; *Sermo de poenitentia*) probably belongs. The *Sermon on Worthy Preparation* is also a counterpart to this, since in a similar way, alongside the old motif of supplication, the new motif of faith in the promise is found, even though a real break can only really be observed in the *Sermon on Penance* (see chap. 4, n. 18). Both sermons are bound together by common formulations. See, for example, the phrase "however imperfect and fallible your own contrition may be" (1:323,28 and 1:331,19). What Luther learned from Matt. 16:19 he tries (in the *Sermon on Worthy Preparation*) to apply to Jesus's call in Matt. 11:28, which he also understands as a promise.

various formulations from the *Sermon on Worthy Preparation* summarized in the (second) scholion on Hebrews 5:1,[11] in which a specific argument that had just been put forward in the *Asterisci* against Eck was also incorporated.[12] If we compare the sentences in the sermon with their summary in the scholion (and with another identical summary[13]) and pay attention to the particular conciseness and remarkably tight design of the scholion as a whole,[14] then we would rather place it chronologically after the sermon than assume the opposite relationship.

From this perspective, the scholion of Hebrews 5:1 is sensibly assigned to the texts associated with it.[15] Accordingly, the lectures as a whole must be dated to the winter semester of 1517/1518 and the summer semester of 1518, which is entirely consistent with all known dates.[16]

---

11. Cf. WA 1:330,36–331,25 [not in LW] with 57/3:170,13–171,8 = LW 29:172–73.

12. Cf. WA 57/3,170,1–4 = LW 29:172 in the context of ll. 1–10 with 1:286,17–19 in the context of ll. 5–24. The two proof texts are still not connected with each other in the "Explanations."

13. It appears as an appendix to the brief interpretation of the Ten Commandments, which was written in Latin and German in 1517 as *Instruction for the Confession of Sins* (with M. Kroeger, *Rechtfertigung und Gesetz*, 176, n. 16, following Th. Brieger, "Kritische Erörterungen zur neuen Luther-Ausgabe" *ZKG* 11 [1890], 101–54, here 130–31, 139–49) and which Luther published in 1518, with this expanded appendix (WA 1:247–56, 257–65). That the appendix (both in its Latin and German versions) presupposes and summarizes the *Sermon on Worthy Preparation* can easily be seen by comparing 1:330,36–331,25 with 1:264,9–18 (completely identical with 57/3:170,14–171,8) or 1:255,24–39 (the last five lines go beyond the Latin version) and the rest of the sermon with 1:264,18–265,11 or 1:256,1–15 (the German version, tighter and more rounded than the Latin one, is probably written after the latter for this very reason).

14. See pp. 233–234.

15. The usual dating to Oct. 1517 (see, e.g., E. Bizer, *Fides ex auditu*, 75) has recently been advocated again by M. Kroeger (*Rechtfertigung und Gesetz*, 1968, 176ff.) in a broad argumentative context, but his arguments are refuted for the literary-critical reasons presented here.

16. What Luther lectured on in the summer semester of 1517, after the Galatians lectures slated for the winter semester of 1516/17 (see K. A. Meissinger, WA 57/2, V), remains an open question, of course—if we reject the assumption of a series on Titus (see, Hirsch/Rückert, XXV, n. 1), which is possible according to the texts supplied in Hirsch/Rückert, XXII f. Looking ahead to the second Psalms lectures, there is no difficulty at all. Luther's interpretation of the first five psalms was already available in print in Mar. 1519 (WA 5:4–5). However, this does not force us to assume that Luther (as, e.g., E. Vogelsang thinks: *Unbekannte Fragmente aus Luthers zweiter Psalmenvorlesung*, 1518, *AKG* 27, 1940) had already started the lectures in the summer semester of 1518. Since this first unit is a quarter of the length of the lectures that were interrupted in Jan. 1521 (see WA 5:6), there is no need to allow more than one semester for them, especially since Luther was less busy elsewhere in 1518/19 than he was in 1519/20. Luther's personal testimony of 1545 ("Meanwhile, that year [1519] I had already returned to interpreting the Psalter a second time": WA 54:185,12 = LW 34:336) cannot be used to argue either for or against the assumed date (the beginning of the second Psalms lectures—that is, the winter semester of 1518/19).

We now turn to the scholia mentioned above that highlight the factors that drive the story of the promise forward. The scholion on Hebrews 7:12 has already been discussed (in chap. 4) in connection with the texts Luther used to prepare the *Pro veritate* theses, to which it directly belongs in terms of its subject matter and theme. The fact that it had to be assigned to the "Explanation" of thesis 7 of the *Theses on Indulgences* and thus, although it was only dictated during the course of the lectures in May/June 1518,[17] appeared in our presentation *before* the "Explanation" of thesis 38 emphasizes that Luther's insight that "the declaration is too little" is still very spotty and incredibly new (indeed, it does not appear anywhere in his letter to Spalatin of February 15[18] or in the theses and proofs of the Heidelberg Disputation) and that what is new is in fact only found in an unambiguous context in the series of theses *Pro veritate*, which the following presentation is also based on.

A) Certainty of Salvation Through Faith in a Specific Word (Scholion on Heb. 5:1)

This scholion stands out from all other texts in the lectures due to its particular conciseness and strikingly succinct design. Repetitions of the same lines of thought are avoided and a digression resulting from a string of Bible passages is missing. The entire text is held together by a single theme, that of the certainty of salvation, which Luther highlighted within the constellation of themes and motifs of March 1518 from Hebrews 4:16 (LET US THEN WITH CONFIDENCE DRAW NEAR TO THE THRONE OF GRACE, THAT WE MAY OBTAIN MERCY AND FIND GRACE TO HELP IN TIME OF NEED). Although the text is linked to 5:1 (EVERY HIGH PRIEST . . . IS APPOINTED TO REPRESENT THE PEOPLE),[19] it is otherwise an interpretation of 4:16, which is not only shown by the gloss on this verse[20] but also by the scholion on 5:1 itself, in that it remains bound to 4:16 both in terms of content and concept.[21]

17. Lectures were cancelled for the whole of April because of Easter and the trip to Heidelberg (see WA 1:350).

18. WA Br 1:144–47, ll. 12–51.

19. WA 57/3:169,10–11 = LW 29:171.

20. WA 57/3:26,7–27,2, but esp. the marginal gloss: 27,18–19. Line 19 (Matt. 11:28!) is obviously in view already in the scholion in 57/3:170,14–171,8 = 29:172–73. [LW does not print the gloss, only the scholion.]

21. Cf., for example, CONFIDENCE (*FIDUCIA*; 4:16) with "to believe with complete certainty" (*certissime credere*; WA 57/3:169,17–18 = LW 29:171), "to have confidence" (*confidere*; 57/3:171,3 = 29:172) and approach "with boldness" (*praesumptio*; 57/3:171,7 = 29:173 [LW has "with confidence"]). The ATTAIN GRACE (*GRATIAM CONSEQUI*; 4:16) appears in the

First, we look at its structure. The composition of the scholion, which is well thought out, begins with a thesis (WA 57/3:169,10–11 = LW 29:171). This is first explained with a quotation from the church fathers, which for Luther is very important ("For, as Bernard says": 57/3:169,11–20 = 29:171). It is then formulated more precisely and reworked (57/3:169,20–23 = 29:172). A conclusion is drawn from this ("From these statements": 57/3:169,23–170,1 = 29:172) whereby the sequence shows that a comprehensive statement is coming, which on the basis of two proof texts ("For it is true" [*verum enim est*]: 57/3:170,1–4 = 29:172), is then made ("From which it follows" [*ex quibus sequitur*]": 57/3:170,4–10 = 29:172) and illustrated twice ("Indeed, any sacrament requires . . ." [*sic*]: 57/3:170,10–13 = 29:172 and "Thus there is also a great error" [*ita*]: 57/3:170,13–171,8 = 29:172). The second illustration, a concise summary of a part of the *Sermon on the Worthy Preparation of the Heart*,[22] forms an effective climax and conclusion.

The scholion begins with the thesis "that it is not enough for Christians to believe that Christ was appointed to act on behalf of people unless they also believe that they are included." In fact, it is not enough even to believe that God *can* forgive *your* sins unless you also believe with complete certainty that they *are* forgiven *you*.[23] The Holy Spirit gives this certainty to our conscience; we do not have it of ourselves.[24]

Here, as in the Romans lectures (on 8:16), Luther uses formulations from Bernard's sermon that are an important factor in the emergence of his reformational theology, which is attested not only by their position here and in the *Acta Augustana*[25] but also, for example, by Melanchthon's view of Luther's development.[26] However, if Luther had only quoted the Bernardine text[27]

---

scholion frequently (57/3:169,24; 170,1,13; 171,3–4 = 29:172). The cultic term *DRAW NEAR* (*ADIRE*; 4:16) is taken up again with "approach" (*accedere*; 57/3:170,14–15; 171,8 = 29:172–73).

22. See pp. 230–231, esp. nn. 11 and 13.

23. WA 57/3,169,10–18 = LW 29:171. See besides the scholion on 9:24 (on that, see pp. 243–245) on 11:6, esp. 57/3:233,10–11 = 29:235: "Faith is needed, namely, the faith by which we believe that *we* are numbered among those for whom God is . . ." (author's emphasis).

24. WA 57/3:169,18–23 = LW 29,171–72. Bernard's opinion is not "objected to" here (E. Bizer, *Fides ex auditu*, 80): The phrase "as Bernard says" must be taken as referring to "the testimony of such a conscience" but not to the "not" (with E. Vogelsang's German translation: *AKG* 17, 81, against that of G. Helbig [Leipzig 1930, 71]).

25. WA 2:15,35–16,3 = LW 31:273–74. See chapter 4, n. 173.

26. Cf. his preface to the second volume of Luther's complete works, Wittenberg 1546 (Scheel, Document No. 532; 199,18–26) and the first sermon on Luther's life by Mathesius (No. 538; 207,20–25).

27. WA 56:370,9–12, 14–16 = LW 25:359–60 = MPL 183:384 A.

in his Romans lectures and had blunted its point with his commentary, which attributed the certainty to "humility" and "remorse,"[28] here he identifies with it, which is also shown by the fact that he freely adopts it in the sense Bernard intended and fully incorporates it into his discussion.

Put another way, the fact that the conscience can only *receive* the testimony of God's grace that gives certainty but cannot bring it about itself means that only *faith* obtains grace. Thus faith is understood here as the posture of pure reception.[29] You cannot make yourself certain of God's forgiveness; you cannot establish the "*pro me*" yourself. Your certainty comes "to you," not "from you" (for this Pelagian!).

It is highly significant that Luther speaks of the institutional sacrament at precisely this point, thus linking the problem of what gives certainty with the question of the function of the sacraments. As much as this can be understood from the "Explanations" of thesis 7 and thesis 38 of the *Theses on Indulgences* (which here open out into statements about the sacraments in general, as it were[30]), it is a *novum*, something new, compared with Luther's earlier theology, for which uncertainty was the fundamental criterion, which is why the sacrament was never considered as a place of haven and certainty.

The concept of the sacrament that Luther develops in the middle of the scholion has a certain inconsistency that cannot be ignored. On the one hand, there are two proof texts that are fused together for the first time in the *Asterisci*[31]—namely, that "very commonly known and highly esteemed" statement 'that it is not the sacrament itself but faith in the sacrament that justifies,' and also the well-known statement of St. Augustine: '(The sacrament) justifies not because it is performed, but because it is believed.'" These proof texts emphasize not only faith but also the sacrament as its basis and object ("faith *in the sacrament*"). On the other hand, however, it is strongly emphasized that faith alone justifies. But clearly faith is not received from the sacrament. For that would then make the latter the effective agent, the very thing that Luther vehemently denies: "The error is to say that the sacraments . . . are effectual signs of grace."[32] In any case,

28. See chap. 3, n. 59.

29. The factual connection between WA 57/3:169,20–23 and ll. 23ff., which at first glance seems unclear, lies in the parallelism of "receive" (l. 23) and "believe" (l. 25).

30. Luther at first arrives at this generalization by listing all the sacraments together ("Therefore, it comes about that no one obtains grace because they are absolved or baptized or communed or anointed, but because they believe they obtain grace by being absolved, baptized, communed, and anointed": WA 57/3:169, 24–170,1 = LW 29:172; trans. alt.); then he speaks in summary fashion of the "sacraments" or "every sacrament" (57/3:170,1–10 = 29:172).

31. Cf. chap. 4, n. 140.

32. WA 57/3:170,5–6 = LW 29:172.

they do not work by themselves alone but require a disposition in the recipient, which of course means something other than that the receiver should put no obstacle in their way. The sacraments specifically presuppose faith. Luther says: "Any sacrament requires a completely pure heart... But the heart is not purified except by faith, as Acts 15[:9] says."[33] This is exactly what he had formulated shortly before in the *Asterisci* against Eck: "The sacraments... do not effect the grace which they signify, but faith is required *before* every sacrament."[34]

If faith, the stance of pure reception, can already exist *before* the reception of the sacrament, then the latter only appears as the fulfillment of its presupposition. To be sure, faith is related to the sacrament[35] but is clearly not based on it nor is it produced by it. Rather, faith is provoked or called forth by a word.

This brings the surprising conclusion of the scholion, the summary of the *Sermon on the Worthy Preparation of the Heart*, into focus. Although it is only added as an illustration of what has been said before, it carries it forward, in contrast to the sermon, in the direction of *The Babylonian Captivity of the Church*.

Faith (on the part of those approaching the sacrament of the Eucharist) is not defined here in a vague and general way as a stance of pure reception or only negatively (without works) but is seen as grounded in a specific word: "This faith alone makes them pure and worthy; it does not rely on those works but on the most pure, holy, and firm word of Christ, who says: 'Come to me, all who labor and are heavy laden, and I will give you rest.' Therefore, we must approach in the boldness and confidence of these words, and those who approach in this way will not be confounded."[36] According to this, faith is based on an invitational call addressed to the uncertain and despairing[37] with the promise[38] of certain help.

---

33. WA 57/3:170,6–10 = LW 29:172.

34. WA 1:286,15–16 (author's emphasis).

35. WA 57/3:169,25–170,1 and 171,3–4 = LW 29:172: "If they believe and are confident that they will obtain grace *there*" (author's emphasis; trans. alt.). See WA 1:330,21–22 (*Sermon on the Worthy Preparation of the Heart*): "Draw near without fear, for you will find them [the fruit of the Spirit] nowhere except in this sacrament."

36. WA 57/3:171,4–8 = LW 29:172–73 (the words of the Luther text up to "I will give you rest" are emphasized; trans. alt.). With the final sentence, what J. Ficker fails to notice is that the psalm verse (Ps. 35:4; Vulgate 34:6; see 57/3:27,18–19) already quoted in the gloss on 4:16 is taken up again.

37. Cf. the line gloss on 4:16: "Let us then with confidence draw near let us not be hindered by any scruple of conscience or fear of sins" (WA 57/3:26,7–8).

38. Cf. the *Sermon on the Worthy Preparation of the Heart*: "Where Christ promises: come..." (WA 1:331,23; see ll. 32–33: "faith in your promise") and the German translation of the Latin "the word of Christ" (WA 57/3:171,6 = LW 29:172 = WA 1:264,16; *Instruction on the Confession of Sins*) with "the word and promise of Christ" (WA 1:255,32; *A Brief Explanation of the Ten*

Faith gains the firmness of this word by relying on it, it obtains its certainty by "claiming" the certainty of this one word, and it purifies the heart by receiving the clarity of this word.[39]

Matthew 11:28, as the epitome of the gospel, had special importance even before the Hebrews lectures: in the sermons for Second Advent 1516[40] and for St. Matthias Day (February 24, 1517).[41] This verse also occurs in the interpretation of the Lord's Prayer from the spring of 1517.[42] With regard to the *Sermon on Worthy Preparation* and its inclusion in the scholion on Hebrews 5:1, the most interesting thing, however, is its use at the end of the interpretation of Psalm 23 from the years 1516/17, because here it is connected with the Eucharist and at the same time with an understanding of the promise[43]—albeit one that is determined by Luther's *early* theology. Thus a connection can be recognized that makes it clear that Luther did not arrive at his reformational understanding of the word completely unprepared during the indulgence controversy. Nevertheless, it should be noted that the starting points for this are

---

Commandments) and the later passage from the *Sermons on Genesis*: "Christ came for this reason, to pardon sin and publicly announce this promise: 'Come to me all you who are heavy laden' etc." (WA 9:388,20–21).

39. In complete contrast to Luther, for Biel, who addresses Matt. 11:28 ("come to me") in a sermon, this word not only means a gift but also requires a preparation to be done by us: see H. A. Oberman, *Spätscholastik und Reformation*, vol. 1, 112, and the quotation in n. 89.

40. Here Matt. 11:28 (alongside Matt. 9:2) is the epitome of the gospel in its proper and true function, from which that of the intensification of the "old law" is sharply separated (WA 1:105, esp. 19–22). See pp. 170–173.

41. WA 1:140,27–34 = LW 51:30. See on that chap. 3, B 5, esp. n. 113.

42. In the divine speech in WA 9:131,1–10 (*Auslegung und Deutung des heiligen Vaterunsers*, 1518), where Matt. 11:20 appears together with Isa. 35:4 and John 1:29 as a word with which God wants to make us certain of his help: "For I had it shouted out by all the prophets, who said loudly and openly . . ."

43. WA 31/1(:464–71):471,14–15. Of the Lord's Supper texts that precede the *Sermon on Worthy Preparation*, this psalms interpretation is the one that comes closest to it. The concept of the promise is of course still determined by the understanding of the crucified Christ as an archetype: "We have nothing but the word and promise about God until we are brought to him. Therefore, those who have learned that we are to ponder nothing but Christ in his death (see ll. 12–13: for in his cross and suffering he was our exemplar) understand that *this itself* is the word and promise of Christ" (31/1:468,36–39; author's emphasis).

Against the proposed dating (1516/17), one could also argue that this interpretation of psalm 23 is in fact *dependent* on the scholion on Heb. 5:1, especially in view of the concluding section of the interpretation of the psalm ("Great confidence is given to us to approach the altar"; see Heb. 4:16. "A table has been prepared for us, surely not against us but for us": cf. 57/3:165,17–18). However, since this would offer the easier solution to the question of dating in terms of the overall view of this investigation, it could not be defended. Cf. above chap. 2, n. 435b.

only found very sporadically, are by no means representative of the tendencies of his theology before 1518, and remain ineffective due to the predominance of other factors.[44]

The *Sermon on Worthy Preparation* (or the scholion on Heb. 5:1), judged from *The Babylonian Captivity*, represents only an interim solution. In contrast to its counterpart, the 1518 *Sermon on Penance*, which in its final part points faith to the specific place of the word of absolution, which already completely defines the sacrament, it does not discuss the place of the word at all. Luther knows at least that faith is related to the sacrament; he knows that grace is obtained there. However, he does not believe this, as later, on the basis of the sacrament understood as a word, so that the preparation for the Mass would coincide with its use,[45] but on the basis of a different word of Scripture that only invites and leads to the sacrament. But it remains unclear what faith receives in the sacrament and from the sacrament itself.

But Luther himself is aware of the question at stake in this ambiguity. For in the final part of the *Sermon on Worthy Preparation* he tries to determine the relationship between the preparation and attitude to the reception of the sacrament, which consists in word and faith, and the sacrament itself:

> You must not neglect it but, on the contrary, must administer it especially so that the memory of Christ's passion is not lost. For what good is it if you are worthily prepared, but do not do that for which you have prepared yourself? For the Lord commanded that this sacrament should be celebrated for no other reason but in remembrance of him. Therefore, you should neglect it only if you want to neglect his remembrance. For he said, 'Do this, as often as you do it, in remembrance of me.' And Paul said, 'As often as you eat this bread and drink this cup, you proclaim the Lord's death until he comes.' Hence, the church decided that mass

44. In the interpretation of the Lord's Prayer of 1517, for example, the text mentioned in n. 42 is a complete exception. The dominant motif becomes clear in the following: "If you know that God wants to have sinners, then take comfort in knowing that you are a sinner yourself. For if you judge yourself inwardly and find within you an unworthy and impure heart, (know that) it is pure before God" (WA 9:150,2–5). See further chap. 10, n. 95.

45. Luther then defends this view in 1520. See the sermon *Concerning the Testament of Christ* of Apr. 8, in which he says of the gifting words of the Lord's Supper: "Those who have meditated well on these words ["*given* for you"] will know the power of the Eucharist and the proper way of preparing to receive it, which is found in them" (WA 9:446,3–4; see p. 321, and see also *The Babylonian Captivity*: "Hence the only worthy preparation and proper use is faith by which we believe the mass, that is, the divine promise" [WA 6:517,22–23 = LW 36:43, trans. alt.]); "the word of promise must reign here alone in pure faith, which is the one and only sufficient preparation" (WA 6:520,5–6 = LW 36:46).

> should not be held without the reading of the gospel. However, this matter of remembrance requires another sermon.[46]

There is an allusion here to the *Sermon on the Passion* of the same time,[47] which follows along the old lines of the sacramental meditation on Scripture.[48] However, Luther does not discuss its relationship to the celebration of the Mass itself. Thus the reference in the *Sermon on Worthy Preparation* to the *Sermon on the Passion* only creates further ambiguity. But if it is Luther's opinion, as the earlier texts suggest, that the celebration of the Mass only *assists* the sacramental meditation on Scripture and that this describes its essential effect,[49] then becoming worthily prepared by penitential meditation on the passion would lead back behind it again. For the certainty gained through faith on the basis of the specific word is destroyed again if it is to be surpassed and obtained instead by meditating on the image of the crucified, which can only lead back to uncertainty as long as it is not made unambiguous (that is, not mediated by the sure promise).

Despite the new interpretation of the fourth petition of the Lord's Prayer in 1518/19,[50] the crucified Christ is presented as our comfort and consolation in the passion sermon of the following year (1519) in only a single place,[51] then quite emphatically in *A Sermon on Preparing to Die* (November 1519), where the "image" of Christ (i.e., the reality of the Christ event[52]) is linked with the sacramental promise and thus seen as attested, given, and made

---

46. WA 1:334,3–11.

47. WA 1:336–39,14; see the abridged version of this sermon preparationin 1:339,15–340,14. Cf. M. Elze, *Das Verständnis der Passion Jesu im ausgehenden Mittelalter und bei Luther*, 134–36, 140–45.

48. Cf. pp. 76–102.

49. Cf. pp. 102–119.

50. Cf. pp. 349–354.

51. Cf. ibid., §13, esp.: "You must dare to stake everything on this [1 Pet. 2:24] and similar sayings" (WA 2:140,11–12 = LW 42:12; trans. alt.).

52. By "image" Luther means a concrete reality that we do not observe as an object from a distance but rather experience firsthand. Death, sin, and hell are the three "images" that "seek to take over the heart completely with their appearance, their arguments, and their signs" (WA 2:688,25–26 = LW 42:103; trans. alt.). Christ's reality is also spoken of as an "image": on the cross, "he himself prepared for us a threefold image to hold up to our faith against the three counter images" (2:691,12–13 = 42:106; trans. alt.), so that "Christ's image may be in us alone and we may argue and deal with him" (2:692,20–21 = 42:108; trans. alt.). Nowhere else in Luther is the word *image* used as often as in this writing.

certain by it.[53] But the idea of the crucified as a source of comfort is only really presented in a decisive way in the *Sermon Concerning the Testament of Christ* of April 8, 1520, which forms the basis of the understanding of the Lord's Supper in *The Babylonian Captivity of the Church*.[54] Luther initially finds the main aspects of this idea in the scholia of the Hebrews lectures, which we will deal with below.

B) Meditation on Christ's Passion and the Words of the Lord's Supper (Scholion on Heb. 9:14)

The scholion straddles the boundary between meditation piety and promise theology and so captures a "fruitful moment" in the whole story of Luther's theology.[55]

In the sense of the meditation piety, as we have seen it, for example, in the interpretation of the fourth petition of the Lord's Prayer of 1517,[56] one might expect the text (THE BLOOD OF CHRIST PURIFIES OUR CONSCIENCE) to prompt Luther to think about "every little drop of Christ's rose-colored blood"[57] from which we "suck what is ours, especially our penitence."[58] The scholion of course speaks of "looking at the blood of Christ in

53. H. Appel, *Anfechtung und Trost im Spätmittelalter und bei Luther* (1938), treats the sermon against the background of late medieval devotional literature, especially the *Ars moriendi*, the art of dying (121–24). In his opinion, "the description of the struggle against the images of death, sin, and hell, which can only be overcome by not looking at them 'in themselves' but in the image of Christ," forms the focal point of the booklet (*Sermon on Preparing to Die*, 122), as found in §§6–14 (LW 42:101-7). However, this is not true insofar as the *strongest emphasis is just as much on this middle section of the sermon* (§§4–5,15–20 = LW 42:100–101, 108–14): *the plea to understand the sacrament as a firm promise and a sign that gives us certainty. Luther stresses that it is the sacrament that really opens access to the reality of Christ, the "image" of Christ, described in the middle section.* "It is therefore necessary not only to look at the three images in Christ and with them to drive out the counter-image and leave it behind, but to remember that we have a sure sign to give us certainty and that this is given to us in the sacraments." (WA 2:695 [6–15], 12–15 = LW 42:111; trans. alt.). Similarly, "in the sacraments, God himself has said to you all the things that are now said of Christ and wants the sacraments to be a sign and testimony that Christ's life has taken on and overcome your death, his obedience your sin, his love your hell" (2:692,27–32 = 42:108; trans. alt.). See, from the context, esp. 2:693,7–15 and 2:694,10–11, 18–19 = 42:109–10.

54. Cf. chap. 6.

55. Cf. the whole section B with chap. 8.

56. See pp. 97–102.

57. WA 9:143,28 (interpretation of the Lord's Prayer, 1517).

58. WA 9:145,31–32.

faith"[59] and of "meditating on his passion."[60] But the pattern of the devotion is immediately thwarted and corrected by Luther's interest in a very specific oral word, which is such that it gives certainty in and of itself and is therefore unambiguous.

Specifically, as in the scholion on 5:1, Luther is concerned about the certainty of the *forgiveness* of sins, whether they *are* forgiven. Speaking of the purity of conscience, he says: "Nothing at all can make the conscience pure except this blood of Christ alone, and even the blood itself cannot do this unless our heart believes that it has been poured out for the forgiveness of sins. For we must believe him who makes the testament when he says: 'This is the blood, which is poured out for you and for many for the forgiveness of sins.'"[61]

Not even the blood of Christ itself can give certainty because as such, as an image and concept, it is not unambiguous. Jesus's actions and suffering cannot remain in the form of an image but need to be expressed orally in words that are precisely defined if they are to create certainty. Luther finds such words in the formulaic *gifting words*[62] of the Lord's Supper, the words of institution. These words, which stress its gift character, are words that Luther tellingly had never paid any attention to until now.[63]

The words of the composite quotation[64] made up of Matthew 26:28 and Luke 22:20 did not come together by accident. For Luther, Matthew speaks "the clearest of all"[65] because of his addition "for the forgiveness of sins." The "for you" used by Luke and by Paul (albeit only in the words about the bread) is very important to him because it not only names the addressees of the saying and the gift in the third person (like Matthew and Mark: "for many") but also directly addresses them in the second person.

59. WA 57/3:207,23–24 = LW 29:209.

60. WA 57/3:209,16 = LW 29:210.

61. WA 57/3:207,26–208,4 = LW 29:209 (trans. alt.).

62. It is presupposed here that it is more in keeping with the New Testament situation, considered from the angle of form analysis and the history of religions, to speak of them as "gifting words" or the "formula of distribution" ["This is my body which is given for you, this is my blood which is shed for you"] than as "interpretative words."

63. See chap. 2, n. 496b.

64. It can also be found in Chrysostom's interpretation of Hebrews, which Luther used throughout his lectures: "This is . . . the blood of the New Testament, which is shed for you for the forgiveness of sins" (chap. 9, Homily 16; MPG 63:124).

65. WA 57/3:212 (8–11),9: "omnium clarissime Matt. 26" = LW 29:213 (trans. alt.).

In the form in which they are presented here by Luther, the gifting words have a double significance. First, they report Jesus's death as a fact of history ("the blood shed"), which "the Jews also saw and of which all the Gentiles also heard, and yet were not cleansed."[66] But it does not somehow have to be meditatively related by the viewers to themselves, nor does it have to be seen to have any significance for them, for the linguistic form itself already articulates its comforting significance ("for the forgiveness of sins"). "For no matter how much we were to see or hear that the blood of Christ was shed, none of this would cleanse the conscience unless the words 'for the forgiveness of sins' were added."[67]

However, the certainty of it is only fully brought out by the second part of the formula: the linguistic allocation of forgiveness to us, which happens with the words "for you" (singular). This unambiguity enables the listener to be certain "that Christ's blood was shed for *his or her* sins,"[68] "as the words themselves declare."[69] Thus in the language of the *Acta Augustana*, it creates the *fides particularis*: the special faith that arises from the special word. Thus Luther can finally say in a statement that fully parallels the contemporaneous *Pro veritate* theses in structure and content: "A good, clean, quiet, and joyful conscience is nothing but faith in the forgiveness of sins, which cannot be had except in the word of God that proclaims to us that the blood of Christ was shed for the forgiveness of sins."[70]

The precise understanding of the word that has now emerged fundamentally contradicts the thrust of the sacramental meditation on Scripture, even if, according to this scholion, both seem to peacefully coexist.[71] For if the precise understanding of the word had its roots in the sacramental meditation on Scripture, and thus belonged to it from the outset, it would be incomprehensible

66. WA 57/3:208,28–29 = LW 29:210 (trans. alt.).

67. WA 57/3:208,26–28 = LW 29:210 (trans. alt.). Luther especially emphasizes the importance of "for the forgiveness of sins" several times. See besides 57/3:208,3–4 = 29:209: 57/3:208,23–24,24–6 = 29:10; 57/3:209,15 = 29:210; 57/3:212,9–11 = 29:213.

68. WA 57/3:209,21 = LW 29:211 (trans. alt.; author's emphasis). Cf. 57/3:208,29–209,2 = 29:210, "Indeed, it is not enough for people to believe that it was shed for the forgiveness of sins unless they believe that it was shed for the forgiveness of their own sins," and 57/3:209,13–14 = 29:210, "We should pay special attention to the pronouns 'his/her,' 'their,' 'my' etc" (trans. alt.).

69. In a later formulation of Luther (from *A Simple Way to Pray*, 1535; WA 38:374,19–20 = LW 43:211 (trans. alt.).

70. WA 57/3:208,22–26 = LW 29:210; trans. alt.

71. Especially in the sentence "We must contemplate his suffering with such earnestness that faith may increase, that is, that the more often we meditate upon it, the more fully we may believe that the blood of Christ was shed for our sins" (WA 57/3:209,19–21 = LW 29:210–11; trans. alt.). Cf. 57/3:207,23–25 = 29:209.

that it only appears here and that the passion sermon preached shortly before,[72] which clearly agrees with our scholion in the matter of the sacramental meditation on Scripture,[73] says nothing at all about the precise understanding of the word that is expressed in it. Evidently, the two aspects that coincide in the interpretation of Hebrews 9:14 are basically pulling in different directions. Luther went in one direction in the passion sermon mentioned above. Even in 1519, in the *Sermon on the Contemplation of Christ's Holy Passion*, he had great difficulty in bringing his new understanding of the word into play,[74] which certainly does not suggest an affinity between the two aspects from the outset. At the time of the Hebrews lectures, Luther did not yet recognize the significance that his new idea had for a new understanding of the Lord's Supper, since he did not yet expressly relate the testator's words to the sacrament as their present *Sitz im Leben*. Only after almost two years of experimentation did the different starting points or organizing centers of the Hebrews lectures result in a new overall conception of the Lord's Supper.

The difference that emerges in the scholion on Hebrews 9:14 is important for determining the distinctive reformational character of Luther's understanding of the word. If this is not properly considered, this distinctive character can only be understood as a deepening of late medieval meditation piety.[75] But according to his reformational understanding, Luther's "for me" means the certainty of a special faith, understood as an echo of the unambiguity of a specific word, which in turn correlates with the loudly proclaimed "for you" (plural). This cuts off the uncertain path of meditative empathy and does not prove its validity through existential concern, thus contradicting the spirit of the tropological interpretation rather than being based on it.

The difference described must be due to a difference in understanding of the church and the sacrament: meditative piety can leave everything institutional and external, take it as an occasion for the real thing, and "interpret" it in this way, like the early Luther did with the Mass. But if the oral word is constitutive and not just an opportunity for meditation, then it must necessarily

72. See n. 47.

73. The immediate agreement, of course, is only in its rejection of the wrong meditation on Christ's passion (cf. WA 57/3:209,16–19 = LW 29:210 with 57/3:338,15–29 [not in LW]) but not in its concrete affirmation: For the sermon, Christ and the story of his passion are material for self-knowledge (1:337,35 and passim), but for the scholion, the blood of Christ expresses itself in the words of the forgiveness of sins.

74. However, it only succeeds to a limited extent: only in a single place (quoted in n. 51).

75. Cf. M. Elze, "Züge spätmittelalterlicher Frömmigkeit in Luthers Theologie," *ZThK* 62 (1965): 381–402, here 400–401, where of course the restrictive n. 75 (in the Elze article) needs to be considered.

demand and bring to bear an understanding of the sacrament and the church that corresponds to it. It does not "interpret" the meditative piety but changes it. Therefore, it is not enough to talk about a deepening of it where there has been a radical change.

C) Against Conjectural Certainty (Scholion on Heb. 9:24)

Luther's interest in the *pro nobis* of Christ's action—words meant to bring us certainty because they stress that what Christ did, he did *for us*—which led him to pay so much attention to the gifting words of the Lord's Supper with their "for you" in the scholion on 9:14, finds a new point of reference in Hebrews 9:24 (TO APPEAR IN THE PRESENCE OF GOD FOR US).[76]

In the "*pro nobis*," we do not know Christ through speculation but through practice.[77] "Therefore, Christians must be certain, indeed, absolutely certain, that Christ appears for them as a priest before God. For as they believe, so it will be done for them."[78] These words prefigure the "if you believe, you have it!" of the freedom tractate, but there of course it is expressly attached to the word of promise. This connection is not clearly specified here but is nevertheless intended, as we can see from the scriptural passages that Luther immediately cites[79] (Mark 11:23–24; Matt. 8:13 and Jas. 1:6–7)[80] and which come up again shortly after the writing of this scholion in his position on the second point of contention in Augsburg, the question of the certainty of faith.[81]

---

76. WA 57/3:215,15–216,19 = LW 29:217–18. Cf. the marginal gloss (57/3:53,13–15) and with it 57/3:165,15–18; 166,14–15.

77. "Some know Christ through speculation, others through practice. The meaning of the former is that Christ appeared in the presence of God for others, but the meaning of the latter is that Christ appeared in the presence of God for us" (WA 57/3:215,16–18 = LW 29:217; trans. alt.). Luther was by no means the only one in his time who pushed for "experience" rather than "speculation" and paid special attention to the "for you" of the words of the Lord's Supper. J. Altenstaig emphasizes in his *Vocabularius Theologiae*, s.v. "memoriale," that in the Sacrament of the Altar, Christ himself offers us his body, "which was slain for us, and his blood, which was shed for us. And this is for tasting, which he understands from the following: so that we may remember his suffering not through *speculation*, as it were, but through a sort of *experience*." (Fol. CXLV/CXLVI; author's emphasis).

78. WA 57/3:215,18–20 = LW 29:217 (trans. alt.).

79. WA 57/3:215,20–216,2 = LW 29:217.

80. E. Bizer, *Fides ex auditu*, 90, is therefore too harsh in his judgment when he says that "strangely enough, there is no mention here of the word, of the certainty of faith."

81. WA 2:14,30–35,24–29; 15,9–14 = LW 31:272–73. Cf. below pp. 371–372.

Up to this point, Luther does not go beyond what he had already said in his Romans lectures on Romans 8:16,[82] even though this, too, is understood differently in the context of the parts discussed in the Hebrews lectures than in the Romans lectures. However, in what follows he clearly abandons the position he adopted in the Romans lectures by vigorously contradicting the traditional understanding of Ecclesiastes 9:1—that is, the doctrine of conjectural certainty, which is based on this passage.[83] This is exactly what he had not yet done when he treated Romans 8:38[84] and so also withdrew his remarks on Romans 8:16.[85] Here in Hebrews 9:24, Luther warns against the opinion of those who relate the verse "people do not know whether they are worthy of love or hate" to their present situation, thereby making them uncertain of God's mercy and of their trust in his salvation. For that means completely destroying Christ and faith in him.[86] Luther finds his exegetical solution in the immediate context of the saying:[87] the preacher (Ecclesiastes) is not speaking of our present state but of our future state, of which we cannot be certain in the sense of 1 Corinthians 10:12, where Paul says, "Let anyone who thinks they stand take heed lest they fall"[88]—a solution that he had already ventured in the "Explanation" of thesis 58 of the *Theses on Indulgences* in order to emphasize the certainty of the words

82. "For we are and have only as much as we believe. Therefore, whoever believes with full faith and trusts that they are the children of God, are the children of God, because we read in Mark 11[:24]: 'Whatever you ask in prayer, believe that you will receive it, and it will be done for you,' and in Matt. 9[:29]: 'According to your faith let it be done for you'" (WA 56:79,2–5 = 57/1:73,12–16 = LW 25:71). That faith here is not yet bound to the word and so is by no means a *particular* faith becomes clear in a somewhat earlier sermon (*Sermon on St. Barbara's Day*, 1514? [see chap. 2, n. 340]). Here Luther opposes the opinion that only certain saints are responsible for certain requests. We can turn to God through anyone, because it is only faith that counts for the answering of our requests. "As you believe, so it will be done for you, 'for all things are possible for those who believe' (4:640,12–13) . . . and help is given to each according to their prayer and faith" (ll. 20–21). Likewise, in the *Dekalogauslegung* (1516): 1:418,23–26 and the *Quaestio de viribus et voluntate hominis sine gratia disputata* (also 1516): 1:150,4–10. See, on the other hand, the Rogate sermon of 1520 (discussed in chap. 10), which is shaped completely by the reformational concept of the promise.

83. Cf. chap. 2, n. 259.

84. WA 56:86,19–24 = LW 25:78 (cited on pp. 72–73).

85. Cf. pp. 72–75.

86. WA 57/3:216,2–6 = LW 29:217 (trans. alt.).

87. WA 57/3:216,9–12 = LW 29:218.

88. WA 57/3:216,6–9 = LW 29:217–18. We find the very same interpretation again in the sermon on Gal. 4:1–7 in the *Church Postil*, published in 1522: WA 10/I/1:332,1–18 = LW 75:368.

of absolution.[89] Thus this scholion also reflects the new understanding of word and faith and is a stage on the way to Augsburg, where Luther had to prove this understanding before Cajetan.

D) A Testament "for the Forgiveness of Sins" (Scholion on Heb. 9:17)

The interpretation of Hebrews 9:17 (FOR A TESTAMENT IS CONFIRMED ONLY AT DEATH) is of particular interest because it provides an important presupposition for that new understanding of the Lord's Supper, which only appeared in complete outline in 1520. Yet our text reveals the extent to which its concept of "the testament of God (or of Christ)" is still bound to the traditional understanding.

In defining the concept of a testament,[90] Luther begins with the general ideas that he gets from Chrysostom:[91] First, the time and heirs must be stipulated, then the inheritance in the sense of "what is to be received" and "what is to be done" (the "promises" and "commands"[92]), and third, the witnesses. Luther then develops these points theologically, although not strictly in order,[93] but

89. WA 1:610,9–26 = LW 31:104 (ll. 25–26 refer to the "Explanation" of theses 7 and 38 of the *Theses on Indulgences*).

90. Previously, Luther had looked back to verse 16 (FOR WHERE THERE IS A TESTAMENT, THE DEATH OF THE TESTATOR MUST INTERVENE): WA 57/3:211,16–22 = LW 29:213. Compare this with 57/3:193,18–24 = 29:194 (scholion on Heb. 7:22). These two texts will be treated below (chap. 9) in a wider context (see pp. 363–370).

91. In *The Epistle to the Hebrews*, Homily 16 (on 9:15–18) in the translation of Mutianus Scholasticus (MPG 63:341; J. Ficker's reference in WA 57/3:211 = LW 29:213 to l. 22 is therefore not entirely correct). Luther quotes three sentences from it (57/3:211,23–25, 25–27, 27).

92. Cf. the definition given by Altenstaig's *Vocabularius theologiae*, where he follows Thomas Aquinas: "A TESTAMENT is properly the disposition of an inheritance to be received . . . Therefore, first, it pertains to the promises, and second, to the commands, which are the way to obtain the promised inheritance. From the blessed theologian, part 3, quest. 78, a. 3."

93. Luther proceeds by first specifying the time ("at the Last Supper") and the inheritance bequeathed (WA 57/3:211,28–212,4; 212,4–23 = LW 29:213–14) before breaking off and reorienting himself on the three points taken from Chrysostom. On the first point, he adds the determination of the heirs (57/3:212,24–213,6 = 29:214), where the difference between the "for all" and the "for many" raises the problem of predestination (see the Romans lectures: WA 56:385,28–31 = 57/1:198,2–4 = LW 25:376), to which Biel's Mass commentary also devotes a special section (Lect. 53 Q, 2:328; cf. Lect. 37 D, 2:60). Then he comes to the witnesses (57/3:213,6–11 = 29:214: the Spirit and the apostles), who according to the exposition (57/3:211,27 = 29:213), should only have been mentioned in the third place, and finally, to complement the second point, to what is to be done.

only occasionally takes up Chrysostom's interpretation.[94] He is mainly interested in the second point, which Chrysostom had dealt with far too briefly for Luther's liking[95]—namely, what Christ gave us with his last meal. There are two things:

a) "What is to be received" (*suscipiendum*).[96] This is not only the future eternal life, as in the theological tradition,[97] but above all, the forgiveness of sins here and now, which Luther sees bequeathed to us according to the gifting words of the Lord's Supper ("This is my body . . . this is my blood . . . for the forgiveness of sins"), which are also the words of institution; this is most clearly expressed in their Matthean form.[98] It is particularly striking how strongly Luther emphasizes the assertoric, indicative character of Christ's present provision for us in the Supper, which he brings out most skillfully

94. When referring to John 17 in connection with the determination of the heirs, the specification of the witnesses, and the stipulation of "what is to be done" in the love command (John 13:34).

95. WA 57/3:212,4–5 = LW 29:213.

96. WA 57/3:212,5–23 = LW 29:213–14.

97. The *Glossa interlinearis* interprets 1 Cor. 11:25 in view of Heb. 9:17 as follows: "This cup is my blood, in which the New Testament is confirmed (i.e., takes effect), by being poured out; for a testament is confirmed by a death. And it is a new promise, not of temporal but of eternal good" (6:50^v). Thomas Aquinas says of Heb. 9:15: "In every testament there is something that is promised, and something by which the testament is confirmed. But in the New Testament, *heavenly* and *spiritual things* are promised. This promise was also confirmed by the death of Christ. And therefore Christ is the mediator of the New Testament so that THOSE WHO ARE CALLED MAY RECEIVE A GUARANTEE of *eternal happiness and* OF AN ETERNAL INHERITANCE" (*Super Epistolas S. Pauli Lektura, Ad Hebr.*; vol. 2, 435, no. 448; author's emphasis). But it is by no means the case that Thomas does not speak of the forgiveness of sins on the basis of the death of Jesus, but the problem is that it bears no relation to the promise, which as something secondary, is separate from it: "The New Testament is superior to the Old because it is confirmed by the death of Christ, through which sins are forgiven, and because it offers a promise" (2:436; no.449). Likewise, for Biel, the "good promises of faith" are the joys of *eternal* happiness" (Lect. 71 G, 3:179; author's emphasis). Lect. 53 Y, 2:334: "In this sacrament, he gave himself to those who eat it as a pledge of the *promise of future glory*." We should compare this with Trent's decree on the Eucharist: "He willed that (the Sacrament of the Eucharist) should be a pledge of our future glory and everlasting happiness" (*Denz.*, 875). However, according to Lect. 53 O (2:325), Christ is "the confirmer of the new and eternal promise, as the Lord himself promises in JOHN 6: WHOEVER EATS . . . HAS ETERNAL LIFE, which is the true inheritance of Christ." For Biel, the forgiveness of sins is not included in the concept of testament: see Lect. 53 Q–T (2:328–31).

98. WA 57/3:212,9 = LW 29:213 (cf. p. 240). Here, and *only* here unfortunately, does this scholion converge with that on 9:14.

on the basis of Luke 22:29: "'I dispose,' he says, not 'I will dispose'; for it is proper to use the verb in the present tense when making a testament."[99]

b) "What is to be done" (*faciendum*).[100] Christ gave us this when he said: "Do this for my remembrance." This means, as the apostle says, that they are to proclaim his death, preach repentance, the forgiveness of sins, and eternal life. Second, they are not to receive the grace bequeathed by the testament in vain but to make use of it against sinful desires. For Christ said, "This is my commandment, that you love one another," as well as the other things that he teaches in a most beautiful discourse in John 12–18 about bearing persecutions in love, and about peace.[101]

Luther therefore sees the *faciendum* of the testament as being directly determined by the command to commemorate it, which he explains from Luke 24:27 and 2 Corinthians 6:1,[102] and, with an echo of Galatians 5:16–17, leading to the love command of John 13:34. This direct reference to the command to commemorate the testament and the understanding of the testamentary mandate first and foremost as a sermon is unknown to the tradition. Apart from the "promise of eternal life," it sees in the testament quite generally the "teaching of the gospel,"[103] or "the faith and law of Christ."[104]

---

99. WA 57/3:212,16–17 = LW 29:214 (trans. alt.). [Legally, "dispose" means as much as "confer" or "transfer"; hence Luke 22:29: "I confer on you or transfer to you a kingdom"; trans. note.]

100. WA 57/3:213,11–18 = LW 29:214–15.

101. WA 57/3:213,11–18 = LW 29:214–15 (trans. alt.). This connection of the eucharistic words in the synoptics and Paul with the farewell discourse in John, which Luther rightly understood as a testament, is noteworthy because it indicates the path that he then pursued in developing his understanding of Christ's vicarious substitution and the doctrine of the Trinity.

102. This is not proved by Ficker.

103. Thus the *Glossa interlinearis* on Heb. 9:17 (6:151^{r}). Cf. Dionysius the Carthusian on Heb. 9:17: "The New Testament . . . is the promise of eternal life, the teaching of the gospel, confirmed with the death of Christ. Hence, he said on the cross: it is finished. Christ wanted to die as he confessed and proclaimed his promise and teaching" (Fol. CXXXIII D).

104. Thus Biel's commentary on the Mass in that well-known definition quoted by Altenstaig s.v. "testamentum dei" (Fol. CCLIII a). H. A. Oberman, *Spätscholastik und Reformation* I, 255, n. 89, and R. Damerau, *Die Abendmahl des Nominalismus, insbesondere die des Gabriel Biel*, 165, n. 49, quote these words: "It must be noted that since a testament is the final distribution of goods, confirmed by the death of the testator, whether it is the arrangement or the actual handing over of the goods, confirmed by lawful attestation, *the faith and law of Christ is rightly the New Testament.* Indeed, in it Christ promises, orders, and distributes an eternal inheritance to his brothers and faithful followers. And this *law* was confirmed by Christ's suffering and

Luther adopted the double determination of the inheritance in the testament as *suscipiendum* and *faciendum* or as "promise" and "command" in his interpretation of Hebrews 9:17 from Chrysostom.[105] But he may also have already been familiar with it from Biel's commentary on the Mass.[106] It serves to sharpen Luther's view if we compare it with that of Biel. Biel does *not* include the words "for the forgiveness of sins" and "do this for my remembrance" in his concept of the testament.[107] Furthermore, for Luther the promise is linked to the command (*mandatum*) in such a way that the forgiveness of sins comes from the preaching of the forgiveness of sins, whereas for Biel it is linked in such a way that eternal life is only given to those who keep the commandments.[108] Thus Luther already shows in his Hebrews lectures, even if not yet with full clarity, the unmistakably distinctive orientation of his own concept of testament, according to which the bequeathed inheritance *is distributed to sinners already now in the present and will not be awarded to those who are worthy in the future.* This unique understanding stems from the fact that, as we have seen, Luther sees the "promise" and "command" of the testament, in contrast to the tradition, as being determined primarily by the gifting words of the Lord's Supper, specifically the words "for the forgiveness of sins."[109]

---

death in which his blood was shed, and this shedding of blood is in turn the lawful attestation and confirmation of his testament" (Lect. 53 N, 2:324–25; author's emphasis). However, Biel deals with the command to commemorate it without any reference to the concept of testament (cf. Lect. 53 U and X, 2:331–34).

105. The second sentence taken over by Luther in his exposition of the scholion (cf. above n. 91) is followed in Chrysostom by this explanation: "After he had *promised* innumerable things, he *demands* something from them saying: A NEW COMMANDMENT I GIVE TO YOU" (MPG 63:341).

106. "Therefore, not only the divine scripture containing the commandments is called a 'testament,' but the promise is also called a 'testament'" (Lect. 53 O with reference to Heb. 9:15, 2:325).

107. Cf. n. 104.

108. The inheritance "is promised and given by the testament, confirmed by the death of Christ. For by this death he made it possible that all who keep his commandments might be granted entrance into the kingdom of heaven. Therefore, he said: IF YOU WOULD ENTER LIFE, KEEP THE COMMANDMENTS": Lect. 53 O, (2:326). Biel explains what has been said here in Lect. 59 T (2:447) in a broad context. According to Oberman, *Spätscholastik und Reformation* I, 20, this text, Matt. 19:17, which is central to the promise, indicates the main theme of Biel's preaching as well.

109. It is true that the gifting words of the Lord's Supper themselves are not yet understood directly as a proclamation of the testament (E. Bizer, *Fides ex auditu*, 88). However, this does not mean that "all the possibilities of a spiritualistic interpretations are still open" (Bizer, 88). Because for Luther, in contrast to Biel, the remembrance is understood precisely from these

E) The Remembrance of the Sacrifice of Christ (Scholion on Heb. 10:2–3)

The gifting words of the Lord's Supper come up again in the last part of the scholion on Hebrews 9:24, which in terms of its content refers to 10:2–3[110] and in retrospect[111] to 9:25–28.[112]

The topic is the sacrifice of the Mass. The text, especially 9:25–26, obviously disputes the statement that "Christ is offered for us every day."[113] With express reference again to Chrysostom,[114] the answer is: "What is offered by us every day is not so much a sacrifice as the remembrance of that sacrifice, as he said: 'Do this for my remembrance.' For he does not suffer as often as his suffering is remembered."[115] "What is repeated"[116] is not the sacrifice of Christ, which happened once for all, but its "remembrance." In this way, Luther answers with the usual information in the tradition in which he stands[117] but speaks in a particularly

---

gifting words (but not exclusively!) as a preaching of the forgiveness of sins—that is, as a preaching of what is bequeathed in the testament (WA 57/3:213,12–14 = LW 29:14; trans. alt.).

110. Heb. 10:2 is in view in WA 57/3:217,25–26 = LW 29:219; 10:3 in 57/3:218,10–15 = 29:220.

111. WA 57/3:217,30 = LW 29:219 ("as in the preceding chapter").

112. The problem discussed in WA 57/3:217,27–218,9 = LW 29:219–20 is linked to these verses.

113. WA 57/3:217,27 = LW 29:219.

114. WA 57/3:217,27–29 = LW 29:219 = In the *Epistle to the Hebrews*, Homily 17 (on 9:24–28); MPG 63:349,14–15 (abbreviated somewhat by Luther). The patristic text was also taken over by the *Glossa ordinaria* (on 10:3; 6.152A).

115. WA 57/3:217,30–218,3 = LW 29:219–20 (trans. alt.).

116. WA 218,3 and 4 = LW 29:220.

117. Lyra's interpretation (on Heb. 10:3; VI, 152 D) largely agrees with Luther: "But you could still say: the Sacrament of the Altar is offered every day in the church, therefore etc. However, it must be said that this is not the repetition of the sacrifice, but a daily remembrance of the one sacrifice offered up on the cross. For this reason, it is said in Luke 22[:19]: 'Do this for my remembrance': for the same thing is offered that he himself bestowed" (With this last sentence Lyra of course differs from Luther, who can only maintain the identity through tropology: WA 57/3:218,5–9 = LW 29:220. On this, see above in the text). Lyra calls the Sacrament of the Altar "a memorial of his sacrifice" (in his general remarks following the interpretation of the individual parts of Heb. 9: see 6:151H) or "a memorial of the Lord's passion" (on 1 Cor. 11:24–26: see 6:50H; see Luther on Heb. 9:2: 57/3:199,16–17 = 29:201). Of course, for him, unlike for Luther, this has a representative character (see on 1 Cor. 11:26: "YOU PROCLAIM THE LORD'S DEATH by representing it through this sacrament"; 6:51D), as also for Biel. It is (according to Lect. 36 F; 2:44) "a memorial sign of his passion" and (according to Lect. 53 U; 2:331) "a memorial and representative sign of this supreme sacrifice that Christ offered on the cross." If the realistic dimension is thus strengthened by the emphasis on the "representation," then the

spiritualistic way, in that he consistently avoids the concept of "representation," which Biel, for example, adheres to.[118]

Luther has two options for defining the memory of Christ's sacrifice in more detail, but he does not consider them because of their problematic relationship to one other.

First, "this sacrifice of the New Testament, when it refers to Christ, the head of the church, is perfect and has ceased completely; but when it refers to the spiritual sacrifice of his body, which is the church, it is offered day by day, while it constantly dies with Christ and celebrates the mystical passover, that is, when it slays lusts and passes over from this world to the future glory."[119]

The sacrifice of Christ is therefore not repeated as such, but in the daily sacrifice of the believer's obedience (that is, understood in its tropological significance). Christians celebrate the "passover"—that is, the "crossing over" or *transitus* of their head (a motif that was very important to Luther![120]). More precise details about the connection between Christ's *transitus* and ours, based on Romans 6, can be found in the scholion on Hebrews 10:19,[121] where "the apostle wants us to imitate Christ who suffered and, in his death, passed over to the glory of the Father."[122] This event is further explained in that sharply

idea of "repetition" is avoided. It is even expressly rejected: "It is offered by us in remembrance of his death. Hence, our offering (oblation) is not a repetition of his, but a representation" (Lect. 53 U; 2:332. Further passages are mentioned in n. 2 of the latter. See further H. A. Oberman, *Spätscholastik und Reformation* I, 255–56, the notes there, and the "critical assessment of Biel's position," 260–61).

118. Cf. n. 117.

119. WA 57/3:218,5–9 = LW 29:220 (trans. alt.).

120. For the time before the Hebrews lectures—for which, apart from the scholion on 10:19 (see n. 123), one should also note WA 57/3:21,4; 57/3:50,2 [glosses are not in LW]; WA 57/3:111,6–8 = LW 29:120; 57/3:118,18 = 29:127; and 57/3:232,3–4 = 29:234—see 3:504,20–25 = 10:447; 3:650,2–3, 30–31 = 29:146,148 (*Dictata*); and 56:80,14–17 = 25:72–73 (Romans lectures). For the time after the Hebrews lectures, the passages to be noted are WA 5:61,21–23; WA 14:331; WA 5:128,32–34 (*Operationes in Psalmos*); WA 2:535,30–536,13 = LW 27:289 (*Commentary on Galatians*, 1519). The best-known parallel passage occurs in the letter to Staupitz of May 30, 1518, introducing the Explanations of the *Theses on Indulgences*: WA 1:526,4–9 = LW 48:65–68 (cf. on this R. Schwarz, *Vorgeschichte der reformatorischen Bußtheologie*, *AKG* 41, 1968, 300, esp. n. 3), which is repeated almost word for word in Luther's contemporaneous sermon for a first Mass (4:658,40–659,5; see chap. 4, n. 19). For an understanding of the topos in Luther's theology denoted by the terms *passover* (*phase*) or *crossing over* (*transitus*), reference should be made not least to its use (documented by J. Ficker, WA 56:80 at l. 15) in the liturgy familiar to Luther.

121. For "dying with Christ," see Rom. 6:4,8; for "mortifying its lusts," see Rom. 6:12, where the reference in each case is to the church.

122. WA 57/3:222,13–14 = LW 29:224.

defined concept of "sacrament" that Luther had advocated in his marginal notes on Augustine.[123]

Second, in contrast to the "remembrance of sins" through the sacrifices of the old covenant (10:3), Luther says that "in our sacrifice, there was and is a remembrance of the forgiveness of sins through the word that Jesus spoke when he said, 'Father, forgive them,' and 'it is finished,' and again, speaking of his blood, 'which is shed for you for the forgiveness of sins.'"[124]

"Offering" (*oblatio*) probably does not refer specifically to the sacrifice but rather to the Mass in general.[125] But what "remembrance" and its accompanying

123. WA 57/3:222,25–223,23 = LW 29:225–26. Cf. esp. 57/3:218,8 = 29:220 ("the mystical passover") with 57/3:223,4–5 = 29:225 ("the mystical and exemplary suffering of Christ").

The *final part of this scholion on Heb. 10:19* (57/3:223,24–224,15= 29:226), *however, goes beyond the old understanding of "sacrament"* (cf. Bizer, *Fides ex auditu*, 79). It is only here that Luther really takes up the intention of the text (SINCE THEREFORE WE HAVE CONFIDENCE TO ENTER THE HOLY PLACE BY THE BLOOD OF CHRIST) and thus enters the sphere of the scholion on 5:1. This is only logical, for it had interpreted 4:16, which (4:14–16) within Hebrews is itself parallel to 10:19–23. The scholion on 5:1 can be compared with the following specific items from the final part of that on 10:19: 57/3:224,5 = 29:226 ("We have confidence to enter"), 57/3:224,6 = 29:226 ("He is our high priest"), and 57/3:224,13–14 = 29:226 ("who rely on Christ through faith"). The scholion on 5:1 also makes it clear that this final part is concerned with nothing other than the *question of certainty*. This evidently has not yet been resolved in the schema of the "sacrament" (57/3:222,12–223,23 = 29:224–25). Luther tries to break out of it by intensifying successive statements: "Christ is not only our companion but also the one who leads the way, not only our leader but also our helper, indeed the one who carries us" (57/3:224,9–10 = 29:226; trans. alt.). So Christ is now no longer presented to us in order to work penitence in us as a spiritual death through his literal death, understood "sacramentally" as an archetype, but rather, *to buoy up our confidence*, [it is pointed out that] he crossed over first of all, and smooths the rough way. Then the apostle points out that Christ not only gave us an example by crossing over, but that he also holds out his hand to those who follow. Therefore he says that 'we have confidence to enter,' for he himself opened this way for us (Heb. 10:20) and at the same time is our high priest who sympathizes with our weaknesses (Heb. 4:15) and can help us when we are tempted" (57/3:224,2–7 = 29:226; author's emphasis; trans. alt.). The Christ of the sacramental meditation on Scripture is not the Christ who stretches out his hand. For the intensification ("not only . . . but also"), Luther refers ("Therefore, he says") to the text of 10:19 ("We have confidence to enter"), which is reminiscent of 4:16. If the two scholia are linked, we can say exactly what the function of the present priesthood or of Christ's mediatorial office is, which goes beyond the initiating effect of an archetype: "For those who rely on Christ through faith are carried on his shoulders (57/3:224,13–14 = 29:226; trans. alt.), or to put it more specifically, 'those who rely on . . . the most pure, holy, and trustworthy word of Christ who says: "Come to me . . . I will give you rest"'" (57/3:171,4–7 = 29:172–73 [Luther emphasizes these lines]; scholion on 5:1). The shift in Christology that is clearly evident here in this final part in comparison to the rest of the scholion (on 10:19) is the subject of chap. 10.

124. WA 57/3:218,10–15 = LW 29:220 (trans. alt.).

125. Cf. the marginal gloss on Rom. 15:16: "The Greeks use the word "liturgy" to describe what we call the mass in Hebrew, which means an offering (oblation), according to John Reuchlin" (WA 56:141,16–18 = LW 25:123; trans. alt.; cf. the note of J. Ficker at l. 17).

phrase "*through* the word" mean is unfortunately not clear. Are we to think during the Mass of the words spoken by Jesus at the time, which refer to forgiveness? Or does the Mass evoke and keep the memory of those words alive? How and in what way does this happen? The later understanding of the "remembrance through the word," according to which this is a giving and receiving of the forgiveness that is granted by the gifting words of the Lord's Supper, cannot yet be assumed here. But the path from here *can* lead to it.[126]

In view of these two ways of seeing the remembrance of Christ's sacrifice, the question remains as to how they fit together. The tension between them is identical to that which we observed in the scholion on Hebrews 9:14 between meditative piety and promise theology. But what is still problematic here seems to be resolved immediately in the following scholion (on 10:5).

F) The Sacrifice of Christ and of the Church
Hearing and Obeying (Scholion on Heb. 10:5)

The interpretation of SACRIFICE AND OFFERING YOU HAVE NOT DESIRED, BUT A BODY YOU HAVE PREPARED FOR ME (Heb. 10:5 = Ps. 40:6) derives its unusual tension and movement from the ambiguity of the Hebrew word underlying the Latin "prepared,"[127] but ultimately from the fact that in the Hebrew the equivalent of "ears" is "body" (LXX and NT). After extensive discussion, Luther allows both expressions to stand at the same time. "Therefore, what the Septuagint (LXX) says about Christ's own body, this the Hebrew text says about Christ's mystical body when it speaks of piercing the ears. But both are the one mystical body, which is constantly offered with Christ. Therefore, each sense can be called one sense."[128]

The similarity of Christ's sacrifice and that of the church lies in hearing and obeying.[129] But the uniqueness of Christ's work emerges far more strongly than this

---

126. See further E. Bizer's comment on the passage: "The notion of remembrance is of course so unclear that it still seems to leave open the possibility of a spiritualistic interpretation. Think of Luther's later remark that he too had considered the significative or symbolic meaning of the words of the Lord's Supper before it was brought to his attention from outside" (*Fides ex auditu*, 91).

127. WA 57/3:220,16–18 = LW 29:222.

128. WA 57/3:221,20–24 = LW 29:223 (trans. alt.).

129. It is interesting how, in a very similar way, Biel can also draw a parallel between a) Christ's sacrifice and b) that of the faithful:

> (a) "But this Christ, who was offered for our sake, was a poor man, when he was offered for you naked on the cross, completely stripped of all temporal things, even necessities and friends, and likewise deprived of their use and enjoyment;

similarity as the basis of the word that creates faith. Through Christ's sacrificial body[130]—that is, his obedience ("through his obedient body offered for us"[131])—God has created the church, which hears, believes, and obeys: Christ's "mystical body."[132] Therefore, Christ prays[133] "actively in this way: 'You have opened my ears,' that is, you have caused[134] me to be obedient to you' . . . and he prays passively thus: 'You have opened my ears,' that is, you have caused people to believe me and to believe in me, and so have brought it about that the forgiveness of sins and salvation for those who believe in me comes through me, not through animals. And this is the sacrifice that is pleasing to God, namely, faith in Christ."[135] God himself[136] works forgiveness and salvation through Jesus's sacrifice, and this only

he was bruised with bruises, blows, and wounds. HE WAS CRUSHED FOR OUR INIQUITIES, AND BY HIS STRIPES WE ARE HEALED (ISA. 53). He also trembled at the words of the Father when he offered his prayer and said: NOT MY WILL, BUT YOUR WILL BE DONE" (Lect. 60 A, 2:345).

(b) We should become like Abel who offered a sacrifice acceptable to God inwardly in his heart because he did not keep himself to himself but submitted and devoted himself entirely to God. Therefore, GOD HAD REGARD FOR ABEL AND HIS OFFERINGS . . . (GEN. 4), first he had regard for Abel, then for his offerings, because the offeror was not pleasing on account of his offering but the offering was pleasing on account of the offeror (an idea that was also very important to Luther: WA 56:277.1–2 = LW 25:264 [on Rom. 4:7]; 1:118,17–18 [*Sermon on Jan. 1*, 1517]; 57/3:230,16–18 = 29:232 [on Heb. 11:4]). In the same way, Abram, with eminent faith, first offered himself wholly to the Most High and therefore offered a pleasing sacrifice" (Lect. 60 C, 2:348).

130. "The apostle . . . understanding the body prepared for Christ to be that which is offered on account of sins instead of the bodies of animals" (WA 57/3:220,20—221,1 = LW 29:223; trans. alt.).

131. This is what Luther had formulated in the *Dictata* on Ps. 40:6 (WA 3:225,34). The whole interpretation of Ps. 40 in the *Dictata* should be considered as background to our scholion since Luther clearly takes it up. The shifts, however, are just as clear: In the interpretation of the psalms, in a different christological mediation, all the emphasis is placed on our obedience: WA 3:227,28 = LW 10:188; 3:228,21–23 = 10:189. Cf. 3:248,15–32 = 10:205–6.

132. WA 57/3:221,26–27 = LW 29:224.

133. Cf. the heading prefixed to the gloss on Ps. 39 in the *Dictata*: "The prayer of Christ as he offers himself as a sacrifice in obedience to the Father" (WA 3:224,9).

134. Cf. on this WA 57/3:219,15–24 = LW 29:221–22; 221,2–5 = 29:223. Since the *Dictata*, the causative meaning of the Hiphil has been particularly important to Luther, because it expresses the main dimension of his tropological interpretation—namely, the power connecting the subject and object. Cf. chap. 4, n. 213.

135. WA 57/3:221,11–15 = LW 29:223 (trans. alt.).

136. "For no one hears Christ unless the Father pierces our ears and opens them, that is, 'draws us'" (WA 57/3:221,19–20 = LW 29:223; trans. alt.).

comes to us through the "hearing of God's word which is faith":[137] through the word to which faith is obedient. For faith is obedience, as Romans 1[:5] says: "for the obedience of faith." And so the meaning will be that in the New Testament, the offering of animals is not pleasing to God. Indeed, it is never pleasing to him. But he takes pleasure in the offering (oblation) and obedience of faith. As in Jeremiah 5[:3]: "O Lord, your eyes are on faith." Therefore, throughout the whole of Scripture, the Spirit has only one aim: that we hear the voice of God (that is, that we believe). For whoever believes will be saved.[138]

Thus that which mediates here between Christ's sacrifice and ours is neither the concept and matter of the "sacrament," nor primarily of the "sacrifice," but only that of "hearing," for which Luther appeals to Mark 16:16 (in *The Babylonian Captivity*, it is the baptismal promise). "What happens physically in the sacrifice of Christ is promised to us through the word."[139] "It is not said that the faithful sacrifice or co-sacrifice in an act of their own kind, independent of listening to the word."[140] "Therefore, the ears are the only organs of the Christian, for it is not by the works of any member, but by faith, that a Christian is justified and judged."[141]

It has become clear in this chapter that (contrary to the usual way of ordering things) the Hebrews lectures do not precede the indulgence controversy insofar as it cannot be said that in the scholion on 5:1, Luther is preparing for the "Explanations" to the *Theses on Indulgences*, in which the new understanding of the sacrament of penance is beginning to emerge. Rather, the lectures presuppose them and from then on, in their second part, they accompany the "Explanations" on their path from the 1518 *Sermon on Penance* via the theses *Pro veritate* to their defense before Cajetan in Augsburg. The reflection of this path offered by the Hebrews lectures is particularly interesting in that they not only overlap thematically with the texts on the sacrament of penance (in the scholion on 7:12) but also show how, with Luther's new understanding of the promise, which is

137. WA 57/3:222,6–7 = LW 29:224 (trans. alt.).

138. WA 57/3:221,5–10 = LW 29:223 (trans. alt.). Cf. the conclusion of a passage in the Sermons on Genesis (1519–1521): "*To sum up:* the whole of Scripture has as its aim to teach that whoever believes will be saved" (9:383,16–17).

139. A. Brandenburg, "Solae aures sunt organa Christiani hominis. Zu Luthers Exegese von Hebr. 10,5f." *Festschrift für G. Söhngen*, eds. J. Ratzinger and H. Fries, 1962 (401–4), here 403.

140. Brandenburg, "Solae aures," 404. If Brandenburg, from a Catholic point of view, has reservations precisely about the one sidedness of putting all the emphasis on Christ's sacrifice alone, this is balanced by the fact that Luther's early theology, which is decisively determined by the very thing that Brandenburg finds missing here (the co-sacrifice of believers with Christ), cannot be described as reformational.

141. WA 57/3:222,7–9 = LW 29:224 (trans. alt.).

first fully expressed with systematic clarity in a reshaping of the sacrament of penance, his understanding of the Mass also immediately begins to change. The Hebrews lectures in the texts examined thus continue the topic begun with the *Sermon on the Worthy Preparation of the Heart for the Reception of the Eucharist*, which should be understood as a counterpart to the 1518 *Sermon on Penance* and can thus also be understood under the heading of the next chapter.

The thrust of the texts examined only becomes apparent in 1520 in *The Babylonian Captivity* after it had failed to be taken up shortly before—in the *Sermon on the Lord's Supper*, published in December 1519. The fact that in the years 1518 to 1520, the entire fabric of traditional motifs only gradually breaks apart is not an objection to the assumption that the breakthrough in its decisive aspect had occurred earlier but rather sheds light on the historical and not mechanical way in which Luther's new approach or organizing principle is being taken up everywhere in his theology. From this point of view, Luther's approach in the *Sermon on the Lord's Supper* just mentioned, which surely must fail if judged by the standard of *The Babylonian Captivity*, deserves particular attention. It shows how theology at a time of radical change slips back into its traditional ways if the starting point or organizing principle (*Ansatz*) of every question is not strictly determined by the new understanding of the promise. Thus, in the language of science, the crucial experiment (*experimentum crucis*)[142] that we undertook has succeeded: it did not reveal the ineffectiveness of Luther's new starting point (*Ansatz*) but precisely its viability.[143]

142. [In science, the *experimentum crucis* is the crucial experiment to determine whether a particular hypothesis or theory is superior to all others and can produce a result that rules out rival hypotheses or theories; trans. note.]

143. In *The Babylonian Captivity*, Luther speaks of the progress he has made between this writing and his *Sermon on the Lord's Supper* of 1519, where he was still very much under the influence of the generally accepted view: "I will tell you now what progress I have made after further study on the administration of the sacrament. For at the time when I was publishing my sermon (= treatise) on the Eucharist, I still adhered to the customary way of understanding it" (WA 6:502,2–4 = LW 26:19; trans. alt.).

CHAPTER 6

The Lord's Supper in the Reformational Upheaval

A) The Blessed Sacrament of the Holy and True Body of Christ (1519)

I. The Sign

IN *A SERMON on Preparing to Die*, published at the beginning of November 1519,[1] Luther expressly points to the sacrament as a comforting means of grace. However, as far as the topic goes, picking out just one sacrament, for example, that of penance, would be arbitrary. So he has to try to speak generally about the sacraments and to bring their constitutive elements to a common denominator, which is understandably done from the angle of his new starting point or organizing principle.[2]

However, since the sacrament of penance is based exclusively on one *word*, the specific word of absolution, and does not have a "visible element," the strength of the starting point or organizing principle that comes with the new understanding of the sacrament of penance has the logical effect that the word does duty for the concept of the sign[3] and, because it is the word that creates the

1. WA 2:680–97 = LW 42:95–115). On the dating, see *BoA* 1:161. For the two main themes of the sermon and their context, cf. chap. 5, nn. 52, and 53, esp. 53.

2. This expansion into the general becomes clear, for example, from the way in which he expands the quotation of Luke 1:38 (which Luther had already cited a year earlier in his defense before Cajetan, along with other scriptural passages, to prove his new understanding of the sacrament [see chap. 4]: WA 2:15,15–16 = LW 31:273): With the sacrament, we should believe "what God says and shows us there, so that we can say with Mary in firm faith, 'Let it be to me according to your words *and signs*'" (2:686,25–27 = 42:101; author's emphasis; trans. alt.).

3. It is defined accordingly: "The sacrament is the external *word* of God spoken by a priest" (WA 2:692,36–37 = LW 42:108; author's emphasis; trans. alt.). When it goes on to say (ll. 37–38) that it "is a great comfort and at the same time a visible sign of God's intention," then "sign" here does not refer primarily to the element but to its function. It should therefore be rewritten with "proof" or "proclamation." "Promise" (or "word") and "sign" together with their corresponding

certainty, we can also speak of a "certain sign"[4] and, important for our context, it makes the elements of the Lord's Supper into an outright "promise."[5]

In *The Sermon on the Blessed Sacrament of the Holy and True Body of Christ and the Brotherhoods*, Luther now tries to take up this result of expanding his new approach to include "the sacraments in general" and—now again quite specifically—to make it fruitful for his understanding of the Lord's Supper.

But this is not done in such a way that the original point of reference, which Luther found in the specific *word* of absolution, is fundamentally taken into account or even, appropriately transposed, chosen as the starting point of the presentation, on methodical and factual grounds.

Rather, Luther begins with a brief statement naming the parts that constitute the Lord's Supper ("The first is the sacrament, or sign. The second is the significance of this sacrament. The third is the faith required with each of the first two. These three parts must be present in every sacrament."[6]), which in their order also form the outline of the whole sermon. After these parts are named, they are briefly defined, and the sermon begins with the *determination of the sign* on the basis of the *elements* of bread and wine and the *act* of eating and drinking together: "The sacrament, or external sign, consists in the form and species of bread and wine," "so that you can partake of the bread and wine as you eat and

---

verbs appear in parallel around twenty times (2:686,26,27,28 = 42:101; 2:693,12,17,25–26, 27,28,31 = 42:109; 2:694,1–2,9,10,18,23–24,29,30 = 42:110; 2:695,7,27,29 = 42:111–12) in a few short sections (§§5,15–18). It becomes clear that "sign," understood as "proclamation," merges into the concept of "word" and "promise," but it still shapes them insofar as it emphasizes their "externality" (see above: "external word")—that is, that they are spoken orally and publically.

4. From 2 Pet. 1:19 ("We have a sure and certain word of God to which you will do well to pay attention") we can say: "God has promised and given me a certain sign of his grace in the sacraments" (WA 2:693,4–13 = LW 42:109; trans. alt.). Cf. 2:693:19 = 42:109 ("a certain sign") and the parallel to it in 2:694,1–2 = 42:110: "a certain sign, the true word of God."

5. Coming from the perspective of the absolution, Luther says of the Lord's Supper that "if the priest has absolved me, I rely on his absolution as on God's word itself" (WA 2:694 [12–16]; 12–13 = LW 42:110; trans. alt.). "Thus you must also say regarding the Sacrament of the Altar that 'if the priest has given me the holy body of Christ, which is a sign and promise . . . then it will and must be that, for the divine sign does not deceive me . . . May my God be certain and true to me in this his sign and promise, whether I am worthy of him or not, whether I am a member of Christianity or not, according to the word and declaration of this sacrament" (2:694,22–30 = 42:111; trans. alt.). This section (§17) and §18 of this sermon on preparing to die overlap directly with the *Sermon on the Lord's Supper*, which we will consider presently (2:695–96 = 42:112–13). Cf. also 2:692,33–35 = 42:108.

6. WA 2:742,7–10 = LW 35:49. The sermon (2:738–58 = 35:73) was published in early or mid Dec. 1519. For this and the dating of the associated sermons on repentance (penance) and baptism, see *BoA* 1:174.

drink."[7] With this explicit determination, the tentative definition, that "the sacrament must be external and visible, having a bodily form or species,"[8] which still keeps the way to the word open,[9] is left behind.

Luther now strongly emphasizes that this sign, consisting of element and action, is a "certain sign"[10] and that in and with it, we really receive[11] and take[12] what is given[13] and bestowed.[14] "Therefore, the immeasurable grace and mercy of God are given us in this sacrament";[15] hence he asserts that "grace is effectually conferred."

With this instrumental and effective understanding, which breaks the earlier sole dominance of the exemplary and significative view of the sacrament,[16] the Thomistic, scholastic position has been reclaimed. That "all the spiritual goods of Christ and of his saints are shared with and become the common property of those who receive this sacrament"[17] can be said just as well by Thomas: "The goods of Christ are communicated to all Christians . . . through the sacraments of the church."[18]

---

7. WA 2:742,15–17 = LW 35:49 (trans. alt.).

8. WA 2:742,10–12 = LW 35:49 (trans. alt.).

9. Cf. n. 3.

10. WA 2:746,2 = LW 35:55 (trans. alt.): "I leave you this sacrament as a certain sign of all this." Cf. 2:745,17 = 35:54 and the following notes.

11. WA 2:743,20–21 = LW 35:51: "To *receive* this sacrament in bread and wine is nothing but to *receive* a certain sign" (author's emphasis). Cf. 2:743,28–29 = 35:51 and 2:742,19 = 35:49.

12. WA 2:744,27 = LW 35:53: "*Take* this sign" (author's emphasis); 2:745,11–12 = 35:54, "I therefore go to the sacrament and *take* a sign from God" (author's emphasis; trans. alt.).

13. WA 2:744,8–9 = LW 35:52: "We are *given* a certain sign by God himself through the priest" (author's emphasis; trans. alt.); 2:745,7–8 = 35:54: "The immeasurable grace and mercy of God are *given* us in this sacrament" (author's emphasis); 2:747,27–28 = 35:57: "In this sacrament . . . we are promised and *given*" (author's emphasis).

14. WA 2:749,23–25 = LW 35:60: "This holy sacrament is nothing but a divine sign, in which is *promised*, *given*, and *bestowed* . . ." (trans. alt.; author's emphasis).

15. WA 2:745,7–8 = LW 35:54.

16. That the two do not have to be mutually exclusive is shown not only by this sermon of Luther, as will become clear below, but also by Thomas Aquinas, which it may be compared with here: "His flesh, and the mysteries accomplished in it, work instrumentally for the life of the soul. But for the life of the body, they not only work instrumentally, but also through a type of exemplar" (*ST* III/q 62/a 5/ad 1).

17. WA 2:743,27–29 = LW 35:51 (trans. alt.).

18. *Expositio Symboli*, Art. 10; Opuscula 6 (quoted according to Paul Althaus, *Communio sanctorum* [1929], 16, n. 35). Cf. the continuation of both passages: "Again all sufferings and sins

If, in Luther's earlier understanding, faith understood as penitence was a constantly oscillating movement, it is now directed to a very specific place, to the bread and wine, to the eating and drinking in the Lord's Supper. Thus the term *sacrament* in the narrowest sense[19] now no longer points to an inner significance but clearly and explicitly to the "external sign" that effectually imparts salvation.[20]

What remains striking in all this is that the term *promise*, which is often used in just this context,[21] does not make sense in its new environment, since it cannot possibly deny its origin in the sacrament of penance structured as it is by the word alone (*solo verbo*).

In short: When Luther speaks of the "certain sign given by God himself through the priest,"[22] "in which are promised, given, and bestowed,"[23] the bestowal of grace in its effectiveness and specific location is understood in exactly the same way as with absolution. The instrumental cause, however, is different. Here in the Supper, the element and action mediate grace, there in the absolution it is the specific word. However, this makes it very questionable whether the expansion of the new organizing principle to include the Lord's Supper has actually taken place here yet.

But first we need to pay attention to defining the actual goods of salvation and their relationship to the act of giving.

II. Significance and Faith

1. The Significance

Strangely enough, the term *gift* does not appear anywhere in the sermon. Instead, the meaning of the sign is discussed in detail, whereby the sign (*signum*) and the thing it signifies (*res*) stand in a peculiarly broken relationship with one other.

---

also become common property; and thus love engenders love in return" (WA 2:743,29–30 = LW 35:51) and "Through this community we obtain two things: one is that the merit of Christ is shared with all, the other is that the good of one is shared with another."

19. Luther retains the general use of the term *sacrament* in the sense of "mystery," although he uses it more sparingly. Cf., for example, the *Operationes in Psalmos* [the second Psalms lectures]: WA 5:76,17–18; 265,33–34; 306,23–24; 365,29–30; 552,10–11; 635,25; 637,31 [slated for LW 64 and 65].

20. WA 2:742,15 = LW 35:49.

21. WA 2:744,27 = LW 35:53: "Take this sign with which I *promise* you" (trans. alt.; author's emphasis); 2:746,13 = 35:55: "This is *promised* to us here, as in a certain sign, by which . . ." (trans. alt.; author's emphasis); 2:747,27–28 = 35:57: "In this sacrament . . . we are *promised* and given" (trans. alt.; author's emphasis). Cf. n. 14.

22. WA 2:744,8–9 = LW 35:52 (trans. alt.).

23. WA 2:749,24–25 = LW 35:60 (trans. alt.).

The sign, which is programmatically determined by the element and action, is not self-evidently "visible" in the simple sense and is itself already a gift of salvation. A relationship between the *res* and *signum* would be possible in three ways: (1) as an arbitrary "divine arrangement," which makes the nature of the sign completely meaningless;[24] (2) as a necessary co-dependency on one another,[25] whereby the sign points to the *res* in its own symbolic power or even communicates it in the image itself ("It effects what it symbolizes," *efficit, quod figurat*[26]), in which case there is a push toward the sensible exterior of the sign;[27] or (3) as a reference leading away from the outside to a somehow different inner testimony. The second and third possibilities, the symbolic and spiritualistic understandings of the sign, do not have to be mutually exclusive. Augustine's spiritualistic concept of the sign is understood thus: "A sign is a thing which, apart from the impression it makes on the senses, causes something else to come into the mind as a consequence of itself."[28] Or even more sharply: "They are called sacraments because in them one thing is seen, another is understood. What is seen is a mere physical likeness; what is understood bears spiritual fruit."[29] However, this still tolerates a weak symbolic understanding to coexist alongside it: "If sacraments

24. In part 4 of the *Large Catechism* (on baptism), Luther says: "No matter how external it may be, here stand God's word and command that have instituted, established, and confirmed baptism. What God institutes and commands cannot be useless. Rather, it is a most precious thing, even though to all appearances it may not be worth a straw" (*BSLK* 692,17–24 = *BC* 457,8).

25. This second type of relationship between the *signum* and *res* is chiefly that of the Thomistic doctrine of the sacraments. Cf., for example, *ST* III/q 65/a 1/resp.: "For spiritual life may have a certain conformity to the life of the body, just as other corporeal things may also have a certain likeness to spiritual things."

26. Cf., for example, Thomas Aquinas, *ST* III/q 62/a 1/ad 1, and Bonaventura IV/d 1/q 5 (in the context of the determination of the relationship of the sacraments of the Old to those of the New Testament): "The difference is commonly explained thus: The sacraments of the new law effect what they signify but not those of the old" (4:24). Also for Biel (Lect. 35 L, 2:26), it belongs to the nature of the New Testament sacrament "that it effects what it signifies."

27. "Now it is a part of human nature to acquire knowledge of the intelligible from the sensible... And so it is that sensible things are required for the sacraments" (Thomas, *ST* III/q 60/a 4/resp.).

28. *On Christian Doctrine*, 2.1.1 (see chap. 2, n. 290).

29. Sermon 272; MPL 38:1247. The memorable formulation "One thing is seen, another is understood," which occurs within a quotation from Gregory, found its way into Biel's commentary on the Mass (Lect. 39 I, 2:92), where (2:93) we also come across the form in which it was influentially adopted by Innocent III: "However, it is called 'the mystery of faith' since also there one thing is believed that is perceived, and another is perceived that is believed" (Denzinger, 31st ed, 414).

did not bear some resemblance to the things of which they are sacraments, they would not be sacraments at all."[30]

Exactly this Augustinian combination can be found in our sermon as in Biel's Mass commentary.[31] To understand this, the two closely intertwined motifs need to be disentangled and presented separately.

a) The *Sign* in Its Significance (the Symbolic Dimension)

The elements: From the bread and wine in the Lord's Supper to the body and blood of Christ needs no translation. Both are in the simple sense "true, natural flesh" and "true, natural blood"[32]—obviously, simply given and so still unimportant: "The natural (in the spiritual) is of no use in this sacrament."[33] We should simply reject it and let it go at that and "just fear and honor Christ as he is present there."[34] Augustine puts it even more emphatically: "Let us not eat Christ's flesh and Christ's blood only in the sacrament, as many wicked people do."[35]

The assumption that the eucharistic elements are transubstantiated is for Luther self-evident and unproblematic.[36] He shares this view with the whole spiritualistic tradition of sacramental piety of the late Middle Ages.[37,38] The body and blood of Christ are themselves not yet the *res* but have symbolic significance. Only at the third level is the pure *res* found: "the mystical flesh of Christ."[39]

---

30. Letter 98,9 (see chap. 2, n. 288).

31. The way the external, visible side of the symbol and the internal, invisible, spiritual participation in the concept of the sign coexist is especially clear in the Hugo passage quoted in Lect. 39 K (2:93–94): "The most divine Eucharist, which is handled visibly and corporally on the altar, according to the species of bread and wine, and according to the truth of the body and blood of Christ, is a sacrament, a sign, and an image of our invisible and spiritual participation in Jesus, which takes place inwardly in the heart through faith and love."

32. WA 2:749,7–18 = LW 35:59; 2:752,4–5 = 35:63.

33. WA 2:751,15–16 = LW 35:62 (trans. alt.).

34. WA 2:751,2 = LW 35:62 (trans. alt.).

35. *Tractates on the Gospel of John*, tract. 27,11; MPL 35:1621.

36. We should not worry about the "how and where" of transubstantiation: WA 2:749,36–750,3 = LW 35:60–61.

37. Note 37 is missing in the original.

38. Apart from Biel's commentary on the Mass, we think, for example, of bk. 4 of the *Imitatio Christi*, in which the term *body of Christ*, obviously used in a formal way, appears very often.

39. Cf. the *Glossa ordinaria* on 1 Cor. 11:24–25 quoted on p. 103 and the passages from the Biel's commentary on the Mass that are referred to in n. 400 on the same page. The definition of the *Glossa ordinaria*, memorable in its clear three-part division, was taken over by Peter Lombard

Luther formulates the symbolic interpretation of the sign programmatically: "(To signify such community), God has also instituted such signs of this sacrament, which everywhere are *added to it* and *with their forms entice and move* us (to such community)."[40] This is developed from three perspectives—namely, from that of their wholeness, their diversity in form, and their constitution through the surrender of their individuality.

The exegetical reason that Christ "saw fit to institute both kinds"[41] hardly plays a role in the demand "that all persons be given both kinds."[42] Rather, it is only raised out of Luther's interest in the full symbolic value of the sign, for "it would be fitting and right if the shape and form or sign of the sacrament were not given piecemeal but as a whole . . . for the sake of the wholeness and completeness of the sign. For this sacrament signifies a complete union and undivided community . . . which is poorly and unfittingly indicated with only one piece or part of the sacrament."[43]

Luther relates the difference in the form of the sign to Christ's incarnation and suffering, to "his life and good work, which are indicated by his flesh," and to "his suffering and martyrdom, which are indicated by his blood."[44]

He also ascribes symbolic power to the way in which the sign is made through the process of surrender and change in which the individual parts lose their individuality, as happens with the production of the bread and wine. Luther here follows in the wake of a long tradition[45] and in the process takes up his

(IV/d.8/c.7); it then gained canonical status when it was accepted and expanded by Innocent III. (*Denz.* 31st ed., 259; trans. alt.): "However, a precise distinction must be made between the three things that are distinct in this sacrament, namely, the visible form, the truth of the body, and the spiritual power. The form is the bread and wine, the truth is the flesh and blood, the power is the unity and love. The first is the 'sacrament and not the *res* (the thing itself).' The second is the 'sacrament and the *res*.' The third is 'the *res* and not the sacrament.' But the first is the sacrament of a twofold *res*. The second however is the sacrament of one, and the *res* of the other. And the third is the *res* of a twofold sacrament."

40. WA 2:748,6–8 = LW 35:58 (trans. alt.; author's emphasis).

41. WA 2:743,5 = LW 35:50.

42. WA 2:742,25–26 = LW 35:50. Duke George found this point highly dangerous (2:738 = 35:47). So Luther had to defend himself in an *Explanation . . . of Several Articles in his Sermon About the Holy Sacrament* (WA 6:76–83) in Jan. 1520 against the charge that he was spreading Bohemian poison. The fact that the criticism only starts at such a peripheral point is proof that the sermon otherwise does not go beyond the traditional understanding of the Mass.

43. WA 2:742,29–743,2 = LW 35:50 (trans. alt.).

44. WA 2:749,17–22 = LW 35:60 (trans. alt.).

45. Cf. Augustine, *Tractates on the Gospel of John*, tract. 27,17; MPL 35:1614: "Our Lord Jesus Christ entrusted his body and blood to these things, which are reduced to the one thing from

own earlier statements:[46] "For just as bread is made from many grains ground together, and the many bodies of grain become one body of bread, in which each grain forfeits its body and form and takes on the common body of the bread, so in a similar way the little grains of wine forfeit their own form and become one common body of wine and drink—so it is and should be with us too."[47]

The symbolic interpretation of the body of Christ (the natural body), which relates it to the body of the church (the spiritual body), cannot begin immediately with the element—here, logically, only with the bread[48]—but actually only with its transubstantiation. But this does not cause any difficulties, since the bread in the Lord's Supper is unquestionably the body of Christ. The point is that, as Augustine says, "from this likeness they often also take the names of the things themselves, just as, therefore, in a certain manner the sacrament of the body of Christ (i.e. his natural body) is the body of Christ (i.e. the body of the church)."[49]

The Act: Eating and drinking also become symbolic signs, "for there is no more intimate, deep, and indivisible union than the union of food with those that are fed. For the food enters them and is changed into their nature and becomes one substance with those that are fed. Other unions, achieved by such things as nails, glue, cords and the like do not make one indivisible substance of the things that are united."[50]

---

many things. For one is made into one thing from many grains, the other flows together into one thing from many grapes." According to the *Glossa ordinaria* (on 1 Cor. 11:24–25; 6.50F), each element has "a resemblance to the thing signified . . . which is the unity of the faithful: because the one loaf is made from the many grains, and the wine flows from the many grapes. Thus the unity of the church consists of the many people of the faithful." In Biel's Mass commentary, cf. Lect. 40 M: "Because one loaf is made from many grains, it signifies the unity of the true and mystical body" (2:108) and Lect. 48 Y (2:248).

46. Cf. the *Sermon on Worthy Preparation* (before Easter 1518): "Community . . . is symbolized in the species of the sacrament, in which many grains, having lost their individual differences, are made into one bread, and likewise, many grapes, having also lost their differences, are made into one wine" (WA 1:329,13–18). For the later period, see the *Sermon for Corpus Christi* of 1520 (4:706,9–12) and the Maundy Thursday sermon of 1523 (12:488–89). This traditional theme is also found in the Württembergian admonition before the Lord's Supper of 1536 (see text in E. Weismann, "Der Predigtgottesdienst und die verwandten Formen" in *Leiturgia*, 3 (1955): 1–97, here 48).

47. WA 2:748,8–13 = LW 35:58 (trans. alt.). Cf. 2:750,33–34 = 35:62.

48. Cf. the transition from v. 16 to v. 17 in 1 Cor. 10.

49. Epistle 98,9 (a continuation of the proof text given at n. 30).

50. WA 2:748,29–33 = LW 35:60 (trans. alt.). Cf. the *Sermon for Corpus Christi* of 1520: "'Eat' and 'drink': these two verbs signify a kind of union between the persons eating and the edible food, and the persons drinking and the potable drink. For those who eat unite the food with

B) The *Significance* of the Sign (the Spiritualistic Dimension)

The symbolic approach asks about the *res* from the angle of the *signum*, while the spiritualistic approach asks about the *signum* from the angle of the *res* by retroactively linking, as it were, the broken relationship to the sign in the sense of "one thing is seen, another is understood." All the emphasis here is on the *res*.

The fourth section of the sermon begins immediately with the *res* and makes it clear that the significance of the sign is something other than the sign itself: "The significance or work of this sacrament (which must be "inward and spiritual"[51]) is the community of all saints. Hence it is also commonly called *synaxis* [Greek] or *communio* [Latin],[52] for "Christ with all his saints is one spiritual body."[53] "The name of this sacrament is communion (*communio*), its *res* is the unity of hearts": this brief earlier formulation (from the *Sermon on Worthy Preparation*)[54] best summarizes the corresponding statements of our sermon.

The *res* is now described in detail: The "true significance of this sacrament" is "real communion,"[55] which is indeed given in the sacrament, not with the sign of the natural body of Christ but only in accordance with its change into another species (*metabasis eis allo genos*). The change of the bread into the natural body of Christ and our change through love into the spiritual body of the church are clearly understood as two different events, which can only barely be held together, "in a makeshift manner," by the symbolic power of the idea of the body (see above). "For just as the bread is changed into his true natural body . . . so we too are truly drawn and changed into the spiritual body, that is, into the community of Christ and all saints."[56] Here, clearly, the ecclesiological

---

themselves, and those who drink unite the drink with themselves, so that the food and drink can also be converted into their nature, so that it is utterly impossible to separate the food from those eating it, and the drink from those drinking it, without corrupting its nature" (4:703,18–22).

51. WA 2:742,12 = LW 35:49.

52. WA 2:743,7–9 = LW 35:50 (trans. alt.).

53. WA 2:743,11–12 = LW 35:51.

54. WA 1:329,13–14 (1518). At the same time, the same determination occurs in the Hebrews lectures (in the scholion on 5:1), in which the "*res* itself" is contrasted with the host (57/3:168,7 = 29:170). Here this "*res* of the sacrament of the body of Christ" is the "people of Christ" (57/3:167,26–168,1 = 29:170).

55. WA 2:748,23–24 = LW 35:58.

56. WA 2:749,10–14 = LW 35:59 (trans. alt.). We should give attention to the "just as–so." See with that the structure of the answer to question 79 in the *Heidelberg Catechism*.

and ethical interest outweighs the christological: "Christ gave his body for this purpose, that the significance of the sacrament, that is, the community and change wrought by love, would be put into practice. And Christ values his spiritual body, which is the community of his saints, more than his own natural body."[57] "Therefore . . . it is more needful that you pay attention to the spiritual than the natural body of Christ; and faith in the spiritual body is more necessary than faith in the natural body. For the natural without the spiritual is of no use to us in this sacrament; a change must occur there and be exercised through love."[58]

Having presented the *res* in its relation to the *signum*, we can now look at the *res* itself in its actual content.

"The community consists in this, that all the spiritual goods of Christ and his saints are shared with and become the common property of those who receive this sacrament. Again, all suffering and sin also become common property; and so love engenders love in return and mutual love unites."[59] The fact that "through the sharing of his goods and our misfortunes, we become one cake, one bread, one body, one drink,"[60] and that here there "is a community and gracious exchange or blending of our sin and suffering with the righteousness of Christ and his saints,"[61] does not mean the same as the "happy exchange" of the freedom tractate,[62] for here Luther is not speaking in the strict sense of Christ and faith but rather of the community of saints, in which Christ is merely the first among many, and of love. This must now be shown in detail.

---

57. WA 2:751,4–7 = LW 35:62 (trans. alt.).

58. WA 2:751,13–17 = LW 35:62 (trans. alt.).

59. WA 2:743,27–30 = LW 35:51 (trans. alt.). Cf. 2:744,9–11 = 35:52; 2:745,16 = 35:54; 2:749,25–26 = 35:60; 2:750,8–10 = 35:61.

60. WA 2:748,17–18 = LW 35:58 (trans. alt.).

61. WA 2:749,32–34 = LW 35:60.

62. "From this marriage it follows, as St. Paul says, that Christ and the soul become one body, and so the possessions of both—fortune, misfortune, and all things—become common property; what Christ has becomes the property of the believing soul and what the soul has becomes the property of Christ. Thus Christ has all the goods and blessings that become the property of the soul and conversely all the vices and sin carried by the soul become the property of Christ. He now takes all our sin and evil on himself through the happy exchange and brings the strife to an end" (WA 7:25,28–34; see LW 31:351). The formulations are closely related, and here as there, Eph. 5:32 is also cited. But this is exactly where we see the difference clearly emerging between the freedom tractate and the sermon with its strong ecclesiological interest. And we cannot explain this difference solely from the topic of "the brotherhoods" treated in the appendix (2:754–58 = 35:67–73).

The "inflow of the head into its members"[63] in the "mystical body of Christ," the "spiritual body," could be understood in three ways, each being the reverse of the corresponding concept of the sign:[64]

1. The head speaks; its members hear and obey (the inflow from the word).[65]
2. From the head flows a substance of grace into its members through the elements "as through instruments" in a supernatural way but now understood again in a natural way (the inflow from the element).
3. The head as example stimulates its members to imitate it as a model (the inflow from the example).

Here, too, the second and third possibilities do not have to be mutually exclusive.[66] Our sermon expressly speaks of the effective implementation of community.[67] This *communio* is determined by love, but it must be able to be demonstrated ("change"[68]) as such. Thus it does not leave the gift as gift but understands it from the outset as a task and demand, and so immediately displaces the soteriological with the ethical, or sees both as existing indistinguishably in one

63. In this summary, J. Heckel (*Im Irrgarten der Zwei-Reiche-Lehre*, *ThEx* NF 55, 6 and *Die Zwo Kirchen*, *ThEx* NF 55, 47) takes up Luther's formulation in *On the Papacy in Rome* that "it is inherent in the nature of every head that it infuses all its life, spirit, and activity into its members" (WA 6:298,6–8 = LW 39:71; trans. alt.).

64. See above pp. 260–262.

65. Cf. the sermon (probably from 1520) in WA 4:715–16, which agrees in subject matter ("Christ the head of the church") with the passage from *On the Papacy in Rome* quoted in n. 63: "The spiritual head of the church is Christ alone, who infuses faith" (4:715,26–27). What is meant here is the faith that "constantly depends on the promises of Christ" (716,1–2). According to the *Operationes in Psalmos*, "the mystical Christ" is the "preached Christ" (5:549,37ff.; 1520). WA 5:550,2–3 speaks of the Christ who rules and is preached and believed on through the gospel.

66. Cf. n. 16.

67. Cf. the concept of sign presented in pp. 258–260, in and with which we really receive what it gives and bestows.

68. "For where love does not grow daily and change people so that they become common property to everyone, there is no fruit or meaning in this sacrament" (WA 2:748,3–5 = LW 35:58; trans. alt.). "In this way we are changed into one another and become common property through love, without which no such change can take place" (2:748,24–26 = 35:58; trans. alt.). Both passages form the end of a section and so emphasize the importance of this idea of "change." Cf. 2:750,27–34 = 35:61–62; 2:751,16–17 = 35:62; 2:754,15 = 35:67.

another. Christ's significance is that of an example and his "remembrance" is an "exhortation to imitate his example," not a proclamation that produces faith but an admonition that demands love.

This becomes clear from Luther's exegesis of the words of institution (*verba*), which twists the plain wording in a strange way to make it say what the whole sermon is saying. However, it was precisely the simple literal sense of these words that Luther later used as the shibboleth or litmus test of the entire doctrine of the Lord's Supper. Therefore, we need to pay special attention to their reinterpretation in our sermon:

> When Christ instituted the sacrament, he said, "This is my body. . . ." It is as if he were saying, "I am the head, I will be the first to give himself for you. I will make your suffering and misfortune my own and will bear it for you, so that you in turn may do the same for me and for one another, allowing all things to be common property, in me and with me. And I leave you this sacrament as a sure sign of all this, in order that you may not forget me, but daily call to mind and admonish one another about what I have done and am still doing for you, in order that you may be strengthened, and also bear one another in the same way."[69]

Further: We should "remember him and exercise ourselves in this community, according to his example. For if his example were no longer kept before us, the community also would soon be forgotten. As we see at present, to our sorrow, many masses are held and yet the Christian community that should be preached, practiced, and kept before us there, following Christ's example, is completely lost."[70]

With the idea of example and imitation, we catch a glimpse of an important motif of the theology of the cross.[71] However, the prototypical power of Christ is now seen not only in individual mortification but also more strongly than before in compassion for others and in love. Nevertheless, self-mortification remains

69. WA 2:745,36–746,5 = LW 35:55 (trans. alt.). See, on the other hand, the completely different way of describing the gift of the Lord's Supper in *The Babylonian Captivity*: 6:515,18–26 = 36:40.

70. WA 2:747,5–9 = LW 35:56 (trans. alt.).

71. There are many writings of Luther around 1519 that document the theology of the cross. Cf. the *Operationes in Psalmos*: WA 5:63,29–64,5 = LW 14:335; 5:64,23ff. = 14:336; 5:69,1ff. = 14:342; 5:70,12ff. = 14:344; 5:70,31–32 = 14:344; 5:71,8ff. = 14:345; 5:71,19ff. = 14:345f. (on Ps. 2); 5:81,5ff.; 5:85,1ff.; 5:91,10ff.; 5:91,17–18 (on Ps. 3); 5:108,9–10, 24ff., 37ff. (on Ps. 4); 5:128,32ff.; 5:141,2ff.,30ff.; 5:154,21–22; 5:164,22ff.; 5:176,22ff.; 5:198,40–199,1–2 (on Ps. 5); 5:217,1ff.; 5:218,14ff. (on Ps. 6); 5:227,34–35,36-37 (on Ps. 7).

the way of salvation—because it is the way of love.[72] Mention of suffering as a necessary disposition in this context[73] can only round off the whole circle of ideas.

The relationship between head and members established by the *exemplum* and *imitatio* paradigm quite logically brings "Christ and all saints," a formula used remarkably often in our sermon,[74] together on the same level without differentiation. Christ appears only as the first among equals,[75] with the saints doing exactly the same as he does: interceding with God for us[76] and sharing with us their spiritual goods, works, suffering, merits, graces, and virtues.[77] These statements still follow the medieval tradition to the letter.[78]

---

72. Becoming "common" (*gemein*) in the sense of common property presupposes mortification, which is what the picture of the crushed grains and grapes wants to convey. We could continue with the interpretation of the heading of Ps. 8 in the *Operationes* without a break: "Surely the word of the cross will crush and humble the people of the world like a great press and gather many into one body like wine into a vat" (WA 5:249,34–36; 1519). For the motif of the "wine press" and its representation in images, see chap. 2, n. 430. Cf. WA 5:71,12–13 = LW 14:345 (on Ps. 2:11): "They (i.e. Christians) are crushed and humiliated between the upper and lower millstone (Deut. 24:6); and after the husks are removed, they become the purest wheat of Christ."

73. WA 2:746,16–28, esp. 23–29 = LW 35:55–56: "Therefore, in order that the disciples might be worthy and well prepared for this sacrament, he [Christ] first made them sad, held before them his departure and death . . . When they were thus full of sorrow and angst . . . they were worthy." This section also appears in the *Sermon on the Worthy Preparation of the Heart for the Reception of the Sacrament of the Eucharist* (WA 1:330): "It is necessary that you offer [God] a soul that is empty and hungry, that is, that you confess that your soul is full of evils and afflictions" (ll. 11–12). This is followed by the quote from Augustine and the Scripture passage (Luke 1:53), which are also quoted in the sermon of 1519 (see WA 1:330,13–15,16–17 with WA 2:746,30–32, 21–22 = LW 35:55–56).

74. There are over thirty such occurrences.

75. Alongside the "I will be the first" of the reinterpretation of the words of institution, we should note the following: "that we might put from us all troubles and tribulation (*anfechtung*) and lay it on the community of saints, and *especially* on Christ" (WA 2:745,9 = LW 35:54; author's emphasis). Indeed, Christ can be counted among the saints in such a way that only of them is it said: "In this sacrament the help, community, and support of all the saints is promised and given" (2:747,27–28 = 35:57; trans. alt.). The distinction between *sacramentum* and *exemplum*, which Luther otherwise emphasized so much, appears almost leveled out in this sermon to the point of disappearing.

76. WA 2:744,23–24 = LW 35:53.

77. Cf. WA 2:743,27ff. = LW 35:51–52; 2:749,25–26 = 35:60; 2:750,9 = 35:61. Cf. the sermon on St. Martin's Day (Nov. 11) 1519: WA 9:422,1–7.

78. Cf. Biel, Lect. 30 E, 1:306, "We must therefore firmly believe and never doubt that the saints in the fatherland intercede for us and support us by their merits and prayers or desires, and likewise, 30 F (1:307), "Since then Christ our head intercedes for us with the Father, why should we not believe this about his members (that is, the blessed saints)? . . . But Christ intercedes for

The spiritual goods and merits of Christ and all saints are exchanged according to the principle of reciprocity, "I give so that you may give" (*do ut des*): "We for our part must make the evil of others our own if we want Christ and his saints to make our evil their own. Then . . . we do justice to the sacrament."[79] But if the gift of salvation is love, then obviously the thought must immediately arise that this needs to be repaid straightaway: "For those who would participate in the gift must also pay for it and recompense love with love."[80] So we find here the idea of an *ius talionis* of love, a law of equal and just repayment, which in turn is made possible by the idea of example (*exemplum*).

In short: The significance of the sign, understood as the actual gift of salvation, the thing signified by the sacrament (*res sacramenti*), indeed its purpose, is love. "This sacrament is a sacrament of love,"[81] whose transforming[82] power shapes the community of the earthly and heavenly saints,[83] in which their participation and sharing is determined by the idea of *exemplum* and regulated by the *ius talionis*, the law of just recompense. In this community, Christ does not yet stand apart from the saints but merely appears as the first among equals.

---

us . . . There is no doubt that the saints will imitate him in this in heaven, just as they faithfully imitated him here on earth."

79. WA 2:748,1–3 = LW 35:57–58 (trans. alt.).

80. WA 2:743,34–35 = LW 35:52 (trans. alt.). Luther speaks of love's principle of recompense, or the law of equal and just reward (*ius talionis*), remarkably often: 2:744,16–17 = 35:52; 2:745,20 = 35:54; 2:746,1ff. = 35:55; 2:747,26ff. = 35:57; 2:754,12 = 35:66; 2:745,31 = 35:54. The thing to note with these texts is the "in turn" and "if you want . . ., then you have to." See on the other hand, the Mass sermon of 1520: "Here there is no duty (*officium*) but a benefit (*beneficium*), no work or service, but . . . pure participation in and reception of the gift" (WA 6:365,10–13).

81. WA 2:745,25 = LW 35:54, which is a thoroughly traditional way of speaking. See Augustine: "O sacrament of piety! O sign of unity! O bond of love! (In *Tractates on the Gospel of John*, tract. 26.13; MPL 35:1613. Cf. MPL 35:1614 and 35:1618. According to Peter Lombard, the *res eucharistiae*, the thing signified by the Eucharist, is the unity of the faithful (IV/d.8/c.7). Compare with the *Glossa ordinaria* on 1 Cor. 11:24–25; 6.51 A, Biel, Lect. 27 D, 1:260: "This sacrament is the bond of love . . . this sacrament is the sacrament of community."

82. Cf. n. 68.

83. "In conclusion, the fruit of this sacrament is community and love . . ., so that the community is twofold: on the one hand, we partake of Christ and of all saints; on the other hand, we let all Christians partake of us too . . . and so through the change wrought by love, we have in common one bread, one drink, one body, one community" (WA 2:754,9–16 = LW 35:67; trans. alt.). The sermon here makes a distinction between certain things, but it nowhere indicates how these things are related to each other in the sense of cause and effect, as will be done later. See, however, 2:752,21 = 35:65 ("after that").

2. Faith

The Lord's Supper is a sacrament of love and therefore leaves faith with only an ancillary function,[84] which is why Luther only discusses it relatively briefly.

Love is the "fruit";[85] faith, merely the "use"[86] that bridges the gulf between *signum* and *res*[87] in order then to focus on the latter, on the significance of the sign, which is what really counts. Of course, faith is also assent to the truth that the elements are changed into Christ's natural body. But this faith, which clings to the external sign, really amounts to nothing, because "faith in the spiritual body is more necessary than faith in the natural body."[88]

"Faith in the same two things," the sign and its significance, means, therefore, in complete agreement with Biel's commentary on the Mass,[89] first, that quite trivial belief in the change of the elements, and second, the step from *signum* to *res* and thus the attempt to grasp the sign's significance, the love that alone fulfills it.

---

84. What Luther says about "FAITH, that power lies in it" (WA 2:749,30–31 = LW 35:60, trans. alt.), "that everything depends on it and that for its sake this sacrament was instituted" (2:750,23–24 = 35:61, trans. alt.), seems to contradict our interpretation. However, these two texts just quoted do no more than simply repeat what Luther had said earlier in the *Sermon on Repentance* (*Bußsermon*), but here in connection with the word(!): "And it depends on faith in the word" (2:715,30–31 = 35:11; trans. alt.); "Everything depends completely on faith in God's word" (2:716,31–32 = 35:13; trans. alt.).

85. "The fruit of this sacrament is community and love" (WA 2:754,9 = LW 35:67; trans. alt.).

86. WA 2:751,32 = LW 35:65; 2:752,8 = 35:64; 2:752,18 = 35:65. The phrase "It must also be used in faith" (2:751,37–38 = 35:63) already presupposes faith, for it says, "in faith" and not "for faith." In this context, the formula *opus operantis* is also retained with material justification (2:751,34,37–38 = 35:63; 2:752,8–11 = 35:63–64) but then rejected as useless (2:752,12–14 = 35:64). See what Luther says about the necessity of faith with Biel, Lect. 29 D (1:291–92), who holds that "faith is required of those present at the altar" (quoted in chap. 2, n. 412).

87. "Faith must make both of them together operative and useful" (WA 2:742,13-14 = LW 35:49).

88. WA 2:751,14–15 = LW 35:62.

89. "First, faith is required to believe that, after the words of consecration, the true body of Christ and his true blood are contained under the species of bread and wine . . . faith is required for the assent to this truth" (Lect. 29 D, 1:291) and Lect. 29 D (1:291–92): "Faith is required of those standing around the altar so that the sacrifice of the offering may be of benefit to them, through which they are received into the unity of the sacrament and remain close to the other members of the mystical body and to Christ the head of this body. And thus they live and can share in the inflow of the spiritual life. For faith working through love purifies the hearts of those standing around the altar so that they themselves may also be offered spiritually in that offering which by its very purity represents the purity of the mystical body, whence ACTS 15: PURIFYING THEIR HEARTS BY FAITH."

Therefore, faith does not remain attached to the sign but escapes from it into its significance.[90] Thus the sign is devalued in a completely Augustinian spiritualistic way,[91] epitomized in Augustine's words, "Believe, and you have eaten already." Just believe in its significance and you no longer need the sign![92]

From this perspective, we can now also understand the anagogical final part of the sermon.[93] The external sign is meant not to comfort and offer firm support, not to make something present in it tangible and communicate it, but to point away from itself to the reality itself, to Christ and all saints, to the things that are unseen and spiritual, to the eternal goods. For, in the language of Tauler, "all temporal and sensible things must fall away, and we must completely separate ourselves from them if we are to come to God."[94]

The sacrament is "a ford, a bridge, a door, a ship, and a stretcher,"[95] in that it transports us across the emergency bridge of faith, from the sensible and visible world to the spiritual and invisible world, but not in that it comes to us by an external sign.

In summary, we can say the following. The tension in the sermon lies in the juxtaposition and interweaving of its emphatic emphasis on the effective and symbolic external *sign*—understood in the sense of the Thomistic axiom that "the sign effects what it signifies"—and the specific location of the gift of grace that it gives, on the one hand, and the strong spiritualistic devaluation of the sign

---

90. That is why, for example, also with §19 (LW 35:61–62), the talk of faith, hardly begun (§18: 35:61), can suddenly change again into talk of love.

91. Cf. also, here again, Biel: "Indeed, the body of Christ is consumed in two ways because it is understood in two ways . . . The true body of Christ is consumed sacramentally, that is, under the species of bread. The mystical body of Christ is consumed spiritually in the faith of the heart" (Lect. 36 G, 2:46. Cf. Lect. 36 L, 2:50). However, the higher esteem for the "mystical body" and spiritual food does not mean contempt for the "true body of Christ," which Biel sharply objects to in Lection 39 (2:85–97). "The usefulness of faith is great because the true body of Christ is contained under the species of bread" (39 B, 2:86).

92. WA 2:742,27–29 = LW 35:50 is the saying of Augustine that Luther takes up: "Why are you preparing your teeth and stomach? Believe, and you have eaten already" (in *Tractates on the Gospel of John*, tract. 25.12; MPL 35:1602. The passage noted in *BoA* 1:196 is incorrect). This is true of Augustine because for him "the sacrament is one thing, the power (*virtus*) of the sacrament another" [where *virtus* like *res* represents the inward part of the sacrament; trans. note] (tract. 26,11; MPL 35:1611).

93. Especially §21 (LW 35:65–66).

94. WA 2:753,6–8 = LW 35:66 (trans. alt.).

95. WA 2:753,17–18 = LW 35:66.

and its certainty through the reference to its actual *significance*—which stands in a broken relationship to it in the sense of the Augustinian axiom "one thing is seen, another is understood"—on the other hand. But the emphasis here falls squarely on the second aspect, the significance, which ultimately binds faith to itself alone.

The significance of the sign, understood as the actual good or benefit of salvation, is love, whose transforming power shapes the community of the earthly and heavenly saints through a mutual receiving and giving of goods, determined by the idea of *exemplum* and regulated by the *ius talionis*, the law of recompense. But in this communion, Christ does not yet stand apart from the saints but merely appears as the first among equals.

The primary determining factor is therefore Luther's interest in ecclesiology and ethics. Love becomes the path to salvation[96] when, instead of belonging entirely to the world, it enters the forum of God and makes this the community of saints.[97] That is, love is directed to God instead of to the world. Faith here can only have an auxiliary function. As a spiritual eye, it looks behind the superficiality of the elements, which initially appear as a means of grace, and sees their real significance, which is shaped by love. But the place where the necessary information about the significance of the sign and also about the sign itself in its significance can be given remains unclear, because the sign, although it is visible, is unable to identity itself.

This sermon says absolutely nothing about the *word*. This means that the reformational approach (*Ansatz*) has not yet come into its own here. The decisive game changer—the thing that determined the sign—was the element, not the word. This is because the sermon was constrained by the medieval system to follow quite traditional paths. And yet the emphasis on the effectiveness and external sensibility of the sign and the specific location of the bestowal of grace are important aspects of the new understanding of repentance, and so these could be carried over to the Lord's Supper, minus the Thomistic stamp that they formerly bore.

However, a decisive change would occur if the sign were understood as a very specific word, as in the 1519 *Sermon on the Sacrament of Penance*. There the sign and its significance coincide because the gift of salvation is exactly what

96. Cf. the clear formulation of the *Sermon for Corpus Christi* of 1520 in the passage in which it is closely related to the *Sermon on the Lord's Supper* of 1519: "We received . . . the truth of love *that we might be saved*, which the sacrament also signifies" (WA 4:706,8–9; author's emphasis).

97. The criterion of this judgment is derived primarily from Luther's treatise on freedom, especially its final thesis (for this, see pp. 340–344. It maintains that faith belongs to God alone and love to the world alone.

the sign says, because the word gives and does what it promises.[98] There faith takes the word in its simple sense and thus grasps the *signum* and *res* at the same time—*which is the essence of the reformational turn in Luther's hermeneutic.*[99] Faith is "use" in that it grasps the word, and faith is "fruit," in that it is grasped by the word. It is sufficient and it is everything, because the word is everything. For as it is with the sign, so it is with faith.[100]

---

98. "There are three things in the holy sacrament of penance. The first is absolution. This is the word of the priest that shows, tells, and proclaims to you that you are free ('loosed') and that your sins are forgiven you before God according to the declaration and power of the above-mentioned words of Christ to St. Peter. The second is grace, the forgiveness of sins, the peace and comfort of the conscience, as the words declare. Therefore, it is called a sacrament, a holy sign, because in it we hear externally the words that signify the spiritual goods within, by which the heart is comforted and set at peace. The third is faith, which firmly believes that the absolution and words of the priest are true, by the power of Christ's words, 'whatever you loose . . . shall be loosed,' etc" (WA 2:715,21–30 = LW 35:11; trans. alt.). As said above, "The sacrament comprises three things: the word of God, that is, the absolution; faith in this absolution; and peace, that is, the forgiveness of sins, which surely follows faith" (2:721,8–11 = 35:19; trans. alt.). *These two texts especially make it emphatically clear how the new approach beginning with the word changes the threefold schema of* signum—res—fides *into the twofold schema with its equation* signum *(=* verbum*)* = res *and* fides. In the second text quoted, faith is already spoken of in the second place. (What is mentioned here in third place is not a third but leads back to the first, in, with, and under which the forgiveness of sins is bestowed. It "follows" faith because faith follows the word.) See chap. 4, n. 199.

99. In the sermon on the Lord's Supper, on the other hand, if we look at it from a specifically hermeneutical point of view, the threatening split between the *signum* and *res*, caused by the absence of the specific word, can only be barely stopped by Luther's use of the old *category of the fourfold sense of Scripture* (which is obviously done unconsciously and seems anachronistic in view of his rejection of it, which has become increasingly decisive since his 1516/17 Galatians lectures). According to this schema, the literal sense of the sign means the natural body of Christ; the spiritual sense, the spiritual body; the tropological, the receiving and giving of love; and the anagogical, the introduction to the invisible things and the food for eternity. On the other hand, in the promise of God ("I absolve you!") uttered by the priest, the literal and the spiritual senses coincide from the outset: The word is what it declares and what it gives us, namely, absolution. The tropological dimension is immediately given with the "you," while the anagogical corresponds to the ultimacy of God's word of judgment, "I absolve you," which lies in the fact that in the final judgment, nothing else is seen other than what the word and faith already give and anticipate. It is hardly necessary to state explicitly that it is *only here, where the unambiguity of the short formula "I absolve you" is taken seriously, that we find the reformational turn in Luther's hermeneutic*. See the *Operationes in Psalmos* on 8:6–7: "The scriptures and the word of God must have one, simple and consistent sense, lest (as they say) we make a waxen nose of the sacred letters" (WA 5:280,36ff.). Luther rejects any diversification or broadening of the sense of Scripture: "Allegory, tropology, and anagogy are all the same . . . for Scripture has no more than one simple sense" (5:645,22–24.; on Ps. 21:19).

100. "The word drives faith," *quale enim est verbum . . . talis fides* (WA 5:259,18–19; on Ps. 8:2).

B) On the New Testament—That Is, the Holy Mass (1520)

The term *promise* seemed strangely foreign in the sermon just discussed, because it cannot logically be linked retrospectively with a sign that is already fundamentally determined by the element and action. "Promise," understood formally, is meant to conceal a *word*.[101] But how and where do we find such a word in the Mass?

In the sermon *Concerning the Testament of Christ* of April 8, 1520[102]—then in the treatise *On Good Works* in its interpretation of the third commandment,[103] again in the *Sermon on the New Testament, that is, the Holy Mass*[104] announced here,[105] and finally, in its tighter Latin version in *The Babylonian Captivity*[106]—hereafter referred to in abbreviated form as the "testament sermon," Luther dares to wrest from the elements and the act their previously undisputed primacy and to attribute this instead to what formerly had been subordinated to them (namely, the words of institution, or more precisely, the gifting words contained in them). This is now the "chief part of the mass."[107] "For in these words and absolutely in none other reside the power, the nature, and the whole substance of the mass."[108] "For these words omit nothing that pertains to the completeness, use, and fruit of this sacrament."[109]

---

101. This becomes crystal clear precisely from the *Sermon on the Lord's Supper* of 1519, where Luther, at the very place where he wants to grasp the element and action in their significance, turns them into words and resorts to direct speech: "God gives us this sacrament, as if he were saying, 'Look, you are attacked by many sins; take this sign by which I can give you a promise'" (WA 2:744,26–27 = LW 35:53; trans. alt.). Here the notion of "promise," which is at home with the new understanding of the sacrament of penance, is able to open up the sign to the word even if it is still determined by the element. However, given the sermon's traditional train of thought, this does not yet lead Luther to take the gifting words of the Lord's Supper in their simple sense as a "promise." Cf. p. 268.

102. WA 9:445–49.

103. WA 6:230,10–231,15 = LW 44:55–56. This part was most likely published in April: see 6:196–97. But its composition *prior* to the sermon of Apr. 8 cannot be ruled out.

104. WA 6:349–78 = LW 35:79–111; probably published in July (see WA 6:349).

105. WA 6:231,14–15 = LW 44:56 ("But more on this another time").

106. WA 6:512,7–526,33 = LW 36:35–57 (this was published with the whole treatise on Oct. 6, 1520).

107. WA 6:355,34 = LW 35:82.

108. WA 6:512,33–34 = LW 36:37 (trans. alt.). See "According to its substance, therefore, the mass is properly speaking nothing else than the aforesaid words of Christ, 'Take . . .'" (6:515,17–18 = 36:40).

109. WA 6:513,9–10 = LW 36:37 (trans. alt.).

The clear and cohesive conception of the testament sermon was not achieved without preparation. As early as the summer of 1518, in the scholion on Hebrews 9:17 (FOR A TESTAMENT IS CONFIRMED BY DEATH), discussed in the previous chapter, Luther, inspired by Chrysostom, had understood the words of institution of the Lord's Supper in terms of the legal category of a "testament,"[110] which he again paid particular attention to in his interpretation of Genesis from 1519 onward.[111] With the help of this concept, he now grasped the nature and function of the Mass in an incredibly one-sided way in comparison to the traditional labyrinth of motifs, such as we have, for instance, in the Mass commentary of Gabriel Biel.

> Thus, if we enquire what a testament is, we shall learn at the same time what the mass is, what its use and fruit is, and what constitutes its abuse. A testament is, without doubt, a promise made by a person about to die, in which they name their inheritance and appoint their heirs. A testament, therefore, involves first, the death of the testator, and second, the promise of an inheritance and the naming of the heir . . . Christ testifies to his death when he says, "this is my body, which is given up, this is my blood, which is poured out." He names and designates his inheritance when he says, "for the forgiveness of sins." But he appoints his heirs when he says, "for you and for many," that is, for those who accept and believe the promise of the testator. For here faith makes us heirs.[112]

Accordingly, this outline drawn up by Luther himself, which surpasses the German version in its clarity,[113] must now be our model for interpreting his

110. Cf. pp. 245–248. We see further preparation for the new conception especially in the scholion on Heb. 9:14 (on this, see pp. 239–243).

111. Especially in the sermon on Gen. 9:9 (cf. above p. 177): "Observe the words used in the Scriptures: 'covenant,' 'pact,' 'promise,' 'testament,' 'ark of the covenant,' 'sign of the covenant,' 'testimony,' 'cup of the new and everlasting testament'" (WA 9:348,9–10). See *The Babylonian Captivity*: "The words that are most common in the Scriptures are 'pact,' 'covenant,' and 'testament of the Lord'" (WA 6:514,4–5 = LW 36:38 (trans. alt.). For more on the term in the Hebrews lectures and the 1519 *Galatians Commentary*, see pp. 363–364, esp. nn. 97 and 103.

112. WA 6:513,22–23 = LW 36:38 (trans. alt.). Cf. the *Galatians Commentary* (1519), esp. on 3:15–18 (2:519,3–521,37 = 27:264–68).

113. The division into six "parts" made there (§12: WA 6:359–60 = LW 35:86–87) is not clear because what is called the third part ("the testament itself, that is, the words of Christ") embraces the whole thing. Parts four and six, the sign and Christ's command to do this in remembrance of him, thus the aspects most important to the tradition, are no longer even mentioned in the

ever-recurring formula that the Mass is nothing but a "testament" or "promise."[114] And so we will first speak of the "death of the testator" (*mors testatoris*), then of the "promise of an inheritance" (*haereditas promissio*), and finally, of the "naming of the heir" (*haeredis nuncupatio*).

1. Death of the Testator

"'Where there is a testament, the death of the testator is necessary' (Heb. 9). Now God made a testament; therefore, it was necessary for him to die. But God could not die unless he became human. Thus, the incarnation and the death of Christ are both comprehended most concisely in this one word, 'testament.'"[115] Formally, this line of thought is undoubtedly based on Anselm's proof ("Therefore, it was necessary"),[116] but in its context turns the argumentative demonstration of the logical necessity of God's incarnation and death at the same time into a thetic answer to the question, "Why did God become human (*cur homo deus*)?" Luther's answer to Anselm is that the *vere homo* is the *vere deus*, that Jesus Christ is truly human and is truly divine, because in and with his human life and death, God spoke his irrevocable, final, and unsurpassable word.

What God's speech reveals is immediately shown by the soteriological flip side of this christological aspect (as we will see, especially in chapter 9).

2. Promise of an Inheritance

"The promise of the forgiveness of sins, made to us by God . . . is confirmed by the death of God's Son . . . For the only difference between a promise and a testament is that a testament at the same time involves the death of the promiser."[117] In the sermon *Concerning the Testament of Christ*, Luther says that "testament" is the general meaning of the word since God makes a pact (*contrahit*) with humans through his promise. In fact, these words usually mean the same thing: *pact* (*pactum*), *covenant* (*foedus*), *testament* (*testamentum*), and *promise* (*promissio*)."

---

structure of the Latin version. This shows how much they are already embraced by the three aspects of the gifting words themselves.

114. WA 6:513,14–15 = LW 36:37; 6:516,13 = 36:41; 6:517,11,19 = 36:42–43; 6:520,22–23 = 36:47; 6:521,6–7 = 36:48; 6:522,4 = 36:50; 6:523,17–18 = 36:51.

115. WA 6:514,6–10 = LW 36:38 (trans. alt.). The German version (6:357,16–27 = 35:84) is more detailed und shows interesting variants, especially the phrase "and resurrection" (l.23), which in this context does not make sense.

116. Cf. Anselm of Canterbury, *Why God Became Man*, ed. and trans. Jasper Hopkins and Herbert Richardson (Edwin Mellen, 1980), 102–3.

117. WA 6:513,34–37 = LW 36:38 (trans. alt.). On the distinction between "promise" and "testament," see pp. 363–364.

He draws this statement from a list of promises growing out of his sermons on Genesis[118] with the programmatic heading: "When God makes a pact with humans, it is done in such a way that God makes a promise and humans believe this promise that he makes."[119]

This describes the relationship of God to humankind in general. "God has *always* dealt with people this way through certain kinds of promises."[120] Already in the old covenant we see that "God promises help to human nature" and that in each case this *one* "promise of God," a very specific word in a concrete situation, preserves and comforts Adam, Noah, Abraham, Gideon, Manoah, David, the prophets, and the psalmists, and saves them from despair.[121] In fact, the "promise" embraces the uniqueness of the Scriptures in general: "For there is nothing more precious in the whole of Scripture than the promise of God. Without this promise, there would not be any place for prayer, work, or faith, in fact, there would be no place for life or anything. For the promise of God sustains and consoles us in all our distress of body and soul."[122]

We would misunderstand Luther if we wanted to see his list of Old Testament promises as proof that he was an early proponent of salvation history (*Heilsgeschichte*) with its schema of "promise and fulfillment." Every time God makes a promise, it happens, the whole thing happens there and then, and salvation is given wholly and completely. For the unity of God is not derived from the totality of a history that is still incomplete but is given entirely in the unambiguousness of his promise and becomes known through the special faith that

118. WA 9:446,30–32 (quotation); the list: 9:446,13–29. See the more detailed list in the sermon on Gen. 9:9 (9:348,12–349,2), in which "promises" do not appear separated from "signs" as in the sermon *Concerning the Testament of Christ* (signs: 9:448,25–31) and *The Babylonian Captivity* (promises: WA 6:514,26–515,4 = LW 36:38; signs: 6:518,2–9 = 36:44).

119. WA 9:446,7–8. See the letter of Dec. 18, 1519, to Spalatin (see p. 177), "Because without the word of the promiser and the faith of the receiver, it is not possible for us to have any dealings with God" (WA Br 1:595; ll. 23–24); the formulations of the programmatic sentence in *The Babylonian Captivity*, "Where God makes a promise in his word, there has to be faith on the part of humans to receive it" (WA 6:514,13–14 = LW 36:39; trans. alt.); but especially, "God does not deal with us, nor has he ever dealt with us, in any other way than through a word of promise, as I have said. We in turn cannot ever deal with God in any other way than through faith in the word of his promise" (6:516,30–32 = 36:42; trans. alt.).

120. WA 9:446,12–13 (author's emphasis). See WA 6:516,30–32 = LW 36:42 (cited in n. 119).

121. The quotation: WA 6:356,24–25 = LW 35:83. For the series of names, see the lists mentioned in n. 118. The prophetic books and the psalms are expressly mentioned in the sermon *Concerning the Testament of Christ*: 9:446,32–34.

122. WA 5:376,2–5: *Operationes in Psalmos*, 1520 (on Ps. 11:6).

makes the listener an individual.[123] Therefore, in the disputation *Concerning the Signs of Grace* that precedes *The Babylonian Captivity*, Luther defends the thesis (which will be treated in more detail in an excursus in chap. 7 [n. 107]) that "the same faith has existed in the elect from Abel throughout the various ages and will continue to exist in them until the end of the world."[124] For Luther, *promissio* is therefore not a category of revelation in salvation history in the sense that any promise is only one of the many promises that are only significant in their totality and their context of reference. According to the theory of *Heilsgeschichte*, God gave his promises one after the other over a period of time in a meaningful way that in retrospect, can be seen to be objectively predetermined in order to fulfill them—that is, to make them become reality—according to a calculable plan that is at least in someway understandable in terms of its necessity. In other words, *promissio* is not a historical or philosophical concept that could shed light on, in Luther's view, the uncanny and confused "masquerade" of history as a whole, and even if it could, it would mean abandoning the individual to their lamentation and despair, to sin and death, because such a concept would allow the kairos to be subsumed into the chronos by distributing the promise and its fulfillment to widely separated stations along the timeline. It would mean that in between these stations, the individual person would disappear completely from view and could not take comfort in the abstract general knowledge that they were already salvifically enfolded by the great passage of time from the outset without any particular knowledge of it.

Promissio is not a category of revelation in the philosophy of *Heilsgeschichte* but the epitome of proclamation. So, as we have seen, Luther cannot understand *promissio* in the Old Testament as a deferred promise but only as a truly comforting and saving promise there and then. "For such a promise, since it is the truth of God, preserves even in hell those who believe it and wait for it."[125] This ubiquitous validity of every promise has its legal basis in the ubiquitous validity of the one Christ event, the *new* testament. This insight also corrects the opinion that the

---

123. Cf. 6:521,19–24 = 36:48–49: "Why did Abraham not believe for all the Jews? Why was faith in the same promise that Abraham believed in demanded of every individual Jew? Therefore, let this irrefutable truth stand firm: where there is a divine promise, each single person must stand for themselves; their own faith is demanded of them, and each will give an account of themselves and carry their own load, as it says in the last chapter of Mark: 'Whoever believes and is baptized will be saved, but whoever does not believe will be condemned'" (trans. alt.).

The human being understood as an individual is therefore not anthropologically self-evident but an effect or result of the promise—that is, of the eschatological situation, created by the promise, that calls for decision. Cf. chap. 4, pp. 224–225.

124. WA 6:471,7–8.

125. WA 6:514:33–34 = LW 36:39 (trans. alt.).

latter could be understood from its Old Testament prefiguration: "This testament of Christ was foreshadowed in all the promises of God from the beginning of the world; *or rather*, all those ancient promises were valid in this new future promise in Christ, whatever they were, and depended on it."[126] For Luther, the difference between the Old and New Testaments does not lie in the promise itself but in how each testament sees the gift of salvation. With the abiding actuality and validity of the promise, the only thing that changes is the "inheritance." In the old covenant, it was the land of Canaan, and so it was "temporal" and "transitory," but in the new, it is "eternal and immortal":[127] "a great, eternal, and unspeakable treasure, namely, the forgiveness of all sins, as the words plainly declare."[128]

With his fundamental understanding of the words of institution as a testament, Luther can now easily press the disempowered *elements* of the Lord's Supper, which he almost only mentions in passing, back into service again.[129] If, according to the traditional view, the word was assigned to the element and so subordinate to it, the relationship is now the exact opposite because, as Luther often emphasizes, "There is more power in the word than in the sign."[130] "The sign may well be lacking, so long as we have the word; for a person can be saved without the sacrament, but not without the testament."[131] The elements themselves are "like a body without a soul, a cask without wine, a purse without money, a type without a fulfilment, a letter without the spirit, a sheath without a knife . . . a jewel case without the jewel."[132]

"A person can have the word or testament and use it apart from the sign or sacrament."[133] Nevertheless, as already in the old covenant—for example, in

126. WA 6:514,1–4 = LW 36:38 (trans. alt.; author's emphasis). The "or rather" (*immo*) indicates the turn in Luther's thinking. This also rules out a *heilsgeschichtlich* understanding of the parallel passage: "So it finally came to the most perfect promise of all, that of the new testament" (6:515,5–6 = 36:39). For more on the problem, see p. 364, esp. n. 104.

127. WA 6:358,5,8 = LW 35:84–85, in the context of the whole section (§9): The "little word 'new' makes the testament of Moses obsolete and worthless;" that is, it makes it nothing but a history bound to the land of Canaan. Over against the legacy of Moses, there stands Christ as "an eternal, divine person" who "speaks of 'a new testament,' so that the other may become obsolete and no longer be in effect . . . The purpose of all this is that the old should be altogether annulled and give place to the new alone" (trans. alt.).

128. WA 6:358,15–16 = LW 35:85 (trans. alt.); cf. 6:359,28–29 = 35:87.

129. WA 6:517,38–39 = LW 36:43: "This is surely true, that to every promise of his, God usually adds some sign."

130. WA 6:374,31–32 = LW 35:107 (trans. alt.); cf. 6:373,32–374,1 and 6:374,21–22 = 35:106.

131. WA 6:363,7–9 = LW 35:91.

132. WA 6:363,14–19 = LW 35:91.

133. WA 6:518,18–19 = LW 36:44.

the case of Noah, Abraham, and Gideon[134]—God added a sign to his promise "as a memorial or remembrance":[135] a "memorial"[136] to "remind" us of the promise[137] and to bind us even more to his word "in order to further safeguard and strengthen our faith . . . For this is also how secular testaments are made. Not only are the words written down, but seals and the marks of notaries are affixed to them, so that they are binding and reliable. This is what Christ has done in this testament. He has affixed a most powerful and noble seal and sign to the words of his testament: his own true flesh and blood under the bread and wine."[138] The fact that Christ gives himself completely and vouches for himself in his word can for Luther only further confirm the seal[139]—although this of course is a wrong understanding of the function of a seal and gives Eck the occasion to ridicule Luther's "ignorance of the law."[140]

The sermon *Concerning the Testament of Christ* clearly shows why the elements are so important to Luther and why he clings to them so stubbornly: The sign is given "so that human nature might grasp God more surely and fasten on to some particular sign by which it grasps him and not wander or waver in its speculations."[141]

The sign thus ensures that we are guided to the specific place of the word, which we must now consider with the third aspect of the gifting words of the testament (*pro vobis*, for you).

---

134. WA 6:518,2–9 = LW 36:43–44. Cf. n. 118.

135. WA 6:518,1 = LW 36:43. The continuation (ll. 1–2): "so that it may thereby keep us the more faithfully and admonish us (i.e. the promise!) the more effectually." See 6:515,22–24 = 36:40: "I shall give my body and pour out my blood . . . leaving you my body and blood as a sign and memorial of this same promise."

136. For Luther, the sign "admonishes." This is clear from his understanding of the elevation. It is "an admonition to us to provoke us to faith in this testament, which he (i.e. the priest) then offers and gives with the words of Christ so that as he shows the sign of this testament, at the same time the offering of the bread properly corresponds to the demonstrative 'this' in the words, 'this is my body,' and the priest addresses those gathered around him with this very sign; in the same way, the offering of the cup properly corresponds to the demonstrative 'this' in the words, 'this cup of the new testament etc.' For the priest is to awaken faith in us by this very rite of elevation" (WA 6:524,24–30 = LW 36:53; trans. alt.).

137. Cf. the *Sermon for Corpus Christi* of 1520: "The word of God is quickly forgotten unless the external sign admonishes us" (WA 4:704,39–40).

138. WA 6:358,36–359,6 = LW 35:86 (trans. alt.).

139. For more, see pp. 359–363.

140. See E. Iserloh, *Die Eucharistie in der Darstellung des Johannes Eck*, 169.

141. WA 9:448,34–6.

3. Naming of the Heir

The Mass is the place where the legacy of Christ is opened and distributed to its recipients in such a way that they experience concretely that "this inestimable promise of Christ belongs *to them*":[142] "The promises are given *to you right here* or proclaimed *to you* through the ministry of the priest."[143] The whole celebration of the Mass must serve this proclamation and distribution. Thus it is Luther's wish that just as the priest "elevates the sign or sacrament openly before our eyes, so he would also proclaim in our ears the word or testament in a loud clear voice, and in the language of the people, whatever it is, in order that faith may be the more effectively awakened."[144] For Luther, the Mass is Christ's legacy and, in accordance with his words, is meant for its recipients ("for you!"), to move them to faith. Therefore, he deplores the "captivity" of the Mass locked away as it is in incomprehensible words and fights against the "perversion"[145] of having the gifting words in a ritual formula in which "the words of consecration . . . are to be said secretly."[146] This perversion, stemming from the fact that the sign has been the sole center of attention, means that the word has been forgotten[147]—although not completely. What is forgotten is that the word is a concrete, oral promise: "Even if they teach these words of Christ, they do not teach them as a promise or testament, and therefore not as a means of obtaining faith."[148]

For Luther, the right understanding of the Mass is necessary for the right understanding of the gospel. "For unless we firmly hold that the mass is the promise or testament of Christ, as the words clearly say, we shall lose the whole gospel and all its comfort."[149] Whether the *whole* gospel is lost or gained depends on whether in the Lord's Supper the promise, but equally whether the promise in the Lord's Supper, is surrendered or retained. For the *promissio* specifically in the Lord's Supper (that is, the gifting word in its three aspects and in its concrete *Sitz im Leben*) is not the only promise for Luther, but—in the context of the

142. WA 6:515,35 = LW 36:41 (author's emphasis; trans. alt.).

143. WA 6:517,31–32 = LW 36:43 (author's emphasis; trans. alt.).

144. WA 6:524,30–33 = LW 36:53–54 (trans. alt.).

145. WA 6:516,27–29 = LW 36:42: "For what more sinful idolatry can there be than to abuse God's promises with perverse opinions and to neglect or extinguish faith in them?"

146. WA 6:516,17–29 = LW 36:41 (trans. alt.). See 6:520,7–19 = 36:46–47.

147. WA 6:518,24–33 = LW 36:44–45.

148. WA 6:516,15–16 = LW 36:41. There will be more on this polemic in the next chapter.

149. WA 6:523,17–19 = LW 36:51.

baptismal promise[150]—it is, however, the epitome of its uniqueness and thus the basic text, summary, and norm of every *sermon*. Thus he can say:

> The mass is a part of the gospel; indeed, the sum and substance of the gospel. For what is the whole gospel but the good news of the forgiveness of sins? Whatever can be said about the forgiveness of sins and the mercy of God in the most expansive and copious way is briefly contained in the words of the testament. Hence, popular sermons should be nothing but expositions of the mass, that is, declarations of the divine promise of this testament.[151]

The inseparable[152] *connection and interpenetration of the sermon and the Lord's Supper, demanded here and also practiced by Luther,*[153] *denotes the origin and center of his reformational preaching. According to this connection, the sermon on the one hand is an exposition of the gifting words of the Lord's Supper, and the Supper, on the other hand, is an opportunity to preach precisely about the promise of the testament.* Luther insists that "had there been no preaching, Christ would never have instituted the mass."[154]

In a broader context, this understanding is expressed in Luther's exegetical writings of the same time, as the following *excursus* shows.

Our starting point is the German version of the text just quoted from *The Babylonian Captivity of the Church*, the last sentence of which takes us further.

> What is the whole gospel but a proclamation of this testament? Christ has comprehended the whole gospel in a short summary with the words of this testament or sacrament. For the gospel is nothing but a proclamation of God's grace and the forgiveness of all sins, granted us through the sufferings of Christ, as St. Paul proves in Romans 10 and Christ

150. See p. 314.

151. WA 6:525,36–526,2 = LW 36:56 (trans. alt.). Cf. the *Treatise on Good Works* on the third commandment:The sermon should be nothing else than the proclamation of this testament" (6:231,16–17 = 44:56).

152. "They too should teach that the Eucharist is connected [with the sermon] so that they are never separated" (WA 4:610,19; the Melchizedek sermon, mentioned by Melanchthon in his letter to J. Hess of Apr. 27, 1520 [CR 1:159; cf. WA 9:317] and thus preached Mar./Apr. 1520).

153. See pp. 288–289.

154. WA 6:373,31–32 = LW 35:106.

in Luke 24. And the words of this testament also contain the same thing.[155]

The reference to Luke 24:46–47 leads to the *Galatians Commentary* of 1519: "Concerning the gospel, the last chapter of Luke says: 'Thus it was necessary that Christ should suffer and rise again from the dead, and that repentance and forgiveness of sins should be preached to all nations in his name.' (Note especially, 'in *his* name,' not 'in *ours*.') Here you see the preaching of the forgiveness of sins through the name of Christ, which is the gospel."[156] What "through the name of Christ" means becomes surprisingly clear from another passage from the same commentary. Here it says of faith that "it is given through the Holy Spirit, because of Christ's merit, in the word and hearing of the gospel."[157] The merit of Christ is expressed in his "name"; it is the abiding foundation for the church's preaching, "the preaching of the forgiveness of sins" here and now in the "promise of absolution." If the death of Christ is the testamentary sealing, the *enactment* of the promise of absolution, then its proclamatory opening, its *coming into effect*, can be nothing other than his resurrection. For the actual apprehension of Christ's death takes place through faith in his resurrection,[158] as a grateful and obedient acceptance of the promise of absolution with which Christ claims to be Lord and asserts his lordship ("ruling, and through the gospel, proclaimed and believed"[159]). The crucified one having been "raised" thus exercises his authority and power as the "proclaimed one,"[160] specifically "through the church's ministry of preaching," which as "the fruit of the resurrection of the crucified Christ" lets us experience the "power of God for salvation."[161]

In his unjustifiably little-known interpretation of Psalm 22 in the *Operationes*, which we use as the basis for the following remarks, Luther goes on to say (on v. 22: I WILL TELL OF YOUR NAME TO MY BROTHERS AND SISTERS; IN THE MIDST OF THE CONGREGATION I WILL PRAISE YOU): "There is a ministry because this word of salvation in the name of the Lord is entrusted not to letters and books, but to the clear and living confession

155. WA 6:374,3–9 = LW 35:106 (trans. alt.).

156. WA 2:466,9–13 = LW 27:184 (on 1:11–12) (trans. alt.).

157. WA 2:518,22 = LW 27:263 (on 3:13–14) (trans. alt.).

158. WA 57/3:193,18–24 = LW 29:195 (Scholion on Heb. 7:22: the guarantor of a testament); 1518. For this in context, see pp. 363–365.

159. WA 5:550,2–3 (*Operationes in Psalmos*; on Ps. 20:6); 1520.

160. WA 5:514,22 (*Operationes*; on Ps. 18:16); 1520.

161. WA 5:514,11–16 (on Ps. 18:15) and 5:658,21–6 (on Ps. 22:22); 1520/21.

of the voice, so that it is not only known but preached publicly, urgently, in season and out of season."[162] Sacred Scripture in itself is not sufficient here. It serves only as a last resort in case the power of the oral word is suppressed.[163] The word is not just meant to be known but "to provoke the whole world"; it should not be read for itself but rather "be made public."[164]

What constitutes the reformational understanding of the word can be judged not least from its contrast to Luther's earlier theology and its high regard for the internal word typical of Augustine. If earlier, the "word" (in the sense of the inner "power of the word") was the "soul of the voice,[165] now the "voice" is the "soul of the word." For writing does not harm or benefit as much as speaking, the spoken word is preeminent over the written word, because the voice is the soul of the word.[166] Nor is it necessary that the words of the Lord should be limited to those taken into our voice from the Scriptures, but the words of the Lord are whatever words God speaks through people, whether they are uneducated or

---

162. WA 5:657,33–35. Cf. the continuation (ll. 36–38): "It is also said in Ps. 8: 'Out of the mouth,' not out of the pen, 'of babies, you have perfected strength.' And again, 'the heavens' do not ponder but 'declare the glory of God.' Therefore, to come forth publicly and preach openly and provoke the whole world, is not within human strength."

163. "For after they had suppressed everything to do with the word and faith, so that neither the power of the vocal word (speech) nor the fruit of faith flourished openly in the church, only that one memorial remained, and only by examining it were we able to remember Christ, and through this remembrance nourish and restore ourselves to word and faith, that is to say, through the sacred scripture, contained not in the voice, but in the letters" (WA 5:643,25–29; on Ps. 22:18).

164. On the quotations, see n. 162. Especially significant for Luther's understanding of the word is the interpretation of Ps. 18:44 (AT THE HEARING OF THE EAR, THEY OBEYED ME): "In the church it is not enough that books be written and read, but they must be spoken and heard. For this reason, Christ wrote nothing but spoke everything. The apostles wrote a few things but said many things. Thus, although David could have said in Ps. 19, 'their book goes out into all the earth,' he said instead, 'their sound goes out,' that is, their living voice. It is not their writings that go out to the ends of the earth but 'their words.' And again, 'there are no speeches or words whose voices are not heard' (v. 3). Notice: it says let their voices be heard not, let their books be read. For the ministry of the new testament is not engraved on dead tablets of stone but entrusted to living voices. From there and elsewhere, it says, 'God has spoken in his holy one.' For now the apostle, who once wrote in the synagogue, speaks in the church, and through the Holy Scriptures promised the gospel (Rom. 1). But through the living word he enacts and performs the gospel. Therefore, we should strive all the harder to ensure that there are many preachers rather than good writers in the church" (WA 5:537,10–22).

165. Cf. esp. the Christmas sermon of 1514 (WA 1:20–29); and, in addition, see chap. 1, esp. pp. 4–11 and p. 17.

166. Of the many texts quoted in the 1514 Christmas sermon, see, for example, WA 1:30,22–23 (Sermon of Dec. 26, 1514): "The letter is a dead voice but the voice a living letter, yet the thought is still dead, although the thought written by the finger of God is the life of the voice and of the letter."

learned, even apart from the use of Scripture, just as he spoke in his apostles and still speaks in his own. Therefore, the words are of the Lord when the Lord speaks in us but not the words that someone simply quotes from Scripture, which even the demons and the ungodly can do, but God does not speak in or through them, nor are they any longer the words of God.[167]

Just like mere Scripture, mere history is also useless. It is not enough to recount the story of Jesus's life and death. "For many preach Christ, but in such a way that they never say or understand anything about his use and benefits, like the crowd of preachers who even at their best preach nothing but stories about Christ."[168] They are mere storytellers who preach Christ's passion purely as historical fact but teach nothing about its use and fruit.[169]

After this excursus, we now return to the text of the testament sermon.

The "naming of the heir," which we must consider here, occurs publicly and orally and is "done physically"[170] at the place of the living voice (*viva vox*) or preached word. This word opens and "bequeaths"[171] to us, by the authority of the risen Christ,[172] the testament that was put into effect by the death of Jesus that took place then and once and for all. For "everything in this testament must be living. Therefore, Christ did not inaugurate it with dead letters and seals, but with living words and signs such as we use every day."[173] This "handing on of

---

167. WA 5:379,6–13 (on Ps. 12:6); 1520.

168. WA 5:543,14–16 (on Ps. 19:2); 1520.

169. WA 5:544,17–18. Both passages should be compared to the freedom tractate of the same time: §18 (7:29) or 7:58,31–59,6; cf. LW 31:357.

170. WA 6:372,25 = LW 35:104 (trans. alt.).

171. Throughout, for example, WA 6:358,15 = LW 35:85; 6:359,28 = 35:87

172. Cf. again the interpretation of Ps. 22:22, which here completely agrees with Luther's Easter sermon of 1521, which we will treat below on pp. 368–370: "For it is true that Christ had to die, since he had foretold so much about his death, lest he be guilty of lying. Again, it must be true that the same name of God will be told about and praised. Therefore, either he is dead and alive at the same time, or he is resurrected from the dead and thus declares and praises God, but not alive and dead at the same time since that would be impossible and absurd. For Christ was neither, nor could he ever have been, a living man and a dead man at the same time, although he was at the same time a dead man and the living God with two different natures in one and the same person, so that it is rightly said that the person was both alive and dead at the same time, but not the nature. Therefore, Christ here foretells his resurrection, or better, the fruit and work of his resurrection, which is the praise and glory of God, that God heard his prayers and saved him from death, for which he says that new and wonderful things will be told of him and that he will praise God's name and give him thanks" (WA 5:657,5–16; 1521).

173. WA 6:359,20–22 = LW 35:86–87 (trans. alt.).

the promise"[174] is what Christ himself expressly willed[175] "when he commanded this testament to be commemorated or remembered, not that he needs it, but because we need it, so that we can remember him."[176] This "duty, remembrance, or commemoration, which we are to carry out for Christ,"[177] is not imposed on us for the sake of a dead man who needs remembering but for our own sake, for our salvation.[178]

With the understanding of the *nuncupatio* (naming) outlined so far, we have also seen Luther's notion of *commemoratio* (remembrance). The sermon *Concerning the Testament of Christ* formulates it briefly and succinctly: "We remember Christ when we confess that he is the one who has destroyed sin, and through whom all spiritual goods (= 'forgiveness of sins, together with righteousness, life, and peace') have been bequeathed to us."[179] As in the section on baptism in *The Babylonian Captivity of the Church*,[180] "remembrance" here is interpreted by "confession." But the confession answers the promise that declares that the crucified Lord has destroyed sin, strife, and death; it is the acknowledgment that the one who died for the world shows himself alive in the comfort of the forgiveness of sins given in his name through the living voice (*viva voce*).

> This is shown by the fact that the Lord, when he instituted the mass, said, "Do this in remembrance of me," as if he were saying, "As often as you use this sacrament and testament you shall be preaching of me." As St. Paul also says in 1 Corinthians 11[:26], "As often as you eat this bread and drink this cup you preach and proclaim the Lord's death until he comes"; and Psalm 102[:21–22], "They shall declare in Zion the glory of the Lord, and in Jerusalem his praise, as often as the kings (that is,

174. Cf. WA 6:517,1–2 = LW 36:42.

175. The fact that, as Luther unquestionably assumes, the "do this" is spoken by the historical Jesus does not make it a theological argument. For Luther, Paul's appeal to proclaim the Lord's death (1 Cor. 11:26) is exactly the same as Jesus's exhortation to celebrate the sacrament for his remembrance (1 Cor. 11:24–25): WA 6:373,16–21 = LW 35:105.

176. WA 6:358,26–28 = LW 35:85 (trans. alt.).

177. WA 6:359,30 = LW 35:86 (trans. alt.).

178. Cf. the interpretation of Ps. 20:1 (WA 5:543,17–21): "It is not yet Christian preaching if you preach Christ purely as a fact of history . . . but you must teach the story of Christ in such a way that it is of benefit to us who believe for righteousness and salvation, and that we may know that he did all things not for himself but for us by the will of God the Father, and that all things that are in Christ are ours."

179. WA 9:447,26–28, 8–9.

180. See p. 313.

> the bishops and rulers) and the people gather together to worship the Lord"; and Psalm 111[:4–5], "He has instituted a remembrance of his wonderful works . . ." In these passages you can see how the mass was instituted to preach Christ.[181]

"Remembering Christ," therefore, means, on the one hand, proclaiming his death, letting him speak for himself as a living person in the promise of the forgiveness of sins: "Take . . . this is my body . . . for you . . . for the forgiveness of sins!" and, on the other hand, taking him at his word ("We remember Christ when we confess"). We can take hold of him in his word, because that is where he allows himself to be grasped by us—and with this Luther genuinely understands the Old Testament word *remember* (*zakar*).[182]

We have already seen the peculiar ambivalence of the remembrance (*commemoratio*) in the first Psalms lectures: "Christ remembers us, that is, makes us remember him."[183] In addition, here, too, it is already emphasized what the Reformation understanding undoubtedly implies, that with "remembrance" (in the psalms), the human ability to remember is not addressed philosophically.[184] But its "reality" and "effectiveness"[185] does not yet lie, as in the testament sermon of 1520, in proclamation and acclamation, thus in a specific oral and binding word, but in the meditation of the "remorseful penitent," and so in the "internal sacrament" described above.[186] It designates the realization of a penitent's penitential existence that actually verifies itself in itself, which is why the two understandings of remembrance quite logically coincide, so that Luther can say, "When we forget him, he has forgotten us, since it is the one and the same forgetting."[187] On the other hand, in 1520 the two sides of remembrance are distinguished by the oral word (of salvation). *In reformational theology, the*

181. WA 6:373,16–26 = LW 35:105 (trans. alt.).

182. Cf., for example, Exod. 20:24: "At the place where I cause my name to be remembered, I will come to you and bless you."

183. WA 3:539,7–8 = LW 11:22 (on Ps. 77:5; trans. alt.); 1513–15.

184. WA 3:531,8–10 = LW 11:11 (on the same psalm): "Memory must not be taken here as in philosophy as a distinct part of the soul. But the most extensive significance for the persistence of any power . . ." (the text here is corrupt).

185. See n. 184.

186. WA 3:539,16–24 = LW 11:23 (on v. 5) in the context of the interpretation of the whole psalm. See on this above, pp. 30–31.

187. WA 3:539,14–15 = LW 11:22 (trans. alt.) (cf. ll. 5–6).

remembrance of Christ is not dependent on the penitential effect, our feeling of repentance, and our neediness, but on the power of the oral word.

In summary, it can said that according to the conception of the testament sermon, the remembrance (*commemoratio*) of Christ is not, as in Luther's early conception of the Mass,[188] an awareness of Christ's suffering through one's self-mortification, let alone a memory that leaps back noetically into history to Jesus's death on Calvary, but the certainty of God's salvific coming to us and his presence with us here and now, which is self-authenticating and at the same time gives us courage. Buoyed by this courage, we listen to the "the naming of the heir," which is grounded in Jesus's death, enacted in the promise of absolution, and thus bound to the specific place of the Lord's Supper and the sermon. As God names us as heirs, he calls us by our name; that is, he addresses us as sinners and at the same time grants us forgiveness. Luther himself gives a striking example of this sort of remembrance in a sermon that, according to his program, is meant to be an exposition and declaration of the promise of the Lord's Supper, revealing Christ's person and work in the word to all who listen. "'Finally, I leave you this, my very self, as a sign that you are mine and I am yours. Be of good cheer: all your sins are now forgiven you. The Father is reconciled. The devil, hell, and death, along with the world, are overcome . . . You are now the blessed children of God.' O how blessed are those who take to heart and cling to this testament."[189]

188. Cf. pp. 102–119.

189. WA 4:618,34–619,2: *Sermon on the Distinction between the Old and New Testament.* This sermon is very close in time to the testament sermon (cf. 4:618,21–32 with 6:357,28–358,13). E. Vogelsang, "Zur Datierung der frühesten Lutherpredigten" (*ZKG* 50 [1931]: 112–45, here 133) would even like to assume its identity with the sermon *Concerning the Testament of Christ* of Apr. 8, 1520.

CHAPTER 7

Promise and Baptism

A) Sermon on Baptism (November 1519)

AS IN THE preceding *Sermon on the Sacrament of Penance* (chapter 5) and in the *Sermon on the Lord's Supper* that follows it (chapter 6), so also here in the *Sermon on the Holy and Blessed Sacrament of Baptism*[1] Luther sees the sacrament as being constituted by three things: the sign, its significance, and faith.

The sign, corresponding to the etymology of the word *baptism* (§1), is to be found in the act of dipping in (immersion) and drawing out. The act itself happened quickly. But its significance, "a blessed dying to sin and a resurrection in the grace of God,"[2] lasts until death or until the last day. As in the Lord's Supper sermon,[3] Luther also tries here to deal with the sign and its significance linguistically, but in this way he initially only arrives at an "interpretation" of the sign ("as the priest says"): "Whoever is baptized is condemned to death, as the priest says when he baptizes, 'Behold, you are sinful flesh. Therefore, I drown you in God's name and in his name condemn you to death, so that all your sins die and perish with you.'"[4] But such an interpretation does not mean that the sign is allegorical, merely a cipher for its lived significance. Rather, the signified event has already begun with the sign, and with it the beginning of this life has been established, which gives space and measure to the new life. Thus, after repeated attempts at formulating this, signaling his special interest in it, Luther can make a *distinction* between baptism understood as a symbolic event that has already taken place, in which the "old Adam" *is* already "completely drowned"[5] and the new person *is* already born, and baptism understood as the time of the baptized—determined by the sign in its significance—the movement of which *will be* fulfilled only with the last day. "And therefore": "As far as the significance or sign of the sacrament is concerned, sin is already dead with the person and

1. WA 2:724–37 = LW 35:23–43.

2. WA 2:272,30–31 = LW 35:30 (§3) and frequently.

3. See p. 258.

4. WA 2:728,17–21 = LW 35:30–31 (§4) (trans. alt.)

5. On these formulations, see WA 2:727,16–17, 31–32 = LW 35:29–30; 2:728,10 = 35:30; 2:729 = 35:31–32 (§6) in various places); 2:734,38 = 35:39.

that person is risen, and so the sacrament has taken place but the work of the sacrament has not yet been fully accomplished, that is, the death and resurrection at the Last Day are still to come."[6] It cannot be denied that the sacrament as a significative event has gained an importance it did not have according to the earlier texts. It is now supposed to mean more than a possibility that always has to be realized anew.[7] But does this not mean that the schema of the sign and its significance must be completely done away with?[8]

Luther is not satisfied with the view just outlined (based on §§1–8) and so, driven by the question, "How does Baptism help me, if it does not blot out and remove sin completely?"[9] he makes a new attempt in section 9 to understand the sacrament of baptism.

The concept that dominates the new conception, which is meant to specify the event outlined in sections 1–8 with its focus on the event,[10] is that of "*covenant*."[11] Luther explicitly refers to it in his Genesis sermons from the same period[12]: "This blessed Sacrament of Baptism helps you because God unites himself with you and becomes one with you in a gracious covenant of comfort."[13]

It turns out that the notion of the covenant as such does not yet help him arrive at a strictly promissional definition of the sacrament as an event of word and faith, such as we find in the 1519 *Sermon on the Sacrament of Penance.* Luther at first stays within the framework of the hermeneutic of signification[14] and

6. WA 2:729,34–730,2 = LW 35:32 (§7) (trans. alt.). Cf. §8: "So half the sacrament is true, that is, the person is without sin and guilt. But because the sacrament is not yet complete, and that person still lives in the sinful flesh, they are not without sin nor are they pure in all things, but they have started to become pure and guiltless" (2:730,7–10 = 35:33; trans. alt.).

7. See pp. 22–25 and p. 309.

8. Can we say of the same thing that it has already "taken place" (§7) and (§8) that it "only signifies"?

9. WA 2:730:18–19 = LW 35:33.

10. "This is the place for a right understanding of the sacrament of baptism" (WA 2:730,19–20 = LW 35:33).

11. Especially instructive is the parallelism of "sacrament" and "covenant" (= *foedus, pactum*) in §10 (WA 2:731,11 = LW 35:34). Obviously, for Luther it is enough at first to define the "sacrament" as "covenant."

12. Cf. see p. 177. It is surprising, therefore, that Luther does not immediately start using it.

13. WA 2:730,20–22 = LW 35:33 (trans. alt.).

14. "First, you surrender yourself to the Sacrament of Baptism and its *significance.* That is, you desire to die, together with your sins . . . as the sacrament *indicates*" (WA 2:730,23–25 = LW 35:33; trans. alt.; author's emphasis).

tries to understand the mutual relationship of God and humans in *it*.[15] But he realizes that clarity cannot be achieved in this way. Thus it is not clear *how* it can happen that after sin, "you rise again and enter into the covenant again" and "it is already gone by the power of the sacrament and covenant."[16] The reference given here to Christ as our advocate before God and to baptism as the place "where Christ is given to us"[17] remains unexplained and is a notion that does not come into play in the whole context.[18]

As the sermon continues (§§11–20), the understanding of *promissio*, which had previously only been mentioned in one place,[19] becomes more and more apparent. It was developed in the outline of the *Pro veritate* theses from the first sermon of the series, the one on penance. The fact that Luther wanted to align himself with his new understanding of the sacrament of penance and thus with a *linguistic*, oral, and public (more precisely, forensic) event is evident from the formulation that through baptism, "we enter into the *judgment* of grace and mercy."[20] If the concept of imputation appears, which is directly related to this,[21] it is understood in a new way compared to the earlier use of the Augustinian quote from *On Marriage and Concupiscence*[22] that includes it. The non-imputation of sin is now no longer longed for and sighed for as something still in the future, as in the series of scholia on 4:7 in the Romans lectures,[23] but has finally come

---

15. The way it is described is quite problematical: "*You* surrender yourself to the Sacrament of Baptism and to what it signifies. . . and *God* will accept this from you"; "*you* pledge yourself to remain in your Baptism, and to slay your sin more and more . . . this too *God* will accept" (§9); and (§10): "So long as you keep your pledge to God, he in turn will give you his grace and pledge not to impute to you your sin" (trans. alt.; author's emphasis).

16. WA 2:731,9–11 = LW 35:34 (§10).

17. WA 2:731,16–17 = LW 35:34.

18. It is then stated in the *Sermon on the Lord's Supper* (WA 2:744,19–30 = LW 35:53; §7), to which Luther himself expressly refers: "as we will hear in the following sermon" (2:731,17 = 35:34; trans. alt.). In §7 of the *Sermon on the Lord's Supper*, we can see the early form of the baptismal remembrance corresponding to this, which Luther in *The Babylonian Captivity* understands to be the Lord's Supper (6:529,3–4 = 36:60; for this, see p. 314).

19. WA 2:728,17–21; cf. LW 35:30–31 (quoted above on p. 291). We should pay attention to the words *condemned* [*urteilen*], *says* [*sprechen*], *condemn* [*Urteil*].

20. WA 2:731,21 = LW 35:34 (§11) (trans. alt.).

21. WA 2:731,22ff. = LW 35:34–35 [Augustine: "Sin is altogether forgiven in Baptism; not in such a manner that it is no longer present, but in such a manner that it is not imputed."].

22. WA 1:25,28 (MPL 44:430): see *BoA* 1:189, note on l. 31, and J. Ficker, WA 56:273 on I. 10.

23. WA 56:273,10–11 = LW 25:261. For the whole context of this passage, see chap. 2 L ("Promise and Supplication") 3.

about with baptism (as a significative event that has taken place). *We no longer need to anticipate it in uncertain hope but can fall back on it in certain faith, indeed "remember" it*[24]—to use the term that then becomes dominant in *The Babylonian Captivity of the Church*.[25] The "calling upon God's grace," understood as a "remembrance,"[26] takes place quite differently to the supplication for grace in the sense of the Romans lectures,[27] in that through his covenant God is bound to baptism. Therefore, we can fearlessly say: "I will remind God of his covenant."[28] "This is why we must boldly cling to Baptism without fear, hold fast to it in the face of all our sin and terrors of conscience, and humbly say, 'I know very well that I cannot do a single thing that is pure. But I am baptized, and through my Baptism God, who cannot lie, has bound himself not to count my sin against me but to slay it and blot it out.'"[29] Understood that way, the "calling upon God's grace" is the "remembrance" of baptism, and the imputation, "the reckoning of God's grace,"[30] is experienced as comfort—"as the prophet says in Psalm 32[:1–2], 'Blessed are those whose sins are forgiven; blessed are those to whom the Lord imputes no iniquity.'"[31]

The opportunity to hear such words of comfort, "turn back from your sins and call on the covenant of your Baptism,"[32] comes specifically in the priestly absolution in section 15. It is undoubtedly the culmination of the rather surprising course of the whole discussion, given the outline of the sermon at the

---

24. WA 2:731,30,35 = LW 35:35 (§11). See 2:733,16 = 35:37; 2:737,19 = 35:43. This "remembrance" on our part is the work of God himself, who remembers his promises and stands by them. "You will notice everywhere in the Scriptures that this is the use of the Spirit, the way the Lord used to remember his promises. Take the promise by which the Lord said to Noah in [Genesis] chapter 6: 'I will make a covenant with you, and you will have a bow as a sign of the covenant' etc. 'For I will destroy the earth.' After the flood ceased, the Lord is mindful of his promise and remembers Noah. Further, just as he saved Noah from the flood by pure mercy, without any merit on his part, so here he cares for Noah out of his gratuitous kindness" (9:345,26–32; Luther's sermon on Gen. 8:1: BUT THE LORD REMEMBERED NOAH etc. This sermon is preached at the same time as the *Sermon on Baptism*).

25. Cf. pp. 311–314.

26. WA 2:731,36 = LW 35:35 (§11). Cf. 2:737,21–22 = 35:43 (trans. alt.).

27. Cf. pp. 146–153.

28. WA 2:737,19–20 = LW 35:43 (§20).

29. WA 2:732,19–24 = LW 35:36 (§12) (trans. alt.).

30. WA 2:732,14 = LW 35:36 (§12) (trans. alt.).

31. WA 2:732,15–16 = LW 35:36 (§12) (trans. alt.).

32. WA 2:737,21–22 = LW 35:43 (§20) (trans. alt.).

beginning (based on the three parts of baptism: sign, significance, and faith), when Luther says here that

> the sacrament of penance thus renews and points again to the Sacrament of Baptism when the priest says in the absolution, "Behold, God has now forgiven you your sin, as he promised you earlier in Baptism and now commands me to do by the power of the keys. So now you are coming again into the essence and work of Baptism, what it is and what it does." Believe it, and you have it. Doubt it, and you are lost.[33]

It has already been shown that the last sentence is Luther's version of Mark 16:16.[34] However, according to *The Babylonian Captivity*, Mark 16:16 is the promise that constitutes the sacrament of baptism. Now we see here in section 15 of the *Sermon on the Sacrament of Baptism* for the first time the formulation of the connection between baptism and penance (repentance). This formulation, in the sense of the reformational understanding of the promise, which was initially attached to the sacrament of penance, culminates in Mark 16:16 and so points to *the place of origin of the reformational view of baptism*. And so at the same time as discovering the connection between the sacrament of baptism and the sacrament of penance, Luther also discovered the shape of the sacrament of baptism, and this has not fundamentally changed since *The Babylonian Captivity of the Church*.[35] From the specific place and the specific manner of the remembrance baptism—namely, the external, oral word of absolution—Luther recognized that the basis[36] and object of this remembrance is constituted by the *promise*. But the promise here is no longer understood in the sense of the promise of judgment, as in the first Psalms lectures and the Romans lectures.[37]

The fact that section 15 is the climax and result upshot of the sermon is proven by its use in *The Babylonian Captivity*, where baptism is clearly defined

33. WA 2:733,31–36 = LW 35:38 (§15) (trans. alt.). The difference to §4 ("Whoever is baptized is condemned to death, as the priest says when he baptizes") is clear: There the symbolic event is interpreted; here in the region of the new understanding of the word about the keys, it is dealt with directly in connection with the oral word of promise.

34. See pp. 224–225.

35. On the slight shifts that occur during the later years, see L. Grönvik, who in *Die Taufe in der Theologie Martin Luthers* presents Luther's doctrine of baptism from the standpoint of *The Babylonian Captivity of the Church* (*Acta Academiae Aboensis*, Series A, Vol. 36:1, 1968).

36. WA 2:733,28–29 = LW 35:38 (§15): "The sacrament of penance . . . has its *basis* in this sacrament" (trans. alt.; author's emphasis).

37. See chap. 2 I ("The Fulfillment of the Promise in Judgment").

as precisely the event of promise and faith according to Mark 16:16. In a move that is decisive for his new understanding of the whole of baptism, Luther here no longer finds its starting point in the visible event but in the audible promise. However, at the beginning of the *Sermon on Baptism*, the visible event still represented the overriding viewpoint, but this is now subordinated to the promise and "comprehended" in it, as Luther will later say.[38]

Finally, a point already touched on deserves special emphasis—namely, the distinction between baptism that has already occurred and baptism that is still occurring. Unlike the understanding of baptism in the earlier texts, according to which "the ongoing spiritual actualization of the baptismal event made the date of the act unimportant,"[39] and where the distinction was therefore made in the sense of that between a possibility and its ever-new actualization, here the distinction is made in such a way that baptism, as an event that has taken place in the past, has and retains primacy over baptism as an ongoing event, not just in an ideal but in a concrete sense. This distinction is specifically addressed in the last part of the sermon. At the same time, it contains the starting point or organizing principle of Luther's reformational ethics, which is of interest here only because of its connection with the promise.

It is no coincidence that the clearest formulation of the above distinction (also in Luther's own judgment) comes in section 15, the section in which Luther arrives at an understanding of baptism in line with his reformational concept of promise: "To put it as plainly as possible, it is one thing to forgive sins, and another to renounce them or drive them out. The forgiveness of sins is obtained by *faith*, even though they are not entirely driven out. The way to drive out sins is *to exercise ourselves against them* and finally die, for in death sin perishes completely. But the work of Baptism is both: the forgiveness of sins and the driving out of sins."[40] Faith according to the early texts[41] was not to be distinguished from mortification because it alone was said to give faith its concrete shape. But now the relationship between faith and mortification is such that faith is the basis and mortification the result. Hence Luther can say: "For so long as I believe that God will not count my sins against me, my Baptism is efficacious and my sins are forgiven . . . *Afterwards* they are driven out through sufferings and dying."[42] Earlier, our relationship with God and

38. The *Small Catechism*, *BSLK* 515,25–27 = *BC* 359,1–2.

39. W. Jetter, *Die Taufe beim jungen Luther*, 341.

40. WA 2:733,39–734, 5 = LW 35:38 (trans. alt.; author's emphasis).

41. Found at various places throughout the first part of this investigation.

42. WA 2:734,7–10 = LW 35:38 (trans. alt.; author's emphasis).

the world in the sense of our self-humiliation are factually identical.[43] But now they are sharply distinguished, so that the second follows from the first. The relationship with God is established with baptism, which took place as a promise "in which forgiveness is bestowed on account of God's pledge with us."[44] The relationship with the world, on the other hand, has been "established by God through many estates in which we are to learn to exercise ourselves and to suffer. To some he has entrusted the estate of matrimony, to others the spiritual estate (that of the clergy), to still others the estate of temporal rule, and to all he has given the command that they toil and work to kill the flesh and accustom it to death."[45]

The "many estates" are the individuations of the one measure of baptism, which as the one "requirement" that follows from the gift of the one baptismal promise is common to all the baptized:[46] "God has given each of his saints a special knowledge and grace to live according to their Baptism. But God has made Baptism and its significance a common measure for everyone. Each of us is called to examine ourselves according to our station in life and to find what for us is the best way of fulfilling our Baptism, namely, to slay sin and die."[47] The consequences of this basic text of reformational ethics, which Luther rightly judges to be a rediscovery[48] when compared to the traditional ethics handed down to him, do not need to be presented here in any more detail, especially since they arise directly from what he has already said,[49] even before he discusses

43. Cf. pp. 337–339 (esp. n. 127) and pp. 341–343.

44. WA 2:734,11–12 = LW 35:38–39 (§15) (trans. alt.).

45. WA 2:734,25–28 = LW 35:39 (trans. alt.). Cf. the continuation (ll. 28–33): "For all who are baptized, their Baptism has made the repose, ease, and prosperity of this life a very poison and hinderance to its work. For in the easy life no one learns to suffer, to die willingly, to get rid of sin, and to live in harmony with their Baptism. Instead, there grows only love of this life and dread of eternal life, fear of death and the unwillingness to blot out sin."

46. WA 2:735,4 = LW 35:40 (§17) (trans. alt.).

47. WA 2:735,18–22 = LW 35:40 (§17) (trans. alt.).

48. "But unfortunately, as we have forgotten about Baptism and what it means, and what we have promised to do, and how we are to walk in it and attain its end, we have also forgotten about the estates and orders and the ways to reach that end, and we almost do not know to what end these estates and orders were instituted or how we are to conduct ourselves in them to fulfil our Baptism": §18 (WA 2:736,25–29 = LW 35:42; trans. alt.).

49. WA 2:735,34–736,1 = LW 35:41 (§18): "From what has been said, this is an easy question to answer. For in Baptism, we all make one and the same vow . . . But we do not all live out our Baptism in the same way or in one special estate or station in life" (trans. alt.).

the question of priestly and monastic vows (see §18[50]). What was ultimately important here was to point out that the relationship with God and the world cannot be distinguished from one another if the relationship with God is understood in an exclusively negative way (as mortification and humiliation) and that this distinction only becomes clear if it is seen positively—that is, in a promise that establishes a sure and certain basis for it.[51]

B) Concerning the Sacrament of Baptism (*The Babylonian Captivity of the Church*, 1520)

How the understanding of baptism in the treatise on *The Babylonian Captivity of the Church* differs from that in the *Sermon on Baptism* has already been highlighted.[52] We noted that in 1519, Luther starts from the visible event, while in 1520 he begins with the audible promise. The fact that section 15 of the sermon is especially included in this starting point is shown not only by the fact that Mark 16:16 immediately appears as a paraphrase and epitome of baptism ("The *first* thing to be considered about Baptism is the divine promise, which says: 'Whoever believes and is baptized will be saved'"[53]) but also by the fact that before and, even more fully and more emphatically, after the reference to Mark 16:16, Luther stresses that the connection between repentance and baptism is such that repentance is determined by baptism in the sense that it is a "remembrance" of the baptismal promise.[54]

Apart from the new outline, the presentation in *The Babylonian Captivity* differs from that in the generally understandable German sermon in that here Luther deals throughout with the fourth book of Lombard and its interpreters, especially with Gabriel Biel's *Collectorium*. There is no earlier text in which the discussion of the sacramental theological tradition was carried out as carefully

50. Cf. esp. "It is true, then, that there is no vow higher, better, or greater than the vow of baptism" (WA 2:736,3–4 = LW 35:41). This should be compared with the treatise *To the Christian Nobility*; with the section on ordination in *The Babylonian Captivity of the Church* (e.g., Luther's polemic against the Romanists, "Clergy and laity [you say] should be separated from each other more than heaven is from earth—but to the incredible injury of baptismal grace": 6:563,29–31 = 36:112; trans. alt.); and finally, with *The Judgment of Martin Luther on Monastic Vows* of 1521 (8:564–669 = 44:243–400).

51. We have the same situation in the concluding thesis of the freedom tractate: see below pp. 337–344).

52. See above p. 295.

53. WA 6:527,33f. = LW 36:58 (trans. alt.). The importance that Luther ascribes to the word can also be seen from a passage from the Gen. sermons: "*In summary*, the aim of the whole of Scripture is to teach that whoever believes will be saved" (9:383,16–17; 1520).

54. WA 6:527,9–32 = LW 36:59; 6:528,8–529,34 = 36:59–61.

and comprehensively as here.[55] His marginal notes on the fourth book of Biel's *Collectorium*, which until now have been dated to 1515/16,[56] were in all probability only written in connection with the preparation[57] and elaboration of the baptismal section in *The Babylonian Captivity*—that is, in the first half of 1520—which is documented in detail below.[58] Luther worked here (this can hardly or not at all be said for the other sections of *treatise*) by directly engaging IV, d, 1ff. of the Biel text that was open before him and let it determine his thinking about the details of the topic as he proceeded.[59]

In the following walk through the baptismal section in *The Babylonian Captivity*, the result of our analysis of the 1519 baptismal sermon will be confirmed and Luther's reformational understanding of baptism will become even clearer. The fact that we have had to repeat what has already been said in the sermon is because of the overlap between the two Luther texts themselves.

Luther sees baptism as being constituted solely by God's promise: "Whoever believes and is baptized will be saved." This sentence of holy law[60] is not a word of institution removed from time and its concrete orality[61] in the sense of the Franciscan-voluntarist pact theology. There the word of institution, in its abstraction

---

55. Even the Lord's Supper section in *The Babylonian Captivity* falls far short of the section on baptism on this point. Here the arguments that are still scattered in the Lord's Supper section fit into a concise context. Since they come into play in its interpretation, it was possible to refrain from explicitly emphasizing the controversial theological aspect (how the arguments differ from Catholic theology) when presenting the chapter on the Lord's Supper. The tighter treatment of the topic in the baptismal section can already be seen formally in the way it is structured according to "promise" and "sign" (WA 6:527,33–531,25 = LW 36:58–64; 6:531,26–535,26 = 36:64–70, whereby 6:534,31ff. = 36:69 again refers back to the main problem that Luther specifies right at the beginning: see n. 54), which the Lord's Supper section as a whole does not have (cf., however, for the details 6:518,13–6,25–26, 27–28 = 36:44).

56. Edited by H. Degering; there 18–19. See pp. 7–12 for the mentioned dating, which has recently been defended, for example, by Heiko A. Oberman (*ZKG* 78 [1967], 232–52, here 246). But why should the marginal notes not have arisen at different times?

57. Cf. the disputations named above, pp. 177–180.

58. Cf. nn. 66, 67, 82, 96.

59. Cf., for example, the reference to "that dangerous saying of Jerome . . . in which he calls repentance 'the second plank after shipwreck'" (WA 6:527,13–15 = LW 36:58; trans. alt.) with IV/d 4/q 2/a 2/concl. 4 (H) and compare the exact description of the Thomistic and Scotist position (6:531,31–34 = 36:64; see n. 123), as well as the discussion of infant baptism (6:538,4–25 = 36:73–74) under the key phrase "the faith of another" (*fides aliena*; 6:538,7 = 36:73) and "the faith of the church" (*fides Ecclesiae*; 6:538,16 = 36:74) with IV/d 4/q 2/a 2/concl. 4 (G) and the other references shown below.

60. Cf. above pp. 224–225.

61. This holds true despite Biel's emphasis on the necessity of "proclamation" (*promulgatio*): see chap. 2, n. 604.

as a written, fixed legal norm, is based on its fulfillment in the performance of the symbolic act in such a way that it makes it possible[62] to think of the necessary presence of God ("who in agreement with his pact, assists with the sacraments that he instituted"[63]) each time the sacrament is celebrated—that is, occasionally[64] (in the sense that the sacramental act itself provides the occasion for the necessary presence of God). Luther rejects this construct of sacramental theology because it does not give effect to the *specificity* of God's salvific will[65] and does not do justice to the wording of the promise, which as the absence of baptism in the otherwise completely parallel curse formula ("Whoever does not believe will be condemned") shows,[66] does not primarily aim at the performance of the symbolic act but rather before this at faith, by granting salvation to those who believe it. Contrary to the wording of the promise, the Sententiarians (who lectured on Lombard's *Sentences*) see in the sacrament "only a sign instituted and commanded by God,"[67] a ritual law

62. Cf. n. 67 and see p. 145.

63. In Luther's treatise: WA 6:531,34 = LW 36:64 (trans. alt.). According to Biel, the effect of the sacrament comes about "when God, by virtue of his pact, assists his sacrament to produce the effect for which he instituted it" (IV/d, 14/q 2/a 1/not. 2 D). Cf. IV/d, 1/q 1/not. 3 E, "God determines to produce the thing signified where the sign is present" (see n. 67), and the Mass commentary in Lect. 47 X (2:228), "For it should be said that God has decided that as often as a priest utters these words (of consecration) in the mass, God will infuse a supernatural power of this kind."

64. It need only be pointed out here briefly that this conception is located within the theological and philosophical context called "occasionalism," especially from one of its later phases. For brief information on this concept, see D. Perler under the head word *Occasionalism* in *Religion Past and Present* 9:269–70.

65. That Luther is concerned with this *specificity* and not with God's will *in abstracto* is very clearly stated in the *Smalcald Articles*: "We . . . disagree with Scotus and the Franciscans, who teach that Baptism washes away sin through the assistance of the divine will, that is, that this washing takes place *only* through God's will and *not at all* through the Word and the water" (*BSLK* 450,18–21 = *BC* 320,3; author's emphasis).

66. WA 6:533,34–534,2 = LW 36:67 (= 9:455,25–30: Sermon on Mark 16 of May 17, 1520). Cf. the marginal note on Biel (see n. 67): "You see what is missing: an understanding (*scientiam*) of the promises and the knowledge (*notitiam*) of faith."

67. WA 6:533,23–24 = LW 36:67. It is this focus on the sign that Luther finds so displeasing in the nominalist concept of promise. By turning their attention to the sign, asking about the relationship between the sign and what it signifies, and at the same time having to take the causal aspect into account (as the definition of the sacraments as effectual signs of grace requires), the nominalists become caught up in the thicket of the distinctions of causes and let the problem of mediation to obscure what is most important—namely, the immediacy and specificity of the promise, of the preached word, in which God himself comes to us. The fact that God binds himself to the sacrament (that is, to the aspect of the promise) is not understood in such a concrete way that God can be grasped with certainty here, as Luther holds, but remains an intangible immanent

that is to be fulfilled by performing it. Luther says, "They tried to turn the sacrament into a command, and faith into a work."[68] They misunderstand the nature and function of the sacraments because, as he notes with almost identical words in his copy of Biel's *Collectorium*,[69] they "took no account either of faith or of the promise in the sacraments but stuck only to the sign and the use of the sign, thus drawing us away from faith to work, from word to sign, by which they not only took the sacraments captive but completely destroyed what was in them."[70]

This devastating judgment on the traditional doctrine of the sacraments is to be understood in its relationship to Luther's own sacramental understanding

---

aspect in the event of the visible sacramental act. God thus becomes just as unknowable in the sacrament as in creation in general. The sacrament therefore loses its specificity and individuality.

This is the sense in which Luther's marginal note on the following text of Biel should be understood: "And so any sign whatever is truly a cause if God himself determines to make the sign point to or signify his presence, just as heat is the cause of heat. And, therefore, this division of causes into causes properly speaking and necessary causes does not seem to be sustainable" (IV/d 1/q 1/a 1/not. 3 E).

Luther now comments: "And so from the sacraments of the church all creatures become sacraments because God assists them all in working, just as within the sacraments there is a power, by which some are effects and others are causes. Therefore, God has as many sacraments as he has creatures because the sacraments cause grace, but the others cause other things. This is disputed by those who are not attentive to the fact that the spoken word in the sacraments is the word of God himself (Degering, 18).

This needs to be seen together with what Luther notes about IV/d 1/q 1/a 3/dub. 3 L ("Every secondary cause is a necessary cause"; Degering, 19): "This is what I said above, that the sacraments are no different from other creatures. You see what is missing: an understanding of the promises and the knowledge of faith."

68. WA 6:533,20–21 = LW 36:67 (trans. alt.).

69. Cf. n. 67.

70. WA 6:533,25–28 = LW 36:67 (trans. alt.). See the corresponding piece in the section on the Lord's Supper: "Here you can see what great things our theologians of the *Sentences* (Sententiarians) have produced! First, that which is the principal and chief thing, namely, the testament and word of promise, is not treated by any of them and so too they have forgotten faith and the whole power of the mass for us. Then, the second part of the mass, the sign or sacrament, is the only part they discuss, yet in such a way that here too they do not teach faith but only their own preparations and the works done without faith (*opera operata*), their participations and fruits, as though these were the mass. When they come to what is profound, they babble on about transubstantiation and endless other metaphysical trifles and destroy the understanding and true use of both sacrament and testament along with all faith" (6:518,24–32 = 36:44–45; trans. alt.). Luther does not mean, to emphasize this again, that the theologians of the *Sentences* knew nothing of the word of Christ that instituted the sacraments and from which they draw their power. (See again Biel, Lect. 26 G; 1:244: The sacraments of the new covenant "get their power from Christ's institution so that after they have been given to some, God assists by causing certain salutary effects in them.") His criticism is precisely that they do not take these words at face value and accept them as they stand and thus do not give the sacrament to the recipients in the way in which it is meant to be given: "for you for the forgiveness of sins!"

in the schema "the letter kills—the spirit gives life."[71] This at the same time can be seen as an authentic explanation of the main keyword (*captivity*) in the title of his complete treatise on the sacraments.[72] The Sententiarians ("the Master of the Sentences in his fourth book with all his scribes") not only took the sacraments captive but also completely destroyed them by ignoring "the spirit, the life, and the use, that is, the truth of the divine promise and our faith." They twist the permission to believe into a command to perform the symbolic act. Not that this is not commanded! But it is meant to be offered as a promise—to impart faith. If its character as a promise is overlooked, it becomes a "dead and death-dealing letter."

If the interest is primarily in the element—that is, the "*materia*" of the sacrament— then even the "form of Baptism, as they term the words themselves,"[73] shifts into the realm of the "dead and death-dealing letter" and so into the realm of "work."[74] For if the words of baptism ("I baptize you in the name of the Father, and of the Son, and of the Holy Spirit") are aligned with the elements rather than the elements with the words ("drawing us away from the words to the sign"), then (as in the Mass,[75] so also here in baptism) the words themselves become a rite, a self-contained ritual formula that has lost its "for me" character and hence its promissional character as well.

For Luther, on the other hand, the words of baptism refer to their recipients, in accordance with the words ("I baptize *you*"). They bind them to the person by whose authority the baptizer claims to act. To call on the triune God with these words does not mean to wait for him or wait to receive something from him, it does not mean to summon or call on him in prayer,[76] but it means to give the recipients of baptism a binding promise on God's behalf to make them certain of their salvation. *Thus, in addition to the fact that the words are oriented to the recipients rather than to the elements, the new understanding of*

71. WA 6:530,5–10 = LW 36:62.

72. Cf. further WA 6:535,27–28 = LW 36:70.

73. WA 6:531,10–11 = LW 36:63.

74. WA 6:530,5–10 = LW 36:61–62 needs to be seen together with 6:533,14–28 = 36:66–67. The polemic is directed against "those who ascribe nothing to faith but everything to works and rituals, since we owe everything to faith alone and nothing to rituals. Faith makes us free in spirit from all those scruples and conjectures" (6:531,23–25 = 36:64; trans. alt.).

75. "And even if they teach these words of Christ (i.e. the gifting words of the Lord's Supper, the words of distribution), they do not teach them as a promise or testament, and thus as a means of obtaining faith" (WA 6:516,15–16 = LW 36:41; trans. alt.; cf. the explication: 6:516,17–29 = 36:41–42).

76. WA 6:531,2–3 = LW 36:63.

baptism is linked to the new understanding of the Lord's Supper by the fact that it is not understood as a prayer but as an assertio, *or proclamation.*[77] We see how the same impulse is effective in the understanding of the Lord's Supper as well as in that of baptism. However, it is also clear that such systematic rigor does not mean monotony!

As an assertoric, unconditional promise from God to the recipient of baptism, the word, "I baptize you," is the concrete enactment of Mark 16:16, its performative word—just as the formula "I absolve you" is the performative word of Matthew 16:19. This word arouses faith, which is why Mark 16:16, in Luther's unmistakable restyling of this verse, is formulated as "If you believe, you have it!"[78] That Luther wants to understand the performative word of baptism as a promise, despite the fact that the presentation given here does not link it very closely with Mark 16:16, is confirmed by the short definition of baptism as "the application of the word of promise and the sign of water to the candidate for Baptism"[79] and by the parallelism between "[the Lord] thrusts you under the water" and "promises you forgiveness of your sins."[80]

The most important thing about the performative word for Luther is that it proclaims the authority of the one who is acting here (cf. "in the name . . ."). For only this authority can guarantee the certainty of faith. The certainty is created by the fact (and this is the point of Luther's whole argument[81]) that the triune God himself is at work in the human word and that this God surrenders himself precisely to the human word. In the word and its accompanying sign, God and humans, "author" and "minister," are indissolubly intertwined. "Beware, therefore, of making a distinction in Baptism such that you ascribe the external part to humans and the internal part to God. Ascribe both to God alone."[82] *If Luther*

---

77. Cf. the Lord's Supper section: "For the mass, or the promise of God, is not fulfilled by praying, but only by believing" (WA 6:522,21–22 = LW 36:50). Prayer is the echo, not the beginning: "The prayers of heart and lips . . . flow from the faith that is received or increased in the sacrament" (6:522, 20–21 = 36:50; trans. alt.). "We must therefore sharply distinguish between the testament and sacrament itself and between their respective prayers" (6:522,30–31 = 36:50; trans. alt.).

78. Cf. p. 225.

79. WA 6:526,5–6 = LW 36:56 (trans. alt.).

80. WA 6:530,29–30 = LW 36:62–63. Cf. from the disputation of Feb. 3, 1520, quoted on p. 179: "In every sacrament the word of God promises us something, such as, 'I baptize you in the name of the Father, etc.'; 'I immerse you and all your sins'" (6:89,4–6).

81. WA 6:530,19–531,6 = LW 36:62–63.

82. WA 6:530,27–28 = LW 36:62 (trans. alt.). Luther here criticizes traditional sacramental theology at the very point at which the unambiguity of God and human certainty are at stake; he criticizes it for making distinctions that destroy both (cf. n. 67): "This is disputed by those

also here sees God's rule "in heaven" as ultimately represented by the creaturely word and its sign "on earth,"[83] *as in Matthew 16:19, then this again expresses that reformational starting point that Luther had developed with his discovery of the linguistic structure of Matthew 16:19 and that he brings to bear against Augustinian spiritualism, on the one hand, and Thomistic immanentism,*[84] *on the other.* It corresponds to the two-part structure of this sentence of holy law and the unity it creates when Luther answers the question, "What is the difference between the human minister and the divine author in the act of baptizing?"[85] with the words "the author and minister are different, but the work of both is the same."[86]

Following Luther's own presentation, his definition of the "sign or sacrament, which is itself immersion in water, from which Baptism derives its name,"[87] must now be treated separately. This definition has always been taken into account.

As has already become clear, Luther's definition of the sign is characterized by the fact that he relates it strictly to the promise, sees it as comprehended by it, and seeks to demonstrate its legitimacy and function solely from it. Thus, right at the beginning of the section on the sign, the opinion of the "more recent" theologians (that is, the Scholastics) that the "sacrament effectually signifies (i.e. grace)"—and so "effects what it symbolizes"[88]—appears forcibly turned into the thesis that the signs added to the divine promises[89] "symbolize what the words signify."[90] On the one hand, this establishes that the performative word of baptism needs a representation that strongly emphasizes its character as an event. On the other hand, however, it is becoming clear that the sign can only represent the *word*.

---

who do not recognize that the word spoken in the sacraments is the word of God *himself*" (author's emphasis).

83. WA 6:530,29–31 = LW 36:62–63 (trans. alt.): "The Lord sitting *in heaven* thrusts you under the water with his own hands and promises the forgiveness of your sins *on earth* by a human voice speaking to you through the mouth of his minister" (trans. alt.; author's emphasis).

84. Cf. n. 92 ("There is some spiritual power hidden *in* the word and the water").

85. WA 6:530,19–20 = LW 36:62 (trans. alt.).

86. WA 6:530,35–36 = LW 36:63 (trans. alt.). Cf. n. 82.

87. WA 6:531,26–27 = LW 36:64. Cf. the 1519 *Sermon on the Sacrament of Baptism*, §1.

88. Cf. chap. 6, n. 26: *efficit quod figurat*.

89. Already this word *added* (see, e.g., WA 6:518,13 = LW 36:44, "He *adds* the sign of immersion to the words of promise," and 6:531,28–29 = 36:64, "*Beside* the divine promises, signs have also been given"; author's emphasis) shows that for Luther the sign is secondary.

90. WA 6:531,29 = LW 36:64 (trans. alt.).

At the beginning of the broad development[91] of his thesis, Luther sets it apart from both the Thomistic-symbolic and the Franciscan-spiritualistic views, which despite their extremely brief description, stand out clearly as different types: "A great majority have supposed that there is some hidden spiritual power in the word and the water, which works the grace of God in the soul of the recipient."[92] "Others deny this and hold that there is no power in the sacraments, but that grace is given by God alone who, because of his pact, assists the sacraments that he instituted."[93] Both views, however, which are also combined later in the same way (e.g., in the *Smalcald Articles*[94]), converge for Luther in the definition that "the sacraments are effectual signs of grace."[95] But he rejects this because it threatens "to jettison faith due to ignorance of the divine promise"[96] and only accepts it in the sense of the efficacy of the word and faith ("Unless you call the sacraments 'effectual' in the sense that they most certainly and effectually impart grace where faith is unmistakably present").[97]

In Luther's view, the traditional definition of the sacraments as "effectual signs of grace" is wrong because it ignores the word and faith. It is also based on a wrong distinction between the sacraments of the Old and New Testaments—which in turn means a wrong understanding of the relationship between the Old and New Testaments in general. Luther believes that the error of the traditional definition of the sacraments as "effectual signs of grace," which ignores the word and faith, is based on the fact that this definition was arrived at in connection with the question of the difference between the sacraments of the Old and New Testaments, but this difference—and thus the relationship between the Old and New Testaments in general—was defined incorrectly. His yearslong preoccupation with the problem, which had lasted since his drafting of the *Explanations of the Theses on Indulgences*, and especially a disputation held specifically on this

91. WA 6:531,31–535,26 = LW 36:64–70.

92. WA 6:531,31–32 = LW 36:64. Cf. Thomas *ST* 3/q 62/a 3 and 4.

93. WA 6:531,32–34 = LW 36:64 (trans. alt.). Cf. the quotations from Biel above, nn. 63 and 67. See chap. 2, n. 498. On Biel in his distinction to Thomas, see W. Jetter's account, *Die Taufe beim jungen Luther*, 80–84, and context, 89–90.

94. *BSLK* 450,1–8, 16–21 = *BC* 320,2–3.

95. WA 6:531,34–35 = LW 36:64 (trans. alt.).

96. WA 6:533,15–16 = LW 36:66 (trans. alt.). Cf. Luther's note on Biel (IV/d 1/q/ 1/a 2/concl. 4 [H]): "And when finally, he also speaks about faith in the sacrament, it is always about the effect of the sacrament" (Degering, 18).

97. WA 6:533,16–17 = LW 36:66–67 (trans. alt.).

matter in 1520,[98] now enabled him to replace the traditional understanding with a new one,[99] in an argument unmatched in its clarity and detail by any previous one.[100]

The decisive aspect of his new understanding is the distinction between "*legal symbols*" ("which Moses instituted in his law, such as the priestly usages concerning vestments, vessels, foods, houses, and the like"[101]), which today correspond[102] to "the outward show of vestments, holy places, foods, and all the endless ceremonies"[103], and "*signs*" ("which God gave to the fathers for a time who were living in the law, such as the sign of Gideon's fleece"), which "at the same time contained a promise that required faith in God."[104] This distinction is strongly emphasized, and the "word of promise" emerges as "the sole and most effective means of distinguishing them."[105] Because of this, the Scholastic distinction that "the sacraments of the new law differ from those of the old law in the effectiveness of their signs" becomes obsolete, "for in this respect they are the same."[106]

98. WA 6:471. The Wittenberg edition of 1545 puts the nine theses of the disputation under the heading *Quaestio circularis de signis gratiae* (6:471, note). Hereafter, we will refer to the title of this untranslated circular disputation by its English equivalent, *Concerning the Signs of Grace* (*De signis gratiae*). The statements in 6:470 need greater precision, as the theses do not have "as many echoes" of *The Babylonian Captivity* as is claimed but are obviously a preparation for a particular part (see n. 100) of the section on baptism.

99. The circle of proof begins in WA 6:531,35 = LW 36:64 ("And they reach this conclusion ") and ends in 6:533,13 = 36:66. After that (6:533,14–15: "Thus it cannot be true"), the conclusion is drawn and at the same time directed back to 6:531,34–35 = 36:64 in order to allow Luther to develop his own position against the thesis referred to there (6:533,15–534,2; 534:3ff). For the traditional understanding, see Biel's presentation: Lect. 87 N (IV, 154–55).

100. Cf. the "Explanation" of thesis 7 of the *Theses on Indulgences* (WA 1:544–45 = LW 31:106–7), the scholion on Heb. 7:12 (57/3:191–92 = 29:192), and theses 44–45 of *Pro veritate* (1:632). The understanding of the relationship between the "old" and "new" sacraments in thesis 45 of the latter ("In the new, the word of the promisor is present but in the old was absent, and so also the faith of the one receiving forgiveness") is even corrected.

101. WA 6:532,12–14 = LW 36:65.

102. Cf. *Concerning the Signs of Grace*, theses 8–9.

103. WA 6:533,6 = LW 36:66.

104. WA 6:532,15–18 = LW 36:65. Cf. the corresponding part in the Lord's Supper section, which in its context admittedly serves a different purpose (6:517,39–518,9 = 36:43–44), as well as earlier in the sermon *Concerning the Testament of Christ* (*De testamento Christi*; WA 9:446,12–29; 448,25–29) of Apr. 8, 1520, and in the sermon on Gen. 9:9 of Nov. 1519 (9:348).

105. WA 6:533,4–5 = LW 36:66 (trans. alt.). Cf. 6:532,19–20 = 36:65.

106. WA 6:532,5–6 = LW 36:65.

Luther's understanding, however, does not assume a unity in salvation history (*Heilsgeschichte*), but in each case the respective promise is believed to be *God's* promise, whose saving will is the same in each case and alone forms the basis of the unity of the Old and New Testaments.[107]

The *distinction* in this excursus of Luther on the relationship between the sacraments of the New Testament and those of the Old Testament aims, in the overall context of the discussion of the Scholastic principle that the sacraments are effectual signs, *at demonstrating the ineffectiveness of the signs, considered in and of themselves, on the basis of the necessity and distinguishing power of the promise.*

> Therefore, let us open our eyes and learn to pay heed more to the word than to the sign, more to faith than to the work or use of the sign. We know that wherever there is a divine promise, there faith is required, and that these two are so necessary to each other that neither can be effectual apart from the other. For it is not possible to believe unless there is a promise, and the promise is not established unless it is believed. But where these two are mutually present to each other, they give a real and most certain efficacy to the sacraments. Hence, to seek the efficacy

107. "The same God who now saves us by Baptism and the bread, saved Abel by his sacrifice, Noah by the rainbow, Abraham by circumcision, and all the others by his signs" (WA 6:532,6–8 = LW 36:65; trans. alt.). See *Concerning the Signs of Grace*, theses 5–6 (WA 6:471): "The gift of grace in Baptism was not the reason for the removal of circumcision or sacrifice (6) but the will of God alone, who has bestowed his grace with different signs for different times and peoples." Luther therefore does not view the times in their diversity from the angle of salvation history and so does not see them forming an overarching unity on the basis of their typological correspondences (such as that between "circumcision or oblation" and "Baptism"). The "diversity of times and peoples" is for him not subsumed into a clear *heilsgeschichtlich* unity, from which God's identity could be demonstrated. Rather, this is nothing other than his saving will, which is defined in Jesus's passion and death (cf. *Concerning the Signs of Grace*, thesis 6, with thesis 1 and see below p. 364). Therefore, Luther can replace "the same God" (6:532,6 = 36:65) with "the same Christ" (thesis 3). Such a saving will is expressed in a concrete promise that is grasped by faith. Therefore, he is always the same in word and faith. This makes it clear why Luther had to reject the idea of progress in salvation history (*Concerning the Signs of Grace*, theses 2–4, esp. 3: "The same Christ and the same faith reigned in the elect from Abel to the end of the world through the various ages") and yet could not accept a unity of salvation history. "Therefore, it is not possible that the new sacraments differ from the old, for both alike have divine promises and the same spirit of faith" (6:533,2–4 = 36:66; trans. alt.). See on this Calvin's interpretation of Heb. 1:1-2 where he makes an astute observation about the identity of the subject (*God*) and verb (*speak*): "But in this diversity however God sets before us one thing . . . that God, who is always like himself and whose word is constant, and whose truth is unchangeable, has spoken of both together" (*In omnes Novi Testamenti epistolas commentarii*, Halle 1834, vol. 2,383).

Cf. on this excursus chap. 6 B, esp. pp. 278–280.

of the sacrament apart from the promise and faith is to labor in vain and to meet with condemnation.[108]

If the promise and faith constitute the effectiveness of the sacrament, then the sign seems to have only one significative function. However, since what the sign "signifies" is "fulfilled" by the promise and faith, it can no longer be spoken of as a "mere" sign. Because it is understood as being tied to the word and faith, the sign is not to be understood allegorically, not as empty but as effective, since it participates in the effectiveness of the event of word and faith, with which it is intertwined.

This can be shown exactly by Luther's interpretation of that "saying" that has been important to him since the *Explanations of the Theses on Indulgences* ("It is not the sacrament but faith in the sacrament that justifies") and by his interpretation of the Augustine quotation, which has been associated with it since the *Asterisci*, both of which appear here again.[109] The interpretation of the saying is particularly important because it clearly demonstrates what could only be deduced from the context above[110]—namely, that Luther does not want it to be understood in the sense of Augustinian spiritualism. It reads: "Faith in the word of promise, to which Baptism is added . . . justifies and fulfils what Baptism signifies."[111] Because it clings to the external, oral word of promise, faith

108. WA 6:533,29–36 = LW 36:67 (trans. alt.) (On the problem of the correlation between word and faith, see above p. 18; here in *The Babylonian Captivity*, the priority of the word over faith is given greater emphasis than the simultaneity ["*simul*"] of word and faith: 6:514,13–25 = 36:39 [cf. 6:356,3–19 = 36:82–83]). After this paragraph, Luther presents his own understanding of the sign, beginning with 6:534,3 = 36:67 ("Baptism, then, signifies two things"), as he develops his thesis formulated in 6:531,29 = 36:64 ("Along with the divine promises, signs have also been given"). *Here, too, Luther is polemical,* although less explicitly than before. In addition, the *opponents* now are not so much the Sententiarians but rather *the representatives of monastic penitential and meditation piety, which Luther himself used to embrace.*

109. WA 6:532,28–29 = LW 36:66 ("that saying . . . ") and 6:533,12–13 = 36:66 ("Not when [the sacraments] are enacted, but when they are believed"; trans. alt.). Cf. *Concerning the Signs of Grace,* thesis 7.

110. See pp. 198–199 and pp. 226–227.

111. WA 6:532,36–533,1 = LW 36:66 (trans. alt.). From the "saying" (6:532,29 = 36:66), Luther goes via lines 29 ("Thus . . .") and 31 ("Because . . .") directly to line 36 ("So . . ."). The formulation of 6:532,36ff. is exactly parallel to that of 6:532,31–32: "Faith in the promise, to which circumcision was added, justified him [Abraham] and fulfilled what circumcision signified" (36:66).

The difference to Augustinian spiritualism becomes clear in the section on the Lord's Supper (6:518:18–23 = 36:44; author's emphasis): "We can have and use the word or testament apart from the sign or sacrament. 'Believe,' says Augustine, 'and you have eaten already.' *But what do we believe, if not the word of the promiser?* Therefore, I can hold mass every day, indeed,

receives the power of the word and is thus in fact "the submersion of the old self and the emergence of the new"[112] and with it "full and complete justification" takes place.[113]

The theological achievement of this conclusive argument can hardly be overestimated. Luther succeeds in *rejecting a sacramental realism based on the sign without countering it with a spiritualism* that sees baptism as signifying a pattern of existence that in itself is only a possibility and that only gains its concrete reality every time it is put into effect. However, the alternative is not superseded by a synthesis of both types but rather by a fundamentally new understanding of the sacrament. This is specifically determined by the concept of *promissio*, which unlike in the Franciscan tradition, is not a decree oriented to the sign but a proclamation oriented to the receiver in the here and now. It thus has its essence in God's will, not abstractly but as an oral and public proclamation, and so is a concrete promise, a word of comfort.

This concept of *promissio* results in a surprising consequence for the understanding of the sign in its "significance." In terms of the historical power of the word that does what it says and what it declares ("Believe, and you have it!"), it can no longer be understood in an improper, tropically broken way. "For Baptism is not a 'false signification.'"[114] Rather, we must now be able to say of it, and of the death and resurrection that it signifies: "The death of sin and the life of grace should not only be understood *allegorically*, as many are wont to do, but also as a true death and resurrection."[115] "We die and rise again. We die, I say, not only affectively and spiritually by renouncing the sins and vanities of this world, but we actually begin to relinquish this bodily life and lay hold of the life to come, so that there may be a real (as they say) and also bodily crossing over from this world to the Father."[116] Luther's powerful polemic also clearly contradicts his own earlier meditative piety, which following the schema of "sacrament and example," understood the text interpreted here, Romans 6:4–11,[117] primarily as

---

every hour, for I can set the words of Christ before me and with them feed and strengthen my faith as often as I choose. This is a truly *spiritual* eating and drinking."

112. WA 6:533,1–2 = LW 36:66 (trans. alt.).

113. WA 6:534,3–4 = LW 36:67. *Thus the sign is drawn into the word and the distinction between the sign (*signum*) and the thing it signifies (*res*) is rendered obsolete. The absorption of the* res *into the* signum, *understood as a word* (see chap. 4, n. 199, and chap. 6, n. 98), *which we observed in the* Sermon on the Sacrament Penance *(1519), is now also evident in the understanding of baptism.*

114. WA 6:534,11–12 = LW 36:68 (trans. alt.).

115. WA 6:534,10–11 = LW 36:68 (trans. alt.).

116. WA 6:534,35–9 = LW 36:69 (trans. alt.).

117. Expressly taken up in WA 6:534,6–8, 12–14 = LW 36:68.

"affectively and spiritually" and only secondarily in a bodily sense.[118] This amazing reversal of emphasis can only be understood if we see it as a consequence of his new understanding of the promise. Its place had previously been taken by the sacramental meditation on Scripture. But now the "significance" of baptism "is fulfilled" in the promise and faith and is obviously better preserved in them than in the "allegorical" understanding of "the death of sin and the life of grace," with which baptism had previously been interpreted existentially. In Luther's new understanding, word and existence are clearly distinguished. And this distinction allows existence and history to be understood and experienced far more realistically than in Luther's early theology.

The baptismal promise not only creates the Christian's being but also keeps it going. Thus, in contrast to his early theology, becoming is based on being and no longer constitutes being. The Aristotelian concept of motion, which appears again here, denoted by the frequent "always," has lost its former dominance. Now it no longer determines the understanding of the promise—as in the phrase "always desiring, always yearning and groaning,"[119]—but is now determined by it. Baptism is no longer fulfilled by the motion of penance, but penance is concretely encompassed by baptism. Luther says:

> Understand . . . that you cannot return either by penance or by any other way but only by the power of your Baptism and to do again what you were baptized to do and what your baptism signified. Baptism never becomes useless or invalid unless you despair and refuse to return to the salvation it bestowed. You may indeed wander away from the sign for a time, but that does not make the sign useless or invalid. You have been baptized once with the sacrament, but you must always be baptized by faith, always die, and always live . . . We are therefore never without the sign of baptism just as we are never without the thing it signifies. In fact, we always need to be baptized more and more, until we fulfil the sign perfectly on the last day.[120]

Although this text from the concluding section of the main part of Luther's presentation on baptism[121] does not yet in itself clearly support our interpretation

---

118. See pp. 76–102.

119. See pp. 135–153.

120. WA 6:535,4–16 = LW 36:69 (trans. alt.).

121. Together with WA 6:535,17–26 = LW 36:69–70, but this section does not contain any new thoughts. What follows, beginning with the thesis "This glorious liberty of ours and this understanding of Baptism has been taken captive in our day" (6:535,27 = 36:70) to the end of

that the promise determines the motion of penance (repentance) and not the other way around, its validity is nevertheless clearly demonstrated by the sections that open the presentation and to which it refers back.

Here Luther laments the way that baptism has been forgotten[122] by his contemporaries. He blames "that dangerous saying of Jerome, either unhappily phrased or wrongly interpreted, in which he calls repentance 'the second plank after shipwreck,' as if Baptism were not repentance."[123] It should be the task of bishops "to make every effort to recall Christians to the true understanding of Baptism, so that they might realize who they are and how they ought to live as Christians."[124] Instead, however, they are leading people away from baptism, so that they forget all about it.[125] After Luther briefly indicated his counter position (using Mark 16:16), he stresses the need for the *remembrance* of this promise with the utmost urgency, which is already expressed linguistically by an accumulation of elaborately stylized synonymous expressions that all underscore the one event of the *sermon* that constitutes the remembrance:

> This message should have been impressed upon the people untiringly, and that promise should have been dinned into their ears without ceasing. Their Baptism should have been called to their minds again and again, and their faith constantly awakened and nourished. For just as the truth of this divine promise, once extended to us, continues until death, so our faith in it must never cease, but be nourished and strengthened

---

the chapter (6:543 = 36:81), is a specific complaint and polemic against the papacy arising from the positive understanding of baptism presented earlier. As already at the end of the *Sermon on Baptism* (cf. pp. 295–298), only more extensively and in some sense more radically, Luther here formulates his reformational idea of vocation, which in due time will gain world-historical significance. This is a direct consequence of his new understanding of the promise over against the special status of monastic vows and the spiritual estate in general.

Only the treatment of the question concerning the meaning of infant baptism (6:538,4–18 = 36:73) is to be taken as an addendum to the main part of the presentation on baptism, because here not only is the conclusion drawn from what has already been said, but a fundamental element of the reformational understanding of the promise also becomes particularly clear: the precedence of the word over faith.

122. WA 6:527,10–11 = LW 36:58 (trans. alt.): "so that now there are scarcely any who remember their Baptism, let alone glory in it."

123. WA 6:527,13–15 = LW 36:58 (cf. 6:529,22–34 = 36:61 and 6:535,1–4 = 36:69). The saying of Jerome that plays an important role in scholastic sacramental theology (cf., e.g., Biel IV/d 4/q 2/a 2/concl. 4 [H]) is found (according to *BoA* 1:460) esp. in epistle 130,9 (MPL 22:1115).

124. WA 6:527,23–25 = LW 36:58 (trans. alt.).

125. WA 6:527,25–32 = LW 36:58.

> even to death, a continual remembrance of this promise made to us in Baptism. Therefore, when we rise from our sins or repent, we are merely returning to the power and faith of Baptism, from which we fell, and to the promise then made to us, which we deserted when we sinned. For the truth of the promise once made always remains—that he will welcome us back with open arms when we return.[126]

The idea of "remembrance" was already apparent in the baptismal sermon. Here it is now developed with full clarity. Coming from the Old Testament via the New Testament's eucharistic tradition related to the liturgy and the theology of the Mass, *Luther introduces it into his understanding of repentance, thus determining its relationship to Baptism*. The boldness and originality of this theological undertaking can only be marveled at:

> Let all penitents first remember their Baptism and the divine promise which they abandoned, and when they remember it with confidence, let them acknowledge the same before the Lord, rejoicing that they are still within the fortress of salvation because they have been baptized, and abhorring their wicked ingratitude in falling away from the faith and truth. Their heart will be wonderfully strengthened and roused in the hope of mercy when they consider that the promise God made to them cannot possibly lie, that it is still unbroken and unchanged, and cannot be changed by any sin, as Paul says in 2 Timothy 2[:13]: "If we do not believe, he still remains faithful—for he cannot deny himself." This truth of God, I say, will guard them, so that even if everything else fails, this truth, if it is believed, will never fail them. Those who are penitent can use this promise as a shield against all the assaults of the insolent enemy, as an answer to the sins that trouble their conscience, as an antidote for their fear of death and judgment, and finally as a comfort in every spiritual attack. Above all, because of this one truth, the penitent can say: "God is true to his promises, and I have received the sign of this in Baptism. If God is for me, who can be against me?"[127]

The importance of this text is already clear from the fact that Luther follows it with three sections, each of which restates the same thing in a new way. It brings together all the characteristics of the reformational concept of promise. God is understood as the one who promises himself to us in the oral word so that

126. WA 6:528,8–17 = LW 36:59 (trans. alt.).

127. WA 6:528,20–35 = LW 36:59–60 (trans. alt.).

we can rely on him. God's truth lies in his faithfulness, with which he stands by his word. He has bound himself to the promise once made to us in baptism so that, when we come under spiritual attack, being empowered and encouraged by the oral word of the sermon, we can always hold him to this one specific promise and insist, against the accusations of our conscience and the horrors of death and the last judgment, "I am baptized!"[128] The nominalist idea of the ordained power of God that Luther took up in the first Psalms lectures, also in connection with Mark 16:16 and 2 Timothy 2:13, in the sense of the promise of judgment as described earlier,[129] now comes into effect here in a new way: in the promise of salvation, which is sharply distinguished from the word of judgment. This promise is not perceived in the confession of sins and prayer of supplication but in the fact that we hold it up to God as a promise already received and grasp hold of his faithfulness in it. Luther calls it "confessing the promise to the Lord"[130] or, in short, "confessing the Lord."[131] Thus in the wake of the new understanding of *promissio*, a new notion of "confession" emerges, which is characteristically different from the earlier one, in which it was primarily "self-accusation" and seen in an entirely negative way. "Confession" in the new sense, being identical with "faith," is an echo of assertoric preaching.[132] In it, we surrender ourselves to God's promise without the negative self-reference. The same change we saw in the understanding of confession is also evident in that of "remembrance." In the first Psalms lectures, Luther had understood it in the sense of meditative piety[133] and even in the Hebrews lectures (on 10:2–3) he saw it—as the "remembrance

---

128. "We also read of a certain holy virgin who in every time of spiritual attack made Baptism her sole defense, saying simply, 'I am a Christian'; and immediately the enemy recognized the power of Baptism and her faith, which clung to the truth of God and his promises, and fled from her" (WA 6:529,6–10 = LW 36:60; trans. alt.). "Christian" can be exchanged for "baptized" (6:529,11 = 36:50).

129. See pp. 123–130. The saying from 1 Tim. 2:13 (LW 6:528,26–28 = LW 36:60) is taken up again in 6:529,15–16 = 36:60–61. See n. 131.

130. Cf. again WA 6:528,20–22 = LW 36:59 (trans. alt.): "Penitents should first take hold of the remembrance of their Baptism and of the divine promise that they abandoned, and remembering it with confidence, confess the same to the Lord."

131. "For no sins can condemn you save unbelief alone. All the rest, so long as faith in the divine promise made to the candidate for Baptism returns or remains, will be absorbed in a moment by the same faith, or rather by the faithfulness of God, because he cannot deny himself if you have confessed him and faithfully cling to him who made the promise" (WA 6:529,13–17 = LW 36:60–61; trans. alt.).

132. Cf. WA 6:535,30 = LW 36:70 ("a proclaimer and restorer of this freedom and knowledge"; trans. alt.).

133. Cf. above p. 288.

of Christ's passion"—as an existential reenactment ("the mystical passover"), though it is unclear how this squares with his initial reformational understanding.[134] *Now the task of reminding us of our Baptism is entrusted to the sermon, which keeps God's promise in baptism alive by a public, audible* assertio, *or proclamation, of what it is and thus ever anew establishes repentance as a "return to Baptism."*[135]

> When the children of Israel were about to return to repentance, they first of all remembered their exodus from Egypt and by remembering it, they turned back to the God who had brought them out. Moses reminded them of this many times and David afterwards did the same. How much more then ought we remember the exodus from our Egypt and by remembering it, turn back to him who led us out through the washing of regeneration, which we are commended to remember for this very reason! This can be done most fittingly in the sacrament of the bread and wine. Indeed, in former times these three sacraments—penance [repentance], Baptism, and the bread—were all celebrated at the same time in the same service, each one supporting the other.[136]

The last two sentences formulate the connection between the three abiding sacraments for Luther and thus *the substantive center of the entire text of The Babylonian Captivity of the Church.* Repentance (penance) and the Lord's Supper have the same task: to lead us back to baptism and let its promise be heard again. In both cases, this happens by means and by virtue of the promise. This promise, understood as the word of absolution or the gifting word of the Supper, constitutes the sacrament and led to its discovery in the first place. But the promise is not exhausted by the sacrament but forms the basic text of every sermon. For this reason it is

> the sum and substance of the gospel. For what is the whole gospel but the good news of the forgiveness of sins? Whatever can be said about forgiveness of sins and the mercy of God in the broadest and richest sense is all briefly contained in the word of this testament. For this reason, popular sermons ought to be nothing else than expositions of the mass, or explanations of the divine promise of this testament.

---

134. Cf. above pp. 249–252.

135. In Luther's summarizing formulation at the end of *The Babylonian Captivity of the Church*: WA 6:572,16–17 = LW 36:124 ("a way and return to Baptism").

136. WA 6:528,36–529,6 = LW 36:60 (trans. alt.). Cf. pp. 282–283.

This is what Luther said in the section on the Lord's Supper.[137] As it turned out, he comes to the same understanding in the section on baptism, with its determination of the remembrance of the baptismal promise.

Thus the reformational concept of promise also yielded a new understanding of preaching, which is a significant event in church history. However, the common opinion that Luther ultimately arrived at his new understanding of the sacraments from an "original propensity for preaching,"[138] being a born preacher himself, is incorrect. Rather, he gave the sermon a new function by making the promise of baptism, repentance, and the Lord's Supper its basic text. *The origin of the reformational understanding of preaching can be seen in the notion of promise,* which grew out of a profound reexamination of the function of the sacraments and cannot be separated from this context either historically or systematically.

How the new understanding of the promise comes to the fore in the use of Scripture, and how Luther thus puts his reformational program of preaching into effect, will be shown in the next chapter, using examples.

---

137. WA 6:525,36–526,2 = LW 36:56 (trans. alt.).

138. A. Brandenburg, *Gericht und Evangelium*, 20. Cf. chap. 2, n. 424.

CHAPTER 8

Promise and Meditation

(The Reformational "For Me")

THE QUESTION OF the reformational "for me" (*pro me*)[1a] is identical to that of the concept of canon that Luther used in his interpretation of Scripture. It is developed particularly clearly in the preface to his September Testament (1522)[1]—that is, in the most journalistically effective place. The essence of a canon is its unambiguity. With regard to the use and effect of the Scriptures, we must therefore be certain "that there is only one gospel, just as there is only one book of the New Testament, and only one faith, and only one God who makes promises there . . . just as there is only one Christ."[2] This unity is the verbal unambiguity of the promise, which we become aware of by listening to it "when its voice comes and tells us, 'Christ is your own, along with his life, teaching, works, death, resurrection, and all that he is, has, does, and can do.'"[3] Behind the Christ event that is expressed, given, and appropriated in such a voice, behind this *word* of Christ, stand his *works* considered in and by themselves. "For the works are of no help to me, but his words give me life, as he himself says."[4] For this reason, Luther gives the Gospel of John priority over the synoptics and places the letters of

1a. For this and the following chapter, see W. Kreck, *Das reformatorische "pro me" und die existentiale Interpretation heute, Studien zur Geschichte und Theologie der Reformation*, Festschrift for E. Bizer, ed. L. Abramowski and J. F. Gerhard Goeters, 283–303.

1. WA DB 6:2–11 = LW 35:357–62. Cf. the preface to the interpretation of 1 Pet.: DB 12:259–60 (1523).

2. DB 6:2,12–22, here 2,21–22; 6:22–28,2, here 6:22–23. Cf. 12:259–60, especially 260,6–7: "the same word and the one gospel, just as there is only one faith and one baptism in the whole of Christendom."

3. DB 6:8,18–19 = LW 35:361; trans. alt. (cf. 6:8,23–24 = 35:361). Cf. 12:259,8–13: "But gospel means nothing else than a preaching and proclamation of God's grace and mercy, purchased and won by our Lord Christ with his death. It is strictly not something found in books or written with letters, but is more an oral sermon and living word, and a voice that rings out across the whole world and publicly proclaims it, so that it can be heard everywhere." For the same idea, with a specific focus on the notion of testament, see 6:4,12–23.

4. DB 6:10,21–23 = LW 35:362 (trans. alt.).

Paul and the First Letter of Peter alongside it.[5] Therefore, "the true touchstone by which to judge all the books of the Bible is this: do they promote Christ (*Christum treiben*) or not?"[6] Luther's "canon within the canon" is therefore not a general christological principle, not even a story of Christ as such, but the precisely defined magnitude of the promise of Christ.

The problem indicated by the juxtaposition of Christ's word and work[7] has occupied Luther indirectly since he wrote that famous gloss on Augustine's *On the Trinity* (*De trinitate*) IV, 3 ("sacrament/example") of 1509.[8] In his early theology he solves it, as we have seen,[9] in the sense of Tauler and sees a "work" of Christ, primarily the passion, as effective in the present in that its significance is perceived through its existential reenactment. Significance is the third thing that mediates between fact and existence, which is either abstracted from the fact or to which the fact is reduced—namely, a possibility of human self-understanding that forms the basis of its realizations and thus always precedes them. It is important to note that, in contrast to most other representatives of late medieval meditative piety, according to Luther, the reenactment is not accomplished by us but by the archetype of this significance (that is, by Jesus, who is the first to realize this self-understanding or significance).[10]

Thus, in Luther's early theology, it is not Christ's works and his word that stand in opposition to one another but rather his works and our apprehension of their significance, which is understood as being brought about by them.

What we have just outlined is summed up by the term *meditation*. It means, in the sense of the early Luther, that process of understanding in which I apply the fact of Jesus's life and suffering to myself, allowing it to become significant for me by recognizing its for-me-ness (*pro me*), which is not inherent in the fact itself but can only be spoken of when I am affected by it or when the fact is applied to me. The "for me" is not an aspect of the perceived fact but of my perceiving existence, which is shorthand for the mode of its appropriation.

A considerable lack of clarity in the presentations of Luther's theology stems from the fact that *this* "for me" is not removed from the *reformational* "for me" but is understood differently. While his early theology understands the "for

---

5. DB 6:10,9–35 = LW 35:362. Cf. DB 12:260,9–32 and before that WA 10/1.1:46,17–47,7 (47,6–7: "St. Paul writes nothing of Christ's life, but he makes it clear why he came and how we should make use of him").

6. DB 7:384,26–27 = LW 35:396 (Preface to James and Jude, 1522; trans. alt.).

7. In the sense of the word–deed (not work or office!).

8. See pp. 78–81.

9. See pp. 95–97.

10. Cf. in the next chap., esp. pp. 347 and 369.

me" mainly in the sense of appropriation (An*eignung*), his reformational theology takes it primarily in the sense of bestowal (Zu*eignung*). This emphasis on bestowal is an echo of an explicit, audibly articulated promise "for you" (both singular and plural), the validity of which does not depend on the strength of its appropriation. The only thing they have in common at first is that in both cases nothing is expected from the fact as such. But beyond that, it should not be overlooked that the early understanding of meditation was profoundly transformed by Luther's reformational understanding of the promise. For this excludes the *fides historica* (historical faith)[11] not only in the form that the early theology rejected.[12] Rather, what now lines up with the *fides historica* is precisely what Luther's early theology considered to be an alternative to it—namely, faith understood as "contrition."[13] The alternative to it now is faith "in relation to the promise."[14]

---

11. This term, known mainly from the *Theses Concerning Faith* (WA 39/1:44–58 = LW 34:109–26), appears in Luther for the first time, to the best of my knowledge, in the text quoted in n. 13. (The issue it raises is, of course, clear to him already early on [see above for my opinion in the text]). Since it is Melanchthon's postscript, he could have used the term spontaneously as a summary of a more extensive work. In any case, we come across it at the same time in Melanchthon himself in his *Capita* ("Headings," see n. 14). The corresponding phrase "to preach in an historical manner," on the other hand, can often be documented in Luther for this time (*Operationes in Psalmos*: 5:543,14–16; 544,17–18; *The Freedom of a Christian*: 7:58,32–33 = 31:357). See the passion sermons of 1517, 1518, and 1519: WA 9:142ff.; 1:336–39, 339–40; 2:131–42. Melanchthon gives an interesting clue to understanding how he uses the term. He says (CR 1:109) of a letter, that he wrote it "candidly and in an historically trustworthy manner" (*simpliciter et fide historica*) and so "in good faith." This use of the term fits perfectly with that of the "Headings" (cf. n. 14). "Historical faith" (*fides historica*), therefore, means the general trustworthiness of human speech, which cannot convey ultimate certainty. Chr. Gestrich's excursus on *fides historica* (*Zwingli als Theologe, Studien zur Dogmengeschichte und systematischen Theologie* 20, 1967, 29–31) needs to be supplemented accordingly.

12. Cf., for example, the gloss on Tauler's sermons, which we have discussed above pp. 95–97.

13. At least that much can be gleaned from the fragments of a disputation-style lecture by Luther titled "On Justification" (probably from Aug. 1520: WA 9:470), which have survived in a collection of Melanchthon: WA 9:470–71. Cf. esp. 471,5–7: "Many who believe are contrite, and yet their sin is not forgiven. Judas believes in a general way and is contrite, yet his sin is not forgiven. Remain steadfast in this conviction: the conscience cannot be pacified by historical faith." The significance of what Luther is saying comes to light later, especially in the Cordatus controversy (see, e.g., W. Neuser, "Luther und Melanchthon—Einheit im Gegensatz," in *Theologische Existenz heute*, NF 91 (1961): 6–13.

14. This is the formulation of Melanchthon's "Headings": "Writers differ in the way they speak of faith. There is faith in miracles (*fides miraculorum*), which does not justify. There is also historical faith (*fides historica*), which is the sort of opinion by which I believe Livy and Sallust and other historians in good faith. Even the ungodly believe that the world was created, that Christ rose again, and many other things, but this faith also does not justify. But *faith that is*

This is by no means to say that the "for me" of the meditation was simply replaced by the "for me" of the promise. Rather, there is an interplay between them. While the sacramental meditation on Scripture, in the sense of Luther's early theology, contributed to the emergence of his reformational theology of promise, it was also changed by it.

The influence of Luther's early understanding of meditation on his reformational theology can be seen from the way in which it individualizes and intensifies the New Testament's *pro nobis* (for us) by turning it into a *pro me* (for me).[15] It is also evident from the fact that Luther reshapes biblical texts so that they are given the character of direct address if they did not have it already. An impressive example of this is the restyling of Mark 16:16 in the second person so that it now reads, "If you believe, you have it."[16] The application of the principle of this restylization can also be seen from the fact that Luther, given the various formulations of the gifting words of the Lord's Supper, clearly prefers the "for you" (*pro vobis*) to the "for many" (*pro multis*).[17] Looking at it this way, we can certainly observe a continuity from the early meditational to the reformational concept of promise and consequently may think that Luther's reformational for-me-ness (*pro me*) is nothing but a deepening of late-medieval meditative piety.[18]

But this only shows one side of the phenomenon. For regardless of the connection just outlined, a decisive shift has taken place. It can be observed in the use of the verb *meditate* or one of its equivalents, such as "*take to heart*" or "*engrave on the heart.*" In Luther's early theology, we see it in connection with the story of Jesus, his birth, passion, and so forth.[19] *But his reformational theology uses it in a new way: in dealing with the literal promise, first in connection with the promise in Matthew 16:19 in the sacrament of penance.*

> This holy, comforting, and gracious word of God must enter deeply into the heart of every Christian, where they may with deep gratitude *engrave*

---

properly related to the promise is the faith that justifies" (CR 21:35–36 [18b]). This, however, does not mean that Melanchthon's use of the phrase "faith related to the promise" in his "Headings" is the same as Luther's.

15. Cf. M. Elze, "Züge spätmittelalterlicher Frömmigkeit in Luthers Theologie," in *ZThK* 62 (1965): 381–402, here 400, n. 71.

16. Cf. pp. 225–226.

17. Cf. pp. 239–240, 289 and n. 26 (*Small Catechism*).

18. Cf. Elze, "Züge spätmittelalterlicher Frömmigkeit," 401, and Elze, "Das Verständnis der Passion Jesu im ausgehenden Mittelalter und bei Luther," in *Geist und Geschichte der Reformation*, 127–51, here 127 and 150–51.

19. See, for example, pp. 97–102.

> *it on their heart*. For the sacrament of penance consists in this: the forgiveness of sins, comfort, and peace of conscience, besides joy and blessedness of heart over against all sins and terrors of conscience, as well as against all despair and spiritual attack at the thought of the gates of hell.[20]

Only when he becomes aware that the promise of Christ is spoken and heard in the present—no longer in the word understood as an image but in the image understood as a word[21]—does Luther think he can escape the "human devotions" that featured prominently in his early understanding; only in this way does he think that God's power and gift can be accepted without human verification. This becomes especially clear in the sermon *Concerning the Testament of Christ* of April 8, 1520, in which the reformational view of the Lord's Supper was formulated for the first time in a form that was no longer superseded, and in exactly the place where Luther's discovery of the word as the real power of the Eucharist is most originally attested:

> The mind must be raised to those things that are signified by the ceremonies, not to those things that are done, that are exposed to the senses—We do not understand the mystery of the Eucharist more easily and more directly from anything else but the words of Christ himself. So do this, fix your eyes on the words of Christ, for they are not to be hidden but made public, so that you may know that they contain the whole of your salvation. Lay aside human devotions. Prepare your mind to meditate on the words of Christ. *Take* . . . Whoever has meditated on these words well will understand from them the power of the Eucharist and see in them the true method of preparation.[22]

As before,[23] Luther initially tries here, too, to move beyond the visual event of the Mass to what it signifies. But this is now not found by refracting the

20. *Sermon on the Sacrament of Penance*, 1519; WA 2:715,15–20 = LW 35:11 (trans. alt.; author's emphasis).

21. Cf. the *Treatise on Good Works*, §17: Faith comes "only from Jesus Christ, freely promised and freely given . . . This is how you must picture Christ in you and see how in him God holds before you his mercy and offers it to you without any prior merits of your own. It is from this image of his grace that you must draw faith and confidence for all your sins" (WA 6:216,15, 26–29 = LW 44:38; trans. alt.).

22. WA 9:445,19–446,4.

23. Cf. the sermon of Sept. 21, 1516, in which the ceremonies of the Mass are taken as a pointer to a hidden meaning: WA 1: 443,17–23 and for that see p. 114.

visual into the interior realm and only finding certainty there but is found externally. The "mystery of the Eucharist" paradoxically lies precisely in the external public word! As in the *Sermon on the Sacrament of Penance* (1519),[24] despite its Augustinian starting point, Luther's former Augustinian understanding of the sign is overcome when he recognizes the power of the sacrament's gifting words ("given for you," "shed for you") and when he pays close attention to exactly what these words say. Accordingly, faith is directly related to the external word, to these words, and as "the true method of preparation," faith is no longer a devotional preparation for receiving the gift"[25] but sees itself as prepared beforehand—"by trusting in these words."[26]

What Luther says here in relation to the visual event of the Mass is exactly the same as he says in 1521 in his sermon on Luke 2 in relation to a visual story about Jesus (in the narrative)[27]: The mystery of the event is revealed in each case in a clear promise. This parallelism allows us to understand why Luther places[28] the "meditation on divine doctrine"—that is, the use of Scripture generally, right next to baptism (, repentance) and the Lord's Supper, and accordingly states in the eighth thesis of the disputation, programmatic for *The Babylonian Captivity*, on the second distinction of the fourth book of the *Sentences* of Peter Lombard: "There are almost as many sacraments as there are words of God. These sacraments arouse faith, even if the sign is missing."[29] But Luther can only say this because he is still thinking of the "promise" as a general word;[30] hence he says

24. §6 and as well see chap 4, n. 199.

25. Cf., on the other hand, the interpretation of the fourth petition of the Lord's Prayer of 1517 (WA 9:146,17–30) and the scholion on Heb. 5:1, which is not yet clear on this point (for the scholion, see pp. 232–239, esp. 212–213).

26. As parallels to this text (WA 9:446,3–4), see in the same sermon (9:447,17–19), "Therefore, this is the right preparation for the Eucharist, that you seize this promise and firmly believe that this testament of Jesus Christ has abolished your sins," and (9:447,24–25), "So come, not as one who has been cleansed beforehand by your prayers and confessions, but come as one who needs to be cleansed by faith in the Eucharist itself and this testament." See WA 6:517,22–23 = LW 36:43; 6:520,6–7 = 36:46 (*The Babylonian Captivity*) and the *Small Catechism*: "A person who has faith in these words, 'given for you' and 'shed for you for the forgiveness of sins,' is truly worthy and well prepared" . . . "and whoever believes these words has what they declare and state, namely, 'the forgiveness of sins'" (*BSLK* 521,4–7 = *BC* 363,9–10), to which reference was made already earlier (chap. 4, n. 199).

27. See pp. 332–339.

28. In the sermon on Gen. 9:9 (WA 9:348–49): see above p. 177 ("Structure of the Presentation").

29. WA 9:313,17–18 (see above pp. 178–180).

30. Cf. theses 3–5 with theses 7–8 (see pp. 178–180, where all the theses are cited).

he could number "among the sacraments" . . . "all those things to which a divine promise has been given."[31]

However, Luther's pan-sacramentalization of Scripture here immediately raises the question of whether it is not an inadmissible extrapolation that destroys the very point it was based on (namely, that the promise is a *specific* word). This question is posed and answered in a particularly dramatic manner *in the series of three sermons on the story of Jesus's birth (1519, 1520, and 1521). At the same time, these sermons give a clear indication of how the sacramental meditation on Scripture, in the sense of Luther's early theology, continues to influence his reformational theology and yet is profoundly changed by it.* As with the Lord's Supper, it will also be shown here that Luther's new reformational approach, his new organizing center (*Ansatz*), does not mechanically gain immediate acceptance everywhere but rather can only be rediscovered or expanded upon in bold experimentation after various attempts.

In December 1519, Luther begins his long-planned[32] ongoing interpretation of "the whole story of the gospel" with a programmatic sermon on the topic of the distinction between law and gospel.[33] In defining the gospel in its distinction from the law,[34] the motifs that are then taken up and clearly outlined in the first sermon in the series are already hinted at. This interesting sermon from December 25, 1519, begins with a preliminary remark of fundamental importance. Its significance is not only evident from the sermon itself but also from the fact that it prefigures the outline of the freedom tractate (its two-part structure),[34a] introduces the Wartburg Postil in an expanded form under the title *A Brief Instruction on What to Look for and Expect in the Gospels*, and continues to act as a determining factor in the previously mentioned preface to the September Testament, where Luther writes: "Here I remind you at the outset that we will treat the whole of Christ's life and all his deeds in two ways: as a sacrament and as an example."[35]

---

31. WA 6:571, (35–572,9) 35–36 = LW 36:123 (*The Babylonian Captivity*).

32. Cf. Luther's letter to Spalatin of Oct. 16 (?) (WA Br 1:538–39; ll. 5–17) and Nov. 7, 1519 (Br 1:553–54; ll. 3–4). In response to many requests, Luther wrote a sermon book to help priests and monks "so that they might cut back on and reject those dirty fables of preachers that proscribe rather than describe Christ, and so popularize the pure theology of Christ among the people, expelling those errors that flood the land like a deluge" (Br 1:538; ll. 8–11; cf. 2:112,21–22). On Nov. 7, Luther is then "ready to work on the interpretation of the epistles and gospels" (Br 1:553; l. 3).

33. WA 9:437–38; cf. Poliander's note: 9:436,34–37.

34. WA 9:437,1ff., 35–39; 438,5,23–5.

34a. See pp. 76–77.

35. WA 9:439,19–21.

The distinction between Christ and Christians (saints) and, in connection with this, between law and gospel[36] is blurred when a sermon presents Christ only as an "example" to be imitated. For we see in him not a model of virtue to be imitated, but he *works* this virtue in us as a "sacrament." A distinction needs to be made between the latter, Christ as a sacrament, who is the primal cause of what we do, and Christ as an "example," whom we are called to imitate. A mistake here means nothing less than gaining or losing the point of the entire gospel.[37]

The sermon itself begins by immediately applying the principle set out in the introductory remarks to the text to be interpreted, Matthew 1:1: THE BIRTH OF JESUS CHRIST. The sermon is intended to be nothing other than a meditation on these words, which are mainly taken as a "sacrament" and, only briefly at the end,[38] as an "example."

"These words are a kind of sacrament by which, if anyone believes, we too are reborn"[39]: Christ's "birth" causes our "rebirth"—by sacramental meditation.[40] "Christ is born, believe that he is born for you, and you will be born again." The importance of this statement is further reinforced by the parallel formulation that immediately follows: "Christ has conquered death and sin: believe that he has conquered them for you, and you will conquer them too."[41]

Luther expressly states that this understanding is based on baptism and absolution,[42] just as the "meditation on divine doctrine" appears in the summary of the sermon on Genesis 9:9 from November 1519 alongside baptism and the Lord's Supper. Only from this perspective, can *all*[43] the words of the gospel be understood as "symbols," "through which we are given the very righteousness, virtue, and salvation that the words themselves declare."[44] This determination covers Luther's new understanding of the sacrament exactly, according to

36. WA 9:437,1ff. (What is meant here is the gospel story of Jesus's entry into Jerusalem [Matt. 21], which Luther preached about on Nov. 27, 1519: 9:425–26).

37. WA 9:439,21–440,5.

38. WA 9:442,28–31.

39. WA 9:440,6–7.

40. WA 9:442,28: "Christ's nativity is the cause of ours."

41. WA 9:442,25–26.

42. WA 9:440,7–10, 17–19.

43. Cf. n. 46, but esp. see chap. 2, n. 370.

44. WA 9:440,11–12: The importance of this definition is evident from the fact that it occurs again in the concluding "summary concept" (cf. 9:442,20) with almost the same formulation: "Indeed, we meditate on the gospel sacramentally, that is, the words work in us through faith the very thing that they declare" (9:442,23–24). See pp. 326–327.

which the word of absolution is a promise[45] and works and gives what it says. However, the question raised above arises as to whether this understanding can be expanded to such an extent that it can be said that "all the words, all the stories of the gospel are sacraments of a kind, that is, sacred signs by which God works in believers whatever those stories signify."[46] *How* can a story of the gospels be preached and believed sacramentally as a whole or in all its individual words? What is the meaning of the insight that we must relate the narrated events to ourselves?[47] Luther does not consider here that the required relationship cannot be established more or less arbitrarily. For it must surely be given immediately if the words and their salvific significance are not to fall apart and thus break the power of the sacramental (= promissional) word.

In his Lord's Supper sermon, published shortly before Christmas 1519, Luther had tried to apply the notion of promise, found in his new version of the sacrament of penance, to the elements and action of the Mass and to understand them as "certain signs."[48] But he felt forced to immediately revise this approach again.[49] This is because his revision showed him that understanding the word as a symbol or sign that does what it says is tied to a very specific word and only applies to another word with the same structure, but it cannot be applied to an *event* that is directly visible, as in the Mass, or indirectly, as in the telling of a story. According to the reformational understanding of promise, such a visible event is not a "word" if it cannot be shown that this means me. What I have imagined and seen may instruct me, delight me, touch me, and thus fulfill all three functions of a speech (*oratio*).[50] But how can I be certain that

---

45. Melanchthon in his Matthew lectures (on 8:2) immediately picks up the definitions from this sermon, especially those cited in the next footnote ("All the stories of Christ are sacraments, that is, promises, by which we can be certain that God will give his grace to all who believe"; *Werke in Auswahl*, ed. R. Stupperich, vol. 4, 166, 14–16). His addition ("that is") quite correctly explains what came before, following Luther's sense, as *The Babylonian Captivity* (WA 6:571,35–36 = LW 36:123–24) confirms. For Melanchthon's special understanding of the promise in the mentioned annotation, see E. Bizer, *Theologie der Verheißung* (119–20), and H.-G. Geyer, *Von der Geburt des wahren Menschen* (189–90).

46. WA 9:440,3–5.

47. It is necessary "for us to consider that [Christ's] deeds are done for us, and that what is preached pertains to us. That is, if I hear a story about Christ and do not think that everything applies to me, namely, that Christ was born, suffered, and died for me, then the proclamation or knowledge of the story is of no benefit" (WA 9:440,21–24).

48. See chap. 6, esp. pp. 257–260.

49. With the sermon *Concerning the Testament of Christ* of Apr. 8, 1520, and the writings that follow from it.

50. See pp. 89–90.

I am encountering *God* in this? Do I have to determine and decide this for myself, look for the answer within myself? Do I not ultimately have to make myself certain of salvation and know for sure that the *pro me* here means me? This means that the problem of certainty is once again raised in all its sharpness by this sermon, although it has already been clearly resolved in the new understanding of the sacrament of penance. But it is not clear here how "Jesus's birth" brings about our "rebirth." The *word rebirth* does not occur here. For the word of the text that I am meant to meditate on ("birth") can certainly not do what it says. But it is suddenly no longer expected to do this. It is meant to do something else—namely, bring about a "*re*birth." That is, in order to arrive at the *effect* of the text as claimed in the basic definition of sacramental meditation, its *wording* must not be understood literally but figuratively. However, this departs from the strict correspondence between saying and doing, which is essential to that definition.

Instead of a spoken promise, which cannot be found in the text either,[51] Luther attempts the mediation in question solely by means of a visible image.

For him, the words THE BIRTH OF JESUS CHRIST encompass a view whose concrete features bear the stamp of tradition, in the sense of and in the motifs of the Bernardine devotion to Christ.[52] For the child in his mother's lap lies before our very eyes, close enough to touch. He is not the unapproachable judge, the *Christus iudex*. Accordingly, Luther wants only one thing in all his new attempts:[53] that we do not lose our trust in God out of fear for the Christ the Judge and the "divine majesty." "I say this so that we are not afraid to embrace this child"[54]; "all this is true of him so that your conscience should not be terrified and you should not be afraid to go to this child and to take comfort from him . . . See with what means God entices you."[55] It is already assumed that the birth of Jesus is the incarnation of *God*. It is meant to enable us to *grasp* God and therefore Luther later allowed it to be "attached" to the promise as a sign.[56]

Here, of course, since the promise is missing, it is not clear that we can even grasp *God* in this child, and if we can, it is not clear how we can do that. Nor is

51. Cf., on the other hand, the Emmanuel sermon treated on p. 362, where the promise is found already in the wording of the text (Matt. 1:21,23).

52. Cf. n. 66.

53. WA 9:440,30–442,22.

54. WA 9:442,21–22.

55. WA 9:441,12–16. Therefore, despite the incidental remark (9:441,30), the entire passage is by no means a "digression" (9:442,20).

56. Cf. the sermon *Concerning the Testament of Christ* (see pp. 359–360).

it clear, as the later Christmas sermons emphasize, that Christ's humanity is of no use to us without his divinity.[57]

In summary, we can say that, on the one hand, this sermon shows a *new approach*, a *new organizing center* compared to Luther's earlier interpretation of the gospels. For with his expansion to include in it "all the words and stories of the gospel," the *concept of the promise*, known from his new understanding of the sacrament of penance, is introduced. Only with it can he say that the "words work in us through faith the very thing that they declare."[58] Of course, the strict correspondence between saying and doing that is established in this and similar programmatic formulations[59] by the underlying concept of the promise is not actually maintained. In fact, in the actual execution of the sermon, it is rather—and this is the other side of the coin that needs to be emphasized—not the promise that is ultimately determinative but the *meditative piety* in its most *developed form*. This piety, which has already found expression in Luther's earliest statements, here represents a final deepening of certain medieval traditions. Hence the *proprium* of the gospel, its unique character, "which is not given in human stories,"[60] lies in the effectiveness of its archetype. Therefore, its causal aspect seems to be immediately identical to the Pauline understanding of the gospel as "the power of God" (Rom. 1:16–17),[61] which in turn means that the causative understanding of the word, which was already important in the early texts, emerges here too.[62] The demonstrative model (*sacramentum/exemplum*) is thus differentiated from the effective archetype and subordinated to it.

Luther would never have extricated himself from his image theology and its problems if his concept of the sacrament, and thus also the way in which the two concepts are related to each other, had not changed. This change, especially in relation to the story of Jesus's birth, occurred in the third of the sermons to be discussed here, in which *sacramentum* is replaced by *promissio*, which in turn is

57. Cf., for example, the Christmas postil published in 1522 on the prologue of St. John: "The humanity would be of no use if the divinity were not inside. But again, God will not be and does not wish to be found except through and in this humanity, which he has raised up as a certain sign (as Isa. 11 says), and with which he gathers to himself all his children from the world" (10/I/1:208,22–209,2).

58. WA 9:442,24–25.

59. See nn. 44 and 46.

60. WA 9:442,26–27

61. WA 9:442,27–28. See 9:440,16–17.

62. It has already been emphasized (see pp. 223–224) that "causative" alone is not enough to describe the distinctive character of the reformational understanding of the word, if it is correct that it signifies a mismatch, with "word" meaning the ideality of Christ or the authority of his promise. See pp. 358, 369–370.

sharply differentiated from meditation in the sense of a devout contemplation of a visual object. This also confirms that we were correct in distinguishing between the two aspects (the "new organizing center" and the meditative piety in its "most developed" form) in our analysis of the 1519 sermon.

Before we turn to the sermon of 1521, we should attend to the Christmas sermons of 1520, whose Janus face once again reveals the problematic nature of the relationship between the earlier meditative piety and Luther's *promissio* theology.

The sermon of December 25, 1520,[63] takes up the motifs from the previous year in its meditation on the birth of Jesus but uses them even more extensively and fervently. The reference to the previously mentioned tradition of piety is even explicit this time:

> Those who invented this song, which is no less delightful than spiritual, were taught by the Spirit: "A child so praiseworthy was born to us."[64] Nothing has been left out of this song that could refer to the spiritual understanding of this nativity. Thus we see . . . that I should believe that the child is mine, that it is a pure child, whose mother is a virgin, that the child is also God, and that my heart can truly say, the Son of God is mine.[65]

In this exegesis of the song, the three points of Bernard's sermon previously mentioned[66] are taken up again. The most important for Luther is the third

63. A detailed version of it is preserved in the Poliander codex (WA 9:517–20; mixed Latin and German text) and a brief transcript in Melanchthon's collection (9:498–99). A purely German printed version of it has also been handed down (7:188–93). See WA 9:516; 7:187–88.

64. "A child so praiseworthy / is born for us today / from a virgin pure / to comfort us poor people." This is a translation of the hymn *Ein Kindlein so löbelich ist uns geboren heute / von einer Jungfrau säuberlich, zu Trost uns armen Leuten . . .*" (*Evangelisches Gesangbuch* 18:2; the German strophe of this Latin hymn comes from the fifteenth century).

65. WA 9:518,22–28.

66. In Melanchthon's transcript, which corresponds to the German edition (WA 7:188,18–189,2): "Bernard recounts three miracles: 1. that God and human being become one person; 2. That a virgin gives birth; 3. That the human heart and the word are able to come together and be united through faith" (9:498,23–26).

Luther does not quote Bernard verbatim but draws together various passages from his sermons for the "Vigil of the Nativity of Our Lord": MPL 183:102D ("These are the miracles . . . she who begets is both mother and virgin; he who is begotten is both God and human") and 183:87D ("The Virgin believes. The virgin conceives by faith. The Virgin gives birth. The Virgin remains a virgin: who cannot but marvel? The Son of the Most High is born, God from God, begotten before the ages; the Word is born an infant: who can ever marvel enough?"). See Sermon 6 (*On the Annunciation of the Lord*); MPL 183:109–16.

point that appears twice here, at the beginning and the end—namely, its for-meness ("is mine") as a pointer to our spiritual birth, which is prefigured by Mary's faith in the words of the angel.

> So if this birth (i.e. the birth of Jesus) is to be of benefit to us and convert us, we must take the example of the Virgin to heart and follow her, for there is no other way to receive the benefits of this birth than by taking to heart the words of the angel, just as Mary did. This miraculous sign must be renewed in us without ceasing. We must all receive the child for ourselves so that each of us can say and believe that this child is mine, as the Virgin did, when she conceived him. Each of us must act as if he were born for us alone; whoever does not receive the child in this way does not have any part in this birth at all."[67]

To conceive and give birth to Christ "in our heart"[68] like Mary in order to be able to say that "God's Son is mine"[69] and thus "become one with Christ in faith"[70] is finally a matter of the right disposition of our affects.[71] From the perspective of the reformational concept of promise, this shows the problem and the limit of Luther's early meditative piety as presented.

"No one conceives Christ, no one becomes the mother of God, unless their heart is free of all affections. Because we cling to creaturely things, our heart is not pure. We cannot obtain this birth. Mary abandoned all creaturely things, was the

---

The treatment of the Poliander codex differs in an interesting way from the other two versions in that, as the text quoted (see n. 65) shows, it immediately understands as the third point ("3. Mary's faith was so great that she believed that this sacrament was going to be *in her*": WA 9:517,16; author's emphasis) what, according to the other versions, is the manner of use of all three *topoi*: "But this is the real miracle, that the Virgin Mary believes that these things are to take place *in her*, which is so great a thing that we cannot marvel at it enough" (German version: 7:189,4–7; author's emphasis).

67. German version: WA 7:189,21–29.

68. Cf. with the text quoted below and referenced at n. 72 the words "to conceive Christ in your heart" and the parallel phrase "to know Christ" from the sermon on Gen. 28 (WA 9:403ff.; quotation: 9:407,29,28), preached shortly before (see 9:517, n. 1; accordingly, Luther continues with the interpretation of Gen. 29 on Dec. 30: see 9:535–37). The sermon on Gen. 28 will be treated on pp. 360–361.

69. WA 9:518,28 (see n. 65). Cf. the Christmas sermon of 1519: "The child is mine" (9:440,28).

70. WA 9:519,18–19.

71. Cf. Poliander's marginal note (WA 9:517): "The disposition of our affects toward God's grace."

most despised of all humans . . . and became as nothing at all."[72] "It must still be like that for us, our heart must first have died if it is to be revived."[73] The sermon consequently concludes: "This child does not speak (literally: is not eloquent) to everyone, but only for those who feel their brokenness, only to hungry, troubled, tortured souls oppressed by their folly and weakness."[74] The Christ event only becomes the "word" for those who feel their need of it. Hence reflection on the part of person for whom this child "speaks" leads from Christology back to anthropology and seeks to determine the goal of the former from the latter. Thus the fruit of the Christ event does not determine its use but its use the fruit.

The next day, St. Stephen's Day,[75] Luther speaks again in the same way about the birth of Christ and how it should be used. This is where he also brings in the example of Stephen:

> Whoever wants to benefit from the birth of this child must, as I said, renounce everything else, must let go of everything that they love and hold dear . . . and with cheerful courage, must give themselves up to shame, dishonor, poverty, and death, if they are to become worthy of gaining the child. The old skin must be peeled off, and the old self with all its desires must be killed, for the child has come to create a new person in us.[76]

We see that the appropriation of Jesus's birth in our spiritual birth, our rebirth, means not only a movement of the mind but also the penitential movement of the whole person in "resignation" and "self-mortification." However, since the sermon says of the new person that it presupposes the death of the old, Luther's early theology at this point has still not yet been overcome.

On December 30,[77] Luther wanted "to say a little more about how it is possible for this Christ child to be born in us and to complete the thought."[78] Since the "sacrament" side of things has already been illuminated—"We have heard how the child must be ours if his birth is to bear fruit in us, and how we

72. WA 9:519,22–29.

73. WA 9:520,6–7.

74. WA 9:520,32–34.

75. WA 9:525–27; Dec. 26, 1520.

76. WA 9:526,30–39.

77. WA 9:530–35.

78. WA 9:531,2–3.

should receive him"[79]—Luther now focuses on the "example" side of the story. For this reason, he refers to Philippians 2: 5–11: "As he [Christ] clothed himself in our flesh, so let us cloth ourselves in the flesh of others *through love*."[80] After the birth of Jesus has been received in faith, it should find its counterpart in love: "Now someone might ask how we can know that we have received the child in our hearts through true faith. That is why we also want to speak about the sign that is certainly there and follows in external works outside the heart when the child is within. This sign is no different than when we dress and cloth ourselves in our neighbor's flesh. For this is also a spiritual birth and incarnation because through it we are born another self."[81]

To execute the theme, Luther uses motifs that are especially well known from the Lord's Supper sermon of 1519. Thus he says: In love Christ wants to "weave us humans together so that we all become one flesh and one body."[82] Love "is a sure sign that Christ's birth has power and space in me. The more such works of Christian love increase in us, the more Christ also increases in us."[83] However, the prevailing tendency of the sermon of 1519 to identify the former with the latter by verifying Christology from ecclesiology seems to be contradicted here by the way it grounds love in faith, the example in the sacrament, according to the conception of the freedom tractate (which is taken up here as in many other sermons of these months[84]).

Although the basic structure of all three Christmas sermons of 1520 undoubtedly repeats that of the freedom tractate, we have to doubt that what we are seeing is exactly the same thing. The point of difference lies in the concept of faith or the understanding of the "sacrament," which here, to put it schematically, is understood in the sense of the early meditative piety, whereas in the freedom tractate it is understood in the sense of the reformational concept of the promise. Luther evidently felt the tension indicated by this himself and appended the promise, as it were, to the sermon (of December 30) that had already been rounded off and completed. Because "enough has been said about how we should use this birth so that it may benefit us,"[85] it must come as a surprise to hear that

79. WA 9:531,3–5.

80. WA 9:499,33–34 (cf. ll. 28–29); Melanchthon's transcript. [The phrase "through love" in the German original is printed in Greek; trans. note.]

81. WA 9:532,3–10.

82. WA 9:533,21–22.

83. WA 9:532,29–31.

84. Cf. n. 129.

85. WA 9:534,9–10.

the gospel "also" teaches this (Luke 2), indeed, that its "summary" (*summa*) is the "promise." For, as Luther says, "The *summa* is contained in the words, 'for you is born this day a Savior . . . Christ, the Lord'. This is the promise the angels gave to the shepherds, a promise that belongs to us all, as the angels said: 'God's favor to his people.'"[86] In the sermon of 1521, as we will see presently, this "promise"[87] becomes the epitome of the "sacrament." But it cannot be said that it is already this here, since the sacrament could be defined independently of it, which is exactly what we find in Luther's early theology.

The fact that Luther appended a schema obtained elsewhere to a sermon that was already complete in itself is also evident from the specific definition of the sign, which of course belongs to the promise. According to the understanding of the sign found in the sermon *Concerning the Testament of Christ* (of April 8, 1520), it should encompass the entire (birth) story. However, starting from the second part of the angel's word, Luther's interest is purely allegorical and fastens on the swaddling clothes, which he takes as symbolizing the "physical word of the gospel and the promise."[88] The "sign" certainly does not refer to the story or the humanity of Christ at all but to the word itself that reveals it. There is "no more certain sign for locating Christ than the place where the gospel is preached"; the word itself "is our sign, there alone we find Christ."[89]

Looking at the sermon as a whole, we would have to say that Luther's *early meditative piety and his reformational theology of promise still stand side by side in a tense juxtaposition and are not yet closely intertwined or clearly set apart from one other. Only on the third attempt, in the sermon written at the Wartburg, does Luther repeat a feat that is on a par with the move he made in the* Pro veritate *theses and the sermon* Concerning the Testament of Christ.

In this sermon, which appeared in the Christmas postil in 1522, the reformational form of the "for me" (*pro me*) is shown, as in its original form in the understanding of repentance, baptism, and the Lord's Supper, with the sharpness of an ideal type.[90]

In clear contrast to the devotional contemplation of the birth story,[91] which Luther wants to partially model for "simple, ordinary Christians . . . so that they

86. WA 9:534,10–14.

87. WA 9:534,14.

88. WA 9:534,19–20.

89. WA 9:535,7–8, 6–7.

90. The only thing missing in comparison with the freedom tractate is an explicit reflection on the doctrine of the two natures.

91. WA 10/1/1:62,17–70,22 = LW 52:9–14.

know how to go about it,"[92] he turns his attention to "the sort of mysteries, secret things, that are presented to us in these stories."[93] If however we expect the concept "mystery" to be an abstraction from the story to its significance that transcends times and people in the sense of the sacramental meditation on Scripture that we find in his early theology, then the explanation that immediately follows, which serves as a comprehensive definition, will come as no little surprise: "All mysteries point to two things especially, the gospel and faith, that is, what is to be preached and what is to be believed, who is to preach and who is to listen. We will see that here too."[94]

What is presented as a mystery, as a "secret thing," in the story of Luke 2:1–14 is—just as in the sermon *Concerning the Testament of Christ*![95]—paradoxically precisely the revealed word, which is not given behind the text but immediately in it, to be grasped in it, and which is articulated verbally with the words "for you" (*pro vobis*): "These words (that is, Luke 2:10–11) clearly show that he is born for us."[96] We only know what faith is from the word of the promise. True faith, "which God's word and deed demands, firmly believes that Christ is born for you, that his birth is yours, and that it happened for your good . . . as the angel says here."[97] *Not the text of "the stories for themselves,"*[98] *but first and foremost God's illuminating commentary on them through the mouth of his messengers. That is, the word that comprehends the event in itself and "gives"*[99] *it to you, makes it yours, is the pivotal point of the whole story.* Only this word can "announce, open up, and illuminate"[100] the birth of Jesus and thus the entire story of the historical Jesus as well as the entire story of the Old Testament—a most remarkable equation! To understand this story in its saving significance, "the gospel must first be heard, and the angel's appearance and voice must be believed. If the shepherds had not heard from the angels that Christ was lying there, they could have looked at him thousands and thousands of times and still not have realized that the child

---

92. WA 10/1/1:62,15 = LW 52:8 (trans. alt.).

93. WA 10/1/1:70,23–24 = LW 52:14.

94. WA 10/1/1:70,24–27 = LW 52:14 (trans. alt.).

95. Cf. p. 321.

96. WA 10/1/1:71,12–13 = LW 52:14 (trans. alt.).

97. WA 10/1/1:71,7–11 = LW 52:14 (trans. alt.).

98. "This is what Isaiah 9[:6] means: 'A child is born to us; a son is given to us.' To us, to us—he is born to us and given to us. Therefore, see to it that you do not just enjoy the stories for themselves without the gospel" (WA 10/1/1:73,12–15 = LW 52:16 (trans. alt.).

99. See the text quoted below (and referenced in n. 106).

100. WA 10/1/1:81,13–14 = LW 52:22 (trans. alt.).

was Christ."[101] This is an unequivocally brilliant insight that is still valid to this day but which had to be discovered again, with the assistance of form analysis (*Formgeschichte*). According to it, not only is revelation not so immanent in history that it would be obvious,[102] but history is also not transparent to a salvific meaning that might be seen running through it, even if it were changed to another kind of genus (*metabasis eis allo genos*), nor could it be understood by means of existential verification on the part of the person meditating on it, even if the salvific meaning of an event in history were reflected in the meditator—and if it could be understood that way, the word would cease to have a gifting function and would only be an interpretative word. But Luther sees history as so closed, so ambiguous—and thus unable to offer any certainty of salvation—that the interpretative word (*Deutewort*) in the narrative of the story is not enough, but attention needs to be paid to the gifting word (*Gabewort*).

Christ does not reveal himself as the historical Jesus "in himself,"[103] nor in that process of appropriation and contemporization (bringing Christ into the present) known from the sacramental meditation on Scripture, in the sense of Luther's early theology, but gives himself in the word bound to the sermon, and only in it, and in that word is recognized as savior. *Faith does not come from the image and its perception, but from the word and its hearing—more precisely, from the gifting word, not the interpretative word* (just as the gifting word in the Lord's Supper can no more be understood as an interpretative word than the angel can be understood as an interpreting angel). "Christ's birth cannot be distributed physically, and even if it could, it would still be of no use. Therefore, it becomes spiritual and is distributed to everyone through the word, as the angel says here."[104] "He does not simply say, 'Christ is born,' but adds 'for you,' 'Christ is born *for you*.' Likewise, he does not say, 'I announce a great joy,' but 'I announce a great joy *for you*.'"[105] Luther goes on:

> What greater joy can a heart hear than that Christ is given to it as its very own? The angel does not just say: "Christ is born," but his birth is for us; he says, he is "your Savior." Thus, the gospel does not merely teach the history and stories about Christ but personalizes them and gives them to all who believe them, which is exactly what the gospel is

101. WA 10/1/1:81,14–18 = LW 52:22.

102. Cf. WA 10/1/1:62,20–21 = LW 52:9 (trans. alt.).

103. See n. 98.

104. WA 10/1/1:72,4–6 = LW 52:15 (trans. alt.).

105. WA 10/1/1:71,14–16 = LW 52:15 (emphasis in LW).

> supposed to do. What good would it do me if he were born a thousand times and if this were sung to me every day with the loveliest airs, if I do not hear that his birth is meant for me and should be mine?[106]

To clearly grasp the reformational form of the "for me," its difference to Luther's early meditative piety needs to be highlighted again at this point. It, too, rejected a *fides historica* (historical faith), which also arose from the insufficiency of "history in itself"[107]: "Literally it is useless, but spiritually it is life."[108] What is new now, however, is the equation of the "spiritual" understanding with the "distribution" through the word of promise, which is to be taken quite literally, according to its wording. As the term (*distribute*) indicates, this equation presupposes the reformational understanding of the sacrament and is specifically applied to the interpretation of the gospels or finds it confirmed there by the text (here by Luke 2:10–11) already. This clearly shows how the concept of the promise, which was obtained from a new way of understanding of the sacrament, helped Luther discover the promise, which opens up the individual stories in the gospels (even if the term *promissio* is not always found in them). It also shows how the concept of the promise is verified in its canonicity by the promise itself. The gifting words of the Lord's Supper are not the only promise but rather—as the verbs *bestow*, *give*, and *distribute* show—the epitome of its uniqueness and therefore the canon of Luther's interpretation of the Scriptures and of the *reformational* understanding of the "for me" (*pro me*). This *pro me*, far from being merely a pointer to a formal epistemological principle,[109] is to be seen as part of the promise itself

106. WA 10/1/1:79,9–16 = LW 52:20–21 (trans. alt.). As for the last sentence, the editor, W. Köhler, recalls that saying of Angelus Silesius in the "Cherub Wanderer": "And if Christ had been born in Bethlehem a thousand times, and not in you, you would be lost forever" (text form according to Köhler). However, the purpose of this whole chapter is to show that this is exactly not the sense in which the reformational *pro me* is to be understood.

107. See n. 98. [The word translated "history" can also be rendered "story"; trans. note.]

108. WA 9:103,28–30; on that, see pp. 95–97.

109. We can only note in passing that this "for me" *also* corresponds in its own way to the insight that Luther formulated in the first Psalms lectures (on Ps. 69:25): "For as long as something is not known to have been done, it has not yet been done to us or with us, but it is done with us when it is known to have been done" (WA 3:435,37–39 = LW 10:377; trans. alt.). But its peculiarity lies in the fact that it is accomplished by a specific promise that tells us it is salvific and at the same time specifies the mode of this knowledge. We thoroughly agree with H.-J. Iwand's polemic "Wider den Mißbrauch des 'pro me' als methodisches Prinzip in der Theologie" (*EvTh* 14 [1954]: 120–25). However, it runs counter to his intention (or at least to that of the reformational Luther, whom he cites as his authority) when he says, indicating his own position, that the "I" meant in the "for me" is "hidden and fixed in the story of Jesus Christ and is waiting to be grasped by me and made the center of my self in faith" ("Wider den Mißbrauch," 121).

and is not the transforming appropriation of the meaning of a story encountered in a vivid narrative. It owes its origin to the gifting word and does not mean the execution ("*exactio*"[110]) of an interpretative word. In this way, reformational theology distances itself from the existential interpretation[111] of Luther's early period as well as from the hermeneutics of signification that is necessarily allied with it.

The fact that the existential interpretation does not go beyond the framework of a hermeneutics of signification, but rather remains completely at home in it, is due to the fact that even in its desire to exclude a historical faith (*fides historica*), its existential concern with the history of Jesus means that it is still occupied with this history, even though, according to this thinking, Jesus can only be made present for us today by a trope. This has to correspond to a basic structure of human existence, and for the early Luther, this is cross and suffering. The way of negation is the mode of contemporization, the way in which the past is brought into the present;[112] it opens up the spiritual significance, the *res*, of the factual history of Jesus. It is this tropical[113] understanding of the history of Jesus that F. Gogarten, for example, praises in Luther as "historical (*geschichtliches*) thinking"[114] that would overcome the "metaphysical thinking" of his

110. WA 9:470:20–25 ("On Justification": see n. 13).

111. It is entirely appropriate, in view of Luther's early theology, to speak with G. Ebeling ("Die Anfänge von Luthers Hermeneutik," *ZThK* 48 [1951]: 172–230, esp. 229–30) of an "existential interpretation." But we must not overlook the fact that Luther later corrected this.

112. "Because Christ is spit upon, killed, scourged, crucified in us to this day" (WA 3:167,24 = LW 10:139; on Ps. 31:9; 1513–15), which Luther mentions as a prerequisite for tropology (see WA 3:167, 20–25). We must agree with G. Metzger's interpretation (*Gelebter Glaube*, 171): "The word of the cross . . . is primarily about the living impression of the person of Christ who implants his effects in the personal breadth of human existence." Thus "Luther's view of conformity remains in the realm of history. The historical figure of Jesus 'addresses' us in the double sense of the word, in that the word, which can be viewed as a testimony of the incarnate one, comes to us and at the same time demands of us the conformity that it alone can bring about." But this is a view that is fundamentally different to Luther's reformational theology, which cannot be said to be characterized by the "certainty that every age has an immediacy to Christ's passion" (Metzger, 167, n. 49).

113. I have deliberately said "tropical" and not "tropological" to emphasize the tropical implication in Luther's tropology.

114. Gogarten's understanding, for which he expressly appeals to Luther (see chap. 9, n. 17), is probably correctly described by H. Fischer ("Die 'geschichtliche Christologie' und das Problem des historischen Jesus. Erwägungen zur Christologie Friedrich Gogartens," *ZThK* 65 [1968]: 348–70): "The relationship of existence that is articulated as faith qualifies the *historical* speech of Jesus and his faith as *christological*" (363). "It is true that christological statements are constituted by the unity of historical knowledge . . . and the personal relationship of existence, that is, the relationship of faith" (363–64).

day—without realizing that what he claims as "historical thinking" is in fact a particular metaphysics of existence that can also be found in Tauler[115] (namely, the way of negation).

How the existential interpretation in the sense of Luther's early theology and its hermeneutics of signification are overcome is best shown, after *Concerning the Testament of Christ*, by this sermon, which understands the "hidden thing" of the story of Jesus, as explained, precisely in the revealed word, the oral promise, that articulates and bestows the fruit of that story. The bestowal determines the appropriation; the appropriation itself does not determine what is to be appropriated.[116]

If we look at what has been bestowed, we see how the *christological* moment is operative in the bestowal. This must now be considered in its hermeneutical aspect. We will see that the correction made by Luther's promise theology to his meditative piety also means a radical correction to his early Christology and ethics.

According to his early Christology, Christ is the archetype, which is seen above all in the crucified Jesus. The effect of this archetype on the existence of believers is that they suffer God's judgment in lifelong penitence. The tropical refraction in the tropological reference to the fact, the death of Jesus, does not exclude a remarkably direct perspective on Christ: he appears as the first among equals. The fact that Christ's divinity and the doctrine of the Trinity were a source of great embarrassment to the early Luther[117] is the result of this *wirkungsgeschichtliche* Christology, which is not interested in Christology as such, but only in its significance for later times.

It is only logical that, together with the correction to the meditative piety by the promise theology, Luther's early Christology, his archetypal Christology, should also be decisively reshaped—into a mediator Christology based on Trinitarian theology.

Now it is not the case that the figure of "mediation," the motif of "exchange," does not appear until 1520. On the contrary, from a formal point of view, we

---

115. This brief comment must remain within the framework selected here. On the dispute over the legitimacy of Gogarten's alternative, see W. Kamlah, "Gilt es wirklich 'die Entscheidung zwischen geschichtlichem und metaphysischem Denken'? Anmerkungen zu Friedrich Gogarten, Entmythologisierung und Kirche," *EvTh* 14 (1954): 171–77, but esp. H.-G. Geyer, "Metaphysik als kritische Aufgabe der Theologie," in *Theologie zwischen gestern und morgen. Interpretation und Anfragen zum Werk Karl Barths*, ed. W. Dantine and K. Lüthi (1968), 247–60, esp. 250–51, 257 and 259–60.

116. Cf., on the other hand, the sermon of 1520 (see p. 329).

117. Cf. pp. 89–92.

have seen it already since the first Psalms lectures,[118] which might suggest that there is an identity between the subject matter of the early passages and that of the freedom tractate. However, while there may be a formal identity, there can be no question of a factual identity, as our investigation of the Christmas Sermon of 1514 has already shown.[119] According to this sermon, the interweaving of God and humanity, as in the statement "the Word became flesh in order that flesh may become the Word," was aimed solely at the Christian's humiliation, which is experienced by all creatures as well as by God. This means that if the "exchange" is actually only defined negatively, as our humiliation, then our relationship to God and the world, to faith and love (to use the reformational distinction), coincide. But if faith is understood positively, more specifically, if it is produced by the (now joyful!) exchange that takes place in the *promise* and *its* "for you" (*pro te*),[120] then our relationship to God and the world, to faith and love, are strictly differentiated. In contrast to Luther's early theology, his new theology of promise therefore also changes the foundation of ethics.

This thesis will be developed in the following from the parts of the sermon on Luke 2 from 1521 that were initially excluded from the presentation above and finally corroborated by the concluding thesis of the freedom tractate. The reshaping of Luther's Christology that we mentioned earlier will be specifically addressed in the next chapter.

In keeping with the spirit of the freedom tractate,[121] according to the sermon on Luke 2 of 1521,[122] Christ's own being is imparted in the promise of the sermon and its "for you": "To you, to you, I announce a great joy" that "does not remain in Christ," but is given "to all people." The promise ("distributed by the word to everyone, as the angel says here") reveals "the true basis of all blessedness, which unites Christ and the believing heart, so that what each has individually becomes common to all." In it we receive Christ's communicative[123]

118. WA 3:412,37–41. See W. Maurer, "Kirche und Geschichte nach Luthers Dictata super Psalterium," in *Lutherforschung heute* [1958], 85–101, here 97.

119. See pp. 12–14. and pp. 18–20, n. 90.

120. Cf. WA 10/1/1:48,11–14 (Sermon on Titus 2:11–15; 1522): "The exchange is presented to you, only with the word and gospel, and illuminates him through your ears for your heart and offers him to you as the one who gave himself for you, for your unrighteousness, for your uncleanness."

121. Cf. pp. 356–359.

122. On the following, see the section WA 10/1/1:71,14–72,18 = LW 52:15.

123. Cf. the freedom tractate: "Now just as Christ by his birthright obtained these two prerogatives, so he *imparts* them to and *shares* them *with everyone* who believes in him according to the law of the above-mentioned marriage" (WA 7:56,35–37 = LW 31:354; author's emphasis).

being. In this self-communication of himself, Christ removes us from ourselves in our sin. In contrast to the sermon of the previous year, the appropriation (namely, "that you make his birth for you your own and exchange yours with him, so that you leave behind your birth and take over his"[124]) comes entirely from Christ's promise and no longer from reflecting on our humiliation as Christians.

If the "sacrament" is thus redefined in the sense of the reformational concept of promise, the "example" is also linked with it in a new way.

> If therefore Christ has now become yours, and you have been cleansed in such faith by him, you have received your inheritance and chief good, without any merit of your own, as you see, but solely out of the pure love of God, who gives you his Son's goods and works as your own possession. Then follows the example of the good works that you can do for your neighbor, as you see that Christ has done for you.[125]

Christ's vicarious action for us results in our vicarious action for our neighbor. Christ grants us faith in the word; we extend love to others by faith. Because different things are given in each case, the actual substitution is different in each case and one cannot be compared with the other. The second follows from the first; the first is the reason for the second. Accordingly, both are not encompassed by a common logos, one and the same human nature, one and the same possibility of human self-understanding, as would be the case with the archetypal Christology. First of all, then, sacrament and example are *not* analogous. The correspondence *follows*.[126] It does not result from something that has always been presupposed but is based specifically on the promise.

The crucial point to note is that the sacrament can only take precedence over the example in such a way that the two no longer merge into each other if the sacrament, constituted by the spoken word, is understood as a promise. But

---

124. WA 10/1/1:73,16–18 = LW 52:16 (trans. alt.).

125. WA 10/1/1:73 (23–74,21),23–74,4 = LW 52:16(–17) (trans. alt.); cf. 10/1/1:75:11–16 = 52:17 ("These are the two things that Christians should do. The one is directed toward Christ . . . the other is directed toward their neighbor") as well as 10/1/1:75:20–23 = 52:18 and the "knowing Christ" (*Christum cognoscere*) as the epitome of Scripture: "What more do you want to know? What more do you need? If you know Christ to the extent (as has been said above) that through him you walk toward God in faith and toward your neighbor in love and if you do to your neighbor as God has done to you, that is indeed the whole Bible in a nutshell" (10/l/1:75:20–23 = 52:22; trans. alt.).

126. We have to conclude, therefore, that Luther genuinely grasps the meaning of John 13:34 and its καθὼς: "Love one another *as* I have loved you" (cf. John 15:12; 17:11), which he quotes in the section interpreted here in terms of its double structure.

as long as the promise has to be won through existential verification, through penitence, it is inevitable that humiliation before God will merge with humiliation for the benefit of the world, as the early Luther texts clearly document.[127]

This result is confirmed in advance by the thesis that concludes and summarizes the *freedom tractate*, which undoubtedly plays a key role in the overall understanding of Luther's theology:

> We conclude, therefore, that Christians do not live in themselves, but in Christ and their neighbor. Otherwise, they are not Christians. They live in Christ through faith, and in their neighbor through love. *By faith they are caught up beyond themselves into God*, and conversely *by love they descend beneath themselves into their neighbor.* Yet they always remain in God and his love, as Christ says in John 1[:51], "Truly, truly, I say to you, you will see heaven opened, and the angels of God ascending and descending upon the Son of man."[128]

When writing the tractate, Luther was so absorbed with its theme that in the last months of 1520, he repeatedly took up and varied the motifs and theses of this work in sermons, especially his Genesis sermons, and with these variations even gives an instructive commentary on them.[129]

One of these sermons clearly reveals which idea guided him in formulating the double movement that unmistakably characterizes the final thesis of the tractate; at the same time, it explains the passage John 1:51, which was added to the thesis as scriptural proof.

The sermon deals with the interpretation of Jacob's ladder in Genesis 28, preserved in Melanchthon's transcript[130] and in a more detailed version.[131] This interpretation "gives the purpose and reason for the church"[132] and dates to December 1520:[133] "Angels ascending and descending: this refers to teachers and heralds of God's word . . . they must first ascend, that is, they themselves must

---

127. Cf., for example, WA 56:199,24–35 = LW 25:183 (Scholion on Rom. 2:11; 1515/16) and the text 56:419,6–17 = 25:411 (Scholion on Rom. 10:10) quoted on p. 46.

128. WA 7:69,12–18 = LW 31:371 (author's emphasis; trans. alt.).

129. Cf. WA 9:395,9ff. (still 1519); 9:477,10–22 (cf. 9:506,5–8); 9:478–79; 9:482,1ff.; 9:484,5ff.; 9:488,10; 9:499,28ff.; 9:506,16ff.; 9:513,3ff.

130. WA 9:494–95, 9:497–98.

131. WA 9:403–11. See 9:494, 497, but esp. 9:517, n. 1.

132. WA 9:497,14.

133. See WA 9:494,97, but esp. 517, n. 1.

first be believers, faithful and godly, then they must descend and bring the divine things to humans."[134] Here Luther's comment is formulated specifically with the preaching office in mind. However, it is found more generally as in the thesis of the freedom tractate in the *Operationes in Psalmos* (on Ps. 14:1) that prepared it,[135] which reads: "Entering into Christ is faith . . . but going out is love."[136]

In his early theology, Luther interpreted the double movement of the angels on Jacob's ladder exclusively in terms of our relationship with God: "For these two things, namely, God's goods and our evils, are the very ladder to God, by which we descend into ourselves and ascend into God."[137] Our relationship to the world is included in this double movement, which on closer inspection turns out to be only one, that of the way of negation. By recognizing our "evils," we recognize God's "goods": self-knowledge and knowledge of God are intrinsically intertwined. However, since the knowledge of God lacks any positive determination, the only thing that remains is negative self-knowledge,[138] both as a relationship with God and as a relationship with the world.

---

134. WA 9:495,13–17. See the parallel passage (9:408,16–17): "First they should be deified (*vorgottet*), then become human again."

135. W. Maurer, *Von der Freiheit eines Christenmenschen*, 159–66, sees the interpretation of Ps. 14 finished already by Easter 1520.

136. WA 5:407,42–408,13 (quotation: 5:408,4–5,7). See Poliander's marginal note to the sermon of Dec. 30, 1520 (see pp. 329–331), on the transition from sacrament to example: "This is to enter into Christ and to come out again, John 14" (but according to 5:408,3–4, the text must be John 10:9); 9:533 on line 2. The fact that Luther could not repeat in the Christmas sermons of 1520 the precise determination of the turning point of the movement of the turn under discussion that he had made in the freedom tractate, and only managed to do so in the sermon of the following year, shows how difficult it was to find it and how difficult it is to hold onto it.

137. WA 1:447,9–11 (Sermon of Sept. 21, 1516): on this, see p. 116. In the Romans lectures (on 12:8: THE ONE WHO RULES, WITH DILIGENCE; WA 56:458,13–17 = LW 25:450), the double movement refers only to the subordination to superiors. "For to ascend means to rule over, but to descend is to be attentive [to the needs of others]. But they do not rule to benefit themselves, since everyone who is exalted is exalted for this reason, so that they do not seek anything for themselves, for they no longer live for themselves but must acknowledge that they have been become servants of their servants" (ll. 14–17; trans. alt.).

138. As a late witness to this early theology, see this insightful interpretation of Ps. 116:11 in the *Operationes in Psalmos* (on Ps. 5:11), 1519: "'I said in my ecstasy: everyone is a liar.' This ecstasy was the tribulation in which we are taught how vain and deceitful every human being is who does not hope in God alone. For humans are human until they become God, who alone is true. By participating in him, they also are made true, as long as they cling to him in true faith and hope after being reduced to nothingness by this ecstasy. For where do they go, who hope in God, if not to their own nothingness? But where do they depart to, who go off into nothingness, if not to him from whom they came? But they came from God and his

This theology of radical negation, which connects the early Luther with a certain form of late medieval mysticism,[139] shares with the final thesis of the freedom tractate precisely the radical negation ("Christians do not live in themselves") that means freedom from the self and from the world, insofar as the latter claims the ultimate dignity for itself. But the place "outside of us" = "in God" is not only gained negatively (= not in oneself) but also in the God for us (= in Christ), who draws us to himself in his word of promise. God's being and acting for us—that is, *the Christ-promise alone—is what establishes the distinction between faith and love.* If the Christ-promise did not appear or appeared only as an internal reversal of the negation, then both our relationship to God *and* our relationship to the world would be seen as nothing more than our self-humiliation. Both relationships would merge into each other without

---

nothingness. Therefore, *they return to God, who return to nothingness.* For they cannot fall outside the hand of God, who fall outside of themselves and every creature, for the hand of God embraces them on all sides" (WA 5:167,38–168,6; author's emphasis. See Luther's answer to Prierias: "The saints . . . reduced themselves to nothingness, that God may be all in all"; 1:654,12–14). God's omnipotence and ubiquity are thus only experienced in the "return to nothingness." Humans are in God, who embraces them and the world, but only as they reflect on themselves as those who have become nothing. Thus, completely contrary to Luther's intention to abandon himself and hope in God alone, the "purest hope in the purest God" (5:166,18) returns to itself in that it actually only has itself. However, with such reflection, humans run the risk of wanting to encompass the very thing that encompasses them (cf. the reception of precisely these ideas in F. Gogarten, who deals with Luther's interpretation of Ps. 5:11 specifically in *Die Frage nach Gott*, 88–112). The extent to which this danger is averted in the broader context where Luther talks strongly about the promise (5:175,11–31) does not need to be discussed here.

139. Cf. the *Deutsche Theologie*, chap. 23,1, "Taulers Predigten" (ed. F. Vetter; 88,7ff.; 370,22–38; 408,12–14) and Gerson's *Sermo factus in coena Domini pro humilitate*, esp. the first meditation of his concluding "commendation of humility" (*Opera*, 1489, vol. 2, 40 T/U), for example, the formulations: "True humility, I say, when it happily leaves God's supreme power and glory and his most magnificent majesty to be seen and considered in all its weakness, shame, and servility, becomes the most powerful and most glorious and most free empress and ruler over all things . . . even over the most truculent of its realm . . . To be sure, it assumes all things for its own facility and use, while for God's sake it has determined to despise itself and all other things. What contempt will satisfy humility more amply? . . . Therefore, how great is the rule of humility to have all things under its feet through noble contempt. It exalted Christ who suffered the greatest humiliation in his passion and gave him the name that is above every name that at the name of Jesus every knee will bow . . . Consider his dominion over all things through humility." These references here are meant to do no more than formulate one *task*: *to present the early Luther's concept of freedom which is included in his theology of radical negation and to compare it with the texts of Tauler and Gerson as well as with the* "Deutsche Theologie." Worthy of consideration here is W. Thimme, "Die 'Deutsche Theologie' und Luthers 'Freiheit eines Christenmenschen.'" Ein Vergleich, *ZThK* 40 (1932): 193–222.

distinction and become one,[140] even though the intention of the way of negation is precisely the opposite: to completely separate and radically abstract God from the world.[141] Only in the *deus pro nobis*, the God for us, in the oral promise of salvation, are God and world, faith and love, not radically separated only to collapse into one another, precisely in their radical separation, but differentiated and materially subordinated to one another—so that love is based on faith and, by virtue of its basis, passes on its received foundation ("then they descend and bring divine things to humans"). This passing on, this love, corresponds in its movement to the movement of its foundation. But this correspondence does not occur as a repetition of its foundation but rather as if it were turned away from it ("above us"—"below us"). However, this turn in the correspondence does not mean a turning away from the basis of the correspondence but a desire to leave it precisely in its uniqueness and without analogy.[142]

While in the theology of pure negation, we humans embrace both God and the world in the negative self-knowledge that we experience; on the other hand, according to the thesis of the freedom tractate, we are between God and the world, or more precisely, "*in* Christ and our neighbor," embraced by God and his "love."[143] This is because faith no longer bends back on itself as the self returning to nothingness[144] but rather is focused on its basis and support namely,

---

140. See, in contrast, the interpretation of Gen. 28 of Dec. 1520 already mentioned (n. 131), the "double structure" of Jacob's dream corresponding to the ascent and descent of the angels: "Here sleep has two phases: we sleep to God and we sleep to the world. They sleep to God, who fearlessly wait on God, listening to what the Lord may say in them . . . We sleep to the world if we are poor in spirit" (WA 9:408,6–9). Thus we see the distinction between the promise, in which Jacob stands "alone under God's power and protection" and "our deduction, from the attendant circumstances, that he was abandoned by all creatures" (WA 9:409,6–29).

141. The reformational Luther will make the judgment (WA 5:108,2–5; see on that below chap. 9, n. 10) that we will not find *God* on the path of such abstraction but will remain most deeply attached to the *world* we are trying to escape.

142. The return of love to faith, which is the constantly renewed connection of love to its origin, has nothing to do with this impossible reversibility. See the *Treatise on Good Works* of 1520: "Then suffering compels faith to call upon God's name and to praise him in such suffering, and thus comes back through the third commandment, and back into the second. And through the same invocation of God's name and praise, faith grows and comes into its own and thus strengthens itself through the two works of the third and second commandments. *Thus faith goes out into works and through works comes back to itself again* (WA 6:249,27–33 = LW 44:79). It is not said here that faith only becomes itself in love, since it is itself before works of love by virtue of God's work. Rather it is emphasized here that faith not only initiates love but *remains* its origin.

143. It goes without saying that this *caritas* is not identical with the love of the neighbor, which is differentiated from faith.

144. "For where do they go, who hope in God, except into the nothingness of themselves?" (WA 5:168,1–2; see above n. 138).

the promise. It is not a duplication of self-abandonment, of love, but its foundation. Insofar as faith is the foundation of love but is itself based on the *deus pro nobis*, on the promise of Christ, it is also the foundation of love. At the same time, the *promissio* we experience the irreversibility of Christ's actions for us and our actions for our neighbor, thus establishing the concrete difference between faith and love.

CHAPTER 9

The New Christology

THIS CHAPTER, TOGETHER with the next, develops the thesis already hinted at in the previous one, that, at the same time as his reformational concept of the promise emerged, the archetypal Christology of Luther's early period was transformed into a new Christology that must be described as a trinitarian mediator Christology. This distinction between two christological types does not mean, however, that the two, regardless of their overall differences, are not connected to each other in detail by a variety of motifs and references. In addition, it is almost impossible to distinguish between primary and secondary christological tendencies in the statements of the years 1517/18–1520/21 to be considered here. For the christological statements have their place in the context of the interpretation of certain texts of Scripture and, accordingly, each has a considerable ability to persist in the history of interpretation. Therefore, we should not expect that the new reformational starting point or organizing principle (*Ansatz*) of Christology that occurs in one place will immediately and consistently be taken up in another or taken up at all, especially since it only became controversial indirectly—namely, in the new understanding of word and sacrament that gave rise to it. The picture is therefore complicated. The fact that the new approach (*Ansatz*) can be discovered in it at all is solely a consequence of the question of how the word is to be understood.

A. Archetypal Christology finds its classical expression, so to speak, in the scholion on Hebrews 2:10 (THE AUTHOR OF THEIR SALVATION)[1]: Christ, the obedient man on the cross, is the sign erected for our salvation.

> This sign beautifully shows the manner in which we are saved, namely, through Christ as through an archetype or pattern, to whose image all who are saved are conformed. For God, the Father, made Christ to be a sign and archetype, that those who cling to him by faith should be transformed into the same image and thus be drawn away from the images of the world. Hence Isaiah 11:[12]: "The Lord will set up a sign for the nations and assemble the outcasts of Israel." Again, in the same chapter [11:10]: "The root of Jesse, who stands as a sign for the peoples, him will the Gentiles implore." Hence this gathering of God's children into one

1. WA 57/3:124–25 = LW 29:131–32 (trans. alt.); cf. 57/3:126,3–5 = 29:132–33.

> happens in the same way as if the town magistrate were organizing a spectacle to which the citizens would flock together, leaving their homes and work behind to gather at this one place. Thus Christ through the gospel, offered to the whole world a spectacle,[2] captivates everyone with his knowledge and contemplation, and draws them away from those things they cling to in the world. In this very way, they are transformed and become like him. For thus it says that Christ is the cause and captain of our salvation because through him God draws and leads his children to glory, for it is commonly said that Christ is the instrument and means by which God leads his children. Since, therefore, he thus determined to draw his children through Christ, it rightly says that "it was fitting that he should make Christ perfect through suffering," that is, make him the most perfect and complete example by which he would move and draw his children.[3]

Luther always maintained that it is the man Jesus, and especially him crucified, in whom God can be *grasped*. In this respect, he continues to maintain the concept of sign clearly developed here. But can God be predicated of the man Jesus? Can Jesus be called God even in his deepest humanity? Do I really climb the ladder of Christ's humanity to *God*?[4] And accordingly, is my forsaking the world as exemplified by the cross[5] and being "conformed" to the mind of Christ really *salvation*? The cross as such does not enable me to see in it the

---

2. How this "offering" is to be understood as a gifting of the crucified can be seen from the explanation of the fourth petition of the Lord's Prayer of 1517 (see pp. 97–102).

3. Christ and believers are then encompassed by the same reality. For the hermeneutical implications, see, for example, Luther's preparation for the interpretation of Ps. 4:8 in the *Operationes*: "Now therefore having heard this exposition concerning the people of Christ, it will be very easy to explain the Psalm in relation to Christ himself, the head, who is the form and model for all his faithful, who are his body. Therefore, the same words and the same meaning are understood of both" (*Unbekannte Fragmente aus Luthers Psalmenvorlesung*, 1518, ed. E. Vogelsang, 56:19–22).

4. Cf. the scholion on Heb. 1:2: "For that humanity is our holy ladder by which we ascend to God in order to know him, as in Gen. 28[:12]" (WA 57/3:99,3–4 = LW 29:111). For an understanding of the history of interpretation of the topos of Jacob's ladder as it relates to the cross of Christ, which we also find in the liturgy and as a motif in art, see the evidence in J. Ficker (57/3:99,4).

5. On the concept "*imago*" (= "image") = "reality," see chap. 5, n. 52. A very concise formulation of the "detachment" (*Entweltlichung*) can be found in the scholion on Heb. 9:23: "To cling to God is to be freed from the world and all creatures; to bear the image of Christ is to live according to the affection and example of Christ" (on 9:23) (WA 57/3:214,20–21 = LW 29:216; but cf. on that 57/3:215,4–5 = 29:216).

glory of God,[6] to see in the rejected the accepted, in the cursed the blessed,[7] in death life,[8] and so in my own case, to see in my request God's answer, and in my need his rescue.[9] With this powerfully presented theology of negation, where the negation turns into an affirmation, it remains unclear how I can be certain that I am actually dealing with God in this negation and that it is God who turns it around. It is also unclear whether calling the negation an affirmation is not just an arbitrary and idiosyncratic assertion on my part. Luther himself later recognized this ambiguity, which is a characteristic of his early theology and for that very reason its decisive weakness, and did not let it appear again.[10]

---

6. "God is strange in his saints, for he hands them over to tribulation and thus crowns them" (on Ps. 4:4a [Latin]: KNOW THAT THE LORD HAS DEALT WITH HIS SAINTS IN A STRANGE WAY; WA 3:62,36–37; 1513–15). [The psalm verse with "strange" is not included in English Bibles, ed.]

7. Again on Ps. 4:4b (THE LORD WILL HEAR ME WHEN I CRY TO HIM): "No one cries unless they are in grave distress. Here, therefore, that cry is said to be loud, because in the days of his flesh, [Jesus] offered up tears to God, who heard him because of his reverence. Therefore, the meaning is this: when you see that I am most rejected, then I will be most accepted. And when you think, according to the foolishness of your senses, that I am cursed by God, then I will be most blessed. And this will be because the Lord has dealt with me, his saint, in a strange way." (WA 57/3:63,10–16).

8. "These are strange things: not so much the miracles that he did, but much more, that he killed death with death, and overcame punishment with punishment, suffering with suffering, shame with shame, so that death in Christ is so precious in the sight of the Lord that it can be eternal life, punishment can be joy, suffering can be pleasure, shame can be glory; and conversely, life can be death, joy can be punishment, pleasure can be suffering, glory can be shame, but according to a different way of viewing God, and of course, human beings" (on Ps. 111:4: WA 4:243,7–13 = LW 11:377–78; 1513–15; trans. alt.). But how does this way of seeing God become mine?

9. WA 3:63,20–23 (Conclusion to the scholion on Ps. 4:4 [Latin]: see nn. 6-7): "Thus it is with all the saints, God does 'strange' things with them in this sense, that they are heard the most when they cry out, when they are in their greatest need, and the ones who feel most abandoned are the ones most accepted." See the sermon on the stilling of the storm pericope: p. 169.

10. This is impressively shown by the revision of precisely the interpretation of Ps. 4:4 [Latin] of the *Dictata*, which we referred to in the previous notes (see nn. 6,7,9), in the *Operationes in Psalmos* (1519): "If you only consider his death and all that is shown to us in Christ's sufferings, and do not recognize the divine will in them, and if you bear it and praise it, you are bound to be scandalized by that cross and flee to your own cross where you will soon become an idolater and give the creature the glory due to God alone" (WA 5:108,2–5). Significantly (see p. 353), with reference to John (16:3), it says: "To know Christ is to know his cross and to perceive God under his crucified flesh. For this is what God wills. This is the will of God, indeed, this is God" (5:108,9–11). "Therefore, we need admonition and exhortation by which we may be raised to recognize God in such cases" (5:108,32–33). On the matter of being answered, Luther says that since the psalmist cannot demonstrate that his prayer is answered because God does not seem

In the sense of the archetypal Christology, it can be said in summary that the way of salvation consists in us individually accepting our allotted suffering as such, which Jesus experienced on the cross more intensely and more radically than anyone else.[11] In viewing salvation this way, we see that the radical nature of Jesus's suffering is a sufficient basis for our own suffering and that therefore it has happened "for us."[12] "For thus 'the Lord dealt with his holy one [Jesus] in a strange way.' But these strange things were done radically and causally in Christ's suffering, and now it is necessary for all people to be conformed to his example."[13]

The christological type outlined seems to still be present even in 1519—in the interpretation of Psalm 5:2 [Eng. 5:1] in the *Operationes in Psalmos*.[14]

---

able to be grasped, he (Luther) will do the best he can: "The psalmist promises, of course, God's help, as if to say: I have this one thing that I can offer you for your comfort: I can promise you with confidence that you will be heard. Therefore, believe it, so that you do not love vanity, that you do not exchange the glory of God, but wait for his answer and be strengthened in this also by my example, for I am most certain that the Lord will answer me, not only at this time, but whenever I cry to him" (5:109,27–35).

11. F. Gogarten rightly says that Luther "understands the cross of Christ from his own experience of God" (*Die Verkündigung Jesu Christi*, 317; likewise, pp. 318, 319, 320). But he overlooks the fact that Luther later corrected himself on this point (cf. n. 17).

E. Wolf, "Die Christusverkündigung bei Luther," *Peregrinatio* 1, 30–80, here 74, correctly sees in the idea of the archetype a "relationship of mutual interpretation of the person and work of Christ, on the one hand, and of the person and life of the believer, on the other," but because he does not make any historical differentiation, he does not recognize the fact that Luther decisively corrected his early archetypal theology with his later mediator theology.

12. WA 4:236,18: Gloss on Ps. 111:4. The scholion on this verse (see n. 8) shows clearly that the "for us" of Luther's early theology is determined quite differently than that of his reformational theology (see chap. 8).

13. WA 4:243,13–15 = LW 11:378 (Scholion on Ps. 111:4; trans. alt.).

14. "Moreover, these two things again describe the sum of our whole life: to have a king and a God. He rules as king when he takes us away from ourselves and leads us to himself. He is God when he accepts us as we come to him and fills us with himself—that is, with his divine goods. His first work is the cross, our passover (*phase*) or crossing (*transitus*), where he leads us away from the world, away from our sins, and completely mortifies us. His second work is our acceptance and glorification . . . For Christ by his two natures does both of these things. By the rule of his humanity or (as the apostle says) of his flesh, which happens in faith, he conforms us to himself and crucifies us, making of us hapless and proud gods true human beings, that is, wretched sinners. For since we ascended into Adam in the likeness of God, therefore he descended into our likeness, to bring us back to a knowledge of ourselves. But this happens in the sacrament of the incarnation. This is the rule of faith, in which the cross of Christ reigns, overthrowing the divinity perversely sought and restoring the humanity and weakness of the flesh that was wrongly despised and abandoned. But by the rule of his divinity and glory, Christ will conform us to his glorious body, where we will be like him, no longer sinners or weak, no longer led or ruled, but kings and children of God like the angels" (WA 5:128,29–129,6).

However, since it is entirely soteriological in thrust, it cannot be demonstrated with certainty but can only be said to be probable that it is based on Luther's early Christology. The fact that Luther presents it here is suggested by the hermeneutical schema that he retained from the *Dictata*,[15] according to which the person praying is Christ, who speaks "in his own person" for all Christians as their archetype. The humiliation and exaltation that Christ underwent is reproduced in them. This double movement corresponds to the two natures in the person of Christ that are understood to bring about our humiliation and exaltation, which is admittedly not a present event (*in re*) but one that lies in the future (*in spe*). This explicitly soteriological statement of the two natures doctrine, which is reminiscent of the factually identical use of the more specific christological figure of the communication of attributes as a cipher for the *simul iustus et peccator* in the Romans lectures and in the interpretation of the *Seven Penitential Psalms*,[16] makes it clear that Luther, while retaining the eschatological reservation, can still say that humiliation and exaltation follow each other in *succession*. Although this is how we must understand his early soteriology, it would contradict his later theology if this, at the same time, were considered a direct statement of his Christology—as it seems to be when Luther says here that "Christ as man must be apprehended first before Christ as God, and that the cross of his humanity must be sought before the glory of his divinity. But if we have Christ as man, he will lead us to Christ as God of his own accord."[17]

B. One of the most interesting phenomena that we encounter when enquiring about the concept of the *promissio* is that at the same moment the Mass is understood in terms of the gifting word; that is, when Luther's concept of the promise, which he first discovered in a reconfiguration of the sacrament of penance, also reshapes the Mass, God and humans are thought of as being together in Christ for the first time with the same rigor that we find in the

15. Cf. WA 3:64,35; 65,2 ("I and my faithful ones").

16. See chap. 2, n. 242, and p. 166.

17. F. Gogarten relies on texts like these when he says: "And if the approach of Luther's christological thinking is correct, namely, that it must begin with the real and true humanity of Jesus, then Christology can only speak about that which has its basis in his humanity and so given this limitation, can only speak about who Jesus is as a human being" (*Christ the Crisis*, 44 [trans. alt.], with reference to Ebeling; see *Crisis*, 1 and the reference there to precisely WA 5:129). The divinity of Christ would therefore be a predicate of his humanity. If one can infer a directly christological statement from the text, which as mentioned, is entirely soteriologically oriented (the very thing we find Luther doing in his early theology), which is questionable anyway (see above), it must be said—and this is certainly true of Gogarten's Luther reception as a whole—that Gogarten bases his historical thinking on precisely that which Luther had just overcome through his reformational theology. This is an astonishing thing, but investigating it would be a task in itself.

writings of the Reformation era. On top of that, for the first time, the traditional formula of the unity of God and humans, in one and the same person, loses the purely illustrative character that it had before and acquires its real objective function. It can be shown that Luther's reformational Christology and his doctrine of the Lord's Supper are originally intertwined. The archetypal Christology and the trinitarian mediator theology indeed overlap in some texts, but in one place the break can be clearly seen. This is important enough to warrant closer examination.

The break is evident in the explanation of the fourth petition ("Give us today our daily bread") when we compare the two interpretations of the Lord's Prayer of 1517 and 1518/19. According to the first version, this meant, as already described,[18] the word, the food of the soul as a means of devotion, and faith as the reenactment of Jesus's archetypal suffering in penitence. In contrast, in the second version Luther speaks of the oral word in the form of a promise. Important now is the question: "When and through whom does the word come to us?"[19] In keeping with the new concept of the promise, the answer emphasizes its oral and public character and, with reference to Isaiah 55:10–11, has the internal word swallowed up in the external word, thus no longer placing it before it, as the original and proper word, as was previously the case.[20] Rather, Luther says the word comes in two ways:

> In the first place, it comes to us through a person; for instance, when God lets a comforting word be heard through a preacher in the church, or otherwise through oneself, which strengthens people and says to them in their hearts: take courage and be bold. For the word of God will surely speak to their hearts in such a way . . . In the second place, the word comes by itself directly, as when God pours his word into the hearts of suffering people, so that they become strong enough to endure everything. For God's word is almighty.[21]

---

18. See pp. 97–102.

19. WA 2:108, 1 = LW 42:52 (*An Exposition of the Lord's Prayer for Ordinary Laypeople*, 1519) (trans. alt.). The question style, known to us from the later catechisms, appears here consistently for the first time in the interpretation of the fourth petition: see 2:106,20 = 42:50; 2:107,21 = 42:51; 2:108,1,21 = 42:52; 2:111,26 = 42:56; 2:113,4–5, 19–21 = 42:58–59.

20. Cf. the use of Isa. 55:10–11 in the *Dictata* in connection with the interpretation of Ps. 45:2–3: WA 3:258–59 = LW 10:215–16. Cf. pp. 8–11 in the context of the whole of chap. 1.

21. WA 2:108,2–20 = LW 42:52 (trans. alt.).

This point is underscored by a parallel passage. Again, Luther says that the word comes in two ways:

> First, outwardly through people . . . Second, inwardly through the teaching of God himself. But this must be with the external word, but the external word is also free. But when the outward word functions properly, the internal word does not remain external. For God will never permit his word to go forth without bearing fruit. He is there and teaches inwardly himself what he gives outwardly through the priest. As he says in Isaiah 55, my word that goes forth from my mouth will not return empty, but like the rain that soaks the earth and makes it fruitful, so will my word go forth and accomplish everything for which I send it.[22]

"What then is the bread or word of God?"[23] As in the freedom tractate,[24] this question refers more specifically to the unity and unambiguity of the word: "But which then is the word, when there are many words of God?"[25] "Word" in the singular can only refer to Christ[26]; the word is the Word—for this Luther significantly relies on a Johannine "I am" formula: "The bread, the word, and the food are none other than Jesus Christ our Lord himself, as he says in John 6[:51], 'I am the living bread.'"[27] There is only one word bound up with Jesus Christ

---

22. WA 2:112,7–113,2 = LW 42:57–58 (trans. alt.). The relationship between the outer and inner word is defined in precisely the same way here as in the *Pro veritate* theses (30–33). See pp. 215–217, esp. n. 173.

23. WA 2:111,26 = LW 42:56.

24. Sections §5 and §6 (WA 7:22–23; German version not in LW) are connected by the question: "You may ask, 'What then is the word of God, and how is it to be used, since there are so many words of God?'" (WA 7:51,12–13 = LW 31:346). This transition corresponds exactly to that of §7 to §§8–9 in the question: "But you may ask, how is it that faith alone justifies . . . since so many works . . . are prescribed for us in Scripture" (7:52,20–22 = 31:348 [trans. alt.]). The unity and unambiguity of the word is answered by the unity and certainty of faith—where faith can only be determined by the promise in distinction to the law (§§8–9). Accordingly, the lines of §§5–6 and §§7–9 converge in §10: "The one who hears the word becomes like the word" [lit. as is the word, so is the soul created by it] (i.e. in faith); 7:53,26–27 = 31:349 (trans. alt.). This completes the first of the three lines of argumentation in the first main part of the freedom tractate (see 7:53,31–4 = 31:350).

25. WA 2:108,21 = LW 42:52.

26. Cf. WA 2:111,27–33 = LW 42:56.

27. WA 2:111,27–28 = LW 42:56. Of the four possibilities for understanding the formula considered by R. Bultmann (*The Gospel of John*, 225, n.3), the fourth would be the most likely. However,

himself: not the intangible, internal word but—and this is the new insight!—the external oral human word that brings the internal word with it. Only this external spoken word is inseparably connected with Christ himself. This intertwining of the two and the unity it establishes is clearly expressed at the end, where Luther summarizes the whole interpretation of the petition[28]: "Christ is the bread, God's word is the bread, and yet there is but one thing, one bread."[29] To stress the interconnectedness once more in all its sharpness, Luther explains it chiastically: "He is in the word and the word is in him."[30] Thus, the idea of the heavenly Christ and the host Christ, previously retained as a reference to a spiritual meaning,[31] is radically rejected. "How does that help you if he sits in heaven or is hidden in the form of bread?"[32] "Thus he is of no use to you, and you will not be able to avail yourself of him."[33] Instead of highlighting the static distance from heaven and the equally static proximity to the bread, Luther stresses the dynamic, functional word that communicates itself to us: Christ himself "must be distributed, served up to you, and become words through the internal and external word, for that is truly God's word."[34] He does not reveal himself, but "God makes him into words so that you can hear him and therefore recognize him."[35]

Luther is now particularly keen to emphasize that *God* communicates himself in the Christ who is present together with the oral word. God is not understood as the one who makes the crucified Christ the archetype of his action under the form of its opposite (*sub contrario*) in order to thus make his proper work

---

Bultmann's definition of the "recognition formula," "that here the ἐγώ is the predicate," is not satisfactory because the ἐγώ is more than a predicate. In such sentences, Luther does not, to use Hegel's words (*The Phenomenology of Mind*, preface, 13), "take the subject as a fixed point to which the predicates are attached as their support, through a movement within the person who knows it and which is not considered as belonging to the point itself; but only through this movement (i.e. belonging to the point and not to those who know it) would the content of the sentences be presented as their subject" (trans. alt.). See Luther's doctrine of the two natures included in the discussion on pp. 363–370.

28. WA 2:113, 35–114, 4 = LW 42:61–62 (*An Exposition of the Lord's Prayer*, 1519).

29. WA 2:114,1–2 = LW 42:59 (trans. alt.).

30. WA 2:114,2–3 = LW 42:59 (trans. alt.).

31. See p. 114.

32. WA 2:113,38–39 = LW 42:59.

33. WA 2:113,37 = LW 42:59 (trans. alt.).

34. WA 2:113,39–114, 1 = LW 42:59 (trans. alt.).

35. WA 2:113,37–38 = LW 42:59 (trans. alt.).

(*opus proprium*) visible in the hidden action of his alien work (*opus alienum*). Rather, God is understood as the one who "distributes" and "gives" Christ in and with his word. God is the one who works with Christ in the same unity as Christ works with the oral word. Thus we can be certain of *God* through Christ in the word. Christ, on the other hand, no longer appears in the oral word as an archetype but trinitarianly as a *gift*, as God's declared will and the present demonstration of his power.[36]

> The fourth little word is *give*. No one can get the bread, Jesus Christ, by himself, neither by studying, hearing, asking, nor by searching. If we are truly to know Christ, all books are too few, all teachers too feeble, and all reason too dull. The Father himself, and only the Father, must reveal him and give him to us, as Jesus states in John 6: "No one comes to me unless the Father who sent me draws them." He says further, "No one can receive me or know me, unless it is given to them by the Father." And "everyone who hears that I am from the Father comes to me."[37]

(A more detailed determination of the gift follows on from these explanations of the external and internal word.)

The striking compilation of three Johannine passages, all from the end of chapter 6, points to the simultaneous interpretation of John 6:37–40 that Luther sent to Spalatin on February 12, 1519, for the elector.[38] It is the authentic commentary on our passage and documents the decisive influence of Johannine theology on Luther's emerging reformational Christology:[39]

> See and pay attention to how Christ declares that he has his divinity and all things in common with the Father. He said that he does all things by the will of the Father. Therefore, there is no doubt that the works that Christ did are the works of the Father. But when he testified that

36. The terminological shift from "sacrament" to "gift" should not be overlooked (cf. pp. 76–77). But it is not the concepts themselves that are decisive but the context that determines them in each case. Luther also speaks of "sacrament" in his reformational theology but uses the word there in a different way than he did in his early theology.

37. WA 2:111,34–112,5 = LW 42:56–57 (trans. alt.).

38. WA Br1:326–31. "I have in my hands a vernacular version of the Lord's Prayer to be published again" (I.12).

39. To examine this influence in detail (cf., e.g., the 1518 Lenten sermon on John 11: WA 1:273–77, esp. 1:274,28–275,37) would be an important task. In general, the Johannine element in Luther's theology is usually given far too little attention.

> he too does the same works, Christ says: "And I will raise him from the dead." Yet surely the power to give life and raise from the dead belongs to God alone. But since it is one and the same work, it clearly shows that Christ is true God and one with the Father, since there are not two Gods. And yet, when he distinguishes himself from his Father, as if speaking of another and calling himself the Son, he beautifully concludes that he is true God from the Father who is truly God, and that both are not two, but one God, equal in power and might, willing and doing the same things.
>
> Again, it is the same argument when Christ says that he will not cast out, will not destroy. For to save life requires the same power as to give life. The Father gives, and the Son does not destroy but saves. Therefore, he is indeed other, but not a different God, having the same power as the Father. Most importantly of all, he proves what he says when he declares "whoever believes in the Son" etc. It is unbelief to believe in anything but the one true God, and yet the Father, the true God, wants to be believed in the Son. And what does the Son want, but to be believed in the true God? For he will not give his glory to another[40] But it is God's glory to be believed in the Son. For no creature is sufficient to be able to support or benefit those who believe in them. For faith, hope, and love are due to God alone, whence they are also called theological virtues. But [John] adds: "Whoever believes in the Son has eternal life." But faith in the Son could not give eternal life unless he himself were the eternal and true God.[41]

The importance of this text is shown by the fact that the interpretation of WHOEVER BELIEVES IN THE SON, according to this line of thought, occurs again in the basic principle of Luther's first *Explanation of the Creed* (1520)[42] and that this principle already represents his christological position as a whole, which is then developed in the sermons of the Wartburg Postil (1521/22), especially those on Titus 2:11–15, Hebrews 1:1–12, and John 1:1–14.[43] However, the context of the interpretation of the Lord's Prayer, which emphasizes the external word, is the place where we see for the first time from his *Sermon on*

---

40. Cf. the use of Isa. 42:8 (see Isa. 48:11) in the same context in the sermon on Titus 2:11–15 in the Wartburg Postil: WA 10/1/1:57:5–14.

41. WA Br 1:330–31. (ll. 118–40). See, however, the sermon of Feb. 24, 1517, on Matt. 11:27: WA 1:139–40.

42. See p. 383 (for the proof passage, see n. 57).

43. WA 10/1/1.

the Prologue of John of 1521/22 the correction he makes to his understanding of the word in his 1514 sermon on the same text.[44]

His new conception of the word, expressed in the two texts under consideration, became the most important principle to determine the design of the first part of the freedom tractate in the next year, but this happens through several intermediate stages.[45] It sets out what happens in faith through the power of the word with a systematic rigor and balance that is astonishing for Luther, who mostly proceeds exegetically. Accordingly, his theme is the "most holy word of God,"[46] which is presented right at the beginning as the only thing necessary for the Christian's life of freedom (§§3–5). However, the administration of this necessary thing to people belongs, in the final analysis, to the office or ministry (*Amt*) of Christ. For only his "office of the word"[47] (§5)—that is, the proclamation of his person and story (§6)—answers the question about the unity and unambiguity of God's word, which as we have seen, already motivated the interpretation of the Lord's Prayer: "But you will ask, 'what is this word, and how is it to be used, since there are so many words of God.'"[48]

This transition from sections 5 to 6 corresponds exactly to that from sections 7 to sections 8–9 in the question: "But you ask how is it that faith alone justifies . . . since so many works . . . are prescribed for us in Scripture."[49] The unity and unambiguity of the word is answered by the unity and certainty of the faith created by it, but this unity and certainty of faith can only be determined by the *promissio*, "the divine pledge and promise,"[50] in distinction to the law

44. See chap. 1.

45. Since our attention here is focused on the concept of promise, important texts for the development of Luther's theology such as the *Sermon on Two Kinds of Righteousness* of the spring of 1519 (WA 2:143–52 = LW 31:297–306) can be disregarded.

46. WA 7:50,34–35 = LW 31:345. The adjective is reminiscent of thesis 62 of the *Theses on Indulgences* (1:236,22–23 = 31:31), the explanation of which (1:616–17 = 31:230–31), a compendium of Luther's understanding of the gospel prior to his discovery of the promise, seems to be identifiable with what is explained in §§5–9 of the freedom tractate. But this is already called into question by the explanation of the following indulgence thesis ("The gospel destroys the things that exist . . . and reduces them to nothing . . . because it teaches humiliation and the cross" (1:617,7–9 = 31:232).

47. WA 7:51,8–9 = LW 31:346.

48. WA 7:51,12–13 = LW 31:346.

49. WA 7:52,20–22 = LW 31:348 (trans. alt.).

50. WA 7:24,10 [German]; see LW 31:348–49 [Latin]. [The phrases "pledge" and "promise" translate the words *vorheyschung* and *zusage*, where *vorheyschung* (= *Verheißung*) stresses the future dimension of the promise, while *zusage* (= *Zusage*) its present aspect, the latter being the reformational emphasis; trans. note.]

(§§8–9[51]): "Come, believe in Christ, in whom I promise you all grace, righteousness, peace and freedom. If you believe, you have it; if you do not believe, you do not have it."[52] Accordingly, the lines of sections 5–6 and 7–9 converge in section10: "The one who hears the word becomes like the word (in faith)."[53] This concludes the first of the three lines of argument in the first main part of the freedom tractate.[54]

The concept of *promissio*, which is most important in the first course of the discussion because it precisely defines the "most holy word of God" and which reorients[55] the aspects of the early theology of immediacy[56] that were included in it, also dominates the second, parallel course of the discussion (§11).

Here the formula "as the word/so faith" (§10) comes into play in the sense of the basic principle of the freedom tractate: "When God makes a pact with people, it happens in this way: God makes a promise and we believe this divine promise."[57] If people receive everything they need in God's promise, then by using it, by clinging to it, they acknowledge what belongs to God alone: the glory of the creator. Faith—here (and even more clearly in §13) the freedom tractate touches directly on the subject matter of the *Treatise on Good Works*—is the fulfillment of the first commandment; it is perfect obedience; it alone gives honor to God. This effect of the "function of the word" on the "function of faith"[58] is described in phrases reminiscent of the earlier descriptions of the correlation of God and faith.

---

51. Cf. WA 7:34,11–22 [LW does not have the German version of the tractate] or 7:63,34–64,12 = 31:348–49.

52. WA 7:24,12–14 [German].

53. WA 7:53,26–27 = LW 31:349 [The formula Luther uses here is *quale est verbum, talis . . . anima* = as is the word, so is the soul created by it]. It is understandable that Luther can only artificially separate the two lines and that just as he cannot speak of faith without speaking of the word, so, too, he cannot speak of the word without speaking of faith. So the question of its use is already included in the question about the one word ("or in what manner is it to be used"); to speak of its function ("to preach Christ") means to describe its effect ("That is, to feed the soul, make it righteous, set it free, and save it, provided it believes what is preached. For faith alone is the saving and efficacious use of the word of God"; 7:51,15–17 = 31:346).

54. Cf. WA 7:53,31–34 = LW 31:349.

55. Initially, already in the explanation of thesis 38 of the *Theses on Indulgences*. On this, see pp. 200–203.

56. Cf. the Hebrews lectures on the texts mentioned in chap. 4, n. 116.

57. In the formulation of the sermon *Concerning the Testament of Christ*: WA 9:446,7–8. Further formulations are referenced in chap. 6, n. 119.

58. Cf. WA 7:51, 9 = LW 31:346 with 7:53,34–35 = 31:349.

How God and faith "belong together,"[59] in fact can only come together, is shown in detail in a third and final part of the description[60] in which the christological aspect is now specifically addressed (§§12–18).[61] The personal union of God and human nature that takes place in faith by virtue of the Word is not illustrated by the two natures of Christ's person, as in Luther's early theology,[62] but is based on them[63] ("*since* Christ is God and human in that person"[64]). They are no longer the cypher and archetype of the change from suffering to salvation,

59. German "*zuhaufe*." This is how Luther formulates it in his explanation of the first commandment in the *Large Catechism* (*BSLK* 560,21–22 = *BC* 386,3; trans. alt.).

60. The theological (in the narrower sense) and christological aspect, which here in the freedom tractate at first unexpectedly stand side by side (§11 next to §12 but compare §11 with §13 in its foundation [WA 7:55,37–38 = LW 31:352–53] given by §12), overlap from the outset in the sermon of Mar. 25, 1520 (dating with E. Vogelsang, *ZKG* 50 [1931]:129): "God, that mighty warrior, with only the word, promised salvation through Christ. If I trust this promise, if I ascribe to God what is his, that he is just, almighty, truthful etc., how could it ever happen that I should be abandoned by him and deceived by false hope? Behold, God is everything, but humans are nothing. What then are their works? Dust and ashes. But these are the works of faith: that we do not recognize or consider those things that are not, that we realize that there are no sins in us, because Christ took them away. Yet there is no health in us from the sole of our foot even to the crown of our head. But this disease does not harm us. Even though we may feel it, we should not dwell on it but only on Christ who conquers it. If we try to fight with sin and strive against death and the devil on our own, we will succumb, like the Israelites, who were killed by the serpents as they fought against them. But those who gazed at the bronze serpent were saved. So too, we will be saved only by the sure promise of God once we have turned our back on all the machinations of the world and the flesh. This is the same promise by which the illustrious prophet David, having grasped it by faith, remained steadfast and unwavering" (WA 4:616,12–25).

61. It was only briefly highlighted before but not developed (WA 7:51:13–15, 31–34 = LW 31:346–47).

62. Cf. especially the scholion on Heb. 7:1: "But this righteousness, which in Rom. 1:17 is said to be from faith . . . is erroneously explained as referring to the righteousness of God by which he himself is righteous, unless it were understood in such a way that faith so exalts the human heart and transfers it from itself into God that the heart and God become one spirit and thus the divine righteousness itself is in a certain way the righteousness of the heart, the 'formative' righteousness, as they call it, *just as* in Christ, humanity became one and the same person through union with the divine nature" (WA 57/3:187,14–188,3 = LW 29:188–89; trans. alt.; author's emphasis). To illustrate the soteriological dimension of the unity of word and faith, the freedom tractate employs the image of the "heated iron" that "glows like fire because of the union of the fire with it" (7:53,27–28 = 31:349), an image traditionally used to clarify the doctrine of the two natures (cf. *BSLK* 1023 n. 1; 1030,20–27).

63. It only confuses the matter when scholars (like W. Maurer, *Von der Freiheit eines Christenmenschen*, 50) use the words "illustrated by" (*veranschaulicht*) and "based on" (*begründet*) synonymously.

64. WA 7:55,8–9 = LW 31:351 (trans. alt.).

which is always possible with the suffering that is always and everywhere present in the world. Rather, the two natures are the inalienable implication of the real coexistence of the righteous God and sinful humans, of God's life and human death, in the promise and only in it. This implication, without which the word would be vacuous, means nothing but its authority[65] (which of course can only be grasped in its uniqueness when seen in contrast to the causation of an existence based on its archetype), nothing but the full power of the God who conquers sin, death, and hell ("His righteousness is greater than the sins of all, his life stronger than any death, his salvation more invincible than any hell"[66]). Of this God, in the unity of the same person, it can be said that he dies and goes to hell in our place. It only becomes the "happy exchange" (*fröhliche Wechsel*) because of the unity of the person of Christ, who is God and human at the same time. For Luther, the doctrine of the two natures is identical with the teaching of Christ's office as mediator.[67]

If we see here the strong emphasis that the happy exchange takes place in Christ, we must not forget that this refers to the promise that specifies the "most holy word of God." The basis of the promise is not without its settled place in the word in which it is expressed. Just as Luther could not speak of the word without speaking about its effect (namely, faith) and already saw in it the Christ figure of the "happy exchange,"[68] so now, in the detailed description of this exchange, he cannot abstract it from its concrete place in the word. It is no coincidence that at the end of the third line of argument, which is also the end of the first part of the tractate, Luther returns to his starting point, the sermon, which is understood as an effective word that, in the sense of his new understanding of the sacrament,[69] means "that Christ works in us what is said about him and what he himself is called."[70]

---

65. The term is introduced here for interpretation from a corresponding context in the Rogate sermon. Cf. p. 383.

66. WA 7:55,16–17 = LW 31:352 (trans. alt.). From this we can understand why Luther, in both the *Small and Large Catechisms*, puts the explanation of the second article completely under the title "Lord" (*BSLK* 511; 650–53 = *BC* 355; 434–35).

67. This thesis, which here serves as a summary of §12, is explained in detail in another context: see pp. 371–385.

68. WA 7:51,31–34 = LW 31:347.

69. Cf. the similar formulations from the Christmas sermon of 1519 quoted in chap. 8 (and documented with proof texts in nn. 58–59).

70. WA 7:58,40–59,1 = LW 31:357 (trans. alt.).

That the importance of the concept of *promissio* was not overestimated in all this[71] will only become fully clear once it has become possible to determine the point of convergence between the first part of *The Freedom of a Christian* and *The Babylonian Captivity*, where the concept of the promise is dominant.

C. To do this, we turn to a second series of texts that are factually related and proceed from the peculiar association of the reformational concept of *promise* with the concept of *sign* known from the scholion on Hebrews 2:10 in the sermon *Concerning the Testament of Christ*, the Easter Sermon of 1520.

If the entire power of the Mass is seen in the gifting words, then the question arises: "Why did a sign need to be added?"[72] As we can see from Noah's rainbow, from the circumcision of Abraham, from the exodus of the Israelites from Egypt, and finally, from the incarnation, the sign, which is added to the promise and attached to it, is necessary because it points faith to the place where the promise can be found, "so that human nature may grasp God with more certainty and fasten on to a particular sign by which it may take hold of him and not wander or waver in its speculations. For since God cannot be reached through them, it therefore makes one thing or another into a god for itself."[73] The sign—meaning here a particular *story* (the exodus from Egypt; the man Jesus)—appears at first entirely subsidiary to the promise. But when Luther mentions the incarnation at the end of his list of signs[74] in order to determine the relationship between what is subsidiary and what is essential, between the sign and the word, he sticks with it and defines the sign's function in exactly the same way and with the same conceptuality[75] as he had previously used in speaking about the testament

71. We must also take into consideration the section WA 7:63,1–5 = LW 31:362–63 from the second part of the tractate, which summarizes the explanations of the first part in short theses.

72. WA 9:448,24.

73. WA 9:448 (,25–449,8),34–37.

74. For this reason, the divinity took on flesh, so that we might now have a certain sign on which to fix our minds, like the Jewish people at the mercy seat. For they were not permitted to worship at any other place than at the mercy seat. Thus, if we are to apprehend God, we will not be able to do so except by a sign—that is, the humanity of Christ; again, we will not grasp him unless we fix the eyes of our mind on his humanity. For Christ is clearly that mercy seat, as Paul says in Rom. 3 (WA 9:449,9–14).

75. "Here, here, fix your mind on Christ, if ever you are tempted to know God by his deeds, or desire to lay hold of God, saying with Peter: 'Lord, show us the Father' . . . Fix your eyes on me: I am the appointed sign by which you may gaze upon the Father. I am the way, the truth, etc. Behold, Christ himself summons errant, wandering, and vagrant reason to a sensible sign, so that by means of that sign it may grasp God through faith" (WA 9:449,15–22).

of Christ, the gifting word.[76] What was at first highly questionable, precisely because of the promise ("Why did a sign need to be added?"), now coincides with it exactly—in the humanity of Christ. And this is how it is understood from now on. From this point of view, we can understand why the elements of the sacrament, while in themselves dispensable,[77] become extremely important for Luther when "comprehended[78] in the word," because they in turn help faith by pointing it to the word, to its goal, and so "fixing"[79] its gaze on the gifting word and thus on the giver. "In the mass, the sacrament is exhibited, which signifies nothing else than: Behold, here is the true Christ, the sign of the new testament and the forgiveness of sins. Here, here is the one by whom you know for certain that sin has been abolished."[80] In this way, the sign and the promise combine to form a unity. The humanity of Christ is understood as a sign "in which you can gaze at the Father,"[81] and thus as a sign of *God's* presence, but nowhere else than in the promise. The elements of the sacrament in turn are linked to the specificity of the promise and derive their necessity solely from the "sensible sign,"[82] the story of Jesus, which they summarize and bear to within themselves.[83]

Christ is almost described in the same way, as a "visible sign,"[84] in the sermon on Genesis 28 of December 1520, which has already been mentioned in another

---

76. WA 9:445,22–24: "Fix your eyes on the words of Christ . . . for the sum of your salvation is contained in them."

77. Cf. WA 6:518,17–19 = LW 36:44 (*The Babylonian Captivity*).

78. Cf., for example, the *Small Catechism* (*BSLK* 515,26–27 = *BC* 359,1–2).

79. Cf. the strikingly frequent use of "fix" ("*defigere*"): WA 9:445,22; 9:448,35; 9:449,10,13,15,19.

80. WA 9:448,13–15.

81. See n. 75.

82. See n. 75.

83. For the strict reciprocity and simultaneity that prevails here, see from the discussion of the doctrine of transubstantiation in *The Babylonian Captivity* Luther's confession, "I firmly believe that not only is the body of Christ in the bread but that the bread is the body of Christ" (WA 6:511,20–21 = LW 36:34; trans. alt.) and pp. 363–370.

84. "In summary: No one can see God except through a visible sign, namely, Christ" (WA 9:405,10). Continuing a tradition of interpretation going back to John (1:51), Luther interprets Gen. 28:12 (JACOB SAW IN HIS SLEEP A LADDER) as a reference to the *Christus homo* (9:404,30), who is the only way to heaven (9:404,33). Here he continues a tradition of interpretation that goes back to John (1:51) (see n. 4). John 3:13 is cited, then the dialogue in John 14:3–14 (as already in the sermon *Concerning the Testament of Christ*: see n. 75) is drawn on extensively. "The good apostle was wavering in his thoughts, so Christ says to him: 'Thomas, come here, do not waver in your thinking, do not turn away, it's me" (9:405,3–5). The conclusion of this first stage of interpretation is then "In short . . ." (see above).

context.[85] For Luther, the concept of "visible sign" sums up the idea of a whole story, which he unfolds as follows:

> There he stands, bearing in his body all the forms of the most lowly human beings. He is poor, a child, an infant, a young lad, born of a virgin. He lets himself be nursed by a woman and carried like any other child. There was nothing about him to suggest that he was something special . . . Not satisfied with the lowliness of his family's business, for which he was despised, he even converses with sinners, tax collectors, and harlots, with Matthew and Mary Magdalene, and hangs around with the loose rabble. Hence, they [the Pharisees] said, "If this man were a prophet, he would surely know what these people are like." To which he responds, "Those who are well have no need of a physician but those who are sick." When Christ breaks the traditions of the elders by healing on the Sabbath, they say, "He must be a scoundrel, for he does not observe any day but considers every day alike." Likewise, when the disciples plucked and ate some heads of grain on the Sabbath, they were accused. Again, [the Pharisees] heard with malicious intent that the disciples were eating bread with unwashed hands. It is true that Jesus did these things while living among people on earth. But in his martyrdom, he becomes subject not only to humans but to Satan, and yet the greatest thing he does is that he becomes a sinner before God the Father and bears our sins for us as if they were his own.[86]

The last sentence here no longer narrates the story of the "historical Jesus" but, as already formally indicated by the change of tense, confesses the reality of the present Christ, who intercedes for us with the Father, so that we can turn to him in our sin and say: "Come on, you are the Christ, and you said that you would graciously stretch out your hand to us in our need. So then, I come to you now on the strength of that promise and ask for mercy."[87] Luther emphasizes with all his might that this Christ, who is God for us, is none other than the man Jesus of that time. Yet historical reason does not see that this man Jesus is *deus pro nobis*, God for us. This must be revealed and asserted in the *promise*, which is clear when looking back at the sermon *Concerning the Testament of Christ*.

Thus only one side of Luther's reformational Christology comes to light when he mocks the commentators on the first book of the *Sentences* and their

---

85. Cf. p. 340.

86. WA 9:405,27–406,6.

87. WA 9:407,5–7.

speculations about the supreme mysteries of the Trinity in an impressive surrealist grotesque full of theological earnestness and threatens them for their godlessness: "If they bore up into heaven with their heads and look around, they will find no one there, because Christ is lying in the manger and on the woman's lap down here, then they will stumble down again and break their necks!"[88] This clearly expresses the thrust of the whole interpretation once again. In view of this emphasis on the humanity of Christ, the visible sign, we almost[89] feel like asking if the promise is even necessary, since in the sermon *Concerning the Testament of Christ*, it was the other way round and the need for the humanity of Christ was questioned with the words "Why did a sign need to be added?" But it is the genius of Luther's reformational Christology that both questions are asked and both are answered at the same time.

This fact is formulated quite sharply at the end of the Emmanuel sermon of March/April 1520,[90] which belongs to the last two sermons discussed: "If Christ had been a mere man, he could not have helped us, or if he had only been God, he still could not have helped us. But Emmanuel, God with us, helps and save us. Emmanuel is his name."[91] This not only rejects predicating the humanity to the divinity but also the divinity to the humanity.[92] In Christ, our Emmanuel, *God* is truly with us, and God is truly with *us* "in the muck and in the toil so that his skin smokes."[93] His "name" means nothing else than the

88. WA 9:406 (13–22),17–20

89. Cf., however, the proof text in n. 87.

90. WA 4:608–9. On Apr. 27, Melanchthon reports on it in a letter to Heß (CR 1 [:155–61],159; see also WA 9:317). Perhaps it belongs to the planned interpretation of Isaiah that Melanchthon speaks about (CR 1:158) but about which no further documents have survived or to the ongoing interpretation of the gospels, to which the Christmas sermon of 1519 (on Matt. 1:1) belongs.

91. WA 609,27–30. See the marginal notes (of Melanchthon?): "This word includes the whole gospel and our whole knowledge of Christ; for it indicates that we are reconciled to God and that we have this reconciliation through faith," and that "wherever Christ is, there God will be known, and God will truly be there and will dwell there" (608); see also Melanchthon's own interpretation of Matt. 1:21 in his lectures on Matthew (*Werke In Auswahl*, ed. R. Stupperich, vol. 4:141–42; Nov. 1519).

92. As a commentator on the *Sentences* of Peter Lombard in his early career (1509/10), Luther considers it "impossible to ascribe the predicates of the infinite, divine being to the humanity of Christ" and thus adopts the Ockhamist position (see R. Schwarz, "Gott ist Mensch. Zur Lehre von der Person Christi bei den Ockhamisten und bei Luther," *ZThK* 63, 1966 [289–351], 345–47, the quote: 345). Yet in contrast to this, in his theology of the cross of the following years, he seems able to predicate the deity of the humanity, the affirmation of the negation (for more on this, see pp. 365–367, esp. n. 112). The third phase of his Christology is the reformational phase, the original shape of which will be presented in this chapter.

93. WA 4:609,1.

act of substitution, whereby God stands in for us and we stand in for God. This happens in the promise in a way that makes it absolutely certain. "Therefore, the voice of Emmanuel offers us the greatest consolation if the terrors of conscience, the affects of sin and the flesh, the fear of the devil and hell should trouble us. 'Take heart,' Christ says, 'for I have overcome them,' and, 'I am with you to the end of the age.'"[94]

Such bold promises and in them the inviolable validity of the "name," its finality and irrevocability, are based on God's *death*: "That we may be certain that Christ is Emmanuel, he gave himself as an eternal testament, ratified by his death. He goes away only to be called back. Therefore, as often as mass is celebrated, this testament is given to us so that there may be nothing deeper inside us than our food. Although it may be absurd to unbelievers that we eat our God, this is the one thing that saves us the most if we believe it."[95]

What is meant by this must now be explained in more detail. This will also give us an insight into the depth of the christological dimension of the reformational concept of promise.

For the first time in the 1516/17 Galatians lectures,[96] and correspondingly in the 1519 *Galatians Commentary*[97] and then again in *The Babylonian Captivity* of 1520,[98] Luther, taking up Jerome's translation of the Old Testament word *covenant* (*diatheke* or *berit*) with "pact" (*pactum*),[99] distinguishes between "pact"

94. WA 4:609,7–10.

95. WA 4:609,19–23.

96. WA 57/2:82,1–15 (Scholion on 3:17; cf. the gloss: 57/2:24,21–25); 1516/17.

97. WA 2:521,25–37 = LW 27:268 (Note: The LW calls the 1519 *Galatians Commentary* the *Lectures on Galatians*). The text of the transcript of the lectures (see n. 96) reappears here in the interpretation of 3:18 almost unchanged: "Note also that the apostle calls the promises of God a testament. The same term is used in other passages of Scripture in which the writer indicates somewhat obscurely that God would die and that thus in God's promise, as in a formally announced testament, God's incarnation and passion were to be understood at the same time. For, as Heb. 9:17 states, 'A testament is ratified only at death.' Hence, God's testament was not to be ratified unless God died. In the same place (Heb. 9:15) it stated of Christ: 'Therefore he is the mediator of a new testament in order that they may receive the promise, since a death has occurred.' And this is the day of Christ that Abraham recognized and rejoiced in when God gave his promise (John 8:56). At the same time, it is possible to harmonize this with Jerome's statement that Hebrews speaks of 'pact' rather than 'testament.' The one who stays alive makes a pact, while the one who is about to die makes a testament. Thus Jesus Christ, the immortal God, made a pact. But at the same time, he made a testament because he was to become mortal. Therefore, just as God and man are the same, so too pact and testament are the same" (trans. alt.).

98. WA 6:513,36–514,1 = LW 36:38.

99. See nn. 96–97. Jerome's translation was mediated to Luther through Erasmus: see K. A. Meissinger, WA 57/2:24 on l. 21 and 57/2:82 on l. 10.

(or promise[100]) and "testament." He does this in such a way as to ascribe life to the former and death to the latter. Anyone who makes a pact, a binding promise, must stay alive in order to be able to keep it. Conversely, anyone who makes a testament must die in order for it to be executed. The new covenant, which is revealed with the gifting words of the Lord's Supper, contains both aspects at the same time. This happens in Christ who is God and man at the same time. "Pact" and "testament" correspond to the deity and humanity of Christ; indeed they are their function: "A testator is the same as a promiser who is about to die, but a promiser is a testator who is about to stay alive (if I may put it that way)."[101] "Jesus Christ, the immortal God, made a pact and at the same time he made a testament because he was to become mortal. Just as God and man are the same, so pact and testament are the same."[102]

What at first seemed like a mental exercise that could overcome a translation difficulty becomes, for Luther, the means of expressing a bold theological conception. But this only happens after he understood that the gifting word of the Lord's Supper is the specific word of a concrete event.[103]

In a way unprecedented in church history, Luther here acknowledges God's irrevocable commitment to the history of Jesus. Jesus's death is co-constitutive of God's name, of God's being. The power of this death, which alone seals God's being and name and his word that has already happened, not only reveals in the gifting words of the Lord's Supper who God always is; but who God always is, he is only in relation to Jesus's death and the plan for this death, and so only in relation to God's will for it, which implies a very specific view of the meaning of the Old Testament.[104] Otherwise, Jesus's death could not be "necessary" and

100. As in *The Babylonian Captivity* (WA 6:513,36 = LW 36:38).

101. WA 6:513,37–514,1 = LW 36:38 (trans. alt.).

102. See n. 97.

103. The "*Cur deus homo*?" motif (Why did God become human?) that already appears in the Galatians lectures (see n. 96) in relation to Heb. 9:17 is further developed in the scholion of the Hebrew lectures on this text ("This passage of the apostle clearly reveals the allegorical understanding of the Law of Moses, by which we know that everything in this law concerning Christ was also promised and figured in Christ, and therefore . . . the death of him who was true God and true human was once explained by the terms 'testament' and 'promise.' For since he cannot die and yet promises [when he makes his testament] that he will die, it was necessary for him to become human and thus fulfill what he had promised": WA 57/3:211,16–22; see already the scholion on 7:22: 57/3:193,18–24, where the context mentions for the first time the words of the Lord's Supper (see chap. 5 D). See further the Emmanuel sermon quoted above (see n. 95), the sermon *Concerning the Testament of Christ* (9:447,2–7,13–15), and the Mass sermon (6:357,14–27 [§8]; see [§9 [357–58]).

104. It is instructive for Luther's view of the Old Testament that he first speaks here of a prefiguration of Christ's testament "in all God's promises from the beginning of the world" (see

necessarily not God's own death. At the same time, its necessity is no longer understood as a postulate of salvation history (*Heilsgeschichte*) or even of soteriology.[105] The necessity of God's incarnation and death is not seen to lie in our need, our sins, and so forth but in God's own will, his will to be bound to his word: "God made a testament; therefore it was necessary for him to die. But God could not have died unless he were a human being. Thus Christ's incarnation and death are most succinctly comprehended in the same word testament."[106]

For Luther, the necessity of God's death lies in the irrevocability and final validity of God's oral and public promise and should be thought of only concretely in view of it and not abstractly apart from it. It is also the same promise that includes for him the necessity of the indestructible life of the crucified Christ (that is, his divinity).[107] Thus the *promise* is the medium in which the truly human (*vere homo*) and the truly divine (*vere deus*) are inseparably united. This means that the "is" that mediates the *vere homo* and the *vere deus*, God's life and Jesus's death, cannot be understood predicatively and apophantically. It does not express the meaning of an already established subject but is the movement that establishes the reality of both at the same time. It does not mean a significative copula ("is") but an effective one, in fact a synthetic copula. If the "natures" are thus dependent on the promise understood as a copula, then the copula in turn is determined solely by the natures. This makes the observed identification of the word and Christ himself as Word completely understandable.[108]

What the promise, the word, is, it is only if it is understood as the presence of the Word in which God is man. The christological discourse about the personal

WA 6:514,26–515,4 = LW 36:39; Luther comes up with this notion already in the sermon on Gen. 9:9 [WA 9:348] before the corresponding sections in the *Sermon on the New Testament* and the sermon *Concerning the Testament of Christ*), then corrects himself and no longer ascribes indicative and predictive power to them but, conversely, asserts that the basis of their validity lies in this one new promise and thus their dependence on it: "Indeed, whatever value those ancient promises had was entirely derived from this new promise that was coming in Christ and was dependent on it" (6:514,1–4 = 36:38; trans. alt.). Accordingly, in Luther's view, we can only speak of the promise from the point of view of its fulfillment! Therefore, it is not possible to derive a concept of God from the Old Testament that could provide a basis for understanding the death of Jesus that would not at the same time need to be corrected by the death of Jesus (understood as the death of God).

105. This is why Luther can speak so vigorously about the prevenience of grace immediately in the following section (WA 6:514,11–25; see especially the version of the Mass sermon: 6:356: §6).

106. WA 6:514,7–10 = LW 36:38 (trans. alt.).

107. Cf. further the Emmanuel sermon cited above ("For an eternal testament . . . he is only absent that he may be called back . . . to eat our God") and the Easter Sermon of 1521, which will be quoted at the end of this chapter.

108. See above pp. 350–354.

union would, for its part, fade into a mere play of ideas or would be a cipher for the hidden true nature of every human being from the outset if it were forgotten that it is only the reflection of that event that constitutively takes place in the space of the oral and public word.[109]

The simultaneity of God and man, life and death, forgiveness and sin that can be captured in such a word, contradicts the assumption of a secret identity of these opposites or of an immanent peripety (reversal). At this point, philosophy and theology part ways, because philosophy can only think of the simultaneity analytically, not synthetically (and if synthetically, then speculatively or existentially but not concretely in terms of language),[110] again, it can only think of substitution as the representation of something absent, not something present.[111] At this point, Luther's early theology and his reformational theology also part ways. He no longer sees death as standing in for life, Christ's divinity for his humanity. Thus he no longer predicates life of death or Christ's divinity of his humanity[112] but rather, using the Aristotelian axiom "An affirmative proposition requires the agreement of the subject and the predicate" (*Metaphysics* 6), he asserts, against its traditional interpretation that understands agreement to be identity (*praedicatio identica*),[113] the simul-

---

109. Cf. further the sentences that conclude this chapter.

110. See below n. 112.

111. Judging from Luther's theological understanding of signs ("A philosophical sign is the mark of a thing that is absent, while a theological sign is the mark of a thing that is present": WA TR 4:666, 8–9 [No. 5106]; 1540), D. Sölle, for example, defends the philosophical concept of the sign when she makes Jesus the representative of the *absent* God (*Christ the Representative: An Essay in Theology After the "Death of God"*).

112. The situation needs to be seen in a differentiated way so that it is clear that in his early theology, Luther operates with a synthetic simultaneity that is thoroughly speculative and non-linguistic (see, e.g., the scholion on Ps. 4:4: "This is a great miracle, that God and humanity, dead and alive, mortal and immortal are the same, and that almost every contradiction here is reconciled in Christ": WA 55/2/1:73,13–15 = WA 3:52,24–26 = LW 10:61; trans. alt.; see on Ps. 69:5: 3:426,31–36 = 10:364–65). But this in practice (*experimentaliter*) means an analytical simultaneity. For we only experience the cross; there is no oral word of salvation to enable us to see salvation in it (but now in the cross of Jesus!). The crucial point is again stated with a quote from the sermon of Mar. 17, 1521: "When Christ says, 'Whoever hears my word will never die again,' he means this: the word of truth that I speak is eternal. Whoever clings to it lives forever; they cannot die but pass beyond death without even realizing it, for death is no longer death for them. *But if the word is not there, we become aware of death, are frightened, and must die.* The word is the bridge from this life to the next; those who cling to it will cross over to the other side before they even realize it. Here we need to use all five senses and cling to nothing but the word" (9:621,34–622,4; author's emphasis).

113. "But perhaps they will say that 'Aristotle teaches that in an affirmative proposition subject and predicate must be identical,' or (to quote the monster's own words in the sixth book of his

taneity in the sense of a composition that is not weakened in any way.[114] He says neither that the life of God remains unaffected by the death of Jesus[115] nor that the death of Jesus as such is the life of God[116] but rather that the latter is not without the former, just as the former is not without the latter: "A testator is the same as a promiser who is about to die, but a promiser is a testator who is about to stay alive."[117] "'Pactum' and 'testamentum' are the same, just as the same Christ is both God and man."[118]

By seeking to determine the christological dimension of the reformational concept of promise, we have simultaneously discovered the constitutively promissional dimension of reformational Christology and how Luther integrates it into his new understanding of the Lord's Supper. In a nutshell, he discovered his reformational Christology and his reformational understanding of the Lord's Supper *at the same time.*

Metaphysics): 'An affirmative proposition requires the agreement of the subject and the predicate.' They interpret agreement to mean identity. Hence, when I say: 'This is my body,' [they say] the subject cannot be identical with the bread, but must be identical with the body of Christ . . . Thus, what is true in regard to Christ is also true in regard to the sacrament. In order for the divine nature to dwell in him bodily [Col. 2:9], it is not necessary for the human nature to be transubstantiated and the divine nature contained under the accidents of the human nature. Both natures are simply there in their entirety, and it is truly said: 'This man is God; this God is man'" (WA 6:510,25–30; 511,34–38 = LW 36:33,35; *The Babylonian Captivity*; trans. alt.). *The investigation by Schwarz* (Gott ist Mensch) *continues at the crucial point by considering this passage from* The Babylonian Captivity, which he discusses (248), together with *Luther's* pactum-testamentum *motif.* Thus Schwarz has worked out the doctrine's setting in life (*Sitz im Leben*) and has clearly presented it.

114. In the important letter of June 12, 1541, to Georg von Anhalt (see Schwarz, 339–42), Luther again quotes the Aristotelian axiom. It means, "according to Luther, the opposite of what scholastic philosophy wanted to infer from it. The condition for the truth of an affirmative statement is not that the concepts of the subject and predicate, taken by themselves, denote the same thing. Rather, the truth is expressed in words by the fact that only when subject and predicate are put together do they 'interpret' or 'say the one thing that is being spoken about. The truth of the sentence cannot be stipulated beforehand with the demand that subject and predicate must each understand the thing for themselves and must therefore stand for the same thing. Only when subject and predicate are brought together, in the synthesis, is the truth of the 'thing' brought to light. The sentence itself, not its individual words as concepts, expresses its truth" (Schwarz, 339–40).

115. This was Luther's earlier position as a commentator on the *Sentences*. See n. 92.

116. This is what the theology of the cross in Luther's first Psalms lectures and the Romans lectures amounts to. See n. 112.

117. See n. 101.

118. WA 57/2:82,14–15 (see nn. 96–97).

D. An impressive confirmation of this finding[119] is found in the Easter sermon of 1521, in which Luther presents the message of the resurrection as a proclamation of Jesus's death in the Lord's Supper.

> Christ says, look at me, "take and eat" etc. These words encompass all the mysteries of death and resurrection. The words, "this is my body," say as much as this: I will die now and yet remain alive; I will make an eternal testament so that your sins may be forgiven. He thus shows that he will not die but remain alive, for he makes it himself, gives it himself, fulfils it himself, and distributes it himself. He does not say to Peter: "You distribute it," but he himself says: "Here, I have it, I will give it to you myself, and I will leave it behind and then die, but I will distribute it myself and thus remain alive." If you are troubled by sin, a bad conscience, or all sorts of evils, sorrows, and misfortunes, then I have all sorts of goods and comfort that I can give you. Therefore, cast all your sin and evil on me freely etc. Therefore, there is no other use for these words that I have spoken than to believe them; faith is all that is required. Now see what rich abundance there is here, which no one can understand, and yet the whole of Scripture speaks about it—there is enough to preach on here for an eternity! Thus in Christ, death, curse, misery, sorrow and all evil, as well as life, grace, peace, and consolation, and everything that can be called good—all these things agrees.[120]

119. WA 9:657–61.

120. WA 9:660,31–661,9. Apart from the matter of the promise, this and the portion of the sermon that follows it (see n. 121) agree with the sermon on Gen. 22 of 1520 (Oct./Nov.), which together with the scholion on 2:14 in the Hebrews lectures (WA 57/3: 127–31 = LW 29:134–38), forms a bridge with Luther's early theology, where it touches on the idea of Christ as the archetype: "The *figure of Isaac* is fittingly turned toward Christ... and just as Isaac, when he was subjected to death, was lifted beyond life and death, so also Christ is Lord of life and death. Hence Paul said in this sense, 'I live, yet not I, but Christ lives in me,' and elsewhere, 'for me, to die is gain.' He also said, 'I desire to depart and be with Christ,' just as he can say, 'the life I live, I live not for myself but for Christ, and just as he spent himself for others, not living for himself, so too I do not live for myself but so that I may gain many for Christ. Paul says: I hate life and yet I love it—he loves it not because he himself is alive but because he lives for others. Since Christ is one person with two natures because God and man are one, that Christ never died, and yet he died once on the cross, thus obtaining [the victory] for us by his blood so that life may remain, and death be devoured. Then was fulfilled what was spoken by the prophet: "O death, I will be your sting" and "Where, O death, is your victory? Where, O death, is your sting? Death is swallowed up in victory" (Hos. 13:14; 1 Cor. 15:54–56). Satan sank his teeth into Christ, but by biting him he is swallowed up and consumed in victory. That is, although he should have won, he was defeated. In this way, Christ defeated death by dying so that we too may conquer death through his example. For the victory over sin, the law, and death has been given to us through faith in our Lord, Jesus Christ (1 Cor. 15). 1 John 5 says: "This is the victory

Here it becomes clear once again how the main elements of reformational Christology that emerged in this chapter—namely, the promise (= testament) motif and the mediator (= two natures) motif—are intertwined.

That the dead live and the living have the last word through their death is not a proposition that can be divided so that its moments could follow from one another—in one direction or another—but rather a unity that does not move in itself but speaks in itself for me: "for you for the forgiveness of sin." What is thus communicated in the promise, understood as Christ's person in the unity of his two natures, is opposed to sin, "death, curse, misery, sorrow, and all evils" and speaks up for "life, grace, peace, consolation and all that can be called good." When the recipient of the gifting word takes it, they exchange "death, curse, misery, sorrow, and all evils" for "life, grace, peace, consolation and all that can be called good." *Thus* "in Christ"—that is, by virtue of Christ's death and life, which come to us as a promise—our death and our life agree. *Thus* his death devours our death, and *so* his life brings us life.[121]

What Luther advocates here is clearly evident when compared with his early Christology, which lacks this aspect of the promise but in which it can also be said "that God and man are the same, dead and alive, mortal and immortal are the same, and almost every contradiction is reconciled here in Christ."[122] The two natures formula acts here as a cipher for the inner reversal of the negation into an affirmation that is to be taken up in each person's own cross and suffering,

---

that overcomes the world, our faith." Read Job 41 about Behemoth, the great sea monster, how he was tricked and drawn out with a hook like a fish'" (9:367,1–27).

121. "Death therefore opens its jaws and wants to devour this person as it has devoured all humankind before, but this time it strikes a person who is both God and man at the same time. God cannot die, yet dies according to his humanity . . . What humankind suffers, is suffered by Christ, and what Christ does, God has done. Thus death is drowned in life, as Paul says, and all our sins and our evil conscience are drowned in Christ. Therefore, you should believe in him so that death cannot harm you. This is clear from Job 40, where it says of Behemoth that 'he [God] will take him by his eyes with a fishhook' etc. 'Can you draw out Leviathan with a fishhook?' It is like a fisher who lowers a hook into the water baited with a worm so that the hook is not seen. Then along comes the fish, sees the bait, and wants to eat it, so it opens its jaws, bites on the hook and is caught. So it is with Christ. The fishing line is the lineage of Jesus Christ from Abraham on, which is tied to his human nature. The hook is his divine nature that he put on with his humanity, which had to suffer and was despised like a worm. Then along came Death and thought: Aha! I will devour him. But nobody saw that he was God. So Death thought that it would eat the man—but met God. Then it was caught, and Christ pulled it out and humiliated it before the whole world. Thus we see what the resurrection of Christ is" (WA 9:661,10–33). Luther's interpretation of Job 40:19–20 is entirely traditional: see Gregory the Great on this passage (*Moralia* 33, chap. 7, n. 14; chap. 9, n. 17; MPL 76:680–81, 682–83 [Reference given by J. Ficker, WA 57/3:129, on l.6]).

122. Scholion on Ps. 4:4 (see n. 112).

which can be seen in all its radicalness in the crucified Jesus, who thus acts as an archetype.[123] In contrast to this, Luther in his reformational Christology, with its doctrine of the two natures, does not emphasize the causality of an image, but the authority of a word in which the difference between Christ and us is perceived differently than in the relationship of a *primus* to his *pares*; that is, Christ is now seen as preeminent and not merely as the first among equals.

123. Cf. esp. the scholion on Ps.111:4: WA 4:243,13–15 and on that see p. 348.

CHAPTER 10

Promise and Prayer

(According to the Rogate Sermon of 1520)

FOLLOWING THE DESCRIPTION of his theology of promise given by Luther himself in his *Babylonian Captivity of the Church*, our final task is to show his understanding of prayer. Since it only appears in a brief thesis[1] in the *Babylonian Captivity*, a further explanation must be sought. This is found in a hitherto unnoticed short text that is just as important as any of Luther's main writings of the year 1520. It shows prayer in a way that is new to the tradition and to his pre-reformational theology. If Luther used to understand *the promise in terms of prayer*, he now sees *prayer in terms of the promise.*[2] According to his reformational theology, prayer subsists in the promise. What this means is shown from what follows: First, we look at (A) the prehistory of the Rogate sermon, then (B) the sermon itself. In conclusion (C), we briefly return to Luther's pre-reformational view of prayer to finally emphasize, against this background, his new understanding of prayer and its trinitarian character.

A. Luther found his new view of prayer to be very closely connected to the notion of promise that he discovered during the indulgence controversy. This notion of promise of course began with his new understanding of the sacrament of penance, which he had to account for to Cajetan in Augsburg in October 1518. After the *Sermon on the Worthy Preparation of the Heart for the Reception of the Eucharist*[3] and the scholion on Hebrews 9:24,[4] it is the *Proceedings at Augsburg* (*Acta Augustana*) where we find Luther's new view of prayer. In the second part of his written answer, Luther quotes Mark 11:24, in addition to other passages, "the most obvious authority" being James 1:6, to demonstrate his theology of the special word that is apprehended through special faith, which Cajetan calls a "new and erroneous theology."[5] Regarding Mark 11:24, Luther says:

---

1. See "Structure of the Presentation," p. 180 and below p. 100. On the question of prayer in the context of baptism and the Mass, see pp. 302–303, esp. n. 77.

2. See especially pp. 135–153.

3. WA 1:331,5–17 (*Sermo de digna praeparatione cordis pro suscipiendo sacramento eucharistiæ*).

4. See chap. 5 C.

5. WA 2:13,10 = LW 31:270. Cf. p. 203.

> "Truly, I tell you, whatever you ask in prayer, believe that you will receive it and it will be yours." Notice, Jesus says "whatever," without exception. Now it is clear that in the sacrament we ask for something (for no one goes to the sacrament unless it is to ask for grace): Therefore, we must listen to Christ when he says here, "believe that you will receive it, and it will be yours," otherwise, everything in the church would be in doubt and nothing would be certain, which is most absurd.[6]

This amazing connection between the sacrament and prayer, which Luther sees given with Christ's promise in Mark 11:24, strikes Cajetan so much in Augsburg that he subsequently expands his treatise dated September 26. As a sixth point to Luther's thesis that (in Cajetan's words) "for a fruitful reception of absolution, faith in the sacrament of penance is necessary by which penitents believe with full certitude that God has absolved them," he adds: "People approach the sacrament of penance asking God for the forgiveness of sins: for it is written, whatever you ask in prayer, believe that you will receive it and it will be yours. And James says, but let them ask in faith, without doubting: Therefore."[7]

In Cajetan's report, we see for the first time, together with the connection between the sacrament and prayer, the collocation of Mark 11:24 and James 1:6.[8] As an index fossil of Luther's new understanding of prayer, we come across it at an important point in each of the following: *An Exposition of the Lord's Prayer* in 1518/19,[9] *Sermon on Prayer and Procession During Rogation Days* in 1519,[10] *Treatise on Good Works* in 1520[11] and *The Babylonian Captivity of the Church* in 1520.[12] It serves to assert Luther's new understanding of the sacrament in his *Defense and Explanation of All the Articles Which Were Unjustly Condemned by the Roman Bull* (1521).[13]

In Cajetan's eyes, Luther overlooks the fact that not every prayer that is certain of being answered is actually answered, as we can learn from Paul (2 Cor. 12). He claims that Mark 11:24 wants to show "that the certainty of our

6. WA 2:14,30–35 = LW 31:272 (trans. alt.). On Jas. 1:6: see 2:15,9–14 = 31:273.

7. *Opuscula*, 1575, 109b,75-8. See chap. 4, n. 135.

8. The 1518 *Sermon on Penance* (*Sermo de Poenitentia*) has no reference to Jas. 1:6, and the scholion on Heb. 9:24 has no connection with the sacrament.

9. WA 2:126–27 = LW 42:76.

10. WA 2:175–76 = LW 42:87–88.

11. WA 6:232 = LW 44:58.

12. WA 6:570 = LW 36:121.

13. WA 7:319 = LW 32:13.

faith concerning particular effects should be such that the certainty lies with God and not with us."[14] With this distinction, however, Cajetan tears apart what for Luther belongs together according to *God's* will. Here, too, he fails to recognize[15] that for Luther the "certainty of faith" is not a manifestation of human self-will or misplaced confidence but solely the presumption borne of an explicit divine promise ("You will receive") corresponding to God's declared will and command ("Ask!").

> Therefore, take note that a prayer is not good and right just because of its length, devoutness, and sweetness, or its plea for temporal or eternal goods, but only because the one who prays it firmly trusts that it will be answered (no matter how small and unworthy it may be in itself) on account of the reliable pledge and promise of God. Not your worship, but God's word and promise render your prayer good. This faith, based on God's word, is also the true worship and without it, all other worship is sheer deception and error.[16]

This concludes Luther's German *Exposition of the Lord's Prayer for Ordinary Laypeople* of 1519, with its final section on "the little word *amen*,"[17] which—shaped by Mark 11:24 (cf. Matt. 21:22), Matthew 15:28, and James 1:6 and therefore clearly reminiscent of the Augsburg answer—highlights with unmistakable clarity its difference to his 1517 Latin interpretation and so indicates what is new about his reformational understanding of the Lord's Prayer.[18] The *novum* is this: For believers, faith and prayer no longer come from the nothingness of their total humiliation as such, only to continually return to it even in the longing of hope, but they see their adversity swallowed up by the divine promise that God will answer their prayer, and find their security in it.

---

14. *Utrum ad fructuosam* . . .; *Opuscula*, 1575, 111a (quotation: 2.28–30; see 2.21–24).

15. Cf. pp. 219–221.

16. WA 2:127:36–128,2 = LW 42:77 (trans. alt.).

17. WA 2:126–28 = LW 42:76.

18. For details of the commonalities and differences between the two versions, see E. Bizer, *Fides ex auditu*, 131–47.

The next interpretation of the Lord's Prayer, *Eine kurze Form, das Paternoster zu verstehen und zu beten* [*A Short Way of Understanding and Praying the Lord's Prayer*] (WA 6:9–19; 1519) is by no means just "the fruit of his earlier labors on the German *Exposition of the Lord's Prayer*" (WA 6:9). It is taken over by Luther without change in his first catechism (WA 7:220–29; 1520). What is new here compared to the *Exposition* is especially his understanding of the invocation (WA 6:11 = WA 7:220; quoted in n. 99).

Following the section on the "amen," Luther gives a "short summary" of his entire exposition of the Lord's Prayer, which is cast in the form of a dialogue between God and the soul, where the linguistic form already highlights the content of the prayer.[19] What grounds and encompasses this dialogue also appears here (according to the interpretation it summarizes) at the end, in the saying of the "amen," where the divine promise is seen as an "expression" of the faith "that we should have in praying every petition."[20] And so Luther himself prays, "Since you taught and commanded us to pray in this way and have promised to answer us, we hope and are certain, O dearest Father, that for the sake of your faithfulness you will graciously and mercifully grant all this to us."[21]

A few months later, in a partly literal overlap,[22] the striking conclusion of the exposition of the Lord's Prayer becomes the programmatic opening of the sermon *On Prayer and Procession During Rogation Days* (May/June 1519). Here, for the first time, Luther *expressly defines* prayer from the point of view of the promise.

> For prayer to be really good and for it to be heard, two things are necessary. *First*, we must have a pledge or promise from God. We must reflect on this promise beforehand and remind God of it, and in that way be emboldened to pray with confidence. If God had not commanded us to pray and promised to answer us, no creature would be able to obtain so much as a kernel of grain, despite all their petitions.
>
> It follows from this that not one of us obtains anything from God by our own virtue or the worthiness of our prayer, but solely by reason of the boundless mercy of God, which comes before all our petitions and desires. Through his gracious promise and command, he moves us to ask and desire, so that we might learn how much more God provides for us and how God is more willing to give than we are to receive or seek. God wants us to pray with boldness and confidence, since he offers us more than we can ever ask for.

---

19. WA 2:128–30 = LW 42:78–81.

20. WA 2:126,30–31 = LW 42:76 (trans. alt.).

21. WA 2:130,10–13 = LW 42:80–81 (trans. alt.). The hope that our prayer will be answered is at the same time the faith that it is answered. God promised it and, true to his promise, has answered it already. But only because of the promise (see 2:127,21–27 = 42:77) can we say that "if you conclude your prayer with the word 'amen,' spoken with heartfelt confidence and faith, you can be certain that your prayer is sealed and answered" (2:127,3–5 = 42:76; trans. alt.).

22. Cf., for example, WA 2:127,34–36 = LW 42:77 with 2:175,9–11 = 42:87. E. Bizer, *Fides ex auditu*, 146, n. 142, already pointed to the connection between these two texts.

> *Second*, it is necessary that we do not doubt the promise of our faithful and trustworthy God. The very reason God has promised to hear us, indeed has commanded us to pray, is so that we can have a firm and certain faith that God will answer us, as he says.[23]

(The following texts are then listed: Matt. 21:22; Mark 11:24; Luke 11:9ff.; and Jas. 1:6).

This clear definition comes into play again at an important point in the *Sermon on Preparing to Die* (November 1519)[24] and in the interpretation of the third commandment in the *Treatise on Good Works* (1520),[25] which, not least because of this is clearly different from Luther's earlier interpretations of the Decalogue.[26] Then it appears together with the other three points of the *Sermon on Prayer* in a text from the Stephan Roth collection printed in WA 4, which deserves special attention.

B. This text is the outline of a *sermon* on *John 16:23–30*, the appointed gospel for Rogate Sunday that opens the Week of the Cross, probably *from March 13, 1520*.[27] It takes up the sermon on prayer with all of its five parts

---

23. WA 2:175,4–22 = LW 42:87 (trans. alt; author's emphasis).

24. WA 2:696,33–697,4; 697,8–13 = LW 42:112–14 (includes both WA passages).

25. WA 6 (232:13–243,4):232,22–233,4 = LW 44:58.

26. Cf. WA 6:229–49 = LW 44:54–80 (Mass: testament: 6:230–31 = 44:55–56; sermon: proclamation of this testament: 6:231–32 = 44:56–58; prayer: constituted by the promise of being answered: 6:232–43 = 44:58–71; "resting" in the sense of stopping our work and letting God do his work in mortifying the flesh, which is strictly distinguished from faith: 6:243–49 = 44:71–80). All this should be compared with the sermon on the third commandment of Sept. 21, 1516 (1:443,3–447,16; on that, see pp. 111–117. Even if no further documents survived, the especially striking difference between these two interpretations alone, despite the commonality of text and theme, would be enough to compel us to assume here a sharp break in the history of Luther's theology.

27. The theme of Rogate Sunday or *Vocem Jocunditatis* is prayer, from the Latin *rogate*, meaning "pray"! The dates are obtained from the content of the text. It agrees with the content of the sermons cited in n. 31, which were all preached on the John 16:23–30 text for Rogate Sunday (see WA 17/1:248,22–24; 45:81,18–20; 46:380,2–4). As for the year, the *terminus a quo* is 1520 (if Luther had preached *two* sermons on prayer in the Week of the Cross of 1519—thus E. Vogelsang, "Zur Datierung der frühesten Lutherpredigten," *ZKG* 50 (1931): 112–145, here 131–32—then the one given in 2:175–79 would probably betray the influence of the sermon previously delivered, on the Sunday, on John 16:23–30). Given the character of the Rothian collection, the *terminus ad quem* is also likely to be 1520. Of course, we cannot entirely rule out the possibility that a postscript from the following years ended up in the older material. However, only the years 1522 and 1523 would be a possibility: In 1521 Luther was at the Wartburg for Rogate, while 1524 is the year of the first reliably dated sermon on John 16:23, and the undated text cannot be directly identified with this or with any of the other sermons mentioned in n. 31.

delivered in the Week of the Cross a year earlier.[28] But now it goes further and expressly points out from the text (John 16) that prayer is bound up with the event of the triune God,[29] a connection that for Luther is constitutive of faith in the promise, thus making it clear that the *theology of the promise* is explicitly a *doctrine of the Trinity*.[30] This is its special significance for the history of the understanding of the word in the early Luther.

On the one hand, its history can be traced back to before the *Proceedings at Augsburg* through the stages already identified. On the other hand, it is the archetype of the numerous sermons that Luther preached on John 16:23–30 over the course of the following years on Rogate Sunday.[31] This sermon reveals the reformational change in Luther's theology at a "fruitful moment."

Our presentation that mirrors the text tries to match the fundamental importance of its fifth section by (a) investigating it first and only and then (b) turning to the remaining sections, taking them in order. Because of its archetypal character, later versions of the text are also taken into consideration.

> Every prayer must consist of five things, otherwise it will be useless.
> *First*: Prayer has God's promise, on which all prayer rests: where there is no promise, our prayer is futile and does not deserve to be answered because it rests on itself.
> *Second*: Prayer states what is needed or the thing to be obtained by prayer so that my scattered thoughts may be gathered up into the

---

The date we have assumed above, which is further supported by the fact that Poliander's otherwise almost complete collection for Rogate 1520 does not offer a sermon (see WA 9:326), seems the most likely.

28. This does not include the second part of the sermon (§§ 6–8), which stands in clear contrast to the first and can be taken as a unit in itself (this matches the fact that the two parts were also handed down separately: see WA 2:174). The five sections in WA 2:175–77 = LW 42:87–90 appear in 4:624 [for which there is no LW translation] and correspond in the following way: 1:1; 5:2; 4:3; 3:4; 2:5.

29. It thus takes up the interpretation of the invocation in the *kurzen Form, das Paternoster zu verstehen* [*A Short Form for Understanding the Lord's Prayer*] of 1519 (quoted in n. 99).

30. Cf. E. Bizer's presentation on justification, "Über die Rechtfertigung" (in *Das Kreuz Jesu Christi als Grund des Heils*, ed. F. Viering, 13–29, esp. 20–29). His question is taken up in what follows.

31. 1. 1524 (WA 15:546–50); 2. 1525 (17/1:248–55); 3. 1526 (20:378–82); 4. 1528 (27:129–31)—there are also weekly sermons on John 16:23–30 from the same year: 28:56–59,59–62—5. 1531 (34/1:379–91,391–400); 6. 1534 (37:391–93; cf. 52:298–302,34); 7. 1537 (45:81–84); 8. 1538 (46:380–88; see the print version: 46:75–111; 1539). WA 4:624 can be considered the archetype because the five characteristics of prayer described in the five sections of this text determine, mostly explicitly, the structure of these sermons.

divine promise, by which I hope to obtain what I need; this is called the gathering of one's thoughts. According to this, little self-chosen prayers, rosaries, and the like are not presbyteral prayers, since they do not gather the mind or hold before it the thing to be obtained.

Third: Faith is necessary, by which I believe that God has promised that I can obtain what I need beyond all doubt. God will supply it, not because of you or your prayer, but because of his faithfulness, by which he has promised to give and provide what I need. And so, trust alone obtains what God's faithfulness compels him to provide.

Fourth: Prayer should be earnest, not offered with a wavering mind, and not as if we do not earnestly desire the thing for which we pray, as if on a frivolous adventure, where whatever happens happens, as when you throw a stone at a pear, hoping to knock it to the ground. But this surely would be mockery of God, as if he were not willing to give what he had promised. Such an attitude to prayer not only fails to obtain what it seeks but provokes God with dire consequences.

Fifth: Prayer should be in the name of Jesus, by whose command ("If you ask anything in my name" [John 16:23]; and again: "Ask, and you will receive" [Matt. 7:7]) and authority we may confidently approach the Father of all things. Thus it cannot happen that our prayer goes unanswered, for the Father promised it through his Son, as through an instrument. Christ grieves for our sins; he prays for them in heaven as if they were his own. So please tell me: How could our prayers possibly be denied? The Son prays in my name in heaven, and I pray in his name on earth. Therefore, Christ's righteousness is mine, and my sins are his. It is, to be sure, an unequal exchange! And each is thus purified: my sins are destroyed in Christ and his holiness has purified me, so that I may be worthy of eternal life.[32]

a) The final section (5^{32}) implies the questions: "Is it not possible that God, who has power over all things, may refuse my request? How can I call on him at all and be certain that he will answer me, and thus be certain that he really does have power over all things?"[33]

32. WA 4:624. In the main text that follows, the sections of this text are only referred to with numbers (1–5). But in the footnotes, we use the abbreviation "sec" for clarity.

33. See in sec. 5 the parallelism between "We may confidently approach the Father of all things," / "so it cannot happen that our prayer goes unanswered," / "how could our prayers possibly be denied?"

Freedom from such uncertainty and from our sin comes to us only in the context of that event in which God brings himself to us and us to himself: the event of the triune God. For we only have security in the identity of God's speech and action, of his declared will and the deed that carries it out, of his promise and its fulfillment, of his mercy and his faithfulness (Ps. 85:10)[34]—identities that for faith and prayer are certain, because of the difference between Father, Son, and Spirit.

In the word of the *human* Jesus, "Ask and you will receive," God himself can be grasped in the command and promise.[35] Conversely, the word of the human Jesus only leads to certainty because it is *God's* command and promise: "Thus it is impossible not to be heard, for the *Father* promised it through his Son who is the instrument."[36] As instrument, the Son represents God—who comprehends all things in himself—to the world. But this does not happen just once in a unique, isolatable, and historic event. Otherwise, Jesus and his word would only have an initiating effect and it would be unclear who would guarantee to us that God is certainly present in the world today. But as it is, the Son continues to stand powerfully with the Father against human unbelief and for his will that he once declared, and he continues to stand for the Father's word, and thus for the possibility and reality of faith and prayer. In doing so, he is doing nothing other than holding the Father to his own word. By thus speaking up for our faith and our prayer, he is an advocate for our unbelief, our sin. Hence he identifies himself with our sin in such a way that he destroys it.[37]

---

34. Cf. WA 2:176,39–177,11 = LW 42:89 (Sermon on Prayer and Procession During Rogation Days, 1519), especially the words "at the same time" (ll. 1–2) [LW: "just as"], and "We also find the link between mercy and faithfulness in Ps. 85. Mercy and faithfulness have kissed, that is, they are joined in every work and gift for which we pray" (II. 9–10).

35. "The promise of God" (sec. 1) happens "by the command and authority of Jesus" (sec. 5). See sec. 5 with sec. 2, 1519 (WA 2:175).

36. Cf. with this the weekly sermon on John 16:25–28 of July 18, 1528: Jesus is not to be taken for a pseudo-prophet but is the one sent by *God*, so that you may receive his words and works *as divine* ... Is this not a great promise? If you consider Christ's words and work as *the work of God*, God the Father is pleased with you" (WA 28:61,25–35; author's emphasis). Luther shows here, almost in passing, that he saw the atonement brought about by Christ as the mediation of God and humans and so of humans and God. This provides the decisive criterion for the meaning and possible shape of a theory of satisfaction.

37. This is meant to match the striking parallelism of intercession and cancelling of sin in sec. 5 (on its structure, see n. 44). It can also be found elsewhere, such as in Luther's *Great Galatians Commentary* (on 2:20): "In these words Paul gives a beautiful description of the priesthood and the work of Christ, which is to placate God, to intercede and pray for sinners, to offer himself as a sacrifice for their sins, and to redeem them" (WA 40/1:297,33–298,12 = LW 26:177).

We take the unceasing prayer of the Son as a sure word of the Lord that lasts forever. For in Christ's role as mediator, both are one and have a single purpose: to stand in for us before God and at the same time to stand in for God before us. Since in this interconnection, the Son and the Lord are one, our prayer and God's answer are also one—after all, our prayer corresponds to the word of the Lord and God's answer to the Son's request. We can be certain that prayer in the name of Jesus will be answered by God. By appealing to Jesus's word—that is, claiming it or, as Luther says in one of his later Rogate sermons, "clothing ourselves with it"[38]—we have our answer already: In the name of Jesus, God does not deny himself.

"Tell me, please, where is the refusal here? The Son prays in my name in heaven, I pray in his name on earth."

This intertwining of two aspects of a single event can best be understood from the coincidence of a word of forgiveness spoken by a human being and God's own forgiveness, as Luther clearly explains when he interprets Matthew 16:19 as a "sentence of holy law." This passage is foundational for Luther because here he discovered his reformational theology.[39] It does not speak about the general possibility that a human word may be identified as divine but about believing that God is savingly present in a *specific human word*, the word of absolution. That is, it speaks about the coincidence of the word of forgiveness spoken by a human being in the name of Jesus and God's own forgiveness. Likewise, there is no certainty ascribed here to human prayer as such, for if we tried to analyze our prayers, it would only make us uncertain. Rather, the coincidence of our prayer and God's answer happens in such a way that I—"I in his name on earth"—may approach the Father *through him* (compare: through Jesus Christ our *Lord*[40]) in

38. Cf. WA 15:548,3–4 (1524): "I must put on the promise so that my prayers may be certain." It is extremely important to see that for Luther the whole Christ is imparted and apprehended in the one promise: "Ask and you will receive." So "putting on the promise" means putting on Christ himself: "Being clothed with his garments, his name, and his gifts so that you may also be Christ; if you do this, you will be heard" (15:547,5–6). "I do not ask, 'Father,' because I am worthy . . . but because your Son, Jesus Christ, has given me his name and all that he has, so that I may stand before you, blameless, with all his goods. Now I claim these goods for myself and stand clothed in his merit" (15:546,26–30). In his sure word, we have the whole "person" of Christ; in it his whole mission is fulfilled, "For he was born for this reason, to give you a certain conscience" (15:548,10–11; see the *Sermon on the Prologue of John* of 1523 in 11:227,7: "For this reason he became a human, that our hearts may be made certain"). For the motif of "putting on," see 27:130,14–15 (1528) in the context of ll. 13–26: "'In the name of Jesus.' This is the clothing and apparel of prayer. That was the basis that you are a priest ordained by the word of Christ."

39. See chap. 4.

40. "Therefore, these words 'in my name' call for faith in prayer so that we know that we do not need to be worthy in order to pray, and that neither should our unworthiness prevent us from praying, but that our certainty of being heard rests solely on Christ, who is our only mediator and

the certainty of being heard and answered, because he at the same time speaks up *for me* ("the *Son* prays in my name in heaven") before the Father. Because Christ intercedes for us, we may approach the Father with confidence.[41]

From here it becomes immediately understandable why Luther in 1525 (in the sermon that is closest to the archetype) rejects Christology as a doctrine of the two natures if it is ossified into a static formula and merely denotes a state of affairs (*Sachbestand*) rather than a living relationship (*Tatverhalt*) epitomized by that movement in which God brings himself to us and us to himself. In a word, Luther wants nothing to do with the doctrine of the two natures if its scriptural—and here Luther specifically means its Johannine—interpretation is not directly informed by the doctrine of the mediatorship of Christ.[42]

What God conveys through Christ is his promise ("The Father promised it through the Son as an instrument"). Thus Christ's function as mediator is

---

high priest before God. And so we give our prayers to him, as does the whole of Christendom, concluding and sealing our requests and appeals with these words: 'through Christ our Lord'" (WA 46:85,17–24).

41. Cf. sec. 5 with its variant from 1525: "The fifth thing we ask him in the name of Christ is nothing else than that we may come before God in the faith of Christ and comfort ourselves in the sure confidence that he is our mediator through whom all things are given to us and without whom we would deserve nothing but God's wrath and displeasure, as Paul says in Rom 5: 'By whom we dare to approach God through this grace in which we stand and of which we boast.' That is, we truly pray in the name of Christ when we rely on him and believe that God accepts and hears us for Christ's sake, not for ours. But those who pray in their own name presume that God should hear them and have regard for them because of their many, long, devout, and sanctimonious prayers. But such prayers merit and obtain nothing but God's wrath and displeasure. For those who pray them want God to have regard for them without a mediator, in which case Christ counts for nothing and is of no use" (WA 17/1:252,23–35; from the remaining Rogate sermons, see esp. 20:381,6–30; 1526).

42. Luther puts it pointedly in a chiasm: "And here we also see that to believe in Christ, that *Christ is one person*, who is God and man, would not help anyone unless *this same person is the Christ* who for our sake went forth from the Father and came into the world and again left the world and returned to the Father. That is to say, *this* is Christ, the one who for us became man and died, rose again and went to heaven. On account of this office (of mediator), he is called Jesus Christ. To believe that this is true of him is to be and remain in his name" (WA 17/1:255,11–18). See 17/1:254,9–16: "[Jesus says] you will see clearly how I, through suffering, enter into the being and kingdom of the Father, that I sit at his right hand and intercede for you and am your mediator, and that I have done all this for your sake so that you may come to the Father also." [Luther continues]: "In saying this about the Father, he does not tell us much about his divine nature, as the Sophists try to do in their writings, which are futile and incomprehensible anyway. All Jesus says is that he is going to the Father, that is, that he will receive the kingdom and rule of the Father."

fulfilled in his "office of the word," meaning his prophetic office.[43] But since by standing in for God before humans, he also stands in for humans before God;[44] his prophetic office is nothing other than his priestly office. This priestly intercession in turn takes place as Christ's final and ceaseless action "in heaven," where he uses God's power and exercises his own vicarious lordship. Thus his prophetic office, and with it his priestly office, is the specific manner in which Christ carries out his kingly office.[45] These three offices thus prove to be interrelated aspects of the one and the same office of mediator (*munus triplex*),[46] with the prophetic office highlighting especially the means of mediation, the priestly office what is mediated, and the kingly office the power of the mediation.[47]

---

43. Cf. *The Freedom of a Christian*: "Christ was not sent for any other office than that of the word" (WA 7:51,8–9 = 7:22,19–20: §5 = LW 31:346; trans. alt.) and see also the weekly sermon on John 16:25–28: "'Because I came from God,' because I am the messenger and Son of God, that makes you dear to the Father. This, he says, is the message that I preach, by which I call all people to myself: 'I am of God and come from God, that is, I descended and became a human being, assumed the office of preaching that I might preach God's word and do the signs that accompany it. That is my office, my mission.' Again, concerning the divine nature of Christ, I understand it simply this way: He came into the world that he might live among people and preach. He spoke God's will and said that he had been sent to them that they might hear it; those who do it are God's dear children: 'My mission is now over; I have finished my work. I will no longer preach but die and assume God's rule so that I might reign forever.' This promise is comforting to those who believe that all Christ's words and works are the works of God, who wants nothing better than that we believe and cling to Christ alone and depend on no other work" (28:62,9–20; July 18, 1528). For an extremely clear and concise formula that includes the doctrine of the Trinity, Christology, and soteriology at the same time, see the interpretation of Luke 2:49 in the Lenten Postil of 1525 (17/2:24–26): "Thus Christ is in that which is of his Father when he speaks with us through his word and thereby brings us to the Father also" (17/2:24,18–19).

44. The fact that in sec. 5 the juxtaposition of the two sentences "The Father promised . . ." and "Christ suffers . . ." can only be understood in this way is confirmed by the reversal of their sequence in the sentence "The Son prays. . ." (where prayer in the name of Jesus on earth, appropriately, appears to correspond to the promise of the Father through the Son). The intertwining expressed in this sentence remains the theme: "Christ's righteousness . . ." and "my sins in Christ." It is thus formulated four times synonymously in sec. 5. The repetition shows the importance it has for Luther.

45. Cf. on the juxtaposition of Christ's session at the right hand of the Father and his intercession (Rom. 8:34) in the understanding of the office of mediator: WA 17/1:254,9–16 (quoted in n. 42).

46. The doctrine of Christ's threefold office was first worked out by Osiander and Calvin, but contrary to the usual view, Luther already knew it and taught it. This is clear from the freedom tractate, which speaks not only of Christ's priestly and kingly office but also of his "office of the word" (see n. 43).

47. These three offices are held together in unity in 1534 in an especially impressive way (according to the House Postil of Veit Dietrich of 1544): "It is true, Christ does not leave us. He sits at the right hand of the Father and intercedes for us, as Paul says. Thus we know that the

This mediation, understood as the epitome of the promise, is therefore the exact determination of the figure of the "happy exchange" (fröhliche Wechsel)[48] *known to us from the freedom tractate,* which is encountered in section 5 of the sermon. By its very nature, this mediation rules out a mere adequation that says Christ's righteousness is mine and my sins are Christ's. "It is, to be sure, an unequal exchange." What humans gain in this transaction through Christ, God loses through Christ; but God gains humans with his loss. That is the only way he can "clean things up" with them ("Each is thus purified"). The "unequal exchange" implies a concept of God according to which God is defined not as one who lives in isolation but as one who comes to people in their need. Luther therefore fights against the concept of God advocated by Aristotle in *Metaphysics* 12, which he refers to in a table talk thus: "The first being sees only himself. If he looked outside himself, he would see the troubles of the world." Luther then immediately asserts: "In that passage, Aristotle tacitly denies God."[49] "I say the opposite: If God looks only at himself, he is a most miserable being."[50]

Luther held that the two natures doctrine only comes into its own in the doctrine of the office of mediator. If this insight is combined with the idea from other texts that the two natures doctrine is aimed at the inalienable unity of the person and thus the unrestricted communication of attributes,[51] then it becomes clear that Luther's interest in the unrestricted *communicatio idiomatum* and the mediatorial office of Christ are deeply intertwined. The person is understood as a function and the function as a person.[52] This means that any metaphysical speculation about the person is just as much rejected as a *wirkungsgeschichtlich* understanding of the function, which wants to see it in terms of the impact it has on later times.

---

prayer he offered for his church and for us poor sinners at the Last Supper over the table and afterwards on the cross has been answered and is still continuing and will remain effectual until the end of the world" (WA 52:299,1–5). Above all, Luther clearly asserts here that the kingly office does not surpass the prophetic office and that the latter is in fact unsurpassable. Jesus's word has universal reach and eschatological validity, because the Father hears his prayer and answers it.

48. See esp. WA 7:53,15–55,36 (= 7:24–26: §§10–12) = LW 31:349–52 and the directly associated sections §§14–16 (see on that pp. 384–386).

49. WA TR 1:57 (no. 135); 1531.

50. WA TR 1:73 (no. 155); 1531/32.

51. On this, see R. Schwarz, "Gott ist Mensch—Zur Lehre von der Person Christi bei den Ockhamisten und bei Luther," *ZThK* 63 (1966): 289–351. Luther's specific view appears for the first time in 1520 (in *The Freedom of a Christian* in connection with his criticism of the doctrine of transubstantiation): see Schwarz, 348.

52. Christ brings about the "happy exchange," according to the freedom tractate, since he is "God and human in one person" (WA 7:55,9 or 7:25,34–35; §12 = LW 31:351; trans. alt.).

Such a Christology is the necessary reflection of the special form of the "authority"[53] *that is consistent with the promise.* For if this means the right and power of the one who impels us to divine certainty and empowers us to be certain ("By whose command and authority[54] we may confidently approach the Father of all things"), then it means the right and power of God himself. For only God himself can make us certain that he alone has power over all things—that is,[55] that he can "answer" us. So the specific words of Christ, "Ask and you will receive," with their promise that our prayers will be answered, contain an implicit divine claim. The divinity of Jesus is therefore not a soteriological postulate but an implication of the promise. It is neither its presupposition nor its extrapolation but is either believed *with* it or denied *with* it in the indissoluble unity of his person, work, and word.[56]

This corresponds directly to how reformational theology first (1520) formulated the trinitarian faith: "We should not put our faith in anyone but God alone. Therefore, we confess the divinity of Jesus Christ and of the Holy Spirit by the fact that we believe in them just as we believe in the Father. And as there is one and the same faith in all three persons, so the three persons are also one God."[57]

The fact that section 5 of the sermon under discussion does not expressly speak of the Holy Spirit like the later Rogate sermons does not change anything about the trinitarian character of the mediation event described there. For Luther, pneumatology is included in Christology, because "the Holy Spirit goes nowhere except into the body of Christ, for the Spirit is the Spirit of Christ."[58] He testifies, in accordance with Christ's own testamentary words,[59] "how it stands

---

53. Thus everything that follows the first sentence in sec. 5 is only the unfolding of its implied Christology ("And *so* it is not possible for our prayer not to be answered").

54. In the semantic field of "authority," "command," and "promise" (*iussus* and *promissio*, or alternatively *praeceptum* and *promissio* [as everywhere in the later sermons]) are combined into a unity.

55. See n. 33. With regard to us, the equation of "making certain" and "answering" (= "fulfilling") still contains the distinction between faith and sight (cf. n. 86).

56. According to the weekly sermon on John 16:25–28 of July 18, 1528 (WA 28:60,12–30), it is nothing less than a denial of Christ's *divinity* if we reject his mediation operative in the promise and so try to come into God's presence by our own will and power. This is an impressive example of how for Luther the two natures doctrine and the doctrine of justification are closely interwoven.

57. *Eine kurze Form der zehn Gebote, eine kurze Form des Glaubens, eine kurze Form des Vaterunsers* [*A Short Form of the Ten Commandments, A Short Form of the Creed, A Short Form of the Lord's Prayer*], 1520 (Luther's first catechism in three parts): WA 7:215, 18–22.

58. WA 20:381,20–21 (1526).

59. What Luther in 1520 includes above all in the gifting words of the Lord's Supper—namely, that Christ's substitution is communicated in the word ("for you") and his testament thus

between me, you, and the Father,"[60] for Christ says: "All come to the Father through me, and without me no one can come, indeed no one knows him except through the only Son."[61] "The Holy Spirit however will not teach us about what goes on in the Godhead."[62] His work is rather aimed directly at us, freeing us from reliance on our own power: "If we are to pray in the name of Christ, we should not be praying in our own name."[63]

In short, for Luther, prayer is a trinitarian word event that includes us in itself; "speaking with God (the Father), listening to the Holy Spirit, who tells us that everything is gathered into Christ."[64]

Excursus

Section 5 of the Sermon and the Tractate Freedom of the Christian

Section 5 is nothing other than a condensed anticipation of large sections of the first part of the freedom tractate.

---

executed—the later Rogate sermons locate in the Johannine farewell discourses, which completely in accordance with the text, are seen as a testament. Only after Jesus's death, and of course his resurrection, is his word revealed. The fact that he goes to the Father means that he guarantees the enduring validity and power of his legacy. And this in turn means nothing other than his coming and his presence with us as the Spirit in word and sacrament: see, for example, WA 46:87,16–26; 88:13–20; 92,28–96,28 (1539).

60. WA 28:60,9–10 (*Wochenpredigt über Joh 16:25–8* of July 18,1528).

61. WA 28:60,11–12.

62. WA 28:60,31–32.

63. WA 28:60,32–33.

64. WA 34/1:385,4–5 (1531). This word event of the economic Trinity is united with the *immanent Trinity* in the same way that the *vere homo* (truly human) is with the *vere deus* (truly divine) in the unity of Christ's promise. It is neither its presupposition nor its extrapolation but its implication. With it nothing else is asserted and confessed than that faith in the word has to do wholly and certainly with God himself: "Some people ask what God was doing before the creation of the world. Moses and John answer that 'he was speaking,' or better, he was preaching: the Word was in the beginning. He spoke with himself, and to himself, and in himself, about himself, and expressed and revealed himself to himself. *Therefore, he is the Word only as much as he is God*" (*Genesispredigten*, 1519–21; 9:329,28–31; author's emphasis). This determination of the immanent Trinity is explicated in the determination of the *economic* Trinity (9:330,29–35): "All things were created and all things are also preserved by the heavenly Word. According to the saying [Heb. 1:3], 'we are upheld by the word of his power,' our soul is sustained by this word and without it, it perishes. Adam was commanded not to eat from the tree. But he fell away from this word and perished with all his posterity. But how shall we return to it, that we may be saved? Not otherwise than through the incarnate Word sent to us and preached throughout the world. By laying hold of him, we can again be saved, but we can only lay hold of him and be saved by faith."

According to the first sentence of section 5, the Christ-promise opens up free access to God, who alone has power over all things and empowers us to be certain of him. What follows is the express demonstration of Christ's mediatorial office, implicit in the promise, and of the exchange that takes place in it.

In the first part of the freedom tractate, which describes what happens in faith by means of the word, Luther discusses Christ's mediatorial office in the "happy exchange," first in general, then specifically in connection with the aspects of his kingly and priestly office[65] bound up with it, understood as the office of the word. This is followed immediately[66] by a discussion of how Christ through his office as mediator *communicates*[67] or shares his kingship and priesthood with us ("Since . . . we are fellow-priests with Christ, let us come boldly with confidence, through the Spirit of faith, into the presence of God and cry 'Abba, Father!'").[68] The freedom of the Christian, which in section 5 of the sermon ("We may confidently approach the Father of all things") is reflected only in a single statement—and thus; in its unity—appears in the tractate in its twofold form, in relation to the world and in relation to God: Through "our kingship we (Christians) have power over all things, and through our priesthood we have power over God."[69] This double dimension finally appears in the conclusion of the whole tractate: "We conclude, therefore, that as Christians we do not live in ourselves, but in Christ and in our neighbor. Otherwise, we are not Christians. We live in Christ through faith, and in our neighbor through love. By faith we are caught up beyond ourselves into God. Conversely, by love we descend beneath ourselves into our neighbor. Yet we always remain in God and his love."[70] Here the conclusion ("Yet we always remain") combines the two different aspects to form a unity, which is addressed in section 5 of the sermon with its "We may confidently approach the Father of all things."[71]

---

65. WA 7:56,15–34 (= 7:26–27: §14) = LW 31:353 (trans. alt.).

66. WA 7:56,35–58,11 (= 7:27–28: §15,16) = LW 31:354–56.

67. "But just as Christ obtained these two prerogatives by his primogeniture, so *he imparts and shares them with* all his faithful according to the law of the above-mentioned marriage, by which the wife owns whatever belongs to the husband. Hence, we are all priests and kings in Christ, whoever we are, if we believe in him, as 1 Peter 2[:9] says" (WA 7:56,35–40 = LW 31:354; trans. alt.; author's emphasis).

68. WA 7:57,29–30 = LW 31:355 (trans. alt.).

69. WA 7:28,14–16: §16 (= 7:57,37–58,1 = LW 31:355 [trans. alt.]: "By our royal power we rule over all things, death, life, and sin etc., but by our priestly glory we can do all things with God, because God does what we ask and desire").

70. WA 7:69,12–16 (= 7:38: §30) = LW 31:371 (trans. alt.).

71. We can dispense with a further discussion of this conclusion in this context, for it is of such importance, systematically, that it warrants a discussion in its right. Cf. pp. 339–344.

At one important point, the tractate goes beyond section 5 of the sermon. It explicitly shows how prayer is intertwined with the sermon. The Spirit-wrought cry of prayer, "Abba Father," takes place through the faith ("through the Spirit of faith") that is born there and kept alive, "where the Christian freedom that we have from Christ is rightly taught and whereby Christians are kings and priests and therefore lords of all and may firmly believe that whatever they have done is pleasing and acceptable in the sight of God."[72] In such preaching, Christ himself acts as a priest and "teaches us inwardly in the spirit through the living instruction of his Spirit."[73] This "teaching" appears as the second aspect of Christ's priestly office, alongside that of intercession.[74] This also brings the unity of the Son's request and the Lord's word as shown in section 5 into focus here.

b) Section 5 made it clear why the *promise* constitutes prayer (section 1) and why it alone is its "basis and power."[75] Prayer that relies on our own will and strength, on the other hand, would be empty and worthless. But as it is, prayer does not get its power from us. Instead, it is enabled and empowered by the fact that God commands us to pray through Christ and at the same time promises to answer our requests.

Luther calls the second point about prayer the necessity, the *palpable need* (section 2). This does not constitute prayer on its own but belongs to it in that the command and promise address the palpable need. It is clear from the command as such that the need itself does not necessarily give rise to prayer, for it can also drive us to despair[76] or prompt us to overcome it ourselves. Prayer does not derive its necessity from our need but from God's command. Even more, our need can only really be recognized and named in view of God's pledge and promise to overcome it. Luther says, "Set God's promise against your need!"[77] Therefore, according to section 2, the concentration ("the gathering of one's thoughts")

---

72. WA 7:59,1–6 (= 7:29: §18) = LW 31:357 (trans. alt.).

73. WA 7:56,31–32 (= 7:27: §14) = LW 31:354 (trans. alt.). This passage would not be correctly understood if it were taken contrary to the interpretation given by §18 (see n. 72).

74. WA 7:56,31–32 (= 7:27: §14) = LW 31:354 (trans. alt.): "Nor does he only pray and intercede for us but teaches us inwardly in the spirit" (ll. 31–34).

75. WA 17/1:249,15 (1525).

76. Cf. the striking reference to Judas and Cain in the sermon on the Lord's Prayer of Mar. 9, 1523: "If this promise is not there, our need is not relieved. For Judas and Cain had a pressing need, but they had no faith in the promise. Remind God that he is our Father and that he promised, 'Ask and you will receive' etc. 'You said that you are our Father. This is your word, not mine. Faith simply relies on your promise'" (WA 11:56,21–25).

77. WA 20:380,9–10 (1526).

on the need that is to be brought to God and on the help expected from God is actually a concentration on "the divine promise."

This concentration on the promise is the *faith* that prevails in prayer. Section 3 sees it as the courage to compel God to stand by his word and honor it.[78] Faith can only do it because God lets himself be compelled in this way. As the Rogate sermon of 1526 says, the "amen" of the Son gives certainty, because "the Lord ties himself down with it." Luther says, "Is it not too much that the [divine] majesty swears an oath? . . . This is the greatest promise, that he says 'amen, it shall be so,' and swears to it by his faithfulness, which is eternal faithfulness. For this reason, you must begin your prayer by *reminding* God of what he has said: 'God, you have twice sworn an oath by your dear Son, that I should pray and that I would be answered. Because of this pledge and promise that you have made through the mouth of your Son, I come now and pray.'" This is the foundation of prayer.[79]

Faith is determined entirely by its content, the promise. The certainty that "caps off" prayer with its "amen" is based on the "amen" of the Son and is nothing other than its echo. The answer to prayer is verified only through the word and "felt"[80] only through the word. The promised answer is more certain than life and death itself.[81]

Since the faith that prevails in prayer is connected with its "amen" to God's promise, which in turn is anchored to his faithfulness, it gains the power of

---

78. Section 3: "Trust alone obtains what God's faithfulness *compels* him to provide" (author's emphasis). This "compulsion" is a crucial aspect of our faith that trusts his promise. The sermon of 1519 speaks of "reminding" God of his promise (WA 2:175,7–8; 178,1–2). See 17/1:249,30 (1525): "Take the promise for yourself and take hold of God at the same time"; 20:380,15–16 (1526): "I am a sinner, full of unbelief and avarice, but I lay hold of you through your promise." See also, in addition to the Rogate sermons, that saying, "We must hold God to his own words" from the famous sermon on the Syrophoenician woman in Matt. 15:21–28 (Lenten Postil, 1525, 17/2:200–4; quote: 204,2).

79. WA 20:379,15–16, 24–29 (author's emphasis; trans. alt.; see l. 33: "holding the promise up to God"); 1526.

80. WA 27:130,27–33 (1528): "Finally, you can cap it off with the 'amen' at the end, so that you are left in no doubt. When you have said your prayer, you should feel something move in your heart to tell you that it has been answered. You can say, 'Lord, you have commanded us to pray and promised to grant our request. Therefore, I know that my prayer has been accepted and answered.' But you cannot base that answer on your moral rectitude, but only on Christ's command and promise. If you do not say this, the prayer does not have an amen. However, if your prayer is true, you will feel it all. But if God does not answer you at the time you would like, then don't worry about it."

81. WA 15:548,6–8 (1524): "God has commanded us to pray and promised to answer us. You should be less certain of your life than you are of being answered. You should rather die a hundred times than doubt that God will answer you."

God's word over all the powers of the world. Therefore, Luther can boldly claim (in his Rogate sermon of 1531):

> Our prayer is God's power. What are all the powers of the world against that word, "*amen*"? Petitionary prayer is a great power, a divine power, which the power of the pope, of Satan, and of the Turk is not. For the whole world against God's word is, as Isaiah says, "as a fleck of dust" [40:15]. All the power of the world is just a little thing. Thus say: I trust God's promise—and what is that promise? The promise that you can rely on his word because it is called, "the power of God," and his power is stronger and more certain and will do far more than all the power of the Turks and popes . . .[82] In Elijah, "you see a single man praying, and yet with his prayer he rules over the clouds, the heavens, and the earth. Here God lets us see the power and force that a true prayer has, and that nothing is impossible for it.[83]

Through the power of Christ's promise, prayer is omnipotent,[84] since God has answered it already.[85] But it is precisely the certainty that God has answered our prayer, as he assures us in his word, that makes the eschatological discrepancy

82. WA 34/1:389,9–14 (1531). In another version: "The amen makes the promise so great that the whole world and its tyrants are nothing, absolutely nothing. For what is the Turk, the emperor, the pope and even the whole world compared to God's power? Our prayer is God's power. And Isaiah says that in God's sight and compared to God, the whole world is like a speck of dust on the scales [Isa. 40:15]. If I could but stick with the word, I would be relying on God's power, and that to me is far more than all the Turks and the pope" (389,19–20). Luther points to 2 Kgs. 6: "This happened to Elisha, who saw that there was a much greater army with him than with the enemy. But he had a different view of things than his servant, who saw only the armor and helmets, but when his eyes were opened, he saw that Elisha was surrounded by horses and chariots of fire. And so there was no substance to what he saw at first (389,25–28).

83. WA 17/1:251,19–22 (1525). This reference to Elijah is found already in the section on prayer in the *Treatise on Good Works* (1520): WA 6:239,20,28–31 = LW 44:67.

84. Cf. WA 28:59,24–26 (1528): "The prayer of a Christian is omnipotent . . . nothing is impossible for it, since the word 'whatever' [as in 'whatever you ask'] exempts nothing but includes everything under God's Yes."

85. The fact that prayer is already answered as soon as it is uttered is because of its basis: see sec. 5 and cf. n. 21. Appealing to 1 John 5:14–15, the Rogate sermon of 1525 likewise speaks expressly of prayer that has been answered already: WA 17/1:250,32–251,14; 253,5–13. See 46:85,31–34 (1539): "And yes, do not by any means cast such a prayer in doubt or uncertainty, but confidently believe that your prayer has come before God and has met with success, and that it is already a Yes. Since it was offered in the name of Christ and concluded with the amen, Christ himself confirms his word here." Likewise: 37:391,14–15; 392,21–22 (1534).

between God's promise and our palpable need so much more painful to bear.[86] Since this discrepancy remains, even when we grasp God by his promise, our desire is stretched to the utmost between our need and his promise. The tension felt, as we desire what is promised, makes for the earnestness of prayer[87] and at the same time reminds us that the essence of prayer is a *longing* (section 4). This longing excludes fearful hesitation[88] no less than frivolous adventure ("Where whatever happens happens, as when you throw a stone at a pear, hoping to knock it to the ground"). Rather, prayer is a reasoned and purposeful venture—where basis and goal are one.[89]

This is not contradicted by the Rogate sermon of 1525, in which the longing appears with the catchword *sighing of the heart* (Rom. 8:23).[90] For this sighing means that fear, need, and attacks (*Anfechtungen*) are not accepted in a spirit of resignation but are impatiently endured while their promised overcoming is unceasingly longed for and desired. However, in section 4 as well as in section 2,

---

86. The interpretation of THAT YOUR JOY MAY BE FULL, which immediately follows the command and promise of prayer, speaks of this in a particularly impressive way in the last Rogate sermon (in the printed version published in 1539): Our "joy cannot be complete (as Christ says here) until we see God's name perfectly hallowed, all false doctrine and sects eradicated, and all tyrants and persecutors of his kingdom subdued. Again, there will be no fullness of joy until the will and schemes of the devil and all the godless are overthrown and God's will alone is done. And yet again, our joy cannot be complete until the cares of the belly or hunger and thirst no longer assail us, sin no longer oppresses us, spiritual attacks (*anfechtung*) no longer weaken the heart, and death no longer holds us captive. But this will not come to pass until the life to come, for there we will feel nothing but perfect joy without even a tiny drop of sadness anymore. But in this life we have it only in part, as St. Paul says in 1 Cor. 13:9, and we have only a tiny drop of it in faith, which is the beginning or foretaste of the perfect joy to come, so that we have the consolation that Christ has redeemed us and that through him we have entered God's kingdom. But its power and effect in us is weak and thus progress is slow, and we cannot be perfect, either in faith or in life. For we keep falling into the mire and are weighed down with sadness and a heavy conscience, so that our joy cannot yet be pure, or it is ever so slight that we can hardly feel that it has even begun" (WA 46:91,26–92,6 = LW 24:400–401; trans. alt.).

87. Section 4: "Prayer should be earnest." Cf. the interpretation of the third commandment in the *Treatise on Good Works* (1520) on prayer: "Follow the words with an earnest heart in deep devotion, that is, with desire and faith, so that the heart earnestly desires what the words say and does not doubt that your prayer will be answered" (WA 6:235,17–19 = LW 44:61–62; trans. alt.).

88. Section 4: "not offered with a wavering mind." See "The majority of our most pestilential teachers have taught people to be hesitant in prayer and still to this day they lead many astray"; WA 4:631,11–12 (W. Maurer, *Melanchthon, 2*:151, has shown that what we have here [4:631,6–633,4] is a revision of Melanchthon from the year 1520).

89. Cf. the sermon on prayer of 1519: You are worthy and fit to pray and receive when "you proceed with bold courage, trusting in the faithful and certain promises of your gracious God" (WA 2:176,37–177,11; on the identity of the basis and goal of prayer, see p. 377).

90. WA 17/1:251,8–252,3; 251,36–252,22.

Luther does not consider the need of the person who is praying in and of itself but in light of the one "who will make good on what he has promised."

It must not be overlooked that the desire created by the promise in its opposition to our need does not become an independent human possibility or an ability within our reach but remains the work of God himself as the unutterable sighing of the Spirit, who intercedes for us (Rom. 8:26–27).[91] As with the origin of the promise, so also its use is an event of the triune God that occurs "solely on the basis of the unfathomable depth of God's goodness which, coming *before* all our prayers and desires, moves us through his gracious promises and commands to pray and desire, so that we learn how much more he cares for us than we will ever realize and that he is always more ready to give than we are to take and seek."[92]

C. The traditional definition of prayer as the "ascent of the mind into God"[93] occurs in the 1525 sermon, embedded in the context of section 4 and interpreted by it. Previously,[94] Luther had seen it from a completely different perspective, which was in no way related to the promise that God would answer our prayers. Rather, he saw it in the context of the double movement of our justification by God and God's justification by us in the simultaneity of the confession of sins and the forgiveness of sins.[95] This double movement was understood as a permanent event, without a fixed basis and a fixed goal in the oral word of salvation. This corresponds to the fact that since this event by its very nature was a prayer

91. See above reference. The "desire" is characterized as a transsubjective power in this way: "Longing surpasses all our words and thoughts. Hence humans themselves do not know the depth of their sighing or desiring" (WA 17/1:252,11–13). The Holy Spirit does nothing other than promote the work of Christ. See pp. 383–384 and the proof text from the freedom tractate quoted in n. 73.

92. WA 2:175,13–17 = LW 42:87 (1519); author's emphasis; trans. alt.

93. See n. 90.

94. WA 1:445,37–38 (*Sermon on the Third Commandment*, 1516): see chap. 2, n. 453. The definition also appears in the 1517 interpretation of the Lord's Prayer (9:127,15–17) and its revision of 1518/19 (2:83,33–34; 85,9–10).

95. See pp. 115–118 and in the context there esp. the quotation from the sermon on the Lord's Prayer of 1516 (117 n. 459). See further the principle of the 1517 interpretation of the Lord's Prayer: "God is praised and honored when we dishonor ourselves" (WA 9:133,31–32. See 133,4–7 [on that, 130,27–29]; 138,13–14; and19–20 in the context of ll. 19–30). It implies the early understanding of promise in the sense of the promise of judgment that we find in 1 Cor. 11:31, which then also emerges explicitly in Luther's words, "If you know that God wants to have sinners, take comfort in the fact that you recognize yourself as a sinner. For if you judge yourself inwardly and find there an unworthy and impure heart, know that it is pure before God" (150,2–5). Here the 1517 interpretation of the Lord's Prayer again completely agrees with the almost simultaneous interpretation of the penitential psalms: see chap. 3 B I (see chap 2 I: "The Fulfillment of the Promise in Judgment").

in which the one who prayed was "always longing and sighing," there could never be any certainty that it would be answered.[96] The fact that Luther's early concept of promise, informed as it is by such an understanding of justification and prayer, differs from his reformational view, can be seen not least by looking at his Rogate sermon of 1520, which was presented here in the context of its pre- and posthistory.[97]

This sermon shows clearly and distinctly the features of Luther's reformational view of prayer. It is remarkable how consistently and rigorously the concept of promise, found in his new understanding of the sacrament of penance, also reshapes his understanding of prayer.

Since the promise determines prayer, Luther was able to understand the sacrament as prayer in 1518 in the *Acta Augustana*. Conversely, when in 1520 he considers including prayer among the sacraments in *The Babylonian Captivity*, he does so for the same reason: because it has God's promise that he will answer it. This is the same promise with which Christ invites us to pray[98] and for which

---

96. See chap. 2 L ("Promise and Supplication"). Obviously, I evaluate the early texts differently than, for example, R. Hermann in "Das Verhältnis von Rechtfertigung und Gebet nach Luthers Auslegung von Röm. 3 in der Römerbriefvorlesung" (1925) in *Gesammelte Studien zur Theologie Luthers und der Reformation* (1960), 11–43, and *Luthers These "Gerecht und Sünder zugleich." Eine systematische Untersuchung* (1930). To deal with these works in the manner they deserve warrants a special study that cannot be done by making comments in footnotes.

97. Luther's brief letter of consolation (*Trostschrift*) of 1521 (WA 7:779–91 = LW 42:183–86) belongs to the immediate posthistory of his 1520 sermon, in addition to the later Rogate sermons. The following words about the complaint of a person in need (as in the prayer of Ps. 142: see 7:787–89 = 42:184–85) form the opening of the letter: "Such a person (suffering grave *Anfechtung* or spiritual attack) must by no means rely on themselves, nor should they be guided by their own feeling, but must take hold of the words offered to them in God's name, cling to them, despite how they feel, and direct all their thoughts and feelings to them" (7:785,3–7 = 42:183; trans. alt.). The letter finishes on the same note as it began: "We must never doubt the promise of our faithful and trustworthy God. For he has promised to answer us, indeed he has even commanded us to pray so that we may know for certain and firmly believe that our prayer will be answered" (Matt. 21:22, Mark 11:24, Luke 11:9–13 follow). "God also wants us to pray (and especially those suffering *Anfechtung*) so that we might know Christ aright and know that it is only through him that all our sins are paid for and that God's grace is given to us, and furthermore that we cannot deal directly with God without this mediator" (7:789,23–791,3 = 42:186; trans. alt.). What a different way Luther has of seeing Ps. 142 here compared with that of the interpretation of the penitential psalms of 1517 (on that, see chap. 3)!

With regard to its posthistory, we should also remember the interpretation of the Lord's Prayer in the *Large Catechism*, which before it treats the individual petitions, singles out the "command" (*BSLK* 662–66 = *BC* 440,1–445,34) and "promise" (666–67 = 443,19–21) and emphasizes our "need" (667 = 443,22–25) and "desire" (668,19–46 = 444,26–27).

98. "There are also a few other things that could possibly be counted as sacraments, namely, all those things to which a divine promise has been added, such as prayer . . . For Christ has promised in many places that those who pray will have their prayers answered. He promises this

he vouches and interposes himself as Son and Lord: to bring God to us and us to God.

It is no coincidence that Luther grasped and understood the trinitarian confession at the same time as his Rogate sermon (1520). His first interpretation of the creed is nothing other than a confession of what is believed in prayer, and as a confession itself, it is already a prayer uttered with the certainty of being answered, as its conclusion especially shows: "I believe . . . and do not doubt at all, that the Father, through his Son Jesus Christ our Lord, with and in the Holy Spirit, will grant me all these petitions. That is to say, AMEN, which means, this is most certainly true."[99]

---

especially in Luke 11:5–13, where in many parables he invites us to pray" (WA 6:571,35–572,3 = LW 36:123–24; trans. alt.).

99. *Eine kurze Form der zehn Gebote, eine kurze Form des Glaubens, eine kurze Form des Vaterunsers*, 1520: WA 7:(194–229), 220,2–5. This ending of the creed corresponds exactly to what is said about the "amen" at the end of the interpretation of the Lord's Prayer: 7:229,18–22. The creed and the Lord's Prayer interpenetrate each other even more in the concrete form of the catechism than the relationship between them outlined in the preface would lead us to expect (204,13–205,3). The prayerful character of the creed is particularly evident in the interpretation of the first article (215–16). With its content drawn entirely from Rom. 8:14–39, it is nothing but an unfolding of what it means, by virtue of Christ's promise, "to confidently approach the Father of all things" (sec. 5). Conversely, we see that prayer is determined by the creed, as is clear from the "intent" of the invocation (see again sec. 5): "O almighty God, since in your boundless mercy you have not left us alone, but have also commanded and taught us through your only beloved Son, our Lord Jesus Christ, that through his merits and mediation, we should respect and call you a father, even though you should rightly be a strict judge over us sinners, according to your justice": 7:220,12–17 (= 6:11,19–23; 1519. See n. 18). If we look back to the corresponding passage in the 1517 interpretation of the Lord's Prayer, according to which "this prayer comes from our Lord Christ who taught it to us so that we should deny ourselves and take up his cross in order that we may become his disciples" (9:124,30–32), then the radical change brought about by the Reformation becomes clear at a specific point, here especially in connection with Christology. In 1517, Christ was still seen as the archetype and model, his work still understood in terms of its impact on us (*wirkungsgeschichtlich*), and the confession "truly God" (*vere deus*) had not yet been given its full weight. In 1520, on the other hand, Christ is understood as our mediator and his work is seen in trinitarian terms.

CHAPTER 11

Summary

THE STARTING POINT and goal of this investigation was the reformational understanding of promise and faith, as first comprehensively presented in Luther's treatise *The Babylonian Captivity of the Church* (*De captivitate*) of 1520. It turned out to be possible and useful to examine his early texts by working backward from the treatise as well as by working forward toward it. In other words, we studied these texts both retrospectively and prospectively relative to the treatise.

1.

As we saw, in the first Psalms lectures and the Romans lectures, word and faith are understood differently than later on. The external, oral word is the word of judgment that demands and brings about the humiliation of the hearer. Grace, on the other hand, does not come to us as "the other word" (as Luther puts it in his 1520 freedom tractate) but only in judgment, which suddenly changes into grace or gradually slips into it. The event of grace is not revealed in the oral, public word but lies hidden beneath its opposite. Therefore, judgment and grace cannot be distinguished from each other on the basis of how they are heard but only on the basis of the different affect they have *in* us—and then only as two aspects of a single movement that finds its unity in the confession of sins and the prayer of supplication, where these two aspects of judgment and grace find immediate expression. In the confession of sins and the prayer of supplication, we die to ourselves, are torn away from ourselves, and placed outside of ourselves—that is, outside of our own abilities and potentialities, outside of our self-realization, and thus precisely into the ground that is operative in us. That means we now live outside of ourselves—that is, in God alone (*extra se in solo deo*). It is important to note carefully that according to this formula, the place and ground of our salvation is derived solely by way of negation (*via negationis*). What "God" is can only be expressed as the negation and rejection of all human attempts at self-realization and can only be spoken of from the standpoint of human neediness. Therefore, God is a "negative essence"; "*We cannot possess or touch him unless we deny all our affirmations about him.*"[1] The way of negation applies not only to the mind but also to the whole person in a life of continual penitence. But we

1. WA 56:393,1–3.

must not let the existential character of this doctrine of God obscure the fact that it is a thoroughly philosophical theology and must be regarded as a metaphysics of existence (assuming it is permissible to describe the movement of life and thought associated with the three ways of the Areopagite as a "metaphysics"). Even if the way of negation is permeated by the notion of "God's ordained power," it still remains a metaphysics. In fact, this permeation takes place in such a way that God can still only be defined negatively, by way of negation. His power can only be spoken of in comparison with human powerlessness. But this powerlessness is experienced in the never-ending, ever-renewed humiliation of ourselves in penitence. The fact that on the path of negation, we are always in motion (*semper in motu*) means that we will always be fundamentally uncertain. Consequently, the Aristotelian motif of *semper in motu* and the Neoplatonic motif of *via negationis* are so interwoven that what God is and what we are is equally shrouded in uncertainty and undergoes an infinite regress. The unity of God is not expressed (as in Luther's reformational understanding) in the unambiguity of the oral word of forgiveness that is meant to make us certain of our salvation. Rather, the unity of God is found in the movement of our constant humiliation (*exinanitio*), in which we are uncertain of our salvation and can never be certain of it, because this movement lasts a lifetime.

In contrast to the Neoplatonic way of negation, the treatise on our inability to choose God (*De servo arbitrio*)[2] makes an important distinction in that things that were said to be undifferentiated and indistinguishable in the early texts—namely, the hidden God (*deus absconditus*) and the revealed God (*deus revelatus*)—are now clearly distinguished. And when Luther says of the latter that "God has bound himself to his word" (*verbo suo definivit sese*),[3] then the earlier definition formulated only by way of negation is excluded and its place taken by the twofold form of the word as law and gospel. Here the law does not change into the gospel, nor does the negation change into an affirmation, but each is distinguished from the other by the way in which its oral form impinges on its hearers. Instead of this distinction between the two forms of the external oral word, the early texts contain the incompatible distinction *between* the external (improper) word and the internal (proper) word—a distinction that locates Luther in unbroken continuity with the tradition of the Augustinian hermeneutics of signification.

The fact that God defines himself by allowing himself to be defined only by way of negation is to be understood in a *christological* sense: he can only be sought in the crucified one, who is the archetypical embodiment of the *via negationis*, the path on which human beings in their totality are led, the path of penitence

2. Often called "The Bondage of the Will."

3. WA 18:685,23 = LW 33:140 (trans. alt).

with its humiliation and worldly detachment.[4] In him, their own cross and suffering is seen concretely in its most intense and radical form and thus finds its sufficient basis. In him, their cross and suffering also finds its strange inner reversal from negation to affirmation, from death to life: "But these strange works were done radically and causally in Christ's suffering, and all of us must necessarily be conformed to his example."[5] The acceptance of cross and suffering that comes our way is the existential dimension that binds Christ and Christians together. This dimension, which we see concretely in the image of the crucified one, shows us Christ's *meaning* and *effectiveness*—both terms are mutually inclusive in the context intended here and can therefore be represented by a single term, *significance.* This existential dimension encompasses the being of Christ as "sacrament." This being is imparted through a certain way of dealing with biblical texts, which is decisively shaped by a meditative piety such as Tauler also employs in his sermons. This "sacramental meditation on Scripture" is the setting in life (*Sitz im Leben*) of Luther's early Christology and at the same time the center of his monastic existence. He says that "this is how we are to suck what is ours from the wounds of Christ, especially penitence."[6]

In the context of this "archetypal Christology," the function of the word is limited to leading the listeners and readers into prayerful contemplation and conveying to them a vivid, pictorial impression of the devotional image that immediately impresses itself on their soul. In this view of things, the image before them only proves to be true when it is reenacted and we can see the effect it has on them, specifically in penitence (contrition). For archetypal Christology, the authority of Christ is the *causal effect of an image* of his existence, which is fulfilled in penitence and humiliation, in which Christians are conformed to his archetype. But his authority is not the *authority of a word*, understood as the promise of the forgiveness of sins and victory over death, for which Christ himself stands as guarantor, the only promise that can give certainty. In fact, it is precisely this dimension of the promise, so constitutive for Luther's reformational Christology, that is completely missing in his early Christology. Accordingly, Luther is nowhere interested in the gifting words of the Lord's Supper ("This is my body given for you"; "This is my blood shed for you for the forgiveness of sins"), where Christ says what he gives us in the sacrament. The Mass is only important insofar as it keeps alive the idea of sacrifice. We become aware of Christ's sacrifice when we perceive it tropologically—that is, when we see it as the sacrifice of ourselves with him. Thus the Mass preserves the idea of the "the

4. WA 57/3:124,13–14: "abstraction from the images of the world."

5. WA 4:243,14–15.

6. WA 9:145,31–32.

mystical cross of Christ on which everyone must be offered."[7] In this sense, the Mass is identical with the "sacramental meditation on Scripture," contrition and the confession of sins, or at least it is interpreted in this way and left behind.[8]

It is clear to what extent this understanding of the Mass resists being harmonized with Luther's later view of the Lord's Supper. The discrepancy evident at this point is precisely reflected in the difference between the early understanding of the *promise* and that which first appears in the *Explanations of the Theses on Indulgences.* One of the main tasks of the whole investigation was to point out and work out this difference, taking into account the common elements stemming from the Franciscan theology of the pact.

The problem with Luther's early view of promise is that it does not go beyond the general understanding of the word—which is seen from its metaphysics of existence and the archetypal Christology identical to it—but fits seamlessly into it. This finding is in keeping with the tenor of the presentation, which started with the core of Luther's early theology and its understanding of word and faith and only then treated the understanding of the promise to make it clear that *promissio* has no fundamental significance for the whole of his early theology. The method used in the second part had to be different. Here the (new) concept of promise had to become the subject and center of every chapter. This was the only way to do justice to the importance it was gaining from the spring of 1518 onward.

Luther's early understanding of *promissio* fits into the whole of his early theology because, in terms of its *content*, the promise is dominated by the *confession of sins* and *prayer of supplication* so that it merely strengthens his early metaphysics of existence derived from the way of negation and for that reason is never able to overcome it.

Concretely, this was able to be demonstrated above all by a tradition-historical analysis of the series of scholia on Romans 3:4–5 and 4:7, which form one of the most striking parts of the lectures. It led once again to the center of Luther's early theology and at the same time to the center of his monastic existence as a professor of biblical theology and showed how deeply his thinking is rooted in various traditions, which he then reshapes in a very specific way.

Considered against the background of its prehistory in the first Psalms lectures, the dialectic of active and passive justification that Luther developed in his interpretation of Romans 3:4–5 is identical with the two-sidedness of God's pact, as formulated in Mark 16:16. This saying, which according to *The Babylonian Captivity* can be taken as a proclamation of the baptismal promise, is interpreted according to Luther's early theology (especially in the scholion on Ps. 51) by

7. WA 3:646,20.

8. *Dekalogpredigt*, 1516.

1 Corinthians 11:31 alone: Whoever believes; that is, whoever judges themselves is saved. In other words, they are no longer judged. This interpretation follows in the wake of a long monastic tradition. The promise is therefore specifically fulfilled in self-accusation and self-annihilation. The definitive declaration of the divine will given with it does not, as later, establish and maintain the certainty of faith but instead makes it necessary for salvation for believers to bend back negatively on themselves, to empty themselves, and to let themselves be led back into their nothingness. But if sinners can only be certain of salvation by reflecting on themselves in an infinite regress by way of negation, and if the forgiveness of sins is identical with the confession of sins, then they are *actually* not certain of their salvation at all and cannot be certain of it.

This is also evident from the prayer of supplication. It is particularly highlighted in the series of scholia on *Romans 4:7* that likewise have a background in the theology of the pact, as could be shown by going back to Biel (in Lection 59 of his Mass commentary) and Luther's scholion on Psalm 113:9 (=115:1): "God decreed that he would impute sin to everyone except to those who lament their sin, are afraid, and continually implore his mercy."[9] This is how we are to understand the *simul peccator et iustus* of Luther's early theology—which settles an old dispute in Luther research. It expresses the double-sidedness of God's pact as formulated in Luke 11:9–10 ("Ask and it will be given to you; seek and you will find; knock and the door will be opened to you"), the understanding of which is again characteristically determined by the Aristotelian motif "always in motion." Thus God's promise can only be fulfilled in the uncertainty of continual supplication ("assidue *implorare*"). Because it does not come to us as a concrete oral promise in time, we can only experience it in hope. We can only really perceive it if we have the right attitude or disposition toward it. The promise itself remains the abstract condition of its fulfillment (in the confession of sins and the prayer of supplication), but this alone is its concrete reality.

It has become clear that Luther's early theology, which we have briefly reviewed, has an impressive systematic coherence and is in a class of its own. It is a negative theology that can indeed be described as a metaphysics of existence, expressed with an archetypal Christology. It works with the sharpest dialectical means of thought and language (for example, in the scholion on Rom. 9:28), yet it is not just a thought structure but the objectification and enactment of a monastic existence that takes the path of radical negation. It is rooted in various traditions that Luther continues but not without sharpening and reshaping them in his own unique way. Therefore, as much as we can demonstrate certain dependencies from the point of view of tradition history,

9. WA 56:281,18–19 = LW 25:268 (trans. alt.).

his early theology as a whole is something unique and comparable only, if at all, to Tauler's sermons, from which it is distinguished among other things by its exegetical character.

No matter how much we may appreciate the originality of Luther's early theology or what we call it, it is *not* reformational in the sense in which Luther understood it. The aim of this investigation was to show that his reformational theology cannot simply be tacked onto it, nor can its relationship to it be understood in terms of the schema of "a bud and its blossoming." But this is not to deny that Luther's early theology is the presupposition for his reformational theology and that the latter cannot be understood without it. We could say in summary that the way of negation that Luther pursued with his early theology forms the prehistory of the reformational exclusive particle. The latter of course does not simply take up that previous history but corrects it at the crucial point, the point of uncertainty, which was said to be principally willed and worked by God. Luther's reformational theology thus presupposes his early theology but not in such a way that it can be detached from it. It presupposes it not only historically but also factually (if such a distinction is even possible), as an unsolved problem, precisely in regard to the question of the certainty of salvation. His reformational theology is the answer that supersedes the question, and yet, as an answer, it is (and remains![10]) related to the question. But it cannot be deduced from the question as such and does not necessarily follow from it, nor can it be expected to do so, at least not directly.

This insight, which is theological, historical, and at the same time systematic, means that the law, even in its most radical form, does not give rise to the gospel; that death does not, of itself, turn into life; the cross into salvation; confession of sins into forgiveness of sins; petitionary prayer into answered prayer; need into deliverance; radical doubt into certainty; and negation into affirmation. Anyone who wants to claim this (such as Gogarten) as a reformational theologian will not recognize the turn described here as "reformational" as such. But that then means that such theologians cannot do justice to what is distinctive about the early texts (by simply superimposing on them the claim that they are "reformational"), nor can they do justice to Luther's treatise *The Babylonian Captivity* and his later retrospections of his reformational discovery, which are characterized by the keyword *promise*.

10. There is a difficult problem that inevitably arises here, and that is this: How could the answer that Luther as an *individual* received to his question—a question that had its own specific context within the history of the church, theology, and piety—become, if at all, the basis and confession of faith for *others*? I tried to give an initial pointer to how I would answer this question in my essay "Die reformatorische Wende in Luthers Theologie," in *ZTK* 66 (1969): 146–47.

2.

As has already been emphasized, the main purpose of this investigation, which can be seen already from its division into two parts, was to demonstrate that Luther's reformational theology, which stresses the word (*promissio*) that gives the certainty of salvation, is found in *The Babylonian Captivity* and singled out by Luther in his later retrospections as his reformational discovery, but is not yet present in his early theology. The second purpose of this work was to demonstrate that the decisive turn in his theology only comes at the time of the indulgence controversy and that his distinctively "reformational" emphasis appears for the first time in his *Pro veritate* theses of 1518. This required two lines of argument that correspond to each other and must verify each other to be convincing. First, a basically negative argument that has to show that Luther's theology from 1520 onward is *not* present in his early theology (part 1) and, second, a basically positive argument that has to demonstrate its purported difference to his early theology in such a way that (a) his reformational theology emerges as a *fundamental* difference, and the story of Luther's theology from the *Pro veritate* theses onward is thus recognizable as a reorientation affecting the *whole* of his theology, and in such a way that (b) the *connection of the reconfigured* concept of the sacrament and hence of the church (especially that of priest and heresy), as well as of the sermon, Christology, prayer, and the approach to ethics, *with its new understanding of the promise*, can not only be constructed conceptually by the interpreter but also demonstrated concretely from the texts themselves (part 2). Both parts could be recognized in the many references running back and forth between part 1 and part 2 in such a way that the negative line of argument becomes compelling from the positive and the positive from the negative.

In the second part of the investigation, to which we now look back in particular, it became apparent in a surprising way how much the concept of the promise (and not that of the righteousness of God[11]) can illuminate the historical

11. Our approach, which takes its bearings from the concept of promise rather than from that of the righteousness of God, makes it necessary (demonstrated in more detail in my article "Die reformatorische Wende in Luthers Theologie," *ZThK* 66 [1969]: 115–21) to interpret Luther's own self-testimonies, which reflect on the reformational turn of his theology, in a way that is consistent with his reformational insights. To be precise, we need to ensure that what is distinctively "reformational" is determined by the understanding of the promise found in *The Babylonian Captivity of the Church*. Furthermore, we must interpret the formulas of the retrospections that are not characterized by the keyword *promise* in the light of its understanding. Bizer in fact has already followed this path in the afterword of the third edition of his *Fides ex auditu* (1966) by using the discovery of the reformational concept of the promise to explain more precisely Luther's discovery described in the *Preface to the Complete Edition of Luther's Latin Writings* (LW 34:327–38; Bizer 180–84)—without of course referring to any of Luther's corresponding retrospective self-testimonies (but see Bizer, 189). This approach now requires us to retroactively

course and factual context of Luther's theology during the years 1518–1520. For the promise alone led not only to the discovery of the significance of the *Pro veritate* theses, to the correct dating of the Hebrews lectures and to the marginal notes to the fourth book of Biel's *Collectorium*, but above all it also led to the discovery of the origin of Luther's reformational understanding of baptism, to the origin of his reformational Christology, and to the origin of his reformational understanding of prayer (together with the localization and significance of his Rogate sermon of 1520), as well as to the starting point or organizing principle of his reformational ethics. (Ernst Bizer has already identified the origin of the reformational understanding of the Lord's Supper and the sermon.[12])

The structure of the second part was given by the texts that determine the overall conception of *The Babylonian Captivity*, especially the theses of the disputations that Luther had used to prepare this treatise (especially the section on baptism, which is the most systematic section of the whole work). The preparation was methodical and scientifically rigorous.

The most important findings of the presentation itself can be summed up in the following outline.

The understanding of promise (*promissio*) and faith (*fides*), as we typically find it in *The Babylonian Captivity of the Church*, is first encountered in the *Pro veritate* theses (in the early summer of 1518) in a new conception of the sacrament of penance. On the one hand, these theses tear apart the context of Luther's earlier theology and, on the other, the entire fabric of traditional sacramental teaching. With his stubborn insistence on the specific *promissio* of Christ used in the verbal promise and the faith subsisting in it, Luther presents the scholastic definition of the sacraments as "efficacious signs of grace" in a completely new way, not by intensifying or deepening it but through a bold recourse to the New Testament, especially its sentences of holy law. Luther overcomes the declaratory understanding of the word, which was still being tested in the "Explanation" of thesis 7 of the *Theses on Indulgences*, and with it the Augustinian distinction between *signum* and *res* (the sign and the thing signified). At the same time, he

change the formal question of Bizer's entire work: If the guiding concept of the "righteousness of God," anchored to the Rom. 1:17 passage, which formally steers his investigation, as the book's subtitle indicates, turns out to be what has to be explained, then the question about the discovery of the reformational understanding of *fides ex auditu*, which factually and materially is Bizer's topic, needs to be framed more aptly from the outset with the help of the interpretative lens of the reformational concept of promise, the significance of which he has brilliantly described ("Die Entdeckung des Sakraments durch Luther," *ET* 17 (1957): 88–89). That was the task I attempted with the investigation undertaken in this book.

12. Bizer, "Die Entdeckung des Sakraments durch Luther," *ET* 17 (1957): 83–87; *Fides ex auditu*, 177–78. (The picture drawn here must of course be differentiated from and also corrected by my own work: see pp. 282–284, 317 and chap. 8.)

rejects the necessity of the disposition of both the giver and receiver and so, too, the basic Aristotelian schema of *forma* and *materia*, even in its highest sublimation, and instead asserts the sufficiency of faith without Augustinian spiritualism because it is based solely on the efficacy of the oral word of salvation.

In October 1518, Luther had to answer to Cajetan in Augsburg for this theology of the word—the word that made him certain of his salvation and, as he confessed at the time, the very word through which he "became a Christian."[13] If we want to recognize the reformational turn in his theology, which is the decisive turn among his many turns, we will need to pay careful attention to Luther's meeting with Cajetan.

The turning point of this turn is clearly marked in his *Pro veritate* theses. That this is not an isolated turn is shown by its mirror image in the Hebrews lectures. Contrary to the usual way of dating them, these lectures do not precede the indulgence controversy in that the scholion on Hebrews 5:1 does not prepare for the "Explanations" to the *Theses on Indulgences*, in which the new understanding of the sacrament of penance is taking shape, but rather the lectures presuppose the "Explanations" and from there on, in their second part, accompany the "Explanations" on their path from the 1518 *Sermon on Penance*, via the *Pro veritate* theses, to their defense before Cajetan in Augsburg. The reflection of this path offered by the Hebrews lectures is particularly interesting because they not only overlap thematically with the texts on the sacrament of penance (in the scholion on Heb. 7:12) but also show how together with Luther's new understanding of the promise, which is first fully expressed with systematic clarity in a reconfiguration of the sacrament of penance, his view of the Mass also immediately begins to change. In the texts examined, the Hebrews lectures continue the topic begun with the *Sermon on the Worthy Preparation of the Heart for Reception of the Eucharist*, which should be understood as a counterpart to the 1518 *Sermon on Penance*. Therefore, the Hebrews lectures document the first phase of the reformational change in the understanding of the Lord's Supper.

However, the thrust (*Tendenz*) of the scholia examined in the Hebrews lectures only really prevails with the Easter sermon (*Concerning the Testament of Christ*) of 1520 after it had failed to be taken up shortly before in the *Sermon on the Lord's Supper*, published in December 1519. The fact that, over the years 1518 to 1520, the entire fabric of traditional motifs is only gradually torn apart is no objection to the assumption that the breakthrough had already occurred earlier at a crucial point but rather sheds light on the historical and not mechanical way in which the new starting point or organizing principle (*Ansatz*) was slowly being taken up everywhere in Luther's theology. From this point of view, Luther's approach in the sermon mentioned above, which proves to be a failure when

13. WA BR 1:217,62.

judged by *The Babylonian Captivity*, was particularly noted. It is an impressive example of how theology at a time of radical change can easily slip back into its old traditional ways if the starting point of every question is not strictly determined by the new understanding of the promise. Therefore, to use the language of science, the crucial experiment (*experimentum crucis*) succeeded and, as the book shows, has demonstrated that Luther's new approach or organizing principle (*Ansatz*) is viable and not at all ineffective.

This is then applied to the understanding of the Lord's Supper in *The Babylonian Captivity of the Church*. Here the sign and significance of the sacrament coincide because the gift of salvation (*res*) is exactly what the sign (*signum*) says it is, because the word gives and does what it promises. Here faith takes the word in its simple sense (and precisely here we should also see the reformational turning point in Luther's *hermeneutics*!) and thus grasps both its *signum* and *res* at the same time. Faith is its use because it takes hold of the word, and faith is its fruit because the word takes hold of it. In both cases, faith is all-sufficient. It is everything because the word is everything. Thus our remembrance of Christ is not dependent on our feeling of penitence, as in Luther's early theology, and does not need to be, but its power resides in the oral promise. What constitutes and defines the Lord's Supper is not our awareness of Christ's suffering in our mortification, but it can only be heard and deduced from his gifting words ("given for you"; "shed for you for the forgiveness of sins"). Contrary to traditional teaching and practice, this word as a ritual formula is not attached to the element. Rather, it is the other way around: The element is attached to the word, which is true both in the case of the hearer and the receiver, and besides that (in contrast to the sense of Luther's early *pro me*), the word in itself already says "for you": "For you for the forgiveness of sins!" God has given himself in this word and has revealed himself in it definitively. It is his "testament," which came into effect through Jesus's death, and it is through its enactment in the Supper that the crucified one lives.

This is how Luther understands *promissio*: as a binding promise (*Zusage*) with immediate effect. For him therefore, *promissio* does not mean a future promise (*Verheißung*); it is not a category of revelation based on a philosophy of salvation history (*Heilsgeschichte*) but rather the quintessence of proclamation (specifically, of "the Lord's death"). Luther here has a very definite understanding of God and history and a very definite view of the Old Testament. The unity of God is revealed not only in the totality of an as yet unfinished story or history but is given entirely in the unambiguousness of his promise and becomes known through its special faith. (This topic was so important for Luther that he made it the subject of a special set of theses, "the signs of grace," which he then incorporated into the section on baptism when he wrote *The Babylonian Captivity*.

Luther came to his reformational understanding of *baptism* in the middle of his baptismal sermon (1519), which in its structure still followed the Augustinian tripartite division of sign, significance, and faith. The specific place and the specific way of "remembering" baptism, which is the external oral word of absolution, reminds Luther that the object and basis of this remembrance is for its part constituted by the promise (in the words of Mark 16:16, which he changes into the second person and turns into the promise "If you believe, you have it!").

Thus along with the connection between the sacraments of baptism and penance, he came to understand the sacrament of baptism itself, which has not fundamentally changed since *The Babylonian Captivity*. That he understood this connection with "remembrance" through the figurative use of a term specific to the liturgy and the doctrine of the Mass, represents a theological achievement that can hardly be overestimated and is testament to the high esteem in which Luther held baptism. According to this understanding, baptism has the same unique character as the death of Jesus himself.

The main part of the baptismal section of *The Babylonian Captivity* repeats the points known to us from the section on the Lord's Supper, but here they are part of one long argument that is carefully structured and self-contained. Luther's examination of the traditional doctrine of the sacrament is impressive, and so our interpretation of it had to pursue the polemical references here in a special way. In contrast to the Franciscan tradition, for Luther the *promissio* in Mark 16:16, which he recognized as a sentence of holy law like that in Matthew 16:19, is not legislated (*legislatorisch*) in a divine decree and oriented to the sign but proclaimed and given (*exekutiv*) in sermon and sacrament and oriented to the receiver.

It has its essence in its orality and is specifically a promise. The sign is drawn into the word; it signifies and "figures" nothing else than what the word says and does. Thus Luther leaves behind the distinction between *signum* and *res* and so opposes not only the entire traditional teaching on the sacraments but also his own "sacramental meditation on Scripture," which he had taught earlier but now rejects as allegorical. In keeping with Luther's new starting point or organizing principle located in the promise, which gives us the certainty of salvation, the Aristotelian concept of motion that appears here again with its frequent *semper* (always), has also lost the sole dominance that it once had. In addition, a new concept of *confessio* (confession) appears that is characteristically different from the earlier one. Confession is now a response to assertoric preaching, in which humans surrender themselves to God's promise without any negative self-reference. The theology of humility has gone!

The substantive center of the entire treatise *De captivitate* lies in the section on baptism, where the sacrament of penance and the Lord's Supper each has the same task: to bring us back to baptism and let us hear again its promise. In both cases, this happens again because of and by means of the promise. And this promise, understood as the words of absolution or the gifting words of the Supper, constitutes the sacrament and even led to its discovery in the first place. However, the promise is not exhausted by the sacrament but, as a "summary and compendium of the gospel," forms the basic text of every sermon. This in turn gave the *sermon* a new function. Thus the origin of the reformational understanding of the sermon also lies in the concept of the promise, which grew out of a profound rethinking of the function of the sacraments and cannot be separated from this context, either historically or materially.

What promissional preaching looks like for Luther was seen from a series of three *sermons on Luke 2 or Matthew 1* (from 1519, 1520, 1521). It became clear how the "sacramental meditation on Scripture" in the sense of Luther's early theology contributed to the emergence of his reformational theology of promise but also how sharply it is corrected by it. Accordingly, the difference between his early *pro me* and his reformational *pro me* clearly emerged. The latter does not immediately mean the appropriation (An*eignung*) of the event of salvation by me, but primarily its bestowal (Zu*eignung*) by God. It is the echo of an explicit, audibly articulated promise *for you* (both singular and plural), the validity of which does not depend on our ability to appropriate it. Because for Luther, not only is revelation not so immanent in history (here: in the story of Jesus's birth) that it would be obvious, but history is also not transparent to a salvific meaning that might be seen running through it, nor could it be understood by means of existential verification, although the word in that case would only have the function of interpretation. Rather, Luther sees history as so closed, so ambiguous—and hence offering no certainty of salvation—that the interpretative word (*Deutewort*) in the narrative of the story is not enough, but attention needs to be paid to gifting word (*Gabewort*). Christ does not reveal himself as the historical Jesus "in himself,"[14] nor in the process of appropriation and contemporization (bringing Christ into the present) that we are familiar with from the "sacramental meditation on Scripture" in the sense of Luther's early theology. But he gives himself in the word bound to the sermon, and only in that word, and it is only in the word that he is recognized as savior. Faith does not come from the image and its perception but from the word and its hearing—more precisely, from the gifting word, not the interpretive word.

When the *promissio* takes the place of the earlier *sacramentum*, it also changes the relationship between *sacramentum* and *exemplum* and with it the *starting point or organizing principle of Luther's ethics*. The sacrament can only precede the example and the two can no longer merge into each other now that the sacrament is constituted by the spoken word, understood as a promise. But

14. WA 10/I/1:73:15.

as long as the promise has to be won through negative existential verification (namely, penitence), it is inevitable that humiliation before God (*coram Deo*) will merge with humiliation before the world (*coram mundo*), as the early Luther texts clearly document. For if our relationship to God lacks any positive determination, our negative self-knowledge alone will remain the sole determinant of our relationship to God as well as our relationship to the world. If the promise of Christ did not appear or appeared only as an inner reversal of the negation, then both our relationship to God and the world would only be perceived as the humiliation (exinanition) of our existence. Both relationships would coincide without differentiation and become one, even though the intention of the way of negation is to radically abstract and remove God from the world completely. Only in the *deus pro nobis* (the God for us), in the oral promise of salvation, are God and the world, faith and love not radically separated, only to merge into one another precisely in their radical separation, but rather differentiated and subordinated to one another in terms of their content so that the one follows the other in proper order, as we have it in the concluding thesis of the freedom tractate.

The question of the *christological dimension* of the new understanding of the promise helped us discover the constitutive promissional structure of reformational Christology and to see that its origin, precisely in the new understanding of the promise, could be determined exactly in this way. In terms of its content, this means that reformational Christology right from the start is so deeply intertwined with the doctrine of the Lord's Supper that it cannot exist without it. Because in the promise of the Lord's Supper, we concretely experience the interconnection of Jesus's death and God's life, of God's death and Jesus's life, and we come to know Christ as one person in two natures ("A testator is the same as a promiser who is about to die, but a promiser is a testator who will remain alive"[15]; "*Pactum* and *testamentum* are the same, just as the same Christ is God and human."[16]). Thus Luther's talk of the "death of God" has its systematic place in the theology of the promise, especially the promise of the Lord's Supper, which asserts that the one who died is alive and that the living one has the final word through his death. Further, it is clear from the promise of the Lord's Supper why for Luther the doctrine of the two natures is identical with the doctrine of Christ's mediatorial office: Christ's person is a communicative event, "for you for the forgiveness of sins."

This new Christology stands out as a special type (a "trinitarian mediator Christology") and clearly differs from Luther's earlier Christology, which in contrast is a "archetypal Christology."

15. WA 6:513,37–38 = LW 36:38 (trans. alt.).

16. WA 57/2:82,14–15.

The fact that for the reformational Luther, Christology was the necessary reflection on the particular form of authority that came with the promise was also shown by the (previously ignored) Rogate sermon of 1520. It testifies with unique clarity to how the new understanding of the promise also comes out in a new conception of *prayer*. Its broader significance lies in the fact that it expressly highlights *promissio* theology as a doctrine of the Trinity and clarifies Luther's first interpretation of the creed by showing that it is nothing other than a confession of what is believed in prayer and, as a confession itself, is prayer uttered in the certainty of being answered. This certainty that prayer is answered is created by Christ's promise and was unknown in Luther's early theology—and impossible.

The investigation concluded with the presentation of his new understanding of prayer. For with it the last of the special forms of the reformational concept of *promissio* has been considered, and at the same time, its thematic framework was made broad enough that it could be made clear that its reorientation that began with the *Pro veritate* theses affects every aspect of Luther's theology. Furthermore, the main themes of *The Babylonian Captivity of the Church* are illuminated by their history in his early theology. The fact that this history is the story of the "reformational turn in Luther's theology" is further attestation of the fundamental importance of this treatise, which after the New Testament, is the most influential and consequential writing in the history of the church.

CHAPTER 12

Retrospective Afterword (2023)

LIKE ALL GERMANS, my first encounter with Martin Luther goes back to early childhood. It took place via my native language, which would not have happened without Luther's translation of the Bible. It makes a difference of course whether it remains an unconscious encounter or whether it goes on to become a real engagement with the Luther Bible itself through reading and studying it. I remember the time when I was eight or nine years old. Every night, before going to sleep, I used to look at the family Bible together with my brother. It was my grandparents' Luther Bible with illustrations by the German painter Julius Schnorr von Carolsfeld. For us of course the dramatic pictures were the most important thing. Yet in the religious instruction at school, in confirmation classes, in the church youth groups, and in divine worship, we heard and read texts from the Luther Bible, sang Luther's hymns, and learned Luther's *Small Catechism* by heart.

I will never forget the moment when our religious instruction teacher wanted to make a point about Luther's understanding of the sacrament. He pulled out a bank note, held it up and asked: "What is this?" We answered: "A hundred-mark note." He said: "No, a piece of paper worth less than a penny. But just as the bank note is not just a piece of paper but rather one hundred marks, because of the government's monetary guarantee, so, too, because of Christ's words of institution, the bread and wine in the Supper are not just bread and wine, but the body and blood of Christ."

To be sure, all these early encounters with Luther do not resemble anything like Luther research, yet they were a good preparation for it.

1.

When I began my theological studies at Tübingen in 1959, Bultmannian Scholasticism ruled supreme there, at least in the Evangelical Stift (Protestant seminary) to which I belonged. Barth was not read; neither was Luther. But I soon found a kindred spirit in Gerhard Hennig, a fellow student and my future brother-in-law, who had studied with Ernst Bizer (1904–1975) in Bonn. He gave me an understanding of Bizer's Luther interpretation and introduced me to the scholarly debates around the relationship between the young and the old Luther, especially around the question of the reformational element in Luther's theology.

Thus I read Luther right at the beginning of my studies and realized that Bultmann's appeal to Luther is problematic. Bultmann claimed that with his existential interpretation—or put negatively, his demythologization—of the New Testament, he is doing nothing more than consistently applying the Pauline and reformational doctrine of justification by faith alone to the relevant field of knowledge. This claim puzzled me. Above all, I was struck by the fact that Bultmann, like Schleiermacher, only wanted to speak of God in the mirror of the human recipient (*homo recipiens*), while Luther, on the other hand, insists that it is necessary to define the human recipient on the basis of the God who speaks (*deus dicens*) and not the other way around. The criticism of Bultmann in my *Theologie* book[1] goes back to that time and is in a sense the oldest part of the book.

In order to become more familiar with Bizer's Luther interpretation, I transferred from Tübingen to Bonn in the summer semester of 1961 and studied there for three semesters. Before becoming a professor, Bizer was a pastor in Württemberg and together with Paul Schempp, Hermann Diem, and others belonged to the Kirchlich-Theologische Sozietät in Württemberg (Society for Church Theology in Württemberg). The members of this society, who participated in the struggles of the Bekennende Kirche (Confessing Church), took their ministry seriously in all its seemingly trivial details in a way that became and has remained for me a model of pastoral care. They were shaped theologically by dialectical theology—which they by no means received uncritically—but above all by an intense study of Luther.

This is the theological tradition in which I grew up. It emphasized especially the word of God in contrast to a type of theology at that time, which was heavily influenced by psychology and other forms of subjectivity that were dominant in the liberal theology of the nineteenth century. In the school of Barth as well as Bultmann, the "I" had no place either in scientific theology or in the pulpit.

The thinking of these theological giants that were so influential during my university years had one thing in common: they all emphasized the word in particular. But if the word does everything, then what is the point of the Lord's Supper? That was the question that prompted me to write a seminar paper under the supervision of Bizer in Bonn. I wanted to explore why the Supper is necessary if the word is sufficient. If the audible word (*verbum audibile*) does what it says, why is there need for a visible word (*verbum visibile*), the Lord's Supper? This question suggested itself to me not least because I am a member of a Lutheran church—the Evangelische Landeskirche in Württemberg—which, with Luther's

1. Oswald Bayer, *Theologie*. Handbuch Systematischer Theologie, vol. 1 (Gütersloher Verlagshaus, 1994). Part of this volume is translated in *Theology the Lutheran Way* (Eerdmans, 2007); for the author's critique of Bultmann's existential approach to theology, see especially pp. 159–68 of the English translation.

approval, has as its normal form of worship the preaching service without the Lord's Supper.

The topic of that seminar paper was a comparison of Luther's 1519 sermon on the Lord's Supper (*Sermon on the Blessed Sacrament of the Holy and True Body of Christ and on the Brotherhoods*) with his 1520 sermon on the Supper (*A Treatise on the New Testament, That Is, the Holy Mass*). This paper, the first document of my Luther research, formed the basis of my doctoral thesis and postdoctoral (habilitation) thesis. Both were published together in a single volume with the title *Promissio: Geschichte der reformatorischen Wende in Luthers Theologie*[2] (*The Reformational Turn in Luther's Theology*).[3] The book deals with the question of what exactly is "reformational" in Luther's theology. This is important for determining our point of orientation in ecumenical conversation and dispute. The thesis of this initial research, which has now been widely received but also disputed, and which I still stand by, can be formulated as follows: The turning point in Luther's Reformation theology coincided with the discovery of a special understanding of the biblical term *promise* (*promissio*), and that turning point can be located precisely in the early summer of 1518 in connection with a radical new version of the sacrament of penance, which Luther was forced to produce as he explained and defended his theses against the sale of indulgences. Here he set himself the challenge of explaining and solving this problem *theologically.*

To start with, Luther discovered the true meaning of the keywords "Whatever you loose (release) on earth will be loosed (released) in heaven, and whatever you bind on earth will be bound in heaven" (Matt. 18:18; see also 16:19). He understood this dominical saying as a "sentence of holy law"; that is, he recognized that the very moment another person looses or binds me, forgives sin or retains sin by means of the human voice, God himself does the same because he has bound and still binds himself to that word in such a way that sin *is* forgiven. God commits himself to a human word. This word is not simply the sign (*signum*) of a thing (*res*) that is different from the sign itself. Rather, the sign *is* the thing itself; the *signum* is the *res*. The word says what it does and does what it says. It *is* (*est!*) God's word. God himself is active and present in the human word, the creaturely word.

The promise is therefore to be understood primarily in the present sense and only secondarily in the future sense. It is not a promise that will only be fulfilled in the future. Rather, it is a speech act that as such enacts reality, constitutes reality, brings it about. The *promissio* is to be understood as a performative word, comparable to the executive word of a legal transaction. When, according

2. Bayer, *Promissio* (Vandenhoeck & Ruprecht, 1971).

3. This English translation of the book is based on the expanded second edition that appeared in 1989, published by Wissenschaftliche Buchgesellschaft.

to Roman law, a cow, for example, changes hands, the farmer says "*promitto ac spondeo*" (I promise and pledge) or just makes and confirms the sale with a handshake. The act of sale is therefore legally binding and has the force of law. The word is valid the moment it is spoken. It establishes a relationship that did not exist before. It is a performative word, comparable to a court verdict that convicts or acquits. The *promissio* is a legally binding promise with an immediate effect.[4]

In a second step, Luther applied his insight into the nature of the word of absolution to baptism. In *The Babylonian Captivity of the Church*, it says that in baptism, God baptized me "with his own hands," naturally through the minister of the divine Word (*minister verbi divini*). Thus the creaturely and external action that happens with water through a human agent is not, as with Barth, merely a pointer to God's inner action and our response to it. Rather, the inner action takes place through the outer, as Augsburg Confession V attests when it says that faith is produced by the word—of course, where and when it pleases God (*ubi et quando visum est Deo*), not automatically. Faith *comes* (Gal. 3:23 and 3:25), and it comes in no other way than through the external word (Rom. 10:17). Luther first discovered this in connection with the sacrament of penance (1518), then transferred and applied this thinking to baptism (1519) and finally (Easter 1520), to the Lord's Supper. He then further applied it to his understanding of the sermon, prayer, and Christology. None of this happened overnight. Luther began to test his new understanding of absolution by applying it to other fields. I have researched and presented this exciting process here in this book.

In short, the book is about the discovery of the word as a means of salvation (*medium salutis*); it has to do with discovering that the word does not function in a significative or constative way but in a constitutive way. If the word of absolution says "You are free!" then you are free indeed.[5] Absolution comes about through hearing. If you hear it and believe it, you have it.

That brings us to the crucial point around which the whole of Luther's theology can be oriented. This new orientation is evident from the first reformational

---

4. This sort of understanding probably suggests that Luther was familiar with medieval Germanic legal thought, in which the self-binding and self-commitment of the ruler when taking office was called a *promissio*. See P. E. Schramm, *Geschichte des englischen Königtums im Lichte der Krönung*, 1st ed. 1937 (Böhlau Verlag, 1970): 179ff. (*Vom Mandatum regis zur Promissio regis* = From the mandate of the king to the promise of the king).

5. This example comes from Ernst Bizer himself, who in his lectures, liked to illustrate the point by talking about an incident from his own life—namely, his release from a French prisoner-of-war camp, when a colonel tapped him on the shoulder and dismissed him with the words, "Vous êtes libre!" ("You are free!"). See J. Mehlhausen, "In Memoriam Ernst Bizer," *Evangelische Theologie* 37 (1977): 306–25, here 323–24; reprinted in J. Mehlhausen, *Vestigia Verbi. Aufsätze zur Geschichte der evangelischen Theologie* (de Gruyter, 1999), 528–47, here 545–46. On the other hand, for the methodological differences in approach between my work and Bizer's, see n. 2 of the summary at the end of the book, immediately before this afterword.

text in the history of his theology, the set of theses *Pro veritate inquirenda et timoratis conscientiis consolandis* (*On Seeking Out Truth and Comforting Terrified Consciences*, 1518). This is a wonderful title because it does not isolate the academic disputation on the investigation of the truth from the consolation of the troubled conscience; it does not separate the intellectual knowledge of faith (*intellectus fidei*) from the affective experience of faith (*affectus fidei*). The scientific study of theology is only a relative end in itself, not an absolute end. It serves life and faith, or at least relates to them. This corresponds to the distinction and relationship between the "monastic" and the "scholastic" sides of theology, between *pietas* and *eruditio*, which plays a key role in my *Theologie* book. This part has been translated in *Theology the Lutheran Way*.[6]

The *Pro veritate* theses provide us with something I consider important, especially for our conversation and dispute with Roman Catholicism, and that is the mention of the infallible work (*opus infallibile*) of the word (thesis 24). The Protestant Church knows of only *one* infallibility (see Isa. 55:10–11), which comes at the point where the gospel is bindingly promised, heard, and believed.

For me that was a tremendous help for the ministry. In researching the reformational turn in Luther's theology, it became clear to me what the pastoral ministry really is: the *ministerium verbi divini* (the ministry of the divine word). This reformational description of the office of the ministry reminds me that, as a pastor, I am called to bring God's promise to people with a troubled conscience. This became clear to me already as a student through that seminar paper.

2.

This also led to my understanding of the sermon. The *promissio* is the one sacramental Word, Jesus Christ himself, who is present, who meets us, and who gives himself to us. This sacramental Word is concentrated in ritual and liturgical forms. The basic language of Christianity is that of baptism as well as the formal absolution and the Lord's Supper. However, if all we had were these concentrated ritual and liturgical forms, there would always be the risk of sterile ritualism. These forms *must* be explicated. That is why the sermon is necessary. But they also *can* be explicated. That is why the sermon is possible.

In the process of explicating the basic language of Christianity, as in the process of interpretation, there is always the danger that the explication ends up losing what is to be explicated and the gospel is diluted. Again, the danger is that the gospel not only loses its concentration but is also transformed (or even more pointedly, deformed) and distorted. The sermon then becomes either a moral appeal or theoretical instruction or the description of a religious feeling.

6. See pp. 9–13.

Because of the constant threat of all these dangers, whether as to ethics, theory, or psychology, it is important to have in mind a critical perspective or, better, a model of true evangelical preaching. As a preacher, I still find that I always do best when I read and hear the text for the sermon with the following questions in mind: "What is its promissional structure? Where is the promise to be found?" It is amazing what you discover when you do this. You find that the biblical texts are full of promises. A *promissio* is not only the explicit word of absolution: "Your sins are forgiven you!" A promise is also, for example, every biblical "Fear not!"

The preacher can and must understand the gift character of God's word and pass on the unconditional, absolute, categorical gift in the promise. The law demands, but the gospel gives. The character of the unconditional gift must be the basic structure of a gospel sermon. This is a clear criterion for an evangelical sermon, for preaching the gospel.

That a sermon meets this criterion is crucial. Thus the preaching of the promise does not have to use the same words every time, such as the formula of absolution. Rather, the *promissio* should be sought in the language dynamics of the text and delivered anew every time by the performance of the sermon.

3.

When all these insights first dawned on me, I could not find much support for them from colleagues. When I was working on my *Promissio* book in Tübingen, Luther was frowned upon—it was the time of the student movement of 1968 and the years following, when there was great agitation for change. I was now a lecturer at the Protestant seminary. My colleagues used to ask: "Why waste time with your medieval monk? Can he change the world today? What are we to do with Luther's magical understanding of the word?" In those days, it was unfashionable to understand the word as an effective word (*verbum efficax*).

So at that time I stood alone with the thesis of my Luther research without any support. Only later, with the insights of J. L. Austin and other Anglo-Saxons, did linguistic analysis become common coin in academic circles. This worked in my favor, because it meant that what I had discovered previously with my analysis of the Luther texts was now seen to be plausible, or at least arguable. It is important for me to stress, however, that the linguistic analysis of the Anglo-Saxon world was not my starting point and that I wrote my *Promissio* book entirely without any knowledge of it. Only later, after the publication of the book, did I present my research and findings in relation and reference to linguistic analysis in the short work *Was ist das: Theologie?* (*What is Theology?*, 1973) that sketches out the topic from the angle of the philosophy of science. Twenty years later, this sketch was incorporated in my above-mentioned *Theologie* book (1994), which appeared in the series *Handbuch Systematischer Theologie*. As already mentioned, the core of this work was later translated into *Theology the Lutheran Way* (2007).

After *Promissio*, the detailed presentation in the *Handbuch* is my second major contribution to Luther research, where I was also able to further develop and clarify my own understanding of theology. I paid particular attention there to the way Luther characterizes theological existence with the triad *oratio*, *meditatio*, and *tentatio* (prayer, meditation, and attack). His comments on these terms had never been thoroughly interpreted in Luther research and reception before this and so their fundamental and far-reaching significance remained undiscovered.[7] And yet the concept of theology characterized by these three terms is far better able to hold university theology and church piety together than any other concept and prevent them from being pulled apart (see 8).

4.

My dissertation was a piece of research in the area of the history of theology; so I actually graduated with a doctorate in the discipline of church history. However, the faculty in Bonn suggested that I do my habilitation (second doctorate) in systematic theology and that I continue working on the topic of my dissertation.[8] That was good news indeed, for it was naturally a great relief to be allowed to continue with the research that I had already begun.

In a word, the *promissio* concept became and has remained the matrix of my entire theological work. Thus, when it comes to what is important, the focus of my attention theologically is consistently on the word of gift and promise,[9] by which God creates and preserves the world. He calls me and all creatures into life and promises to bring me and all believers into new and definitive community with himself. He does this in and through baptism, the Lord's Supper, and every

7. Gerhard Ebeling (*Studium der Theologie. Eine enzyklopädische Orientierung*, Mohr Siebeck, 1975, pp. 176–78 [= *Nachwort. Luther über das Studium der Theologie*]), and Rolf Schäfer ("Oratio, meditatio, tentatio: drei Hinweise Luthers auf den Gebrauch der Bibel," in Schäfer, *Gotteslehre und kirchliche Praxis*. Ausgewählte Aufsätze, ed. Ulrich Köpf and Reinhard Rittner [Mohr Siebeck, 1991, pp. 671–81]), certainly refer to the triad, but they do not attempt to interpret it comprehensively.

8. I gave a brief account of the significance of my transition from church history to systematic theology in the preface to the second edition of this book (1989).

9. Already in the context of this *Promissio* book in 1971 and afterward, the language of gift and promise were key concepts in my work, long before the beginning of the discourse around the concept of gift in philosophy (especially J. Derrida, M. Godelier) and in theology (J. Wohlmuth, K. Wenzel, V. Hoffmann, and others) that became established in the 1990s and 2000s following Marcel Mauss's writings.

sermon related to them. It is through these means that he restores the perverse world by turning it back to himself. We only properly understand the justification of the ungodly (Rom. 4:5) by the word alone, by grace alone, by Christ alone, and by faith alone when we see it within the framework of this concentration and breadth. The positive aspect of *promissio* makes theology a positive but by no means a positivistic science.

It took a long time, however, for it to dawn on me that the *promissio* concept is fundamental not only for the understanding of the sacrament and the sermon but also for the doctrine of creation. In my book *Schöpfung als Anrede* (*Creation as an Address*), which appeared in 1986,[10] *promissio* then became the dominant category, as the title ("address") suggests.

Applying this category to the doctrine of creation naturally raises questions. Can God's saving action and his action in creating and preserving the world both be designated with the same category? Nevertheless, the heuristic application has proven itself. It has shown that there is also much in the doctrine of creation that can be opened up and made accessible, if it is approached from the angle of the promise—for instance, the idea of the "readability of the world," to borrow the title of a book by Hans Blumenberg.[11]

I was astonished at how fruitful the question of the promise can be for hermeneutics, the doctrine of creation, and ethics—as my ethics book, *Freiheit als Antwort* (1995),[12] shows, which explicates freedom as a response to God's address in creation.

Freiheit als Antwort combines with *Schöpfung als Anrede*, *Autorität und Kritik* (*Authority and Critique*, 1991), and *Leibliches Wort* (*Bodily Word*, 1992) to form a set of books where each of the latter three has its own distinctive emphasis as indicated by its respective subtitle (in English): *Hermeneutics of Creation*, *Hermeneutics and Philosophy of Science*, and *Reformation and Modernity in Conflict*. Regardless of this, however, they are linked together not only by an homogeneous conception, as set out in the *Theologie* book, but also thematically. Thus each book also deals with theological ethics, which is the focus of *Freiheit als Antwort*. So, then, this book fits into a context that explicates the implications that the theology of creation, hermeneutics, and the philosophy of science have for theological ethics and also indicates their place within the history of theology and philosophy.

---

10. First edition, 1986, and second edition (expanded by two chapters), 1990.

11. Hans Blumenberg, *Die Lesbarkeit der Welt* (Suhrkamp, 1979), trans. Robert Savage and David Roberts under the title *The Readability of the World* (Cornell University Press, 2022).

12. *Freedom in Response. Lutheran Ethics: Sources and Controversies*, trans. Jeffrey F. Cayzer (Oxford University Press, 2007).

5.

Overall, the aim of my work is to make systematic-theological judgments in relation to the interweaving of Luther's *Promissio* theology and the problems of modernity. Making judgments in this area, riddled as it is with conflicting views and interpretations, is only possible by means of a "metacritique." I have learned this from a Lutheran who lived at the time of the German Enlightenment, Johann Georg Hamann, the friend and "metacritic" of the redoubtable philosopher of the *Aufklärung*, Immanuel Kant. Hamann, considered by Goethe to be the brightest mind of his day, was a journalist and gifted thinker. He lived at the center of the problems and opportunities of modernity and, in my judgment, played an important bridging role. He promoted Luther's theology in the context of the Enlightenment and, where necessary, in contradiction to it. In fact, he single-handedly overturned Kant's critical philosophy by means of his metacritique, as I have shown in my book *Vernunft ist Sprache* (*Reason is Language*, 2002).

When we want to learn from Luther, we cannot simply repristinate his theology because Luther did not deal with the problems of modernity in advance. We can only learn through engagement with him, by relating his questions and answers to our contemporary problems and by freely responding to the challenge that his theology still offers today. In connection with this, it is necessary to find "concepts of critical mediation" (as I call them), such as freedom, responsibility, and so on. And this is what Hamann helps us to do.

In this sense, the presentation of Luther's whole theology in my above-mentioned book *Leibliches Wort: Reformation und Neuzeit im Konflikt* is distinguished by its attempt to set out the truth sought with Luther by means of contrastive comparisons. Luther is brought into conversation, and where necessary into contention, with influential modern truth-seekers like Kant, Hegel, Schleiermacher, and others. This approach is not anachronistic but is aimed at truth claims that span the epochs and that people cannot simply fob off or distance themselves from by means of historical explanation. And in my opinion, Hamann's assistance in this task is irreplaceable. Hamann knows the modern era like no other. As a sensitive, perceptive, and cosmopolitan person, he registers everything new. But he does it critically and is not afraid to raise objections where necessary.[13] Looking through Hamann's glasses, I have discovered something new in Luther, especially when it comes to the linguistic character of reality.

---

13. This comes from the title of one of my Hamann publications, *Zeitgenosse im Widerspruch. Johann Georg Hamann als radikaler Aufklärer* (Pipo, 1988), trans. Roy Harrisville and Mark Mattes under the title *A Contemporary in Dissent. Johann Georg Hamann as a Radical Enlightener* (Eerdmans, 2012).

6.

How did I become a Luther scholar? What first led me into Luther research and has allowed me to persist in it to this day is the factuality, precision, and visual power of the reformer's theology. For me, Luther is not a formal authority but a material authority: He helps me stick to the subject matter of the gospel. He fascinates me as a witness to the truth.

The only possible way I could imagine investigating this witness to the truth in a theologically responsible way was to employ the historical critical methods that I had learned already as a student. And so in this *Promissio* book, I let myself be guided by the standards of New Testament exegesis, which as an assistant lecturer in the New Testament between the years 1965 and 1968, I was responsible for teaching to students at Tübingen. I wrote this book—as the subtitle, *The Reformational Turn in Luther's Theology*, indicates—primarily from the perspective of tradition history as well as form and literary criticism. Thus I mainly analyzed larger units of text rather than working with the isolated Luther quotations used by the respective interpreters, which was a very common practice in Luther research at the time. As far as the tradition-historical method is concerned, my aim was to read as many sources as possible that Luther himself is known to have used in preparing his lectures.

At the Fourth International Luther Research Congress in St. Louis in 1971, I presented a paper together with Martin Brecht on "Newly Discovered Texts from the Young Luther." I spoke about the texts discovered by Brecht that I identified and dated as genuine Luther texts and that have finally been edited and published in the Weimarana, the original edition of Luther's works (WA 59). The scientific ethos that I am committed to and that governs all my Luther and Hamann research has been aptly described by Max Weber in his *Science as a Vocation* as follows: "Anyone who lacks the ability to don blinkers, so to speak, and convince themself that the destiny of their soul depends upon whether they are right in making precisely this or that conjecture about a given passage in their manuscript should keep well away from science."[14]

7.

My later studies of Luther texts following this book, including sermons, catechetical segments, and a hymn, are all detailed synchronous interpretations and should be judged accordingly. As a systematician, I have of course always been

14. Max Weber, *The Vocation Lectures: Science as a Vocation; Politics as a Vocation*, ed. with an intro. by David Owen and Tracy B. Strong, trans. Rodney Livingstone (Hackett, 2004), 8 (trans. alt.).

interested in the exemplary character of the selected Luther texts and their significance for today. My goal in working with them has been to bring them into critical engagement with the present. This work led to a paradigmatic presentation of Luther's entire theology, which I offered in a series of lectures in 2001/02 to students of all faculties at Tübingen. These lectures were published in book form in 2003 and since then the German original has gone through four editions.[15] It has been translated into English[16] as well as into six other languages.[17] This presentation of Luther's entire theology is in a sense the culmination of forty years of work on and with a multitude of Luther texts. There is no denying that its author is a systematician. Its subtitle, *A Contemporary Interpretation*, raises the question of the relationship between historical and systematic theology in Luther research. This research cannot be reduced to a "purely" historical question and has also been pursued, as the more recent history of theology shows, not least by systematicians, such as Althaus, Wingren and Ebeling.

8.

Theology, however, not only operates in the tensile unity of present and past, bringing them together in conversation, but what is crucial for it—if we follow Luther's understanding of theological science—is precisely the interweaving of doctrine and life that stands in direct opposition to the all too common neo-Protestant tendency to separate them. In his characterization of theological existence as *oratio*, *meditatio*, and *tentatio* (prayer, meditation, and spiritual attack), Luther holds both doctrine and life together.

The historical-critical method also has its place within the framework of meditation, since for Luther meditation takes place "not only in the heart, but also externally through the spoken and written words of Scripture, when we keep on working at them and rubbing them like an herb, reading and re-reading them, diligently paying attention to the words themselves and thinking about what the Holy Spirit means by them."[18] Meditation is not simply a disposition of the heart, but an active "grappling," a craft that includes all available methodological tools,

15. Bayer, *Martin Luthers Theologie* (Mohr Siebeck, 2003, 4th ed. 2016).

16. Bayer, *Martin Luther's Theology: A Contemporary Interpretation*, trans. Thomas H. Trapp (Eerdmans, 2008).

17. In Portuguese (Sao Leopoldo, 2007), Chinese (Hong Kong, 2011), Danish (København, 2017), Korean (ca. 2018), Spanish (Salamanca, 2020), and Italian (Torino, 2020).

18. WA 50, 659, 22–25 = LW 34:286 (Preface to the Wittenberg edition of Luther's German writings, 1539) (trans. alt.)

and so also the work of historical criticism. This, too, is how I have understood my work with the Luther texts.

So it should come as no surprise if the historical critical method used in Luther research, as a form and aspect of meditation, also has consequences for the personal faith-life of the Luther interpreter. Thus, for instance, my own prayer life changed through my scientific analysis of Luther's Rogate sermon of 1520. There I discovered the constitutive connection between *promissio* and lament, or complaint, and in the period that followed I tried, as a systematician, to highlight the significance of complaint and lament for theology.[19]

Equally significant, and unheard of in the history of the church, is Luther's idea that *tentatio*[20] does not sit somewhere on the margins but belongs to the very center of theology as one of its main aspects. The theologians' situation is best characterized as struggling faith because faith is never without a struggle; their situation is like that of Jacob on the banks of the Jabbok (Gen. 32), struggling all night with whom or what he does not know! A theologian is someone who, driven by *Anfechtung*, goes to Holy Scripture in prayer in order to interpret it to others who are also under attack themselves, so that they too can prayerfully go to Scripture, interpret it, and become certain of salvation.

Anfechtung is profoundly risky because it is something irregular and unforeseeable that cannot be manipulated and can never be finally mastered, nor can it ever be overcome by any method or strategy but must be endured in all its offensiveness and strangeness and appreciated in its significance as a constitutive element of theological work.

It is my wish for the future of the church that Luther's triadic understanding of theology is rediscovered anew; that theology retrieves its genuine character through *oratio*, *meditatio*, and *tentatio*; and that the unfortunate modern split between theological research and the life of faith is once again overcome.

9.

I return to the concept of *promissio*. From the discovery of the promissional structure of the word of absolution—via the discovery of the promissional structure of baptism, the Lord's Supper, and the sermon—I have gradually learned, as

19. Bayer, "Toward a Theology of Lament" in *Caritas et Reformatio: Essays on Church and Society in Honor of Carter Lindberg*, ed. David M. Whitford (Concordia Publishing House, 2002): 211–20; "Erhörte Klage," *Neue Zeitschrift für Systematische Theologie* 25 (1983): 259–72. Cf. Gregory Schulz, "Bayer's Twenty-First-Century Disputation Concerning Lament," in *Promising Faith for a Ruptured Age*, ed. John T. Pless et al., 195–208.

20. [Even though the Latin literally means "temptation" (as in the Lord's Prayer, "lead us not into temptation"), it is best translated, like its German equivalent *Anfechtung*, with words like *spiritual attack* or *trial*, depending on the context; trans. note].

a pupil of Luther, to understand the whole of reality, not only that of redemption but also that of creation and the consummation under the category of promise. As has become clear, even my understanding of the philosophy of science and of ethics, which itself must be developed as an ethics of the gift, did not remain unaffected by this. Indeed, the promise became the root and matrix of my entire work in systematic theology. The fact that in a certain respect, this comprehensive expansion of the meaning of the term and its application to include all areas of theology retrospectively also has Luther's "blessing" fills me with particular joy.

It was only much later that I discovered what I had already claimed many times but could never really defend without a lingering sense of uneasiness, because I could not provide any explicit evidence for it—namely, that in Luther's mind, also the first commandment with its divine *self*-identification, "I am the Lord, your God, who brought you out of the land of Egypt, out of the house of slavery," is to be understood first and foremost as a promise—and not just as the original promise that creates Israel and the church, because for Luther the *promissio* also has a universal breadth and depth that goes beyond this. In his glosses on the Decalogue, written at the Coburg in 1530, Luther emphasized this point with great precision and concision and also explicitly designated God's self-identification as such a promise: "[This] promise [is] the source of all promises and the origin of all religion and wisdom, including the gospel, the promised Christ."[21]

He has also impressively described this comprehensive meaning of the first commandment elsewhere. This is what he says in an expository sermon from 1525: "Everything flows out of that mighty ocean of the first commandment and back into it. No more fruitful and fuller voice of consolation has ever been heard and will never be heard, but neither has any harsher nor more severe voice ever been heard than that of the first commandment: 'I am the Lord your God.'"[22]

In this sense, *promissio* stands for the concrete, particular divine *speech*, in which God commits himself to the bodily word of the Lord's Supper, as well as for the wide-ranging, universal divine *speech*, reaching beyond the church and Israel, that he utters in creation and redemption and that creates and upholds the whole of reality.

21. "Promissio omnium promissionum fons & omnis religionis & sapientiae caput, Evangelium Christum promissum complectens" (WA 30/2: 358, 1–4; gloss on "Ego sum dominus deus tuus," 1530).

22. "Omnia enim haec fluunt ex oceano illo magno primi praecepti et rursus in ipsum refluunt, ut non sit solatio foecundior ac plenior audita vox nec audienda unquam, rursus nec durior nec severior quam vox illa primi praecepti: Ego sum Dominus Deus tuus." (WA 14:640,30–33; on Deut. 10:18; 1525).

Addendum

The Promise and the First Commandment

I crave the reader's indulgence to allow me to include a note to the Luther text "Promissio omnium promissionum fons & omnis religionis & sapientiae caput, Evangelium Christum promissum complectens," which in my opinion, is too important to omit but too long to include in note 21.

Luther also makes clear elsewhere that he wants the promise contained in God's self-identification, which he often counts as part of the first commandment, to apply not only to the Jews but also to all people. Consider the following Luther text:

> I am the LORD your GOD. These words alone, rather than the adjacent words [the prelude] about God bringing Israel out of Egypt, which should really be crossed out, are the words that need to be studied carefully because they concern us all, the whole world in general and every person in particular, Jews and Gentiles alike, not because Moses wrote them, but because God created all people, and still preserves and rules them.[23]

On the question about what exactly the gloss refers to, and also on questions about its translation, see the very detailed essay, "Streiflichter auf Luthers Erklärung des ersten Gebots im Kleinen Katechismus" by Otto Albrecht, which seems to me to have so far received little attention.[24] Amongst other things, Albrecht clearly points out against misinterpretations, that what the gloss characterizes as a promise is only God's self-identification and not the first commandment as a whole, including the words, "You shall have no other gods before me." In regard to the latter, the following gloss says, "This is properly the first commandment because it is determined by the former words, 'I am the Lord your God.'"[25] However, later interpreters of the passage do not seem to have taken any notice of this. So, for example, Heinrich Bornkamm,[26] with reference to these glosses in particular, thinks "that Luther, to express the *sense of*

23. WA 16:432,18–24 (Sermon on Exod. 20:2–5a [Sept. 24, 1525]), edited in 1528 along with other sermons on Exod.). See also WA 16:436,21–24 and in addition Otto Albrecht's explanations of the *Small Catechism* in WA 30/1:637.

24. See *Theologische Studien und Kritiken* 90 (1917): 421–95, esp. 438.

25. WA 30/2:358,5–7.

26. *Luther and the Old Testament* (Fortress, 1969).

promise of the First Commandment, could deny its character as a commandment altogether," or—not surprisingly, of course—Friedrich-Wilhelm Marquardt[27] holds that "actually, this gospel is the first commandment. . . . Indeed, even the gospel itself is actually a commandment."

In the Latin text quoted at the beginning of the addendum, I have deliberately put the comma after *promise* (*promissio*) rather than after *promises* (*promissionum*). In doing so, I have decided against Bornkamm and Albrecht—who in support of his option also cites August Hardeland and Karl Thieme—as well as against my own earlier paraphrases and instead follow Johannes Meyer[28] and Eilert Herms.[29] The resulting parallel sentence structure (*omnium promissionum fons—omnis religionis et sapientiae caput*) suggests this. To put the comma after *promises* seems extremely forced to me. The *fons* would then remain without a genitive determiner. It is grammatically impossible to take *fons* with *caput* and to understand both as antecedents of *religio* and *sapientia*, and it is also impossible to take *sapientia* with *caput* and *religio* with *fons* because of the *et* between the latter two words.

The translation of the quote is by no means a trivial matter, which is why it is almost always only reproduced in Latin in the literature. The question of the antecedent of *complectens* (*promissio*, or *Evangelium*) cannot be decided grammatically either. However, the decision regarding its content has no bearing on this point.

This text is a modified and expanded version of a lecture given in Hong Kong in 2013 on the occasion of the 100th anniversary of the Lutheran Theological Seminary. The lecture, titled "How I Became a Lutheran Scholar," is published in Theology and Life. Annual Theological Journal No. 36, Exploring Bible, Church and Life: Essay in Celebration of the 100th Anniversary of Lutheran Theological Seminary Hong Kong, *China (2013): 373–81. Used with permission. The topic of the lecture was given to the author and was not of his choosing. It was also published (and used with permission) in* Lutheran Quarterly *27, no. 3 (Autumn 2013): 249–63.*

27. "Gott oder Mammon—aber: Theologie und Ökonomie bei Martin Luther," in Marquardt, *Auf einem Weg ins Lehrhaus. Leben und Denken mit Israel*, ed. Martin Stöhr (Lembeck, 2009), 100–40, here 102.

28. "Das erste Gebot bei Luther," *Monatschrift für Pastoraltheologie* (1917): 357–76, here 362.

29. *Luthers Auslegung des Dritten Artikels* (Mohr Siebeck, 1987), 8.

BIBLIOGRAPHY

PRIMARY SOURCES

Aquinas, Thomas. *Catena Aurea in quattuor Evangelia*. Edited by Angelico Guarienti. 2 vols. Marietti, 1953.

———. *Summa Theologiae*. 5 vols. Biblioteca de Autores Cristianos, 1956–1961.

———. *Super Evangelium S. Ioannis Lectura*. Marietti, 1952.

———. *Super Epistolas S. Pauli Lectura*. Marietti, 1953.

Altenstaig, Johannes. *Vocabularius theologiae*. Hagenau, 1517.

Anselm of Canterbury. *Opera Omnia*. Edited by Franciscus Salesius Schmitt. 6 vols. Thomas Nelson, 1938.

———. *Why God Became Man*. Edited and translated by Jasper Hopkins and Herbert Richardson. Edwin Mellen, 1980.

Aristotle. *Aristoteles*. Edited by Immanuel Bekker. Vol. 3, *Aristoteles Latine Interpretibus Variis*. Berlin, 1831.

Augustine. *Enarrationes in Psalmos*. Vols. 36–37, *Patrologia Latina*, edited by J.-P. Migne. Paris, 1865.

———. *Epistolae ad Galatas expositionis liber unus*. Vol. 35, *Patrologia Latina*, edited by J.-P. Migne. Paris, 1864.

———. *De doctrina christiana*. Vol. 34, *Patrologia Latina*, edited by J.-P. Migne. Paris, 1865.

———. *De spiritu et littera*. Vol. 44, *Patrologia Latina*, edited by J.-P. Migne. Paris, 1865.

———. *De trinitate*. Vol. 42, *Patrologia Latina*, edited by J.-P. Migne. Paris, 1865.

———. *In Ioannis Evangelium tractatus CXXIV*. Vol. 35, *Patrologia Latina*, edited by J.-P. Migne. Paris, 1864.

Bernard of Clairvaux. *Sermones Super Cantica Canticorum*. Vols. I and II, *Opera*, edited by Jean Leclercq, Charles Hugh Talbot, and H. M. Rochais. Editiones Cistercienses, 1957.

———. *Sermones*. Vol. 183, *Patrologica Latina*, edited by J.-P. Migne., 35–748.

Biblia: cum glosa ordinaria (et interlineari) et expositione (Nicolai) Lyrae literali et morali necnon additionibus (Pauli Burgensis) ac replicis (Matthiae Thoring). Basel, 1506–1508.

Biel, Gabriel. *Canonis Misse Expositio*. Edited by Heiko Oberman and William Courtenay. Parts I–IV. F. Steiner, 1963–1967.

———. *Collectorium in quattuor libros Sententiarum*. Edited by Wendelin Steinbach. 4 vols. Basel, 1508.

———. *Sacri canonis missae expositio resolutissima*. Basel, 1510.

Bonaventure. *Opera omnia*. 10 vols. Quaracchi, 1882–1902 (Editio maior).

Cajetan (Thomas de Vio). *Opuscula omnia*. Lyon, 1575.

Chrysostom, John. *Homiliae XXXIV in Epistolam ad Hebraeos* (in the translation of Mutianus Scholasticus). Vol 63, *Patrologia Graeca*, edited by J.-P. Migne. Paris, 1862.

Dionysius the Carthusian. *In omnes Beati Pauli Epistolas Commentaria*. Cologne, 1532.

Franckforter, *Theologia Germanica of Martin Luther*. Translated with an introduction and commentary by Bengt Hoffman. SPCK, 1980.

Gerson, Jean. *Oeuvres Complètes*. Introduction, text, and notes by Paul Glorieux. 11 vols. Desclée, 1960–1973.

———. *Opera*. 3 vols. 1489.

———. *Opera Omnia*. Edited by M. L. E. Du Pin. Antwerp, 1706.

Hegel, Georg Wilhelm Friedrich. *Phenomenology of Mind*. Introduction by George Lichtheim. Translated with an introduction and notes by J. B. Baillie. Harper and Row, 1967.

Jacobus de Voragine. *Legenda Aurea*. 3rd ed. Edited by Theodore Graesse. Gotha, 1890.

Lombard, Peter. *Sententiarum libri quattuor*. 2 vols. Quaracchi, 1916. (Cited in the Bonaventure edition; see above.)

Ludolf von Sachsen. *Vita domini nostri Jesu Christi e sacris quatuor evangeliorum sanctorumque patrum fontibus derivata*. Augsburg, 1729.

Luther, Martin. *Dokumente zu Luthers Entwicklungen (bis 1519)*. Edited by Otto Scheel. Sammlung ausgewählter Kirchen- und dogmengeschichtlicher Quellenschriften. Neue Folge 2. 2nd ed. J. C. B. Mohr, 1929.

———. *Dokumente zum Ablaßstreit von 1517*. Edited by Walther Köhler. Sammlung ausgewählter Kirchen- und dogmengeschichtlicher Quellenschriften, 2. Reihe, 3. Heft. 2nd ed. J. C. B. Mohr, 1934.

———. *Luthers Vorlesung über den Hebräerbrief nach der vatikanischen Handschrift*. Edited by Emanuel Hirsch and Hans Rückert. Arbeiten zur Kirchengeschichte 13. de Gruyter, 1929.

———. *Luthers Vorlesung über den Römerbrief 1515/16*. Edited by Johannes Ficker. *Vol. 1, Anfänge reformatorischer Bibelauslegung (I. Glosse, II. Scholien)*. Dieterich'sche Verlagsbuchhandlung, 1925.

———. *Luthers Werke*. Kritische Gesamtausgabe. 57 vols. Edited by J. K. F. Knaake et al. Weimar, 1883ff.

———. *Luthers Werke in Auswahl*. 4 vols. Edited by Otto Clemen in collaboration with Albert Leitzmann. de Gruyter, 1929.

———. *Randbemerkungen zu Gabriel Biels Collectorium und zu dessen Sacri canonis missae expositio*. Edited by Hermann Degering. Böhlau, 1933.

———. *Unbekannte Fragmente aus Luthers zweiter Psalmenvorlesung 1518*. Edited by Erich Vogelsang. Arbeiten zur Kirchengeschichte 27. de Gruyter, 1940.

Mauburnus, Johannes. *Rosetum exercitiorum spiritualium et sacrarum meditationum*. Basel, 1504.

Melanchthon, Philipp. *Melanchthons Werke in Auswahl.* Edited by Robert Stupperich. Mohn, 1951–1983.

———. *Opera.* In *Corpus Reformatorum,* Vols. 1 and 21. Edited by Karl Bretschneider and Heinrich Bindseil. Halle, 1834–1854.

Nicholas of Cusa. *Predigten 1430–1441.* Translated by J. Sikora and Elisabeth Bohnenstädt. Edited by Ernst Hoffmann. Kerle, 1952.

———. *Early Sermons: 1430–1441.* Translated and introduced by Jasper Hopkins. Banning Press, 2003.

Nicholas of Lyra. *See Biblia.*

Paltz, Johannes von. *Celifodina.* Erfurt, 1502.

———. *Das büchlin wirt genant die hymelisch Funtgrub.* Strasbourg, 1503.

Paul of Burgos. *See Biblia.*

Reuchlin, Johannes. *De Verbo mirifico.* Lyon, 1552.

Staupitz, Johannes von. *Sämtliche Werke.* Vol. 1, edited by J. K. F. Knaake. Potsdam, 1867.

———. *Tübinger Predigten: Hiobspredigten.* Edited by Georg Buchwald and Ernst Wolf. Eger and Sievers, 1927.

Tauler, Johannes. *Predigten.* Edited by Ferdinand Vetter. Vol 11, *Deutsche Texte des Mittelalters,* edited by der Königlich Preußischen Akademie der Wissenschaften. Weidmann, 1910.

Thomas a Kempis. *De imitatione Christi: Latein und Deutsch.* Translated and edited by Friedrich Eichler. Kösel, 1966.

Theologia deutsch: *Der Franckforter* ("Eyn deutsch theologia"). *Kleine Texte für theologische und philosophische Fakultät Vorlesungen und Übungen,* No. 96. Marcus and Weber, 1912.

Vitae Patrum. Vols. 73–74, *Patrologia Latina,* edited by J.-P. Migne. Paris, 1849–1850.

Verzeichnis der im deutschen Sprachbereich erschienenen Drucke des XVI. Jahrhunderts [*VD* 16]. Bayerische Staatsbibliothek, Herzog August Bibliothek, and Hiersemann, 1983–.

SECONDARY SOURCES

Aland, Kurt. *Der Weg zur Reformation: Zeitpunkt und Charakter des reformatorischen Erlebnisses Martin Luthers.* Theologische Existenz heute, neue Folge 123. Chr. Kaiser, 1965.

———. *Hilfsbuch zum Lutherstudium.* Luther-Verlag, 1996.

Althaus, Paul. *Communio sanctorum: die Gemeinde im lutherischen Kirchengedanken.* Chr. Kaiser, 1929.

Andresen, Carl. "Zur Entstehung und Geschichte des trinitarischen Personbegriff es." *Zeitschrift für die neutestamentliche Wissenschaft und die Kunde der älteren Kirche* 52 (1961): 1–39.

Appel, Helmut. *Anfechtung und Trost im Spätmittelalter und bei Luther.* Schriften des Vereins für Reformationsgeschichte 165. M. Heinsins, 1938.

Asheim, Ivar, ed. *The Church, Mysticism, Sanctification, and the Natural in Luther's Thought: Lectures Presented to the Third International Congress on Luther Research, Järvenpää, Finland, August 11–16, 1966*. Fortress Press, 1967.

Auer, Albert. *Leidenstheologie im Spätmittelalter*. Kirchengeschichtliche Quellen und Studien 2. Eos Verlag der Erzabtei, 1952.

Bainton, Roland. *Here I Stand: A Life of Martin Luther*. Abington-Cokesbury Press, 1950.

Bandt, Hellmut. *Luthers Lehre vom verborgenen Gott: Eine Untersuchung zu dem offenbarungsgeschichtlichen Ansatz seiner Theologie*. Theologische Arbeiten 8. Evangelische Verlagsanstalt, 1958.

Baring, Georg. "Luther und die 'Theologia Deutsch' in der neuesten Forschung." *Theologische Zeitschrift* 23 (1967): 48–62.

Bauer, Karl. "Das Entstehungsjahr von Luthers *Sermo de indulgentiis pridie Dedicationis*." *Zeitschrift für Kirchengeschichte* 43 (1924): 174–79.

_______. *Die Wittenberger Universitätstheologie und die Anfänge der deutschen Reformation*. J. C. B. Mohr, 1928.

Becker, Eucharius. "Untersuchungen zu dem Tauler zugeschriebenen Lied 'Es kumpt ein Schiff geladen.'" In *Johannes Tauler, ein deutscher Mystiker: Gedenkschrift zum 600. Todestag*, edited by Ephrem Filthaut. H. Driewer, 1961.

Beintker, Horst. "*Phase Domini*: Zu Luthers Interpretation der *metanoia*." In *Solange es "Heute" heißt: Festgabe für R. Hermann zum 70. Guburtstag*. Evangelische Verlagsanstalt, 1957.

_______. "Zur Datierung und Einordnung eines neueren Luther-Fragmentes." *Wissenschafttliche Zeitschrift der Ernst-Moritz-Arndt-Universität Greifswald* I, Nr. 2/3, (1951/52): 70–80.

Bayer, Oswald. "Die reformatorische Wende in Luthers Theologie." *Zeitschrift für Theologie und Kirche* 66 (1969): 115–50.

Bizer, Ernst. "Besprechung von W. Jetter, Die Taufe beim jungen Luther." *Zeitschrift für Kirchengeschichte* 67 (1956): 341–44.

_______. "Die Entdeckung des Sakraments durch Luther." *Evangelische Theologie* 17 (1957): 64–90.

_______. Fides ex auditu: *Eine Untersuchung über die Entdeckung der Gerechtigkeit Gottes durch Martin Luther*. 3rd expanded ed. Neukirchener Verlag, 1966.

_______. "Lutherische Abendmahlslehre?" *Evangelische Theologie* 16 (1956): 1–18.

_______. *Luther und der Papst*. Theologische Existenz heute. Neue Folge 69. Chr. Kaiser, 1958.

_______. "Neue Darstellungen der Theologie Luthers." *Theologische Rundschau*, neue Folge 31 (1966): 316–49.

_______. "Römisch-katholische Messe und evangelisches Abendmahl." In *Ecclesia semper reformanda: Theologische Aufsätze, Ernst Wolf zum 50. Geburtstag am 2. August 1952*. Chr. Kaiser, 1952.

_______. *Theologie der Verheißung: Studien zur theologischen Entwicklung des jungen Melanchthon (1519–1524)*. Neukirchener Verlag, 1964.

_______. "Über die Rechtfertigung." In *Das Kreuz Jesu Christi als Grund des Heils*, edited by Fritz Viering. Gerd Mohn, 1967.

———. "Zur Methode der Melanchthonforschung: Bemerkungen zum Melanchthonbuch von R. Schäfer." *Evangelische Theologie* 24 (1964): 1–24.

Boehmer, Heinrich. *Der junge Luther*. Koehler and Amelang, 1939.

———. *Loyola und die deutsche Mystik*. B. G. Tuebner, 1921.

———. *Luthers erste Vorlesung*. Unknown publisher, 1924.

Bornkamm, Heinrich. *Luther als Schriftsteller*. Sitzungsberichte der Heidelberger Akademie der Wissenschaften, Philosophisch-Historische Klasse, 1965, 1. Abhandlung. C. Winter, 1965.

———. *Luther and the Old Testament*. Translated by Eric W. and Ruth C. Gritsch. Fortress Press, 1969.

———. "Luther I. Leben und Schriften." *Religion in Geschichte und Gegenwart*. 3rd ed. 7 vols. J. C. B. Mohr (Paul Siebeck), 1986, 4:480–95.

———. *Luther im Spiegel der deutschen Geistesgeschichte: mit augewählten Texten von Lessing bis zur Gegenwart*. Quelle and Meyer, 1955.

———. *Luthers geistige Welt*. 4th ed. C. Bertelsmann, 1960.

———. *Luther und das Alte Testament*. J. C. B. Mohr, 1948.

———. *Thesen und Thesenanschlag Luthers: Geschehen und Bedeutung*. Theologische Bibliothek Töpelmann 14. Töpelmann, 1967.

———. "Zur Frage der *Iustitia Dei* beim jungen Luther." *Archiv für Reformationsgeschichte* 52/3 (1961–62). Part I, 52: 16–29; Part II, 53: 1–60.

Brandenburg, Albert. *Gericht und Evangelium: zur Worttheologie in Luthers erster Psalmenvorlesung*. Konfessionskundliche und kontroverstheologische Studien 4. Verlag Bonifacius-Druckerei, 1960.

———. "*Solae aures sunt organa Christiani hominis*: Zu Luthers Exegese von Hebräer 10:5f." In *Festschrift für Gottlieb Söhngen*, edited by Joseph Ratzinger und Heinrich Fries. Unknown publisher, 1962.

Brieger, Theodor. "Kritische Erörterungen zur neuen Luther-Ausgabe." *Zeitschrift für Kirchengeschichte* 9 (1890): 101–54.

Bultmann, Rudolf. *The Gospel of St. John. A Commentary*. Translated by G. R. Beasley-Murray, R. W. N. Hoare, and J. K. Riches. Westminster Press, 1971.

Courcelle, Pierre. *Les Confessions de Saint Augustin dans la tradition littéraire*. Antécédents et Postérité. Études Augustiniennes, 1963.

Cranz, Edward F. *An Essay on the Development of Luther's Thought on Justice, Law, and Society*. Harvard Theological Studies 19. Harvard University Press, 1964.

Damerau, Rudolf. *Die Abendmahlslehre des Nominalismus, insbesondere die des Gabriel Biel*. Studien zu den Grundlagen der Reformation 1. W. Schmitz, 1964.

Debongnie, Pierre. *Jean Mombaer de Bruxelles, abbé de Livry: ses écrits et ses réformes*. Librairie universitaire, 1928.

Duchrow, Ulrich. *Sprachverständnis und biblisches Hören bei Augustin*. Hermeneutische Untersuchungen zur Theologie 5. J. C. B. Mohr, 1965.

Ebeling, Gerhard. "The Beginnings of Luther's Hermeneutics." *Lutheran Quarterly* 7 (1993): 129–58, 315–38, 451–68.

———. "Die Anfänge von Luthers Hermeneutik." *Zeitschrift für Theologie und Kirche* 48 (1951): 172–230.

———. *Evangelische Evangelienauslegung: Eine Untersuchung zu Luthers Hermeneutik.* Wissenschftliche Buchgesellschaft, 1962.

———. "Luther II. Theologie." *Religion in Geschichte und Gegenwart.* 3rd ed. 7 vols. J. C. B. Mohr (Paul Siebeck), 1986, 4:495–520.

———. *Luther: Einführung in sein Denken.* J. C. B. Mohr, 1964.

———. *Luther: An Introduction to His Thought.* Translated by R. A. Wilson. Fortress Press, 1970.

———. "Luthers Auslegung des 14. (15.) Psalms in der ersten Psalmenvorlesung im Vergleich mit der exegetischen Tradition." *Zeitschrift für Theologie und Kirche* 50 (1953): 280–339.

———. "Luthers Auslegung des 44. (45.) Psalms." In *Lutherforschung heute: Referate und Berichte des 1. Internationalen Lutherforschungskongresses,* edited by Vilmos Vajta. Lutherisches Verlagshaus, 1958.

———. "Luthers Psalterdruck vom Jahre 1513." *Zeitschrift für Theologie und Kirche* 50 (1953): 43–99.

Elze, Martin. "Das Verständnis der Passion Jesu im ausgehenden Mittelalter und bei Luther." In *Geist und Geschichte der Reformation: Festgabe für Hanns Rückert zum 65. Geburtstag.* Arbeiten zur Kirchengeschichte 38. de Gruyter, 1966.

———. "Züge spätmittelalterlicher Frömmigkeit in Luthers Theologie." *Zeitschrift für Theologie und Kirche* 62 (1965): 381–402.

Fausel, Heinrich. *D. Martin Luther: Der Reformator im Kampf um Evangelium und Kirche. Sein Werden und Wirken im Spiegel eigener Zeugnisse.* Cawler Verlag in collaboration with the Quell-Verlag, 1955.

Ferel, Martin. *Gepredigte Taufe: Eine homiletische Untersuchung zur Taufpredigt bei Luther.* Hermeneutische Untersuchungen zur Theologie 10. J. C. B. Mohr, 1969.

Franz, Adolph. *Die kirchlichen Benediktionen im Mittelalter.* 2 vols. Herder, 1909.

———. *Die Messe im deutschen Mittelalter: Beiträge zur Geschichte der Liturgie und des religiösen Volkslebens.* Herder, 1902.

Fünten, Wiltrud von der. *Maria Magdalena in der Lyrik des Mittelalters.* Schwann, 1966.

Geyer, Hans-Georg. *Von der Geburt des wahren Menschen: Probleme aus den Anfängen der Theologie Melanchthons.* Neukirchener Verlag, 1965.

Gogarten, Friedrich. *Christ the Crisis.* SCM Press, 1970.

———. *Die Frage nach Gott: Eine Vorlesung.* J. C. B. Mohr (Paul Siebeck), 1968.

———. *Die Verkündigung Jesu Christi: Grundlagen und Aufgabe.* Hermeneutische Untersuchungen zur Theologie 3. J. C. B. Mohr (Paul Siebeck), 1965.

———. *Jesus Christus Wende der Welt: Grundfragen zur Christologie.* J. C. B. Mohr, 1966.

———. *Luthers Theologie.* J. C. B. Mohr (Siebeck), 1967.

Grane, Leif. *Contra Gabrielem: Luthers Auseinandersetzung mit Gabriel Biel in der* Disputatio Contra Scholasticam Theologiam *1517.* Acta theologica Danica 4. Gyldendal, 1962.

———. "Luthers Kritik an Thomas von Aquin in *De captivitate Babylonica.*" *Zeitschrift für Kirchengeschichte* 80 (1969): 1–13.

Greschat, Martin. "Der Bundesgedanke in der Theologie des späten Mittelalters." *Zeitschrift für Kirchengeschichte* 81 (1970): 44–63.

Grönvik, Lorenz. *Die Taufe in der Theologie Martin Luthers*. Acta Academiae Aboensis, ser. A, vol. 36/1. Åbo Akademi, 1968.

Gyllenkrok, Axel. *Rechtfertigung und Heiligung in der frühen evangelischen Theologie Luthers*. Acta Universitatis Upsaliensis 2. Lundequistska bokhandeln, 1952.

Hacker, Paul. *Das Ich im Glauben bei Martin Luther*. Styria, 1966.

———. *The Ego in Faith: Martin Luther and the Origin of Anthropocentric Religion*. Franciscan Herald Press, 1970.

Hagen, Kenneth. "The Problem of Testament in Luther's Lectures on Hebrews." *Harvard Theological Review* 63 (1970): 61–90.

Hägglund, Bengt. "Luther und die Mystik." In *Kirche, Mystik, Heiligung und das Natürliche bei Luther*. Vandenhoeck and Ruprecht, 1967.

———. *Theologie und Philosophie bei Luther und in der occamistischen Tradition: Luthers Stellung zur Theorie von der doppelten Wahrheit*. Lunds Universitets Årsskrift, neue Folge, avd. 1, 51/4. C. W. K. Gleerup, 1955.

———. "Voraussetzungen der Rechtfertigungslehre Luthers in der spätmittelalterlichen Theologie." *Lutherische Rundschau* 11 (1961): 28–55.

Hamel, Adolf. *Der junge Luther und Augustin: Ihre Beziehungen in der Rechtfertigungslehre nach Luthers ersten Vorlesungen 1509–1518 untersucht*. 2 vols. C. Bertelsmann, 1934–1935.

Hausammann, Susi. "Realpräsenz in Luthers Abendmahlslehre" In *Studien zur Geschichte und Theologie der Reformation: Festschrift für E. Bizer*, edited by Luise Abramowski and J. F. Gerhard Goeters. Neuenkirchener Verlag, 1969.

Heckel, Johannes. *Im Irrgarten der Zwei-Reiche-Lehre: Zwei Abhandlungen zum Reichsund Kirchenbegriff Martin Luthers*. Theologische Existenz heute. Neue Folge 55. Kaiser, 1957.

Heintze, Gerhard. *Luthers Predigt von Gesetz und Evangelium*. Forschung zur Geschichte und Lehre des Protestantismus 10/21. Chr. Kaiser, 1958.

Hennig, Gerhard. *Cajetan und Luther: Ein historischer Beitrag zur Begegnung von Thomismus und Reformation*. Arbeiten zur Theologie. Cawler Verlag, 1966.

Hering, Hermann. *Die Mystik Luthers im Zusammenhange seiner Theologi und in ihrem Verhältniß zur älteren Mystik*. Verlag der J. C. Hinrichs'schen Buchhandlung, 1879.

Hermann, Rudolf. "Das Verhältnis von Rechtfertigung und Gebet nach Luthers Auslegung von Röm 3 in der Römerbriefvorlesung (1925)." In *Gesammelte Studien zur Theologie Luthers und der Reformation*. Vandenhoeck and Ruprecht, 1960.

———. *Luthers These "Gerecht und Sünder zugleich": Eine systematische Untersuchung*. Gerd Mohn, 1930.

Hilburg, Johannes. "Luther und das Wort Gottes in seiner Exegese und Theologie." PhD diss., University of Marburg, 1948.

Hirsch, Emanuel. "Initium theologiae Lutheri." In *Festgabe für D. Dr. Julius Kaftan zu seinem 70. Geburtstag 30. September 1918*. J. C. B. Mohr, 1920.

———. *Lutherstudien*. Vol. 1, *Lutherstudien*. C. Bertelsmann, 1954.

Holl, Karl. *Gesammelte Aufsätze zur Kirchengeschichte*. Vol. 1, *Luther*. J. C. B. Mohr, 1921.

_______. *Gesammelte Aufsätze zur Kirchengeschichte*. Vol. 3, *Der Westen*. J. C. B. Mohr, 1928.

Iserloh, Erwin. *Der Kampf um die Messe in den ersten Jahren der Auseinandersetzung mit Luther*. Katholisches Leben und Kämpfen im Zeitalter der Glaubensspaltung 10. Ashendorff, 1952.

_______. *Die Eucharistie in der Darstellung des Johannes Eck: Ein Beitrag zur vortridentinischen Kontroverstheologie über das Meßopfer*. Reformationsgeschichtliche Studien und Texte 73/4. Aschendorff, 1950.

_______. "Luthers Stellung in der theologischen Tradition." In *Wandlungen des Lutherbildes*. Studien und Berichte der katholischen Akademie in Bayern 36. Echter-Verlag, 1966.

_______. "Luther und die Mystik." In *Kirche, Mystik, Heiligung und das Natürliche bei Luther*. Vandenhoeck and Ruprecht, 1967.

_______. *Luther zwischen Reform und Reformation: Der Thesenanschlag fand nicht statt*. Katholisches Leben und Kämpfen im Zeitalter der Glaubensspaltung 23/4. Ashendorff, 1967.

_______. *Reformationsgeschichtliche Studien und Texte*, supplemental vol. I. Ashendorff, 1965.

_______. "*Sacramentum et exemplum*: Ein augustinisches Thema lutherischer Theologie." In Reformata Reformanda: *Festgabe für Hubert Jedin zum 17. Juni 1965*, edited by Erwin Iserloh and Konrad Repgen.

Iwand, Hans Joachim. *Glaubensgerechtigkeit nach Luthers Lehre*. 3rd ed. Chr. Kaiser, 1959.

_______. *Rechtfertigungslehre und Christusglaube: Eine Untersuchung zur Systematik der Rechtfertigungslehre Luthers in ihren Anfängen*. J. C. Hinrich, 1930; Theologische Bücherei 14. Chr. Kaiser, 1961.

_______. "Wider den Mißbrauch des "pro me" als methodisches Prinzip in der Theologie." *Evangelische Theologie* 14 (1954): 120–24.

Jedin, Hubert. *Geschichte des Konzils von Trient*. Verlag Herder, 1949f.

_______. "Luthers Turmerlebnis in neuer Sicht: Bericht über E. Bizer *Fides ex auditu* (1958)." *Catholica* 12 (1958): 129–38.

Jetter, Werner. *Die Taufe beim jungen Luther: Eine Untersuchung über das Werden der reformatorischen Sakraments- und Taufanschauung*. Beiträge zur historischen Theologie 18. J. C. B. Mohr (Paul Siebeck), 1954.

Joest, Wilfried. *Gesetz und Freiheit: Das Problem des* Tertius usus legis *bei Luther und die neutestamentliche Parainese*. Vandenhoeck and Ruprecht, 1951.

_______. *Ontologie der Person bei Luther*. Vandenhoeck and Ruprecht, 1967.

Käsemann, Ernst. *New Testament Questions of Today*. Translated by W. J. Montague. SCM, 1969.

Kattenbusch, Ferdinand. "*Deus absconditus* bei Luther." *Festgabe für D. Dr. Julius Kaftan zu seinem 70. Geburtstag 30. September 1918*. J. C. B. Mohr, 1920: 170–214.

Köhler, Walter. *Luther und die Kirchengeschichte nach seinen Schriften: zunächst bis 1521*. Part 1: *Die Ablassinstruktion, die Bullen, Symbole, Concilien und die Mystiker*. Beiträge zu den Anfängen protestantischer Kirchengeschichtsschreibung. Fr. Junge, 1900.

Krause, Gerhard. *Studien zu Luthers Auslegung der Kleinen Propheten*. Beiträge zur historischen Theologie 33. J. C. B. Mohr, 1962.

Kreck, Walter. "Das reformatorische 'pro me' und die existentiale Interpretation heute." In *Studien zur Geschichte und Theologie der Reformation: Festschrift für E. Bizer*, edited by Luise Abramowski and J. F. Gerhard Goeters. Neukirchen: Neukirchener Verlag, 1969.

Krodel, Gottfried. "The Lord's Supper in the Theology of the Young Luther." *Lutheran Quarterly* 13 (1961): 19–33.

Kroeger, Matthias. *Rechtfertigung und Gesetz: Studien zur Entwicklung der Rechtfertigungslehre beim jungen Luther*. Vandenhoeck and Ruprecht, 1968.

Kropatschek, Friedrich. *Das Schriftprinzip der lutherischen Kirche: Geschichtliche und dogmatische Untersuchungen*. Vol. 1, *Die Vorgeschichte*: *Das Erbe des Mittelalters*. Diechert, 1904.

Lausberg, Heinrich. *Handbook of Literary Rhetoric: A Foundation for Literary Study*. Translated by Matthew T. Bliss, Annemiek Jansen, and David E. Orton. Brill, 1998.

———. *Handbuch der literarischen Rhetorik: Eine Grundlegung der Literaturwissenschaft*. M. Hueber, 1960.

Link, Wilhelm. *Das Ringen Luthers um die Freiheit der Theologie von der Philosophie*. Forschung zur Geschichte und Lehre des Protestantismus. Chr. Kaiser, 1940.

Loeschen, John. "The Function of Promissio in Luther's Commentary on Romans." *Harvard Theological Review* 60 (1967): 476–82.

Loewenich, Walther von. *Die Eigenart von Luthers Auslegung des Johannesprologes*. C. H. Beck, 1960.

———. "Lutherforschung in Deutschland." In *Lutherforschung heute: Referate und Berichte des 1. Internationalen Lutherforschungskongresses, Aarhus 18–23. August 1956*, edited by Vilmos Vajta. Lutherisches Verlaghaus, 1958.

———. *Luthers theologia crucis*. Chr. Kaiser, 1954.

———. *Luther's Theology of the Cross*. Augsburg, 1976.

———. "Zehn Jahre Lutherforschung in Deutschland." In *Von Augustin zu Luther: Beiträge zur Kirchengeschichte*. Luther-Verlag, 1959: 307–78.

Lohse, Bernhard. "Die Bedeutung Augustins für den jungen Luther." *Kerygma und Dogma* 11 (1965): 116–35.

Loofs, Friedrich. "Der articulus stantis et cadentis ecclesiae." *Theologische Studien und Kritiken* 90 (1917): 323–420.

———. *Leitfaden zum Studium der Dogmengeschichte*. 2 vols. M. Niemeyer, 1959.

Lubac, Henri de. *Exégèse médiévale: Les quatre sens de l'Ecriture*. Aubier, 1959–1964.

———. *Medieval Exegesis*: *The Four Senses of Scripture*. Translated by Mark Sebanc. Eerdmans, 1998.

Maurer, Wilhelm. *Der junge Melanchthon zwischen Humanismus und Reformation*. 2 vols. Vandenhoeck and Ruprecht, 1967–1969.

———. "Die Anfänge von Luthers Theologie: Eine Frage an die lutherische Kirche." *Theologische Literatureitung* 77 (1952): 1–12.

———. "Die Einheit der Theologie Luthers." *Theologische Literatureitung* 75 (1950): 245–52.

———. "Kirche und Geschichte nach Luthers *Dictata super Psalterium.*" In *Lutherforschung heute: Referate und Berichte des 1. Internationalen Lutherforschungskongresses, Aarhus 18–23. August 1956*, edited by Vilmos Vajta. Lutherisches Verlaghaus, 1958.

———. *Von der Freiheit eines Christenmenschen: Zwei Untersuchungen zu Luthers Reformationsschriften 1520/21.* Vandenhoeck and Ruprecht, 1949.

Mauser, Ulrich. *Der junge Luther und die Häresie.* Schriften des Vereins für Reformationsgeschichte 184. G. Mohn, 1968.

Meinhold, Peter. *Luthers Sprachphilosophie.* Lutherisches Verlaghaus, 1958.

Metzger, Günther. *Gelebter Glaube: Die Formierung reformatorischen Denkens in Luthers erster Psalmenvorlesung dargestellt am Begriff des Affekts.* Forschung zur Kirchen- und Dogmengeschichte 14. Vandenhoeck and Ruprecht, 1964.

Metzke, Erwin. "Nikolaus von Cues und Martin Luther." In Coincidentia oppositorum: *Gesammelte Studien zur Philosophiegeschichte*, edited by Karlfried Gründer. Luther-Verlag, 1961.

———. "Sakrament und Metaphysik: Eine Lutherstudie über das Verhältnis des christlichen Denkens zum Leiblich-Materiellen, 1948." In Coincidentia oppositorum: *Gesammelte Studien zur Philosophiegeschichte*, edited by Karlfried Gründer. Luther-Verlag, 1961.

Meyer, Hans Bernhard. *Luther und die Messe: Eine liturgiewissenschaftliche Untersuchung über das Verhältnis Luthers zum Meßwesen des späten Mittelalters.* Konfessionskundliche und Kontroverstheologische Studien 11. Verlag Bonifacius-Druckerei, 1965.

Moeller, Bernd. "Tauler und Luther." In *La Mystique Rhénane: Colloque de Strasbourg 16–19 Mai 1961.* Presses universitaires de France, 1963: 157–68.

Müller, Alphons Viktor. *Luthers theologische Quellen: Seine Verteidigung gegen Denifle und Griesar.* Töpelmann, 1912.

———. *Luthers Werdegang bis zum Turmerlebnis.* Friedrich Andreas Perthes, 1920.

———. *Luther und Tauler auf ihren theologischen Zusammenhang neu untersucht.* Wyss, 1918.

Müller, Gerhard. "Die Einheit der Theologie des jungen Luther." In Reformatio *und* Confessio: *Festschrift für Wilhelm Maurer zum 65. Geburtstag am 7. Mai 1965.* Lutherisches Verlaghaus, 1965.

———. "Neuere Literatur zur Theologie des jungen Luther." *Kerygma und Dogma* 11 (1965): 325–57.

Müller, Hans Martin. "Luthers Kreuzesmeditation und die Christuspredigt der Kirche." *Kerygma und Dogma* 15 (1969): 35–49.

Oberman, Heiko Augustinus. *The Harvest of Medieval Theology: Gabriel Biel and Late Medieval Nominalism.* Harvard University Press, 1963.

———. "'Iustitia Christi' und 'Iustitia Dei': Luther und die scholastischen Lehren von der Rechtfertigung." In *Der Durchbruch der reformatorischen Erkenntnis bei Luther*, edited by Bernhard Lohse. Wege der Forschung 123Wissenschaftliche Buchgesellschaft, 1968.

———. "Simul gemitus et raptus." In *Kirche, Mystik, Heiligung und das Natürliche bei Luther.* Vandenhoeck and Ruprecht, 1967: 20–59.

———. "Spätscholastik und Reformation." Vol. 1, *Der Herbst der mittelalterlichen Theologie*. Zurich, 1965.

———. "Wir sein pettler. Hoc est verum: Bund und Gnade in der Theologie des Mittelalters und der Reformation." *Zeitschrift für Kirchengeschichte* 78 (1967): 232–52.

———. "Wittenbergs Zweifrontenkrieg gegen Prierias und Eck: Hintergrund und Entscheidungen des Jahres 1518." *Zeitschrift für Kirchengeschichte* 80 (1969): 331–58.

Østergaard-Nielsen, Harald. "Die Bedeutung der Gleichzeitigkeit für die Christologie bei Luther und Kierkegaard." *Evangelische Theologie* 24 (1964): 642–54.

———. Scriptura sacra et viva vox: *Eine Lutherstudie*. Chr. Kaiser, 1957.

Ozment, Steven E. Homo spiritualis: *A Comparative Study of the Anthropology of Johannes Tauler, Jean Gerson and Martin Luther (1509–1516) in the Context of their Theological Thought*. Studies in Medieval and Reformation Thought 7. E. J. Brill, 1969.

Pesch, Otto. "Zur Frage nach Luthers reformatorischer Wende." *Catholica* 20 (1966): 216–43, 264–80.

———. "Zwanzig Jahre katholische Lutherforschung." *Lutherische Rundschau* 16 (1966): 392–406.

Pfürtner, Stephan. *Luther and Aquinas on Salvation*. Translated by Edward Quinn. Darton, Longman and Todd, 1964.

———. *Luther und Thomas im Gespräch: Unser Heil zwischen Gewißheit und Gefährdung*. Kerle, 1961.

Pinomaa, Lennart. *Register der Bibelzitate in Luthers Schriften in den Jahren 1509–1519*. Unknown publisher, unknown year (ca. 1956).

Prenter, Regin. *Der barmherzige Richter:* Iustitia dei passiva in Luthers *Dictata super Psalterium 1513–1515*. Acta Jutlandica 33/2. Universitetsforlaget, 1961.

———. *Spiritus Creator*. Translated by John M. Jensen. Fortress Press, 1953.

Preus, James Samuel. *From Shadow to Promise: Old Testament Interpretation from Augustine to the Young Luther*. Belknap Press, 1969.

———. "Old Testament *Promissio* and Luther's New Hermeneutic." *Harvard Theological Review* 60 (1967): 145–61.

Raeder, Siegfried. *Das Hebräische bei Luther: Untersucht bis zum Ende der ersten Psalmenvorlesung*. Beiträge zur historischen Theologie 31. J. C. B. Mohr, 1961.

Schäfer, Ernst. *Luther als Kirchenhistoriker: Ein Beitrag zur Geschichte der Wissenschaft*. C. Bertelsmann, 1897.

Schäfer Rolf. *Christologie und Sittlichkeit in Melanchthons frühen Loci*. Beiträge zur historischen Theologie 29. J. C. B. Mohr, 1961.

———. "Zur Datierung von Luthers reformatorischer Erkenntnis." *Zeitschrift für Theologie und Kirche* 66 (1969): 151–70.

———. "Zur Praedestinationslehre beim jungen Melanchthon." *Zeitschrift für Theologie und Kirche* 63 (1966): 352–78.

Scheel, Otto. "Taulers Mystik und Luthers reformatorische Entdeckung." In *Festgabe für D. Dr. Julius Kaftan zu seinem 70. Geburtstag 30. September 1918*. J. C. B. Mohr, 1920.

Schempp, Paul. "Das Abendmahl bei Luther." In *Gesammelte Aufsätze*, edited by Ernst Bizer. Theologische Bücherei 10. Chr. Kaiser, 1960.

______. "Der Mensch Luther als theologisches Problem." In *Gesammelte Aufsätze*, edited by Ernst Bizer. Theologische Bücherei 10. Chr. Kaiser, 1960: 258–95.

Schindler, Alfred. *Wort und Analogie in Augustins Trinitätslehre*. Hermeneutische Untersuchungen zur Theologie 4. J. C. B. Mohr, 1965.

Schwarz, Reinhard. *Fides, spes und caritas beim jungen Luther: Unter besonderer Berücksichtigung der mittelalterlichen Tradition*. Arbeiten zur Kirchengeschichte 34. de Gruyter, 1962.

______. "Gott ist Mensch: Zur Lehre von der Person Christi bei den Ockhamisten und bei Luther." *Zeitschrift für Theologie und Kirche* 63 (1966): 289–351.

______. *Vorgeschichte der reformatorischen Bußtheologie*. Arbeiten zur Kirchengeschichte 41. de Gruyter, 1968.

Seeberg, Erich. *Luthers Theologie in ihren Grundzügen*. Kohlhammer, 1940.

______. *Luthers Theologie: Motive und Ideen*. Vol. 1, *Die Gottesanschauung*. Vandenhoeck and Ruprecht, 1929.

______. *Luthers Theologie: Motive und Ideen*. Vol 2, *Christus: Wirklichkeit und Urbild*. Kohlhammer, 1937.

Seeberg, Reinhold. *Lehrbuch der Dogmengeschichte*. Vols. 2–4. Wissenschaftliche Buchgesellschaft, 1959–1965.

______. *Text-book of the History of Doctrines*. Translated by Charles E. Hay. Baker Book House, 1954.

Selge, Kurt-Victor. "Die Augsburgen Begegnung von Luther und Kardinal Cajetan im Oktober 1518. Ein erster Wendepunkt auf dem Weg zur Reformation." *Jahrbuch der hessischen kirchengeschichtlichen Vereinigung* 20 (1969): 37–54.

Strauß, Gerhard. *Schriftgebrauch, Schriftauslegung und Schriftbeweis bei Augustin*. Beiträge zur Geschichte des biblischen Hermeneutik 1. J. C. B. Mohr, 1959.

Süß, Theobald. "Über Luthers 'Sieben Bußpsalmen.'" In *Vierhundertfünfzig Jahre lutherische Reformation 1517–1967. Festschrift für Franz Lau zum 60. Geburtstag*. Vandenhoeck and Ruprecht, 1967.

Thimme, Wilhelm. "Die 'Deutsche Theologie' und Luthers 'Freiheit eines Christenmenschen': Ein Vergleich." *Zeitschrift für Theologie und Kirche* 40 (1932): 193–222.

Thomas, Alois. "Christus in der Kelter." *Reallexikon zur deutschen Kunstgeschichte* 3 (1954): 673–87.

Vajta, Vilmos. *Die Theologie des Gottesdienstes bei Luther*. Vandenhoeck and Ruprecht, 1952.

______. *Luther on Worship: An Interpretation*. Translated and condensed [from *Die Theologie des Gottesdienstes bei Luther*] by U. S. Leupold. Muhlenberg Press, 1958.

Vogelsang, Erich. *Christusglaube und Christusbekenntnis bei Luther*. Kirche in Bewegung und Entscheidung 16. Scheur, 1935.

______. *Der angefochtene Christus bei Luther*. Arbeiten zur Kirchengeschichte 21. de Gruyter, 1932.

______. "Der confessio-Begriff des jungen Luther 1513–22." *Luther-Jahrbuch* 12 (1930): 91–108.

———. *Die Anfänge von Luthers Christologie nach der ersten Psalmenvorlesung, insbesondere in ihren exegetischen und systematischen Zusammenhängen mit Augustin und der Scholastik dargestellt.* Arbeiten zur Kirchengeschichte 15. de Gruyter, 1929.

———. *Die Bedeutung der neuveröffentlichten Hebräerbrief-Vorlesung Luthers 1517/18: Ein Beitrag zur Frage, Humanismus und Reformation.* Sammlung gemeinverständlicher Vorträge und Schriften aus dem Gebiet der Theologie und Religionsgeschichte 143. J. C. B. Mohr (Paul Siebeck), 1930.

———. "Luther und die Mystik." *Luther-Jahrbuch* 19 (1937): 32–54.

———. "Zur Datierung der frühesten Lutherpredigten." *Zeitschrift für Kirchengeschichte* 50 (1931): 112–45.

Wehrung, Georg. "Fides specialis." *Theologische Literaturzeitung* 77 (1952): 193–290.

———. "Verheißung und Glaube: Zur Frage der Subjekt-Objekt-Korrelation im reformatischen Denken." In *Solange es "Heute" heißt: Festgabe für R. Hermann zum 70. Geburtstag.* Evangelische Verlagsanstalt, 1957: 293–304.

Wicks, Jared. "Martin Luther's Treatise on Indulgences." *Theological Studies* 28 (1967): 481–518.

Widmann, Sören. "Die Wartburgpostille: Untersuchungen zu ihrer Entstehung und zu Luthers Umgang mit dem Text." PhD diss., University of Tübingen, 1969. Summarized: *Theologische Literaturzeitung* 95 (1970): 77–78.

Wolf, Ernst. "Die Christusverkündigung bei Luther." In *Peregrinatio: Studien zur reformatorischen Theologie und zum Kirchenproblem.* Chr. Kaiser, 1962.

———. *Staupitz und Luther: Ein Beitrag zur Theologie des Johannes Staupitz und deren Bedeutung für Luthers theologischen Werdegang.* Quellen und Forschung zur Reformationsgechichte. M. Heinsius Nachfolger, 1927.

INDEX OF SCRIPTURE REFERENCES

INDEX OF NAMES

INDEX OF SUBJECTS

LIST OF DISPUTED DATES OR NEW DATES OF LUTHER TEXTS

1.	*Sermon on the Assumption of the Blessed Virgin Mary* (WA 4:645–50): Aug. 15, 1545	87n.316
2.	*Sermon on St. Barbara's Day* (Dec. 4) 1514 (WA 4:639–44)	92n.340; 91n.340
3.	*Sermon on the Prologue of John* (WA 1:20–29): December 24/25, 1514	17n.1
4.	*Sermon 2 on the Passion* (WA 1:340–45): Lent 1515	87n.316
5.	The Romans Lectures: Easter 1515–September 1516	21n.1
6.	*A Fragment of Luther's Readings* (WA 1:347–49): 517 (at the latest)	151n.635
7.	*Instruction for the Confession of Sins* (WA 1:257–64): Lent 1517;WA 1:264,9–265,11 is an appendix and comes from Lent 1518	118n.463; 231n.13
8.	The Hebrews Lectures: October 1517–September 1518	229–31
9.	*Sermon on Indulgences on the Eve of the Dedication of the Church* (WA 1:94–99): October 31, 1517	181n.2
10.	*Treatise on Indulgences* (WA 1:65–99): November 1517	182n.10
11.	*Sermon for Candlemas* (WA 1:130–32 = 4:636–39): February 2, 1518	124n.496a (= 230n.7)
12.	*Interpretation of Psalm 23* (WA 31/1:464–71): Easter 1518 (at the latest)	21n.1; 111n.435b
13.	*First Mass Sermon* (WA 4:655–59): Spring/Summer 1518	184n.19
14.	*Interpretation of Psalm 4:9* [Vulgate] (WA 5:124,20–125,5): the earliest date is the conversation with Cajetan in Augsburg (Oct. 1518)	220,197
15.	*Disputations on Questions of Sacramental Theology* (WA 6:30–31; 6:470–71; 6:472–73; WA 9:312–13): Spring/Summer 1520 (t. ad quem is the composition of *The Babylonian Captivity of the Church*)	178; 306n.98,99; 307n.107

16.	*Marginal notes on Biel*, Collectorium 4 (edited by Degering): Spring/Summer 1520	111n.435c; 179; 298–306
	(The recently published work by H. Volz ["Luthers Randbemerkungen zu zwei Schriften Gabriel Biels. Kritische Anmerkungen zu Hermann Degerings Publikation," *ZKG* 81 [1970]: 207–19) confirms rather than rules out this dating.)	
17.	*Sermon on John 16:23–24* (WA 4:624): Rogate (May 13) 1520	375n.27

Lutheran Quarterly Books

Living by Faith: Justification and Sanctification, by Oswald Bayer (2003).

Harvesting Martin Luther's Reflections on Theology, Ethics and the Church, essays from *Lutheran Quarterly*, edited by Timothy J. Wengert, with foreword by David C. Steinmetz (2004).

A More Radical Gospel: Essays on Eschatology, Authority, Atonement, and Ecumenism, by Gerhard O. Forde, edited by Mark Mattes and Steven Paulson (2004).

The Role of Justification in Contemporary Theology, by Mark C. Mattes (2004).

Bound Choice, Election, and Wittenberg Theological Method: From Martin Luther to the Formula of Concord, by Roberg Kolb (2005).

The Captivation of the Will: Luther vs. Erasmus on Freedom and Bondage, by Gerhard O. Forde (2005).

Luther's Liturgical Music: Principles and Implications, by Robin A. Leaver (2006).

A Formula for Parish Practice: Using the Formula of Concord in Congregations, by Timothy J. Wengert (2006).

The Preached God: Proclamation in Word and Sacrament, by Gerhard O. Forde, edited by Mark C. Mattes and Steven D. Paulson (2007).

Theology the Lutheran Way, by Oswald Bayer (2007).

A Time for Confessing, by Robert W. Bertram (2008).

The Pastoral Luther: Essays on Martin Luther's Pastoral Theology, edited by Timothy J. Wengert (2009).

Preaching from Home: The Stories of Seven Lutheran Women Hymn Writers, by Gracia Grindal (2011).

The Early Luther: Stages in a Reformation Reorientation, by Berndt Hamm (2013).

The Life, Works, and Witness of Tsehay Tolessa and Gudina Tumsa, the Ethiopian Bonhoeffer, edited by Samuel Yonas Deressa and Sarah Hinlicky (2017).

Luther's Outlaw God: Volume 1: Hiddenness, Evil, and Predestination, by Steven D. Paulson (2018).

The Wittenberg Concord: Creating Space for Dialogue, by Gordon A. Jensen (2018).

The Essential Forde: Distinguishing Law and Gospel, by Gerhard O. Forde, edited by Nickolas Hopman, Mark C. Mattes, and Steven D. Paulson (2019).

Luther's Outlaw God: Volume 2: Hidden in the Cross, by Steven D. Paulson (2019).

Lutheran Quarterly Books

The Augsburg Confession: Renewing Lutheran Faith and Practice, by Timothy J. Wengert (2020).

Luther's Outlaw God: Volume 3: Sacraments and God's Attack on the Promise, by Steven D. Paulson (2020).

Minister's Prayer Book: An Order of Prayers and Readings, revised edition, edited by Timothy J. Wengert, Mary Jane Haemig, Chris Halverson, and Robert Harrell (2020).

Stories from Global Lutheranism: A Historical Timeline, by Martin J. Lohrmann (2021).

Teaching Reformation: Essays in Honor of Timothy J. Wengert, edited by Luka Ilić and Martin J. Lohrmann (2021).

Experiencing Gospel: The History and Creativity of Martin Luther's 1534 Bible Project, by Gordon A. Jensen (2023).

Face to Face: Martin Luther's View of Reality, by Robert Kolb (2024).

A New Song We Now Begin: Celebrating the Half Millennium of Lutheran Hymnals 1524–2024, edited by Robin A. Leaver (2024).

Sola: Christ, Grace, Faith, and Scripture Alone in Martin Luther's Theology, by Volker Leppin (2024).

Promissio: The Reformational Turn in Luther's Theology, by Oswald Bayer, translated by Jeffrey G. Silcock (2025).

United with Christ: Martin Luther and Christian Mysticism, by Volker Leppin (2025).